Non-Western Popular Music

The Library of Essays on Popular Music
Series Editor: Allan F. Moore

Titles in the Series:

Non-Western Popular Music

Edited by

Tony Langlois

Mary Immaculate College, University of Limerick, Ireland

ASHGATE

Published by
Ashgate Publishing Limited
Wey Court East
Union Road
Farnham
Surrey GU9 7PT
England

Ashgate Publishing Company
Suite 420
101 Cherry Street
Burlington
VT 05401-4405
USA

www.ashgate.com

British Library Cataloguing in Publication Data
Non-Western popular music. – (The library of essays on
  popular music)
  1. Popular music–Asia–History and criticism. 2. Popular
  music–Africa–History and criticism.
  I. Series II. Langlois, Tony.
  781.6'3'095-dc23

Library of Congress Control Number: 2011938374

ISBN 9780754629849

MIX
Paper from
responsible sources
FSC® C013056
www.fsc.org

Printed and bound in Great Britain by
TJ International Ltd, Padstow, Cornwall.

Contents

PART III MUSIC INDUSTRIES

PART IV HISTORICAL APPROACHES

Acknowledgements

The editor and publishers wish to thank the following for permission to use copyright material.

American Anthropological Association for the essay: Galit Saada-Ophir (2006), 'Borderland Pop: Arab Jewish Musicians and the Politics of Performance', *Cultural Anthropology*, **21**, pp. 205–33. Copyright © 2006 by the American Anthropological Association.

Cahiers d'Etudes africaines for the essays: Brian Larkin (2002), 'Bandiri Music, Globalization and Urban Experience in Nigeria', *Cahiers d'Études Africaines*, **168**, XLII-4, pp. 739–62; Dorothea E. Schulz (2002), '"The World is Made by Talk": Female Fans, Popular Music, and New Forms of Public Sociality in Urban Mali', *Cahiers d'Études Africaines*, **168**, XLII-4, pp. 797–829.

Cambridge University Press for the essays: Martin Stokes (1992), 'Islam, the Turkish State and Arabesk', *Popular Music*, **11**, pp. 213–27. Copyright © 1992 Cambridge University Press, reproduced with permission; Stephen Blum and Amir Hassanpour (1996), '"The Morning of Freedom Rose up": Kurdish Popular Song and the Exigencies of Cultural Survival', *Popular Music*, **15**, pp. 325–43. Copyright © 1996 Cambridge University Press, reproduced with permission; Christopher Ballantine (2004), 'Re-thinking "Whiteness"? Identity, Change and "White" Popular Music in Post-Apartheid South Africa', *Popular Music*, **23**, pp. 105–31. Copyright © 2004 Cambridge University Press, reproduced with permission; Jocelyne Guilbault (1997), 'Interpreting World Music: A Challenge in Theory and Practice', *Popular Music*, **16**, pp. 31–44. Copyright © 1997 Cambridge University Press, reproduced with permission; Wai-Chung Ho (2003), 'Between Globalisation and Localisation: A Study of Hong Kong Popular Music', *Popular Music*, **22**, pp. 143–57. Copyright © 2003 Cambridge University Press, reproduced with permission; Peter Manuel (1991), 'The Cassette Industry and Popular Music in North India', *Popular Music*, **10**, pp. 189–204. Copyright © 1991 Cambridge University Press, reproduced with permission; John Baily (1981), 'Cross-Cultural Perspectives in Popular Music: The Case of Afghanistan', *Popular Music*, **1**, pp. 105–22. Copyright © 1981 Cambridge University Press, reproduced with permission; Judith Ann Herd (1984), 'Trends and Taste in Japanese Popular Music: A Case-Study of the 1982 Yamaha World Popular Music Festival', *Popular Music*, **4**, pp. 75–96. Copyright © 1984 Cambridge University Press, reproduced with permission; Suzel Ana Reily (1996), 'Tom Jobim and the Bossa Nova Era', *Popular Music*, **15**, pp. 1–16. Copyright © 1996 Cambridge University Press, reproduced with permission; Yngvar B. Steinholt (2003), 'You Can't Rid a Song of its Words: Notes on the Hegemony of Lyrics in Russian Rock Songs', *Popular Music*, **22**, pp. 89–108. Copyright © 2003 Cambridge University Press, reproduced with permission; Szu-Wei Chen (2005), 'The Rise and Generic Features of Shanghai Popular Songs in the 1930s and 1940s', *Popular Music*, **24**, pp. 107–25. Copyright © 2005 Cambridge University Press, reproduced with permission.

Series Preface

From its rather modest beginnings in the 1950s, the study of popular music has now developed to such a degree that many academic institutions worldwide employ specialists in the field. Even those that do not will often still make space on crowded higher education curricula for the investigation of what has become not only one of the most lucrative spheres of human activity, but one of the most influential on the identities of individuals and communities. Popular music matters, and it matters to so many people, people we can only partially understand if we do not understand their music. It is for this reason that this series is timely.

This is not the place to try to offer a definition of popular music; that is one of the purposes of the essays collected in the volumes in this series. Through their Popular and Folk Music series of monographs, Ashgate has gained a strong reputation as a publisher of scholarship in the field. This Library of Essays on Popular Music is partly envisioned as a complement to that series, focusing on writing of shorter length. But the series is also intended to develop the volume of Critical Essays in Popular Musicology published in 2007, in that it provides comprehensive coverage of the world's popular musics in eight volumes, each of which has a substantial introductory essay by the volume's editor. It develops the Critical Essays volume in that it makes overt recognition of the fact that the study of popular music is necessarily inter-disciplinary. Thus, within the limits set by the genre coverage of each individual volume, and by the excellence of the essays available for inclusion, each editor has been asked to keep an eye on issues as diverse as: the popular music industry and its institutions; aspects of history of their respective genres; issues in the theories and methodologies of study and practice; questions of the ontologies and hermeneutics of their fields; the varying influence of different waves of technological development; the ways markets and audiences are constructed, reproduced and reached and, last but not least; aspects of the repertory without which there would be no popular music to study. As a result, no disciplinary perspective is privileged. As far as possible, no genre is privileged either. Because the study of rock largely led the growth of popular music study, the genre has produced a very large amount of material; it needs a volume to itself. Much writing on jazz tends to circumscribe the genre clearly arguing that it, too, needs a volume to itself. Other forms of music have been distributed across the remaining volumes: one on electronica; one on forms of mainstream pop (still frequently omitted from academic surveys); one on specific North American forms which lead to hip-hop; one on the appearance of popular music within other (particularly visual) media; and two final volumes covering 'world' and 'roots', musics whose relationship with more obviously industrialized forms is most particularly problematic. While this categorization of the world's popular musics is not perfect (and is variously addressed in individual volumes), it is no worse than any other, and it does enable the inclusion of all those academic essays we feel are worth reproducing.

The field of study has grown to such an extent that there is now a plethora of material available to read, and the growth of the internet makes it increasingly available. Why, then, produce this series of essays? The issue is principally one of evaluation. Where does one start? It is no longer possible to suggest to new entrants in the field that they should read everything, for there is much which is of lesser value. So, what you will find collected in these volumes is a selection of the most important and influential journal articles, essays and previously-published shorter material on the genre area concerned. Editors were given the brief of choosing not only those essays which have already garnered a great degree of influence, but essays which have also, for whatever reason, been overlooked, and which offer perspectives worthy of greater account. The volumes' editors are all experts in their own fields, with strong views about the ways those fields have developed, and might develop in the future. Thus, while the series is necessarily retrospective in its viewpoint, it nonetheless aims to help lay a platform for the broad future study of popular music.

ALLAN F. MOORE
Series Editor
University of Surrey, UK

Introduction

Since the advent of recording and broadcasting technologies facilitated its flows, the interaction between 'Western' popular music and the 'rest of the world' has been effervescent. Initially tracing the routes of colonial and, later, mercantile power, local and global musics have cross-fertilized, creolized, stimulated or polluted (depending upon your perspective) each other's traditions for well over a century. Musics that, not long ago, 'the West' mostly encountered on the crackling periphery of the short-wave spectrum are now easily accessed through the internet or, thanks to continued migration, among our own communities.[1] This growing proximity has perhaps made many 'Westerners' more conscious of 'non-Western' popular musics than previously, but it is only comparatively recently that this awareness has led to serious attention from academics. The reasons for this late development will be explored shortly in this introduction.

At the outset it is necessary to clarify the focus of this collection of essays, which is primarily concerned with the local practices that constitute popular music in non-Western locations and contexts. Although these musics are far from being untouched by global influences (and in fact this will be a core theme of this collection), we will not dwell upon the 'roots' or 'world music' phenomenon that for many decades has drawn 'foreign' musics into the sphere of Western audiences. 'Roots music' is the subject of another volume in this series; here we will concentrate on non-Western music industries and societies as much as on the music itself.

The central objective of a collection such as this is to provide a practical, useful resource for researchers and students, one that offers a diversity of both regional case studies and disciplinary approaches. In so doing, the volume aims to provide, editor's personal preferences notwithstanding, a reasonably representative overview of the field in question. This selection will outline the areas of most interest to contemporary researchers, and also indicate where their perspectives differ. Scholars are expected to cast a critical eye upon work that has been carried out by others before them, and also upon that of their contemporaries where they have divergent points of view. So unlike edited volumes that are compiled with the intention of establishing a particular agenda or of promoting a certain explorative approach, this collection of essays has been selected with the intention of encompassing geographical and disciplinary diversity in order to evoke a sense of the lively debates existing within the busy academic field. As this collection addresses the theme of 'non-Western' 'popular music' I also consider it necessary, in this introduction, to interrogate both of these terms and consider the implications of our working definitions of them upon the kind of research that has been carried out over the last thirty or forty years. As popular music studies is still a relatively young discipline and 'non-Western' genres have not, so far, been a central feature of its development, it will be important to place this research in its historical context, especially for the benefit of readers who are new to this subject.

---

[1]   See Slobin (1992) for a key study of this phenomenon.

Readers may observe that researchers in this field have come from a range of academic traditions and that those backgrounds have influenced both the kinds of questions asked and the methods used in asking them. It is, however, possible to group their work into a few broad categories according to the central attention of their writing, and this book is organized around these main themes.

The first theme concerns the relationships between **music, power and identity**. Musics around the world are frequently associated with particular sections of society, and as social groups compete for recognition or dominance their music may also become an instrument of cultural politics. Contributors to this book may, for example, ask how a particular music conveys a message of protest or defiance, or, on the other hand, if it is more associated with maintaining the political status quo. On many occasions and in many locations, popular music has been banned, constrained and censored; musicians who do not conform to the accepted norms and tastes of the society in which they live may lose the right to be heard at all. Several case studies in this volume consider the political circumstances in which music is made, and how those norms contribute to the formation of social identities.

As the networks between musician and audience exist at an increasingly international level, **globalization** is also a recurring theme in the study of non-Western pop. The 'world music' phenomenon has brought disparate musical products into a global market, which has cultural influences upon both producer and consumer. Although this book doesn't dwell upon world music per se, local musicians are inevitably influenced by the global media and ideas they encounter. These influences are often understood and interpreted through a prism of decidedly local cultural factors. The musical negotiation of 'tradition' and 'modernity', structure and agency, the local in the context of the global, is a seam that runs through a number of the essays found in this collection.

Other essays look in more detail at local **music industries** themselves. Production, consumption and performance practices are shaped by available technologies and economic networks, as well as the strategies of entrepreneurial musicians. The recording, distribution and everyday use of music products are well documented here in case studies, along with descriptions of their close relationships to other popular media, particularly film and television.

A few essays also discuss the relationship between musician and audience; 'fandom', the identification of enthusiast with performer, might be considered a crucial product of the music business, which is itself dependent upon increasingly interactive technologies.

Historical studies form the basis of other contributions in this selection. These use the benefit of archival resources and hindsight to describe entire systems of musical production, some of which have since disappeared or mutated beyond recognition. Such research allows us to identify the processes of change that take place over time and to compare these examples to contemporary activities. Where an individual's musical career has been shaped by important historical or cultural events, biographical studies are often an excellent way of illustrating music's historical engagement with wider social movements.

Running through each of these broad themes, readers will of course find many theoretical threads, as authors reflect upon the implications of their observations with regard to current academic debates. As these essays are drawn from a period of over thirty years, it is interesting to observe how these debates and approaches have themselves changed over time. Each of the areas I have outlined will be looked at in more detail shortly. At this point, before introducing the essays themselves, it may be useful to consider the developmental background of this field of research, its roots in other, longer established disciplines and the very concepts of 'popular music' and 'non-western' that afford purpose to this collection.

Although the authors included here share an interest in a common field of cultural activity, they may well have converged here from different academic starting points and so diverge in methodology. Those with a background in social anthropology and ethnomusicology may have gleaned their information from a long period of solitary immersion in the society which they are studying – learning the local language and instruments, participating as much as possible in the everyday life of music-making in order to gain insights from the emic, or 'insider's', perspective. Other authors included here may take a more historical or technological perspective – supporting their views with detailed investigations of the literature and records relating to their case study, which afford the longitudinal perspective that anthropological writing can sometimes lack. Music sociologists may have conducted comprehensive surveys of substantial population samples before arriving at the broad patterns of audience taste and musical consumption that they describe. Each discipline brings with it concerns with particular issues and preferences for certain research techniques, and will derive its perspective from humanist or political concerns that prevailed at the time of writing. In short, readers should remember that research into popular music is itself largely a product of Western society and so reflects concerns that are contemporary and regional.

The earliest academic writing that considered popular music to be important was influenced by the work of a cluster of researchers based at the Centre of Contemporary Cultural Studies, in Birmingham, UK. This 'Birmingham school' included, among many others, Stuart Hall, Dick Hebdige, Paul Gilroy and Angela McRobbie, all of whom were concerned with the political and social aspects of popular music consumption and production rather than with the musical material itself. Other important writers such as Simon McReynolds and Simon Frith came into serious writing about pop music from music journalism rather than academia. None of these writers claimed to be musicologists, and in fact they all wrote on many other unrelated subjects. Nevertheless, the academic seriousness with which they approached popular culture was very new in the late 1960s and early 1970s, and was influential upon the way that popular music studies emerged as a discipline. Hall (1981), Hebdige (1987) and Gilroy (1993) did in fact look at non-Western musics, although they focused, in their different ways, upon issues of identity and migration. Each placed the musical practices they described in a historical context, showing how constructions of gender, class and race were constructed and challenged within discourses sustained by popular music. Their application of the recently discovered (or rediscovered) theoretical ideas of Theodore Adorno, Antonio Gramsci and Michel Foucault was combined with an eclectic approach to sociological methodology, leading to a cultural studies that was both critical and very much rooted in 'real life'. In the early 1980s as writers like Simon Frith (1998), Andy Bennet (2003) and Philip Tagg (2009) spearheaded popular music studies as a discipline in the UK they drew upon the radical Birmingham school approach rather than a primarily musicological one. Likewise, the new journals (*Popular Music*, *Popular Music and Society*) and organizations (IASPM – International Council for the Study of Popular Music) that emerged in the same period reflect broadly similar concerns. The Anglo-American origins of popular music studies, with its roots in a 'cultural sociology' led, understandably, to an early focus upon urban Western musics. These were not only readily accessible, but also better suited to debates taking place at that time about subculture, cultural resistance, alienation and identity construction. Even when migrant musics *were* considered, this was usually from a standpoint of their consumption in the West rather than the context of their production elsewhere in the world.

What is Popular?

The definition of popular music itself is surprisingly hard to pin down, given that most of us have a fairly good common-sense understanding of what pop 'sounds like'. This definition has become harder to formulate because the forms of production and dissemination that were once relatively unique to pop have become common to many other types of music. Even if we were to limit our field to encompass the pop musics of just 'the West', so including songs from the Victorian music hall, the experimental work of the Beatles, hard-core dance tracks, black metal, breakcore and Roy Rogers, it would be evident that even at this surface level we are in complex territory. If one considers what these musics actually 'mean' to the range of individuals who encounter them, and how those meanings have changed over time, it is clear that simple definitions and conclusions are wholly inadequate.

A more pragmatic classification of popular music might include a combination of a number of factors. Most music fitting this generic description subscribes to most, if not all, of the following possible criteria:

1. It is *intended* to be enjoyed by the masses, rather than an elite.
2. As a consequence it is *mass-produced and disseminated*, using a wide variety of media broadcast technologies.
3. It is promoted by a *publicity infrastructure*, which commodifies (typically young and attractive) performers as 'celebrities' as a means to sell music products.
4. The pop music industry's need for novelty and a consistent flow of income means that the music (and often the careers of its performers) is *short-lived*.
5. Although since the 1960s its appeal to youth markets has also drawn upon the trappings of anti-authoritarianism, pop songs have been largely concerned with *uncontroversial romantic subjects*.
6. It is overwhelmingly based upon short, *highly formulaic* and catchy songs.
7. As popular music is very often produced for *social dancing*, its rhythm tends to be particularly foregrounded compared to other genres.

Although its component structures might be conservative, even predictable, it should be noted that most of the above criteria relate to pop's modes of production and dissemination, not to its musical qualities. Going further, persuasive critics of popular music such as Adorno ([1947] 1991) and Frith (1981) draw our attention to the music's intimate connection to the project of global capitalism, and even to the illusion of creative authenticity and community with which the industry clothes popular music.

Such critiques are explored in considerably more depth in other volumes in this series, but nevertheless it is useful for our present purpose to note the theoretical context and other parameters that shape the present selection of essays. For example, as well as avoiding world music, this collection will not deal directly with non-Western traditional music (another concept that is proving to be increasingly difficult to pin down),[2] although there are inevitably many areas of overlap between pop and other regional styles. Instead these essays focus upon those local musics that have been adapted for mass consumption or have otherwise been appropriated into such a field.

One very important outcome of recording and broadcasting technology is that the process effectively dislocates music from any specific performance context, such as a concert hall or nightclub. As the mainstay of radio programming, mp3 downloads and pirating, popular music is arguably more subject to dislocation than other genres. At the same time, the technologies of consumption have become ever more amenable to relocation at the discretion of the consumer. Despite this dislocation from fixed time and space, musics nevertheless retain signifiers that are strongly evocative of 'real' performance contexts and places. This process of dislocation consequently renders music open to a wider range of potential meanings than if it was played 'live' by musicians who we can observe, for an audience we know and whose culture we share.

As a consequence of this process, the rich layers of meaning that the performance context itself adds to the music's sonic 'text' are absent. Attending a music festival, for example, may be a very different experience to listening to the same music at home. Upon audition, a listener's understanding is dependent upon their personal familiarity with it, and, if there is little firsthand experience, then upon whatever discursive associations they are able to make with it. To take a case study from Kenya, Edouard Massengo's guitar-based Benga music could be 'read' as coming from Nairobi, Kenya or Africa, or simply as 'non-Western' depending upon the listener's previous levels of familiarity. Indigenous consumers may make very different associations, based upon a more detailed knowledge of Massengo's biography, the location and period of recording. Dislocated as recordings are from 'real time' and place, it is nevertheless an established international convention that recordings generally aim to sonically emulate an ideal *performance* context. In a common stereo spatial arrangement, the lead singer and lead guitar are located near the centre of the mix with drums and bass to the left and right. Other instruments are placed on the fringes of the spatial arrangement as if the performers were positioned in front of the listener on a wide stage. The relative volume and tone of each track is carefully balanced to ensure that even the quietest sounds can be heard clearly and any mistakes are easily erased or repaired. The lead singer's voice is almost always at the dead centre of the mix, and loud enough to be heard clearly, despite the volume of the instruments on either side. The illusion of a 'real time' group performance is created despite the fact that recordings are usually the product of a complex process of repeated 'takes' for each instrument in turn, multi-tracking procedures, digital sampling and considerable studio manipulation. Much popular music can therefore be considered a *representation* of an ideal performance, liberated from a live context and available to listeners who then create a meaning that is shaped by their own experience, social activities and imagination. Although it can be argued that *all* recorded music, 'popular' or otherwise, is nowadays subject to similar production procedures and electronic dissemination, these techniques are more closely

---

[2]   Although it should be noted that the term 'popular' is equated with 'folk' in other languages. Here I will use the term 'traditional' to refer to music that is primarily played by and for a distinct 'folk' community, typically employing non-electronic instruments.

associated with popular music than other genres, to the extent that they might reasonably be considered an additional criterion for its definition.

The history of the recording and distribution of indigenous popular musics began at the start of twentieth century, as colonial routes developed markets for new recreational technologies. Gramophones were followed from the 1920s onwards by radio stations, which were immensely powerful symbols of modernity and identity, as for the first time they enabled the broadcast of local musics to an entire *nation*. From the very outset of our contemporary era, then, popular musics have been technologically mediated throughout the world, though this was primarily for regional audiences with particular tastes and languages. The requirements of recording and broadcasting have not only brought about the contextual dislocation I've already discussed, but they inevitably had an influence upon the structures of the musics themselves and in most situations changed the economic environment in which musicians worked. From the point at which recording appeared on the scene there was a more tangible musical product available for purchase than simply the entrance fee to a performance. The increased professionalization of musicians, and competition between them at local and national levels, owes much to this process of musical industrialization.

The period in which most of the essays contained in this volume were written witnessed both an exceptional growth in electronic transmission of music beyond national boundaries and a decentralization of recording and transmission technologies. Record production plants, which were once the property of international industries or governments, have been largely supplanted by cheaper, small-scale facilities that allow the musician more control of the finished result. Likewise, the gate-keeping function of national radio stations has been largely circumvented, first by pirate producers and broadcasters, and more recently through online broadcasting. Such developments, which have dramatically changed the accessibility and diversity (and 'popularity') of music, have also had an impact on the working practices of musicians and the economic environment in which they operate. In such a fluid situation it has been inevitable that researchers into non-Western pop have been concerned with the complexities of globalization, as musicians in different parts of the world experience and respond to them. Many of the contributors to this volume have addressed, directly or indirectly, the changes that new technologies have brought about.

One of the reasons why popular music studies is a relatively recent field of serious study may be that its subject material has been perceived as ephemeral. It is easy to argue that music that comes and goes out of favour in a matter of months, or even weeks, could not be of enduring aesthetic value or socially significant. However, from the perspective of the twenty-first century it is clear that not only do some popular musics sometimes achieve the status of 'classics', but that over time they can acquire a new patina of meaning for subsequent generations that rediscover them. Dislocated as recordings are from the place and time of their production, every personal collection of music recordings is in effect an archive, whether this goes back ten, twenty or seventy years. In practice all recorded musics co-exist in the present, bearing meanings that continually develop as contemporary productions respond to, or react against, either their structural components or what they have come to represent.

Disciplinary Boundaries

Readers who come to this volume from the field of popular music studies may have noted from the contents page that many of the authors they are most familiar with are not to be found here. In fact until fairly recently the non-Western area of popular music studies has been largely neglected in academia, and in part this is because it fell between at least two disciplinary stools. As I have already indicated, the most influential academic champions of popular music as a serious academic discipline built upon foundations laid in sociology and cultural studies. Their debates around subcultures, identity and postmodernity, along with their research methods, were most obviously applicable to the industrialized, urban societies of the West. There were exceptions to this trend of course, but it is telling that the first books directly to address the subject, Wallis and Malm's *Big Sounds from Small Peoples* and Peter Manuel's *Popular Music of the Non-Western World*, were not published until 1984 and 1988 respectively. Of course there are dozens of other books that consider world musics today, but even now most of these fall into one of two categories: introductory (Bohlman, 2002; Nidel, 2005; Taylor, 1997) or encyclopedic (Broughton *et al.*, 1999; Hartong, 2006). The 'popular', however has been a steadily increasing theme in a number of good ethnomusicology textbooks (for example, Alves, 2008; Bakan, 2007; Nettl, 1996; Stone, 2008; Titon and Fujie, 2008; Turino, 2008).

Despite this recent growth of interest it is fair to say that non-Western popular musics did not appear on the popular music studies radar until the 1980s. For this reason alone, few of the essays included here are more than twenty years old. However, the neglect of the non-Western popular was not just an omission by popular music studies. Ethnomusicologists, who one might imagine would have been keenly interested in this area, were also slow to take popular music seriously. With their anthropological focus upon the *social practices* of music-making in other cultures, ethnomusicologists have tended to concentrate on live performative contexts. The cultural significance of real-time, real-life events are more apparent and accessible to researchers than those involved in the (largely internal) experience of listening to recorded or broadcast music. It is possible to film what is going on at a performance, to question the audience about their experiences, and an ethnomusicologist's ideal is to take part in the performance themselves, so learning about the music from the insider's perspective.

Alongside this methodological preference for participant observation, until recent decades there was a sense that popular music could seldom be thought of as 'authentic' in the way that folk or art traditions might be. Ethnomusicology, like folklore studies, has often been concerned with identifying the definitive, or most typical, example of a musical practice. This enables the establishment of a classificatory baseline against which other historical and cross-cultural phenomena can be compared and measured. Identifying an ideal form, which is reproducible on multiple occasions, makes it possible for researchers to identify the local generative rules of musical construction and performance. It also allows the lone ethnographer in the field to feel more confident that what they may be observing or participating in is a firmly rooted part of that culture and not a unique aberration. This research approach makes perfect sense, but it is not obviously applicable to the production or consumption practices relating to popular music.

Whatever the reasons, it does seem that until fairly recently neither popular music studies nor ethnomusicology were methodologically equipped or philosophically disposed to working with the popular music of other cultures. The earlier essays included in this volume should thus be understood to be the outstanding exceptions to both disciplines rather than their norm. Most of the authors represented in this book would probably consider themselves to be ethnomusicologists, simply because all musical investigation carried out in non-Western locations tends to fall into this default category. However, the current generation of researchers would be as familiar with relevant literature in cultural studies or sociology as they are with the classical anthropological theorists of the 1950s. Consequently it could be argued that this field, which increasingly includes media studies and cultural geography, has become truly multidisciplinary, and hopefully this book reflects something of this diversity.

Where is 'Non-West'?

The matter of geographical diversity is inevitably central to a collection concerned with non-Western musics, and my curatorial objective has been to cast as wide a net as possible, so long as the essays were of the highest quality and germane to the topic in hand. 'The West' in this context has been understood to refer to Europe, North America and Australasia, regions that will be covered in appropriate depth in other volumes in this series. For the sake of practicality the 'non-West' is inevitably 'everywhere else', a classification that though logical for the project in hand is of course riddled with contradictions in the real world of music-making. As Slobin (1992), among many others, has pointed out, the music of migrants has always brought a steady stream of unfamiliar flavours and sounds into host societies, with sometimes unpredictable consequences (see also Aubert, 2007; Ragland, 2003). 'Foreign music', can, in some circumstances, be appropriated into new cultural hybrids, but it might also remain for many years an impenetrable sign of 'otherness' in its new environment. The music of migrants can evolve to accommodate changing attitudes and markets, or remain an obstinate indicator of cultural difference, oblivious to contemporary developments in its original place of origin. The increasing ease of travel and especially of electronic transmission has further rendered irrelevant regional distinctions. Music from *everywhere* is now accessible *anywhere*, via common distributive technologies and means of paying for (or otherwise procuring) it. Likewise, Western music has a history of influencing other cultures that is as long as global exploration itself. These comments are not intended to undermine the contention that such a concept as non-Western music can exist, but rather to acknowledge that its parameters are highly negotiable. These subtle musical and cultural relationships are explored in many of the essays in this collection, as they are in other volumes in this series. Here it is sufficient to note that all prescriptive boundaries, including the concept of non-Western popular music itself, are largely arbitrary. We will find (in chapters by Steinholt and Herd, among others) that even where cosmetic acoustic similarities exist between Western and non-Western popular musics, this does not imply that they convey the same meanings to all listeners. All musical consumption is local, and listening practices and ways of hearing music can vary widely.[3] On the other hand, even when non-Western musics may be very dissimilar from one another

---

[3]   Christopher Small (1998) explores the social process of listening particularly well.

in their form and social use, on an international level they may yet occupy common cultural ground; Taylor (1997), Wallis and Malm (1984) and Olsen (1982) have shown how the Western world music industry has brought together quite disparate fellow travellers.

Given the subject matter of this collection, where, for the most part, Western researchers attempt to investigate the cultures of 'other societies', it becomes necessary to mention the political and ethical context of the research itself. Isn't the exchange of information from field to researcher only in one direction? Might this be construed as a continuation of post-colonial relationships between privileged geographical centres and dependent peripheries?

While unequal power relations existing between different parts of the world are certainly a contextual feature underlying such research (after all, not every region can afford the resources required to conduct such work), I should also note that these circumstances are themselves a matter of considerable debate in the academic field.[4] As we shall see, several of the essays included in this volume (see particularly those by Turino (Chapter 9) and Guilbault (Chapter 10)) deal directly with issues of globalization; most of the others also acknowledge the context of international politics and capital in which the music is produced and disseminated. The authors contributing to this collection are by no means all Western (though they may, of course, be deeply immersed in the tropes of Western academia) and as the regions they investigate are not limited to those that have been subjected to European colonization, it would be an oversimplification to consider their research post-colonial. Nevertheless the ethical and political dimension of intercultural research is regularly drawn to the attention of students and investigators involved in this kind of investigation.

For the purposes of this collection, it has been important to balance geographical diversity with a range of thematic interest and stylistic approaches. I have also avoided overlaps with those other volumes in this series dedicated to particular geographical regions or to subjects such as 'roots music', which are clearly contiguous with the theme of 'non-Western pop'. Consequently readers will find that I have included two essays on music in Eastern Europe, four on Central Asia, five on Africa, three on the Middle East and another three on the Caribbean. Seven essays considering musics in Eastern Asia are included, although this is itself an enormous geographical space. South America has only one representative essay although Latin American popular musics will be found in many other volumes in this series. Although most continents and many approaches have been included here, it should be remembered that the focus of this collection is upon Anglophone sources and that the range of scholarly writing available in the English language is not evenly distributed across all regions of the world. Historically, the emergence of the academic study of other cultures roughly parallels the development of other colonial interests in the late nineteenth century. In our (arguably) post-colonial world, such linguistic and cultural connections retain strong historical links, and so there is a tendency for research in the English language to have been carried out much more in some parts of the world than in others. For example, a good deal of published material is available on the popular musics of South Africa and Japan, as these countries have long been open to the documentation of their traditions by the academies of the West. Other regions that readers may notice are less strongly represented here could well be the subjects of considerable research carried out in French, Portuguese or Dutch, while little of academic value may have been translated into English. As this is a collection of essays that

4   See Barz and Cooley (2008), Feld (1996) and Stone (2008) for considerations of this issue.

have previously been published in English language journals, some effort has been made to cover the widest range of non-Western cultures, but readers should bear in mind that for the above reasons some geographical regions have been studied in considerably more depth than others. No compromise has been made regarding the quality and importance of the essays selected for this volume, however regions that appear to have been neglected here may well be thoroughly explored in other European and, indeed, indigenous languages.

Having established the objectives, context and some limitations of this collection, I would now like to consider some of the broader themes that form connections between individual contributions. Although, in the 'real life' in which music exists these elements are tightly intertwined it is nevertheless possible to identify the broad analytical strands of politics and identity, technology and globalization, that run through many of the writings collected here.

Pop, Power and Identity

It is has long been acceptable in academic spheres to concede that popular music has a political significance, if only (following the Marxist Frankfurt school of criticism) in that it serves as a smokescreen, masking the degree to which its listeners are held in thrall to the forces of capitalism. On the other hand, popular musics have frequently been employed in the crystalization of social movements of every kind, whether as nationalistic songs or in protest movements. Lily Kong's essay on Singapore (Chapter 4) serves as an excellent illustration of this kind of musico-political engagement. She describes how the state-sanctioned song book is parodied, not only undermining the government's ability to promote a nationalist discourse, but in doing so also drawing attention to unpopular or failed state policies. Martin Stokes also shows us, in a Turkish context (Chapter 1), how a young state struggles to contain musical material that is suggestive of ethnic or religious alterity. The very dislocated nature of recorded music from a specific time and space allows it to avoid censure while challenging a dominant regime, even though the explicit lyrical content itself may be vague or its meaning heavily veiled (see also Stokes, 1992).

Stokes's is one of several contributions to this volume in which we see how the very audibility of music can amount to an assertion of cultural difference. By extension it could be argued that *any* musical expression is to some degree an assertion of identity; an assumption of a political position that is in a discursive relationship with the prevailing political regime. In Chapter 8 Galit Saada-Ophir provides an example of music's role in negotiating multiple identities in Israel's borderlands, and Christopher Ballantine, in Chapter 7, looks at the relationship between pop and ethnic identity in South Africa. He argues that white musicians, alienated by ethnically divisive constructions of national identity, employed popular music to define themselves and critique state discourses. Stephen Blum and Amir Hassanpour observe in Chapter 5 that for the Kurds, an ethnic group without a state, music has played a significant role in simply positing a coherent sense of cultural identity. In Chapter 3 Donna Buchanan draws our attention to the strong links that can exist between national identity, popular music consumption and other areas of mass entertainment practices, while in Chapter 6 Ted Swedenburg focuses on Danna International, an individual performer who self-consciously embodies contradictory and ambiguous signs of identity. This example reminds us that while the technological dislocation of popular music facilitates its dissemination across cultural boundaries (in this case between Israel and Egypt), this transmission can also be highly transgressive. The most extreme illustration of the political repression of identity is provided by Stephen Mamula in Chapter 2, which shows how the Khmer Rouge effectively erased all popular music in Cambodia during the 1970s. In Pol Pot's Year Zero, popular music, alongside every other symbol of cosmopolitanism, was considered a corrupt influence and most of its practitioners were executed. Mamula explains how, a generation later, Cambodian pop has been rebuilt from pre-terror recordings.[5]

Global Perspectives

As popular music is typically disseminated technologically and is easily transmitted across borders, it is inevitable that the issue of globalization is common to many of the essays included here. Many explore the extent to which the world's most powerful regions exercise hegemonic influence over their weaker neighbours, or how 'local' musics might otherwise be drawn into the sphere of an international recording industry. In an important critique, Thomas Turino tackles the subject head on in Chapter 9 by questioning whether the concept of globalization has itself become too simple a concept in academic writing. He argues instead that as the precise 'scapes' and 'flows' of intercultural engagement are unique to any one context, the term 'globalization' should only be employed for the rare circumstances where the entire world is equally touched by a phenomenon. Elsewhere, the concept still finds traction, with Wai-Chung Ho (Chapter 11) and Brian Larkin (Chapter 13) looking at Hong Kong and Nigeria respectively. In each situation they demonstrate that despite the strong superficial influence of international musical forms, it is the local process of interpretation and consumption that remains most significant. In Hong Kong, Canto-Pop needs to be understood as existing in a specific cultural niche between popular music sung in Mandarin and in English. In Nigeria, Bandiri occupies a sometimes uncomfortable space between Indian music and Hasua traditions – Islam here serving as the common cultural factor. Other essays that consider the relationship between national politics and popular culture also discuss the extent of international cultural influence. Geoffrey Baker's essay on Cuban Hip-Hop (Chapter 12) provides an example of the adoption of 'foreign' protest music, employed here to address a local nationalist agenda. Here, not only is rap used to promote Cuba's revolutionary ethos, but the music is claimed as the *most* authentic form of hip-hop, asserting that the US version has developed away from the radical social critique with which it is associated. In each of these case studies, the immediate context has contributed towards distinct local meanings, despite the fact that the identifiable sound of the music has persisted. The song words, indeed the language itself, may have changed in the process of adaption, but the musical structures of the genres are still recognizable. In Chapter 10 Jocelyne Guilbault discusses the complex interaction between a Caribbean popular music and globalizing tendencies, but in this case she uses the example of Zouk to challenge academic assumptions about this relationship.[6]

---

[5]   Beyond this volume, readers might wish to further explore the relationship between political power and popular music in Averill (1997), Slobin (1996), Stokes (1992) and Tenaille (2000).

[6]   For other ethnographic studies of specific genres, see also Guilbault's book, *Zouk: World Music in the West Indies* (1993), Goodman (2005) on Berber popular music, Waterman (1990) on Nigerian Juju

Music Industries

Because of their presumed transient nature, popular musics have long been considered particularly more prone than other genres to technological and stylistic innovation. Consequently, many studies of pop, whether in a Western or non-Western context, have focused upon the mode of production. A number of essays included in this selection consider the interconnections between musical innovation and other media technologies. As Larkin shows in Chapter 13, Hindi film songs have been an important influence upon Nigerian Bandiri music, and in Chapter 15 Scott Marcus describes the cinema's impact on the relatively fixed canon of melodies employed in North Indian folk music (see also Dudrah and Desai, 2008). Each melody, we are told, has traditionally served as a signifier of a particular caste, social event or gender, so when new song words are put to these melodies a tension is created between linguistic and musical meanings. Marcus explains that although melodies adopted from film music are relatively poor in extra-musical references, musicians nevertheless strive to incorporate them into their performances. In Chapter 14 Peter Manuel discusses the musical changes brought about in India by the introduction of cassette production technology. In practice, cassettes devolved control over musical reproduction from large international companies such as HMV to local micro-producers. This resulted in a growth of pop musics that employed minority ethnic languages and covered previously taboo subjects such as sex and sectarian politics. John Baily, in Chapter 17, stresses the central importance of radio broadcast networks in maintaining a popular music industry in 1970s Afghanistan, while in Chapter 19 Bart Barendregt and Wim van Zanten examine the impact of a range of contemporary media on Indonesian indie music. DVD piracy, music TV and the internet have all influenced pop music here, in a period where conservative religious views have clashed with a political impetus towards deregulation. Just as broadcast music seems capable of crossing all kinds of physical and moral boundaries, so it is itself increasingly bound to visual media such as films, videos, phone ringtones and games.[7]

Christine Yano reminds us in Chapter 16 that the music industry is not just a system for the production of songs and marketable performers, but to some extent also shapes its own audience. This Japanese case study explores the voluntary bonds formed between fan club and singers of sentimental *enka* songs, demonstrating that their extramusical modes of communication have much in common with other formal relationships, for example the duties observed between an individual and their family or employer. Although the artists' charisma is produced industrially in this case, the reciprocal obligations existing between performer and fan are both formal and emotional. Female music fans in Mali are the focus of Chapter 20 by Dorothea Schulz. Here she discusses the centrality of music in everyday conversations and networking between individuals. Although links between popular music, media, fashion, sexuality and commerce are far from unique to Mali, this case study explores the ethnic and gender aspects of fandom that are highly localized (see also Duran, 1995; Fairley, 1984; Racy, 1976; Taylor, 2000; Veal, 2007).

---

and Cyrille (2002) on Creole popular music in Martinique. Valuable discussions of non-Western popular musics, identity and politics include Al Tee (2002), Shade-Poulsen (1999) and Smith (1975).

[7]   For comparative material from the region, see Becker (1975), Luvass (2009) and Williams (1990).

Returning to Japan, in Chapter 18 Judith Herd observes the process of image creation in the pop music industry. She shows how, in a major televised music competition, even though the music itself is highly standardized and even very Western sounding, the performers' visual images and deportment still conform to traditional communicative formulae. Once again, the music itself might be considered just one aspect of the meaningful material that is available for the listener to interpret and enjoy.

Historical Approaches

In recognition of the fact that popular musics have a temporal as well as a geographical context, a number of essays have been included that describe historical periods, popular musics and local scenes that perhaps no longer exist. Such works allow a certain longitudinal perspective and also mark a gradual methodological convergence between popular music studies, ethnomusicology and historical musicology. Unlike the situation that prevailed throughout the twentieth century, all these academic approaches are presently concerned with both the cultural and the political contexts of music-making, and also with the retrospective appraisal of individual composers or musicians. In the case of Mamula's essay (Chapter 2), the disappearance of a Cambodian popular music culture is tragically poignant, and similar circumstances might be said to prevail in Baily's Afghanistan (Chapter 17) or in Blum and Hassanpour's Iran (Chapter 5), where sudden and extreme political shifts have placed the livelihoods, and sometimes the lives, of musicians in jeopardy. Popular music's potential to function as a potent political sign renders musicians particularly vulnerable and exposed to intimidation.

In Chapter 22 Gage Averill covers roughly fifty hectic years of musical and social change in Haiti, explaining how the concept of cultural authenticity was negotiated through popular music in the midst of the political turmoil that occurred during this period. Invasion by the USA brought musical innovation, but this music was tainted by resentment towards outsiders. The emergence of authentic Haitian bands has been marked by competition between class- and race-based social groups, making popular culture a battleground for alternative notions of identity. An understanding of these divisive issues and of the political context over such a long period provides an invaluable baseline for contemporary research and cross-cultural comparison.

In Chapter 21 Suzel Reily reviews the career of a single composer who was highly significant in the history of Brazilian popular music. Tom Jobim is widely credited as the originator of bossa nova, the 'new style' that transformed Brazil's soundscape in the 1960s.[8] This music drew upon established samba traditions, combining its rhythmic essence with a novel melodic approach and a distinctly languorous lyrical mood. Bossa nova is one of many examples (reggae and salsa are notable among these) where non-Western popular musics have come to be highly influential at a global level. Reily shows how, given a strong case study, a biographical approach enables the exploration of history, politics, ethnicity, and musical

---

[8]   See also Béhague (1973) for a discussion of this genre and Reily (2002) for her work on popular religious music elsewhere in Brazil. Another excellent biographical study is Virginia Danielson's book on the Egyptian singer Umm Kulthum (1997).

and technological development. While Gage Averill's case study considers somewhat similar issues with broader brushstrokes, Reily is able to link contemporary circumstances in Brazil directly to one person's musical journey.

Lara Allen, in Chapter 25, does likewise in her description of Dorothy Masuka's musical career in 1950s South Africa, when ethnic polarization effectively politicized all music-making. Describing Masuka's journey affords Allen valuable insight into the local music industry in the apartheid era. Historical and biographical accounts like these provide important case studies of musical dissidence, yielding valuable information that can then be compared to similar contexts around the world or with other periods in the same location. Their biographical nature shows the musician as a social actor, adopting strategies in response to shifting circumstances in order to maintain their creative freedom or simply to stay in employment.

In Chapter 24 Szu-Wei Chen describes a form of popular music from Shanghai that disappeared decades ago, swept aside by China's Cultural Revolution and since then largely forgotten. *Haipai* was a fusion of Chinese pentatonic melodies and lyrical symbolism, combined with Western jazz instrumentation and arrangements. It was not just another example of musical creolization, but also a multimedia genre in the contemporary sense as it featured prominently in the first Chinese sound films. Before the commercial culture industry moved to Hong Kong in the 1960s, Shanghai was China's centre of musical and media innovation. Chen's historical study reminds us that cultural flows are perfidious, perhaps especially where popular musics, which are not supported by centuries of tradition, are concerned. Political shifts, technological modifications or simple changes in taste can render popular musical practices obsolete overnight.

Yngvar Steinholt reminds us in Chapter 23 that academics and musicians sometimes share views about what is important in music. In the Russian pop he describes it is the literary value of the songs that is prized above other musical elements. Songs that have profound, well-crafted lyrics imbue the author with an aura of authentic artistry and this contradicts the predictability of much of pop's musical structures and the industrial mode of dissemination it is subject to after creation.[9] Gestural reactions against the music industry are frequent elsewhere in the world – Bob Dylan in the 1960s and the 1970s punk rock scene in the UK are examples of popular turns towards a musically simple 'authenticity' and against a musically sophisticated 'false consciousness'. However in this case, it seems that the regional emphasis on language can also be linked to folk aesthetics and values.

Conclusion

The scope of this collection is deliberately broad, in the hope that this diversity will allow readers to find their own ways to explore and find connections between popular musics from very different places and times. There are inevitably many ways of comparing these case studies other than the order in which they are presently organized, and each might be considered a starting place for further research, whether on a regional, theoretical or

---

[9]   Gronow (1975) discusses a similar field in Russian pop, but concentrates on its references to various constructions of ethnicity.

thematic basis. Many of the authors featured here have expanded their ideas into book-length publications, and the journals in which these essays first appeared are also invaluable resources. Researchers should also note that the amount of high quality online material provided by the *New Grove Dictionary of Music and Musicians* (www.oxfordmusiconline.com) and the *Garland Encyclopedia of World Music* (glnd.alexanderstreet.com) is growing steadily and often offers media-rich illustrations. The question of how non-Western popular musics are distinct from any other form is complex – relations between musical, political, technological and cultural spheres change constantly. What these examples provide are detailed snapshots of the circumstances prevailing at specific times and places. Taken together they allow us to comprehend the local significance of an increasingly deterritorialized cultural field.

References and Further Reading

Adorno, T.W. ([1947] Reprinted 1991), 'On the Fetish Character in Music and the Regression of Listening', in *The Culture Industry: Selected Essays on Mass Culture*, London: Routledge, pp. 1–29.

Al-Tee, N. (2002), 'Voices of Peace and the Legacy of Reconciliation: Popular Music, Nationalism, and the Quest for Peace in the Middle East', *Popular Music*, **21**, 1, pp. 41–61.

Alves, W. (2008), *Music of the Peoples of the World*, Andover: Cengage Learning.

Aubert, L. (2007), *The Music of the Other*, Aldershot: Ashgate.

Averill, G. (1997), *A Day for the Hunter, a Day for the Prey*, Chicago: University of Chicago Press.

Bakan, M. (2007), *World Music: Traditions and Transformations*, Columbus, OH: McGraw-Hill.

Barz, G. and Cooley, T. (2008), *Shadows in the Field*, Oxford: Oxford University Press.

Becker, J. (1975), 'Kroncong, Indonesian Popular Music', *Asian Music*, **7**, 1, pp. 14–19.

Béhague, G. (1973), 'Bossa & Bossas: Recent Changes in Brazilian Urban Popular Music', *Ethnomusicology*, **17**, 2, pp. 209–33.

Bennet, A. (2003), *Cultures of Popular Music*, Milton Keynes: Open University Press.

Blum, S., Bohlman, P.V. and Neuman, D.M. (eds) (1991), *Ethnomusicology and Modern Music History*, Chicago: University of Illinois Press.

Bohlman, P. (2002), *World Music: A Very Short Introduction*, Oxford: Oxford University Press.

Broughton, S., Ellingham, M. and Trillo, R. (eds) (1999), *World Music: The Rough Guide*, London: Rough Guides.

Cyrille, D. (2002), 'Popular Music and Martinican-Creole Identity', *Black Music Research Journal*, **22**, 1 (Spring), pp. 65–83.

Danielson, V. (1997), *The Voice of Egypt: Umm Kulthum, Arabic Song and Egyptian Society in the Twentieth Century*, Chicago: University of Chicago Press.

Dudrah, R. and Desai, J. (eds) (2008), *Bollywood Reader*, Milton Keynes: Open University Press.

Duran, L. (1995), 'Birds of Wasulu: Freedom of Expression and Expressions of Freedom in the Popular Music of Southern Mali', *British Journal of Ethnomusicology*, **4**, pp. 101–34.

Fairley, J. (1984), 'La Nueva Canción Latinoamericana', *Bulletin of Latin American Research*, **3**, 2, pp. 107–15.

Feld, S. (1996), 'Pygmy POP: A Genealogy of Schizophonic Mimesis', *Yearbook for Traditional Music*, **28**, pp. 1–35.

Frith, S. (1981), '"The Magic That Can Set You Free": The Ideology of Folk and the Myth of the Rock Community', *Popular Music*, **1**, pp. 159–68.

Frith, S. (1998), *Performing Rites: On the Value of Popular Music*, Cambridge, MA: Harvard University Press.

Frith, S. (2007), *Taking Popular Music Seriously*, Aldershot: Ashgate.

Gilroy, P. (1993), *The Black Atlantic: Modernity and Double Consciousness*, London: Verso.

Goodman, J.E. (2005), *Berber Culture on the World Stage*, Bloomington: Indiana University Press.

Gronow, P. (1975), 'Ethnic Music and Soviet Record Industry', *Ethnomusicology*, **19**, 1, pp. 91–99.

Guilbault, J. (1993), *Zouk: World Music in the West Indies*, Chicago: University of Chicago Press.

Hall, S. (1981) 'Notes on Deconstructing the Popular' in Raphael Samuel (ed.), *People's History and Socialist Theory*, London: Routledge, pp. 227–40.

Hartong, J.L. (2006), *Musical Terms Worldwide*, The Hague: Semar.

Hebdige, D. (1987), *Cut 'n' Mix*, London: Commedia.

Kubik, G. (1981), 'Neo-Traditional Popular Music in East Africa since 1945', *Popular Music*, **1**, pp. 83–104.

Luvass, B. (2009), 'Dislocating Sounds: The Deterritorialization of Indonesian Indie Pop', *Cultural Anthropology*, **24**, 2, pp. 246–79.

McMichael, P. (2005), '"After All, You're a Rock and Roll Star (At Least, That's What They Say)": Roksi and the Creation of the Soviet Rock Musician', *Slavonic and East European Review*, **83**, 4, pp. 664–84.

Manuel, P. (1988), *Popular Musics of the Non-Western World: An Introductory Survey*, Oxford: Oxford University Press.

Manuel, P. (1995), *Carribean Currents*, Philadelphia: Temple University Press.

Middleton, R. (1990), *Studying Popular Music*, Milton Keynes: Open University Press.

Nettl, B. (1996), *Excursions In World Music*, Harlow: Prentice Hall.

Nidel, R. (2005), *World Music: The Basics*, London: Routledge.

Olsen, D.A. (1982), 'Japanese Music in Brazil', *Asian Music*, **14**, 1, pp. 111–31.

Racy, A.J. (1976), 'Record Industry and Egyptian Traditional Music: 1904–1932', *Ethnomusicology*, **20**, 1 (January), pp. 23–48.

Ragland, C. (2003), 'Mexican Deejays and the Transnational Space of Youth Dances in New York and New Jersey', *Ethnomusicology*, **47**, 3, pp. 338–54.

Rasmussen, S.J. (2000), 'Between Several Worlds: Images of Youth and Age in Tuareg Popular Performances', *Anthropological Quarterly*, **73**, 3, pp. 133–44.

Reily, S. (2002), *Voices of the Magi: Enchanted Journeys in Southeast Brazil*, Chicago: University of Chicago Press.

Reynolds, S. (1990), *Blissed Out: The Raptures of Rock*, London: Serpent's Tail.

Reynolds, S. (2005), *Rip It Up and Start Again: Post Punk 1978–1984*, London: Faber and Faber.

Shade-Poulson, M. (1999), *Men and Popular Music in Algeria*, Austin: Texas University Press.

Slobin, M. (1992), 'Micromusics of the West: A Comparative Approach', *Ethnomusicology*, **36**, 1, pp. 1–87.

Slobin, M. (ed.) (1996), *Retuning Culture*, Durham, NC: Duke University Press.

Small, C. (1998), *Musicking*, Middletown, CT: Wesleyan University Press.

Smith, B.B. (1975), 'Chinese Music in Hawaii', *Asian Music*, **6**, 1/2, pp. 225–30.

Stokes, M. (1992), *The Arabesk Debate: Music and Musicians in Modern Turkey*, Oxford: Clarendon.

Stone, R.M. (2008), *Theory for Ethnomusicology*, Harlow: Pearson.

Tagg, P. (2009), *Everyday Tonality: Towards a Tonal Theory of What Most People Hear*, New York and Montreal: Mass Media Scholars Press.

Taylor, T.D. (1997), *Global Pop: World Music, World Markets*, London: Routledge.

Taylor, T.D. (2000), 'World Music in Television Ads', *American Music*, **18**, 2, pp. 162–92.

Tenaille, F. (2000), *Music is the Weapon of the Future*, Chicago: Laurence Hill.

Titon, J.T. and Fujie, L. (eds) (2008), *Worlds of Music: An Introduction to the Music of the World's Peoples*, Andover: Cengage Learning.

Turino, T. (2008), *Music as Social Life*, Chicago: University of Chicago Press.

Veal, M.E. (2007), *Dub: Soundscapes and Shattered Songs in Jamaican Reggae*, Middletown, CT: Wesleyan University Press.

Wallis, R, and Malm, K. (1984), *Big Sounds from Small Peoples: The Music Industry in Small Countries*, London: Constable.

Waterman, C.A. (1990), *Juju: A Social History of an African Popular Music*, Chicago: University of Chicago Press.

Williams, S. (1990), 'Current Developments in Sundanese Popular Music', *Asian Music*, **21**, 1, pp. 105–36.

Part I
Pop, Power and Identity

[1]

Islam, the Turkish state and arabesk

MARTIN STOKES

The relationship between ideology and popular culture has largely been discussed in the context of developed industrial societies, in which the ideologies that might be considered to have most bearing on society in general and popular culture in particular are capitalism and socialism in the context of specific nationalisms. On the Muslim peripheries of Europe, however, the situation may be different. The appearance of 'Islamic' motifs in Turkish popular music and the ambiguous but conspicuous attempts by a populist government in Turkey to control and co-opt this music over the last eight years suggests that Islam has also played a powerful role in shaping the experience of popular music in Turkey. The extent to which Islam constitutes an ideology distinct and separable from capitalism and socialism has been debated at length within and outside the Muslim world. It is clear that Islam has proved less of an obstacle to the development of capitalist economies than that of socialist economies (Rodinson 1977; Gellner 1981). It is also true that the collapse of world markets in the 1970s resulted in crises which reverberated throughout the Muslim world, in which a pristine and 'traditional' Islam has become a focus, in various ways, for resentment at the cultural and economic dependency of the Muslim upon the non-Muslim world. Islam projects itself now as a rival and ultimately superior alternative to the nationalist ideologies within which capitalist or socialist formations have been articulated. In Turkey, the dominant and competing discourses of nationalist Turkism on the one hand and Islam on the other have framed the terms in which Turkish social and political history has been seen in and outside Turkey. The popular music known as arabesk apparently defies both of these ideologies and provides a useful case-study of the way in which they operate 'on the ground', shaping the identities and strategies around which people organise their social existence.

Arabesk is reputedly the invention of one of its star singers today, Orhan Gencebay, whose record '*Bir Teselli Ver*' was the first to capitalise on the increasing availability of media technology and achieve mass sales (by the standards of the day) in 1970. The heroes and heroines of this music and its films are – in fact or fiction – labour migrants, representatives of a society in the grip of cultural and economic transformation, but at the same time powerless as outsiders to protect their sense of value and cultural integrity. Many of the singers are migrants from a remote and barbarised Turkish 'orient', the Arab speaking and Kurdish regions of south east Anatolia, who occupy the urban spaces between squatter town and metropolitan centres. The texts, films and remarkable personalities of the singers, many of whom are transvestites and transsexuals, play with markers of gender identity, emphasising the liminality and powerlessness of the subject. The musical language and texts celebrate an interior world of turbulent and violent emotions, in which the ultimate symbol of the pervasive themes of alienation and powerlessness is the junction of unrequited love and fate – the lover and fate inseparable in the distant, remote and genderless Turkish third person singular, *o*. The songs advocate a path of total inaction calling on their listeners to light another cigarette, pour another drink, and curse the world and their fate.[1]

These themes are familiar in the popular music, literature and films of many of the modernising states around the Mediterranean and Middle East, on the peripheries of world economic systems: in particular, we identify the figure of the migrant outsider, the cultural construction of an inner alterity in the context of national identity, an exotic and threatening 'other' existing within the cultural or political boundaries of the state, the obsessive portrayal of powerlessness and alienation, and the play on gender construction in societies which see themselves as too traditional to be fully or properly modernised.[2] In Turkey the statements made by this music in society which is predominantly Muslim, and in which an authoritarian state tradition is accustomed to prescribing and enforcing cultural policy, are inflammatory in the extreme. If the totalising claims of religious and statist ideologies are taken at face value, the mere existence of the music in modern Turkey is surprising. As it is, it has enjoyed enormous popularity over the last decade.[3] In this article I look at two questions: firstly, the way in which the Turkish state has simultaneously continued to condemn but also to co-opt popular music; secondly, the ways in which musicians and their audiences have responded to this. I argue that what makes arabesk particularly problematic, not just for observers, but for musicians and listeners alike, is the fact of its existence in a Muslim society.

The condemnation of music in the Muslim world is well known (see Al-Faruqi 1985), and Turkey is no exception. This condemnation relies on a few key, but entirely ambiguous passages in the Koran and the Hadith, and the association of music with drink, dance and sexual impropriety. In the Koran, music is not directly mentioned, meaning that it cannot be canonically forbidden (*haram*), but is equated with the voice of Satan (Al-Najm 59–61, Al-Isra 64), 'ludicrous stories' which divert the attention of the faithful from prayer (Lokman 6) and the whistling and clapping of idolators during worship (Al-Anfal 35).[4] The Hadith traditions of Buhari and Muslim are more explicitly critical of music. These traditions can be contested and the four principal schools of Islamic jurisprudence cannot condemn music on their evidence alone. This does not stop them from assigning music to the category of *mekruh*, things which are 'disagreeable' even though they are not explicitly condemned. Whilst the opinion of city and village *imams* (mosque functionaries) on the subject of music are widely known, and overtly acknowledged, their pronouncements do not carry a great deal of weight. Reform in the early years of the Turkish republic associated Islam with backwardness and the Ottoman past, relegating Islam to the domain of private morality. The main thrust of these reforms was directed at removing the web of local networks and hierarchies defined and articulated by religion which stood between the direct relation of the individual citizen to the new state. For the most part village *imams* do not constitute a powerful voice in village affairs. Being state paid and state appointed, with their promotion through the official hierarchy largely under the control of the state, village *imams* are usually young men from the immediate locality. In cities, mosque functionaries have a significant voice amongst the urban religious confraternities (*tarikat*), but one which is in direct and unequal competition with statist discourses propagated by the official media. Under these circumstances condemnations of music do not in practice carry a great deal of weight outside relatively limited circles in rural or urban contexts.

Muslim apologists for spiritual music (*sema*) argue their case in the context of the same set of verbal categories and rules of debate as their opponents. In other words, they acknowledge the condemnation of music (*musiki*) by Sunni orthodoxy, but claim that *sema* is not music, and provide Koranic evidence for the prophet's acknowledgement of the practices associated with *sema*.[5] *Sema* thus covers a wide range of musical and spiritual practices legitimised in this way, from the ecstatic bodily techniques of *zikr* to the highly formalised recitations of *Mevlevi* music and dance.[6] So two factors dilute the force of orthodox Muslim criticism of music. One is the lack of political and legislative power of Islam in the modern Turkish state. The other is ambiguities within the discourse which theoretically allow for the practice of music and the spiritual techniques associated with it as long as they are not actually called music.

The condemnation of arabesk by the ideology which officially continues to dictate Turkish cultural policy is also apparently total but riddled with contradictions and ambiguities. Arabesk continues to be banned from the official media airwaves as a 'foreign' music, even though European art and popular musics do not fall into this category. Arabesk is considered to be unambiguously 'Eastern' through its close relationship with Egyptian film music. Egyptian films enjoyed unrivalled popularity in Turkey as elsewhere in the Middle East, but were banned in 1948. The translations of their songs into Turkish was however permitted, and no legislation could effectively stop people tuning radio sets to Egyptian radio. Egyptian and Lebanese popular music consequently exerted a powerful influence over the development of Turkish urban popular music. Furthermore, arabesk apparently parades an orientalist sophistication in the use of sitars and rhythmic techniques learned from India *tabla* playing.[7] Its melodic constructs are drawn from the repertoire of Middle Eastern modal theory, known as the *makam*. Turkist ideology identifies this *makam* theory as a crucial element of the pan-Islamic civilisation which had swamped and debilitated Turkish culture and society. Music in the Turkist state was, in the opinion of early republican ideologues such as Ziya Gökalp, to be a mixture of 'uncontaminated' rural folk music and Western polyphonic techniques (Gökalp 1967). The official activities of the music conservatories and the state media are still orientated in terms of these goals, and arabesk is entirely excluded as a result.

The state has not however made any attempt to ban arabesk in its entirety. Its legislation concerning music only extends to the prohibition of performance and commercial recordings sung in Arabic and Kurdish. This means that arabesk thrives in the commercial market in the form of cheap cassettes, and the state broadcasting organisation, TRT, which propagates its own brand of purified folk and art music, is widely criticised for being out of touch with popular tastes. The state's legislation has extended at times to the withdrawal of the right to perform of a number of leading singers, mainly for 'moral' reasons. Since cassette sales do not guarantee a livelihood (as a result of cassette piracy), this has meant that a number of singers have been obliged to lead their lives in virtual exile in Germany. Following a sex change operation in Britain, Bülent Ersoy's application for a live performance permit was turned down, ironically under the Police *Vazife ve Salahiyetleri*

216   *Martin Stokes*

Figure 1. *Orhan Gencebay with sitar.*

(Duties and Authorities) Law in 1981, which controls stage performance by women, but is not applicable to men. Bülent Ersoy worked in Germany for eight years, whilst debate raged over whether or not this law could be applied to a transsexual.

Undoubtedly a less overt agenda in the exclusion of arabesk by the TRT is the fact that arabesk has pointed to migration and class issues as lying at the heart of Turkey's social and economic problems. State endorsed folk music deals in the official administrative units of provinces and sub-provinces, constructing differences primarily between regions (excluding the Kurdish regions of the East) in such a way as to continually assert that the only relevant divisions in Turkish society exist between regional groupings and not class. It is certainly true that regionalism did become politically divisive in the late 1970s, as chain migration led to regional specialisations in the labour market, and migrants from particular regions converged on particular localities in the cities. Political rivalries built upon these divisions (Keyder 1987, p. 206). However, the TRT's presentation of regionalism suggests a potential transcendence through the characterisation of regional difference in terms of a centralised style of musical performance emphasising the role of the *bağlama* (long-necked lute) orchestra, 'correct' Turkish pronunciation and vocal techniques associated with the microphone and recording studio rather than unamplified singing (Stokes, in press). Through this centralised style of performance, the state signifies its ability to transcend regional divisions precisely through the carefully controlled presentation of these constructed differences. In their exclusion of arabesk, TRT programmers and policy makers conform to the traditional elitist orientations of the Turkish bureaucracy, but they also identify the disruptive role that arabesk might play in the context of the TRT construction of regional identity. So there is a language of condemnation from the state, and an exclusion of arabesk from the official media airwaves, but together these do not add up to much. As a result, arabesk continues to dominate the commercial market. There are reasons for this ambivalence.

'Arabesk politics'

To a great extent Islam and the state tradition in Turkey are antagonistic, and mutually exclusive in their claims. Islam only recognises the existence of the Muslim community, the *umma*, in which authority is vested in the received word of God. Turkism recognises only the existence of the state, in which religion is a private affair, and authority is vested in 'the people'. Mustafa Kemal, the architect of the Turkish revolution and the political arm of Turkist theory from 1923 to his death in 1938, was working within a long tradition of bureaucratic reform which dates back to the Tanzimat era (1839–1876) (Heper 1985). In spite of this, his secular and Westernising outlook was resisted by many, for many different reasons. Turkey's role in the emerging cold war balance of power was accompanied by external pressure to establish a Western-style democracy. For an industrial bourgeoisie emerging from state tutelage and for the mass of landowning petty-commodity producing villagers this was an attractive proposition. The first free elections in Turkey in 1950 saw Mustafa Kemal's party immediately voted out of power in favour of a government dedicated to setting back the clock of the reforms, promoting economic liberalism and reinstating Islam at the centre of public life. Turkish politics have apparently oscillated between these two poles, with elected populist governments being periodically ousted by the military seeking to check the slide away from bureaucratic reformism and economic control in conformity with a pattern familiar in South American political history. This process culminated in a period of intense political violence in the late 1970s, and the most recent military coup in 1980.

Whilst the present government is tied by the 1983 constitution (engineered by the military) to the overt ideals of Kemalist statism, its politics are those of the free market. This political stance is held in academic, journalistic and popular discourses alike to account for the resurgence of both 'fundamentalist' Islam, and arabesk; both are aspects of what is often described as the 'hegemony of the periphery'. The Turkish state is seen by sociologists in Turkey, following a certain reading of the Weberian concept of patrimonialism, to be clearly bifurcated into a central bureaucratic state tradition and a 'traditional' periphery hostile to imposed reforms (Heper 1985; Mardin 1973). In this model, arabesk is clearly aligned with a reactionary periphery. With its cultural needs excluded by the process of reform, the periphery has developed a mixture of foreign music (easily available on Egyptian radio) and its own traditional cultural resources to create a music which answers its own needs – this argument underpins much of the recent Turkish literature on arabesk (Eğribel 1984; Güngör 1990). Because of the prominence that the music had assumed in the 1980s, I heard arabesk invoked as an explanation for confusion, cynicism and disorder in everything from the state of the Turkish language to the traffic in Istanbul. In particular, the politics of the Anavatan government are often described by its opponents as '*Arabesk politikası*' – 'Arabesk politics'.[8]

The equation of arabesk with 'the periphery' in terms of this binary model seemed to make a great deal of sense between 1985 and 1990. Press concern in Turkey with 'religious reaction' (*irtica*) and its links with leading members of the Özal government (Akin and Karasapan 1988) coincided with the religious content of many arabesk songs during this period. In many cases this religious content was more apparent than real. An *ilahi* (hymn) on a cassette by Fahrettin Karaardıç provided a striking, though unusual example. Whilst it bore little relation to any recognised genre of religious music, particularly the *ilahi*, it played with signifiers of religiosity in an obvious way. The opening invokes *Mevlevi* ritual through a slow rhythmic ostinato and a suggestion of the beginning of a *ney* (end-blown flute) improvisation. This gives way to an ecstatic vocal improvisation, whose vocal delivery owes much to *Mevlut* recitations, but whose formal outlines conform to the essentially secular genre of vocal improvisation known as *gazel*.[9] This is preceded by a spoken recitation of the opening lines, in which the fated and alienated nature of the human condition is outlined in a choking voice, implying extremes of torment. (Such spoken openings are characteristic of arabesk songs.[10]) The terms in which this is done can only be described as flagrantly un-Islamic, but the use of motifs which evoke the notion of Islam to a Turkish audience is unambiguous.

These motifs were even reflected in arabesk films of this period. İbrahim Tatlıses's film *Sevmek* (To Love, 1985) ends with İbrahim as a returned migrant who has squandered his family's wealth in the city singing *ilahi* in the central mosque in Urfa, the 'capital' of the south east. As in many films, fact, fictionalised biography and the film plot overlap: the 'real' İbrahim Tatlıses migrated from this province to Istanbul. The promotional material for this film drew attention to the fact that 'İbrahim Tatlıses sings *ilahi*' in captions which actually dwarfed the title of the film and information concerning the other actors. This religious theme was clearly considered a major selling point. Earlier arabesk songs tended to avoid the use of the word 'Allah', as if maintaining a coy distance from the suggestion that God is entirely to blame for man's situation by referring instead to the creator (*yaratan*), the writer (*yazan*), or the pre-Islamic (and therefore more secular) word for God (*Tanrı*). This reluctance has been replaced by a startlingly direct mode of address, reflected in the titles of a number of more recent songs, such as Ferdi Tayfur's 'Allahım Sen Bilirsin' (My God, You Understand, 1989) and İbrahim Tatlıses's 'Allah Allah' (1988).

Those who identified themselves closely with the bureaucratic traditions of the centre felt that there was much evidence to justify associating the Özal government with the cultural expression of reactionary peripheral forces in their society. Musicians working in the TRT with whom I discussed the issue pointed to the highly publicised attendance of the Prime Minister at arabesk concerts, the repeal of the ban on Bülent Ersoy, the use of arabesk tunes as electoral jingles,[11] and the appearance of well-known arabesk stars singing on prime time television on holiday programmes deemed special, and thereby exempted from normal rules by programmers who were seen to be bending with the political climate. Most recently, İbrahim Tatlıses sang an *uzun hava* (a free rhythm recitation that falls within the accepted folk repertory for SE Anatolia, examples of which he includes on all of his arabesk cassettes) on a special TRT holiday programme in 1990. For TRT musicians, this 'hegemony of the periphery' constituted a significant threat to their livelihoods. Many work outside of their TRT jobs singing in *gazino* clubs at rates – for single evening performances – which compare favourably with their monthly TRT salaries. Whilst peak time appearances as solo singers on TRT programmes do not earn them very much more money, they are essential to singers as advertisements for their skills in the commercial market (in many cases actually as arabesk singers), enabling them to command higher fees for their evening performances. This incursion of arabesk star singers into 'their' air space therefore did constitute a very direct threat.

This identification of the Anavatan government with arabesk was however seen in simplistic terms which obscure a much more ambiguous relationship. This ambiguous relationship was made clear in attempts by the Anavatan government to reform arabesk. In February 1989 a conference was appointed in Istanbul by the Minister of Culture and Tourism, Mustafa Tınaz Titiz, to attend to Turkey's musical problems. The final result was the official endorsement of a kind of arabesk which was purged of its grief and fatalism, literally 'arabesk without pain' (*acısız arabesk*). The results of the conference went no further than the official endorsement of the new arabesk, and the half-hearted promotion of a song created especially for the occasion by Hakkı Bulut and Esin Engin: the former an arabesk singer once but no longer in the public eye and the latter a successful composer of Western-style light (*hafif*) music.[12] The fact that this highly publicised conference took place at all, however, suggests a conscious attempt to reconcile diverging tendencies towards cultural policy within the Anavatan government which are not recognised by the centre-periphery model.

Radical analyses of the Turkish political economy have emphasised the continuity between civilian and military governments rather than their polar opposition. Keyder argues that the nature of military interregnums have been determined by the external circumstances of the world economy and the activity of foreign capital in Turkey (Keyder 1987). Towards the end of the 1950s the collapse of food export prices necessitated a period of import-substituting industrialisation which

Figure 2. *Ferdi Tayfur in Gulhane Park, Istanbul.*

occasioned an alliance between the industrial bourgeoisie and the military. This made the 1960 coup which replaced Menderes both necessary and possible. In 1980 a similar alliance took place at a time when sources of long-term foreign aid were drying up, and controls needed to be exercised over the work force in order to maintain the internal market. The economy during the military interregnum of 1980–3 was managed by the industrial bourgeoisie through Turgut Özal, who won the 1983 election (representing one of three parties which were allowed to stand), and subsequently became president, exercising power through puppet prime ministers, in 1990. The continuity between the military regime and the civilian government in the 1980s has been particularly apparent: that the Anavatan government should proclaim the overt ideals of Kemalist statism and also promote free-market liberalism should be seen as a logical consequence of the circumstances which led to the 1980 coup.

The 1989 music conference responded to this new alliance of Kemalist ideology and market forces. Much in arabesk undoubtedly appeals to the state managers, quite apart from the taxation on cassettes secured by legislation and action against cassette piracy in 1987. The lifestyles of the stars, often described in promotional material as the Kings, Queens, Princes and Princesses of arabesk, suggest possibilities of social mobility which are quite unrealistic for most of the population, and obfuscate the processes of class stratification which are continuing to emerge in modern Turkey.[13] At the same time, the Anavatan government is committed to the language of Kemalist reformism. In appointing a conference to reform arabesk (a task which had absolutely no chance of succeeding, particularly since its avowed aim was to remove precisely that component which makes it most attractive to its listeners, its 'acı' (pain)), the government made a gesture in the tradition of centrist cultural reform but ultimately endorsed the musical *status quo*.

The state is therefore in a strong position to pursue a strategy which manipulates the ideologies condemning arabesk to its own advantage. Musicians have to manage the gap between state policy and their audiences and at the same time to argue and justify their professional activities in ways which render them legitimate and meaningful. The total condemnation of arabesk by Turkist and Islamicist discourses puts singers in a difficult situation. Certainly, all singers have everything to gain from having their music marketed and consumed as arabesk, but they justify this association by distancing themselves as far as possible from the idea that what they are doing is 'just arabesk'. Because the positions occupied by singers in the music business are riddled with contradictions and ambiguities, the ways in which they do so are complex.

Musicians and audiences

Mustafa Keser is a successful arabesk singer in his mid-thirties, working every night with a band in *gazino* clubs, and producing solo cassettes every year. However he also draws an income from the TRT as a singer of Turkish classical music. For him, the similarities in the classical and arabesk repertoires pose particularly difficult questions. Both are closely identified with 'peripheralist' tendencies in the minds of critics and, as such, are considered to enshrine traditional Islamic values. Mustafa Keser, as he told me in an interview in September 1990, distinguishes carefully between the legitimate spiritual concerns of the classical sacred repertoire, and the legitimate secular concerns of arabesk. Whilst there is a significant overlap between the two repertoires, in the vocabulary of separation, loss and ecstatic abandonment, he is insistent that there is no more than a superficial similarity in meanings. In classical music, this vocabulary expresses a form of light flirtation between the singer and God, in the latter a separation between the lover and beloved. Distinguishing carefully between the two, the singer renders his arabesk more legitimate by identifying it closely with the *makam* theory of the classical repertoire. Whilst his performance, orchestration and production are those of arabesk, he points out that they are full of musical complexities, subtle modulations and so on, which distinguish his music – for those who are capable of appreciating the sophistication – from 'real' arabesk. This claim to musical complexity contains another assertion, namely that his music should not be criticised as irreligious. Many art music performers and theorists cite a chain of medieval Islamic theological and mathematical speculation in which music plays a central role. This 'science of music' (*ilmi musiki*) underpins the claims of proponents of *sema* that music has a role to play in the 'audition' of God in the spiritual quest. Keser's argument distances him from the blasphemous notion of using a religious vocabulary to articulate temporal and secular concerns, and at the same time, allows him to separate himself critically from the ideologically undesirable qualities of what he can describe as the mediocrity and commercialism of 'market' (*piyasa*) arabesk.

In common with Mustafa Keser, many arabesk musicians are able to identify themselves with other genres. Whilst the image of the singer elaborated in arabesk films is that of the impoverished migrant who finds fame through the 'discovery' of an innate, individual and untrained talent, the reality is more mundane. Well-known arabesk singers such as Bülent Ersoy and Zeki Müren have come to arabesk from art music, having received a thorough training in *makam* and the classical repertoire in established music conservatories. Many of their supporters continue to think of them as art music singers, even though the orchestration and production of their cassettes conforms entirely to the aesthetic of arabesk, with large string choruses and strong percussion emphasising *darbuka*, *hollo* and *def*.[14] For others, these singers have created a genre of 'arabesk-ised' (*arabeskleştirilmiş*) art music, singing pieces identified with the art music repertoire but in an arabesk manner. A number of singers, including Muazzaz Abacı, move with apparent ease from one genre to the other, maintaining their integrity as singers of art music, but singing arabesk whenever it is economically attractive or necessary. A number of the best-known art music singers move in and out of arabesk for reasons often associated with longer term career plans. It was particularly noticeable that when the debate over the stage performance ban on Bülent Ersoy was at its height in 1987, the singer produced a cassette simply entitled *Konseri* (Her Concert), with two sides of classical *fasıl*, instrumental *taksim*, and the entire apparatus of musical decorum and austerity associated with the art music style.[15] This undoubtedly strengthened the case for the repeal of the ban, following which Ersoy released a number of cassettes which have taken their place amongst the 'classics' of arabesk (*Süskün Dünyam*, *Biz Ayrılamayız*).

The relationship of arabesk singers with official TRT folk music is no less intense. Orhan Gencebay secured a highly prized place as a TRT trainee in 1967. He left the TRT to take up an apprenticeship with Ahmet Sezgin and pursue a career playing music which mixed art music song structures with rural folk and Western instruments, a music which, as Güngör has pointed out, allowed an entrepreneurial migrant bourgeoisie to appropriate urban leisure patterns in the *gazino*, and reflect on the rural lifestyles from which they had escaped (Güngör 1990, p. 60). Whilst the term 'arabesk' was first applied to Gencebay's individual development of this music, his position in relation to official musical hierarchies has been sufficiently strong for him to claim that his music has nothing to do with arabesk. His defiant, but somewhat ambiguous assertion that he is simply a composer and performer of 'Turkish music' (Gencebay 1990) maintains a claim to a legitimacy that he would not have if he were to accept that his music is arabesk – as it is perceived to be by almost everybody in Turkey. Because the TRT provides a stepping-stone upon which rural musicians can find employment and acceptance as musicians in Istanbul, Ankara and Izmir, many instrumentalists, singers, composers and producers have either had, or continue to maintain links with the folk music department of the TRT. Those who try to maintain a professional identity entirely separate from arabesk find it impossible to do so. Many of those who helped me with my research in Istanbul were TRT singers who identified themselves closely with the TRT critique of arabesk. At the same time, they finished their *gazino* shows with currently popular songs drawn from the arabesk repertoire, or folk songs which had become 'arabeskised' through association with particular arabesk stars.

The recording of commercial cassettes which are marketed as folk music invariably conforms closely to the production aesthetic of arabesk. This is a deliberate strategy. Folk music singers are obliged to produce recordings which satisfy TRT folk music conventions, employing 'traditional' percussion and ensembles of Turkish instruments. To save time and expense in the studio, two mixes of songs are made; one for inclusion in the TRT repertoire and the other for commercial distribution. The latter includes synthesiser, electric bass and an arabesk percussion ensemble. The first mix is sent to the TRT, who select the pieces that they can use for dubbing onto filmed 'concerts' in well known Istanbul beauty spots or instantly recognisable regional locations associated with the singer and the music. The second mix is sent to the recording company for distribution on the commercial market. In other words, the music is marketed as folk music and presented by the TRT as folk music, but is consumed, and often thought of as arabesk. When I asked people who their favourite arabesk singers were, their lists would often include the names of established folk music singers such as İzzet Altınmeşe, Burhan Çaçan and Mahmut Tunçer.

So there is enough ambiguity about what arabesk 'is' to allow singers and musicians to exploit the popularity of the genre, but maintain an identity which allows them to distance themselves from 'the market'. Even those with absolutely no claim to involvement with any other kind of music can describe their music as '*fantezi*' rather than arabesk. Definitions of *fantezi* by musicians emphasise solo instrumental participation at the expense of the string chorus and emphasis on verbal text. Exactly where the line is that distinguishes *fantezi* from '*koy*' (heavy) arabesk, is seldom clear. All arabesk features a degree of antiphony between solo and chorus instruments, and contains an element of musical material performed only by the instruments and not taken up by the voice. Here as elsewhere, genre definitions should be seen as strategies maintaining identities which allow the singer to involve themselves with, but simultaneously to distance themselves from arabesk.

States and singers are by necessity well versed in the art of self-justification. Whilst official ideologies condemn arabesk, ambiguities and tensions within these ideologies can be manipulated. As social anthropologists have frequently argued, the ambiguities within ideologies are a critical factor in their operation (see Leach 1970). Without the ambiguities, ideologies cannot 'breathe'. Audiences are in a very different situation. The ease with which people construct their identities in relation to official ideologies depends on their positions within the overall power structure of Turkish society. Arabesk is listened to by a mass audience which includes those at the bottom of this structure. Here I would argue that the force of Islamist and Turkist condemnation shapes and gives meaning to the very subject matter of arabesk: powerlessness. Popular music, in Turkey as elsewhere, 'articulates differing cultural realities' (Shepherd 1985, p. 95) and, to paraphrase Shepherd's point, permits the differing interpretations associated with a subcultural group, the music industry and the state. I will develop this point with a final, brief case study.

Okkan, a sixteen-year-old migrant worker in Istanbul from a province in the north east of Turkey, is an arabesk enthusiast working as an assistant in a music club whose owner I knew. Even when I had got to know him well, the fact that he, along with most other arabesk enthusiasts, had been totally deprived of any critical language with which to talk about the music, made his attempts to articulate his thoughts about arabesk awkward and often contradictory. Using language clearly borrowed from his boss, he would dismiss arabesk – 'it's rubbish', 'it's all made up', 'it doesn't reflect real events' – at the same time as he would talk at length about the songs, films, personalities around which he organised his entire existence. He would come back repeatedly to the point that his favourite singer, Burhan Çaçan, had been an *imam* – possibly meaning little more than that he had briefly acted as a functionary in a village mosque. I was clearly putting him in the peculiar situation of having to verbally justify arabesk. What emerged from this interaction, however, was a clear statement that arabesk mattered precisely because it could not be talked about easily, and that it mattered because it was making a statement about the human condition which had to be seen in terms of the claims made by Islam.

It was never possible to discuss music without being drawn into a discussion of frustration, irritation, boredom and obstacles to doing what one wanted. These discussions focused on the gap between the dominant ideologies and the social realities that they purported to explain. Accounts of the nature of this gap can be paraphrased in the following way. The cultural telos of the Turkish people as outlined by Mustafa Kemal has been perverted or undermined. Kemal envisaged cultural Westernisation and economic development progressing smoothly towards eventual integration into the multi-party democratic system of Western Europe. The end of this process, which constitutes one of the founding myths of the republic, would be EEC membership. Instead, it is argued, recent events in Eastern Europe have put Turkey's potential membership back thirty years, and a growing view exists in Turkey that EEC membership is a perpetually postponed sweetener used to maintain Turkey's policeman role for the Western powers in the Middle East. The scripturalist Islam of the Koran and the Hadith enjoins individual hard work, charity and justice and promises rewards in this world as well as the next. Many Turks argue that the entire Muslim world is in fact culturally and economically dependent upon the Christian West. Conspicuous and repeated failure in the Eurovision Song Contest and the international sporting arena sums up this relationship with the outside world in the most painfully embarrassing way. What is intended as a demonstration of the extent of Turkey's participation in an international arena is experienced as bitter humiliation and failure.[16]

Initially this irritated me. As a fieldworking research student I needed crisp, clear statements about the music and what it meant to my informants. Eventually it became clear that arabesk and these accounts of powerlessness were closely intertwined. Arabesk attempts to articulate exactly what Turkism and Sunni Islam fail to articulate and in doing so provides a non-discursive explanation for the state of powerlessness which many Turks believe to be their lot. In providing a narrative in which the protagonists of the songs and dramas are outsiders subjected to injustice at the hands of remote and manipulative objects of an ambiguous desire, arabesk provides what Weber described as a theodicy – an explanation for why things are not as they should be. A theodicy of this nature fills the gap between ideology and its apparent inversion in social experience. The use of religious tropes in arabesk emphasises its implicit commentary upon Islam as an ideology, and it is not surprising in this context that these tropes emerged at a time when public attention was focused upon the power of this particular ideology to challenge the state. Arabesk exists and means what it does to people like Okkan not in spite of but because of the totalising claims made by the official discourses of Turkism and Islam.

Conclusion

Together, Turkism and Islam have a number of significant implications for the experience of popular music in Turkey. Both ideologies exclude the other, and both contain significant and substantial contradictions and ambiguities in their pronouncements upon culture (through defining what culture is), and upon the role of music in culture. This has allowed the state to simultaneously formulate policy concerning popular culture, endorse the *status quo* and exploit the fact of arabesk's popularity. It has allowed musicians to negotiate an identity for themselves and make sense of what is in fact and in their perceptions a situation full of contradictions. For audiences, arabesk provides images and scenarios which elaborate a world turned on its head, in which the increasingly anomic conditions of Turkish urban life which Sunni Islam and Turkism totally fail to address can be rendered meaningful and shared.

Acknowledgement

Illustrations courtesy of Kervan Plakçılık ve Kasetçilik and Ferdifon Plakçılık ve Kasetçilik, Unkapanı, Istanbul.

Endnotes

1 The songs of Müslüm Gürses contain perhaps the starkest assertion of this message, indicated by titles such as 'Dertliler Meyhanesi' (The café of the afflicted), 'Bir Kadeh Daha Ver' (Give me another glass), 'Sigaramda Duman Duman' (The smoke in my cigarette), 'Yeter Allahım' (It's enough, my God).

2 Elements of these themes recombine in Algerian *Rai* and Greek *Rebetika*, in ways which bear comparison with arabesk.

3 Research carried out by the Turkish daily *Cumhuriyet* in 1987 stated that out of the 200 million cassettes produced every year by the Turkish recording industry, 150 million are

226   *Martin Stokes*

arabesk cassettes (see Güngör 1990). Figures are hard to obtain, and these should be taken as an extremely rough indication.

4 These verses of the Koran can be found in the Penguin translation under the chapters 'The Star' (Al-Najm), 'The Night Journey' (Al-Isra), 'Luqman' (Lokman), 'Al-Anfal'.

5 Evidence from the Koran and Hadith for and against *sema* is presented in Uludağ (1976). For European language summaries of the *sema* polemic, see Molé (1963) and Rouget (1985).

6 *Zikr* is the ritual 'mentioning' of the names of God. It is practised collectively at *tarikat* gatherings in sessions that may begin shortly after Friday prayers and continue all night. The *Mevlevi* are a Sunni *tarikat*, historically based in Konya but with a following in many Western Turkish cities. Their concept and practice of *sema* is closely associated with a regional development of the classical art music repertoire.

7 What is for its critics 'Eastern' is for its adherents 'cosmopolitan' (*kozmopolit*). Reyhan Dinlettir, bongo player for Ferdi Tayfur, demonstrated *tabla* rhythmic patterns and techniques on the bongo that he had learned from studying the *tabla* players on a Ravi Shankar video. For a number of arabesk musicians Indian classical music is considered the height of cosmopolitan sophistication. A promotional postcard of Orhan Gencebay shows him playing the *sitar*. Ali Osman Erbaşi (an arabesk producer and composer) told me that he bought a *sitar* from a 'penniless hippy' returning from the East to Europe, and was trying to teach himself by studying a Ravi Shankar video.

8 This paper was based on research in Turkey between 1981 and 1990. The Anavatan government was replaced in the 1991 elections by their right-wing rivals, the *Doğru Yol Partisi* (True Path Party) of Mr Süleyman Demirel.

9 *Mevlut* refers to the ceremony in which a poem

written by Süleyman Çelebi (dated 1409) was recited for the Ottoman sultans in celebration of the Prophet's birthday. Today it is an expression of popular piety, sung by professional '*mevlidhan*' at the death of prominent men in the community, and in the domestic gatherings of neighbourhood women. The term *Mevlut* refers to the poem, the ceremony and the birth of the Prophet.

10 The spoken introduction to '*Gariban*', recorded by Dündar Yeşiltoprak, music by Özer Şenay and words by Ahmet Selçuk İlhan, is typical in many ways:

'If I am a stranger (*gariban*) in this strange place, am I at fault?
If I wander in turmoil night and day, am I at fault?
If I am alone, am helpless and without hope, am I at fault?'

11 Küçük Ceylan's hit song from 1986, '*Seni Sevmeyen Ölsün*' (May they that do not love you perish) was reformulated and released by a number of pro-Anavatan arabesk singers as '*Özal, Seni Sevmeyen Ölsün*' (Özal, may they . . .) in the run-up to the 1988 election.

12 *Hafif* music is approved by the TRT and included in its programming.

13 Waterman concludes his study of *Jùjú* with a similar point. *Jùjú* 'simultaneously legitimates inequality and argues that all actors may become wealthy and powerful' (1990, p. 227).

14 Arabesk rhythm sections today consist of three core elements: the goblet drum (*darbuka*), a frame drum with a deep frame (*hollo*) and a tambourine-type frame drum with or without cymbals (*def* or *zilli def*).

15 The classical suite, consisting of instrumental improvisations (*taksim*), instrumental preludes (*peşrev*) and a sequence of songs (*şarkı*) in related *makam*.

16 In 1987, Turkey came last in the Eurovision Song Contest with no points, resulting in protracted media debates.

References

Al-Faruqi, L. I. 1985. 'Music, musicians and Muslim law', *Asian Music*, 17:1, pp. 3–36

Akin, E. and Karasapan, Ö. 1988. 'The Rabita affair', *Middle East Report*, 153, p. 15

Eğribel, A. 1984. *Niçin Arabesk Değil?* (Why not Arabesk?) (Ankara)

Gellner, E. 1981. *Muslim Society* (Cambridge)

Gencebay, O. 1990. Interview, *Boom*, January, pp. 34–5

Gökalp, Z. 1968. *The Principles of Turkism*, trans. R. Devereux (Leiden; originally published in Ottoman Turkish, Ankara, 1923)

Güngör, N. 1990. *Arabesk: Sosyokültürel Açıdan Arabesk Müzik* (Arabesk Music from a Socio-Cultural Perspective) (Ankara)

Heper, M. 1985. *The State Tradition in Turkey* (Beverley)

Keyder, Ç. 1987. *State and Class in Turkey* (London)

Leach, E. 1970. *Political Systems of Highland Burma: A Study of Kachin Social Structure* (London)

Mardin, Ş. 1969. 'Power, civil society and culture in the Ottoman Empire', *Comparative Studies in Society and History*, 11, pp. 258–81

  1973. 'Centre-Periphery Relations: A Key to Turkish Politics?', *Daedalus: Post-Traditional Societies*, Winter, pp. 169–90

Molé, M. 1963. 'La danse ecstatique en Islam', *Les Danses Sacrées* (Sources orientales no. 6) (Paris) pp. 145–280

Rodinson, M. 1977. *Islam and Capitalism* (Harmondsworth)

Rouget, G. 1985. *Music and Trance: A Theory of the Relations between Music and Possession* (Chicago)

Shepherd, J. 1985. 'Definitions as mystification: a consideration of labels as a hindrance to understanding significance in music', *Popular Music Perspectives*, 2 (Gothenburg and Exeter), pp. 84–98

Stokes, M. (in press). *The Arabesk Debate: Music and Musicians in Modern Turkey* (Oxford)

Uludağ, S. 1976. *İslam Açısından Mûsikî ve Sema* (Music and Sema from an Islamic Perspective) (Istanbul)

Waterman, C. 1990. *Jùjú: A Social History and Ethnography of an African Popular Music* (Chicago)

Discography

The following is a highly personal selection of Arabesk and 'popular' Halk and Sanat music from the last six years. An asterisk indicates that they are available as mostly German manufactured import CDs. Distributors in England include Turkish Language Books, Shacklewell Lane, London E8, who can provide a list of currently available CDs and order them rapidly from Germany, and Müzik Dünyası, Newington Green, London.

Muazzez Abacı, 'Vurgun'*
Bergen, 'Yıllar Affetmez'
Burhan Çaçan, 'Ayaz Geceler'*
Ceylan, 'Bırakmam Seni'
Emrah, 'Sevdim'
Bülent Ersoy, 'Süskün Dünyam'
    'Biz Ayrılamayız'*
Orhan Gencebay, 'Cennet Gözlüm'*
Müslüm Gürses, 'Gitme'
Mustafa Keser, 'Bana Kötü Diyen Diller Utansın'
Zeki Müren, 'Yağdır Mevlam Su'*
Coşkun Sabah, 'Anılar'*
İbrahim Tatlıses, 'Fosforlu Cevriyem'*
    'Allah Allah'*
Ferdi Tayfur, 'Allahım Sen Bilirsin'

[2]

Starting from Nowhere? Popular Music in Cambodia after the Khmer Rouge

Stephen Mamula

Introduction

To study the resilience of a people victimized by abject terrorism and genocide illuminates the power of culture. By "culture," I denote a traditional way of life, a rubric of familiar phenomena that include indigenous ritual, ideology, belief systems, and the spatial and temporal rhythms to which these systems move and integrate. Yet, also revealed in such a study is the power of cultural *change*—change fueled by a growing market economy, tourism, and affordable mass media and communication technology. At the crossroads of such dynamism lies present-day Cambodia, a postmodern nation utilizing centuries-old fishing and rice harvesting techniques alongside popular consumption of MTV and the Internet. Cambodia is likewise, and infamously, a nation recovering from years of war, political instability, and acute social suffering. A chief operative of such was the Red Khmer or "Khmer Rouge," a radical polity that methodically purged over two million Cambodian citizens between 1975 and 1979, including 90 percent of the country's popular singers and musicians.

This research examines processes of resurgence and re-indigenization of a people devastated by tyranny of the most brutal kind. It is a pertinent topic due the recent and not so recent state of global affairs, whereby indigenous peoples of Darfur, Palestine, Afghanistan, Iraq, Bosnia, and epically, the European and Russian Jews before them, among others, have all been violent targets of political hegemonies or sectarian groups that endanger, and in some cases decimate, vital expressive traditions.[1] Of these occurrences, Cambodia is one of the extreme. Under the leadership of Saloth Sar—a.k.a. "Pol Pot"—the Khmer Rouge government rigidly forbade all practices and institutions of indigenous culture. These included religious worship, marriage and family relationships, education, intellectualism and professionalism, artistic expression, fashion, cosmetics, displaying emotion, most conversation or verbalization, and any discussion of the past. In short, all forms of social and personal behavior not directly serving the strict tenets of revolutionary doctrine were judged treasonous and punishable by death.

Critical circumstances such as these trigger disruptions of expressive culture that prompt vital questions, most fundamentally: How is a nation's popular

Figure 1. Photos of condemned "enemies of the revolution,"
taken immediately prior to execution, circa 1978.

Figure 2. Toel Slang Prison ("S-21"). The central torture
and execution center during the Khmer Rouge era.

music practice, decimated by warfare and genocide, (re)constructed in the early 21st century? Do such conditions produce a cultural "tabula rasa," a clean slate upon which new economic and national policy (manipulated by capitalist priorities and widespread governmental corruption) is imposed on surviving peoples and their musical expression, with little resistance? What strands of pre-genocidal,[2] popular music culture do Cambodians experience today and how is it experienced? Additionally, to what extent have the contexts, demographics, and identifying values of Cambodian popular music been altered as a result of the country's past?[3]

I contend that electronic broadcast and consumer media, specifically that accessible to Cambodians since the mid 1990s (television, radio dissemination, compact disc, video compact disc, DVD) has been instrumental in regenerating indigenous culture; i.e., "re-indigenizing" a people to native expressive forms of music and dance. Throughout Cambodia in the past decade such technology, particularly television broadcasts and commercial video (either legitimate or pirated), has served purposes of circulating both traditional *and* popular musics, producing a degree of re-stabilization to the former and a syncretic conduit for the latter whereby vernacular, non-vernacular, native, and non-native styles are dynamically hybridized. Cambodia's rich, pop music culture of the 1950s and 1960s—itself largely a syncretic production of mass media—has been similarly rekindled, adding a further expressive layer to the current discourse.

These musical-technological conditions, added to the ironic complexities of the Khmer Rouge political genocide—in which both perpetrator and victim were linked through ethnicity, race, nationality, language, and even family—generate an exceptional investigative scenario with few directly applicable research precedents or theoretical models. Therefore, I choose to deliver this piece as an ethnographically-based historical account designed as a reference for further studies on the topic of human genocide and expressive behavior as applied to Cambodia, the Asian continent, and elsewhere.

In approaching these questions, I draw on ethnographic data personally collected in the Cambodian capital city of Phnom Penh, with a population of just over one million; Siem Reap, a much smaller, tourist-oriented city adjacent to the Angkorian temples; Battambang, a regional capital and the country's second largest city near the border of Thailand; and in various rural provinces, during the summers of 2004, 2005, and 2006. The scope of the study entails a diachronic time line, a before-during-after trajectory of Cambodian popular music culture with the Khmer Rouge era of 1975–1979 serving as the main reference or pivot point. Within this trajectory, I examine Cambodian popular music primarily as human experience; as performed, danced and listened to, identified with, ritualized, and spatialized by living cultural bearers in their indigenous land.

Definition

As applied to my research in Cambodia, popular music is defined as expressive performance culture that is secular, aurally/orally learned and transmitted, and communicated in the vernacular. It typically employs amplification with or without western electronic instruments, is commodified for a prescribed demographic or "market," and disseminated through mass mediated formats and technologies such as vinyl,[4] audio cassette, conventional (AM-FM) radio, and compact disc (CD). Additionally, visual imagery and, specifically, the moving image of music video is an increasingly defining—and possibly redefining—constituent of Cambodian popular music.

Historical Background

The historical lineage of Cambodian popular music is rich and multifaceted. Western musical instruments were introduced during the late 1800s by the French, who, as colonists or technically "protectors," established institutions for the training of Europeanized concert performers. Privileged Cambodian youth sent to be educated in France returned with popular chanson and cabaret music.[5] In the early 20th century, the people of the Philippines, by this time considerably Westernized due to Spanish and North American contact, provided a concert band of professional musicians to the Cambodian royal court, a gift that exposed and disseminated marching and brass music. From the 1930s, Caribbean genres such as rumba, cha-cha, bossa nova, tango, and others began emerging on Phnom Penh's dance floors. These genres, originating in the African diasporic South Atlantic, were diffused by sea trade to Manila. In the Philippines they were acculturated and soon rendered accessible via direct culture contact and (early forms of) mass media to neighboring Cambodians, who in turn, adopted these styles syncretically. Such music became known as *phleng Manil* or "Manila music."

Both economically and artistically, the most prosperous decade for pre-Khmer Rouge Cambodian pop music was the 1960s. Major popular musicians of the era included Sinn Sisamouth, Ros Serly Sothea, Pen Ran, Mao Sareth, Hudy Meas, and Sos Moth. Norodom Sihanouk, who ruled as the nation's king and later head of state from 1953 to 1970, was additionally an avid popular singer (recording prolifically), amateur saxophonist, and accomplished filmmaker—an identity that rendered him relatively tolerant of popular music culture and its industry underpinnings. Affordable consumer technologies such as the transistor radio and audiocassette, along with the rise of discothèques in urban areas such as Phnom Penh, galvanized interest in new music and dance styles. Access to mass-produced musical instruments such as electric guitar, bass, and drum kit further enabled popular music participation and the formation of indigenous combos of primarily Western instruments. Several Cambodian recording companies, such as Chan Chaya, Heng, Vann Chann, Wat Phnom, Chab Meas, and Nokor Beach were in full operation, as well as radio stations—the latter reaching high levels of listenership by the end of the decade. Supplementing indigenous radio transmission in Cambodia was Voice of America, which regularly programmed jazz and popular music, and United States Armed Forces Radio ("USAFR") based in nearby Saigon, now Ho Chi Minh City. USAFR streamed a continuous flow of Top Forty hits directed at American military troops deployed in Viet Nam, yet was likewise accessible, as was VOA, to Cambodians through the station's extensive broadcast range.

Though some French cabaret influence is heard in slow tempo ballads of this period, the most salient aspect of Cambodian popular music in the 1960s was a clear and pulsating rhythmic framework fueled largely by Afro-Caribbean dance. Dance rhythms such as the rumba, cha cha, and others were absorbed syncretically by the Cambodian public (more efficiently so, I maintain, due to the integral, *body-to-music* relationship inherently shared by African and Southeast Asian expressive traditions). Popular singers, such as Sinn Sisamouth, recorded many Caribbean-influenced hits. Re-issues of 1960s Cambodian pop songs feature numerous anthologies of these genres. Further evidence of Africanisms in Cambodian popular musics of this era may be observed in the adoption of dances such as the twist and the jerk (the former introduced by popular singer Chum Kem upon returning from Italy, where the dance was likewise fashionable). Significantly, what was beginning to emerge syncretically in Cambodian popular dance was a unique hybrid technique crossing African derived hip movement with indigenous *apsara* gestures of hand and upper body.[6]

In 1970, the relatively permissive Sihanouk government was overthrown by a military dictatorship—led by General Lon Nol—minimally tolerant of popular culture and music. Criticism of Lon Nol's corrupt practices could be heard in Cambodian song lyrics of the period, contributing to governmental censorship. More significantly, war with North Vietnam and a concurrent civil war with the Khmer Rouge, in addition to the half million tons of cluster bombs secretly dropped on Cambodia by the U.S. government, created horrific social circumstances that led to an erosion of popular music production and its media infrastructure until 1975 when it ceased to exist entirely.[7]

With the takeover of Cambodia by the Khmer Rouge in April 1975 came a strict banning of all popular music activity. During its regime, the Khmer Rouge was systematic and brutal in dismantling institutions perceived oppositional to revolutionary practice and ideology, including radio and television transmission, cinema houses, theatres, record stores, as well as nightclubs and discothèques. Crucially, an estimated nine in ten of all Cambodian musical

Figure 3. Jacket covers of 1960s Cambodian popular
singers. The male figures are of Sinn Sisamouth.

performers—vocalists, instrumentalists, instrument makers, and dancers—were
executed or starved to death by the end of the Khmer Rouge era. Survivors, at
various points, either fled the country as refugees, hid in seclusion, or in very
rare instances, survived by playing/singing revolutionary song.[8] Cambodia was
in complete shambles when the Vietnamese army defeated the Khmer Rouge
and seized control of the capital and government in early 1979. The concept of
"city" had been rendered obsolete through the firm agrarian strictures of Khmer
Rouge doctrine. Phnom Penh lay in ruins as survivors returning from forced
labor camps ("farm collectives") in the outlying provinces occupied gutted
buildings while battling hunger, disease, and extreme trauma.[9] Cambodia's self-
imposed isolation during the Khmer Rouge era rendered its aftermath all the
more horrifying to an outside world largely ignorant of the atrocities. Following
eight years of Vietnamese occupation and a temporary government brokered by
the United Nations (UNTAC), the "Kingdom of Cambodia" was reestablished
as an independent nation state in 1993.

Cambodian Popular Music Today

Present day Cambodia consists of lush rice paddies and equatorial forest criss-crossed by a desolate tangle of dirt roads, rusted, tin shanty houses, and swarms of motor scooters often carrying entire families. When arriving, a musical vitality is sensed as one enters the dense sphere of outdoor sounds produced by the radios of awaiting airport taxis, many with colorful CD jewel cases strewn on their front seats and dashboards. The CD format is the most universal mass medium in Cambodia, having surpassed cassette technology because of its ease of duplication, storage capacity, and efficiency in mercantile exchange both legal and otherwise. Single, album length CDs of indigenous popular music legitimately retail in stores for $1.50 to $2.00. However, pirate versions of the same CDs are abundant and sell openly to foreigners for half the retail price. Cambodians themselves may pay forty cents or less. The compact disc industry specializing in Cambodian popular music consists of a considerable network of production companies based in Phnom Penh and in the Cambodian diasporic communities of California and Rhode Island. These companies include Rasmey Hang Meas, Chlangden Productions, Cambodian Rocks, and Khmer Rocks. Because of greatly increased revenue expedited by Internet commerce (and the severe competition from local pirates it eliminates), marketing focus is aimed primarily at diasporic communities throughout the United States, Canada, France, and Australia. Cambodians typically utilize home duplicates of compact discs or pirated versions purchased locally in small bodegas or large, centralized, mercantile exchanges such as the Russian Market and Central Market in Phnom Penh.

As in many third world cultures with low literacy rates, visual communication plays an important role in Cambodia. Complementing the audio (music) CD is the video compact disc or "VCD" (compatible with DVD players but of lower resolution), which has similarly gained popularity due to its reduced consumer cost. I contend that the video component naturally appeals to the Khmers' highly evolved visual culture, as represented abundantly by phenomena such as the ornate architecture, sculpture, and general iconography of the Angkor temples, the living tradition of shadow puppet theatre, and in the profound spiritual and mythical world expressed through traditional court dance with its complex vocabulary of stylized body movements and gestures.[10] Moreover, for centuries, Cambodians were practitioners within a rich oral tradition of enacted folk tales and storytelling, a process that has reinforced cultural sensitivity to visual phenomena. These sensitivities have naturally facilitated adaptation to new visual mass media and as a by-process facilitated exposure to the popular music content (local, national, regional, and global) these media carry. Television transmission, largely returning to Cambodia in the mid to late 1990s, is

increasingly accessible also owing to its declining consumer cost, which consequently has enabled both an increase in private home viewing and is sustaining
ad hoc, communal TV viewing enclaves in both urban and rural locales. While
traveling through the Cambodian countryside, one sees a myriad of television
antennas sprouting from even the smallest hut.

Importantly, ample data suggest that mass media in Cambodia over the past
decade is serving the overlapping roles of "disseminating the popular," while
popularizing the traditional. Televised and VCD produced performances of
classical and court music (especially those featuring precious instruments not
destroyed by the Khmer Rouge), are common. Native classicisms, including
highly stylized vocal melisma, utilization of struck idiophones and specifically-
tuned pentatonic scales, and a seemingly timeless, non-dialectical formal quality
are prominent qualities of these performances. One of the most widely viewed
television channels, CTN—Cambodia Television Network—broadcasts a daily
menu of diverse musical and dramatic shows. During a several hour monitoring
period of CTN, one will experience an assorted stream of genres such as classical
dance with pin peat (traditional court instrumental music), disco, narrative folk
poetry, light romance songs in Karaoke format, mohori (folk ensemble) music, and, frequently, current cover versions of the vast 1950s–1960s Cambodian
popular song repertory.

Shown regularly over CTN is "Best of the Best," a taped, live music performance directed to a crowded Cambodian youth audience housed in a large
outdoor stadium. Typically, several of Cambodia's current popular singers, such
as Preab Sovath, Kio Pich Chandra, and Hem Sivom, perform imitative interpretations of Western styles such as disco, rap, power balladry, and innocuous
love songs with choreographed couple and ensemble dancing. Sponsored by
Pepsi and Angkor Beer, the production quality is high by Cambodian standards,
with featured singers paraded grandly in automobiles and motorcycles onto a
massive, smoke swept, proscenium stage beaming with spotlights and professional sound technology. Alternating with these elaborately staged pop song
and dance performances are dramatic presentations of traditional folk tales and
myths, often enacted by indigenous elderly to the rapt and highly interactive
youth audience. Such enactments of tradition are not intended as casual, interim
amusement but rather as self-contained historical narratives. They are delivered
allegorically, stressing deeply entrenched moral codes informed by centuries of
(Theravada) Buddhist teaching and native traditions of myth and animism.[11]
Video formats of such performances are widely available in Cambodian record
stores. Cambodian youths interviewed in Phnom Penh maintain that vernacular
and court dances, including the challenging hand, wrist, and head movements
of the traditional *apsara* dance (cultivated during the Angkor period, circa the
9th to 15th centuries AD), are learned by rote through watching VCDs and often

Figure 4. Iconographic carvings of celestial, *apsara* dancers
on the Angkor Wat temples, circa 12th century.

incorporated into popular social dance. Inversely, such performance broadcasts
enable Cambodian elders to reinforce their folkloric traditions while also accul-
turating themselves to current popular music styles. Thus, electronic mass media
is serving to re-indigenize both Cambodian survivors and youth by encoding
traditional folkloric practice, mythic history, and religious beliefs, and by disseminating both new and familiar—syncretic—flows that become dynamically
interpreted as native, i.e. "indigenous," popular expression.

Regarding a pure sound analysis of current Cambodian popular music it is
in the *compositional* process where the lack of resources is apparent. The period
of the late 1950s through early 1970s produced one of the most vibrant popular
music scenes of its time in Southeast Asia largely due to the idiom's openness to
musical hybridization. The natural beauty and phonetic nuances of the Khmer
language, along with indigenous musical pitch and rhythmic structure (featuring pentatonic scales and cyclic temporality) integrated organically with European harmonies, song forms, and African-derived rhythms from the Caribbean
and North America. Rich syncretic styles were beginning to establish solid roots.
Fueling this syncretic compatibility, I maintain, were the well-cultivated bimu-
sical skills of pre-Khmer Rouge musicians (equally versed in indigenous and
Western musics), as well as the kinesthetic orientation of these musicians and

Figure 5. Cambodian syncretic popular dance
incorporating *apsara* movement, July 2006.

their listeners to musical time as manifested through the direct human experience of drumming, dancing, and live performance. Consequently, hundreds of
finely-crafted popular songs were being composed by stylistically ambidextrous,
rhythmically insightful composers sensitive to the nuances of instrumental and
vocal timbre and performed by those sharing similar aptitudes.

Through its genocide, the Khmer Rouge effectively severed the creative link
between this rich generation of popular song composers—those possessing vast
professional experience and teaching skills—from the generation that followed.
The basic social experience of indigenous peoples playing live music to one another, vital for the transmission and maintenance of any oral tradition, remained
dormant in the immediate post Khmer Rouge period. Audio recordings primarily in cassette form did survive; however, the active production of innovative
syncretic styles such as those of the 1960s had been virtually decimated. As a
partial result, stylistically, current Cambodian popular music is dominated by
superficially diverse genres heavily linked to Western pop styles both current
and past. Several such genres are often associated and marketed through a single
artist. Arguably the most popular singer in Cambodia today, Preab Savath, has
appeared on CD covers in many guises: as a rural folk musician in overalls, wearing black tuxedo tails behind a piano, as an urban rapper in hip hop garb, and
as suave disco crooner swaggering with open silk shirt, to name a few.

Clearly, the diverse, constructed personas of such artists and their light interpretations of Western pop repertory have not yet matched the syncretic and

Figures 6 and 7. Current Cambodian popular
singer Proeb Savath in contrasting guises.

musical depth of earlier performers. Though some salient differences regarding tempo and mood exist among Cambodian pop today (for example, those differences between a romance ballad and rap song), a heavily derivative and homogenous sonic quality pervades, as most songs utilize highly clichéd, 1980s electronic textures such as synthetic drums and keyboard washes that effectively neutralize any uniqueness of style.

In addition to the homogenization of sound, censorship of lyrical content that includes profanity, critique of the government, and statements counter to the moral teachings of Buddha (a recent song about a Monk falling in love created much controversy), along with implicit codes of conduct and dress, also constrain a recovering popular music culture and its creative resourcefulness. Music as expression of political ideology is likewise forbidden in present day Cambodia, a reality that has helped galvanize a generation of politically active popular musicians in the diaspora. Some of these musicians are constructing oral histories of the Khmer Rouge through underground CD distribution in Cambodia, thus educating indigenous youth about a recent past of which they are rampantly ignorant. Long Beach diasporic musician Prach Ly has been rapping on issues concerning the Cambodian genocide since 2001. He addresses the history of the Khmer Rouge in "Power, Territory and Rice," which instantly sold several thousand pirated copies in Phnom Penh and garnered much underground radio play:

> It's about POWER, TERRITORY, and RICE,
> And of course that comes with a hefty price.
> Whenever there's WAR, there's always sacrifice,
> And it's usually the innocent who lose their life.
> They target all intellectuals, survivors.
> Prisoners often ditch their eyeglasses,
> Teachers try to pass as taxi drivers.
> No one was told who was running the country but ah,
> Only that those in power was call "Angka."
> Children's was brainwash into believing in them,
> They was taught that: "there's no such thing as parents."
> At camps, most executions occurred at night.
> Soldiers awoke prisoners suspected of any crimes . . .
> It's about POWER, TERRITORY, and RICE,
> And of course that comes with a hefty price.
> Whenever there's WAR, there's always sacrifice,
> And it's usually the innocent who lose their life.[12]

Conclusion

In summary, Cambodia's popular music culture virtually ceased to exist for a twenty-year period. From the early 1970s to the early 1990s, the country suffered through a succession of disasters: massive carpet bombing perpetrated by

American forces under the Nixon administration, the repressive government of General Lon Nol, the Khmer Rouge genocide, and finally a sub-continental war with the Vietnamese. The 1960s represented a high period for Cambodian popular music, producing a wealth of syncretic genres that have since become contemporary classics in Cambodia and are covered widely by current singers. Recently accessible technologies such as television, radio, CD, VCD, and incipient Internet, are actively and interactively exploited in the process of regenerating indigenous culture, providing a means for direct absorption and recreation, i.e. re-indigenization—of dance gestures and musical structure. Mediated popular music performance (and often live performance) is organically linked with traditional culture by its juxtaposition with ancient Khmer folklore and myths. Current popular music styles in Cambodia are superficially broad—drawing heavily on Western models—and compositionally weak, as a virtual generation of highly skilled song writers and singers were lost in the Khmer Rouge genocide, thereby critically severing an educational link between generations.

At the present time, multifaceted socioeconomic, political, and creative forces observably direct the flows and dynamics of popular music in Cambodia. Though mass-mediated musics serve both as a compositional reference for exploring new styles and to re-indigenize Cambodians to more historical ones, eighty percent of the nation's inhabitants are subsistence farmers and have little leisure time for mediated culture of any kind. Moreover, corruption is rampant at many levels of government and commerce, rendering a fragile stability to Cambodia's incipient constitution and the many options for cultural expression it presently enables. Due to these competing forces, the state of Cambodian popular music is precarious. There is great interest and enthusiasm among Cambodian youth, especially in urban areas, but the continued evolution of a vital, original, popular music idiom, once a flourishing reality during earlier decades, is uncertain because of the volatilities of national government and the economic forces it controls. It is hoped that through their natural skill, sensitivity, and resourcefulness, and with the aid of mass-mediated communication, Cambodian popular music bearers may continue to rekindle vital connections to their past and reestablish indigenous popular music as a unique cultural phenomenon.

The questions that remain are complex: If a nascent, indigenous pop music culture continues to evolve in Cambodia, what forms will it take? Do traditional Khmer music and dance continue to weave their way into mass-mediated Cambodian popular music, thus defining a hybridized incarnation that is recognizably Cambodian? How culturally independent will Cambodia be in years to follow, considering that, although its tradition is rich, the powerful cultures of its Asian neighbors, particularly China and Japan, along with those of the West, will continue to strongly assert their influences? And even if Khmer culture does resist conquest from outside forces, can its own internal struggles—nagging poverty, corruption, and a continuous potential for political unrest—be overcome to sustain the fragile new beginnings of a vibrant popular culture? Those answers will be revealed in the decades to come.

Manhattan College and Rhode Island College

Notes

[1] For other ethnographic research investigating relationships between music and war-politics-censorship, please consult Baily (2003), Misdaq and Baily (2004), and Pettan (1998).

[2] Due to the desperate conditions of the country under the Lon Nol military government of 1970–1975—largely affected through civil war and massive U.S. bombing during the period—"pre-genocidal" culture refers to circa 1968 and before.

[3] "Value" references the significance of a musical *process* to an indigenous people. This process is largely generated through direct participation in culturally informed music phenomena such as singing, playing a musical instrument, dancing, and body movement/gesture. To further clarify, musical *process* is often termed in the social science literature as "event," or "text." Rather than either (by turn, static, and formulaic) I prefer "process" as it underscores the dynamisms, both temporal and spatial, of musical expression. It is through these dynamisms that culture, and popular musical culture, evolve.

[4] Vinyl music recordings in this region of Southeast Asia, with its heavy tropical climate, were not as durable as elsewhere in the world. Moreover, phonographic technology was prohibitively expensive (Manuel 1988).

[5] Please refer to Sam (2005), and Sam, Roongruang, and Nguyen (1998).

[6] *Apsara* refers to the centuries-old tradition of Cambodian court dance, a genre that features over four thousand gestures of body movement. Its iconography remains on the temples of Angkor.

[7] For a revealing understanding of atrocities committed by the U.S. government in their Cambodian bombing campaigns, the reader is directed to Shawcross (2002).

[8] Such a rare instance is documented in Lafreniere (2000).

[9] Refer to Piersath (2000).

[10] For excellent discussions of indigenous Cambodian court dance, refer to Shapiro (1994) and Phim and Thompson (1999).

[11] Such myths are translated into English in Carrison and Chhean (1987).

[12] From Ly (2001).

References

Baily, John
    2003   *Can You Stop the Birds Singing?: The Censorship of Music in Afghanistan.*
             Copenhagen: Freemuse.
Barton, Cat, and Cheang Sokha
    2006   "Songwriters and Composers Rare in Cambodian Music." *Phnom Penh Post,*
             November 17–30, 15:23.

40 *Asian Music:* Winter/Spring 2008

Becker, Elizabeth
 1998 *When the War Was Over: Cambodia and the Khmer Rouge Revolution.* New York: Public Affairs.
Carrison, Muriel Paskin, and Kong Chhean
 1987 *Cambodian Stories from the Gatiiloke, Retold by Muriel Paskin Carrison from a Translation by the Venerable Kong Chhean.* New York: Charles E. Tuttle.
Chandler, David
 2000 *A History of Cambodia.* Boulder, CO: Westview Press.
Chon, Gina
 2001 "Hard Rap on the Rouge: A Pirated CD Stuns Young Cambodians about their History." *Asiaweek* (Hong Kong), April 20.
Cohen, Patricia
 2005 "If Cambodia Can Learn to Sing Again." *New York Times,* December 18.
Daravuth, Ly, and Patricia Shehan Campbell
 1991 *Silent Temples, Songful Hearts: Traditional Music of Cambodia.* Danbury, CT: World Music Press.
Lafreniere, Bree
 2000 *Through the Dark: A Tale of Survival in Cambodia.* Honolulu: University of Hawaii Press.
Lockard, Craig A.
 1996 "Popular Music and Politics in Modern Southeast Asia: A Comparative Analysis." *Asian Music,* 27(2):149–87.
Madison, Oliver
 2005 "Of Sounds and Survival—Khmer Music." *Freemuse,* October 28.
Madra, Ek
 2006 "Wartime Bombs Killing More and More Cambodians." *Reuters,* May 24.
Mamula, Stephen
 2006a "A Fragile Now in Cambodia: Returning Musical Expression to the Terrorized." Paper for the Annual Conference of the Society for Ethnomusicology, Honolulu.
 2006b "Musiking in Post-Genocidal Cambodia: Starting from Nowhere?" Paper for the Annual Conference of the Society for Ethnomusicology, Mid Atlantic Chapter, Baltimore.
Manuel, Peter
 1988 *Popular Musics of the Non-Western World: An Introductory Survey.* New York: Oxford University Press.
McKinley, Kathy
 2005 "Cambodian Popular Music in the Diaspora: Transnational Business and Imaginings of Home." Paper for the Annual Conference of the Society for Ethnomusicology, Niagara Chapter.
Medans, Seth
 2006 "Cambodian Leader Cracks Down in Bid to Solidify Power." *New York Times,* January 9.

Misdaq, Nabi, and John Baily

2004   "Music Censorship in Afghanistan Before and After the Taliban." In *Shoot the Singer: Music Censorship Today*, ed. Marie Korpe, 19–28. London: Zeo Books.

Muan, Ingrid

2001   *Citing Angkor: The Cambodian Arts in the Age of Restoration, 1910–2000*. Ph.D. dissertation, Columbia University. Ann Arbor: UMI.

Pettan, Svanibor

1998   "Music, Politics and War in Croatia in the 1990s: An Introduction." In *Music, Politics and War: Views from Croatia*, ed. Svanibor Pettan. Zagreb: Institute of Ethnology and Folklore Research.

Phim, Toni Samantha, and Ashley Thompson

1999   *Dance in Cambodia*. New York: Oxford University Press.

Piersath, Chath

2000   *Coping Methods: Personal and Community Resources Used Among Cambodians in Cambodia and Cambodian-Americans in Lowell, Massachusetts*. M.A. Thesis, University of Massachusetts, Lowell. Ann Arbor: UMI.

Piore, Adam

2000   "Hip Hop about Pol Pot: A Pirated CD Introduces Rap Music to Cambodia." *Newsweek* (International ed.), July 2.

Sam, Sam Ang

2005   "Cambodia." In *Continuum Encyclopedia of Popular Music of the World, Vol. V: Asia and Oceania*, ed. John Shepherd, David Horn, and David Laing. 167–71, London: Continuum.

Sam, Sam Ang, Panya Roongruang, and Phong T. Nguyen

1998   "The Khmer People." In *Garland Encyclopedia of World Music, Vol. 4: Southeast Asia*, ed. Terry Miller and Sean Williams. New York: Garland.

Shapiro, Toni

1994   *Dance and the Spirit of Cambodia*. Ph.D. dissertation, Cornell University. Ann Arbor: UMI.

Shawcross, William

2002   *Sideshow: Kissinger, Nixon, and the Destruction of Cambodia*. New York: Cooper Square Press.

Steedly, Mary Margaret

1999   "The State of Culture Theory in the Anthropology of Southeast Asia." *Annual Review of Anthropology* 28:431–54.

Turnbull, Robert

2004   "Music Rises in the Killing Fields." *BBC Music Magazine*, 42–47.

Discography

Ly, Prach

2001   *Dalama: The Education of the Lost Chapter*. Self produced and distributed compact disc.

[3]

Soccer, popular music and national consciousness in post-state-socialist Bulgaria, 1994–96

DONNA A. BUCHANAN

This article investigates how sports and popular music contributed to the forma-tion of national consciousness during the immediate post-state-socialist period in Bulgaria. Throughout the difficult summers of 1994 and 1996, Bulgaria's success in international soccer championships briefly restored hope, confidence and national pride to many. Significantly, during the championships musicians produced new songs that celebrated the home team's victories in language and musical styles that referred overtly to the nation's shifting position vis à vis the Balkans, the European Union and the western world.

Introduction

Shortly after midday on 12 June, 1996, I set off to attend a rehearsal of the Bulgarian National Radio's folk orchestra as part of my continuing research on traditional instrumental music.[1] I had just arrived in Sofia for a month of field-work and had not seen these musicians, many of whom were old friends, in two years. After initial greetings were exchanged I asked them when their rehearsal would begin. "We've already finished playing for today," they told me. "But what time did you start?" I asked in confusion, for usually this group rehearsed in the early afternoon. "Two o'clock," they responded. I looked at my watch. It was just 2.25 p.m. They burst out laughing at my bewildered expression. "We used to figure that we made the equivalent of $150.00 a month," explained one musician, "but now, with inflation and changes in the exchange rate, we're only making about $45.00 a month." "Therefore," he exclaimed, quoting a popular phrase, "so much pay, so much work." "If inflation keeps up the day will come when we arrive, greet other and go home," he continued. "We already spend more time commuting to and from work than we do working!" "Well then," I said, when the laughter had died down, "should I come back tomorrow?"

---

[1] This article represents a greatly expanded and substantially modified version of Buchanan in press, which is a more preliminary, conference paper presentation of the material discussed here. I warmly thank my research assistant, Andrew Granade, for his unstinting assistance with both articles.

2   BRITISH JOURNAL OF ETHNOMUSICOLOGY VOL.11/ɪɪ 2002

"No, we'll be in the recording studio," I was told. "Ok, what about Friday?" I persisted. "We're not sure if we'll work at all on Friday," they chuckled, "because it's the beginning of the weekend." "And Monday?" I inquired. "Better that you wait until Tuesday," they said, "because Monday is the first day after the weekend – and besides, there's a soccer game!"[2]

Democracy in Absurdistan

My friends referred to the 1996 EuroCup championships, in which Bulgaria had played Spain to a 1–1 tie three days earlier.[3] Now they were to take on France, and it was the musicians' hope that their team's performance would match its success at the 1994 World Cup tournament, in which Bulgaria took fourth place. The fact that my friends altered their rehearsal schedule to suit that of the EuroCup signified more than a weakening work ethic born of economic despair. Even leading government figures appeared to focus more attention on soccer than the severe economic hardship, skyrocketing crime rate and political instability that had plagued the nation since 1989. The parliament was currently engaged in a plenary session that called for the Prime Minister's resignation, with new elections to be held the following week. Yet even though numerous parliamentarians publicly proclaimed these events crucial to the country's future, they had completely suspended their discussions during the Bulgaria–Spain match and now proposed that a vote be taken on the matters at hand prior to the next phase of the championships, which Bulgarian National Television (hereafter BNTV) would air that evening. "The people", they said, wanted to watch the game – not the plenary session. Thus, at 7.00 p.m. BNTV interrupted its plenum coverage to broadcast a match between Italy and Russia while Bulgarian National Radio continued to carry the legislative proceedings.

"When will we put the future of our country before soccer?!" despaired my friend Tsenka Iordanova, a musicologist who was also my hostess during this short trip. "The economy is so bad that people can no longer take their children out of the city for a week's vacation, let alone to a Black Sea resort for an entire summer, the way they used to," she added. Inflation was rampant and, despite massive salary increases, costs of food and material goods continued to outstrip earnings. Whereas in 1989 a good annual salary totalled 4,800 leva, by 1994 20,400 leva was considered a poor wage, while a good job brought in 60,000 leva. Yet, by mid-June 1996, meat cost 500 leva/kilo, a bag of rice, 95 leva, a litre of milk, 40 leva, and a bottle of mineral water, 10 leva. Gas had become so prohibitively expensive that most people left their vehicles in their garages. The fee for an oil change was 10,000 leva, and this did not include the cost of the oil

---

[2] For a discussion of this anecdote as it pertains to the post-state-socialist history of folk ensembles in Bulgaria, see Buchanan forthc. b: Ch. 12.

[3] Unless otherwise indicated, general information on Bulgarian soccer and the 1994–96 international soccer tourneys is taken from my fieldnotes and a variety of websites listed in the References section that concludes this article.

itself, which was only sold in German marks. Pyramid schemes had wiped out personal savings and numerous banks had folded. Bread had all but disappeared from the marketplace due to an unprecedented grain shortage, prompting the cost of a loaf to rise from 18 leva to 22 leva in a single weekend. Worse yet, local experts predicted that another 23% price hike was imminent.

For many the "bread crisis", as it was christened, epitomized the abject failure of post-1989 economic policy. That Bulgaria, the purported breadbasket of Europe, was forced to import grain was simply unthinkable – even humiliating.[4] At the same time, the slow implementation of a democratic legal code spawned a large number of new millionaires seated behind the wheels of equally new, shiny black Mercedes, many the result of illegal activity.[5] This was "*krivorazbrana demokratsiya*" (crookedly understood democracy), said one friend, in which people believed that they could do as they liked, whenever they liked, giving little consideration to ethics or law, and this attitude had promoted criminal and mafia operations of every conceivable sort, from money laundering to trafficking in women. This was not "*svoboda*" (freedom), she added, but "*slobodiya*" (the abuse of freedom; licentiousness). In fact, the situation compelled one journalist, in a 3 July televised news editorial, to christen Bulgaria "Absurdistan", a particularly chilling comment given its etymological connection to the border republics of the CIS and its recognition of just how tragically comic life had become.[6] Thus, various political leaders broadcast their concern during the otherwise dead airtime separating BNTV's live coverage of the EuroCup semifinals (England vs Germany and France vs the Czech Republic). "Will we have bread on the tables? Will there once again be long lines on the streets?" one inquired solemnly, the last in regard to the interminable queuing for material goods that typified late socialism and the immediate post-Zhikov era. To my astonishment, a second speaker then actually apologized for discussing this and other unsavoury topics, specifically narcotics, "during the tense period between the two soccer matches".

---

[4] Some believed that the government was in fact importing, at a higher price, exactly those products that it usually exported in abundance at a lower price, as evidenced by the following anecdote. One musician related how a harvest worker from the agriculturally rich region of Dobrudzha (in northeastern Bulgaria) accidentally dropped his hat in a truckful of wheat destined for export. But a few weeks later, when Dobrudzha received a wheat shipment from the Middle East, he found his hat mixed in with the grain!

[5] One friend laughingly remarked that even though the economy was in shreds, there were still more people driving Mercedes in Sofia than in New York City. And even though there was little money there were still many people earning it easily and in huge amounts. "Look here," he said, "in Bulgaria we've learned how to become richer much more quickly than in the States. Look how long it took you to become a rich nation – gradually, little by little, this happened. Here we have people who have learned in six years what it took you 200 to learn!"

[6] According to one friend, at some point in the mid-1990s the Bulgarian Socialist Party (the former Communist Party) approached the Russian government about incorporating Bulgaria as a successor state. Public outcry quickly quelled the idea, but the fact that it was even suggested adds another interpretative dimension to the "Absurdistan" remark.

4   B R I T I S H   J O U R N A L   O F   E T H N O M U S I C O L O G Y   V O L . 1 1 / ɪɪ   2 0 0 2

Sport, music and national consciousness

How was it that soccer, while always popular in Bulgaria, had now attained a significance so monumental that it induced employees to overturn work schedules,
the government to suspend its meetings and a political figure to excuse himself on
national television for discussing threats to the public's welfare near game time?
The early 1990s witnessed intense social transformation that redefined Bulgaria's
identity, public image and policy objectives, which included an array of joint
regional projects with other Balkan countries and, eventually, membership of the
European Union and NATO. In this respect, the public's insatiable appetite for
soccer, even when the home team was not playing, connected the country to a
larger European – and with US hosting of the 1994 World Cup – American orbit.
Like the American soap operas (namely, *The bold and the beautiful*) that some of
my Bulgarian friends consumed with relish, soccer provided a "point of contact
with a global audience for people whose capacity to travel [was] extremely limited", and a glimpse into relatively luxurious and glamorous lifestyles fostered
by the fantastic sums awarded to both sports heroes and movie stars (Stokes
1996:26). Mainstream Bulgarians embraced soccer as a cosmopolitan sport that
united them with a global community of fans (cf. Turino 2000:15). Moreover,
amidst the troubled summers of 1994 and 1996, they viewed the unprecedented
success of the Bulgarian team as effectively putting the emergent nation on the
map, briefly restoring a sense of national dignity and confidence in the process.
The team's victories were interpreted as an index of national progress, both in
informal conversation and in political rhetoric (cf. Rowe 1995:122).

In fact, so strongly were soccer wins equated with the debut of post-1989
Bulgaria on the world stage that pop music artists began enshrining the team's
achievements in new songs composed specially for the game of the day. In their
romanticized account of star players' epochal feats and of sporting conflict
between nations, they were not unlike the historical ballads of old. But these
new praise songs celebrated the role of young *voivodi* (legendary heroic chief-
tains or leaders) locked in a contemporary battle – that of winning the respect
and recognition of those superpowers whose political systems and free market
economies Bulgaria now struggled to emulate. In so doing they utilized language and musical styles that referred overtly to the nation's ongoing identity
transformation and its shifting position *vis à vis* the Balkans, the European
Union to which it aspired and the western world, for which the USA was
employed as an especially potent symbol.

Specifically, the songs' styling reflected the increasingly cosmopolitan nature
of post-socialist popular music and Bulgarian life in general. Some pointed to
older traditions of *estrada* (light socialist pop performed by bands employed by
the state radio and recording industries), the cabaret, or lyrical, early twentieth-
century urban song. Others were rock songs similar to American "top 40" hits. A
large number, however, illustrated new ethnopop (*etno-pop*) trends, or popular
music combining the electrified instrumentation (especially bass, electronic keyboard, synthesizers and electronic drums) and technology of western European
and American pop with stylistic elements of local Balkan ethnic musics. As I
have written elsewhere (Buchanan forthc. a, b), Bulgarian ethnopop is a large

and diffuse category that arose in tandem with glasnost and perestroika in the mid-1980s, began to dominate the popular music scene in the early and mid-1990s, and embraces a number of sub-genres, many of which have analogues in other Balkan nations. Some of these sub-genres include the jazz-oriented wedding music (*svatbarska muzika*) promoted first by clarinetist Ivo Papazov and his band, "Trakiya"; rock songs incorporating traditional instruments or singing styles for a bit of local colour; techno and disco remakes of earlier socialist folk ensemble repertory; "*avtorska Makedonska muzika*" (authored, or newly composed Macedonian music), or pop songs influenced by the folk and early twentieth-century urban song traditions of the Pirin–Macedonia region of southwestern Bulgaria and the Republic of Macedonia; and, most notably, "*chalga*" or "*popfolk*" (pop folk), which draws on Rom musicianship and Middle Eastern – especially Turkish – modes, rhythms and performance idioms.[7] The widespread popularity of ethnopop, and particularly the latter two sub-genres, is important not just as a marker of post-socialism, but also because it signifies, among Bulgarians, an emergent sense of regional Balkan consciousness within the European continent.

This article therefore analyses the convergence of two powerful expressive discourses, sports and popular music, as they relate to the continuing formation of national consciousness during Bulgaria's immediate post-state-socialist period. As David Rowe has observed (1995:122), the politics germane to both of these discourses may "support or undermine structures of power that are deeply embedded in our practical consciousness" and assist in the "everyday construction of ideologies" through which "dominant groups seek to symbolize and naturalize their power". In this case, what we will find is that the new songs aided the mythologization of Bulgarian soccer to promote an ideology of international dominance and hence, a more positive national image during a period of extreme domestic civil strife (*ibid.*:140). No longer was a sports team to symbolize the tough, athletic, well-muscled body image formerly prescribed by socialist realism, a testament to state-funded scientific advancements and an image also valorized as a militaristic symbol of the socialist nation's brute strength or technological might, for certainly, under Zhivkov Bulgarian soccer never achieved such acclaim (*ibid.*:126–27). Rather, this team was a testimony to free competition, and its players were the underdogs – the brave *yunatsi* (sing. *yunak*; heroes or champions of song and story) called upon to outwit their oppressor-opponents through courage, virility and sheer cunning.

USA '94

To demonstrate my remarks I will focus primarily on the 1994 World Cup tournament. At this time I rented a room in the well-appointed apartment in southern Sofia of a highly educated, middle-aged couple whom I will call Kalina and Asen. While Kalina worked as a prominent architect whose career included

---

[7] On wedding music see Buchanan 1996, Rice 1994:237–60 and 1996, and Silverman 1989; on "authored Macedonian music" see Buchanan 1999 and Peters 2000; on "pop folk" see Buchanan forthc. a, Dimov 2001, and Rice 2002.

6   BRITISH JOURNAL OF ETHNOMUSICOLOGY VOL.11/ıı 2002

several of the city's trademark buildings, during my stay Asen was at home recovering from a knife wound sustained one night a few weeks before my arrival, when a pair of thugs assaulted him to steal his gold neck chain as he walked home from the nearby tram stop. As we talked it soon became clear that Asen was as much psychologically as physically debilitated by this attack. In fact, for him the mugging had become a profound personal symbol of the social disintegration that he saw around him and of his own increasing disempowerment as the totalitarian state dissolved. Although he had voted for "the democrats" (i.e., the Union of Democratic Forces party, or UDF) and attended their meetings, he now believed that democracy was ruining the country. Echoing the observations of my other friends, he cited as evidence inflation, the hoarding of scarce goods, the poisoning of household products like liquor and vinegar, a general decline in honest, courteous interpersonal relations, and, of course, crime. His own attempts to exercise his new-found civil rights after the mugging had brought no results; the police would not even take his statement. For Asen this only confirmed that the new system did not work and augmented his feelings of helplessness in a culture that has always valorized overt displays of machismo and virility. "You should have seen me, Donna, I was out drinking every night with the most important people in the Party, every night at the Sheraton – at the Sheraton, every night with these people.[8] All I had to do was pick up the phone and I could make things happen." Once a powerful engineer, he was now, in his own words, "just an administrator".

By early July, as Bulgaria began to win steadily in the tournament, local papers dedicated whole sections to the country's participation, including endless armchair analyses of every play. Likewise, BNTV featured special programmes devoted to game highlights and interviews with key players, some conducted as they relaxed next to their hotel pool, to provide the public with a more intimate view of the team's activities and American life. Because the games themselves were broadcast live, many occurred in the middle of the night local time. But no matter what the hour, when a goal was scored or another victory won, the public (predominantly men – many of them drunk) spilled out into the street, yelling at the top of their lungs, leaning on their car horns, singing "Bulgaria in America" (a new pop song aired before each match) and shooting firecrackers or, worse, guns, into the night sky. The festivities strongly resembled older Balkan men's celebrations, in which alcohol consumption, singing, firearms and aggressive displays of emotion were typical.

Over coffee my friend Nora said that she found herself wondering how I, as a foreigner, might perceive the soccer hysteria. "Things are so difficult here," she explained, that soccer offers an "escape to a different reality, a kind of fantasy." "America represents a sort of paradise," she continued, and the fact that the team was succeeding there boosted national pride. "The soccer team," she said, "is carrying the weight of nationalism at a time when there are no laws against crime and people sense that anarchy is ruling their lives." Other female friends

---

[8] Asen refers to the Sheraton Balkan, the most exclusive hotel and restaurant in Sofia, and probably the country, during the socialist era.

agreed: Tsenka interpreted fan behaviour as a sign that Bulgaria was emerging from its "black hole of depression", while a third woman, the mother of a teen-aged son, emphasized that the team provided a healthy, positive role model with which young men could identify. The youths were thus "proud to call themselves Bulgarians", she said. The team's victories bound the country together, creating collectivity out of chaos by shifting definitions of "us" and "them", occluding local differences in favour of an overarching sense of unity. As Greg Downey (2000:4) observes for Brazilian *capoeira*, Bulgaria's "champions bore the nation in their bodies; the nation's accumulated skill and pugilistic knowledge resided in their athletic artistry and technical abilities".

"Ole-le, ole-le, ole-le": Bulgaria vs Germany

When Bulgaria met Germany in the quarter finals at 7.00 p.m., local time, on 10 July, 1994, the entire country held its breath. Germany was the former world champion and a European superpower whose lifestyle, technological savvy and reputation for efficiency Bulgarians admired to such an extent that they became the basis of two related maxims: *"Bai Doicho vsichko znae"* (*Bai Doicho* knows all) and *"Bai Doicho vsichko mozhe"* (*Bai Doicho* can do all), where *"Bai"* is a term of respect used to address esteemed older men and *"Doicho"* is a nominal gloss for "Deutsche".[9] But Germany was also the nation that had embroiled Bulgaria on the wrong side in World War II and which a few friends – Kalina among them – accused of arrogantly using their Black Sea riviera as a playground while simultaneously adopting a supercilious attitude towards the local population. There was much at stake.

As usual, in the days leading up to the game Radio Signal +, an innovative new station devoted to *narodna muzika* (folk or traditional music) of all sorts, aired several songs composed for the tournament. Such songs, as discussed above, generally reflected a wide range of styles, from rock to *estrada* (light socialist pop music) to rap to local ethnic traditions. Some went so far as to parody opponents by employing easily recognizable tunes or characteristics of their own national musics. For example, the song *"Adios, Meksiko"* (Farewell, Mexico) is accompanied by a mariachi band, while *"Ex, che vesel karnival"* (Oh, what a joyous carnival), which refers overtly to Mexico, sets new lyrics to the well-known Mexican song *"La cucaracha"* (Excerpt 1).

Many others illustrated the new *popfolk* ethnopop genre. My second example (Excerpt 2), which I recorded from Radio Signal + on the morning of the Bulgaria vs Germany game, falls into this category. The verses are chanted in rap fashion over a reggae beat. These elements are set to an accompaniment that combines electric piano, a synthesized drum track, electric bass and alto saxophone and that exhibits several prominent Turkish features. These include the ornamentation and wailing timbre employed by the saxophone, and the *taksim*-like solo improvisation performed on this instrument in *makam Hicaz* following

---

[9] My sincere thanks to Richard Tempest for bringing these expressions to my attention and for his many supportive comments on this article.

Excerpt 1 Part of *"Ex, che vesel karnival"*.[10] Text and arrangement by Mihail Shopov; performed by Asen Kisimov

La kukaracha, la kukaracha –	La cucaracha, la cucaracha –
Tozi tants i e poznat:	She's familiar with this dance:
Bŭlgari skachat, Meksiko plache,	Bulgarians jump, Mexico cries,
No tants i radost se priznat.	but [this] dance and joy are well known.
La kukaracha, la kukaracha,	La cucaracha, la cucaracha,
Pochne futbolniya bal,	The soccer ball begins,
Fenove skachat, ot radost plachat,	Fans jump, they cry from joy,
Ex, che vesel karnival.	Oh, what a joyous carnival.

Excerpt 2 Recorded 10 July, 1994, from Radio Signal +, Sofia; performers unknown

V devetdeset i chetvŭrta godina	In the year '94
shte ni sreshtne pak s Arzhentina.	We will meet again with Argentina.
Maradona shte bŭde Madona,	Maradona[11] will become Madonna,
i Stoichkov shte vkara tri gola.	and Stoichkov will score three goals.[12]
Na finala shte sreshtnem Germantsi,	At the final we'll meet the Germans,
no nali, sme polvin Amerikantsi!?	but we're half Americans, right!?
Shte napravim desant na vratata,	We'll make a landing on the goal,[13]
i shte vzemem prosto igrata.	and simply take the game.
USA, USA, USA,	USA, USA, USA,
Shampioni sme.	We are the champions.
Tsyal narod proslavikha futbolistite.	The entire nation celebrated the soccer players.
USA, USA, USA,	USA, USA, USA,
Shampioni sme.	We are the champions.
Tsyal narod proslavikha futbolistite!	All the people celebrated the soccer players!

---

[10] From *Peite s nas: haide nashte! Evro '96: 11 pobedni pesni* (Sing with us: let's go team! Euro '96: 11 victory songs).

[11] Maradona is Argentina's Diego Maradona, prohibited from competing in some of the 1994 World Cup championship games because of drug use.

[12] This verse predicts the potential outcome of games that had not yet been played when the song was produced. Ultimately, Bulgaria beat Argentina 2–0; legendary Bulgarian attacker Hristo Stoichkov scored the first goal. However, strangely enough, he scored a total of three goals in his team's victories over the teams in their tournament group before they advanced to the top eight competition.

[13] The implication of this line is that the Bulgarian team would make a parachute-like landing on the goal cage.

the chorus, each of which imitates similar techniques used by Turkish *zurna* and clarinet players. The text, which attributes the skill of the Bulgarian team to the fact that they are now "half-American", reveals the then widely held local belief that Bulgarians, now a free people, exhibited a fundamental affinity with Americans, and that the USA, as a champion of democracy, would extract Bulgaria from its current predicament. As one friend later remarked, "we had such grandiose illusions".

"Stoichkovsko horo"

While some songs glorified the entire team, others praised key players. *Orkestŭr Kristali*, one of two bands responsible for creating the *popfolk* style, dedicated an entire album to Hristo Stoichkov, who later became the tournament's joint-top scorer (six goals).[14] Like the previous example, the album's title song, "Ole, Stoichkov", exhibits Middle Eastern influence (Excerpt 3). The piece begins with a *taksim*-like solo sounded by synthesized strings, and during verses three and

Excerpt 3 "Ole, Stoichkov"

Barcelona zamina to –	He left for Barcelona –
mach igrae veche tam.	he already played a game there.
V Katalonskiyat otbor	In the Catalan team
toi ya stanal shampion.	he became a champion.[15]
Ole, pod ispanskoto nebe	Ole, under the Spanish sky
vsichki znaeme dobre	we all know well that
che Stoichkov za sega	Stoichkov currently
toi e futbolna zvezda.	he is a soccer star.
Radvame se ni sega	We're celebrating now
na sportmenska to igra.	at his sportsmen-like game.
S nomer osem na gŭrba	With number 8 on his back
pole Stoichkov na sveta.	Stoichkov threw himself on the world.
"Stoichkov," duma Malagu [?] –	"Stoichkov," said Malagu[16] –
priyateli sa edin za drug –	They're friends with one another –
"Vsichki v Barsa igraete –	"Everyone in Barca that you play –
chak zavizhda im Pele."	even Pelé[17] envies them."

---

[14] The dedication reads: "This album is dedicated to our beloved Hristo Stoichkov. We wish him and the entire national soccer team success in USA '94." Stoichkov's other achievements include Best European Player (1991–92, 1993–94), 1994 FIFA Footballer of the Year and Bulgarian Sportsman of the Year (1993–94).

[15] Stoichkov scored the single and victorious goal against Club Español, a second Catalan team, as a member of Barcelona's Club Barca in his September 1990 debut game.

[16] Indistinguishable – perhaps the name of a Barca teammate who also played for the national Spanish team.

[17] Brazil's legendary Edson Arantes do Nascimento, better known as Pelé.

10   BRITISH JOURNAL OF ETHNOMUSICOLOGY VOL.11/ii 2002

four this "orchestra" supplies brief interjections between phrases that comment on the vocal part in a manner not unlike the *lawazim* of Arab music or similar passages in *arabesk*, a Turkish pop music genre emulated by some Bulgarian groups.[18] In addition, flamenco influence is evident in the tune's modality and in the use of synthesized brassy trumpets preceding each verse, which impart the flair of a Spanish bullfight. Some of the group's members are Rom, and the vocal style (diction, timbre, inflection and ornaments) reflects Rom influence. While the Spanish elements can be interpreted as a musical reference to the fact that Stoichkov first achieved international acclaim while playing for Barcelona's Club Barca in 1990–95 and 1996–98, the incorporation of specifically flamenco influences illustrates that Bulgaria's Rom musicians recognize, and align themselves with, the music of other European Gypsy groups. This, too, is an important characteristic of some *popfolk* and speaks to a Rom musical circuit that transcends state borders.

Some may find it ironic that Bulgarians would so resoundingly champion a team whose starting lineup emigrated immediately after the 1989 collapse of communism to play for clubs in France, Portugal, Germany and Spain; indeed, in February 2001 Stoichkov landed a coveted multi-year contract with the USA's Chicago Fire, for whom he has played since March 2000 (Zoomsoccer 2001). However, such contracts only enhanced the players' appeal. The fame and prestige accorded them as national symbols derived in part from their ability to move into the western European (or American) arena and succeed there. They became a novel type of transnational guest worker, whose wealthy lifestyles and residence abroad typified the new Bulgarian dream perfectly. Just as basketball came to represent a way out of the inner city for many impoverished American youngsters, for the average Bulgarian soccer began to symbolize an exit, literally and figuratively, from life's problems. As yet another soccer song from the 1994 tournament states, "Now, when there are no visas/the USA is one to me/ Bulgaria is living in crisis/but it's still a soccer nation."

"Lilies" of many valleys

About thirty minutes before the Bulgaria vs Germany game began, BNTV programmed several soccer songs to heighten the public's anticipation. My next example, *"Zdravei, Lili Marlen"* (Hello, Lili Marlen), was one of these. As its title suggests, this work's melody is that of *Lili Marlen*, the controversial song composed by Norbert Schultze and popularized by Lale Anderson and Marlene Dietrich, among others, in German, French and English-language versions during the Second World War (alternative titles include "Lilli Marlene", "Lili Marleen",

---

[18] On *arabesk* see Stokes 1992.

[19] A diminutive nickname for Hristo Stoichkov.

[20] Bulgarian forward Emil Kostadinov. The version of stanza 3 presented in the text is that recorded on game day. An alternative rendition, released on a commercial cassette in 1996 (discussed below), reads: *"Itso be, pochakai,"/smee se Leche tam,/ "che ti lyubovnik si velik otdavno tova go znam,"/no neka i az sled zlaten pas/s gol krasiv, v mig shtastliv/da kazha*

Excerpt 4 "Zdravei, Lili Marlen". Text and arrangement by Mihail Shopov; performed by Asen Kisimov

Tam na stadiona	There at the stadium
v Nyu-Iorkskiya pek,	in the New York heat,
se vikhiri Maradona	Maradona is whirled
na 20-ti vek.	to the twentieth century.
Sreshta goreshta s Germaniya	Bulgaria plays a hot match
igrae dnes Bŭlgariya –	with Germany today –
igrae v yulski den	plays on a July day
za teb, Lili Marlen.	for you, Lili Marlen.
Krai starata laterna,	Near the old organ grinder,
pred nemskata vrata,	before the German goal cage,
znam shte stoyat nad tebe	I know that above you will stand
prochuti svetila.	renowned luminaries.
No moita levachka s ostŭr shut	But my left-hander with a sharp shot
shte gi napravi v mig "kaput",	will render them in a flash "kaput",
i moya v tozi den	and mine in this day
shte si, Lili Marlen.	will be you, Lili Marlen.
"Itso be, pochakai,"	"Itso,[19] be, wait,"
smee se Emil,	smiles Emil,[20]
"ne znaekh, che takŭv velik	"I didn't know that you were such a great
lyubovnik ti si bil,	lover,
no neka i za sled tvoya pas,	but let me, too, after your pass,
i moya sprint okichen s fint,	and my fancy sprint with a feint,
da kazha otkroven' –	say frankly –
'Zdravei, Lili Marlen'."	'Hello, Lili Marlen'."
Trifon pŭk zhelezni	And Trifon,[21] of iron,
shepne im vŭzglas,	whispers to them in a cry,
"Tozi pŭt momcheta, otnovo sŭm	"This time, my boys, I'm once again
sŭs vas."	with you."
A Berti Vogts si misli, "Znam,	And Berti Vogts[22] thinks to himself, "I know,
tez bŭlgari si nymat sram!	these Bulgarians have no shame!
Dano Lili Marlen spasi	Let's hope Lili Marlen
te v tozi den.	saves you on this day.
Lili, Lili Marlen,	Lili, Lili Marlen,
dano ostanesh ti pri men."	may you remain near me."

---

otkroven ... ("Itso, *be*, wait"/smiles Leche there,/"that you're a great lover I've known for a long time,"/but let me, too, after a golden pass/with a beautiful goal, in a happy flash/to say frankly ...). Here Leche is a diminutive nickname for Bulgarian forward Iordan Lechkov.

[21] Trifon Ivanov, Bulgarian defenseman.

[22] Coach of the German national team.

12   B R I T I S H   J O U R N A L   O F   E T H N O M U S I C O L O G Y   V O L . 1 1 / i i   2 0 0 2

Excerpt 5 Lili Marlen, verses 1 and 2. German lyrics by Hans Leips. (© By permission of the Publisher APOLLO VERLAG, Paul Lincke GmbH, Mainz; cf. Jackson 1979:10–11)

vor der Kaserne	In front of the barracks
vor dem grossen Tor	in front of the heavy door
stand eine Laterne,	stood a lantern
und steht sie noch davor,	and if it still stands there
so wolln wir uns da wieder sehn,	let's see each other there again
bei der Laterne wolln wir stehn	let's stand by the lantern
wie einst, Lilli Marleen.	as once, Lili Marleen.
Unsre beiden Schatten	Both of our shadows
sahn wie einer aus;	looked like one;
dass wir so lieb uns hatten,	that we love each other
das sah man gleich daraus.	that one saw it quickly as the same,
Und alle Leute solln es sehn,	and all people shall see it
wenn wir bei der Laterne stehn	when we stand by the lantern
wie einst, Lilli Marleen.	As once, Lili Marleen.

"The girl under the lantern" and "My Lili of the lamplight").[23] Its presence in the Balkans is explained by the fact that, once the German occupation of Yugoslavia was established, Radio Belgrade's director, Karl-Heinz Reintgen, incorporated it into the station's broadcasts to the Afrika Korps (Brock n.d.:2; Jackson 1979:21–2; see also Rhodes 1997).[24] It was transmitted nightly, just before the station signed off, as well as in response to listener requests and messages, despite the firm opposition of Propaganda Minister Joseph Goebbels (Jackson 1979:22–3). In that context the song's romantic lyrics and sentimental, cabaret-like presentation signified home, hearth, sweetheart, domestic bliss – the ideals for which every soldier fought. Here in the soccer war, however, the figure of Lili Marlen became a musical personification of the German nation – its feminine saviour, or muse – wooed away by the advancing Bulgarians and, especially, Hristo Stoichkov (see Excerpt 4).

It is also significant that the parody's character points to a second Bulgarian music trend popular at this time: a resumed interest in the "old urban songs" (*starogradski pesni*) that the socialist regime suppressed shortly after it came to power, and the creation of newly-composed popular songs, primarily from the Pirin–Macedonia region of southwestern Bulgaria, which display many of the same qualities (see Buchanan 1999 and forthc. b: Ch. 12). Many of the new "authored Macedonian songs", which were popularized at two major festivals called "Pirin Folk" and "Pirin Fest" in the early and mid-1990s, retain the lyrical

---

[23] The German version of the song may be heard on *Marlene Dietrich overseas: American songs in German for the O.S.S.*

[24] The Afrika Korps was a World War II German tank regiment stationed in North Africa under the supreme command of General Rommel. Radio Belgrade broadcast entertainment to troops in the Korps, to which residents of Belgrade and surrounding areas could also listen.

Excerpt 6 Lili Marlen, verses 1 and 2 (*The girl under the lantern; my Lili of the lamplight*). English lyrics by Tommie Connor and John Turner Phillips (from Jackson 1979:52)

Underneath the lantern
by the barrack gate
Darling I remember
the way you used to wait,
'Twas there that you whispered tenderly
That you loved me, you'd always be
My Lili of the lamplight,
My own Lili Marlene.

Time would come for roll call, time for us to part
Darling I'd caress you
and press you to my heart
And there 'neath that far off lantern light,
I'd hold you tight,
we'd kiss "good night,"
My Lili of the lamplight,
My own Lili Marlene.

melodies, dramatic vocal style and sentimental, nostalgic texts typical of the older genre, which itself was strongly related to similar urban songs found in turn-of-the-century Germany, Russia and old Vienna (cf. *Songs of old Vienna*). Thus the vocalist, Asen Kisimov, performs the soccer parody in the manner of a cabaret bard – now spoken, now sung – while the lyrics employ the romantic conquest of Lili Marlen as a metaphor for Bulgaria's sports victory. A comparison of the German and English texts (Excerpts 5 and 6) with that of the parody reveals further pertinent associations. For example, the English line "Underneath the lantern, by the barrack gate" becomes, in the Bulgarian version, "Near the old *laterna*, before the German goal cage". Here lyricist Mihail Shopov's use of the word "*laterna*" could be interpreted as a Bulgarianization of the English "lantern" or the German "Laterne", for the romantic image of an amorous rendezvous in the glow of a streetlamp figures strongly in both of the latter texts. However, the Bulgarian term for lamp is "*fener*"; "*laterna*" translates as hurdy-gurdy or organ-grinder, both of which are alluded to, musically and textually, in the contemporary Macedonian popular songs as a means of capturing the sonic ambiance of the country's "old cities", such as old Plovdiv.

Importantly, this is not the only contemporary use of this controversial tune in the Balkans. In conjunction with the 1996 EuroCup, "*Zdravedi, Lili Marlen*" was released on an album of soccer songs produced by Shopov (*Peite s nas: haide nashte! Evro '96: 11 pobedni pesni* (Sing with us: let's go team! Euro '96: 11 victory songs; see Figure 1)) produced by Shopov. The cassette includes a second parody, "*I pak zdravei, Lili Marlen*" (And hello again, Lili Marlen), which extols a second Bulgarian victory over Germany on 7 June, 1995 (Excerpt 7).

Figure 1 Sing with us: let's go team! Cassette liner for Konstantin Shopov's collection of 11 soccer victory songs, released in conjunction with the 1996 EuroCup championships

While the musical accompaniment of the latter version, rendered primarily on synthesizer, is exactly the same, Shopov altered some of the lyrics to accommodate the new situation. By this time the vanquishing Bulgarians had grown so strong that Lili Marlen deserted the Germans entirely.

According to Naila Ceribašić (1995:99) and Svanibor Pettan (1998:21), during the Yugoslav civil war in 1991–92 one of the two songs most frequently requested by Croatian soldiers was *"Čekam te"* (I am waiting for you), sung by a group of seven female actresses from Zagreb to the *Lili Marlen* melody. It was thus broadcast regularly on Croatian radio and television, particularly on "Gardijada", a TV programme for soldiers (*ibid.*). From Ceribašić's perspective, in this case the tune did not symbolize antipathy to Germany (or things German), but rather Croatia's self-identification with Western Europe and, hence, in the language of orientalism, with a more "civilized" society by virtue of its history within the Austro-Hungarian Empire and general geographic proximity to that area. This distinguished Croatia from its Serbian opponent, whose "oriental" past under Ottoman rule – once more in the gendered language of orientalism – was perceived as possessing uncivilized, brutish male behaviour (torture, rape, invasion, crimes against civilians) of which Croatia was the more feminine, passive victim. The song's nostalgic, sentimental properties, conventional German harmonies and legato character underscored this interpretation.

Excerpt 7 "*I pak zdravei, Lili Marlen*", verses 3–4 ("And hello again, Lili Marlen"). Text and arrangement by Mihail Shopov; performed by Asen Kisimov

Vitosha sinee,	Vitosha shines blue[25]
nad stadiona NAK.	above NAK stadium.[26]
Razvyava se pobedno	Victoriously waves
tri bagridniyat flag.	the tri-coloured flag.[27]
Sreshta goreshta s Germaniya	A hot game with Germany
igrae dnes, Bŭlgariya,	Bulgaria plays today,
igrae v yunski den,	plays on this June day,
za teb, Lili Marlen.	for you, Lili Marlen.
Itso, Lyubo, Leche, Krasyu –	Itso, Lyubo, Leche, Krasyu – [28]
Persiya kadril,	a Persian quadrille,
zhongliraha s topkata,	juggled with the ball,
poznati ya sŭs stil.	familiar with its style.
I Berti Vogts si misli, "Znam,	And Berti Vogts thinks to himself, "I know
te nyamat si ni strakh ni sram.	they've neither fear nor shame.
Zashto Lili Marlen	Why, Lili Marlen,
i dnes izbyagakh ti ot men?	did you flee me today, too?
Lili, Lili Marlen,	Lili, Lili Marlen,
shte pomnya dŭlgoto ti den.	I'll remember your long day.
Lili, Lili Marlen,	Lili, Lili Marlen,
shte pomnya tozi yunski den."	I'll remember this June day."

Pettan's findings provide additional insight. His analysis of Croatian war songs reveals that they may be divided into two categories, which he calls "official" and "alternative" (1998:19). These relate to two opposing approaches to the war that "served different, but almost equally important roles within the context of Croatia's defense" (*ibid.*:24). The former featured pre-existing songs associated with earlier conflicts, as well as new repertory. "Official" songs were well produced and professionally performed, and were disseminated widely through the mass media and music stores. Their refined lyrics, sung in Croatian and/or English to cosmopolitan, Euro-pop arrangements, cultivated positive

---

[25] "Vitosha" refers to Mt Vitosha, the highest peak in the vicinity and an important symbol of Sofia and its population. It overlooks the city and its central stadium complexes from the south. On a clear day it often appears blue-violet against the skyline.

[26] I believe that NAK is an acronym referring to a pair of stadiums that sit side by side along Boulevard Tsarigradsko Shose near downtown Sofia: the stadium of the National Army (*Natsionalnaya Armiya*) and the Kolodrum, or cycling arena. Both are part of a larger complex of sports bowls that also includes Vasil Levski Stadium, where many important matches are held.

[27] Bulgaria's flag features three broad stripes of, from top to bottom, white, green and red.

[28] These nicknames refer, as far as I can tell, to Hristo Stoichkov, Luboslav Penev, Iordan Lechkov and Krasimir Balakov, respectively.

Excerpt 8 "Čekam te" (I am waiting for you), final verse (Pettan 1998:21–22)

"Official" version

And the destroyed houses will be built again,
and every child will laugh again,
And our song will be heard everywhere,
because Croatia – that is all of us,
let love be our winner.

Alternative version

The day slowly replaces the night,
Chedo[29] was unable to pass the Bosut River,
He will stay dead in the cold Bosut forever,
while I live and defend my Croatia.

depictions of the Croatian homeland, mourned her suffering at the hands of an ambiguous foe, and appealed for peace. In music, text and image they aligned Croatia with Western Europe and petitioned the international community for assistance (*ibid.*:18–26). By contrast, "alternative" songs were produced anonymously for a domestic audience by amateur musicians and were distributed by *pirati* – street vendors associated with the sale of pirated recordings. Sung only in Croatian, in what Pettan describes as a "Balkan" style characterized by a more guttural vocal timbre associated with rural mountain communities, their belligerent, often coarse and politically problematic lyrics portrayed a military poised for action against the Serbian aggressors (*ibid.*).

"*Čekam te*" appeared not just in the "official" version described by Ceribašić but also in an "alternative" version which, from Pettan's perspective, parodied the former. His translation of each song's concluding stanza illustrates the sharply divergent approaches to the war signified by the two categories (Excerpt 8).

Given Bulgaria's immediate geographical proximity to the former Yugoslavia, it is quite possible that Shopov's soccer songs were inspired by one of these Croatian hits. The 1990s witnessed the increased dissemination and interchange of local popular musics within the Balkans through radio, television, live performances and, often, pirated recordings; Shopov's parodies might thus be indicative of these emerging regional circuits.[30] Whatever the case, the Bulgarian songs should be considered against the backdrop of the earlier versions and their accumulated militaristic associations. Indeed, there may not be a better example of how a single musical composition can unite diverse populations while simultaneously taking on local/specific – and even chauvinistic – meanings.

---

[29] *Chedo* is slang for *Chetnik*, the term used to describe Serbian anti-communist, nationalist forces during World War II.
[30] In fact, although I purchased my recording of 11 Bulgarian victory songs in a legitimate music store, it was a pirated version. The liner notes were duplicated to resemble the original

"*Chestita pobeda!*": Victory songs

At about 9.00 p.m., when Bulgaria's victory was assured, the entire country erupted in a celebration that lasted until well after midnight. Following local custom, which dictates that intense joy is expressed best through intense caco-phony, people cheered and fired guns from their roof tops and balconies. They set off firecrackers, blew into noisemakers and horns, activated car alarms and sang "*ole, ole, ole*" in the streets. Crowds dispersed up and down Vitosha Boule-vard, one of downtown Sofia's main thoroughfares, and thronged public squares. As they marched they chanted "*Bŭl-gar-ski, yu-na-tsi!*" (brave Bulgarian heroes; brave Bulgarian champions), employing the language of heroic ballads.

Meanwhile, back at the BNTV studio phone calls were placed to various players. President Zhelyu Zhelev addressed the nation, applauding the team on its accomplishment. Commentators began to speculate about the remaining games, even turning to the supernatural for guidance. The country's most famous medium, *Baba* Vanga, had predicted earlier that two countries whose names began with B would meet in the finals; the journalists now awaited her phone call confirming this prophesy.[31]

Music, too, was integral to the festivities. Wedding bands and folk ensembles performed spirited *narodna muzika* as congratulatory messages flashed across the bottom of the television screen.[32] To crown its coverage the TV studio invited a female vocal trio led by renowned folk singer Yanka Rupkina to give an impromptu performance of a hastily written victory song. This trio, whose other members included Yanka Taneva and Elena Kamenova, was modelled on an earlier group, the Trio Bŭlgarka, in which Rupkina had performed with Stoyanka Boneva and Eva Georgieva. Like the soccer team, the original trio symbolized a positive dimension of the political transition, for they had attained international recognition in the late 1980s while touring widely with the group Balkana (see Buchanan forthc. b: Ch. 10).

Perhaps to emphasize this relationship, the current trio presented new lyrics to a love song called "The *sedyanka* has been ruined", which appeared on the Trio Bŭlgarka's 1988 Hannibal Records release, *The forest is crying* (see Excerpts 9 and 10). In keeping with the times, the threesome performed the new version in a more contemporary, studied arrangement that featured the tradi-tional song melody, performed by Rupkina, over text fragments (derived from *tai, aide nashte, tai, tai*) repeated rhythmically by the remaining vocal duo, largely in major and minor seconds. Within a few days Radio Signal + aired the

---

wrapper, but the cassette itself bore no information whatsoever – neither title, performers, producer, distributor, date, nor even any indication of which side was A or B. As a commodity the cassette therefore speaks to the larger problem of copyright law infringement that has plagued the entire region, but especially Bulgaria, in the last decade.

[31] *Baba* Vanga was half correct, for Brazil conquered Italy to take the title. That journalists would incorporate soothsaying into their broadcast was a sign of the times, as local interest in the supernatural, strongly prohibited under Zhivkov, surged after 1989.

[32] This included a performance by Ensemble Naiden Kirov from Ruse and an amateur Shop folk ensemble.

Excerpt 9 Sedyankata ye na razvala, verses 1–2, From *The forest is crying*; performed by the Trio Bŭlgarka

Sedyankata ye na razvala,	The work bee has been ruined,
Edin dodi, drug si hodi,	One comes, another leaves,
Tai, tai, tai, i tai, byalo Rade,	*Tai, tai, tai, i tai,* fair Rada,
Tai, tai, tai, i tai, byalo Rade,	*Tai, tai, tai, i tai,* fair Rada,
Edin dodi, drug si hodi,	One comes, another leaves,
Tai, tai, tai, i tai, byalo Rade,	*Tai, tai, tai, i tai,* fair Rada,
Tai, tai, tai, i tai, byalo Rade.	*Tai, tai, tai, i tai,* fair Rada.
"Moito lube shtŭ li dodi?"	"My love, will he come?"
"Edo yego chiito ide."	"There he is, that's him coming."
Tai, tai, tai, i tai, byalo Rade,	*Tai, tai, tai, i tai,* fair Rada,
Tai, tai, tai, i tai, byalo Rade,	*Tai, tai, tai, i tai,* fair Rada,
"Edo yego chiito ide."	"There he is, that's him coming."
Tai, tai, tai, i tai, byalo Rade,	*Tai, tai, tai, i tai,* fair Rada,
Tai, tai, tai, i tai, byalo Rade.	*Tai, tai, tai, i tai,* fair Rada.

same piece in a more polished version whose new middle section interpolated a solo *bavna pesen* (unmetred, lavishly ornamented "slow song") performed by Rupkina over a similar vamp. The song's text was simple, pairing a few lines of praise (Victory! Let's go team!/Eleven young men/eleven on the field/They left for far away/to [disperse] their male strength/Like a whirlwind from the Balkans/like a wind above the field/May you be strong, may you be healthy/ courageous Bulgarian boys) with a repetitive chorus that was clearly based on the original work. The resulting arrangement sat at the juncture between socialist *narodna muzika* and post-1989 ethnopop trends, especially those which remake older folk ensemble repertory into rhythmic *"disko folk"* productions. Together with several other members of Balkana, Rupkina had been at the fore-

Excerpt 10 Soccer victory song (excerpt) sung by Yanka Rupkina, Yanka Taneva and Elena Kamenova. Composed 10 July, 1994, and performed on same day on Bulgarian National Television

Pobeda! Aide nashte!	Victory! Let's go team!
Tai, aide nashte, tai, tai,	*Tai,* let's go team, *tai, tai,*
Tai, aide nashte, tai, tai.	*Tai,* let's go team, *tai, tai.*
Edinaiset mladi momtsi,	Eleven young men,
Edinaiset po poleto,	Eleven on the field.
Tai, tai, tai i tai, aide nashte,	*Tai, tai, tai i tai,* let's go team,
Tai, tai, tai i tai, yunacheta,	*Tai, tai, tai i tai,* heroic leaders,
Tai, tai, tai i tai, aide nashte,	*Tai, tai, tai i tai,* let's go team
Tai, tai, tai i tai, yunacheta.	*Tai, tai, tai i tai,* brave youths.

front of the latter movement in the late 1980s; the trio's soccer victory song seemed an extension of this earlier style.[33]

By this time television journalists had mobilized in the streets. On the spacious plaza in front of the National Palace of Culture they strolled amidst the euphoric mob, interviewing the many celebrities gathered there. Here the power of sport to unite a diverse public by provoking national sentiment was strikingly clear. These "golden boys" have brought the nation together, remarked one person. "They've driven the whole nation to sing a national hymn" added another. An ecstatic journalist, likening the soccer victory to the birth of a new nation, shouted that Bulgarians would no longer celebrate the tenth of November (the day that former Premier Todor Zhivkov was deposed) but the tenth of July.[34] And, in a clear illustration of how "sport and nation" may "articulate with economic, technological, military, demographic and other discourses of 'development'", a second commentator observed that, given that Bulgaria was now a "*futbolna natsiya*" (soccer nation), perhaps in the coming years it would also become a "*tehnicheska natsiya*" (technical or technological nation) (Rowe 1995:136–37).

As for Kalina and Asen, they arrived home about 11.30 p.m., hoarse from yelling with the rest of town. "This victory represents a little joy in a country that has been completely beaten up by the politicians," Asen remarked. "All I could think about" said Kalina, taking me aside, "was that your relatives will now think to themselves, 'look at Donna in the great nation of Bulgaria!' Perhaps they didn't know where Bulgaria was before, but now they will know where to find it."

The next morning Asen spent two and a half hours telephoning his friends to wish them "*chestita pobeda*" (happy victory), now a household phrase both in casual conversation and official press. He used this sporting event as a means of pulling his social circle together, a metaphor of soccer's effect on the nation in general. He clearly felt empowered by the victory, which was as much an ethnic triumph over the Germans as a marker of international athletic prowess; in the post-game words of forward Iordan Lechkov ("the Bald Eagle"), "It always feels good to win . . . but to beat the Germans . . . is like a drug" (quoted in Klein and Hornung 1994). Indeed, Kalina observed that all day long, everywhere she looked, she saw men parading around with their chests puffed out.

In media interviews over the next several days President Zhelev echoed Asen's reaction and summarized the country's attitude, which I paraphrase here. The team's success was a success for Bulgarian soccer, for the Bulgarian nation and for the Bulgarian people. It had raised the public's confidence and spirits. In fact, through their playing the team had accomplished what diplomacy had failed to do: to situate Bulgaria among the world's most influential nations in a way that hundreds of millions of people would never forget. "We want our country to be recognized by the American citizens to whom we feel very friendly

---

[33] On *disko folk* see Buchanan 1995:406–7, forthc. b: Ch. 10; and Rice 1994:258–60.
[34] "*Nyama 10-ti noemvri, ima 10-ti yuli!*"

and open, and we want for the Americans to know where Bulgaria is on the map, at least on the football map!" declared Zhelev's foreign policy advisor, Carmen Vlichkov, in an interview with National Public Radio's Robert Siegel (NPR 1994). Importantly, Zhelev also attributed the team's accomplishment directly to democratic reform, for this allowed Bulgaria's best players to compete in Western Europe, where they gained experience and acclaim impossible under state socialism (*ibid.*). In fact, like many journalists at home, Vlichkov went so far as to equate the significance of Bulgaria's victory over Germany with that surrounding the events of 1989 (*ibid.*):

> RS: So, you're comparing, or commentators in Sofia compared, two momentous events – the advent of democracy and a quarter-final victory in the World Cup?
> CV: I say that these are comparable in terms of the emotional approach and the high spirits which the citizens of the Bulgarian towns and villages [have exhibited] throughout the country; [these events are] something that we expect to have an impact altogether on the very image of Bulgaria throughout the world.

To take advantage of the positive international exposure Zhelev therefore flew to the US for the semi-final competition.

All of my female associates also remarked, however, on the negative aspects of what they witnessed around them. Kalina noted that on the day after Germany's defeat every man in Sofia either went to work inebriated or did not go at all. Asen was no exception; he had arrived home in a highly intoxicated state and remained so for the next several days. As the hours of celebrating lengthened, the festivities took on an ugly tone; young men expressed themselves by engaging in acts of vandalism and assault: upsetting garbage cans, destroying public property and overturning cars, smashing their windows and then looting the contents. Tsenka described the mood on the streets as "dangerous", adding that the energy unleashed by this event was unprecedented in her experience. "I don't think the country can take another win," she laughed.

"This was a lesson for Germany," Kalina declared, repeating rumours that the German press had maligned Bulgaria in its pre-game releases, "but I can't understand celebrating by breaking things or hurting people." She worried that the victory had influenced people's behaviour adversely. It was as if all the resentment and frustration harboured by Bulgarian men, whose "self-confidence was completely stripped by the system" (and here I think she meant both by state socialism and its successor governments), had been cathartically released by the team's achievements in the world sporting arena. "When democracy arrived," she exclaimed bitterly, "everyone celebrated, screaming and yelling in the streets. Everyone expected that someone would wave a magic wand and change things overnight. This wasn't right, but it was what we expected."[35] When these expectations went unmet, many people gave up, feeling crushed and

---

[35] See Buchanan forthc. b: Ch. 1.

Figure 2 The 1994 victory parade approaches the city centre and Vasil Levski Stadium along Tsarigradsko Shose Boulevard

helpless. In soccer, however, men found a more favourable national image, and by assimilating this image – this metaphor of sport as nation – into their own personal identities, a new sense of self-importance became apparent in their very bodies. "I'm sure not one man will go to work tomorrow afternoon, even though the game [Bulgaria's semi-final match with Italy] will not begin until 11.00 p.m.," Kalina chuckled. "They'll prepare themselves for the match [i.e., drink, discuss odds]. And given this, if Bulgaria wins again our economic policy will amount to nothing!"

Parade of champions

Kalina need not have worried, for Bulgaria lost its semi-final match to Italy 2–1 and the ensuing consolation round with Sweden 4–1, falling to fourth place in the tournament. Nevertheless, when the players returned home at midday on 22 July they were treated like visiting royalty. At the airport journalists pointing microphones descended on them as they stepped off the plane. Time and again the press asked, "Your first words on Bulgarian soil?" and then added ominously, "All of Bulgaria is watching you at this moment". A brief ceremony followed. The team was then paraded through town in appropriately decorated cars and floats along a boulevard lined with cheering fans to a packed Vasil Levski Stadium (Figure 2), where a second ceremony and victory "megaconcert" featuring practically every soccer song produced during the tournament awaited them.

To begin the festivities the federal government and local businesses showered gifts on the players, contributing to their movie star images.[36] Hristo Stoichkov and Boris Mihailov were awarded cars – a red Volvo and blue-green Renault, respectively. Two other team members received apartments in Sofia. Every player received a gold medal, insurance, state pensions at a generous percentage rate and a week's vacation in Varna for themselves and their families. City officials also placed their names in the "golden book of Sofia", in which the names of visiting dignitaries are supposedly written. In addition, to my great surprise, the State granted every player "*Sofiisko grazhdanstvo*" (Sofia citizenship), or the right to reside in the capital. This privilege, the event's emcee announced, had been passed by the legislature and forwarded to the city council, where it would be officially registered. That residence in Sofia was still strictly controlled in 1994 testifies to the continued strength of pre-1989 policies far into the transition period.

The many speeches extended the patriotic fervour of the previous days in ways that bracketed contemporary foreign policy objectives. You drove Americans to chant "*bŭlgarski yunatsi*", said President Zhelev, emphasizing the novel international alliance that this demonstrated, even though it was difficult to explain to them what a *yunak* was. You moved your "Macedonian brothers to cheer for Bulgaria", he continued, indicating a sense of unity with a people whose ethnic legitimacy many Bulgarians have challenged for decades (especially under state socialism), but whose right to statehood was also quickly acceded by the Bulgarian government in 1992.[37] The post-1989 state was being built according to new principles that required new coalitions, Zhelev seemed to be saying, and soccer was facilitating this process.

Despite their lengthy journey from the US, the soccer team was made to stand throughout the speeches and awards in the scorching July heat at the stadium's centre, not taking seats in the stands until the megaconcert began. For this event each song was performed by a lead vocalist to a pre-recorded accompaniment. Initially entertaining, the concert continued at such length that almost everyone left the stadium before it concluded – including the team. In fact, it seemed clear that the entire gala was orchestrated not so much to applaud the team or its accomplishments but to celebrate the nation. As one television news journalist observed, the tourney had made every citizen feel Bulgarian, rather than as a member of "the red party" (i.e., the Bulgarian Socialist Party, or BSP) or "the blue party" (the UDF).

---

[36] In fact, one friend told me that a wealthy Bulgarian-American allegedly promised each player a large sum of money for every major victory – $10,000 if the top eight competition was reached, $30,000 for getting into the quarter finals, and $100,000 for reaching the semi-finals. Supposedly this benefactor hoped that his offer would serve as a financial incentive, but I have been unable to independently verify this information or his identity.

[37] Independently of this event, one friend told me that several residents of FYROM (Former Yugoslav Republic of Macedonia) had flown the Bulgarian flag in honour of the team's success but had been reprimanded by local authorities for this act, probably because it could be interpreted as advocating a Bulgarian claim to Macedonian territory.

But not everyone found soccer so inspiring. One couple, both academics, insisted that the soccer fervour was not nationalism but "cheap populism". For them, nationalism represented a force that drew all citizens together. They viewed soccer as a mass culture phenomenon but stressed that not everyone was a fan. They credited the team's popularity to nihilism – to the fact that citizens had become so disillusioned that they believed in nothing any more. For some, soccer became a new national icon to worship, but this couple was not among them. They thought it ridiculous – even shameful – that Zhelev had flown to the US to watch the semi-finals in this time of crisis. "So be careful about calling this nationalism," they cautioned, "because for us it is the opposite." In fact, they found the whole affair terribly alienating.

Conclusions

I have argued that an analysis of sport and music in mid-1990s Bulgaria reveals how the transition away from state socialism affected governmental policy as well as the lives of everyday citizens. First, during this period aspects of soccer culture touched upon or embraced topics that previously had been closely monitored or repressed between 1944 and 1989, including emigration, urban folklore, the supernatural, capitalism, materialism and democratic freedom. In addition, the Turkish and Rom flavour of some soccer songs points to important issues of ethnic identity and minority group relations that are not addressed here but which are crucially related to the formulation of a democratic Bulgarian national identity as well as the shifting sands of regional Balkan politics.

Second, both song lyrics and the behaviour and commentary of soccer fans, including that of political leaders, demonstrate the nation's profound desire to be recognized by, allied with and included in the Western world. Although the evidence presented here pertains especially to the events of 1994, this yearning continued to be voiced long afterwards. For example, following a rehearsal of Radio Sofia's folk orchestra in late June 1996, amidst the excitement surrounding the EuroCup games, one musician approached me eagerly and said, "Donna, all of America recognizes Bulgaria now because of our soccer players, right?"

Third, my investigation also shows that the soccer craze both nourished and fed on a fantasy of material wealth and glamour inseparable from the public's aspiration to a democratic, capitalist lifestyle most commonly symbolized in song texts and conversation by the United States ("Now, when there are no visas/the USA is one to me ...") and personified by the team's star players. The latter's sporting accomplishments, evidenced in song and story as national progress towards this lifestyle, suggested that Bulgaria, twice victorious over Germany, might deserve or soon earn EU membership alongside its economically superior but vanquished foe.

Fourth, this study discloses the shattering economic, social and psychological impact of democratic reform through 1996, and how the Bulgarian public and its leaders employed popular culture as a coping mechanism directed at regaining a positive national outlook and unified sense of national consciousness. Both music and sport are powerful forms of cultural performance that possess the ability to generate national sentiment, and even to transform that sentiment into prescriptions for nationalist action. In other words, soccer and soccer songs were implemented as types of "cultural nationalism" to facilitate state building – in this case, that of a democratic Bulgaria (Cronin and Mayall 1998:2; Turino 2000:14–15). As national emblems, such phenomena create "a collective gaze" and then shift it "onto issues of the deepest ideological importance", namely, those of identity, belief and values (Rowe 1995:140). Thus, when Zhelev declared the soccer team's achievements to be a direct result of democratic reform and an effective means of gaining Western recognition, he gave mainstream Bulgarians logical, positive and tangible reasons to stay his government's course. The national sentiment that resulted became literally internalized, affecting people's emotional well-being, psyches and even postures, as well as their behaviour or actions. In short, through their engagement with the soccer craze, many Bulgarians experienced the nation in their very bodies.

Yet the disenchantment with the whole fad professed by some of my associates shows that nationalism of any sort (civic, cultural, ethnic, religious) is a razor-sharp sword with a double edge – my fifth point. It both binds and divides, simultaneously casting a thin veneer of unity over a social reality of extraordinary difference and diversity. To wit, during the 1996 EuroCup several colleagues rooted for France because they could no longer endure the civil disturbance that followed a Bulgarian win; they did not want to face the riots in the streets and on public transport, or to hear the chanting and gunshots. Still others backed France because a few players, as representatives of the nouveau riche, were thought to be connected with mafia organizations, particularly mafia-run private security services whose guards had begun to assume police powers (like putting lights on their cars and ignoring traffic laws). The fact that civil laws did not obtain made patrolling such activity nearly impossible, and this generated great resentment among some fans.

Thus, while scholars devoted to this troubled region might fruitfully reflect on what and how other types of cultural performances are marking the construction of the new Balkan states, we must also consider that the sentiments and alliances provoked by such phenomena are inherently as exclusionary as they are inclusionary, and that individuals (or groups) may espouse or reject them for a whole host of reasons, personal or otherwise. Perhaps this is an obvious point, but its implications are far-reaching. I would propose, for instance, that it is important to think not only about how the Balkan nations envisage themselves in regard to the potentiality of a united Europe, but also about what such an affiliation would *ex*clude and *oc*clude. Bulgaria's fervent pitch for EU membership marks a clear move away from the Russian power orbit (historically a strong influence even before World War II), for example, yet relations between the two countries have not disintegrated as a result but merely changed. Moreover, Turkey is a major player in regional politics, military strategy, religion and, as my second and third musical examples demonstrate, the construction of contemporary expressive culture. Team Bulgaria's success on the soccer front may have served to rally nationalistic aspirations towards the EU and distract citizens from the economic devastation surrounding them. The eclectic, often overtly Turkish character of those soccer songs written in a *popfolk* vein, however, reveals that these aspirations are held in tension with a growing awareness of what it means to be Bulgarian in a Balkan context. When we think about the Balkans, then, we must cast our gaze east as well as west, and south as well as north.

This brings me to my last point. As I write these words in October 2001, Bulgaria's dedication to peace, stability and political and economic change, as well as to joint regional and international security and trade coalitions, is being rewarded with continued IMF support, meaningful overtures from both the EU and NATO, and a coveted seat on the United Nations Security Council. It is fair to say that Western powers do now know where the nation is – and not just because of its soccer players! At the same time the international nature of these developments, like the cosmopolitan inflections of Bulgarian soccer songs and fan commentary, demonstrates that when analysing the Balkans we must always think in terms of multiple alliances, whether military, economic, cultural or political. We must think both inside and outside the region, and both inside and outside Europe, to consider how local perceptions of transnational or global influences also drive the hopes, dreams, motivations, policies, images and identities of these nations and their citizens.

References

Books and articles

Brock, Gordon, sponsor (n.d.) "The official Lili Marleen page." http://ingeb.org/garb/lmarleen.html.

Buchanan, Donna A. (1995) "Metaphors of power, metaphors of truth: the politics of music professionalism in Bulgarian folk orchestras." *Ethnomusicology* 39.3:381–416.

—— (1996) "Wedding musicians, political transition, and national consciousness in Bulgaria." In M. Slobin (ed.) *Retuning culture: musical changes in Central and Eastern Europe*, pp. 200–30. Durham and London: Duke University Press.

—— (1999) "Democracy or 'crazyocracy'? Pirin folk music and sociocultural change in Bulgaria." In B. Reuer (ed.) *New countries, old sounds? Cultural identity and social change in southeastern Europe*, pp. 164–77. Munich: Verlag Südostdeutsches Kulturwerk.

—— (in press) "Soccer songs and the construction of national sentiment in post-state-socialist Bulgaria." In B. Reuer (ed.) *United Europe – united music? Diversity and its social dimensions in Southeastern Europe*. Munich: Verlag Südostdeutsches Kulturwerk.

—— (forthc. a) "Bulgarian ethnopop along the old *Via Militaris*: Ottomanism, orientalism, or Balkan cosmopolitanism?" In D. A. Buchanan (ed.) *Balkan popular culture and the Ottoman ecumene: music, image, and regional political discourse*.

—— (forthc. b) *Performing democracy: Bulgarian music and musicians in transition*. Chicago: University of Chicago Press.

26   B R I T I S H   J O U R N A L   O F   E T H N O M U S I C O L O G Y   V O L . 1 1 / I I   2 0 0 2

Ceribašić, N. (1995) "Gender roles during the war: representations in Croatian and Serbian popular music, 1991–1992." *Collegium Antropologicum* 19.1: 91–101.

Cronin, Mike, and Mayall, David (1998) "Sport and ethnicity: some introductory remarks." In M. Cronin and D. Mayall (eds) *Sporting nationalisms: identity, ethnicity, immigration, and assimilation*, pp. 1–13. London and Portland, OR: F. Cass.

Dimov, Ventsislav (2001) *Etnopopbumŭt*. Sofia: Bŭlgarsko Muzikoznanie Izsledvaniya.

Downey, Greg (2000) "Domesticating an urban menace: efforts to reform *capoeira* as a Brazilian national sport." Unpublished manuscript.

Jackson, Carlton (1979) *The great Lili*. San Francisco: Strawberry Hill Press.

Klein, Gioffrido Z., and Hornung, Riccardo (1994) "Brave Bulgars! We, who are about to defeat you, salute you!" *Village Voice* 19 July:187.

National Public Radio (1994) "Bulgarian soccer victory an historic event." Transcript of Robert Siegel interview with Carmen Vlichkov, Bulgarian foreign policy advisor, on the NPR programme *All things considered*, 11 July 1994.

Pettan, Svanibor (1998) "Music, politics, and war in Croatia in the 1990s: an introduction." In S. Pettan (ed.) *Music, politics, and war: views from Croatia*, pp. 9–27. Zagreb: Institute of Ethnology and Folklore Research.

Peters, Karen (2000) "Representations of Macedonia in contemporary ethnopop songs from southwest Bulgaria." *Balkanistica* 13:131–63.

Rhodes, Robbie (1997) "The saga of 'Lilli Marlene'." *Mechanical Music Digest Archives*. http://mmd.foxtail.com/Archives/Digest/199707/1997.07.12.

Rice, Timothy (1994) *May it fill your soul: experiencing Bulgarian music*. Chicago: University of Chicago Press.

—— (1996) "The dialectic of economics and aesthetics in Bulgarian music." In M. Slobin (ed.) *Retuning culture: musical changes in Central and Eastern Europe*, pp. 176–99. Durham and London: Duke University Press.

—— (2002) "Bulgaria or chalgaria: the attenuation of Bulgarian nationalism in a mass-mediated popular music." *Yearbook for Traditional Music* 34.

Rowe, David (1995) "Ideologies in competition." Chapter 6 in his *Popular cultures: rock music, sport and the politics of pleasure* (pp. 122–43). London: Sage Publications.

Silverman, Carol (1989) "Reconstructing folklore: media and cultural policy in Eastern Europe." *Communication* 11:141–60.

Stokes, Martin (1992) *The arabesk debate: music and musicians in modern Turkey*. Oxford: Clarendon Press.

—— (1996) "'Strong as a Turk': power, performance and representation in Turkish wrestling." In J. MacClancy (ed.) *Sport, identity, and ethnicity*, pp. 21–41. Oxford: Berg.

Turino, Thomas R. (2000) "Introduction." In his *Nationalists, cosmopolitans, and popular music in Zimbabwe*. Chicago: University of Chicago Press.

Zoomsoccer (2001) "Stoichkov signs for Chicago Fire." http://www.zoomsoccer.com/news/USA/ 981652693.52.html; 7 February.

Websites (without cited authors)

http://www.angelfire.com/tx2/Stoichkov/Bulgaria.html
http://www.angelfire.com/tx2/Stoichkov/FCBARCELONA.html
http://www.angelfire.com/tx2/Stoichkov/personalinfo.html
http://www.angelfire.com/tx2/Stoichkov/WSC.html
http://www.angelfire.com/tx2/Stoichkov/euro96.html
http://www.ukans.edu/carrie/docs/texts/lilieng.htm
http://www.worldcuparchive.com/CUPS/1994/wc94index.html

Recordings

Bulgarian National Television broadcast, World Cup Soccer Championship, 10 July, 1994.

Marlene Dietrich overseas: American songs in German for the O.S.S. Columbia Records GL 105 LP 9405, n.d.

Ork. Kristali, Montana: Ole, Stoichkov '94. Folkton-EOOD, n.d.

Peite s nas: haide nashte! Evro '96: 11 pobedni pesni (Sing with us: let's go team! Euro '96: 11 victory songs). Music, texts and arrangements by Mihail Shopov. Performed by Asen Kisimov. Distributed by Unison Music Company, n.p., n.d.

Radio Signal Plus (+) broadcasts, 10 July, 1994, and 17 June, 1996.

Trio Bŭlgarka, *The forest is crying (lament for Indje Voivode).* Hannibal Records HNBC 1342, 1988.

Note on the author

Donna A. Buchanan gained her Ph.D. from the University of Texas at Austin in 1991 and is currently Assistant Professor of Musicology at the University of Illinois at Urbana–Champaign. Her research interests include the music of Bulgaria, the Balkans, the Mediterranean and the CIS, especially Russia. Address: School of Music, University of Illinois, 2136 Music Building, 1114 West Nevada St, Urbana, IL 61801, USA; email: buchana1@uiuc.edu.

Music and cultural politics: ideology and resistance in Singapore

Lily Kong

This paper focuses on popular music written and produced by Singaporeans to illustrate the nature of social relationships based on ideological hegemony and resistance. Analysis is based on two groups of music: 'national' songs supported by the government in the 'Sing Singapore' programme; and songs brought together in *Not the Singapore song book*. Interviews with local lyricists and analysis of video productions provide supplementary information. Music is used by the ruling élite to perpetuate certain ideologies aimed at political socialization and to inculcate a civil religion that directs favour and fervour towards the nation. Music is also a form of cultural resistance against state policies and some social-cultural norms. Music embodies social commentaries on aspects of Singapore society, such as controversial government policies and the ostentatious lifestyle of many Singaporeans.

key words popular music cultural politics ideology resistance Singapore

Department of Geography, National University of Singapore, 10 Kent Ridge Crescent, Singapore 0511

revised manuscript received 24 May 1994

Introduction

In their introduction to *Inverting places: studies in cultural geography,,* Anderson and Gale (1992) drew attention to the recent focus in cultural geography on the relationship between 'culture and power' and 'culture and resistance'. Such a focus has arisen out of a recognition of the plurality of culture groups in any one society and the consequent control, conflict and contestation between groups, sometimes arising from cultural differences, sometimes (mis)appropriating cultural differences. Indeed, the explicit attention paid to cultural politics in the various essays in Anderson and Gale's volume form part of the growing geographical literature scrutinizing these issues in theoretical and empirical, historical and contemporary ways.[1] Much of this reinvigoration within the sub-discipline draws inspiration from, *inter alia,* cultural studies where music too has received some research attention (Hebdige 1979). Particularly associated with the Centre for Contemporary Cultural Studies at the University of Birmingham, cultural studies in postwar Britain have stressed nations of ideology, hegemony and

resistance, and illustrated how culture groups are related to each other in terms of dominance and subordination along a scale of 'cultural power' (Clarke *et al.* 1976, 11). Culture groups will appropriate the resources of other groups, transforming and often exaggerating them as a form of protest and resistance (Hall and Jefferson 1976; Hebdige 1979). These ideas will inform my discussion of popular music in Singapore.

Alongside the repositioning of Cultural geographical attention to include notions of power and resistance, has been the focus on the question of national identity and the explicit recognition that such identities are often, if not always, deliberate constructions rather than 'natural' givens. The political discourses that seek to define hegemonic vision of 'nation' and 'national identity' have been explored in a growing literature by geograghers, amongst others. For example, in Jackson and Penrose's (1993) collection of essays, we find, *inter alia,* discussions of how policies on immigration and refugees reinforce nationalist and racist ideology and of how nationalist rhetoric plays a role in the construction of nations Whilst, in *Fields of vision,*

448

Daniels (1993) illustrates how landscapes in various media have articulated national identities in England and the United States from the later eighteenth century. The message here is of the explicit and de&berate construction and deconstruction of national identity, achieved via a variety of strategies, from political rhetoric through specific government policy to cultural production. This paper is situated within such a discourse on the constructed nature of 'national identity' and will illustrate how a cultural form (music) is harnessed in the construction of a hegemonic vision of a specific nation, Singapore.

A third development within cultural geography in recent years has been a movement away from privileging élite culture in research to a more explicit recognition of the significance of popular culture, defined as the 'everyday practices, experiences and beliefs of what have been called "the common people" ' (Burgess and Gold 1985, 3). The hegemony of elite culture - based traditionally on 'a view of the relative "worth" of élite versus popular culture' *(ibid.,* 15) - has been challenged through the realization that the very ordinariness of popular cultures masks their importance as 'wellsprings of popular consciousness' (Harvey 1984, 7).

My exploration of music and cultural politics in this paper takes off from these recent repositionings within cultural geography. By focusing on two groups of popular music in Singapore, I will illustrate their embodiment both of ideologically hegemonic intentions of constructing a version of the 'nation' and of manifestations of resistance. Specifically; I will examine 'national' songs commissioned and encouraged by the state in the 'Sing Singapore' programme, promoted by the Psychological Defence Division of the Ministry of Communications and Information in 1988. The various texts of the programme, including the *Sing Singapore* book containing the lyrics and scores of 49 songs, the two accompanying tapes and the video clips aired on national television, are examined. While these songs do not represent 'popular music' as the term is commonly understood, they are 'popular' in the way in which they are a part of the everyday lives of many Singaporeans. For example, these songs are taught in schools and are aired on national television and radio. The fact that many young children are learning them and that they are becoming so much a part of their learned culture is reflected in Dick Lee's (a local composer and artiste) comment that these could well be the folksongs for future

generations (talk show at National University of Singapore, 23 July 1993).

Apart from examining such national songs, I will also analyse songs contained in a volume entitled *Not the Singapore song book* (1993), which contains new lyrics set to popular tunes, including some national songs. The tongue-in-cheek, 80-page book containing a collection of 53 songs by seventeen Singaporeans, a tape by entertainer Najib Ali titled 'Born in SIN (that is, Born in Singapore; SIN is used to mimic 'Born in the 'USA), featuring ten songs from the book, as well as Najib Ali's live stage show, act as a form of resistance to official cultural representation.

My argument is built on two bases. On the one hand, music is used by the ruling elite to perpetuate certain ideologies aimed at political socialization and the development of a sense of national identity or to inculcate a civil religion that directs favour and fervour towards the 'nation'. On the other hand, music is a form of cultural resistance, both against state policies and certain socio-cultural norms.

While I begin by situating my work within broader developments in a retheorized cultural geography, I also depart from other cultural geographical impulses pertaining to popular music in the United States. By emphasizing cultural politics, I diverge from the American tradition of 'musical geographies' that spotlight the identification of musical hearths and paths of diffusion and the perception of places in music (see, for example, Carney 1987). An intellectual tradition that is more pertinent to the development of my arguments is a concern with how and why '[s]ongs have been composed to teach, convert, seduce, pacify, and arouse' (Denisoff and Peterson 1972, 1). Abudant research exists on classical music and how it acts as propaganda in Czechoslovakia, Finland, England and Germany, for instance.[2] Here I draw inspiration from those studies which explore the use of popular songs for a variety of ends: to reinforce an ideology and legitimize a ruling élite (for example, Warren 1972); to act as a rallying call to others so as to establish and reinforce group identity;[3] and to voice dissatisfaction with society, including social norms and political conditions. Political dissatisfaction is captured, for example, in American 'protest songs',[4] while opposition to social norms has been expressed in rock 'n' roll (Frith 1983; Perris 1985).

One final body of literature that sets the context of this study is the small collection of writings on music in Singapore. Research here is both sparse and diverse, dealing variously with music education (Nguik 1991), the uniqueness of particular local musical styles (Thomas 1986) and rock music as a sub-culture (Ho 1981). This paper will contribute to local research by highlighting the role of music in capturing and contributing to the sense of place and society in Singapore.

Contextualizing the case study: nation-building in post-colonial Singapore

Singapore acquired internal self-governing status from the British in 1959.[5] Full independence was attained in 1963 as part of Malaysia, comprising the Federation of Malaya, Singapore, Sabah and Sarawak, but this merger was to be short-lived. In 1965, Tunku Abdul Rahman, Malaya's Prime Minister, decided that separation was necessary to avert serious political tension and communal upheavals," and it was under such circumstances that Singapore became a fully independent state. The uncertainties and justified fears of the time are poignantly captured by Yong (1992). How was a small island with no natural resources, high un-employment, low levels of income and skills, overcrowded conditions and a potentially divisive multiracial population[7] to survive? The tasks ahead were enormous.

Since those early days, Singapore has come a long way in its economic development. The problem of chronic unemployment has long been solved[8] and labour shortages have developed in certain sectors. Most of the population is housed in subsidized, public-sector high-rise flats[9] replacing the slums of the 1960s. Singapore's GNP has grown from S$2193 million[10] in 1960 to S$63 905·1 million in 1990 *(Singapore 1991* 1991), while foreign exchange reserves have catapulted from S$1068·6 million in 1965 to S$48 033·9 million in 1990 *(ibid.).* Singaporeans today generally enjoy a high standard of living and have a per capita income second only to Japan in Asia. In 1991, there were three persons per telephone in Singapore and eleven per private *car (Singapore facfs and pictures* 1992 1992); the latter figure was achieved only after stringent actions were taken to reduce the car population.

How has such an economic miracle been possible? A large part of it is certainly due to the shrewdness of the People's Action Party (PAP), not only in its economic strategies but also in its social engineer-ing, including its conscious attempts to shape social values and political cultures. It is this pre-eminent role of the PAP in Singapore, its attempts at social engineering and the resultant political culture that provides the more immediate context for this paper. The PAP came into power soon after independence in 1966 and has remained in power ever since. Indeed, for a long time (1966-81), Singapore had the dubious distinction of having only one party (the PAP) in a democratically elected parliament. There were few signs of serious political opposition and, even today, there are merely four opposition members from two different parties in an 81-seat parliament. With this stranglehold on the govern-ment of the country, the PAP has actively sought to develop an 'administrative state' (Chan 1975) in which the citizenry is depoliticized (Chan 1989), where public participation in decision-making is minimal - if nut nun-existent - and mobilization of the people to support state policies is the norm (Chan 1976, 1989).

Depoliticization is valued as desirable and neces-sary fur social stability and economic growth Com-petitive political struggle is actively discouraged, if only because of the belief that

> time spent by groups and counter-groups to lobby, influence and change policy outcomes are a waste of time that detract from the swift implementation of the plan and programme. (Chan 1975, 55)

As a consequence, there is not so much public participation as public mobilization 'which may have no impact on the reshaping or resharing of power as far as the participants are concerned' (Chan 1976, 39). Such mobilization is made possible by the establishment of local-level institutions such as Citizens' Consultative Committees, Residents' Committees and community centres entrusted with the task of socializing participants to 'accept basic values aimed at creating a consensual political base in the country' (Seah 1973, 119). The outcome of such forces is the development of a political culture in which open conflict, confrontation and bargaining have been markedly absent.

Yet, by the 1980s, certain social and political circumstances were construed as potential threats to the existing hegemony and there emerged a cau-tious, if forced, acknowledgement that the electorate was now demanding more consultation and public participation. The first political 'setback' was when the ruling PAP candidate lost to a Workers' Party candidate in the October 1981 single ward by-election. In December 1984, the PAP lost two seats to the opposition for the first time in a general

450

election[11] and suffered an overall decrease of 12·6 per cent in votes cast. This was a decline from 75·5 per cent in the 1980 general election to 62·9 per cent in 1984, with a further drop to 61·8 per cent in 1988 (Quah and Quah 1989). Although this would qualify as a landslide victory in any other context, it was considered a major blow to the PAP given its long, unbroken monopoly of both parliamentary seats and percentage votes. In the meantime, in 1987, the government uncovered an alleged Marxist conspiracy said to have used the Roman Catholic church as a cover for its activities aimed at overthrowing the government.

Beyond the assault on political legitimacy, the government also identified the erosion of Asian values amongst Singaporeans and the threat of becoming a 'pseudo-Western society'[12] as assaults on the socio-cultural order. Such a society is generally thought to be 'motivated by individualism', promoting 'personal freedom, [lindulging] in sensual pleasures and [lacking] a sense of responsibility to the family and society' (Straints *Times Weekly* Overseas Edition 22 October 1988).

The assaults on the PAP's political legitimacy and the perceived erosion of important values led to the development of policies geared towards re-asserting its hegemony. It began to proclaim its version of the nation and to rally Singaporearts behind it. Various measures were adopted. For example, the Education Ministry identified ten schools to which it would give special assistance to help keep alive the best Chinese traditions and core values, believed to include filial piety and family and society above self[13] *(Straits Times Weekly Overseas Edition* 25 March 1989). A national ideology was developed which spelt out clearly the country's ethos and core values so that a national identity would evolve, thought to ensure the long-term viability of the country. These cure values include community over self; upholding the family as the basic building block of society; resolving major issues through consensus instead of contention; and stressing racial and religious tolerance and harmony. In addition, the idea of total defence, first given publicity in late 1982; was developed and amplified through diverse channels in the mid-1980s. Borrowing from the Swedish experience, total defence comprises military, civil, economic, social and psychological defence, and is designed to prepare the country for any eventuality. Despite its pre-eminent importance (Seah 1989), military defence alone will not suffice in times of trouble. Civil defence forces are necessary to maintain the internal administration of the country under adverse circumstances, whilst adequate economic defence ensures that government, business and industry will be able to organize themselves such that the economy will not break down during or under threat of war. Whilst military, civil and economic defence take care of the material realm of existence, more pertinent to this discussion are social and psychological defence. The former refers to the promotion of cohesion amongst Singapore's diverse groups so that external subversion through the exploitation of primordial sentiments would be minimized, while ideals are fully shared by all Singaporeans. Psychological defence is defined as 'the means of winning the hearts and minds of the people and preparing them to confront any national crisis' (Seah 1989, 956). As I will illustrate in the next section, national songs are an important weapon in social and psychological defence, aimed at encouraging Singaporeans to celebrate a particular desired version of the nation and to develop a strong national identity: to bond ourselves with our identity and destiny' (Buang 1989, 1).

While the attempts at social engineering continue, the government has also acknowledged, perhaps belatedly, the population's quest for a more active voice in decision-making by setting up the Feedback Unit in 1985. Headed by a PAP Member of Parliament, the unit is meant to

> gather feedback on Government policies and receives suggestions from the public on national issues. It ensures swift and effective response by Government departments on public suggestions and complaints. *(Singapore facts and pictures 1992* 1992, 92)

In effect, the Feedback Unit is an 'approved channel' of participation, indicative of how involvement is allowed only if directed through 'proper' and indeed 'managed' routes. It is in this context of conscious depoliticization, ideologically hegemonic intents, negligible organized opposition and overt resistance, and managed 'participation' that the two sets of Singapore popular music discussed below are to be understood.

The cultural hegemony of national songs

As Miller and Skipper (1972) have exemplified, lyrics are not the only ways in which meanings are communicated through songs. Indeed, music may convey its meanings and values through visuals, rhythms, titles of songs and albums, the timing of releases and sometimes through the lifestyles of the performers. In this section, I will illustrate how such processes around the 'Sing Singapore' package combined in the attempt to achieve an ideologically hegemonic effect. Through various means of dissemination (including constant airing on national television and radio; the organization of community singing sessions in community centres; and, at the directive of the Ministry of Education, teaching the songs to schoolchildren during school assembly time[14]), the objective is to convince Singaporeans of the idea that Singapore has come a long way since its founding (in 1819) and independence (in 1965) and that they must continue to play their part in maintaining this dramatic development. The ultimate concern is to develop in Singaporeans a love for their country, a sense of patriotism and a willingness to support the ruling elite who have led the country through the short years since independence, As Dr Yeo Ning Hong, Ministry for Communications and Information, wrote in his message for the *Sing Singapore* (1988) songbook,

> Singing the songs will bring Singaporeans together, to share our feelings one with another. It will bring back shared memories of good times and hard times, of times which remind us of who we are, where we came from, what we did, and where we are going. It will bring together Singaporeans of different races and backgrounds, to share and to express the spirit of the community, the feeling of togetherness, the feeling of oneness. This, in essence, is what the 'Sing Singapore' programme is about.

Evidence of the state's hegemonic intentions abound in the lyrics of national songs which have been written in all four official languages in Singapore - English, Mandarin, Malay and Tamil. Through national songs, Singaporeans are encouraged to express feelings of love and pride for and of belonging to their country. These emotions are captured in a variety of ways. For example, in *This is my land,*, Singaporeans are encouraged to proclaim that

> This is our island
> O Singapore, We love you so, love you so. *(ibid.,* 116)

In turn, pride for the country is expressed in Sing a **song for Singapore:**

> I want the world to know about my island in the sun
> Where happy children play and shout, and smile for ev'ryone. *(ibid,* 109)

Such pride stands alongside a sense of belonging, expressed, for example,-in *We are* **Singapore:**

> This is my country
> this is my flag
> this is my future
> this is my life
> this is my family
> these are my friends
> We are Singapore Singaporeans
> Singapore our homeland
> it's here that we belong. *(ibid.,* 95)

and in We *the people of Singapore:*

> We the people of Singapore . . .
> Find in it ev'ry joy and hope
> As 'tis our very home. *(ibid.,* 105)

Feelings of love, belonging and pride must, however, be translated into more active man&stations and, in the national songs, Singaporeans are exhorted to attain excellence for Singapore. This idea of excellence encompasses various concepts such as unity, commitment to Singapore, productivity, hard work and teamwork. The message in brief is this: if Singaporeans can ensure that they have these qualities and mindsets, excellence can be achieved for the country and Singapore may stay ahead of other competitors, if not serve as their model. To make sure that the message is adequately conveyed to the populace, it is also promoted in a variety of ways apart from the official songs. For example, it pervades much of the existing state rhetoric, with ministerial speeches to public audiences emphasizing time and again the need to keep ahead by achieving excellence. Thus, the then First Deputy Prime Minister Goh Chok Tong (1988, 10) intoned:

> Singapore is safe so long as we strive for excellence in all that we do. Once we become a mediocre society, we are in peril . . . we have no margin for error. A single mistake can mean the end of us.

The achievement of excellence in practical terms is also given much public airing as a way of encouragement and of instilling pride, Thus, newspaper headlines publicize the fact that 'Sinapore [is the] top investment site for Western businessmen' *(The Straits Times* 8 April 1991); that the 'Republic remains best-rated Asian country outside Japan' in terms of risk *(The Business Times* 17 April 1991); and that Singapore companies are 'rated among Asia's best-managed (The Straits *Times* 18 August 1992). The overall effect is that a vision and common goal for the future - to maintain the record, if not better it - is established.

452

These messages are encoded in the lyrics of many national songs. For example, to achieve excellence for Singapore, Singaporeans are told that they must stand up to be counted *(Stand up for Singapore* and *Count on me Singapore, Sing Singapore* 1988, 95), 'serve [Singapore] with all our might' and 'guard it *with our very lives' (We the people of Singapore, ibid.,* 105). At the same time, the ideological message purveyed is that excellence is possible only when Singaporeans remain united, for it is by standing together that the 'lion's roar' can be heard *(We are Singapore, ibid.,* 95); it is also by 'steering together' with drive and unity' that the vision of excellence *can be* achieved *(Undaunted, ibid.,* 107). *This unity,* it is emphasized, is particularly important in multi-*racial Singapore (Untuk rakyat dan Negara, ibid.,* 102). In addition, it is possible to achieve excellence only if Singaporeans develop the virtue of hard work and this ethic is reinforced in several songs which eulogize the worker who is diligent and persevering. For example, in the Chinese song *Kuai le gong ren* (literally translated 'Happy workers') *(ibid.,* 106), the virtues of teamwork, cooperation and hard work are extolled and good workers are reliable and happy Singaporeans who work hard to deliver their promises. That these ideas pervade both national songs and state rhetoric and serve to reinforce one another is reflected in the parallel between the lyrics of *Undaunted* and Prime Minister Goh Chok Tong's speech:

With our spirit undaunted
More than ever we will try
To be the best we ever can be
For us and posterity
Day by day, year by year
Together we steer
With drive and unity
Our vision we'll achieve
EXCELLENCE FOR SINGAPORE. *(ibid.,* 107, original emphasis)

The key to our long-term survival is the spirit and equality of our people and then. leaders . . . if we work with one heart, share one common vision, then in our lifetime we can be that Nation of Excellence. (Goh 1986, 11)

To encourage Singaporeans to play these various roles and to help attain excellence for Singapore, national songs appropriate past and present conditions. Specifically, past achievements are glorified; the role of the government is exalted; and both the built and natural environments are used to extol

Singapore's beauty and achievements. In highlighting these achievements Singaporeans are encouraged to continue to give of their best for their country, to defend it and to support the ruling order.

The appropriation of the past is designed to remind Singaporeans of how successfully the state has been steered from struggling Third World conditions to newly industrialized status and to arouse a sense of pride and loyalty. For example, in *We are Singapore* (Sing *Singapore* 1988, 95), Singaporeans are reminded that

There was a time when people said
that Singapore won't make it
but we did
There was a time when troubles
seemed too much for us to take
but we did.
We built a nation strong and free.

Through this reminder, Singaporeans are encouraged to think that no problem would ever be too difficult to handle as long as they continue to uphold the spirit of the pioneers. This spirit, as intoned in the songs, belongs to 'loyal people with a rugged past' *(Reach out, reach out, ibid.,* 103) who had served the country 'in love and trust' *(This is our country, ibid.,* 106). It is embodied in the 'seeds of strength and mirth' sown by brave and loyal men' *(Sing* a *song* of *Singapore, ibid.,* 109) who took the country 'through the years calm and stormy' and 'shaped our destiny' *(Undaunted, ibid., 107).*

Part of Singapore's successes, we are reminded, would have been impossible if not for the government for, as pointed out in the Tamil songs *Engkal Singapore* ('Our Singapore') and *Paduvom Varungal* ('Come let's sing'), Singapore has a 'strong and effective' government that 'cares about the welfare of her people' *(ibid.,* 115, 97). *The* result of such good government is that 'Me is joy and harmony' *(Voices from the heart, ibid.,* 100). Indeed, to reflect the good life that Singaporeans are said to enjoy, elements of the built and natural environment conjure images of progress, peace, joy and harmony. For example, in *Sing a song of Singapore (ibid.,* 109), happy children are said to be playing

In city streets in parks so green in highrise housings *[sic]* too
In every place so fresh and clean On sunny beaches too.

In those two lines, the urban environment of 'buildings . . . climbing all the way to the sky'

(Singapore town, ibid., 100) *and* the rustic peace of (practically non-existent) natural environments in Singapore are appropriated for ideological ends, namely to remind Singaporeans that if they did not continue to support the status quo and strive together with their leaders towards excellence, they stand to lose the beauty and prosperity of their 'fair shore' *(The fair shore of Singapore, ibid.,* 110). The images of skyscrapers are particularly important as symbols of modernization and development as well as of triumph over an environment that offered nothing towards economic progress by way of natural resources. At the same time, the emphasis on the 'fresh, 'clean', 'green' and 'sunny' can work at two levels. On the one hand, it represents a recognition of the value of the natural alongside the developed. The lyricist was determined to recover 'sunny beaches' as part of Singapore's natural heritage, despite the fact that land reclamation and seafront construction over the last two decades have left few beaches untouched. Here the tension between urban development and conservation of the natural environment that has recently been voiced in public arenas (see, for example, Savage and Kong 1993) is ignored, whether in innocence or for ideological ends. On the other hand, the portrayals may represent a proud acknowledgement of the consciously created manicured parks in 'clean and green Singapore,[15] so glossing over the irony that the many parks and 'instant trees' of the 'Garden City' could be created and planted only by rolling back the natural heritage that had existed before (see Kong and Yeoh 1992).

While the lyrics of many national songs illustrate the state's ideological intentions, other factors also serve to support these intentions. The music tends to be anthermic, designed to arouse a sense of patriotism. At the same time, new national songs tend to be released just before National Day during which Singapore's independence is celebrated. This is intended to intensify the fervour of nationalistic emotions. Furthermore, the music videos aired on national television have carefully selected visuals, all of which serve to enhance pride, reflect harmony and encourage togetherness. For example the images of smartly clad, combat-ready soldiers and sophisticated defence machinery are designed to evoke a sense of pride and strength, while happy images of the various ethnic groups in Singapore (such as the Chinese, Malays and Indians) are designed to remind Singaporeans of the harmony between different groups and the sense of unity that

must prevail At the same time, the soaring skyscrapers and other modern buildings are often backdrops that remind Singaporeans of the significant development and modernization that Singapore has undergone in a short period of time, reinforcing the effect intended by the lyrics. In all these ways, the state attempts to persuade Singaporeans of the 'naturalness' of one reading of these texts, when it is a preferred rather than the only reading. As Anderson and Gale (1992,7) point out,

> [p]owerful institutions (including nations) can. . . work to ensure that what are partial culturally-bound interpretations of reality are accepted as 'natural' and 'correct' by the public at large.

To cast the use of music for hegemonic intentions in Singapore in a larger context, I would suggest that music contributes to an attempt to develop what may be called a 'civil religion' (Bellah 1970). In a general sense, a civil religion is 'any set of beliefs and rituals, related to the past, present and/or future of a people . . . which are understood in some transcendental fashion' (Hammond 1976, quoted in Stump 1985, 87). In the American context, Stump *(ibid.,* 87) suggests that a civil religion exists in a nation when its people believe that their 'values and beliefs are . . . superior to those of other nations' and that their 'nation [has] a special mission to serve as a model for the rest of the world'. In Singapore, the state attempts to create such a civil religion by using various ideological tools. Apart from music, other symbols - such as the state flag, pledge, chants and cheers, as well as constant reinforcement in ministerial speeches and press reports spotlighting Singapore's superiority in a variety of fields - all serve to direct favour and fervour towards the state and, in the process, construct a version of the 'nation'. However as Gramsci(1973) has pointed out, hegemony is never total and the dominant group's preferred reading of texts can often be met with contested meanings. In the next section, I will examine this contestation by using the example of *Not the Singapore song book.*

Not the Singapore song book: parody as resistance

While the government's national songs are clearly ideological and the timing and release of the various texts and intertexts are powered by hegemonic

454

intents, the lyrics contained in *Not the Singapore song book* (1993) reflect how popular music can be a form of subtle cultural resistance as well. Many of the lyrics are written with a humour often parodying national songs and Singapore life. Yet, the humour belies several more deep-seated concerns of the lyricists. Indeed, the lyrics are largely concerned with government policy on the one hand and the 'ugly Singaporean' on the other.

The appropriation of melodies of national songs and the setting of new lyrics to them is particularly powerful as a means of symbolic opposition; this despite the fact that the lyrics do not express explicit opposition to government policies. Their success lies in the way in which resources of other groups are transformed and exaggerated as a form of resistance and protest (Hall and Jefferson 1976; Hebdige 1979), and the way in which new, subtly resistant lyrics are set to familiar tunes meant to arouse patriotism and respect for and gratitude to the ruling order. In the revised version, the lyrics draw ironic attention to controversial government policies. The best example of this is Ong Cheng Tat's *Count! Mummies of Singapore* set to the tune of *Count on me, Singapore*. While the original lyrics exhorted Singaporeans to stand up and be counted amongst those who would give their best and more' to the country *(Sing Singapore* 1988, 95), Ong's version translates the exhortation for Singapore women in particular, urging them to reproduce:

> We have the ova in our bodies,
> We can conceive,
> We can conceive.
> We have a role for Singapore,
> We must receive,
> We must receive. *(Not the Singapore song book* 1993, 35)

The lyrics are a reference to the government's concern that Singapore's fertility level is below replacement rate[16] - a reflection of trends towards later marriages, postponement of child-bearing and smaller family sizes. The urgency with which the government has sounded the alarm about fertility is revealed, in particular, in the frequent public pronouncements by no less than the Prime Minister Goh Chok Tong and Senior Minister Lee Kuan Yew.[17] Ong satirizes this sense of urgency:

> There's a spirit in the air,
> Telling us to be a pair!
> We're going to get our hubbies, start a family . . .

> We must conceive!
> We MUST conceive!! *(ibid.,* 35, original emphasis)

Apart from setting lyrics to the melodies of national songs, other popular tunes (such as *Sixteen going on seventeen, Rose, Rose I love you* and *If you're happy and you know it)* are used. In such cases, the sense of irony may be missing but the impact of the symbolic resistance is not. A range of government positions on national issues are pilloried. Like Ong's contribution, the population issue is the target of many other lyricists, some of whom focus their assault specifically on the Social Development Unit (SDU). The SDU was initiated and sponsored by the government to act as a matchmaking body for the increasing number of non-married graduates. In addition, the SDU organizes many functions and courses which provide opportunities for graduates to get to know one another. The focus on graduates stems from the former Prime Minister's view that it is nature rather than nurture that produces intelligent, hard-working offspring in the mould of the 'excellent Singapore'. Hence, to ensure that the gene pool is not depleted, graduates (with presumably the 'desirable' genes) must continue to reproduce. As one example, Ee Kay Gie's *The SDU march*, to be sung 'vigorously and with conviction' *(ibid.,* 5) to the tune of *Colonel Bogey* exhorts Singaporean women to get married for the sake of the nation. Nowhere in the revised lyrics is there any hint that marriage is for any reason other than as a service to the nation:

> Hey girl!
> Why aren't you married yet!
> You girl!
> A man's not hard to get! . . .
>
> Now's the time for you to choose your mate!
> Don't delay! Do not procrastinate!
> Wed now and do your nation proud -
> Then do your part, spread the word clear and loud!
> *(ibid., 5)*

True to official positions, other revised lyrics also reveal how marriage is not an end in itself but a means to an end - child-bearing. Mary Loh, one of the main contributors to *Not the Singapore song book,* highlights the government position that the rich who can afford it should have more children, while Colin Goh takes the income tax rebates for successive children designed to encourage larger families to ridiculous proportions. Sung to the tune of

Raindrops keep falling on my head, Goh's *Babies keep formin' in my bed* is an exaggeration about how income tax rebates are expected to persuade people to have more children:

And for that
Tax rebate,
I won't be even stoppin'
Reproducin' -
'Cause when it comes to income tax
There's no way like sex.
Babies keep formin' in my bed,
But that doesn't mean
I really wanna keep 'em fed,
Kids are not for me -
'Cause all I wanna do is just keep on savin',
Till my life's free, no more taxes for me . . . *(ibid., 43)*

Other lyricists capture the sense of resignation and helplessness amongst those affected by government policies such as the car policy and streaming in schools. The government's attempts to deal with the severe traffic congestion have prompted the introduction of a quota for the number-of new cars allowed on the roads. Potential car owners are expected to bid for a certificate of entitlement (CoE). The large number of aspiring car owners has raised CoE and hence car prices and many people have been forced out of the market, disappointed if not disgruntled. Desmond Sim captures this disappointment in his version of *What I did for love,* entitled *What I bid for love (ibid.,* 18). Similarly, the way in which the constant streaming in Singapore's education system puts examination pressure on students is captured in the lyrics of Sam Wan's *What we always do is stream (ibid.,* 47), sung to the tune of *All I have to do is dream.* Written into the song is the idea that such streaming exercises have added to the workload and hence have worked to the detriment of students.

On the basis of such examples, I submit that there is a cultural politics at work in *Not the Singapore song book.* The expression of dissatisfaction reflects a certain groundswell in the demand for more open consultative government. That the lyricists represent the better-educated - many of them are lawyers, publishers, playwrights and ex-teachers - reveals how this segment of the population is finding its voice of dissatisfaction, resistance and social commentary.

When set against the ideological messages of national songs, it is not difficult to couch cultural resistance in terms of opposition to the hegemony of the state. However, as Frith (1983) was at pains to illustrate in his iconoclastic work *Sound effects: youth, leisure and the politics of rock,* music (in his case, rock 'n' roll) may also represent opposition to peer-group and adult middle-class norms. Adopting the logic of his argument, I will illustrate how the contributors to *Not the Singapore song book* oppose the norms of two groups, the yuppies and the *nouveau riche* (sometimes they are one and the same), which have arisen out of the rapid economic development in Singapore and the struggle for excellence. These norms are the everyday practices of the 'ugly Singaporean' (one who is greedy, spoilt and ungracious) indulging in an ostentatious lifestyle." Indeed, they have sometimes been cited as constituting a distinctive Singapore culture, although not all agree with this view ('Sunday Plus', *The Sunday Times* 15 August 1993). Certainly, they receive no support from the seventeen lyricists of the *Not the Singapore song book.* By casting some of these norms in a questionable, if not negative light, the lyricists are making a pitch for the development of alternative norms.

The ostentatious lifestyles of many Singaporeans are described in taunting style; many of the lyrics highlight the fixation of Singaporeans with material trappings, such as the 'three cs': condominium, credit card and car *(Three Cees, Not the Singapore song book* 1993, 23), or with brand-name goods such as Gucci, Dior, Fellini, Balmain and Bruno Magli *(My favourite things, ibid.,* 20). Most of the time, the constant effort to keep up with the ostentatious lifestyle is for no better reason than because it is 'chic' or 'stylo[19]' *(Hand phone, I carry hand phone, ibid.,* 7). Unfortunately, it often means 'payin' [f]or what I can't afford *(Cash, ibid., 37).* The result is the need to take anti-stress pills *(Cash, ibid.,* 38) or the *Gold Card blues (ibid.,* 50), as goods are confiscated when the bills cannot be paid. Certainly, the ostentatious lifestyles and the continual attempts to 'live it up' and upgrade already comfortable if not luxurious lifestyles[20] are not uniquely Singaporean traits. They are part of a more widely developed consumer culture. The constant striving for excellence (so strongly encouraged in the national songs) is leading to the alienated and showy lifestyles frowned upon in songs like *Cash.* Other effects of this constant encouragement to do well are the various forms of greed and *'kiasuism'* which are said to characterize the Singaporean. For example, Goh Eck Kheng's *Oh my kiasu (ibid.,* 71), sung to the tune of *Oh my darling Clementine,* vividly portrays the ugliness of the *kiasu* Singaporean:

456

Mr Kiasu, Kiasu King
scared to lose out, always must win;
Number One in everything!
Grab first; don't talk,
Always jump queue,
Help yourself to sample things.
Look for discounts, free is better,
Never mind what they all think!
Must not give face,[21]
Winner takes all,
Hamtam[22] everyone you know.
Take but don't give, bide the best things;
Get there first or else don't go!
Always quit while
you are ahead.
Pushing helps to set the pace.
I want! Give me! First in all things!
That's the way to win the race!

Apart from the ostentatious lifestyles, other traits including, for example, the ugliness of a spoilt yuppie's child *(I'm a yuppie's kiddie, ibid.,* 21) and the inconsiderate, unsociable and irresponsible act of littering (especially of heavy, sharp or breakable material that can cause physical harm, or what is colloquially termed Killer litter') are opposed *(Killer litter, ibid.,* 29).

Taking the cue from Frith (1983), I would suggest that, through these songs, the lyricists are expressing their resistance to some social norms developed, as one lyricist pointed out (personal interview, 16 August 1993, as a consequence of values, such as excellence and hard work, promoted in the national songs. Although positive in themselves, such values become ugly When pushed to extreme limits. While couching his opposition to such extreme interpretations of exemplary values in humorous terms, he maintains that his message is of resistance to 'state and peer-group pressure to excel in everything', even at the expense of 'good mental health and basic courtesy and concern for others'. At the same time, he is at pains to reiterate that the values of striving for excellence and hard work are in themselves positive but, because they are being pounded home' all the time, there is an overkill and people either adopt the ideology or become cynical about the messages. Through satire, many of the writers hope to express resistance to the 'overkill' but. at the same time, they hope to make the original messages more palatable so that people can accept them 'in the right spirit' (telephone interview, 17 August 1993).

This use of satire is a recent phenomenon, dating from the 1980s and involves other cultural forms apart from music, such as literature and drama. For example, in recent years playwrights have become holder in discussing important local social issues, such as race, gender, alternative sexualities, nationalism, censorship and political control, and the question of what makes a country like Singapore home. As pointed out by Heng (1992, 28)

> [m]any of these issues are painful, complex, and fraught with danger . . . [and] . . . playwrights must be careful not to instigate (or be accused of instigating) racial strife, for instance, when they analyse racial prejudices and problems on the local stage.

Hence, humour and, particularly, satire is adopted as the means by which to explore such issues. Yet, as Heng *(ibid.,* 28) also pointed out, the effect may be to 'acclimatise us to accepting, rather than questioning existing social conditions'.

Conclusion

> Over the ages, kings and princes, revolutionaries and priests, peasants and slaves, have expressed their hopes and fears through music. While aiming to convince, they have used music to reassure the faithful as much as to persuade the unbelieving. (Denisoff and Peterson 1972, 13)

While some (Barzun 1958; Greenberg 1957) have argued that popular music is 'simply kitsch background noise' (Denisoff and Peterson 1972, 6), I have sought to argue that ideologically hegemonic intentions as well as voices of resistance can well be detected in popular music. In the case of the 'Sing Singapore' programme, the national songs form part of a total defence strategy in which Singaporeans are organized to defend their country against all forms of attack, military and non-military. This is to happen in two ways. First, Singaporeans are persuaded in the national songs, *inter alia,* to unite as one, differences (racial, religious, cultural, class, etc.) notwithstanding. Once this likelihood of sectoral division is diminished, the possibilities of internal fissures are concomitantly reduced Secondly, Singaporeans can then be prepared to face external threats. Here again, national songs are the ideologically hegemonic tools by which to persuade Singaporeans and reinforce in them a love and patriotism for their country as well as in support for the ruling élite that has succeeded in taking the country from poverty to prosperity. Music is thus used to whip up the patriotic feelings of Singaporeans so that, should they need to be called upon in any way to defend the country, their support will be forthcoming, In this way, social and psychological defence (via the national songs) create the fundamental psyche necessary before economic, civil and military defences can be effected. This, as Lee Kuan Yew pointed out, is what the state wants:

> to produce a community that feels together . . . on certain things it responds together: this is my country; this is my flag; this is my President; this is my future. I am going to protect it. (quoted in *total defence: the total picture* 1987, 10)

In the context of Singapore, therefore, the place of music in the construction of 'nation' is important. Through music, the state is constructing its version of the nation, one in which the citizenry is bound by 'core Asian values', chief of which must be the notion of society above self. It must be noted, of course, that the 'Sing Singapore' programme is neither the first instance of harnessing music in the construction of hegemonic discourse in Singapore, nor indeed is music the only instrument in such a construction. From the first days of independence, the state has attempted to employ music to develop a sense of national identity and patriotic verve. From the organization of national song-writing competitions {to encourage the production of distinctively Singapore songs) to hosting Asia-Pacific song competitions (in which the representative participation of Singaporeans will hopefully whip up a sense of nationalistic support from fellow Singaporeans), music has been part of the state's arsenal in the symbolic construction of nation.

The 'Sing Singapore' programme is hence not singular in the history of state exploitation of music. It is, however, singular in its degree of organization and commitment as well as in the extent of its reach and influence. Whereas allegiance to the state and ruling élite could be relatively well achieved in the past via delivery of economic goods, such allegiance has become more d&cult to gain in recent years with a more sophisticated populace. The state has therefore had to step up its efforts in the hegemonic construction of 'nation'. Music, like some other cultural forms (such as dance (see Chua 1989) and religion (see Kong 1993a)) and non-cultural forms (such as political rhetoric), has therefore been developed to form part of a multiprong strategy.

Neverthelss, the political culture of Singapore does not encourage open conflict and confrontation.

Singaporeans have had to find other ways to express their opposition to preferred meanings (Kong 1993b) and it is in this context that the latent meanings in *Not the Singapore song book* may be appreciated Resistance may be expressed through approved channels such as newspaper columns and the Feedback Unit but here it may be managed and its threat to the status quo nullified. However, while Singaporeans are not weaned on a staple of open conflict, a more educated populace is beginning to discover its political voice and is beginning to express opposition both to government policies and to some Singaporean cultural traits, albeit in symbolic and latent, even supportive, rather than overt or confrontational ways. *Not the Singapore song book* is the outcome of the discovery of such a voice and is one manifestation of an emergent cultural politics of music in Singapore.

Notes

1. See, for example, Baker and Biger (1992); Duncan (1990); Jackson (1989); and Kong (1993a and b).
2. See, for example, Hughes (1989); Meyer (1991); Pen-is (1985); and Stradling (1989).
3. See Hebdige (1979); Maultsby (1983); Tanner (1978); and Winders (1983).
4. See Auslander (1981); Denisoff (1972); Miller and Skipper (1972); and Rodnitzsky (1969).
5. This meant that the British controlled foreign affairs and defence of Singapore and still had a decisive say in internal security, while all other matters were decided by a local government.
6. Disquiet among Malaysian leaders stemmed from communal fears that the predominantly Chinese People's Action Party (PAP) from Singapore intended to supplant the Alliance leaders as the most important political party in Malaysia. This atmosphere of intercommunal bickering and tension was compounded by racial riots in 1964 which left 35 people killed and 563 wounded. Tunku Abdul Rahman proposed separation as a solution to such troubles.
7. Singapore's population comprises a Chinese majority (77·7 per cent) and substantial Malay and Indian minorities (14·1 and 7·1 per cent respectively) The last group, categorized in census reports as 'others', constitutes 1·1 per cent (Lau 1992).
8. Unemployment stood at 1·7 per cent in 1990 *(Singapore* 1991 1991).
9. Indeed, in 1993, one of the new towns, Tampines, won a United Nations Habitat Award in the developed countries section for offering good housing design and amenities. In 1991, the Urban Redevelopment Authority was also awarded the

458

Habitat Scroll of Honour by the United Nations Centre for ,Human Settlements for its achievements in improving Singapore's living environment.

10. At the time of writing, £1·00 is approximately equal to S$2·30.

11. The PAP had won all parliamentary seats in the April 1968, December 1972, December 1976 and December 1980 general elections.

12. *Straits Times Weekly Overseas Edition* (20 August 1988, 4 September 1988, 3 November 1988).

13. Dr Tony Tan, former Education Minister, was quoted as saying that some values like honesty and hard work are universal values, while filial piety and society before self find greater expression in Asian than in western societies *(Straits Times Weekly Overseas Edition* 26 November 1988).

14. While the songs do not enter the official school curriculum, they are played and taught to students during assembly periods.

15. See Savage and Kong (1993) for a discussion of the efforts to-make Singapore a dean and green garden city.

16. Replacement-level fertility (the level of fertility necessary for a given generation of woman to replace themselves with a new generation of women) was reached in 1975. This rate of about 2·1 has since dropped even further to reach 1·6 in 1985 (Yap 1989).

17. *Straits Times* (17 June 1984, 2 March 1987, 22 April 1987, 5 August 1987).

18. whilstthe origins of this concept are unclear, the reality of the phenomena is certainly unquestionable today and takes the form of *kiasuism,* a colloquial term meaning a grabbing mentality, borne of the fear of losing out and the urge to always stay ahead.

19. Singlish word for stylish.

20. This phenomena has recently been labelled the Singapore paradox' by the second Minister for Trade and Industry, Lim Boon Heng *(The Sunday Times* 15 August 1993, 24).

21. 'Give face' is a colloquial term meaning to do someone a favour and to give him/her some consideration.

22. 'Hamtam' is used in Singlish to mean pulverize.

References

Anderson K and Gale F eds 1992 *Inventing places: studies in cultural geography* Longman Cheshire, Melbourne

Auslander H B 1981 'If you wanna end war and stuff, you gotta sing loud' a survey of Vietnam-related protest music *Journal of American Culture* 4 108-13

Baker A R H and Biger G eds 1992 *Ideology and landscape in historical perspective* Cambridge University Press, Cambridge

Barzun J 1958 *Music in American life* Doubleday, New York

Bellah R N 1970 *Beyond belief: essays on religion in a post-traditional world* Harper & Row, New York

Buaug Z 1989 A matter of survival *Mirror* 1 April l-2

Burgess J and Gold J eds 1985 *Geography, the media, and popular culture* Croom Helm, London

Carney G O ed. 1987 *The sounds of people and places: readings in the geography of American folk and popular music* University Press pf America, Lanham

Chan H C 1975 Politics in an administrative stage: where has the politics gone? in. **Seah C M** ed *Trends in Singapore* Singapore University Press for Institute of Southeast Asian Studies, Singapore 51-68

Chan H C 1976 The political system and political change in Hassan R ed. *Singapore: society in transition* Oxford University Press, Kuala Lumpur 30-51

Chan H C 1989 The PAP and the structuring of the political system in **Sandhu K S and Wheatley P** eds *The management of success: the mudding of modern Singapore* Institute of Southeast Asian Studies, Singapore 70-89

Chua S P 1989 Cultural pluralism in dance: the changing scene in Singapore *Performing* Arts 5 52-4

Clarke J, Hall S, Jefferson T and Roberts B 1976 Subcultures, cultures and class: a theoretical overview in **Hall S and Henderson J** eds *Resistance through rituals* Hutchinson/Centre for Contemporary Cultural Studies, London 9-74

Daniels S 1993 *Fields of vision: landscape imagery and national identity in England and the United States* Polity Press, Cambridge

Denisoff R S 1972 Evolution of the American protest song in **Denisoff R S and Peterson R A** eds *The sounds of social change* Rand McNally and Company, Chicago 15-25

Denisoff R S and Peterson R A eds 1972 *The sounds of social change* Rand McNally and Company, Chicago

Duncan J 1990 *The city as text: the politics of landscape interpretation in the Kandyan Kingdom* Cambridge University Press, Cambridge

Frith S 1983 *sound effects: youth, leisure, and the politics of rock* Constable, London

Goh C T 1986 *Speeches* Ministry of Communications and Information, Singapore

Gramsci A 1973 *Letters from prison* Harper and Row, New York

Greenberg C 1957 Avant-garde and kitsch in **Rosenberg B and Manning White D** eds *Mass culture* Free Press, New York 98-107

Hall S and Jefferson T 1976 eds *Resistance through rituals youth subcultures in post-war Britain* Hutchinson/Centre for Contemporary Cultural Studies, London

Harvey D 1984 On the history and present condition of geography: an historical materialist manifesto The *Professional Geographer* 36 1-10

Hebdige D 1979 *Subculture: the meaning of style* Methuen, London

459

Heng G 1992 Singapore: an eastern fashion-driven society *The Straits Times* 2 May 28

Ho W C 1981 The subculture of rock music in Singapore Unpubl. academic exercise, Department of Sociology, National University of Singapore

Hughes M 1989 The Duc d'Elgar': making a composer gentleman in **Norris C** ed. *Music and the politics of culture* Lawrence & Wishart, London 41-68

Jackson P and Penrose J eds 1993 *Constructions of race, place and nation* University College Press, London; University of Minnesota Press, Minneapolis

Jackson R 1989 *Maps of meaning Unwin Hyman*, London

Kong L 1993a Ideological hegemony and the political symbolism of religious buildings in Singapore *Environment and Planning* D: *Society and Space* 11 23-34

Kong L 1993b Negotiating conceptions of 'sacred space': a case study of religious buildings in Singapore *Transactions of the Institute of British Geographers* NS 18(3) 342-58

Kong L and Yeoh B S A 1992 The practical uses of nature in urban Singapore *Commentary* 10 36-46

Lau K E 1992 *Singapore census of population 1990: demographic characteristics* Department of Statistics, Singapore

Maultsby P K 1983 soul music; its sociological and political significance in American popular culture *Journal of Popular Culture* 51-60

Meyer M 1991 *The politics of music in the Third Reich* Peter Lang, New York

Miller L and Skipper J K 1972 Sounds of black protest in avant-garde jazz in **Denisoff R S and Peterson R A** eds *The sounds of social change* Rand McNally and Company, Chicago 26-37

Nguik S Y C 1991 General music education in the primary schools in Singapore 1954-1990 Unpubl. EdD thesis, University of Illinois, Urbana-Champaign

Not the Singapore song book 1993 Hotspot Books, Singapore

Perris A 1985 *Music as propaganda: art to persuade, art to control* Greenwood Press, Westport, CT, and London

Quah J S T and Quah S R 1989 The limits of government intervention in **Sandhu K S** and **Wheatley P** eds *Management of success: the moulding of modern Singapore* Institute of Southeast Asian Studies, Singapore 102-27

Rodnitzky J L 1969 The evolution of the American protest song *Journal of Popular Culture* 3 35-45

Savage V R and Kong L 1993 Urban constrains, political imperatives: environmental 'desing' in Singapore *Landscape and Urban Planning* 25 37-52

Seah C M 1973 *Community centres in Singapore: their political involvement* Singapore University Press, Singapore

Seah C M 1989 National security in **Sandhu K S** and **Wheatley P** eds *Management of success: the moulding of modern Singapore* Institute of Southeast Asian Studies, Singapore 949-62

Sing Singapore 1988 Psychological Defence Division Ministry of communications and Information, Singapore

Singapore 1991 1991 Ministry of Information and the Arts, Singapore

Singapore facts and pictures 1992 1992 Ministry of Information and the Arts, Singapore

Stradling R 1989 On shearing the black sheep in spring the repatriation of Frederick Delius in **Norris C** ed. *Music and the politics of culture Lawrence & Wishart*, London 69-105

Stump R W 1985 Towards a geography of American civil religion *Journal of Cultural Geography* 5(2) 87-95

Tanner J 1978 Pop, punk and subcultural solutions *Popular Music and Society* 6 68-71

Thomas P L 1986 *Like tigers around a piece of meat: the Baba style of Dondang Sayang* Institute of Southeast Asian Studies, Singapore

Total defence: the total picture 1987 Kim Seng Constituency, Singapore

Warren R L 1972 The Nazi use of music as an instrument of social control in **Denisoff R S an Peterson R A** eds *The sounds of social change* Rand McNally and Company, Chicago 72-8

Winders J A 1983 Reggae, rastafarians and revolution: rock music in the *Third World Journal of Popular Culture* 17 61-73

Yap M T 1989 The demographic base in **Sandhu K S and Wheatley P** eds *Management of success: the moulding of modern Singapore* Institute of Southeast Asia Studies, Singapore 455-76

Yong M C 1992 Singapore: the city-state in history in **Ban K C, A and Tong C K** eds *Imagining Singapore* Times Academic Press, Singapore 24-45

[5]

'The morning of freedom rose up': Kurdish popular song and the exigencies of cultural survival

STEPHEN BLUM and AMIR HASSANPOUR

In the final scene of Harold Pinter's play *Mountain Language* (1988), a guard informs the prisoners that they are now permitted to speak in their own language, at least 'until further notice'. The guard is an agent of an unnamed state that pursues a policy of linguicide, summarised in an earlier scene by an officer who tells prisoners that 'Your language no longer exists'. In 1993 the Kurdish *Tiyatora Botan* (based in Cologne) began to present Pinter's play to audiences of immigrants from Turkey, where Kurds were long called 'mountain Turks' (*dağli Türkler*) by the government.[1]

All the arguments and techniques that states can deploy in attempting to suppress languages and cultures have become familiar to Kurds, who constitute the largest non-state nation in the world.[2] Kurds living in Turkey, Syria, Iraq and Iran have yet to obtain unrestricted rights to education, publishing and broadcasting in Kurmanji and Sorani, the two main dialect groups of Kurdish.[3] Kurdish broadcasting and publishing remain tightly controlled by the government in Iraq and Iran; in Turkey the distribution of Kurdish publications and cassettes was legalised in 1991, but distributors and purchasers face various types of interference from officials and others. We do not write as dispassionate observers of this situation but as active participants in the continuing struggle to maintain and cultivate all Kurdish dialects wherever they are spoken. To recognise an existing plurality of languages, and the rights of citizens to express themselves in their native tongue, would not endanger the interests of any democratic state: only despotic states insist on denying basic language rights to their subjects.

Those who tell Kurds that their language does not exist create conditions in which singing or listening to a popular song are a sign of life. In such conditions, every performance of a Kurdish song conveys the same message as the refrain of the nationalist song 'Ey, Reqîb' (O, Enemy!): 'Let no one say that the Kurds will die; Kurds will live on' (Example 1). For exactly this reason, in 1967 the Turkish government made it illegal for Kurds to own or distribute recordings in 'a language other than Turkish'. Police in many parts of Kurdistan have searched houses looking for Kurdish-language recordings.[4] Listening behind closed windows is a well-

326   *Blum and Hassanpour*

Example 1. 'Ey Reqîb' with the original Sorani text (from Nebes 1969, p. 52) and the Kurmanji text sung by Şivan Perwer (on his Tape 3).

Ey re-qîb her ma-we qew – mi Kurd zi-
Ey re-qib her her ma-ye qew – mê Kurd zi-

man, Nay-şi-kê – nê da – ne y to-pî zeman, Na-şi-kê û da – na-yê to-pê ze-

REFRAIN

man Keş ne – îê Kurd mir-du – we,
man Keş ne-bê Kurd di -mir-in

Kurd zîn – du – we Zîn – du – we, qet
Kurd jin di – bin Jin di – bin, qet

na – ne – wê a – îa – ke – man
na – ka – wê a – la Kurd – an

Sorani (from Nebez 1969, p. 52)
Ey reqîb her mawe qewmî Kurdziman (or: Kurd zuban)
Nayşikênê dane y (or: danerî) topî zeman

Kes nelê Kurd mirduwe, Kurd zînduwe,

Zînduwe, qet nanewê, alakeman.

(O enemy, the Kurdish-speaking people are still alive,

The creator of the cannon of time cannot destroy them.
Let no one say that the Kurds will die; Kurds will live on.
They will live, the flag of the Kurds will not fall down.)

Kurmanji (from Bayrak, p. 137)
Ey reqîb her maye qewmê Kurd ziman,
Naşikê û danayê topê zeman.
Keş nebê Kurd dimirin, Kurd jin dibin.
Jin dibin, qet nakavê ala Kurdan.

established practice; ownership of tapes counts as evidence of 'separatism' just like ownership of printed materials.

Important though it is, language is not the only distinctive feature of 'Kurdish popular song' – the music that Kurds most readily accept as their own when they participate in weddings and concerts, listen to radio broadcasts, and purchase or make copies of cassettes. The 'listening public' is, of course, much larger than

Nasir Rezazi in concert.

the reading public addressed by Kurdish publications. We define the latter as 'a population of individuals capable of independent reading' (Hassanpour 1992, p. 444), which excludes the many Kurds to whom native-tongue education has been denied. The listening public includes anyone who expresses approval or disapproval of performances offered by Kurdish musicians. The Diaspora of well over half a million Kurds in Europe, North America and Australia constitutes an important segment of both publics.

Formation of a listening public

The formation of reading publics requires standardisation of languages and stimulates further efforts at language reform (see Hassanpour 1992, pp. 439–68). In contrast, the circumstances in which music is produced do not always favour standardisation of the musical idiom, and a listening public may or may not desire a high degree of standardisation.

In Kurdistan, as in other oral societies, songs were performed, heard and transmitted in face-to-face encounters between singers and audiences. During the activity known as *geřelawije* in Mukri Kurdistan (the area around Mahabad in Iranian Kurdistan), which is still a part of many social gatherings, each listener becomes a performer when it is his or her turn to sing. Dependence on face-to-face encounters, in which the number of listeners is necessarily limited and every performance is in some respects a new act of musical creation, inhibits the development of a listening *public*. Nonetheless, songs and other musical forms have crossed dialect and even language barriers as they were carried by individuals from region to region. The late Tawfiq Wahby remembered numerous songs performed in the early twentieth century in Sulaimaniya (then part of the Ottoman Empire, now in Iraq) by mule-riders and others in caravans coming from Mahabad.[5] In the 1930s listeners in Mahabad heard summer performances by the great singer Seyd 'Elî 'Esẍer Kurdistanî from the Sanandaj region (which has a distinctive dialect, although 'Esẍer's lyrics were usually not of local origin and were influenced by Sulaimani and Mukriyani literature).

More often than not, urban singers like Seyd 'Elî 'Esẍer were born in villages and attracted to cities by the presence of instrumentalists, tea-houses, and more sizeable and affluent audiences. Villages generally remained the most important source of songs. Until quite recently it was rare for members of the urban and upper middle classes to become singers: the family of Şemaî Sa'ib (born in Sulaimaniya) opposed his decision to pursue this profession, and in the 1950s Menîc Heyran of Mahabad had to abandon her (wealthy) family before she could accept invitations to sing at weddings. The advent of gramophones and the broadcast media, and of limited music education in schools, helped to raise the status of singers and musicians. Several prominent contemporary singers (Nasir Rezazi, Şahrux, Mezher Xaliqî) are from urban (though not necessarily upper- or middle-class) backgrounds. Most singers today are male; the proportion of female singers is higher in Kurmanji-speaking areas than elsewhere.[6]

Songs called *goranî* or *stran* are potentially more popular than other vocal genres, since they are short, non-narrative and easier to learn. They are found all over Kurdistan, unlike the more specialised genres *beyt* (narrative), *lawik* and *heyran*, which are not performed in the regions of Kirkuk, Sanandaj and Kirmanshah. Every *goranî* has a refrain, which may be considerably longer than the verses (see Example 2). Dance songs, lyric songs and political songs are all considered *goranî*, although some singers specialise (to the point of avoiding dance songs, or singing almost nothing else). One who sings for the dancing at weddings will call out lines praising individual male dancers, who are expected to reciprocate with donations. One who sings after the dancing is paid by the bridegroom's family and enjoys a higher status. This distinction is no longer relevant at concerts in the Diaspora where listeners will expect to hear some dance songs and will probably wish to dance in the aisles.

The initial impetus towards creation of a nationwide public, joining together the local audiences that still exist, came from the introduction of gramophones in 1908 and years following. The owners of gramophones were landed nobility in the villages, merchants and top government officials in the cities. Recordings were in Turkish, Arabic and Persian since, as usual, the dominant nations were the first to make use of the new medium. Kurdish songs did not appear on phonograph records until the late 1920s, when several companies in Baghdad (His Master's Voice, Baidaphon, HomoKord and Polyphon) produced dozens of records with songs performed by Kurdish singers from Iraq, Iran and Syria. Seyd 'Elî 'Esẍer's

Example 2. 'Hêdî, Hêdî' (Gently, Gently) as sung by Sahrux on Az dast-e 'eshq.

La dû- re- we   na- wit bîs - tûm,   Na- şu- re-

za   xo- şit wîs-   tûm,   Gwu-ye le-   gel

şi'- re- kan-   ma   zor ji- ya - wî,   ji- ya -

REFRAIN

wî   we- re şe-   mal, we- re   we- re şe-   mal, we- re,

Ma-yey ji -   nim,   a-   wa- tî gya-   nim,

ma-ye- y ji- ya-   nim, a-   wa-tî gya-   nim   Hê- dî, hê-

dî, hê- dî,   we- re des- tî, we-re,   dil şi- kis - ti, we- re,

A- wa-   tî jî-   nim   ma-ye-y ji- ya-   nim

A - wa-   tî jî -   nem, a- man, ma-ye -y ji- ya-   nim

Le dûrewe nawit bîstûm	(From afar you have heard my name
Naşureza xosjt wîstûm	Without knowing (me) you have liked me
Gwuye legel şi 'rekanma zor jiyawî, jiwayî	It is said (that) you have lived with my poems, you have lived . . .
Were şemal, were (2)	Come, North Wind, come (2)
Mayey jiyanim, awatî giyanim (2)	(You are) the substance of my life, the yearning of my soul (2)
Hêdî, hêdî, were destî, were,	Gently, gently come into my hands [i.e. join me in dance], come
Dîl şikisti, were	My broken heart, come,
Awatî jînim, mayey jiyanim	Yearning of my life, substance of my life.)

thirteen recordings are largely responsible for his continuing influence on Kurdish music in all Sorani-speaking areas.[7]

Radio broadcasting has contributed, more than any other factor, to the formation of a listening public with access to music on a daily basis. Broadcasting in Kurdish began in the 1920s in the autonomous Kurdish region in Soviet Caucasia. In Iraq, Kurdish broadcasting began in 1939 and during World War II there were two wartime stations from Jaffa and Beirut playing music in their propaganda programming. The size of the public for these broadcasts was obviously quite small, since only the wealthy could afford a radio set. In 1938, the Iraqi government installed radio sets with loudspeakers in public places in a number of Kurdish cities. But radio did not become a popular medium until the 1960s, when affordable transistor sets penetrated homes in the urban and rural areas.

While copyright was never a problem (since no country in the region had signed a regional or international copyright agreement), the Soviet, Iranian and Iraqi governments exercised political and ideological controls over the types of music that were broadcast. Radio Yerevan in Soviet Armenia, Radio Tehran and Kirmanshah in Iran, and Radio Baghdad only aired songs recorded in their own country. Radio Yerevan, broadcasting in Kurmanji, had more female singers than Radio Baghdad. All these stations preferred *goranî* or *stran* to other musical genres, although Radio Baghdad also played *heyran* and *qetar*. Songs with a political content were not played on these government-run stations except during a brief period following the fall of the Iraqi monarchy in July 1958. After Radio Cairo initiated a propaganda campaign against the pro-Western regimes of Iraq, Iran and Turkey in 1957, its Kurdish programme regularly aired the nationalist song 'Ey, Reqîb!' (O, Enemy!) and other political songs such as 'Ey Kurdine' (O, Kurds).

From 1947 to the present, clandestine stations have been a major source for political songs. Despite being officially suppressed in Turkey, Kurdish music survived in the countryside. The airwaves from Yerevan, Baghdad and Kirmanshah carried music into private homes, despite the fact that listening to Kurdish broadcasts was considered an act against the Turkish state.

Today, the listening public has access to a diverse universe of songs through radio, television, audio and video stores and their own VCRs and tape recorders. The first Kurdish-controlled television stations (located in Sulaimaniya, Erbil and Zakho) broadcast locally produced programmes that reach more than half of those living in the area governed by the Regional Government of Kurdistan (Hedges 1992, Zimmerman 1994). Artists living outside Kurdistan return for concerts attended by enormous numbers of listeners (e.g., Nazir Rezazi's July 1991 concerts in Ranya, Rawandiz, Diyana and Shaqlawa). The autonomous war of Kurds in Iran since 1979 made it possible for many activists (belonging to several political parties) to move to other regions, heightening the exchange of linguistic, cultural and musical influences. In the Diaspora, singers and instrumentalists from all parts of Kurdistan perform for audiences comprised largely of emigrants from Turkey, Iran and Iraq.

Musical life in the Diaspora

Conditions in the Diaspora are especially conducive to interaction among musicians from Kurmanji- and Sorani-speaking regions. The singer Delal (born in Istanbul and now living in Sweden) told an interviewer for the bilingual (Kurmanji and

Nasir Rezazi in concert.

Sorani) publication *Dîdar* that 'Kurdish music is one music'; hence she has 'tried to become more familiar with Sorani music during the last four years' by listening to recordings of such outstanding singers as Hesen Zîrek (from the Mukryan region) and Tahir Tofîq (from Koy Sanjaq in Iraqi Kurdistan), and by collaborating on her fourth cassette with a young Sorani instrumentalist, Murad Kawa (Bêkes 1994, p. 11). Had she chosen to remain in Turkey, her opportunities for exposure to Sorani music would have been limited to recordings and radio broadcasts from outside the country.

It is the scope and intensity, not the mere fact, of contact that distinguish the present from earlier periods of Kurdish cultural history. Emigrants keep in touch with current styles of dancing and of 'Kurdish dress' as they receive video-tapes of weddings, television programmes and concerts from Kurdistan; tapes of events in the Diaspora are also sent back home. Wedding videos usually include footage of live musical performances as well as songs (in various languages) added during production to provide a soundtrack for scenes like those of the wedding party travelling in cars, or the montage of family photos of bride and groom that normally precedes the scene in which the marriage documents are signed.

The listening public is eager to hear singers from all regions of Kurdistan. It has become much more than a mere 'confederation' of smaller publics, each inclined towards songs in its own dialects. Certainly, individual listeners may be quick to complain when songs from their region are not performed. As a new ensemble was making its debut at a Stockholm restaurant in October 1993, a man from Kirmanshah (in the southernmost part of Iranian Kurdistan) shouted 'Imam 'Ali! if you do not play any songs from Kirmanshah . . .'. All the same, the activities of the singers who are recovering and expanding the repertoire of Kurdish song are greatly appreciated by most segments of the listening public.

A good example of the type of programme that is more easily produced in the Diaspora than in most parts of Kurdistan is the 'Kurdish Concert' held on Saturday 4 June 1994 at the Haus der Begegnung in the eighth district of Vienna. It was organised by the Association of Democratic Students from Iranian Kurdistan with additional support from the society of 'Friends of the Kurdish People' and the 'Wiener Integrationsfonds', which sponsors cultural events for various immigrant groups under the motto 'Wir alle sind Wien' ('*All* of us make up Vienna'). Nazê Deborian (b. 1968 in the Armenian SSR and now living in Denmark), one of two featured singers, was accompanied by her husband Newroz, who plays Western flute and Kurdish *balaban* (a cylindrical oboe with a broad reed, *pîk*). The other singer Ala Salahiyan (b. 1952 in Sanandaj and living in Vienna since 1988), was accompanied by an ensemble of three musicians ('*ūd*, electric bass, and piano) led by Rizgar Xoşnaw (b. 1952 in Shaqlawa and now living in Graz). Many of Ala's songs have been composed by Xoşnaw, whose ensemble used notations of the melodies (single lines in the treble clef). Instrumental introductions on '*ūd*, flute, or piano were never as long as they sometimes are on cassettes.

Announced for 17.00, the concert began shortly after 18.00 and ended at 21.30. An intermission of about 75 minutes gave the audience a good chance to socialise over drinks and snacks. Children in the audience were more active than their parents in moving to the music, sometimes turning in their seats to face one another and clap hands, or moving their shoulders to the right on one bar and to the left on the next.

The singers performed separate sets on each half of the programme, largely made up of songs from their most recent (privately produced) cassettes, which were on sale in the lobby. Interestingly, the arrangements on Nazê's cassette are the work of Sulaimaniya musicians with whom she collaborated in 1993. Both singers refreshed their memory of the lyrics by glancing at song-sheets written in the modified Cyrillic alphabet (for Nazê's Kurmanji) or in the modified Arabic alphabet (for Ala's Sorani). When Stephen Blum asked Ala whether the differences between Sorani and Kurmanji have much significance for singers, he replied that 'there is only a little difference', comparable to the variations in German as spoken in Berlin and Vienna. It is true that some songs are performed in both languages: for example 'Lûrke, Lûrke' and 'Ez Kevokim' ('Kaboke' in Sorani; versions of this song are performed in every region where Kurds reside, including the province of Khorasan in north-eastern Iran).

In this concert, each singer presented a rather different repertoire. Nazê made her entrance singing the conventional syllables '*loi loi*', and many of her songs included long strings of similar vocables (e.g., '*oi dele, dele min*' and '*yar Gulê Gulêk, Gulê Gulêk, Gulê Gulêk*'). Her sets stayed closer than Ala's to the repertoire identified in Kurdish publications as 'folklore' and in this respect were consistent with the slogan 'Biçînewe bo Kurdistan' (Let's go back to Kurdistan), printed on the flyers that advertised the concert.

Nationalist songs composed by Xoşnaw (e.g., 'Ême Heyn' (We Live)) hold an important position in Ala's repertoire. His cassette also includes another composer's setting of a poem by the nationalist poet Hêmin. On the whole, popular song in Sorani makes greater use of lyrics by major twentieth-century poets than does popular song in Kurmanji. Such poets as 'Ebdulla Goran (1904–62) have intended for some of their verses to be sung rather than read; poems designed more for reading have also been appropriated by singers and composers.

Singers, topics and repertoires

At a concert in the Diaspora and in the territory controlled by the Regional Government of Kurdistan, the listening public can hear whatever songs the singers wish to present. This state of affairs marks a welcome change from the circumstances in which public performance of political songs was a risky undertaking (except during such brief periods as the cessation of hostilities between the Iraqi government and the Kurds in the early 1970s, when the late Şemaî Sa'ib performed his song in honour of the nationalist leader Mela Mistefa Barzanî).

The celebrated singer Miĥemedî Mamilî of Mahabad (b. 1925 or 1926 in a family of musicians) is said to have performed more than 700 songs during his long career (Ehmed 1983, p. 9), and his large repertoire has never included dance songs. Although most of Mamilî's songs are non-political, a song based on Hêmin's poem *Gulî Hîwa* (The Flower of Hope) celebrates the struggle of a female *peshmarga* named Exter (Hêmin 1974, pp. 142–3; Ehmed 1983, p. 348):

Exter kiçî Kurdî çaw mest
Ilhambexşî şi'rî piî' hest
Ey pêşmergey millet perest
Ke dîtimî tifeng bedest
Zanîm gulî hîwa pişkût
Beyanî azadî engût

(Exter, Kurdish girl with beautiful eyes,
Inspirer of poems full of feeling,
O you patriotic peshmarga,
When I saw you with a rifle in your hands
I knew that the flower of hope blossomed.
The morning of freedom rose up.)

Mamilî performed the song only in private gatherings and did not allow any uncontrolled taping of it; all the same, he was repeatedly arrested and deported (for political activism as well as for specific songs) during the last two decades of the Pahlavi monarchy (terminated in 1979 by the Iranian Revolution).

Another prolific singer, Tahir Tofîq, sang a number of political songs such as 'Gulî Serbestî' (The Flower of Freedom) and 'Şîrîn Behare' (Shirin, It is Spring!). The repertoire of Mela Kerîm (1885–1938), one of the first singers to be recorded, included at least three patriotic songs: 'Fexre bo ême Kurdistan' (Kurdistan is our Pride), 'Dil le Derdi Weten' (My Heart from the Pain of my Homeland), and 'Çend Şîrîne Lam Dar û Berdî Wetenim' (How Sweet are the Trees and Stones of my Homeland) (Şarbajêrî 1985, p. 144). It is hoped that current singers will revive some of these songs.

Of the eleven *sirûd*-s ('anthems' designed for group singing) printed in the collected poems of Goran (1980), 'Berî Beyane' (It is the Beginning of Morning) and 'Demî Raparîne' (It is the Time of the Uprising) have been most popular. His *sirûd* 'Kurdistan' was regularly aired from the late 1960s to the mid-1970s by the clandestine station Radiyoy Peykî Êran (operated by the Iranian Tudeh Party in Eastern Europe). Goran's verses have probably been more popular with singers than those of any other Kurdish poet, owing in part to his creative transformation of the syllabic rhythms of folk poetry (see Khaznadar 1967; Hitchins 1993). His narrative poem *Bûkêki Nakam* (An Unfulfilled Bride) can be effectively sung using the traditional melody-types known as *meqam*, a word borrowed from the Arabic

334   *Blum and Hassanpour*

Example 3. Sivan Perwer, 'Hevalê bargiranim' (from his Tape 2).

Hevalê bargiranim
Hevalê şoreşvanim,
Hozane geli bin dest,
Hozane Kurdistanim,
Az denge Kurdistanim,
Endame Kurdistan

(I am a friend of the toilers,
I am a friend of the revolutionaries,
The singer of the oppressed people,
I am the singer of Kurdistan,
I am the voice of Kurdistan,
A member [i.e. a citizen] of Kurdistan)

maqâm, used in both Kurmanji and Sorani (see the transcription of four lines in Blum 1980, p. 303).

Singers can dramatise the continuing vitality of Kurdish culture by reviving songs and verses that had almost vanished, by reproducing and adapting rural songs in new performance contexts, by continuing to perform the songs associated with Kurdish nationalism, and by composing new songs on topics of current interest. Şivan Perwer, a prominent singer who began his career in the Diaspora, is deeply engaged in all of these activities. His first cassettes of the late 1970s and his 1976 performances at the eighteenth congress of the Kurdish Students Society in Europe emphasised nationalist songs, such as 'Ey, Reqîb!' (O, Enemy!, see Example 1) and his own 'Hevalê Bargiranim' (I Am a Friend of the Toilers, see Example 3). These tapes became popular among Iranian leftist groups immediately after the Revolution; a booklet containing the full text and a Persian translation of his *Tape One* was issued in 1979 by the Association for Defence of the National Rights of the Kurdish People (Kirmanshah) (Jami yat-e Dafa' 1979). The Kurmanji translation of 'Ey, Reqîb!' sung by Şivan is close enough to the original Sorani verses (by the poet Dildar, 1918–48) so that both versions can be sung simultaneously (as sometimes occurs at *Newroz* – New Year's – festivities and at funerals for members of the *peshmerga*).

Şivan drew on a wide range of Kurmanji poetry from the seventeenth century to the present as he expanded his repertoire, which now includes somewhere between 400 and 500 songs. He had produced twenty-five cassettes by 1991. The compact disc *Chants du Kurdistan* (1989) includes a song attributed to the poet Feqiyê Teyran (1598–1660) as well as Şivan's setting of 'Ey Firat' (O Euphrates!) by Cigerxwîn (1903–84), the most important Kurmanji poet of this century (whose verses have been largely neglected by other singers). Verses that might occur in many traditional songs (e.g., 'Canê, Canê, Canê, Were Meydanê' (My Soul, Come Out into the Open Space)) are joined by Şivan with new verses, in this case 'Dilana Me Şoreş E' (Our Wedding Ceremony is a Revolution). Several songs evoke common social relationships, such as marriage between a man and the daughter of his father's brother ('Lê Dotmam' on the compact disc; cf. the lyrics in Bayrak 1991, p. 201) or the plight of a wife and children who are deported after the husband and father is arrested ('Mala Min' (My Family, My House), also on the compact disc). Şivan accompanies all his songs on the *tanbur* (a plucked lute with three courses), which provides a series of strong accents that are co-ordinated with the articulation of the sung syllables.

Popular song necessarily draws heavily on the conventional topics, verbal formulas, rhythms and melody-types that have long been associated with the Kurdish way of life. Kurdish singers use conventional rhythmic patterns to combine groups of three or four syllables into lines of 4 + 4, 3 + 4, 3 + 4 + 4, 4 + 3 + 4 etc (see Examples 1 and 3). Most words are easily understood no matter which syllables receive longer durations or coincide with strong beats (this is what is usually meant by the term 'syllabic rhythm'). However, many two-syllable words are most often sung so that the initial accented syllable falls on a beat and has a higher pitch than the second syllable (cf. *were* (come) and *hêdî* (gently) in Example 2).

The common birthday greeting *'pêpîroz'* or *'Be Pîroz, be pîrozbê'* (Congratulations!, All the Best!) is nicely accommodated by the rhythmic pattern shown in Example 4, which Nasir Rezazi selected for the 'Kurdish birthday song' he composed in order to meet the need for such a song at birthday celebrations (Example 5). We do not know of any other song that includes the birthday greeting; another composer would be free to set these words to a different rhythm. Rezazi's cassette *Be Pîroz* also includes a song addressed to a *bêrî*, one of the women who milks the sheep and goats after the shepherds bring them back to the fold. This is such a common topic of Kurdish song that lines addressing a *bêrî* are sung to a number of rhythmic patterns (Example 6). Kurds born in urban areas who have not spent some time in villages would not have experienced this aspect of village life. Yet the *bêrî* songs and poetry are still viable, in part as reminders of a rural way of life. Whatever activities members of the listening public may pursue in their daily lives, most have at least a residual awareness of the importance of herding animals in the traditional economy of Kurdistan.

Rezazi (b. 1955 in Sanandaj and now living in Sweden) has composed about sixty new songs and knows at least another 1,000. He has produced thirty-three cassettes. The rhythms and melodic shapes of his songs make them immediately identifiable as Kurdish, however much he may have transformed traditional musical resources in a new song. Of the nine songs on his cassette *Razyane* (Anise), one is identified as the traditional genre *lawk* and the melodies of the others are described as 'folklore'. The lyrics, however, are credited to Rezazi himself (three songs) and to the important Sorani poets Şêrko Bêkes (two songs) and Hêmin (one song) as well as to 'folklore' (two songs). Rezazi was active in the nationalist movement and has lived in different regions of Kurdistan. He sings Kurdish poetry in Kurmanji, in Hawrami and in the southernmost Kirmanshahi dialect as well as in Sorani, and he is one of the few singers who also write on Kurdish music and culture (cf. Rezazi 1990, 1991).

336   *Blum and Hassanpour*

Example 4.

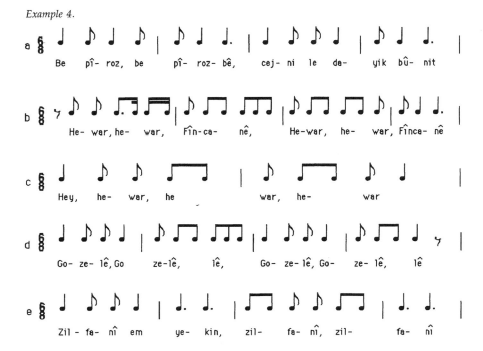

Sources:

a) Nasir Rezazi, Be Pîroz, A/1
b) Cewarî 1983, no. 26
c) Celîl 1973, no. 34
d) Celîl 1986, no. 46
e) Cewarî 1983, no. 12

The ability to create new lyrics for existing melodies and melody-types (an activity in which Rezazi excels) has long been one of a singer's most important skills in Kurdistan and in neighbouring regions. One way that Mamilî would prepare himself for the season of weddings was to create new words in Kurdish for some of the Azerbaijani songs he heard on broadcasts from Baku (capital of the Azerbaijan SSR). When asked in the late 1960s by Amir Hassanpour why he chose to do this, Mamilî replied that he had 'also revived many old Kurdish songs', which was true (and would also have entailed the creation of new lyrics).[8] Azeri songs never amounted to more than a small fraction of his vast repertoire (estimated, as stated earlier, at over 700 songs).

Mamilî is by no means the only singer to have made Kurdish adaptations of songs from other languages. A notable recording by Mela Kerîm, 'Ke Delên', was based on the Turkish song 'Adalar Sahilinde' (On the Shores of the Islands) with new Kurdish lyrics by the poet Pîremêrd.[9] 'Ke Delên', which was probably recorded in Baghdad in the 1930s, was still being played in Mahabad tea-houses

Example 5. Nasir rezazi, 'Be pîroz, be pîrozbê' (Congratulations! or All the best!).

Be pîroz, be pîrozbê cejni le dayik bûnit

Dinya be towe xoşe ke manay heye bûnit

Jîn bizey ketwe ser lêw ke toy de xowe bînî

Şiney ewîn helî kird pîroztirîn owînî.

(All the best (on the occasion of) the celebration of your birth!

With you the world is pleasant, your life has meaning.

Life had a smile on its lips when it found you with it.

The breeze of love . . .)

during the 1950s and was reissued in the 1960s. It remains a standard, recently performed by the Kāmkār family with a different set of lyrics ('Hewraman' on their cassette no. 14). 'Ke Delên' may serve as an excellent example of how foreign components of a repertoire may become 'Kurdish' as they are reproduced and altered by Kurdish singers.

Influences and 'authenticity'

Conceptions of what is 'essentially Kurdish' vary according to differences in working and living conditions and in response to various ideological constraints. Performances by the Kāmkār family, including a concert of 'Kurdish Folk Music' presented by Bijan Kāmkār and the *Dāstān* ensemble in Stockholm on 13 November 1993, have been criticised by some listeners as 'too much under the influence of

338   *Blum and Hassanpour*

Example 6.

Sources:
a) Bayrak 1991, p. 167
b) Nasir Rezazi, Be Piroz, A/2
c) Celîl 1986, no. 73
d) Celîl 1986, no. 3

Persian music', and it is undeniable that the family has long been intensely involved with Persian classical music. Responding to one of his critics on a Stockholm Kurdish radio programme, Bijan Kāmkār (b. 1949, Sanandaj) argued that his music remained 'essentially Kurdish' despite the Persian influences. The concerts and cassettes of the Kāmkārs are often arranged so that the music on each half or side remains within one Persian *dastgāh* or *āvāz*. For example, the two sides of Pashang Kāmkār's 'Bārāne' (1990), a recording of solo improvisations on the *santur* (a hammered dulcimer, one of the central instruments of Persian music), are in the *dastgâhs* of *Māhur* and *Bayāt-e Esfahān*. A review of the cassette in the semi-official Persian-language newspaper *Keyhān* praised Kāmkār for bringing 'local melodies' closer to 'national music' by means of his fast passage work (Keyhān Havā'i 1990).

Musicians who are active in the Islamic Republic of Iran often justify their interest in Kurdish culture by speaking of its 'antiquity' and its 'authenticity' (*eṣālat*), while in the Diaspora the emphasis is on the independence of Kurdish music from Persian, Arabic or Turkish music (Kurds in the Diaspora never refer to their music as a 'local' species of another nation's music). Cassettes issued in Iran are licenced by the Ministry of Culture and Islamic Guidance, which requires popular songs to be 'non-Western' and evidently prefers those with some claim to 'authenticity'. The composer Jalil 'Andalibi introduces his arrangements of Kurdish songs from the Mahabad and Badinan regions with the remark that 'the Kurdish language may be considered the most authentic (*'aṣiltarin*) Iranian form of speech, comprising numerous dialects that have left traces on music and its meanings' ('Andalibi n.d.). One of the two songs he has arranged from 'the folklore of (Kurmanji-speaking) Badinan' is 'Hêdî Hêdî' (Gently, Gently, see Example 2), first aired on Baghdad radio in the 1960s, sung by Gulbehar; the newer arrangement combines Gulbehar's Kurmanji version with some older and newer lyrics in Sorani.[10]

The introductory essay to another of 'Andalibi's projects, a recording in the *dastgāhs* of *Abu-'atā* and *Dashti*, emphasises the 'simple and fluent nature' (*tebi'yat-e sādeh va ravān*) of Kurdish folklore, symbolised in his view by the frame drum, *def*. As part of his compositional plan in this work, 'Andalibi asked the singer, Behruz Tavakkoli, to sing Persian verses with a Kurdish accent for the purpose of 'forging a link between Persian-speaking listeners and the local (*maḥalli*) music of Kurds' ('Andalibi 1990).

Kurds would prefer situations in which they were not providing others with 'folklore' and 'local colour' – situations of cultural autonomy, to be explicit. Although an attempt to describe current conditions of musical production in the Islamic Republic of Iran would greatly exceed the scope of this article, we can note that prominent use of the *def* and emphasis on qualities deemed 'natural' and 'indigenous' are consistent with the prevailing ideology, which supports a 'national culture' based on the 'national language', Persian.[11]

The point is not lost on the musician Kawe, born in 1972 and raised in camps operated by Komala, the Kurdish Organisation of the Communist Party of Iran. In 1988 he resettled in Sweden. Kawe describes the cassette *Step 1* as his 'first step . . . to develop and modernise and simultaneously present Kurdish music to other nationalities hoping that there will be other steps ahead'. Insisting that 'Kurdish music has always borrowed' and that 'looking for pure music doesn't fit in today's world', he rejects the thesis that 'the ruled nations should protect themselves from those who rule', regarding it as the slogan of the Islamic Republic (Kawe 1994). He wishes to avoid not only the *def* (widely used in religious ceremonies) but also any imitation of the genre *marsiye* (lament for Shi'ite martyrs), so as not to associate his music with the controls exercised by the Islamic Republic (which, in its early years, made religious ceremonial music the model for all to emulate).

Kawe and other young Kurdish musicians in Sweden (Ciwan Haco, for one) have been criticised by older immigrants for having 'destroyed Kurdish music'. In performances from which traditional instruments have been eliminated (the *def* to be sure, but also the *tanbur* and *balaban*), the articulation of sung syllables may easily lose some of the qualities that older listeners value. It is not so much language as the ways it is treated that makes songs recognisably Kurdish. Arguments about what songs and ways of singing can be accepted as 'Kurdish' are an inevitable consequence of the different situations in which Kurds must recognise themselves.

Conclusion

From the authors' point of view, a 'Kurdish popular song' is a *goranî* or *stran* that is reproduced for a shorter or longer period of time via the mass media as well as in public concerts and at weddings (in both rural and urban areas). In this sense, 'popular song' draws continually upon 'folklore' but also serves to construct 'folklore'. Popularity is inevitably a matter of degree, ranging from ubiquitous reproduction at a given moment to total failure (when no one wishes to hear or reproduce a song). Songs addressed to clearly circumscribed groups of listeners do not become 'popular' until they are accepted by members of the larger listening public.

The Kurdish word *gel* means both 'the people' and 'the public'. Although *gel* is in many respects synonymous with Turkish *halk* (a word borrowed from Arabic), its musical connotations are quite different. *Halk mûsikîsi* (folk music) is regularly contrasted with *sanat mûsikîsi* (classical music) in Turkish publications and institutions (see Markoff 1986; Stokes 1992). One reason that no such distinction is relevant in Kurdistan is the absence of a state. The Regional Government based in Erbil has made no effort to establish a conservatory for 'Kurdish classical music', and any such effort would be ill-advised. A few of the ways in which musicians from Iranian Kurdistan deal with the conceptions and institutions of 'classical music' in the Islamic Republic have been discussed.

As the world's largest non-state nation, Kurds are the heirs of musical practices that have not been developed into instruments of hegemony (the fate of more than one practice in Istanbul, Tehran and Baghdad). Kurdish cultural survival requires visions and representations of national culture, but these need not be defined through such oppositions as 'classical' versus 'folk', nor do they need to be controlled through the centralised institutions of a state bureaucracy. Kurdish musicians have shown a deep creative interest in aspects of many musical practices inside and outside of their homeland, and we are confident that they will continue to do so.

Endnotes

1. Programme books distributed by the *Tiyatora Botan* include Mehmet Uzun's Kurdish translation of Pinter's play, *Zimanê çiya*. S Blum attended one of the group's performances in Vienna on 1 June 1994.
2. McDowall (1992, p. 12) gives the following estimates of the Kurdish population in 1991 (in millions):

Country	Total Population	Kurds	% of total
Turkey	57	10.8	19
Iraq	18	4.1	23
Iran	55	5.5	10
Syria	12.5	1.0	8
Former			
USSR		.5	
Elsewhere		.7	
TOTAL		22.6	

3. Kurmanji dialects are spoken by most Kurds in Armenia, Turkey, Syria, the Badinan region of Iraq, Khorasan (in Iran), and Turkmenistan. Kurds living south of the language boundary that runs north-east along the Great Zab river (in northern Iraq) to Oshnaviyeh (in Iran) speak Sorani dialects, with certain exceptions. Sorani publications generally use a modified Arabic alphabet. The Cyrillic alphabet is used in Armenia for writing Kurmanji (and the Arabic alphabet is used in northern Khorasan), but it is most often written in a Roman alphabet that resembles the one adopted in 1926 for Turkish. Our examples use this alphabet for both languages. For a table showing all three alphabets, see Hassanpour (1992, p. 375).
4. Amir Hassanpour acquired collections of books and phonograph recordings that were destroyed by his parents on four occasions, since they were afraid of house searches that

were common in Iranian Kurdistan during the 1960s and 1970s.

5. The importance of caravans in transmitting songs from Mukri Kurdistan to Sulaimaniya is also discussed in Şarbajêrî (1985).

6. Important female singers listed in Abdulhekim (1990, p. 24) include Miyrem Xanê, Eyşa Şanê, and Gulbehar.

7. One of these is reproduced on *Sharakam Sna* (My City, Sina), cassette 1, beginning of side B (see Discography under Haqshenas). Ayazi (1992, p. 663) gives information on Seyd 'Eli 'Esẍer's career. The Kāmkārs perform some of his songs on their cassette no. 6, *Zardi-ye Xazān* (The Yellowness of Autumn), named after Esẍer's song 'Zerdî Xezan'.

8. A recording of one of Mamilî's songs, made when he was 32 years old, is included on the recording *Kurdish Folk Music from Western Iran*. The importance of Azeri songs in his repertoire is also noted by Ehmed (1983, p. 372).

9. Egyptian musicians are also familiar with a song that sets Arabic lyrics to the melody of 'Adalar Sahilinde'.

10. The phrase *'hêdî hêdî'* (gently, gently) is one of the many verbal formulas used in Kurmanji song (but not, to the best of our knowledge, in Sorani); see, for example, the texts recorded by Volland (1909, p. 185) and Bayrak (1991, p. 259). Asking the gentle north wind (*şemal*) to 'come' is a common topic throughout Kurdistan; singers never invite the evil south wind (*vîryan*) to come, but it comes anyway.

11. Under the Pahlavi monarchy, Iranian policies for internal broadcasting in Kurdish consistently favoured local dialects (often falsely described as 'dialects of Persian') over the more standardised forms of Sorani and Kurmanji that were necessarily used in the broadcasts of Iranian propaganda aimed at the Kurds of Iraq and Turkey. In 1974 supervisors (*modirān*) of Kurdish programmes in Iran were told by a high official that 'Kurdish is nothing but a dialect of Persian; but the enemies of Iran are creating a nation and a language for the Kurds' (quoted in Hassanpour 1992, p. 288). For a full discussion of Kurdish broadcasting, see Hassanpour (1992, pp. 282–303).

References

Abdulhekim, S. 1990. *Mehmed Arifê Ciziri: kewê ribad e* (Stockholm)

'Andalibi, J. 1990. 'Vizhegi-hā-ye musiqi-ye kordi va ahemiyat-e sāz-e daf dar asar-e hāzer' (The specific qualities of Kurdish music and the importance of the *daf* in the present work). Note to cassette *Hay Gol* (see Discography)

n.d. 'Dar bāre-he musiqi-ye asar-e hāzer' (Concerning the music in the present work). Note to cassette *Az dast-e 'eshq* (see Discography)

Ayazi, B. 1992. *A'ineye Sanandaj* (The Mirror of Sanandaj) (Tehran)

Bayrak, M. 1991. *Kürt Halk Türküleri (Kilam û Stranên Kurd): Inceleme – Antoloji* (Ankara)

Bêkes, H. 1994. Interview with Delal, *Dîdar* (Stockholm), no. 10–11 (July), pp. 10–11 (Sorani section)

Blum, S. 1980. 'Iran, II. Folk Music', in *The New Grove Dictionary of Music and Musicians*, ed. Stanley Sadie (London), vol. 9, pp. 300–9

Celîl, C. 1973–86). *Kurdskie Narodye Pesni i Instrumental'nye Melodii* (Moscow), 2 vols. (vol. 1 repr. Stockholm, 1982)

Cewarî, N. 1983. *Kilamêd Cimaeta Kurdaya Govendê* (Uppsala)

Ehmed, M.H. 1983. *Bazî Bêryan ya Jiyan û Goranîyekanî Mihemedî Mamilê* (The path of the milkmaids, or the life and songs of Mihemedi Mamilê) (Baghdad)

Goran, E. 1980. *Dîwanî Goran* (vol. 1, ed. Mihemedî Mela Kerîm) (Baghdad)

Gowhari, H. 1994. (Book of interviews with Rezazi and other Kurdish singers)

Hassanpour, A. 1992. *Nationalism and Language in Kurdistan, 1918–1985* (San Fransisco)

Hedges, C. 1992. 'Hungry and cold, Kurds turn to TV', *The New York Times*, 12 February, p. A12

Hêmin. 1974. *Tarîk û Rûn* (Twilight) (place of publication not known)

Hitchins, K. 1993. 'Goran, Abdulla', in *Encyclopedia of World Literature in the 20th Century*, vol. 5, ed. S.R. Serafin (New York), pp. 263–4

Jamiyat-e Dafa' az Hoquq-e Melli-ye Khalq-e Kord (Kirmashan) (Association for the Defence of the National Rights of the Kurdish People (Kermanshah). 1979. *Doktor Shivān: Matn-o Tarjome Navār Shomāre Yek Doktor Shivān* (Doctor Shivan: text and translation of his Tape Number One)

Kawe. 1994. 'Mosîqay Pêşkewtû Kameye?' (What is progressive music?), *Dîdar* (Stockholm), no. 10–11 (June), p. 21 (Sorani section)

Keyhān Havā'i. 1990 'Bārāne, ejrā'iye jadid az Pashang Kāmkār', *Keyhān Hava'i*, 24 October, no. 902, p. 21

Khaznadar, M. 1967. *Ocherki Istorii Sovremennoï Kurdskoï Litertury* (A history of contemporary Kurdish literature) (Moscow)

342   *Blum and Hassanpour*

Markoff, I. 1986. 'Musical theory, performance and the contemporary bağlama specialist in Turkey', PhD dissertation, University of Washington

McDowall, D. 1992. *The Kurds: A Nation Denied* (London)

Nebez, J. 1969. *Kurdische Schriftsprache: eine Chrestomathie moderner Texte* (Hamburg)

Pinter, H. 1989. *Mountain Language* (London and New York)

Rezazi, N. 1990. 'Hunermendî bîîmet Hesen Zîrek' (The talented artist Hesen Zîrek), *Berbang*, 77, pp. 35–9

1991. *New le Komelî Kurdewarîda* (Names and titles in the Kurdish Community) (Stockholm)

Şarbajêri, 'Usman. 1985. 'Karwanî mosîqa wa goranî le şarî Silêmanî' (The caravan of music and song in the city of Sulaimaniya), *Roşinbîrî Nö*, 106, pp. 128–60

Stokes, M. 1992. *The Arabesk Debate: Music and Musicians in Modern Turkey* (Oxford)

Volland. 1909. 'Beiträge zur Ethnographie der Bewohner von Armenien und Kurdistan', *Archive für Anthropologie*, 36, pp. 183–96

Zimmerman, A. 1994. 'Kurdish broadcasting in Iraq', *Middle East Report* (July–August), pp. 20–21

Discography

Dates and manufacturer's catalogue numbers are given only when these are included in the item, which is rarely the case. When the cassettes issued by one artist or ensemble are numbered in sequence, these numbers are included. Many of these cassettes can be obtained from the following dealers or institutions:

Institut Kurde
106, Rue La Fayette
75010 Paris, France
Fax: (1) 47 70 99 04

Khayyan Books
Nordhemsgatan 44A
413 06 Göteborg, Sweden
Fax: (031) 24 63 22

Kitab-i Arzan
B. Jarls G. 9B
554 63 Jönköping, Sweden
Fax: (036) 11 09 99

Navar Co.
P.O. Box 392
North Hollywood, CA 91603, USA
Fax: (818) 762 2001

World Music Institute
49 West 27th Street
New York, NY 10001, USA
Fax: (212) 889 2771

'Andalibi, Jalil (composer), *Az dast-e 'eshq*. Mowlana Ensemble, no. 1, n.d.

Hay Gol. Mowlana Ensemble, no. 9. 1990

Deborian, Nazê, *Nazê 2: Nenê*. Produced by singer (Krathuset 3, 1. tv., 2670 Greve, Denmark), 1993

Hāqshenās, Mohieddin, *Shārakam Sna (Şarakem Sine/*My City, Sina). 2 cassettes (Nay soloist: jamshid 'Andalibi. Producer and author of notes: Majed Mardukh Ruhani).

Kāmkār Family, *Zardi Xezān: Qat'āti az Arsalan Kāmkār bar Esās-e Tarāne-hā-ye Seyd 'Eli 'Esẍar Kurdestāni*. No. 6. n.d.

Awrāmān: Musiqi-ye Mahalli-ye Kordi. No. 7. 1989

Bārāne. No. 10. 1990

Konsert-e Musiqi-ye Kordi Ejrā-ye Festivāl-e London va Almān. no. 14. n.d.

Kawe, *Step 1* (issued in Sweden). n.d.

Komkar: Federasyonsa Komelên Karkerên Kurdistan li Elmanya Federal (Hansaring 28-30, 5000 Cologne 1, Germany), *Kilam û Stranên Gel, 1: Heseniko*. n.d.

Kilam û Stranên Gel, 2: Ehmedo Roni. n.d.

Kurdish Music from Western Iran (includes *Behare* by Mihemedî Mamilî), comp. Dieter and Nerthus Christensen. Ethnic Folkways Library FE 4103. 1966

Mîkaêl, *Slaw.* Arranged and produced in Sweden by Kawe.

Perwer, Şivan. *Şivan 1, 2, 3 and 4.* Produced in late 1970s

   Sivan Perwer: Chants du Kurdistan. Auvidis A 6145 (Musiques Traditionelles). 1989

Persian Spiritual Music, Kurdish Folk Songs (includes songs performed by Amir Ali Vahazadeh, Azad Naghsbandi and Khaled Othman). World Music Institute WMI 011 (The New Americans). 1989

Rezazi, Nasir. *Be Piroz.* Komkar

   Gomê Şin. Komkar

   Nayalê Cudayi. Komkar

   Râzyâne. Pars Video (5585 Reseda Blvd., Suite 103, Tarzana, CA 91356)

Sa'ed, Mohammad, *Golāra: Naghme-hā-ye Mahalli-ye Kordi-ye Kermānshāhi.* Āvāz-e Janub, no. 23. Singer: Mohammad Reza Darabi

Salahiyan, Ala. *Menu Saghi* (compositions by Risgar Xoşnaw). 1994 (issued by the performer, Fuchs-röhrenstr. 32/28, 1110 Vienna, Austria)

[6]

Saida Sultan/Danna International: Transgender Pop and the Polysemiotics of Sex, Nation, and Ethnicity on the Israeli-Egyptian Border

Ted Swedenburg

Disputes over sexual behavior often become the vehicles for displacing social anxieties, and discharging their attendant emotional intensity. Consequently, sexuality should be treated with special respect in times of great social stress.

> —Gayle Rubin, "Thinking Sex: Notes for a Radical Theory of the Politics of Sexuality." In *Pleasure and Danger: Exploring Female Sexuality*, ed. Carol S. Vance

In the fall of 1994 one of my Egyptian graduate students at the American University in Cairo (AUC) handed me a music cassette which she was sure I would want to hear given that, as she explained, it was all the rage among Cairene youth. The tape contained two numbers, sung in English, Arabic, and (I thought) Hebrew, by an Israeli artist whose name my student did not know. It was poorly recorded and the lyrics hard to make out, so I filed it away in a drawer after listening to it a few times. Over the next months I would hear it occasionally blaring from cars and from a cassette player at the AUC snack bar, and I eventually learned, through conversations and various lurid articles in the opposition press here and there, that the singer's name was Danna International; she was also known in Egypt as Sa'îda Sultân; she was a Mizrahi, a Jew of Arab origin; and "she" was a transsexual.[1]

In August 1995 my interest in Danna was reignited by the discovery of a sensationalistic exposé entitled *A Scandal Whose Name Is Sa'îda Sultân: Dânnâ the Israeli Sex Artist*, penned by Muhammad al-Ghaytî and published by a reputable nationalist (Nasserite) press. The book's cover features a photo of Madonna bending toward the camera in a metallic gold bustier and black net stockings, her cleavage and eyes blacked out, in the style of local scandal magazines. The upper left-hand corner announces, "For Adults Only"; the black cover informs us that although the Zionists failed in their efforts to conquer Egypt politically, they have now succeeded, through the agency of Danna International's sexuality, in invading Egypt's bedrooms. The book elaborates on many of the issues that both the Egyptian opposition and public-sector media started to raise about Danna/Saʿîda and her illicit cassette (known locally as *Bûsnî Yâ Sûsû*, or "Kiss Me Sûsû") in December 1994.[2] We learn that Danna International's given name is Yaron Cohen, that he was born to a Yemeni family that migrated to Israel after 1948, and that, while growing up, he learned traditional Arabic songs of Yemen and the Arabian Gulf from his mother (al-Ghaytî 1995: 18–20).[3] As a teenager, Yaron frequented the "perverts clubs" (*nawâdî al-shawâdh*) of Tel Aviv, where his "deviant" tendencies were affirmed and developed. Eventually Yaron underwent hormone treatments and a sex change operation and launched a singing career under the stage name Danna International, with the encouragement of the prominent Israeli-Yemeni singer Ofra Haza and devoted fans in the "perverts' clubs" of Tel Aviv (F, 21–22, 32–33, 35).[4] Although she aroused controversy among extremist rabbis who considered her sex change contrary to Jewish law, Danna nonetheless enjoyed the backing of the Israeli leadership. It was only due to the support of Zionist power brokers, in fact, that her music was able to "penetrate" Egypt via the Sinai peninsula and "master" the ears of twenty million youths (F, 12–13).

The author goes on to inform us that Danna's inspirations in the world of show business are Elvis, James Dean, Michael Jackson, and, especially, Madonna, all of whom are major stars in Egypt.[5] Al-Ghaytî describes all of these international icons of popular culture as "deviants" (F, 38) and proceeds to rehearse some of their perverted adventures. We discover that Elvis, late in his career, spent hours indulging in "disgusting" sex at an S & M club, where he died; that James Dean used to bugger young black men in his dressing room; that the "disfigured black pig" Michael Jackson favors the company of children; and the biggest "deviant" of them all, Madonna, is a prominent supporter of civil rights for "perverts" (F, 40). Moreover, we learn that, according to her gynecologist, Madonna is not a 100 percent biological woman. "Can you imagine," the author asks, "Madonna, the global symbol of the naked woman, is not a complete female?" (F, 44).[6] We are informed as well that both Michael Jackson and Madonna are closely tied to and enjoy the strong backing of the Zionist lobby in the United States (F, 42, 46–47). Moving beyond vilification by association, al-Ghaytî proceeds to illustrate Danna's depravity through an examination of her lyrics, sung in what he describes as a "devilish blend" of Arabic (in various regional dialects), English and Hebrew (F, 58). The themes of her songs, he claims, are all sexual adventures, and their words are so scandalous that the author on occasion feels compelled to leave blank spaces and simply describe what they mean. One of Danna's songs is an "unambiguous call for prostitution and immorality"; another features a sordid encounter between a woman and a dog; others are composed chiefly of "scandalous [read: orgasmic] groans" (F, 62). The final number of the cassette, sung in Hebrew and English, is said to exemplify how Danna's shameless voice and lyrics constitute a deviation from all morality and tradition and constitute an attack on all the monotheistic Semitic religions and their principles and laws (F, 64).

According to al-Ghaytî, Danna is merely one element of a larger Zionist cultural torrent which includes other Israeli female pop singers, such as Ruthie, Nancy, and Suzanna Ma'ariv, who have employed "sexual shouts" in order to win an Egyptian audience and to "penetrate . . . like a plague" the circles of innocent Arab youth. Several even used the devious tactic of making "corrupted" Hebrew recordings of tunes by revered neoclassicist Arab singers like Umm Kalthûm, 'Abd al-Halîm Hâfiz, and Farîd al-Atrash and punctuating them with orgasmic moans (F, 66). It should be emphasized that the latter are nationally revered, canonical figures in Egypt for which there are no comparable examples in American popular culture. (To get a sense of the cultural capital of such singers in Egypt, imagine that Frank Sinatra passed away and millions of weeping fans showed up at his funeral, that he is a central figure in U.S. nationalist mythology, that his music is constantly played on radio, that his concerts and movies are endlessly aired on television, that video clips of Sinatra singing in concerts or movies are interspersed as fillers between television programs on a daily basis, and, finally, that all popular music is measured in relation to Frankie's standard of excellence. Then imagine that an artist from a currently vilified country, say Iran, began to record "versions" of Sinatra's songs and that they were embraced by American youth.) Although Danna has in fact "stolen" only from the lesser Egyptian pop star Hasan al-Asmar, a figure whom the nationalist intelligentsia consider "vulgar," according to al-Ghaytî, these corruptions of beloved Egyptian classics by Israeli singers manage at once to "penetrate" Arab youth and to destroy the Arabs' deep-rooted musical heritage (F, 66). This sort of theft and perversion of Arab heritage, we are informed, dates back to the days of Jewish presence in Egypt. The author tells, for instance, of Rachel Qattâwî, the female scion of a poor branch of Egyptian Jewry's leading family, the Qattâwî, known for its wealth and for its collaboration with British colonialists. During World War II, Rachel worked as a barmaid at Cairo's Continental Hotel, where she befriended the great (and canonical) singer Ismâhân as well as other Egyptian artists and mastered Ismâhân's repertoire, all the while working undercover for Jewish and British intelligence. When she immigrated to Israel, Rachel "stole" Ismâhân's legacy (Ismâhân died in 1944), and she recorded an album of Ismâhân's songs in 1967 (F, 92–94).[7]

Ultimately, for al-Ghaytî, the entire Danna phenomenon boils down to a Masonic-Jewish conspiracy. Danna, who is accused of being a Freemason, advocates the individual's right to happiness and sensual delight, both of these being prototypical Masonic principles, invented by Zionist Jews, whose aim was to destroy society (F, 50–52). This philosophy accords, as al-Ghaytî argues with reference to such noted authorities as Wagner and Hitler, with the nature of the Jews, a parasitic and rootless people whose eternal aim is to destroy civilization (F, 106, 115–16). Therefore Danna's influence must be resisted vigorously in order to defend and protect Egypt's youth from her poison. Although by the time we reach his conclusion al-Ghaytî's argument has come to resemble the rantings of a neo-Nazi rather than cultural criticism, with the trope of the Jewish-Masonic conspiracy stemming from the notorious *Protocols of the Elders of Zion* and Hitler's anti-Semitic propaganda, the Western reader should be aware that the notion of a Masonic-Zionist plot is commonplace in Egypt, particular in Islamist versions but also in Marxist and nationalist variants. Several books have been published on the theme and can be purchased in "respectable" bookstores: Freemasonry, moreover, is banned in much of the Middle East.

Israeli "Penetration"

Running throughout al-Ghaytî's arguments, in fact, are a number of ideological threads that are frequently articulated by members of Egypt's nationalist intelligentsia. One theme is the danger posed by Israel. Although the Egyptian government signed a peace treaty with Israel in 1977, most of the intelligentsia has vigorously opposed normalization (*tatbî'*) of Israeli-Egyptian relations. Egyptian universities, for instance, continue to boycott Israeli scholars, and although Israel established an academic center in Cairo in the early 1980s, it remains unthinkable for an Israeli scholar to deliver a public lecture at any Egyptian university. Indeed, numerous significant issues continue to animate anti-Israeli feelings and receive extensive coverage in the press.[8] However, while there is considerable apprehension regarding Israeli policies and its interest in dominating Egypt, there is not much coverage of Israel's considerable economic activities in Egypt. It is hardly known, for instance, that Israeli investors are leasing land and growing commercial agricultural produce in the Egyptian Delta, and it may well be that the government tries to prevent such activities from being publicized. Instead, anxieties about Israel's aims and power are displaced onto the domain of culture, such that the press is constantly churning out inflammatory stories, many of them delusionary, about Israel's efforts to conquer Egypt and the Arab world culturally.[9]

Typical of such incendiary sensationalism is the report which appeared in the Nasserite newspaper *al-'Arabî* in February 1996 discussing an Israeli cigarette sold within the Palestine National Authority and said to be about to appear on the Egyptian market.[10] The article, which reproduces the emblem on the cigarette pack depicting two men driving a chariot, tells us that the men are wearing distinctive American hats, that they are riding in an Egyptian chariot drawn by Arabian horses, and that one holds a whip whose lash hangs so as to form the Arabic word *Misr* (Egypt). In sum, Uncle Sam is deploying an Egyptian whip to control the Arabs, and the entire scenario is devised by the Israelis. One encounters the same Israeli arrogance and vision, the piece concludes, in the statements of the former Israeli foreign minister Ehud Barak and in the trademark on an Israeli cigarette packet. Although the notice is bizarre and the interpretation of the emblem fanciful, it is symptomatic of Egyptian fears (especially as articulated by the national intelligentsia) about official Israeli attitudes, policies, and designs. These must be kept in mind in order to understand both the appeal of and the resistance to Danna International in Egypt.

In a similar vein, al-Ghaytî elaborates quite obsessively on another aspect of the perceived Israeli aggression: the sexual threat it poses to the Egyptian bedroom. One of the means he uses to convey this "danger" is to misrepresent the sexiness of Danna's lyrics both through wild exaggeration and by means of strategic mistranslation. The song that al-Ghaytî calls an "unambiguous call for prostitution and immorality," for instance, is in fact a wedding song, sung from the position of a woman. This is made obvious not only by the lyrics—Danna sings in Arabic, " 'ânâ al-'arûsa" (I'm the bride), and in English, "Going to a honeymoon"—but also by the music (which features the ululations typical of Arab wedding celebrations) and by the very name of the song, which—as I learned once I obtained the CD from Israel—is " 'Arûsa" ["Bride"]. If the song is in any way "deviant" it is perhaps because the singer is not "really" a woman, a fact al-Ghaytî seems either to overlook or to ignore. Al-Ghaytî's notion that another song concerns an encounter between a woman and a dog is the product of the fertile imagination of the antipornographer. As for the number that is supposed to represent an attack on all Semitic religions, it is simply a remake of Queen's inoffensive "The Show Must Go On": the English lyrics Danna sings are "Show must go on / Inside my heart is breaking / My make-up may be flaking / But my smile still stays on." This is not to say that the tape is devoid of sexiness (al-Ghaytî is correct to interpret Danna's screams as orgasmic, but these are much less ubiquitous than he claims) but to underscore the symptomatically hysterical and displaced character of al-Ghaytî's attack.

Curiously, al-Ghaytî's account of the classical homophobic topos of sexual *penetration* focuses on the aggressive and wanton Western-Israeli *female* who seduces the innocent young Egyptian *male*. Although the theme of the Egyptian man victimized by a predatory Western woman is to be

found in works of modern Egyptian fiction dating back at least to the
1940s,[11] today's moral-sexual panic about the voracious and corrupting
Western (and now, Israeli) woman is much more virulent and widespread.
AIDS, for instance, is widely represented by the agencies of public meaning
as a disease that Egyptians contract when male nationals are ensnared by
loose Western women. A 1992 film called *Love in Taba*, which, despite its
artistic wretchedness, airs frequently on state television, is typical of this
official story. It recounts the tale of three naive Egyptian youths who are
willingly seduced and entrapped by three young libertine Western women
while on holiday in Taba, a small resort in the Sinai Peninsula that sits right
on the border with Israel. When the foreign women depart for home, each
leaves a note informing her lover that he is now infected with AIDS. It is
significant that these events occur at Taba, for the Sinai Peninsula is often
depicted in the media as a wild and dangerous frontier zone through which
Israeli corruption enters the Nile Valley, and al-Ghaytî explicitly names it
as the corridor through which Danna's cassettes have "penetrated."[12] Meanwhile, the opposition press and word-of-mouth assert that AIDS is being
broadcast in Egypt by prostitutes dispatched there for that purpose by the
Israeli government.[13] A public service announcement shown frequently on
state television manages simultaneously to provide accurate information
about HIV transmission and to suggest, through its visual imagery, that the
main danger of infection occurs when Egyptian males go abroad and are
stalked by prostitutes. The iconographic message is reinforced by an explicit
statement that AIDS is a "foreign" phenomenon, that the Egyptian traveler
should beware, and that "Abroad they use such things as condoms and
other methods to help prevent AIDS, but here there is no fear of such
things because the principles which our youth believe in protect them from
such evil." The spot concludes with a verse from the Qur'ân.[14]

The announcement's anxious tone, however, undercuts the confident
assertions about Egyptian youth and their deep-seated moral principles.
And for al-Ghaytî, the "evil" does not just lie in foreign lands or frontier
regions but menaces the very heart of the nation. The focal point of the
danger, however, is strictly *heterosexual* cross-cultural encounters. Al-
Ghaytî does not suggest that "perverts" (homosexuals or transsexuals) constitute the true threat to Egypt, for he assumes that such people simply do
not exist there. What Danna's transsexuality and deviance serve to underscore instead is simply the repulsive character of her sexual success in
Egypt. In this regard the transgendered Danna is like her hero, the international sex symbol Madonna, who is also both very popular and highly controversial in Egypt and, although more or less legal,[15] equally loathsome—
not least, as al-Ghaytî notes, since Madonna herself is not "really"
biologically female. Transsexuality and queerness serve here to underscore

the fact that the Western-Israeli sexual assault is not merely corrupting but that its very foundations are perverse and deviant. The challenge posed by Western mass culture, as exemplified by Elvis, Michael, James Dean, Madonna, and Danna, is essentially moral and sexual.

Youth as "Problem"

If al-Ghaytî's diatribe can be read as a catalog of interlinked themes that run through the discourse of Egypt's nationalist intelligentsia concerning the threatening and corrupting influences posed by Israel, westernization, sexuality, and Western mass culture, another important and related motif in this nationalist discourse concerns precisely *who* is at risk. Those said to be most threatened by these dangers are youth, the *shabâb*, and particularly the young *men*. On 21 August 1995, *Rûz al-Yûsif*, Egypt's leading weekly magazine, a sensationalist but well-regarded nationalist public-sector vehicle, published an exposé about advertisements that had appeared in Egyptian magazines, promoting phone numbers that promised to connect callers with "new friends." It turned out that such calls were quite expensive and that they connected the consumer to sex professionals in Israel.[16] Under the banner "Normalization by Sex with Israel," the issue's seductive cover photo of Tina Turner wearing a miniskirt and exposing considerable cleavage is intended to convey the dangers of "phone sex." In the predictably melodramatic account of the arrival of Israeli phone sex, we learn that once the peace treaty was signed with Egypt, Israeli intelligence agencies turned away from Egypt's military secrets and began to study Egypt's social ills with the aim of exploiting them. What they discovered is that Egyptian youth are afflicted by sexual problems that are traceable to the country's economic difficulties and make it difficult for youth to marry and satisfy their sexual needs. Phone sex, along with AIDS, counterfeit money, and heroin, are all Israeli exports designed to take advantage of Egyptian youth's difficulties.[17]

Despite its propagandistic exaggerations, the *Rûz al-Yûsif* article does nevertheless point to some of the concrete causes of the "youth crisis." Youth in Egypt do indeed face a crisis of opportunity, which particularly affects those from the lower and lower-middle classes who manage to get university degrees. An advanced degree is supposed to guarantee a government job, but today the waiting period for actually getting such a position is about ten years. In any case, the pay for such sought-after jobs averages a pitiful 100 L.E. ($30) per month, and legions of state employees must moonlight to make ends meet. Opportunities for work in the private sector, especially respectable jobs that educated youth will accept, are also limited.[18]

Such economic obstacles in turn make getting married a laborious and much-delayed process.[19] Marriage, however, is a requirement for any young person who wishes to become a social adult, to achieve independence within a nuclear family, to move out of his or her parental abode, and to gain sexual access. Because marriage requires considerable outlays of money and families of prospective brides demand the whole package (i.e., a furnished apartment, etc.) in order to ensure that their daughters are well settled, unless a youth comes from a wealthy family he will frequently not marry until he reaches his early thirties. Many young men migrate to work in the Gulf countries and toil there for as long as five to ten years in order to save up enough money for marriage. The Central Agency for Statistics estimates that four million Egyptians have "missed the train of marriage" because they are well into their thirties, beyond the accepted marrying age; and some have calculated that the number of marriages registered in the country has declined by nearly 1 percent, an astonishing fact for a country with such a young population.[20] As a result, the social category of "youth" in Egypt includes large numbers of men (and some women) in their late twenties and early thirties. It is widely recognized that the crisis afflicting them is in part sexual due to the fact that sexual outlets outside of marriage are limited, proscribed, and usually prohibitively expensive, and because "dating" is generally unacceptable unless one is already engaged.[21] Such factors contribute to making sex a major topic of discussion and controversy in Egypt today.[22]

Youth are also considered a problem in the domain of culture. Nationalist, especially oppositional, intellectuals commonly assert that youth are the victims of a general moral decline in Egypt that is the by-product of *infitâh*, the economic liberalization launched in the 1970s by the late President Anwar al-Sadat, and the consequent advance of materialism and decline of traditional values.[23] The *infitâh* is also regarded as indelibly linked to normalization with Israel and to the consequent Zionist penetration. Youth are seen as especially susceptible to the corruptions of both Western mass culture and "vulgar" indigenous culture (so called because it is regarded as rooted in "low" cultural values), both of which are said to be outcomes of the *infitâh* and the attendant rise of a boorish nouveau riche and decline of noble cultural values. "Vulgar" or "fallen" Egyptian culture fails to meet the nationalist cultural idea of a synthesis of the high neo-classicist culture (which in addition to elite Arab traditions can also include elements of refined Western culture, such as ballet or Beethoven) and the best of folk cultural values (represented by the stereotypical "authentic Egyptian," the son of the people or *ibn al-balad*). With regard to music, the canonical figures who serve to epitomize ideal national values and to represent the musical high points of Egyptian culture's "golden age" include the late Umm Kalthûm, 'Abd al-Halîm Hâfiz, and Muhammad 'Abd al-Wahhâb. Cheap Egyptian culture is both "low" (because there is no synthesis with "elevated" culture) and, frequently, contaminated by "cheap" Western mass culture. In their ideological combat against the tidal waves of base culture, the national intelligentsia's cultural mandarins therefore frequently condemn contemporary musicians who do not conform to canonical values, asserting that they represent the "fall" of Egyptian music from its glory days and describing them as *jîl al-ghinâ' al-hâbit* (the generation of the vulgar song).[24] The frequent press attacks on "debased culture" and condemnations of "vulgar" musicians who threaten the authenticity of the Arabic song are responses to the fact that, although many Egyptian youth will publicly assert their admiration for Umm Kalthûm and 'Abd al-Halîm, they primarily listen to contemporary "vulgar" Egyptian pop music. Thus the makers of public meaning invoke the shining example of a figure like Umm Kalthûm in order to articulate a critique of the effects of privatization, structural adjustment, and normalization with Israel, and at the same time, to put forward a blanket condemnation of contemporary youth culture, which can never equal but can only, at best, imitate past glories. As a result, many of the most popular musicians are consigned to the margins of public space, are never aired on television or radio, and are sometimes forced to resort to underground and illegal releases which are marketed in the same cassette kiosks that deal in Danna's contraband cassettes.[25] This marginalization of a significant component of contemporary musical life in Egypt is yet another symptom of the general absence of autonomous public spaces (whether youth clubs, media, or dance halls) where youth might publicly articulate their desires or demands. The popularity of "vulgar" music, the object of so much thundering from nationalist intellectuals straining to shore up neo-classicist cultural values, can in turn be understood as a sign of a general disaffection on the part of Egyptian youth, of their tremendous skepticism concerning the economic and social possibilities awaiting them, and of their lack of interest in the great modernist projects of nationalism and development that were hegemonic until the mid-1970s.[26]

The nationalist intelligentsia, therefore, recognize Egypt's social fragmentation and the alienation of youth from the once-revered projects of national liberation and development and cast themselves as youth's savior. Although intellectuals condemn youth for their cultural predilections, they are occasionally empathetic and assert that young people cannot really be blamed for their cynicism, since the government and the economy offer them so little.[27] Even such sympathetic analyses, however, deny Egyptian youth any agency and depict them as mere victims of government dereliction or dupes of foreign plots. Young people's own cultural concerns have no role to play in this rescue operation, for it is the national tradition and culture, as understood and articulated by the intelligentsia, that is to be their salvation.

Arab Jews

The final link between al-Ghaytî and nationalist discourse has to do with
the place of Arab Jews, whether in the Arab countries or inside Israel. In
al-Ghaytî's text, as in most nationalist discourse, this subject is essentially
an absence. Although al-Ghaytî notes Danna International's Yemeni origins, he pays minimal attention to the question of the Mizrahim in Israel
and basically assumes that Arabs and Jews are diametrically opposed categories. He does mention in passing that Jews of Arab background occupy
the lower rungs of Israeli society and that the singer Ofra Haza faced many
difficulties due to her Yemeni origins, but on the whole he manages to
depict Israeli Jewish society as homogeneous and monolithic. The author
assumes that Danna sings in Arabic simply because her "target" is Arab
youth outside Israel and so never takes into account other possible audiences such as the roughly 16 percent of Israel's five million citizens who are
Palestinian Arabs, the 54 percent of the population who are of non-European and mostly Arabic-speaking origin like Danna herself, or the many
Israeli Ashkenazis (Jews of European origin) who are familiar with Arabic
and Arabic culture.

      Al-Ghaytî also treats the Egyptian Jews "within" as national traitors,
collaborators with British colonialism, and agents of Zionism. He ignores
the rich and varied nature of this now all-but-vanished community, which
included rich and poor, Communists and Zionists, and a majority of apolitical non-Zionists. Out of a population of seventy-five thousand to eighty
thousand, only about fourteen thousand immigrated to Israel between 1948
and 1951 after the new Jewish state was created.[28] It was only in the wake
of the June 1967 war that this community was finally decimated, but even
then only about one-third to one-half of Egyptian Jews immigrated to
Israel.[29] Nor does al-Ghaytî discuss any of Egypt's major cultural figures who
were Jewish, like the singer-actress Layla Murâd, a still revered icon of
Egyptian film and music from the late 1930s to the early 1950s who was
raised as a Jew and converted to Islam when she married the well-known
actor Anwar Wagdî.[30] Also conveniently absent from al-Ghaytî's account is
any mention of other well-known Jewish cultural figures such as Layla
Murâd's famous musician father, Zâkî Murâd, the pioneering cinema director and producer Togo Mizrahi (responsible for some of the early landmarks
of Egyptian film), and the musician Dâ'ûd Husnî, remembered as one of the
great artists who along with Sayyid Darwîsh revitalized Egyptian music in
the early part of the century and who was responsible for Egypt's first full-
length opera, *Cleopatra's Night*, in 1919.[31] In al-Ghaytî's account, the Jews
in Egypt (not *of* Egypt), as represented by Rachel Qattâwî, are simply
thieves of Arab culture and Zionist undercover agents.

Danna's Egyptian Fans

Just who is actually listening to Danna in Egypt? How can one characterize the massive and heterogenous social category of "youth" whom nationalist intellectuals like al-Ghaytî want to "protect" from the dangers of Danna International? The difficulty of such a task is compounded by the fact that since there is no public space for Egypt's young people to articulate their perceptions of "vulgar" pop music, there exists no real vocabulary in which to voice favorable views.[32] There are no magazines or broadcasts that represent alternative views of or by Egyptian youth; youth- and pop-culture-oriented magazines tend to be either of the gossip variety or public-sector vehicles through which "responsible" adults address youth. Almost nothing of real concern to youth percolates up the cultural hierarchy from the bottom. Moreover, open discussion is severely constrained by official condemnations that create a sense that listening to Danna signifies immorality, an absence of patriotism, and a lack of respectability. Many thus simply repeat what the press says about Danna: asked if he had ever heard of Danna International, a taxi driver bringing a friend into town from Cairo airport replied, "You mean the singer that brings AIDS from Israel?"

Although Danna's tape is sold strictly on the black market and for high prices (four to eight times that of a regular prerecorded cassette), she appears to enjoy an extensive audience of youth and students, from among both the westernized upper and upper-middle classes and the lower-middle and working classes.[33] One of Danna's appeals is that she is "forbidden," both as a "sex" artist and as an Israeli, and the uproar in the press has simply served to drive up both the price and the desirability of her cassette.[34] High-priced versions of the cassette are sold under the counter in many of the numerous Cairo kiosks that specialize in prerecorded music tapes as well as contraband cassettes by "vulgar" Egyptian pop singers. In addition, enterprising kids have made lesser-quality versions that they hawk in the streets for lower prices, sometimes disguising them, to avoid police harassment, as Qur'anic recitation cassettes. (Police raids on cassette shops increased after it was learned that Danna's tape had appeared on the market.) Although the buzz on the streets is that *Bûsnî Yâ Sûsû* is a "sex" tape, it is less well known that Danna is a transsexual, and this does not appear to be part of Danna's attraction nor to matter much to consumers. Most of the Egyptian audience is familiar with the Western pop musical sources—such as Whitney Houston, Gloria Estefan, Donna Summer, Queen, and the Gypsy Kings—that Danna draws on and does "versions" of, since these are *international* pop stars known and consumed in both Israel and Egypt. Danna's practice of blending Western dance beats and textures with oriental vocalisms and modes is equally familiar in Egypt and in fact is characteristic of a great deal of contemporary Egyptian pop music (as discussed below).[35] But many in this audience do *not* understand Danna's English lyrics.

My chief sources regarding Danna's reception in Egypt are westernized upper-middle-class students at the American University of Cairo who are quite familiar with the Egyptian and Western pop musical traditions Danna draws on, patronize the nightclubs where Danna's singles are played (going to discos is almost exclusively an upper- and upper-middle-class phenomenon), and—unlike most of the audience—are fluent in English. These students dismiss the attacks on Danna in the opposition press, saying that the nationalist opposition tends to describe *everything* as Israeli plots. But, reflecting the absence of public spaces for youth to assert positive views about sexuality and gender relations, they are rather defensive about claims that *Bûsnî Yâ Sûsû* is a sex tape—it's not really "bad," at least most of the songs are not, they say. Their response also resembles the posture of youth interviewed in an exposé published in the public-sector magazine *al-Shabâb* [Youth] about the popularity of Western "sex" pop (Danna, Madonna) and "satanic" music (heavy metal). Most youth joined the chorus of condemnation; the few who defended their interest in such music claimed that they did not really pay attention to the lyrics and that it was ludicrous to suppose that merely listening to satanic rock would turn them into worshippers of Satan.[36]

Bûsî/Pussy

A closer look at one of Danna's songs will serve to suggest some of the pleasures her music might offer a young Egyptian consumer. I assume here a listener who understands English, but someone with even a smidgen of English knowledge would get some of the lyrics and suggestions. Of the four Arabic-language songs on the contraband cassette, the most popular is probably "Sûsû Yâ Sûsû" [Sûsû Oh Sûsû], which was a favorite in the dance clubs of Cairo and Sharm al-Shaykh as well as on the street in 1995. As its "real" Israeli title, "Danna International," is unknown in Egypt, the hit was known simply as "Sûsû," itself a pet name, a diminutive of Yûsif (Joseph), and a type of nickname employed mainly by the older, educated generation. While a friend of lower-class background insists that Sûsû could *not* be a nickname for a male, my AUC students say it *could* be a term of endearment for a man, but one who is somewhat *fâfî* (effeminate).

"Sûsû Yâ Sûsû" opens with a vocal chorus chanting "wa abîba ay" (with no apparent meaning). An Arab drum beat from a *tabla* quickly backs up the chanting, which is then joined by a (Western) "house" bass dance beat until finally a "pure" house rhythm together with electronic keyboards overrides the "oriental" rhythms. As the Arabic name Sûsû is chanted above the house beat, the entire song modulates between Arabic, house, and Arabic-house blended rhythms, modes, and textures.[37] The song is equally heterodox linguistically, constantly shifting between and combining English and Arabic, and occasionally using Mediterranean European languages, but, contrary to al-Ghaytî's claims, not Hebrew. Many phrases combine two or more languages, some are nonsensical (but fit the rhythm), some are articulated in such heavily accented English that I did not understand them until I procured the CD and read the lyric sheet,[38] and many words are ambiguous. In addition, there is considerable bilingual punning.[39]

The opening verse (to house backing) contains the phrases (in Arabic and English): "Khudnî lil Monaco [Take me to Monaco] / Khudnî lil Mexico [Take me to Mexico] / Jublî bil taxi [Bring me in a taxi] / I'm feelin' sexy / Danna International." The subsequent verse includes the phrase "Kiss me, mon cheri." The third verse also mixes English and Arabic: "Inta al-milyûnayr [You (masculine) are the millionaire] / And I have a golden hair [the grammatical error here seems deliberate] / I'm feelin' [givin'?] bussy [bûsî] / Come on and bussy." This set of phrases is extremely polysemic, for *bûsî* (long u and long i) means "kiss" in Egyptian Arabic (hence the origin of the name by which the song, and entire cassette, is known in Egypt, "Bûsnî Yâ Sûsû" or "Kiss me Sûsû," even though the line appears nowhere in the song). In addition, *bûsî* is the form of command used to address a female, whereas the previous verse used the masculine form of address (*inta*). "Bussy" also suggests "pussy," since the "p" sound is pronounced "b" in Arabic, as in Bîbsî (Pepsi) Cola.[40] The verse continues as follows: "Shtaraytu bil duty free [I bought it in duty free] / Shampoo Mal Givenchy / And expensive pantaloni [trousers, in Italian, here pronounced "bandaloonee"] / Compact disc and telefoni [telephone in pidgin Italian]."[41] Then, following the Arabic shout, "Yâ lahwî!" (oh disaster), the rhythm shifts, and the rapid beat of the solo *tabla* backs up Danna as she chants in almost perfectly accented Egyptian Arabic and an enticing, charmingly feminine lilt punctuated by hiccups, a style that is stereotypical of the cute sexy female of Egyptian cinema: "Sûsû Yâ Sûsû" and " 'Albî yâ Sûsû" (my heart Sûsû). The next line, interestingly, Egyptian non-English speakers hear as "Gismî yâ Sûsû" (my body Sûsû) but English speakers hear as "Kiss me." The phrase therefore sounds "sexier" to the monolingual Arabic speaker. The rest of the song more or less repeats these moments, but adds "Yalla [come on] yâ Sûsû" and "Touch me yâ Sûsû" during the "Sûsû" sequence.

Danna as "Local"

Contrary to al-Ghaytî's polemical claim that the Danna phenomenon is a case of foreign penetration and corruption, I want to argue that we should view Danna's music (at least her Arabic songs) as an intervention *within* the local culture. For I think it is this very indigenousness—operating on a number of levels—that accounts for much of her appeal in Egypt. This is already manifest in the tone of Danna's singing. While the grain of the voice is clearly provocative, the seductiveness is not "foreign" but rather is recognizable on local terms, recalling as it does the prototypical coy, alluring, and usually blonde starlet of the Egyptian movie screen. What is simultaneously shocking and appealing is that this coquettish and "forward" female tone of voice is asserted more publicly and openly by Danna than it is in the cinema. The "dirty" lyrics of Danna's songs are not foreign to contemporary Egyptian pop either; salaciousness, in fact, is one of the chief charges that cultural mandarins level against Egypt's "vulgar" pop singers. At least in Arabic, Danna's lyrics suggest nothing more audacious than those of 'Adawiya's famous and extremely successful number, "Bint al-Sultân," or songs by other "unrefined" singers who are massively popular with lower- and middle-class Egyptian youth.[42] Indeed, the sexiness of Danna's lyrics, I would suggest, works mainly by implication: along with the crucial role played by the tone of her voice, Danna's pronunciation and her use of multilingual combinations and nonsensical expressions render her meaning vague and open to multiple readings. In this regard "Sûsû Yâ Sûsû" recalls "Louie, Louie," the famous Kingsmen hit of the early 1960s, which all adolescents at the time "knew" was a dirty song even though, or perhaps because, its lyrics were virtually indecipherable.[43]

While there are elements in the lyrics that hint at Danna's transgendered status—"Sûsû Yâ Sûsû" vacillates between *bûsî* (kiss!, feminine form) and *inta* (you, masculine)—as far as I can determine, Sûsû's possibly effeminate character is not a significant issue for fans, or at least not one that is openly voiced. Although, as in much of the Middle East, open discussion of homosexuality is quite circumscribed in Egypt, as a practice it is hardly rare.[44] Nor is it entirely absent from the public arena, as evidenced, for example, by Yusri Nasrallah's wacky 1994 film *Mercedes*, which, directly inspired by the cinematic campiness of Pedro Almodovar, deals frankly and sympathetically (although not centrally) with homosexual characters.[45] Although Danna's transsexuality does not seem to be a major issue for Egyptian fans, sex change operations are not unthinkable in Egypt. In fact there has been an ongoing controversy regarding a man named Sayyid 'Abdallah who had a sex change operation in 1988 and applied as Sâlî (Sally) for admission to al-Azhar Islamic University. In November 1995 the Shaykh al-Azhar, Jâd al-Haqq (the country's leading religious authority), finally issued a *fatwa* (religious edict) stating that sex change operations were permissible,[46] thereby regularizing the status of other transgendered individuals in Egypt.[47] The sad footnote to the Sâlî case, however, is that after her sex change operation was ruled permissible, she was denied admission to the women's section of al-Azhar for having performed as a belly dancer. Just as with Danna, it is Sâlî's overt sexuality that is more offensive to the powers that be than her transgendered status. Thus, for Danna's Egyptian fans in any case, "Sûsû Yâ Sûsû" is principally a *heterosexual* "sex song" whose "transgressive" scenario is that of the cosmopolitan Western or westernized Arab woman who is traveling, feels sexy, has "a golden hair" (the quintessential sign of feminine beauty in Egypt), and makes advances toward Sûsû in a mixture of Western languages and impeccable Arabic. Although the singer's forwardness is rather shocking in the local context, it is appreciated by Egyptian youth, and this response no doubt in part reflects changing gender relations and the increasing role of women in Egyptian public life.

In terms of their musical style, Danna's Arabic numbers combine Western and Eastern rhythms, modes, and textures in a manner that is hardly foreign to Egypt, since many of the country's most interesting pop musicians engage in similarly innovative, syncretic, and hybridizing experiments and in the indigenization of foreign pop styles.[48] Two examples, chosen somewhat at random, of similar attempts to articulate an alternative vision of cultural modernity are the 1995 cassette *Râb mûsîk li-al-shabâb faqat* [*Rap Music—For Young People Only*], produced by Ashraf 'Abduh (Al-Sharq), and Muhammad Munîr's 1996 hit "Al-layla dî" [Tonight]. *Rap Music—For Young People Only* garnered negative reviews from the mandarins, who saw it as another example of "vulgar" pop, but as usual youth ignored the literati's admonitions, and the tape was a hit all over Egypt in 1995, particularly in working-class neighborhoods. The songs on the cassette are not really rap music at all but instead a shameless and delightful blending of Egyptian pop vocalizations and melodies with well-known recent U.S. and U.K. house and dance beats and samples: the melody of one tune, "Sikkat al-salâma" [The Road of Peace], is in fact from a well-known Coca-Cola advertisement. Muhammad Munîr, on the other hand, is an Egyptian pop singer with a "respectable" reputation, whose music videos and concerts are broadcast on television, and whose lyrics are often penned by well-known national poets. Munîr has been syncretizing Western and Eastern music for years and has recorded with the German rock bands Embryo and Logic Animal. Munîr's latest hit, "Al-layla dî," features funk beats, electric keyboards and electric guitars, "oriental" rhythms from a drum machine and a *tabla*, and an oriental flute.[49] The song's instrumental hook is played in a Western scale, while Munîr sings the vocals in an oriental mode. Such hybridizing of Eastern and Western musics, which works through the indigenization of Western pop styles, is entirely typical of much popular music heard throughout the Arab world. Because Munîr has a reputation as a serious artist, and since this song's lyrics are penned by one of Egypt's premier "folk" poets, 'Abd al-Rahmân al-'Abnûdî, this sort of musical syncretism is considered acceptable by the cultural establishment.

Indeed, some of Danna's tunes function in such an acoustically indigenous manner that they have even been employed in an advertisement for an Egyptian shampoo called Luna 2.[50] Stylistically, therefore, Danna's music is far from foreign but rather, like much contemporary Egyptian pop, falls into the category of what mainstream nationalist intellectuals label "vulgar" (*hâbit*) or "cheap" music. It combines lower-class or "popular" Egyptian and Arab musical traditions with Western pop motifs without concern for neo-classicist conventions of synthesizing the "best" in high and low culture.[51]

Just as issues of homosexuality do not seem to be a significant factor in the reception of Danna on the part of Egyptian youth, the same can be said about another striking characteristic of her work and her cultural identity—her Arab Jewishness. Danna is by no means the first and only Israeli Mizrahi artist to enjoy underground success in Egypt. A tape by Ofra Haza entitled *Yemenite Songs*—later released in the United States under the title *50 Gates of Wisdom* (Shanachie Records, 1987)—circulated widely in Egypt in the late 1980s. Ofra Haza had first established her reputation in Israel singing mainstream pop, and it was only after she was thoroughly confirmed as a respectable artist that it was safe for her to return to her Mizrahi roots and record this set of traditional Arab-Jewish Yemeni music. Because the Ofra Haza cassette was understood in Egypt as "folk" music, and not as "cheap" or "vulgar," and because it had no sexual overtones,[52] its circulation in Egypt did not provoke the controversies that Danna's cassette has ignited. The point is that Danna's music issues from a wider and extremely rich phenomenon of Mizrahi pop music in Israel that is Levantine and Middle Eastern (and as such is marginalized in Israel), and is therefore comprehensible and "local" to Arab audiences in the Eastern Arab world.[53] Mizrahi pop music, for instance, is heavily consumed and appreciated by Palestinian youth in the West Bank and Gaza, a phenomenon little appreciated or noted by observers of Palestinian culture. Moreover, Zehava Benn, an Israeli Jewish singer of Turkish origin who sings the (canonical) repertoire of Umm Kalthûm to the backing of a Palestinian Arab orchestra from Haifa, was invited to give a concert in Gaza City, inside the Palestinian National Authority, in fall 1995. Although she was ultimately unable to perform because of security concerns, her popularity among Palestinians and the fact that the National Authority invited her once again suggests the existence of a lively but underground Levantine expressive culture that can be shared by Arabs and (oriental) Jews. Such a phenomenon is incomprehensible if one thinks of the region as starkly divided into the polarities Arab (East) and Jew (West).

It is only once one has grasped the elements of Danna's sonic indigenousness sketched above that one can understand that what makes Danna's cultural interventions in Egypt so effective is the fact that she works *within* musical and cultural trends that are thoroughly familiar to Egyptian youth. She pushes at the edges *from inside* a vibrant and innovating tradition, and this makes her music lively and exciting for many Egyptian young people. This is also precisely what makes her seem so dangerous to many nationalist intellectuals, much more threatening in fact than a Madonna or a Michael Jackson, since she communicates with Egyptian youth *in Arabic*. Indeed, the title track from Danna's latest release, "Maganona" (*magnûna*, "crazy" in Arabic), from the CD of the same name—a brilliantly wacky dance number sung aggressively in Egyptian dialect and the only Arabic number on the entire CD—can be read as a response to Danna's underground success in the Arab countries.[54] Danna's liminality, the fact that she is at once Arab and Jew, is precisely what makes her dialogue with Egyptian youth possible and is also what is so offensive to mainstream nationalists of all stripes, for whom nationalist ideology presupposes an essential *difference* between Arab and Jew. A nationalism that conceives of Egyptian society as homogeneous, unitary, and self-identical has no room for a border figure like Danna.

"That Mutant . . ."

Danna's significance and positioning in Israel is rather different.[55] She is popular and highly successful, at least among certain, but mainly marginalized, segments of the population, but she is also highly controversial and looked on with disfavor by the cultural elite. One sense of the associative baggage attached to her name is conveyed by Yigal Amir, who, just before he assassinated the Israeli Prime Minister Yitzhak Rabin in November 1995, is said to have remarked to a nearby policeman, "Today, they give us the spectacle of Aviv Gefen; next time, they'll make us listen to that mutant, Diana [sic] International."[56] Amir was stalking Rabin at a Peace Now rally, at which the Prime Minister spoke and during which he joined the featured singer, Aviv Gefen, for a singalong on stage. Gefen, a major new Israeli rock singer whose long, dyed-orange hair, heavy makeup, and androgynous clothing project a "radical" image, performs songs whose lyrics express "existential meaningless" and criticize the military establishment. But Gefen is also the offspring of elite circles, a close relative of Moshe Dayan, and his onstage gender ambiguity is entirely nonthreatening. His "rebelliousness," in short, is firmly located within the national tradition and represents the "respectable" face of dissent.[57] It would have been simply unthinkable for Yitzhak Rabin to have appeared on stage for a singalong together with a "trashy" gender- and culture-subversive like Danna International. Yigal Amir's remark does, however, underscore one of the major issues in Israel with regard to Danna. When I asked an Israeli

correspondent whether her Arab-Jewish identity was of any concern in
Israel, she replied that the media focuses almost exclusively on the issue of
Danna's "sexuality, sexuality, and sexuality," and in particular, her *transsexuality*. After Danna was chosen as a contestant in the competition to represent Israel in the 1995 Eurovision pop song contest, Ya'ir Nitsani, one of
Israel's leading comedians, proclaimed that Danna should not represent
Israel in this major international event because her transsexuality was a
"shame."[58] This sentiment appears to be widely shared and to have played a
role in Danna's failure to take first place in the competition (she placed second). When Danna appeared on one of Israel's major talk shows, hosted by
Dudu Topaz (Israel's Phil Donahue cum Oprah Winfrey), Topaz interro-
gated her about her orgasms—they're *my* orgasms, she replied—and asked
(with a look of horror on his face) if she had really had "it" cut off during
the sex change operation. Recent Israeli media speculation is that Danna
did not *really* undergo a sex change operation (although her breasts, an
important part of her image, cannot be denied) and that rumors to this
effect had inspired Danna to drop her lesbian girlfriend and take up with a
boyfriend, an officer in the Israeli navy, in order to prove her femaleness.
But, the story continued, this new relationship was a sham, really a gay relationship and not a heterosexual one.[59]

Perhaps it is this sexual undecidability (does she have a lesbian girlfriend? a gay boyfriend? a heterosexual boyfriend? what *kind* of sex and what
kind of anatomy does she have?) that makes Danna so wildly popular
among gay Ashkenazi men, who see her as a "heroic" role model.[60] Her rise
to fame also coincided with the growing popularity of drag queen shows in
Tel Aviv. But Danna's Arab identity remains more a matter of campy exoticism for the Ashkenazi gay community than one that poses critical questions about Israel's Eurocentric racial hierarchies. However, Danna does also
enjoy a substantial audience among the Mizrahim. According to correspondents, it is mainly the "disco youth" who are Danna's fans, and the majority
of Israelite-Jewish youth are Mizrahim.[61] Dance music in Israel, however,
has a rather low position in the cultural ranking system. As in Egypt, the
Israeli cultural elite promotes "quality" music (in Hebrew, *eikhoot*), which is
what the educated Ashkenazim (like the Egyptian elite) listen to.[62] The
fact that Danna sings in Arabic doubly disqualifies her music from the category of "quality," for Arabic music is severely ghettoized in Israel, consigned
to the lowest rungs of the country's Eurocentric cultural hierarchy, much
lower than dance music.[63] This is compounded by Danna's Mizrahiness,
which further positions her at the bottom of the prestige system.[64] A review
in the daily *Ma' ariv* of Danna's 1995 release, *E.P. Tampa*, exemplifies the
entirely commonplace stigma attached to Israeli Jews of Arab background.
The reviewer labeled her music *frehiyoot-bivim*, from *frehiyoot*, a derogatory

term that Ashkenazim frequently use to denote a young Mizrahi woman, meaning slut, and *bivim*, meaning gutter.[65] The Mizrahi community, however, is relatively unaffected by such Ashkenazi Eurosnobbism, and Danna has a somewhat mainstream appeal among Mizrahim as a successful ethnic insider. For instance, a friend of mine took her son to see Danna perform a concert of children's songs for kids in Holon, a poor Mizrahi town near Tel Aviv.

Among Danna's songs sung in Hebrew, which are more responsible for her fame in Israel than her Arabic numbers, are heterosexual love ballads that function as parodies in light of her sexuality. She has also recorded covers that, from a queer and Mizrahi position, poke fun at canonical Israeli popular music from the 1950s and 1960s, including "songs of the beautiful Israel" and "military songs." According to Smadar Lavie, when you hear a macho Israeli soldier song like "Yeshnan Banot" coming from the mouth of a "black" Mizrahi woman rather than from a muscular, blonde, square-jawed Ashkenazi, the effect is hilarious. Moreover, the fact that such songs emanate from a "trashy"-looking Mizrahi who appears hyperfeminine but whose very femininity is ambiguous adds another dimension to their uproariousness. There is also an Israeli dimension to Danna's song "Sûsû Yâ Sûsû" that highlights the country's disavowed but complicated and intimate connections to Arab culture. When Israel started broadcast television in the early 1960s, it had more programming in Arabic than in Hebrew, and one of the programs developed in the Arabic section[66] was a children's show called "*Sami and Susu*," a kind of Arabic "Mr. Rogers" mixed with "Sesame Street." There were no good children's shows at the time in Hebrew, so in the late 1960s "Sami and Susu" was given Hebrew subtitles and rapidly gained great favor with Israeli Jewish kids. According to one of my correspondents, the name Sûsû therefore "evokes cuddly memories" among a certain generation of Israelis. The Sami character was played by the young actor George Ibrahim, a Palestinian leftist who eventually lost his job during the intifada when he started to express his political views openly. Sami used to tell Susu, "khudnî yâ Sûsû" (take me Susu), a phrase that reappears in the lyrics of Danna's song, and the two characters were then transported to a new site as an "airport/spaceship" soundtrack played, a theme also evoked in Danna's "Sûsû Yâ Sûsû."[67]

Local Transnational

Commenting on Danna's "sexual invasion" of Egypt, one Egyptian newspaper article described the stakes as follows: "Thus Israel tries to destroy us by any means. Will she succeed or will our youth establish that they are really Egyptian?"[68] Such alarmism on the part of the intellectual elite, as well as police raids on cassette vendors, indicate the presence of some sort

of resistance. But not the overt resistance characteristic of a social movement—rather, resistance that is underground, inchoate, indirect, and
often not even conscious of itself as resistance. Nonetheless, it is critical
to attend to such apparently marginal cultural phenomena, for as Melucci
suggests, it is here, in the realm of submerged and everyday cultural practices, that alternative frameworks of meaning are produced.[69] Melucci
terms this the domain of "movement networks," and he goes on to claim
that the submerged, daily practices characteristic of such networks constitute the normal state of affairs for contemporary social movements. Overt
social movements *as such*, he claims, only emerge episodically and for limited durations. When we examine the sorts of alternative meanings that
are being forged through the consumption of Danna, we are examining
potential spaces for the emergence of movements and autonomous activity.

It would be a mistake, I would argue, to read these phenomena solely
through the theoretical lens of postmodernism. The popularity of Danna in
Egypt is indicative of widespread skepticism on the part of many Egyptian
youth regarding the version of modernity being offered up by the state and
nationalist ideologues, a skepticism that Walter Armbrust has labeled anti-
modernist.[70] But Danna's circulation in Egypt also suggests youth's desires
for an *alternative* modernity, one that would expand the accepted limits
regarding gender behaviors and roles and the articulation of pleasure.
Danna-in-Egypt also indicates visions of a modernity that is able to participate, without a sense of inferiority, in global popular cultural trends, not by
the passive consumption of the likes of Madonna and Michael Jackson, but
by the active reworking and rearticulating of transnational cultural forms,
by assimilating or domesticating such forms within indigenous culture. It
should be noted that such resistance, as currently articulated, does not seem
especially focused on female or queer desires and demands, but it does por-
tend an openness on the part of Egyptian youth with regard to these issues.

What is also significant about Danna-in-Egypt is that this is not merely
an instance of transnational cultural flows from West to East, the subject of
much of the academic work on global cultural movements. Although this is
certainly one dimension of the dynamics at work here, this is principally a
case of what I want to call *local* transnationalism. The cultural transactions
between Israel and Egypt at work here are not, in the main, *vertical* flows
(North-South or dominant-subordinate) or the products of the workings of
global capitalist forces, but *lateral* flows, products of underground exchanges
and affinities that traverse the borders of neighboring but hostile countries.
Danna is not (yet) a world music artist with substantial audiences in the
West.[71] Unlike Madonna or the rai star Khaled, she does not arrive in Egypt
via established circuits of advanced capitalism. She is a *local* star, whose
product is recorded and distributed by a *local* Israeli company (IMP Dance),

not the branch of a multinational firm. Moreover, it is not Danna and her record company who have reaped financial gain from the sale of a half million Danna cassettes sold in Egypt; instead, the profit has been shared by Egyptian bootleggers, black marketeers, and street peddlers. Contrary to the claims of the nationalist intelligentsia, Egyptian young people who identify with or relate to Danna are neither identifying with Israel nor being captured by Zionist ideology. My AUC students, who come from elite backgrounds, enjoy Danna *and* are angered by Israeli actions against the Palestinians and the Lebanese and feel ashamed at their government's kowtowing to the American and Israeli governments (a phenomenon known in the United States as "moderation"). Likewise, many Egyptian youth are simultaneously fans of Madonna and Michael Jackson *and* strong critics of the U.S. government's unwavering support for Israel and its policies toward Iraq. Egyptian youth "identification" with Danna instead is an inchoate and perhaps unwitting identification with the Mizrahim, the Israeli Jews who originate from the Arab countries. Mizrahi culture, as scholars like Ella Shohat, Smadar Lavie, Shlomo Swirski, and Ammiel Alcalay have demonstrated so well, is a lively, vital, complex cultural reality inside Israel, despite its marginalization by Israel's Ashkenazi elite. It is encouraging, therefore, to find echoes of Mizrahi culture in Egypt, where the Jewish strains of national culture have been so heavily suppressed and officially forgotten. I therefore regard the phenomenon of Danna International in Egypt as a hopeful sign, not the pathological effect of Israeli and Western cultural imperialism and the resultant corruption of Arab culture. But this potential will probably remain merely latent, underground, and proscribed, in the absence of other political and social developments in Egypt and Israel that might be congenial to the complicated and open identity and sexual politics that Danna International portends.[72]

Notes

Thanks are due, first of all, to Saba Mahmood for urging me to take up this project. Mona Maursi first alerted me to Danna International and gave me a tape with two of her songs. Nirvana Said and Dina Girgis provided complete versions of "*Bûsnî Yâ Sûsû*" and information about Danna's reception in Egypt. Bob Vitalis brought me Danna's CDs from Israel and continues to be a source of inspiration and timely anecdotes. I am grateful to Joel Beinin, Clarissa Bencomo, Sandra Campbell, Elliott Colla, Smadar Lavie, Don Moore, and Muhammad El-Roubi for their comments on earlier versions of the paper; to Elliott Colla and Hosam Aboul-Ela for their help on the theme of the predatory Western woman in Egyptian literature; to David McMurray for calling my attention to the Yigal Amir connection; to Motti Regev for sending his articles; and to Tom Levin for his encouragement and sparkling editorial suggestions. Yael Ben-Zvi and Smadar Lavie served as invaluable resources on Danna's place in Israel. Special thanks are due to Clarissa Bencomo and Gamâl 'Abd al-'Azîz for assistance in tracking down articles, help in transcribing and translating lyrics, and helping me contextualize Danna in Egypt.

102   *The Musical Quarterly*

1.   A wealth of information on Danna International—including pictures and samples of her music—was available at the unofficial Danna homepage (http://www.netvision.net.il/~optic/ Danna.htm), which, unfortunately, was no longer operating at press time, ostensibly due to lack of funds. Danna's CD discography includes *Danna International* (IMP Dance, Tel Aviv, 1993), *Umpatamba* (IMP Dance, Tel Aviv, 1994), and the E.P. *E.P. Tampa* (IMP Dance, Tel Aviv, 1995). Danna's latest CD is entitled *Maganona* (Helicon/Big Foot Records, Tel Aviv, 1996). While difficult to find in the United States, they are available from Hataklit, an Israeli import company in Los Angeles (800/428-2554).

2.   See Hamdî Rizq, "Sậ'îda Sultân tathîr dajja fî Misr wa juhûd 'amanîya li-muwâjaha 'al-ghazw al-jinsî' al-Isra'îlî" [Saida Sultan Stirs Up a Clamor in Egypt and Security Efforts to Counter the Israeli "Sexual Invasion"], *Al-Hayât*, 4 Oct. 1995, 1; Tawhîd Majdî, " 'Bûsnî Yâ Sûsû' yubâ' sirran fî Misr bi khamsîn gînayh" ["Kiss me Susu" Is Sold Covertly in Egypt for Fifty Pounds], *Rûz al-Yûsif*, 12 Dec. 1994; *Rûz al-Yûsif*, 16 Oct. 1995, 27; *al-Jamhûr al-Masrî*, 18 Feb. 1995, 12; *al-Hayât al-Masrî*, 31 Dec. 1995.

3.   Hereafter, the book is referred to in the text as F.

4.   The author uses terms like "perversion" and "deviance" throughout to describe gays and lesbians.

5.   The upscale McDonald's in my neighborhood in Cairo featured posters of Madonna, James Dean, and Marilyn Monroe. According to al-Ghaytî, Marilyn Monroe was both an inspiration for Danna as well as a "deviant" (F, 40) (see below).

6.   Al-Ghaytî's claim is that Madonna is not "complete" because she is unable to bear children. As the entire world knows, Madonna has recently given birth to a child.

7.   The year 1967 is clearly meant to resonate as the year of the Six-Day War and Israel's overwhelming defeat of the Syrian, Jordanian, and Egyptian armies. But given the very low status of Arabic music in Israel, especially as recorded by Mizrahim, Rachel Qattâwî's recording must have been a very marginal phenomenon and not, as al-Ghaytî implies, an Israeli theft of a valuable treasure.

8.   These include the nature of the Israeli-Palestinian "peace," which many regard as tanta-mount to Palestinian surrender and as a complete sham, Israel's refusal to dismantle its nuclear arsenal and make the Middle East a nuclear-free zone, and the Israeli government's failure to bring to trial the military officers responsible for carrying out the massacres of forty-nine Egyptian prisoners of war near al-'Arîsh during the war of 1956 and of over one thousand Egyptian POWs during the 1967 war. More recently, public anger in Egypt was aroused by Israel's attacks on Lebanon in April 1996, the IDF's targeting of the U.N. Qana base and resulting death of over one hundred civilians, and what is seen as the successful U.S. pressure to torpedo any censuring of Israeli actions. Needless to say, Israel's policies and actions appear very different from the vantage point of Egypt than they do from inside the United States. A sense of that quite different perspective can be gained in the United States from the various writings of Edward Said and Noam Chomsky. On the Qana affair, see the reporting in the *Independent*, especially Robert Fisk, "Massacre Film Puts Israel in Dock," *Independent*, 6 May 1996; for my own views on the question of Palestine, see Ted Swedenburg, *Memories of Revolt: The 1936–1939 Rebellion and the Palestinian National Past* (Minneapolis: University of Minnesota Press, 1995), especially chapters 1 and 2.

9.   For instance, see recent articles in *Rûz al-Yûsif* exposing Israel's efforts to steal and destroy Egyptian music and cinema: Khâlid Abû Jalâla, "Sarqat al-mûsîqa al-Misrîya" [The theft of Egyptian music], *Rûz al-Yûsif*, 28 Mar. 1995, 62 63; and 'Amrû Khafâjî,

"Al-tatbî': Ghazw Isrâ'îlî li-al-sînamâ al-Misrîya!" [Normalization: An Israeli Assault on Egyptian Cinema!], *Rûz al-Yûsif*, 21 Nov. 1994, 68 71.

10. "Wiqâhat Isrâ'îlî fawq 'albat sijâ'ir: 'al-khayl 'arabî' . . . wa 'al-kurbâj masrî'. . . wa 'al-qâ'id 'Amrîkî' . . . !" [Israel's Impudence on a Cigarette Packet: "Arab Horses" and "Egyptian Whip" and "American Commander"!], *Al-'Arabî*, 19 Feb. 1996. The claim, of course, is rather ludicrous, since virtually no Israeli products are sold on the Egyptian market, and there is no compelling economic reason for Egyptians to desire more expensive Israeli cigarettes. Indeed, as of press time, the cigarette had yet to appear in Egypt.

11. See, for instance, Yahya Haqqi, *The Saint's Lamp and Other Stories*, trans. M. M. Badawi (Leiden: E. J. Brill, 1973); Tawfiq al-Hakim, *Bird of the East*, trans. R. Bayly Winder (Beirut: Khayats, 1966); and Sulayman Fayyad, *Voices*, trans. Hosam Aboul-Ela (New York: Marion Boyars, 1993).

12. The press reports frequently on army campaigns against heroin and hashish production in the Sinai, whose 'Aqaba Gulf beaches are known as freewheeling resort areas: Sharm al-Shaykh (site of the recent antiterror summit) caters to upscale Western tourists and the westernized Egyptian bourgeoisie, while Dhahab and Nuwayba' are the mecca for scantily clad, drug-seeking Euro-hippies and Israelis. For a description of South Sinai's even wilder days under Israeli occupation, see Smadar Lavie, *The Poetics of Military Occupation: Mzeina Allegories of Bedouin Identity under Israeli and Egyptian Rule* (Berkeley: University of California Press, 1990).

13. See "Isrâ'îl tuhârib Misr bi-al-jins fî al-tilîfûn" [Israel Wages War on Egypt by Telephone Sex], *Rûz al-Yûsif*, 21 Aug. 1995, 18, 20–22.

14. One could read the closing scene of this TV announcement—the opening of the Pan African Games held in Cairo in 1991—as an implication that the AIDS threat also emanates from Sub-Saharan Africa.

15. See the books on Madonna in Arabic that are sold at Cairo newsstands, like *Madonna's Diet Book* and *Confessions of Madonna*.

16. "Isrâ'îl tuhârib Misr bi-al-jins fî al-tilîfûn," 18, 20–22.

17. "Isrâ'îl tuhârib Misr bi-al-jins fî al-tilîfûn," 21.

18. Since the mid-1980s, Egypt's most prestigious professional syndicates (doctors, engineers, lawyers) have been lobbying for limits on the numbers accepted into their professions' university programs in an effort to combat increasing unemployment. The engineers' syndicate has even attempted to block the government from opening new university programs and technical institutes. Thanks to Clarissa Bencomo for this point.

19. Before a young man can marry, he must, at the minimum, own an apartment, furnish it, purchase an acceptable amount of gold jewelry for his fiancée as an engagement gift (the *shabka*, which is the bride's property and serves as a form of insurance for her), and be able to finance a decent wedding party. A significant wedding party expense is the *firqa* or music group, and wedding gigs constitute one of the major sources of income for Egyptian popular musicians and are often much more lucrative than recording. Thus, paradoxically, the same weddings that are a major source of support for the music that youth love also function—by virtue of their great expense—to oppress that same generation.

20. Firas Alatraqchi, "Tied in a Knot," *Pose*, Mar.–Apr. 1996, 21.

21. Still, young people's sexual adventures outside of marriage are more frequent than one would imagine from official representations. One survey of one hundred high-school

104   *The Musical Quarterly*

and college girls in Cairo reported that 8 percent had had full sexual intercourse, 20 percent had held their lovers' hands, 23 percent had kissed, and 37 percent had experienced sex without intercourse. See Ayman M. Khalifa, "The Withering Youth of Egypt," *Ru'ya* 7 [Spring 1995]: 7.

22.   It is also often claimed that the crisis of youth is a significant factor in the rise of Islamist movements. Government-style propaganda, such as the famous 1994 film *al-Irhâbî* [The Terrorist], which stars Egypt's leading comedian, 'Âdil Imâm, asserts that innocent youths are attracted to Islamic militant groups because their perfidious leaders provide women to marry, at no cost. See Walter Armbrust, "How the Egyptian Establishment Declared Victory in the War against Islamicists," paper presented at the American Anthropological Association Annual Meetings, Washington, D.C., 17 Nov. 1995. Although such propaganda is simplistic, it is the case that youth, so heavily affected by the crisis of opportunities, constitute the main adherents of Islamist movements. Whereas in the late 1970s and early 1980s the militant Islamist groups that employed violent means mainly attracted university-educated youth (see Saad Eddin Ibrahim, "Egypt's Islamic Militants," *MERIP Reports* 103 [1982] 5–14), today such groups are also gaining lower-class youth adherents. The Muslim Brotherhood, Egypt's main Islamist organization and a mass movement that, although technically illegal, attempts to mobilize through legal channels and aboveground, successfully recruits university-educated youth. Although the Muslim Brotherhood has not found a "solution" to the wedding crisis, it does enjoin simple wedding ceremonies, where music groups and dancing are not permitted, and thus ensures that what Muslim Brothers call "Islamic weddings" are much cheaper than those that are the norm for the rest of the population.

23.   This paragraph draws heavily on Walter Armbrust, *Mass Culture and Modernism in Egypt* (Cambridge: Cambridge University Press, 1996).

24.   Kamâl al-Najmî, "Da'wâ hisba did fann al-ghinnâ': hakadhâ kân al-'amr" [The Charge of *Hisba* against Singing: The Matter Was Thus], *Al-Hayât*, 18 Nov. 1995, 20.

25.   See Armbrust, *Mass Culture and Modernism in Egypt*, and Khalifa, "The Withering Youth of Egypt," 9. The censorship and banning from radio of songs by "respectable" artists is also routine; see Fâtima Hasan, "Jadal fî Misr hawla hazr 199 ughnîya li-54 mutriban wa mutribât" [Controversy in Egypt about the Banning of 199 Songs by 54 Male and Female Artists], *Al-Hayât*, 1 July 1993, 23.

26.   Although class divisions within Egyptian society are gaping and getting wider, and although the upper-class youth who are the direct beneficiaries of *infitâh* do not face the same problems as lower-middle- and lower-class ones regarding employment and marriage, the former are also alienated from the classical nationalist project and are negatively affected by the absence of public spaces for youth. One should, of course, make some distinctions. Some middle- and lower-class youth want to bring back the "golden age" of culture and politics represented by the Nasser era, while others wish for the return of the public-sector safety net through the halting or slowing down of the pace of privatization and structural adjustment and for an expansion of the possibilities of working in the Gulf. Upper-class youth meanwhile are somewhat more focused on cultural liberalization.

27.   See 'Abd al-Latîf Wahba, "Tashîlât Isrâ'îlîya li-jadb al-shabâb al-Misrî" [Israeli Facilitations to Attract Egyptian Youth], *Al-Ahâlî*, 8 Nov. 1995, 2.

28.   See Gudrun Krämer, *The Jews of Modern Egypt* (Seattle: University of Washington Press, 1989).

29.   The rest emigrated to Brazil, France, the United States, Argentina, England, and Canada; see Joel Beinin, *The Dispersion of Egyptian Jewry* (Berkeley: University of California Press, forthcoming).

30.   Murâd's films are regularly aired on Egyptian television, her music is played on the radio and readily available on cassette, and her death in November 1995 brought forth a wave of laudatory obituaries and tributes in the Egyptian press. The exclusion of Egyptian Jews from nationalist discourse was also noticeable in the favorable tributes to Layla Murâd that appeared following her death in the Egyptian press during November and December 1995: almost all of them failed to mention her Jewishness.

31.   See Beinin, *The Dispersion of Egyptian Jewry*, chapter 3; Sasson Somekh, "Participation of Egyptian Jews in Modern Arabic Culture, and the Case of Murad Faraj," in *The Jews of Egypt: A Mediterranean Society in Modern Times*, ed. Shimon Shamir (Boulder, Colo.: Westview Press, 1987); *Bulletin of the Israeli Academic Center in Cairo* 10 (July 1988).

32.   Ironically, much of the coverage of Danna in the press is written by badly paid young stringers who have no real "voice" but merely ventriloquize official discourse.

33.   Danna's claim, in an interview with *Jerusalem Report*, that a half million of her cassettes had been sold in Egypt is credible; see Daniel Grynberg, "A Natural Woman," *Jerusalem Report*, 22 Feb. 1996, 35.

34.   While one of my students who purchased *Bûsnî Yâ Sûsû* before the media offensive against Danna paid only 8 L.E. (just slightly above the average price of a prerecorded cassette), her friends who bought it after the onset of "moral panic" had to pay 50 L.E.

35.   The Algerian rai star Khaled's 1992 hit, "Didi," also reached the top of the charts in both Israel and Egypt.

36.   See Ilhâm Rahîm, "Sharâ'it fî-al-mamnû' " [Forbidden Cassettes], *Al-Shabâb* 219 (Oct. 1995): 54–55.

37.   Whereas house music in the West normally uses major keys, Danna's dance music deploys oriental modes; thanks to Smadar Lavie for comments on comparative musical modes.

38.   I am told that Danna is parodying the parodies of Mizrahi- and Palestinian-accented English by Israeli Ashkenazi comedians like Shaike Ofir.

39.   Such polylingual linguistic play is a long-standing tradition for Levantine Jews, going back at least to Andalusian Spain; see Ammiel Alcalay, *After Jews and Arabs: Remaking Levantine Culture* (Minneapolis: University of Minnesota Press, 1993).

40.   The lyric sheet of the CD Danna International, available only to the Israeli consumer, is more explicit, transcribing the phrase as "I'm giving pussy." For the Arabic-speaking listener, however, the meaning remains more ambiguous.

41.   Telephone in Italian is *telefonare*, but *telefoni* rhymes nicely here with *pantaloni*.

42.   Consider, for example, the following quite representative lines from 'Adawiya's "Bint al-Sultân": "The water's in your hand / And 'Adawîya is thirsty . . . / Why don't you look at me / My little fruit, my pineapple /Water me, water me more / The water in your hand is sugar." Quoted in Armbrust, *Mass Culture and Modernism in Egypt*, 132.

43.   The song's supposedly lewd lyrics, in fact, got it banned from sales and airplay in Indiana and elsewhere and inaugurated an FBI investigation. But the controversy only

spurred greater sales, and the record hit number two on the Billboard and number one on the Cashbox charts (http://www.eskimo.com/~raigb/kingsmen.html).

44.   On the peculiar contradictions of Egypt's homosexual community, see, for example, Neil Miller, *Out in the World: Gay and Lesbian Life from Buenos Aires to Bangkok* (New York: Vintage, 1993), 68–69. Miller describes the complex situation of Egyptian gay life as follows: "Making contact with a gay or lesbian community in Egypt was difficult. There was essentially no such thing. Egypt was the place I visited where there was the strongest social sanction against an openly gay or lesbian life, where a sense of homosexual identity was weakest, where there was the least degree of AIDS awareness. Paradoxically, in a society where the sexes remain strictly segregated, same-sex relations were commonplace, at least among men. But you didn't talk about the subject, except to your very closest friends, and perhaps not even then. In Egypt, sex had to be kept secret, and homosexual sex in particular was *haram*— taboo. Categories of sexual identity and orientation were slippery, elusive in Egypt and in the Arab world in general. Once you crossed the Mediterranean, the terms 'gay' and 'straight' revealed themselves to be Western cultural concepts that confused more than they elucidated. In modern-day Cairo, male homosexual sex was everywhere and nowhere."

45.   This is also true of some of the work of Egypt's most celebrated director, Youssef Chahine. See in particular his film *'Iskandarîya Layh?* [Alexandria Why?].

46.   The Mufti of Egypt, Dr. Muhammad Sayyid Tantâwî, opposed sex change operations on the basis that what God has created should not be changed (see Hamdî Rizq, "Shaykh al-'Azhar yuftî bi-jiwâz tahwîl al-jins" [The Shaykh al-Azhar Gives a Formal Legal Opinion Permitting Sex Change], *Al-Hayât,* 10 Nov. 1995, 24). Tantâwî replaced al-Haqq as Shaykh al-Azhar after the latter's death.

47.   See Rizq, "Shaykh al-'Azhar yuftî bi-jiwâz tahwîl al-jins," 24, and *Middle East Times,* 31 Dec. 1995. Incidentally, sex change operations are also performed in Saudi Arabia (the cases I have read about are female-to-male), again with *fatwas* from religious leaders.

48.   See Armbrust, *Mass Culture and Modernism in Egypt,* 173–84.

49.   The track is from a cassette by Munîr entitled *Mumkin?!* (Digitec Records, Cairo, 1995).

50.   I have seen the ad on the video monitors that run a nonstop mix of music vids, adverts, movie trailers, cartoons, snippets of soccer matches, and bits of "America's Favorite Home Videos" for passengers waiting to board the metro at downtown Cairo stations. The promotion of Luna 2 opens to the strains of Danna's song "Sa'îda Sultân" (a remake of Whitney Houston's "My Name Is Not Susan") and shows ordinary-looking (somewhat chubby by U.S. standards) Egyptian women dancing around and mouthing Danna's opening words, "Wa t'ûlû ay, wa t'ûlû ah" (And you [plural] say what, and you say yeah). Danna's tune rumbles in the background as the ad promotes the shampoo's virtues, and then the volume of the music comes up again as the spot closes with another chorus of "Wa t'ûlû ay, wa t'ûlû ah." I am unaware of any press attacks on Luna 2 for its use of Israeli sex and corruption in the marketing of its product.

51.   See Armbrust, *Mass Culture and Modernism in Egypt,* 181–82.

52.   Al-Ghaytî, however, claims that Ofra Haza's tape was "licentious" (F, 34–35).

53.   On Israeli "Oriental" music, see Motti Regev, "Music Cultures and National Culture: The Israeli Case," *Popular Music* (forthcoming); Alcalay, *After Jews and Arabs,* 253–255.

54.   Here are just two of the many amusing lines from this single: "Who do you think my husband is? / I'm a respectable woman [*sitt muhtarma*]," and, "You all think I'm crazy / I'm not

crazy [*ana mish magnûna*]." The last line of the song goes, "*ana mish magnûna* / *ana magnûna*" [I'm not crazy / I'm crazy].

55. I depend in this section primarily on the Israeli correspondents Yael Ben-Zvi and Smadar Lavie.

56. Marcus Schattner, "Un certain Israel en danger de paix," *Liberation*, 13 Dec. 1995, 2.

57. Regev, "Music Cultures and National Culture"; Yael Ben-Zvi, personal communication; Smadar Lavie, personal communication.

58. Note that it would be unthinkable for an Arab country to participate in the Eurovision contest, while Israel's "European" identity simply goes without saying.

59. Yael Ben-Zvi, personal communication; Smadar Lavie, personal communication. Perhaps in an effort to put rumor to rest, Danna recently revealed in a published interview that she does indeed have a penis and has no plans to have it "cut" in an operation. She has, however, had hormone injections for breast development and will soon have silicone implants. In response to the question of her sexual preference, Danna—who calls herself a "woman and a man"—divulged that she has a boyfriend and is not and has never been physically attracted to women. When asked about her politics, Danna asserted that while she does not consider herself to be political, she is in favor of "peace"; see Yoav Birenberg, "What Can I Tell You, Yoav, We Have a Wonderful State and a Wonderful People" [in Hebrew], *Yediot Aharanot*, weekly supplement (*7 Nights*), 23 Aug. 1996, 6–7.

60. But according to Smadar Lavie, Ashkenazi gays' real role models are the same as those of straight Israelis, because they are so mainstream.

61. It should be noted, although the point cannot be developed here, that Mizrahi youth, due to their place in the economic-racial hierarchy in Israel, are not benefiting from the country's current economic boom in the wake of recent peace deals with Arab countries, and that their hopelessness and alienation resembles that of lower- and lower-middle-class Egyptian youth.

62. The extreme importance accorded to Western classical music in Israel, for instance, should be understood as part of Israeli Ashkenazis' unceasing efforts to project a Western identity. It is also noteworthy that the Israeli national leadership also occasionally warns against U.S. cultural imperialism, with reference to precisely the same icons of "trashy" cultural domination invoked by Egyptian nationalists. For instance, Israeli President Ezer Weizman in August 1995: "The Israeli people are infected with Americanization. We must be wary of McDonald's; we must be wary of Michael Jackson; we must be wary of Madonnas" (Mid-East Realities, MIDDLEEAST@aol.com, 11 Aug. 1995).

63. See Motti Regev, "Present Absentee: Arab Music in Israeli Culture," *Public Culture* 7, no. 2 (1995): 433–45; Regev, "Music Cultures and National Culture."

64. For an introduction to the position of the Mizrahim in Israel, see Alcalay, *After Jews and Arabs*; Smadar Lavie, "Blow-Ups in the Borderzones: Third World Israeli Authors' Gropings for Home," *New Formations* 18 (1992): 84–105; Ella Shohat, "Sephardism in Israel: Zionism from the Standpoint of its Jewish Victims," *Social Text* 19–20 (1988): 1–35; Ella Shohat, *Israeli Cinema: East/West and the Politics of Representation* (Austin: University of Texas Press, 1989); and Shlomo Swirski, *Israel: The Oriental Majority*, trans. Barbara Swirski (London: Zed Books, 1989).

65. Although the word literally means "chick" (the related word *farkha* has the same meaning in Arabic), it is more derogatory than the term "chick" (for young woman) in English. *Freha* can also be used to refer to an Ashkenazi woman, usually working class, but is usually used to

describe Mizrahim. (Yael Ben-Zvi, personal communication). See Guy Assif, "When There's a Haircut There Are Friends," (Hebrew), *Tarbut Ma'ariv* issue no. 82, 27 October 1995, 13.

66.   The administration of Palestinian-Arab citizens in Israel is essentially apartheid, with separate (and unequal) Arab sections in the Education Ministry, the Histadrut (Israeli Trade Union Federation), and other institutions.

67.   There is even an "Airport Version" of the song on the Israeli CD, which is not found on the contraband cassette sold in Egypt. It opens with the following spoken announcement:

> This is Saudi Arabian airport / May I have your attention please / All passengers on flight no. six o sex / To Monaco please approach to / Gate No. four two / Shukran [thank you, Arabic]

The version then closes with another spoken announcement as follows:

> Ladies and Gentlemen / Attention please / Five minutes before landing / In Ben Gurion airport / No kiss kiss no miz miz [fondling, Hebrew; snacking, Arabic] / And no business allowed / Shukran

68.   "Al-jins salâh Isrâ'îl al-jadîd did Misr" [Sex is a New Israeli Weapon against Egypt], *Al-Hayât al-Misrîya*, 31 Dec. 1995, 4.

69.   Alberto Melucci, "The Symbolic Challenge of Contemporary Movements," *Social Research* 52, no. 4 (1985): 789–816.

70.   See Armbrust, *Mass Culture and Modernism in Egypt*, 217–18.

71.   This may well be changing, however; in December 1996 Danna made what I believe was her U.S. debut with concerts at the Palladium in New York City and in Miami and Los Angeles.

72.   The continued threat posed by Danna was again emphasized as this article was going to press in the fall of 1996 by the journalistic response to Danna's visit to Egypt for a fashion shoot where she modeled a new line of dresses from the mainstream Israeli department store Hamashbir. The Egyptian weekly *Rûz al-Yûsif* described the trip as a propaganda coup for Israel, reporting that Israeli press accounts of Danna's visit revealed Egyptians to be bribetakers (Danna's party pays off a policeman so that they can continue shooting at the pyramids) and pervert lovers (Egyptian men profess that Danna is pretty and that they like her music). The article featured several fashion photos of Danna posing alluringly in slinky outfits: with Egyptian policemen, in the Khân al-Khalîlî bazaar, and together with a boatman beside the Nile. The captions—such as "This Pervert Exploits Us"—attempt to ensure that the Egyptian reader will not be fooled, for the alluring Israeli women is, so one learns, really a pervert, a man! See "Al-Misriyyûn murtishûn yabî'ûn ayya shay' wa yu'ashiqûn al-shadhûdh" [Bribe-Taking Egyptians Will Sell Anything and Love Perverts], *Rûz al-Yûsif*, 5 Aug. 1996, (unnumbered pages).

[7]

Re-thinking 'whiteness'? Identity, change and 'white' popular music in post-apartheid South Africa

CHRISTOPHER BALLANTINE

Abstract

In South Africa, the prospects for social integration were auspicious after the first democratic elections in 1994. As the popular music of the time shows, it was not only blacks who exulted in the new 'rainbow' euphoria: many whites did so too. But for millions of black and white citizens, this moment was short lived. The government's adoption of neo-liberal policies had severe social consequences – which it and the new elite sought to conceal behind populist calls to 'race' solidarity, a new racial typecasting and slurs aimed at whites in general. 'White' popular music has responded to these reversals in a variety of ways – including direct criticism, sharp satire, humour and the expression of 'fugitive' identities. Perhaps more remarkably, white musicians have stressed the need for self-reinvention in music that is ironic, unpredictable, transgressive. These songs play with malleable identities; tokens of a disdain for fixed or essential identities, they are hopeful signposts towards a more integrated future.[1]

No one today is purely one thing. Labels like Indian, or woman, or Muslim, or American are no more than starting-points, which if followed into actual experience for only a moment are quickly left behind. Imperialism consolidated the mixture of cultures and identities on a global scale. But its worst and most paradoxical gift was to allow people to believe that they were only, mainly, exclusively, white, or black, or Western, or Oriental. (Said 1994, pp. 407–8)

There is no Negro mission; there is no white burden. . . . There is no white world, there is no white ethnic, any more than there is a white intelligence. . . . The negro is not. Any more than the white man. Both must turn their backs on the inhuman voices which were those of their respective ancestors in order that authentic communication be possible. . . . Why not the quite simple attempt to touch the other, to feel the other, to explain the other to myself? (Fanon 1986, pp. 228–31)

What is the authority by which claims about an individual's identity are warranted? To what extent does this authority reside in the will of the individual? If individual will is not a sufficiently authoritative basis for identity, to whom belongs the authority to ascribe identity to an individual, and what is the theoretical foundation for that authority? And on the basis of what considerations do these 'ascribers' select, even to their own satisfaction, one identity rather than another to assign to a given individual? . . . Even when identity is conceived as a consciousness, or subjectivity (as in 'the Chicano subject' or 'the white subject'), the ordinance of perceived shared physical descent over proclaimed individual consent is strong. . . . At stake in choosing to address 'identity' in the foregoing terms is the amount of influence individuals have over their own fate. (Hollinger 2000, pp. 22–6)

Can we avoid having to choose between two equally destructive solutions: living together and setting aside our differences or living apart in homogeneous communities which communicate only through the market or through violence? (Touraine 2000, p. 48)

I

In the mid-1990s – long after Nelson Mandela's release from prison, and a couple of years beyond South Africa's first democratic elections, a new graffito appeared on a wall in central Johannesburg. It read: 'Re-release Mandela – the disco version'. I like to think that the writer of this graffito had something more in mind than simply a clever pun: that what was being signalled, rather, was the need to re-energise a project that had lost its way, or been hijacked – a suggestion that symbolically Mandela, its icon, was once again prisoner of forces beyond his control, and was now awaiting release in another 'version'. What the contents of this metaphorical new version might be have become increasingly clear. Within South Africa, voices critical of the African National Congress (ANC) government, and of the new social order in general, have grown in volume, articulacy and anger – particularly in the post-Mandela era, under the presidency of his successor Thabo Mbeki. These criticisms highlight many issues. One has been the topic of some profound reflections by the eminent black South African writer Njabulo Ndebele. Focusing on what he called 'the blinding sterility at the centre of the ''heart of whiteness'' ', he argued that 'whiteness' had to 'undergo an experiential transformation by absorbing new cultural experience as an essential condition for achieving a new sense of cultural rootedness'. This, he suggested, was a world-historic opportunity: whites in South Africa could reclaim their humanity by assisting in 'a humanistic revival of our country through a readiness to participate in the process of redress and reconciliation'. But this involved one essential condition: that the 'heart of whiteness' restore 'dignity to the black body'. Ndebele went on:

We are all familiar with the global sanctity of the white body. Wherever the white body is violated in the world, severe retribution follows somehow for the perpetrators, if they are non-white, regardless of the social status of the white body. The white body is inviolable, and that inviolability is in direct proportion to the global vulnerability of the black body. This leads me to think that if South African whiteness is a beneficiary of the protectiveness assured by international whiteness, it has an opportunity to write a new chapter in world history. It will have to come out from under the umbrella and repudiate it. Putting itself at risk, it will have to declare that it is home now, sharing in the vulnerability of other compatriot bodies. South African whiteness will declare that its dignity is inseparable from the dignity of black bodies. (Ndebele 2000, p. 12)

Of course, this process was never going to be easy. For a start, within the anti-apartheid struggle itself the concept of 'race', though nothing other than a social invention, was never deconstructed. 'Races' were assumed to be real, natural entities; thus race-thinking remained entrenched, and a non-racial future simply meant that the future would be 'multiracial': at best a co-existence free of racism. As Gerhard Maré has argued:

'Non-racialism' was the commitment, but races remained the building blocks, not only of apartheid society, but also of resistance organisations and the theoretical and strategic thinking that informed analysis and practice within attempts to restructure society. (Maré 2003, p. 11)

More obviously – the 'miracle' of the 'rainbow revolution' notwithstanding – it has recently become clear just how close South Africa came to the brink of civil war nine years ago when, in the run-up to the first democratic elections, a tiny but organised minority of 50,000 white conservatives, in collusion with units of the South African Defence Force, stood armed and poised for war. Disgruntled arch-conservatives have continued to plot – in exile for instance, where the racist, white South Africans of the London-based 'Springbok Club' have used the Internet to enlist other white supremacists in their campaign to recolonise South Africa and Zimbabwe and restore 'civilised' white rule. And as if in grotesque (though not, sadly, isolated) echo, two white rugby players were recently convicted of murdering a black youth they caught poaching on a farm: they severely beat the boy, left him to die under a tree, and later threw his body into a dam. As the erstwhile black premier of the Free State Province, Winkie Direko, put it: 'I have sympathy with whites. Yesterday you were the *baas* and I was the *kombuismeid* [kitchen maid]. Now I stand here as the premier of the province. It must be a bitter pill to swallow, but it has to be done' (*Mail & Guardian*, 23–29 March 2001).

Indeed it does. But how is it to be done? What is involved here? What are the implications for white – and surely also for black – identities? At a recent conference in South Africa, Stuart Hall argued that we ought to avoid 'monumentalism' and instead think hard about how to introduce *new subjects*. 'We are talking', he said, 'about the production of a new subjectivity. Something which has never yet been seen on earth in this part of the world, which will not forget the terrors out of which it has been constructed and the violence and the horror but which will also make something creative out of it' (Hall 1997, p. 16).

I think there is a role here for music – the 'last and best source of participatory consciousness', as Charles Keil described music, with its 'capacity not just to model but maybe to enact some ideal communities' (Keil 1994, p. 20). If part of what is involved is a battle not just against racism but also against ethnic absolutism, then it seems to me that music can join that battle; that it can become part of a new cultural politics, enabling a set of aesthetic practices that will fortify such struggles and, as Hall says, permit 'new subjects to be introduced'. This is not a new idea: Paul Gilroy (1993), George Lipsitz (1994), Les Back (1996), David Hesmondhalgh (2000) and others have made similar points about music and identity. Gilroy's example is, of course, Britain, where, against all the evidence of complex, ongoing social and cultural change, racist attitudes have constructed blackness and Englishness as incommensurable. Gilroy thus looked towards a new cultural politics that would defy primordialism and give life to an aesthetic at once English and black. And in similar vein, Back has shown how music can play a role in undermining the ideology that socio-cultural groups – including nations – are hardened, reified categories. Citing work that shows how in Birmingham, for instance, reggae music has created sites where interaction between black and white people can occur, he notes that such musical cultures have developed aesthetics and practices that starkly oppose the dominant, racialised views of the nation. Instead, these musical cultures 'imagine new types of association that transcend the divisions of race, class and gender' and thus redraw the 'map of nationhood' in radically different ways. And so, as black culture tends to become a class culture, '[w]hites in this situation may have more in common with R. Kelly than John Bull' (Back 1996, p. 10).

II

In South Africa, whatever the difficulties, the prospects for such integrations were particularly auspicious after the first democratic elections in 1994. The struggle against apartheid was a struggle against racism; thus anti-racism and the experience of 'interracial' solidarity were among its greatest legacies, and they found victorious embodiment in the country's progressive new Constitution. They have, moreover, remained fundamental commitments for many people, not just black but white as well: a significant minority of whites, after all, had participated in the struggle against

108   *Christopher Ballantine*

apartheid, expressing their opposition through a wide range of political and cultural styles, ideologies, practices and movements, often at great personal cost. For these, as for other whites who followed their example, this post-1994 mood was summed up by the Afrikaans-speaking editor of the *Citizen* when he wrote: 'I've got a white skin. But otherwise, I'm an African. . . . [As white Afrikaners] we're a group of people in the process of becoming a new nation, part of an inclusive nation of South Africans' (*Mail & Guardian*, 15–21 October 1999). And the white, Afrikaans editor of *Beeld* made a similar point: 'We're from Africa not from Europe. We regard ourselves as Africans with paler skins . . . This is where we want our children to live and we want to make this country great for all its people' (van Rooyen 2000, p. 38–9). To the same end, the *Mail & Guardian* devoted a long feature to the work of the white South African artist and poet Wopko Jensma, whose importance was summed up in the claim that he was the first local artist in any medium to transcend the barriers of language or colour: his work was neither English nor Afrikaans, neither Black nor White. This made him, the article said, 'a terrifying, new sort of human. He is the first South African' (10–16 March 2000). More sensationally, and much more irreverently, white Afrikaans performance artist Piet Pienaar made a well-publicised, dramatic visual statement about his changing identity when he submitted himself to a circumcision rite derived from Xhosa practice. He announced that a black woman doctor would carry out the operation, and that it would take place in an art gallery, in front of cameras linked 'live' to the Internet. Viewers around the world would be able to log on to the Webcast at the cost of one US dollar a time, and then join in the auction of his foreskin. Posterity, Pienaar argued, would understand the event as belonging to 'a time when white male Afrikaners were feeling oppressed by their identity. Most Afrikaners aren't circumcised – it's a Jewish, Muslim or Xhosa thing – and this is a symbol of me broadening my identity' (*Mail & Guardian*, 20–26 October 2000).

Signs that whites were exulting in the 'rainbow' euphoria of the new South Africa were especially evident in the popular music made and largely bought by them just prior to the first democratic elections, and for a couple of years afterwards. White singers and bands found numerous ways of identifying with the liberatory post-apartheid social order. They wrote songs – some of them anthemic – that welcomed the 'new beginning' (Phillips 1993); or celebrated the fact that 'the freedom of Madiba[2] brought dancin' in the streets/tiekiedraai and toyi-toyi with a mellow beat/so we're all part of the old and of the new' (Goosen 1996); or prayed that the 'rainbow nation/shine on' (*ibid.*); or hailed (in what has since become a local popular classic) 'all the world in union/the world as one/as we try to reach our destiny/a new age has begun' (Powers 1995); or inverted a colonial term of racial abuse by telling a white audience that '*jy's net 'n wit kaffir van Afrika*' [you're just a white kaffir from Africa] (Goosen 1996); or made use of local black languages (Goosen 1992; Rauch 1995); or pleaded for all South Africans to let go of fear and work towards uniting the country (Rauch 1995); or incorporated black performers (Kerkorrel 1992; Rauch 1995); or, in only faintly disguised reference to the incoming president Nelson Mandela, welcomed back Moses and wished him the best of luck (Phillips 1993):

Hey Moses you're back with a smile, huh!
who's gonna say it's from the Sacred Cow?
say Moses I think you're the best
please don't turn out like all of the rest

Hey Moses you put a smile on my face
can you save this place?
say Moses I think you're the best
please don't turn out like all of the rest

Musically, these white bands sought, to a limited degree, to overcome ancient separations by fusing rock or other 'white' styles, such as *boeremusiek* (ethnically Afrikaans country dance music), with local 'black' idioms. These idioms included, principally, *marabi* (the generic, pan-ethnic music that took root in the country's urban slums in the first three decades of the twentieth century) or *marabi*'s sequels (such as township jazz, *kwela* and *mbaqanga*) (Ballantine 1993); sometimes a neo-traditional style such as *isicathamiya* (a migrant-worker idiom made famous by Ladysmith Black Mambazo) was brought into the mix. In Laurika Rauch's 'The Flying Dutchman' for example, the integration is with the cyclical guitar riffs and looping bass lines of *mbaqanga*; in her song 'Falcon', a Western popular ballad style is interleaved with *isicathamiya* (Rauch 1995).

Frequently, too, the iconography of the album covers underscores such messages – as in James Phillips's gospel-inflected *Sunny Skies* (1993). With every song in its own right a small masterpiece, this is one of the finest, most beautifully crafted albums in the history of South African popular music, and – as political art – one of the most explicitly committed to fundamental social transformation. On its front cover is a reproduction of *Huis Met Witboom*, an oil painting by Water Meyer; a picture of a typical middle-class white home, it suggests a death-like aridity. On the back cover is a photograph of another kind of home – a squatter shack, with an old car parked outside. At a moment of transformation in South Africa's history, both scenes cry out for regeneration. But there is an important difference between them. Unlike the suburban home, the shack dwelling – poor though it is – is alive with colour, humour and sense of creativity: painted on the shack's door, for example, in homage to the spirit of change, is the legend, 'Mikhail Gorbachev seems to be beautiful'. In an unexpected gesture of identification, James Phillips himself leans against the wall; he strikes a pose becoming of a proud homeowner.

In making such statements, these songwriters and performers used – and extended – the methods and procedures of 'protest' music devised by various white popular musicians during the last decade or more of the apartheid era. Johnny Clegg is the best-known member of that earlier cohort. He first came to prominence in South Africa at the end of the 1970s as a young white guitarist and singer who had mastered *maskanda*, a neo-traditional musical style developed by Zulu-speaking migrant workers. His musical partner was master *maskanda* musician Sipho Mchunu; as Juluka, they sought ways to combine *maskanda* with typically Western idioms, and gave performances around the country to mixed, rapidly growing audiences. At a time when the inhumanity and the contradictions of the apartheid system were reaching breaking point, Juluka thus embodied a number of potent cultural transgressions. And so they offered hope: an often euphoric promise that the final struggle against apartheid could be won. Yet from the start the band's musical integrations were awkwardly worked. Certainly, symbols for 'white' and 'black' met in the songs' own interiors – but typically as binary, and often unequal, oppositions: 'white' represented largely by an English folk-rock style derived from the 1960s, which carried the song's narrative, and 'black' virtually relegated to the choruses. The lyrics addressed topics relevant to the anti-apartheid struggle, but commonly in two languages (English and Zulu) split along the same lines.

Still, it was a winning formula. Juluka (and later Savuka, thus renamed after Mchunu went back to farming in the mid-1980s) quickly became an international band, with, for example, the 1982 hit 'Scatterlings of Africa' (reissued on Clegg 1999) reaching the top fifty in the UK and then number one in France and elsewhere. More curiously still, growing fame meant that it did not seem to matter that the 'African' part of the musical equation sometimes dropped out altogether, resulting in straightforward, if often delightful, rock songs. World fame, evidently, came at the price of a smoothing-over of some of the grain that *maskanda* had brought to the band's style.[3]

Clegg and other white anti-apartheid musicians set the example. They established patterns, methods, and continuities of influence that extended not just into the 'rainbow' moment of the early 1990s, but far beyond – into the work of many white groups who identified with the new democratic order long after the euphoric early years had given way to an era of disillusionment, ambiguity and anger. The contours of that era will be discussed later. For now, we must begin by delving a little more deeply into the ways that, during the post-apartheid years, white musicians and groups have sought to signal their break from the past and their identification with the new, non-racial democracy.

A concept of prime importance for these white, post-apartheid performers is *integration*, and they suggest it in a number of ways. First, through music. The Transformers, for example, are primarily a white, Afrikaans-speaking band underpinned by an aesthetic rooted in white Afrikaans music, and with wide appeal to a similar audience. But they include black musicians, and their 1997 album seeks explicitly to integrate aspects of *marabi*, pennywhistle *kwela*, *mbaqanga*, Cape Malay *goema* and the blues, with traditional Afrikaans music and lyrics, to produce a transformed, or transforming, hybrid. Singer-songwriter Eugenie imports elements from the realm of neo-traditional Zulu music to produce arresting Afrikaans–Zulu musical and linguistic combinations. For example, 'Koebaai' (2000) promises to be another traditional Afrikaans *liedjie* (literally, 'little song') until – startlingly – a black backing vocal group appear and introduce Zulu phrases along with an idiom seemingly derived in equal measure from *isicathamiya* and the Enja repertoire! In other examples, Tananas (1996) allude to *marabi*, pennywhistle *kwela*, *maskanda* and *goema*, Janjie Blom en die Bushrockbandvriende (2000) invoke the looping bass lines and the electric keyboard stylings of *mbaqanga*, and Syd Kitchen and AmaKool (1999) strikingly inflect a folk-rock ballad with some of the guitar characteristics, and the male backing-group incantations, of *maskanda*.

Sometimes it is 'pre-colonial' black South African music that is selected for the blend, as when Tony Cox (1999) draws upon Xhosa root-progressions, or Marimba! (1999) use cyclical guitar phrases to conjure the sound of the Xhosa mouth-resonated *uhadi* bow, or David Ledbetter (1999) sings a Tswana ballad to his own 'African-jazz'-style piano accompaniment. Indigenous instruments from various parts of the continent might also be used – for instance the *hosho* rattle (Tananas 1996), or marimba, kudu horn and *djembe* drum (Marimba! 1999). Moreover, as is already evident, nominally white bands sometimes also include black or so-called 'coloured'[4] members, whether permanently, as with Tananas, or temporarily, as when 'coloured' rap artists Brasse Vannie Kaap sit in with Not My Dog (2000), and Isaac Mtshali (of Stimela), Gito Baloi (of Tananas) and Black Moses (of the Soul Brothers) play with Janjie Blom en die Bushrockbandvriende (2000).

If strategies of musical performance are one way of embracing integration as a socially important concept in the post-apartheid era, verbal strategies are another. For many white musicians, song lyrics, titles, band names and, though less frequently, the inclusion of a 'black' language or dialect, are crucial. Syd Kitchen, for example, calls attention to the challenge of the new order by titling a recent album *Africa's not for Sissies* (2001); he names one of its songs 'Settler', and writes lyrics that oppose colonial attitudes and signal a commitment to the new democracy:

Now here I am, you are, each in Afrika
You are my brother this is my home
I offer love – I ask redemption
I offer all – I ask no question
I sing this loud – no hesitation

Elsewhere on the album he rejoices in the overcoming of apartheid:

Stand up for our time is now
Stand up we all made it somehow
Everywhere, it's in the air

Stand up lest the tide subside
Stand up we've got nothing to hide
All those years
Choked in fears
Now no more tears

To the same end, Koos Kombuis (1997) proclaims the theme of egalitarianism in the provocative song-title 'Almal kaffers' (All kaffirs); bands choose names like White Trash, Transformers, and Marimba!; and singers opt to include an indigenous 'black' vernacular (Coleske 2000; Eugenie 2000), or to use a 'coloured' dialect (Koos Kombuis 2000).

Similarly, and perhaps even more strikingly, some young whites have recently started to identify with the modish new musical idioms produced and consumed by black South African youths: *kwaito* in particular. This is evident, in part, from the way 5fm and other radio stations geared to white audiences have increasingly broadcast the music of popular black performers such as TKZee, Bongo Maffin and, especially, Mandoza. Yfm's head of programming, Greg Maloka, has observed that although they don't understand its 'culture', 'a lot of white kids like *kwaito*'. As one fan said, 'Me and my school friends learn the words off by heart even though we don't know what they mean' (*Sunday Independent*, 6 May 2000). Moreover, the growth of white interest in *kwaito* can also be observed in clubs and on dance floors. The idiom has, for instance, 'gatecrashed' the Roxy Rhythm Bar in Melville, Johannesburg – a venue catering to white rock fans (*ibid.*). More remarkable still are those clubs that are consistently multicultural, such as Axis, a gay club, and Angelo's Cantina, both in Durban. Both cater to many different kinds of dancers and musical tastes – including *kwaito*. As one enthusiastic young clubber put it: 'At Angelo's there is no racism and all cultures mix freely. It's a warm and friendly atmosphere. The DJs play Hindi, rave (house), *kwaito* and even Turkish music. Listening to different music, going to different clubs is what we need' (*Sunday Independent*, 26 March 2000 and 6 May 2001; *Independent on Saturday*, 18 March 2000). Although integrations such as this – we could think of them as heuristic transgressions – are still in the vanguard among clubbing audiences, they are clearly on the increase.[5] And not just in the clubs: indeed, the first white *kwaito* singer to achieve prominence appeared on the scene early in 2000, in the form of Francois 'Lekgoa' Henning: he sings in Sotho, English and Afrikaans, and appeals to both black and white audiences. These integrations, and

112   *Christopher Ballantine*

these tendencies towards integration, point us in the direction of a new, emergent identity. We might say that its bearers are becoming 'white Africans'.

None of this, of course, is to deny the stark fact that there remain many white popular musicians and audiences whose connection to South Africa in the post-apartheid era is at best mythical, tentative or confused, and at worst self-serving or non-existent. For the purposes of the present discussion, we might speak of them as 'whites in Africa'. In a book on South African literature, J.M. Coetzee coined the term 'white writing', which he characterised thus:

> Nor does the phrase *white writing* imply the existence of a body of writing different in nature from black writing. White writing is white only insofar as it is generated by the concerns of people no longer European, not yet African. (Coetzee 1988, p. 11)[6]

Mutatis mutandis, exactly the same might be said of the popular music made by, and for, 'whites in Africa'. One can discern here at least four different tendencies.

First, there are those performers who allude, musically or verbally, to Africa, but in such a way as to make the continent an abstraction, without real content. Typically this is done through the use of vague, floating signifiers – signs that connote 'Africa' amorphously, non-specifically. Wendy Oldfield's *On a Pale Blue Dot* (1999), for example, makes free use of such signifiers within a context marked by techno-trance features. There are mythologically 'African' chant-like vocalisations, and Oldfield's vocal style has features that her audience would most readily associate with Angelique Kidjo, the Paris-based Beninois singer whose 'Africa' already exists as a commodity for a world-music audience; she also uses the West African *djembe* drum, the Brazilian *berimbau* (a bow derived by way of the diaspora from an Angolan predecessor) and – as if to confuse matters still further – an Australian didjeridoo. Somewhat similar is *New Anthem* (1998) by Egyptian Nursery. This subtle, delicate techno-based music involves French rap, Lingala (from the Democratic Republic of Congo), English, and black and white musicians. On the one hand, it conjures a symbiosis of white South Africa and black francophone Africa; on the other, it signals a vague, modernised pan-Africa, rather than any particular view of its southern territory.

Secondly, there are white groups for whom Africa is a source of New-Age spiritualism and a variety of cognate fascinations – the primitive, the tribal, the exotic, the trance. Qcumba Zoo are a case in point. Their *Wake Up & Dream* (1996) resonates with phony, mystical identifications with the primitive and the earth, reinforced by simulations of 'ancient voices [that] sing to me'. Through such devices, Africa is present mythologically; South Africa, despite the inclusion of tongue clicks, is hardly present at all except perhaps evasively, as a silence: the album includes a version of Bright Blue's classic anti-apartheid hit, 'Weeping' (1988), but without the original, stirring background strains of 'Nkosi Sikelel' iAfrika' (once symbolic of the struggle against apartheid, now the first section of the new national anthem), and without the original, evocative references to *marabi* and to a *marabi*-jazz saxophone style. More problematic yet is the unashamed ethno-tourism – voyeurism by another name – of the largely white audiences that patronise some of the offerings at a festival such as Rustler's Valley. *Sound Journey* (*ca.* 1999) is a record of one of those events: it presents black South African 'pre-colonial' music as romantically exotic, linking it implausibly to markers of 'primitive' music (panpipes, didjeridoos) from elsewhere in the world, and exploiting it for the entertainment of modern, global, middle-class sensibilities. Most bizarre, perhaps, is the work of a group called Arapaho (1995). They too seek to valorise tribalism: not, however, by claiming any connection to historical South African musics or cultures, but rather through an identification with images drawn from the culture of Native Americans.

Thirdly, for some white audiences the popularity of particular groups seems to be inseparable from the fact that at least in part they assert values traditionally associated with conservative white South Africans. Included here would be a masculinist pursuit of the 'good life' of money, sex and power, as affirmed in Squeal's 'Man and woman' (1997), and a triumphant egocentricity, as celebrated by Watershed (2000).[7] Fourthly, just as some South African whites think of themselves as somehow 'American' or 'British', so too do some popular-music groups shape themselves according to foreign sounds and images. For instance, Just Jinger's *Something for Now* (1998) is clearly rooted in US rock and valorises 'jumpers, coke, sweet Mary Jane'; Sugardrive's *Sand Man Sky* (1997) is a grunge album; while Amersham (1998, 2000), Tree (1999) and Point Sirens (1999) all decisively orient themselves towards The Beatles – and, in the case of Point Sirens, towards Crosby, Stills and Nash as well. For Matthew van der Want and Chris Letcher (1997), on the other hand, this sort of derivativeness presents an opportunity for scathing satire:

Give me a country-and-western song
And I'll be happy all night long.
I won't be on my barstool – I'll be dancing.
Dolly Parton – what a heroine!
She's right when she says that love is a butterfly.
What do you do when you are feeling low?
Read a book? I don't think so.
I play my Hank Williams tapes.
I'm so tired of alternative angst
Play me some Willie Nelson.
Give me a country-and-western song
Make it catchy and not too long
And please, no more eight-minute guitar solos.

III

The moment of euphoria around 1994 was short lived. It was in jeopardy from the beginning, and moribund within little more than two years of the election. At the heart of this decline was sustained pressure from the US and some of its partners (Britain, Germany, Italy and Japan) that the ANC, and after 1994 the new government, should abandon the socialist elements in its economic policies, give up on nationalisation, and submit to the imperatives of neo-liberalism and the West's idea of the free market. In macro-economic terms, the left was in serious retreat by as early as 1994; the rout was confirmed in June 1996 when the government announced its neo-liberal economic programme, known as Growth, Employment and Redistribution (GEAR). ('Just call me a Thatcherite', Mbeki quipped at the time [Saul 2001, p. 28]). John Saul, one of the most eminent commentators on South Africa, has analysed the implications of this shift, and described its consequences. He calls it a 'tragedy'. While not denying the country's signal achievement – a peaceful transition from racially based authoritarianism to liberal-democracy – he argues that there is

absolutely no reason to assume that the vast majority of people in South Africa will find their lives improved by the policies that are being adopted in their name by the present African National Congress (ANC) government. Indeed, something quite the reverse is the far more likely outcome. (Saul 2001, p. 2)

114   *Christopher Ballantine*

These reversals have many facets, but they certainly include the current unemployment rate, recently estimated to be 45 per cent (Norwegian Institute for Applied Social Science, 2002),[8] as well as the number of jobs lost – more than 500,000 in the formal sector since 1994, and 700,000 in the informal sector during 2001 alone, according to estimates by the research wing of the Congress of South African Trade Unions. Currently 50 per cent of all school-leavers are unable to find jobs; the country's biggest labour consultancy has calculated that this figure will rise to 60 per cent (*Mail & Guardian*, 30 March–5 April 2001). Unsurprisingly, crime has escalated to almost anarchic proportions: South Africa's rates of rape, murder, car hijacking and violent crime are now among the highest in the world. A further twist in this unfolding tragedy is that while the ANC government has done little to prevent the HIV/Aids epidemic from spiralling out of control and has regularly blamed its own lack of financial resources for not doing more, it decided in 1999 to procure armaments on a massive scale – despite evidence from its own Finance Ministry that the bill would seriously impede its ability to address the urgent needs of the poor. (The bill recently amounted to more than R50–billion; some economists estimate that it will rise to R500–billion within ten years [*SouthScan* 17/2, 25 January 2002].) For many, this has been one of the government's most serious moral failures. 'Nothing', argued one labour commentator,

serves to indict the government more than the fact that while it said it could not afford to provide HIV-positive pregnant mothers with anti-retroviral drugs, it could afford to purchase arms at a staggering cost. To prioritise arms over the lives of children is an inexcusable evil that will be one of the biggest blights upon this government. (Ebrahim Harvey, *Mail & Guardian*, 16–22 March 2001)

It's a blight that is inseparable from Mbeki's notoriously perverse views on the Aids epidemic and his refusal to acknowledge the causal link between HIV and Aids; in consequence, as an editorial in the *Sunday Independent* argued, the Aids crisis has become 'the new apartheid: pernicious, genocidal, and bureaucratic' (22 April 2001).[9]

Another 'inexcusable evil' arguably comes to light when one looks at the cost of the arms deal alongside the situation in South African schools, the vast majority of which are black. In 2001, more than 45 per cent of all schools still had no electricity, 80 per cent no libraries, 27 per cent no clean water, 34 per cent no telephones, 60 per cent no adequate sanitation, and 11.7 per cent no sanitation at all (*Mail & Guardian*, 11–17 January 2002, and 15–25 April 2002). Indeed, the country's biggest-ever cholera epidemic occurred in 2000, six years after the ANC came to power. It is no surprise, then, to discover that public disappointment at the quality of life in the new South Africa has reached alarming levels. A recent report by Statistics SA revealed that fewer than one in five South Africans think that life has improved since the first democratic elections. More shockingly, one in three South Africans feels that life has actually got worse – a perception that cannot be ascribed to the fact that some have lost their unfair (racial) advantage, as there is little difference in the figures for each 'race' category (*Mail & Guardian*, 3–9 August 2001). As someone who had been disadvantaged under apartheid and had hoped for a better future put it in a letter to the press: 'What we thought would be the Promised Land has become Babylon' (*Mail & Guardian*, 16–22 March 2001).

This is a disappointment of vast scale, but in the history of the postcolonial era certainly not a singular event. In trying to understand it, Saul and others have had recourse to Frantz Fanon's notion of false decolonisation, in which 'the rising African middle-class, both entrepreneurial and political and bureaucratic in provenance, merely [slides] comfortably into their political positions as, yes, intermediaries of global Empire' (Saul 2001, p. 24). And Saul identifies another feature found both locally and elsewhere on the continent: that of the government coming to 'resemble a club of old party militants who are more concerned to reap the rewards of their own earlier sufferings than to effect major changes in society' (p. 29). Not only is the 'coolly self-satisfied, self-righteous, and profoundly ideological thrust' with which this has been carried out 'the single most depressing attribute of South Africa's transition'; more to the point, it amounts to the squandering of 'an opportunity of world-historic proportions' (p. 33). What has occurred, in short, has been mainly a project to fast-track a new, racialised 'African' capitalist class. As recent reports on income and labour have revealed, a huge and growing gap has opened between this new black elite and the vast majority of the black population. Members of this relatively small group almost trebled their incomes within five years; by 2001 they were earning twenty-one times as much as those in the poorest stratum of income-earners (*SouthScan* 16/6, 23 March 2001; Norwegian Insitute for Applied Social Science, 2002).[10]

Significantly, black workers and intellectuals themselves have made many of the sharpest criticisms of the ANC government's economic and social policies. Both the Congress of South African Trade Unions (Cosatu) and the South African Communist Party have consistently blamed those policies for the massive job losses, creeping poverty and poor economic growth. Putting the matter particularly acutely, a leading black intellectual, Mamphela Ramphele, has argued that the government's vaunted black economic empowerment strategy has in fact targeted black men, 'some of whom have become instant millionaires': with the result that, as the disparities between rich and poor increase, 'the poorest sectors, who missed out on education and skills training in the apartheid era, continue to bear the largest burden of poverty' (*Sunday Independent*, 22 April 2001). Academic and columnist Sipho Seepe has considered the scale of the Aids pandemic and the depth of the associated human suffering, and made the point that 'if African lives were cheap under apartheid, they are certainly cheaper under the ANC government' (*Mail & Guardian*, 11–17 January 2002). He has also drawn attention to the 'callousness' of the government's decision to spend R600–million on buying a jet for the president: money that could have been used

to purchase the desperately needed anti-retroviral drugs to prevent mother-to-child transmissions. Instead the president's comfortable travelling arrangements take precedence over saving babies' lives. ... Those who fought valiantly for democracy are not immune to betraying and sacrificing the masses on the altar of political expediency and power. (*Mail & Guardian*, 7–13 September 2001)

Such observations have led Seepe to comment that

not even the most sceptical could have foreseen that a mere seven years later, the very masses that Mandela thanked for bringing the new dispensation would be questioning the government's commitment to a 'better life for all'. ... Instead of the struggle achieving the liberation of both the oppressed and the oppressor, it has simply replaced the oppressor. The oppressed are assuming the role of the oppressor. (*Mail & Guardian*, 30 November–6 December 2001)

In similar vein, another prominent black academic and commentator, Xolela Mangcu, has asked why billions should be spent on arms 'when our population is being devastated by unemployment, hunger and homelessness, when poor black children walk long distances to dilapidated schools; when babies are being orphaned by the

116   *Christopher Ballantine*

scourge of Aids?' The answer, he says, is that 'lies have become the truth in the halls of power' (*Sunday Independent*, 7 October 2001). Even Winnie Madikizela-Mandela has joined the ranks of trenchant critics of the government: 'Today', she has said, 'when I walk in the squatter camps, I see more hungry people than I did during the apartheid era' (*Sunday Independent*, 24 June 2001). Her observation appears to be corroborated by recent research showing that, between 1989 and 2001, the proportion of black households living below the breadline rose from around 50 per cent to almost two-thirds (Schlemmer 2002, p. 21).

How has the government justified this new agenda? Since it cannot really do so, any more than it can reconcile it with earlier revolutionary promises, it has sought to conceal the new thrust behind populist calls to 'race' solidarity. As black unemployment and poverty have worsened, the Mbeki government has diverted attention by racialising the immense problems it faces – certainly a powerful strategy, given the racial character of South Africa's past. In short, the government and some of the new elite have sought to organise what has been called a 'blood bond' and to line up a 'blood enemy': all 'Africans' – racially defined – against, in particular, all whites.[11] As the *Washington Post* observed in February 2001, any black who supports the opposition is now branded a 'race' traitor, and any criticism of the government is equated with racism. This, an editorial in the *Mail & Guardian* commented, is 'Mbeki's most shameful contribution to our society over the past 22 months . . . [W]hat Mandela made a country of hope, confident it could overcome its tremendous difficulties, Mbeki has, in just 22 months, rendered a land of fractiousness and despair' (April 26– 3 May 2001).

Many of these issues are picked up in the work of white popular musicians. The theme of betrayal of the poor is articulated in, for instance, a song which goes: 'We love Madiba . . ./but we don't trust no politicians./Politicians sold us down the drain/They ride on the gravy train/But for the poor there's nothing gained/Except the chance to vote again' (*White Trash* 1997). Bands have criticised the selfish, anti-social, scheming, money-driven lifestyles that have accompanied the rise of the new elite; or they've attacked crime (in the words of Buckfever Underground [1998/ 99], 'if you sit still for long enough, they'll steal your kidneys'). Trans.Sky meaningfully named one of their albums *Killing Time* (1998); on it they sample local idioms such as *isicathamiya* and the *toyi-toyi* protest genre from the anti-apartheid era, and blend these into a song about 'living in a country that's blown apart'. Or in a gentle manner they rap powerful, critical lyrics about a place of 'looting and burning', where 'the future is no longer filled with certainty' and where the poor must still build shacks:

running from the cities from the fires and the shouting
looting and the burning through the night they're taking everything
confusion driving everybody mad from dusk to dawn
come with me together we need shelter from the storm
we need some flimsy apparatus to pull over our heads
watch your back
let's build a shack

walking through the rivers of the dying and the dead
shooting and shouting that is happening ahead
there was a time before the war when we were being drowned
by the sound of diesel engines from the garden next door
collapsing shelters redesigned existing over years
at the back

let's build a shack
picture of the future is no longer filled with certainty

Powerful musical criticisms have come, *inter alia*, from Afrikaans-speaking singers, including several – such as Johannes Kerkorrel – who first rose to prominence during the 1980s as leaders of the anti-apartheid *alternatief* song movement. Kerkorrel's 1996 album *Ge-trans-for-meer* (Transformed), for example, presents a sharply critical perspective, its celebratory references to Mandela and to transformation notwithstanding. Nowhere is this clearer than in 'Sê-sê' (Say say): the song is a litany of pain, where the gospel overtones help signify the suffering of the people addressed in the lyrics – the starving, those made homeless by the demolition of squatter camps, those with Aids, exploited prostitutes, and others. The singer blames *'die vet sotte op die rooi tapyt'* (the fat fools on the red carpet) and, in a gesture of solidarity and support, identifies with those who suffer:

o sê 'n gebed
sê dit vir almal in pyn
ons verloopte skepsels
wat nie meer kan luister
na mekaar se droewige gefluister

oh say a prayer
say it for everyone in pain
for us down-and-out creatures
that can't listen anymore
to each other's mournful whispering

In a later album (2000), Kerkorrel's criticism of the new South Africa erupts in vivid images. The song 'Die stad bloei vanaand' (The city bleeds tonight) suggests everything that was beautiful has burnt to ash (*'alles wat mooi was, het tot as verbrand'*); a dream has been spoiled, debased, even stolen:

Die hemel word daagliks in advertensies beloof
Gooi jou geld in die gleuf by die munt-outomaat
Die droom was beloof, ja, maar net nog 'n leuen is verkoop
Stoot jou kaart deur die gleuf dit kan help die pyn verdoof

. . .

Slaap liggies vanaand, wees waaksaam vanaand
Die kriminele kom sag soos 'n dief in die nag
Steel die huis rot en kaal en hardloop weg in die nag
Met die droom van ons nuwe Suid-Afrika

Heaven is promised daily in advertisements
Put your money in the slot of the vending machine
The dream was promised, yes, but just another lie is sold
Push your card through the slot and it can help ease the pain

. . .

Sleep lightly tonight, be watchful tonight
The criminals come softly like thieves in the night
Steal the house bare and run away in the night
With the dream of our new South Africa

Similarly, another prominent member of the old *alternatief* movement, Koos Kombuis, has corruption and crime in his sights, but he emphasises the cynical avoidance of

118   *Christopher Ballantine*

accountability that accompanies such features. A hard-driving rock song, 'Blameer did op apartheid' (Blame it on apartheid) is the sarcastically named title track on his 1997 album:

Belê jy geld in Masterbond
Verloor jy dit te gou
Pos 'n brief by Telkom
Dan verwyn dit in die blou
Die regering gee nie om nie
Die ministers bly stil
Selfs die Matie-rektor
Het sy vingers in die till

Blameer dit op apartheid
Blameer dit op de Klerk
Blameer dit op Satan
Of blameer dit op die kerk
Die hele land vol onrus
Fokkol werk en fokkol kos
Die Here is op holiday
En die duiwel is nou los

If you invest money in Masterbond
you lose it too soon
post a letter at Telkom
then it disappears into the blue
the government doesn't care
the ministers keep quiet
even the Matie-rector
has his fingers in the till

blame it on apartheid
blame it on de Klerk
blame it on Satan
or blame it on the church
the whole land full of unrest
fuckall work and fuckall food
The Lord is on holiday
and the devil is loose[12]

Now one of the country's most prominent Afrikaans singers and songwriters, Valiant Swart can stand as an example of a typical, younger, white-Afrikaans musician. Too young to have been a member of the *alternatief* movement, he nevertheless shares the current, critical perspectives of his older, anti-apartheid colleagues. In a bleak song about corruption, for instance, Swart (1999) likens the country's two, big northern cities (Johannesburg and Pretoria) to Sodom and Gomorra. And the Biblical metaphor continues:

pandemonium
in die gange van Babylon
brabbel almal in brabbeltaal
en niemand wil luister nie . . .
en daar's niemand wat verstaan
hoekom alles vergaan
langsamerhand

pandemonium
in the passages of Babylon

everyone gibbers in gibberish
and no one wants to listen . . .
and there's no one who understands
why everything decays
gradually

Criticisms such as these are further evidence of the theme of disappointment and betrayal that white singers developed so arrestingly after the mid-1990s. Yet it is worth noting that some musicians who strongly supported the new order had nevertheless – even in the heady moments of the decade's early years – seen the omens suggesting the possibility of corruption and failure. One of these, again, was Johannes Kerkorrel. *Cyanide in the beefcake* (1994) was recorded shortly before the first democratic elections; but the title suggests that the food is already poisoned. Indeed, while the album firmly sides with the need for an end to the apartheid order and for fundamental social change, it is not optimistic about the capacity – or even the commitment – of the post-apartheid government-in-waiting to make a fundamental difference: capitalism and greed, Kerkorrel suggests, remain deeply entrenched. In 'Waiting for Godot', as in Samuel Beckett's play, the longed-for future is endlessly postponed: 'No job, no hope, no mercy, man/No read, no write, no way to speak,/No way to let out all the rage inside/And I'm waiting, yes, I'm waiting'. The tragic side of this predicament is evoked in 'Speel my pop' (Play my doll), a rock song that is also a powerful, funereal dirge with features of both heavy metal and soul. The song signifies its historico-political moment, and the contradictions within that context, by inserting samples from well-known statements by famous politicians: avoidance from former white cabinet minister Pik Botha ('We can make a list of the wrongs of the past; I'm interested in the future'); progressive exhortation from Nelson Mandela ('Go back to school'); and a rabidly ethnic form of white resistance from Afrikaans Weerstandsbeweging leader Eugene Terreblanche ('You see, I'm not a white man, I'm a *boer* [right-wing white Afrikaner]'). Meanwhile, passionate melismata, redolent of soul music, add a culturally 'black' sensibility.

In the work of some groups, these sentiments are projected within more 'selfish' perspectives: with feelings of personal bitterness, anger or alienation. Battery 9, for instance, an Afrikaans group working in an 'industrial dance' genre, have an album called *Wrok* (1998), a word connoting grudge, hatred, spite or resentment. The song '*Blaas hom*' (Blast him) begins with the familiar South African city sounds of sirens and barking dogs; in Afrikaans the singer raps about his rage at being robbed again, and about taking his revenge by shooting the two burglars he finds at his home. (The disc went on to win a South African Music Award in the annual 'Best Rock Album' category.) A quite different example is the powerful 'Special Agents', a track by Matthew van der Want and Chris Letcher on their remarkable album *Low Riding* (1999). In a complex song that nightmarishly connotes an invasive investigation of the personal, there is deliberate ambiguity as to whether the 'special agents' are state officials or mere criminals busy with a night-time burglary. The point is that it makes little difference: their judgement of the 'guilt' of those they are investigating is a foregone conclusion. There is no escape: against a background of ominous walkie-talkie or police-radio sounds, the melody's tendency towards fixity and repetition enhances the feeling of being trapped; and the predominance of falling melodic lines underlines not only a deep personal melancholy, but also the bitter foreboding of the lyrics:

120   *Christopher Ballantine*

the truth is I'm

cut-up all
sheep-faced got
caught by the snipers
i'm hurt . . .

lights down there're
killers in the house –
special agents
checking sentence

Most commonly, however, white musicians deliver these critical sentiments with a sharply satirical edge. The group Sons of Trout (1998), for instance, place a premium on originality and humour; when they think of crime, as they do in 'Siren', they don't think of revenge, guns or disaster, but simply of the fact that 'I cannot sleep, I've got monsters under my bed, I cannot dream/Sirens comin' from the hills' – and they associate this, in the song 'Mercedes Benz', with elite lifestyles: 'You're living in your golden palace, your little castle on the hill./So strung up in your automatic wealth, watcha gonna do with it, watcha gonna do'. In the context of tracks such as these, a third song, 'Kom Psalm', is a deeply ironic assertion of a triumphalism easily associated with the posture of the present government. For a start, the Afrikaans title is a pun: it invokes the spectre of the old politico-religious order, offering both a religious invitation to join in congregational Psalm-singing and a political exhortation to '*kom saam*' (come together). But then in deft, clever parody, the song references a number of musical symbols that remain at once culturally potent and contradictory in the new South Africa: the patriotic strains of 'Nkosi Sikelel' iAfrika', *boeremusiek*, the bent-tones of black South African 'traditional' music, and Pentecostal song. The musical interpellations are conflictual, unreconciled. Read on their own, the lyrics use the language of victory ('I feel that I have been shined upon. I know that all my bad days have gone. So stand up, rise up, get out. Stand tall!'); but heard in this setting, the music tellingly voids the lyrics of any superficial or simplistic sense of triumph. And 'Nkosi Sikelel' iAfrika' occurs also in Danny de Wet's 'New National Anthem', which appears on an album (1998/99) abrasively critical of the rampant consumerism of the post-apartheid order. In satirical juxtaposition, parts of the anthem sound alongside the relentless blare of all-too-familiar burglar alarms and sirens.

Wittier still is the satire of Boo!, an immensely talented group that has enjoyed chart-topping success. Their quicksilver lyrics conceal more than they reveal, feigning a strange dialect of English, a kind of doggerel, nearly every word deliberately misspelt, hovering on the edge of sense:

i herd a wsl of a brd koment owr luving
an wot it sed was that my luv had had enuf
and sumbodi sed that soon i wood reseev my letter
2 tell me that another brothe went 2 get her

o.o.a.a.

i herd a rsl in the wind wspr its over
an that the lyt of our luv was a supernova
i'm getting nervis bout the stait of my posishin
is it worri or is it an intuishin

o.o.a.a.

i herd the brd but i don't by that
i reed the papr but i don't by that
i saw the news but i don't by that
i reep the graipvyn but i don't i don't by that

o.o.a.a. ('Monki Punk', 1999)

Boo!'s lyrics are supported by a lively panoply of musical styles that move in unpredictable directions and make deft use of parody and humour. Their work points to the difficulty of a stable reality to depend on, or a reliable truth to believe in, or even a meaningful way of being: which seems fitting for a society where 'reality' is apparently so easily redefined, or where priorities that affect life and death can so quickly be re-ordered. I referred earlier to comments by Njabulo Ndebele: Boo!'s music seems an exemplar of another recent observation by Ndebele – that despite our new constitution, with its bill of rights and its recognition of our rich diversity, something important is missing. 'When', said Ndebele, 'I pose the questions today, "Who are we?" and "What drives us towards co-operative action?", silence stares back at me. It is not the silence of emptiness, it is the silence of too much sound yielding little meaning' (*Sunday Independent*, 25 February 2001). The music of Boo!, it seems to me, helps us to make sense of that silence.

Much less subtle, more populist, but arguably no less meaningful in this context, are the satirical songs of famous white comedian and film-maker Leon Schuster. *Gautvol in Paradise*[13] (1997) is a humorous criticism of the new order and its failure to deal adequately with issues such as crime, minority rights, the provision of equality of opportunity, and the brain drain. (It is, incidentally, also a hilarious satire of the attitudes and prejudices of some whites in the new era.) Schuster uses sing-along *boereliedjies* (Afrikaans folk songs) and the melodies of famous local and imported popular songs – tunes so well known that they are now virtually community songs – to evoke a musical idiom with a strong implication of 'tradition' among conservative white Afrikaners. 'Gautengeleng', co-authored by humorist Gus Silber, is an example. The song's title, a play on the provincial name 'Gauteng', is an onomatopoeic alarm bell; the music itself is a parody of a *boereliedjie*; and the song is yet another in the long line of recent South African tracks that incorporate the sounds of barking dogs and sirens – but here there are also shouts and the noise of breaking glass as a hijacking takes place:

Hello good morning
Thank you please
Wind down your windows and give me your keys
Put up your hands as I open the door
Of your luxury vehicle
Or your four-by-four

The most politically astute satirist, however, is the veteran singer-songwriter Syd Kitchen. In booklet notes accompanying his 1999 album, *AmaKoologik*, he sets the scene by referring explicitly to the 'veneer concealing the deep divisions still perennial to a South Africa ... [W]hile political democracy has been won by the majority voice in this country, economic democracy is non-existent in the retention of the county's wealth by the minority'. The title track is a somewhat bluesy piece in which elements of rock are crossed with traces of *maskanda* – a synthesis that is highly apt for the biting satire of the political lyrics:

Step up, we got violence in the air, hijacking in the street,
anger and despair in everyone you meet,
polarisation, marginalisation, keeping it going on
we got rape for fun, kids with guns, paedophiles
with sickly smiles
in Heaven
'Does anyone know who won the game?'

This way for bourgeois fears, the electric fence, 'neighbourhood watch',
middle-class defence
patrol-car cruising, the fear of losing, keeping them going on
we got guard dogs, battlements, social testaments, sounding an alarm
that all's not calm
in Heaven
'Do you need any more sauce with your chicken?'

Kitchen's satirical theme – a disintegrating social fabric and an escapist middle-class recoil that accompanies it – is one he brilliantly amplifies in the more recent 'Africa's Not for Sissies' (2001), a stylistically original, bluesy piece with a *marabi* harmonic foundation:

Well I dunno 'bout you – feel like I'm living in a zoo
I don't go out any more
I just sit by my TV – with my poodle Evie
And we bolt up the door
I'm an ordinary man – I got a wife and a life to keep
Yes I'm an ordinary man – but I take a gun to bed every night when I sleep
Well my friend Stan – they hi-jacked his van
Just the other day
Put a gun up his nose – told him to take off his clothes
Then they drove away
Well well I'm an ordinary man – got a wife and a life to keep
Yeah I'm an ordinary man – but I think I'll go to Australia and maybe raise some sheep

IV

Yet perhaps nothing in the democratic era has stung white South Africans as deeply as the government's re-racialisation of the public sphere: the steady emergence of a new racial typecasting and, with it, a rising chorus of slurs aimed at whites in general. As indicated earlier, the propensity for this derived in part from an historic weakness in the ANC's own theoretical stance – a weakness that resulted in a failure to transcend race-thinking, or to give real meaning to non-racialism. Gerhard Maré has argued that this failure is prefigured in the ANC's own historical analysis of the old South African state as an instance of 'internal colonialism' or 'colonialism of a special type' (CST). According to this theory, the economic and political relationships in South Africa were similar to those of colonialism, but without any territorial separation between the colonisers and the colonised. However, as Maré points out,

because the organising principle of the CST-approach is 'race', democracy has also been inadequately theorised and hence remains racialised – the achievement of democracy in South Africa . . . is the inclusion of *races* within a common political process, a common argument within various positions over the years, 'fixed' strongly within the Freedom Charter . . .; or else, within the notion of the national democratic revolution, the achievement of a racialised majority and the advancement of a racialised bourgeoisie. Within this argument democracy will reflect the 'demographics of society', and not political choice – unless, of course, political choice has been racialised effectively. (Maré 2003, p. 9)

Thus, within this paradigm, democracy is the victory of a *'race'* majority – the coming to power of a racialised bloc. Furthermore, as the political order founded on this paradigm unfolds, its intrinsic racial and cultural essentialisms come into stark relief. Zimitri Erasmus has shown this vividly, particularly with respect to 'coloured' identities in the new South Africa. One of the 'dominant discourses of national identity in South Africa', she argues, is

an emergent discourse of African essentialism. In its terms blackness is understood in terms of Africanness, and black or African identity is simply associated with authenticity, resistance and subversion, while whiteness is associated with Europe, in-authenticity, domination and collusion. This discourse denies creolization and hybridity as constitutive of African experiences, thus excluding coloured identities from those defined as black and African. It has shaped the ANC's continued inability to successfully articulate a broader black identity able to include and mobilize coloured people, particularly in the western Cape. (Erasmus 2001, p. 20)

So indiscriminate has the recidivist tendency to essentialist racial typecasting become, that not even anti-apartheid activists have been exempt from its 'blanket insults', as one white activist called them. Noting her deep resentment about this, she went on to say that this 'racial profiling of all white South Africans as "morally depraved" . . . comes dangerously close to racist hate speech' (*Sunday Independent*, 1 September 2000). Other commentators have looked at this tendency in the grim light of recent world history. One of these is Rhoda Kadalie, anti-apartheid activist and former member of the Human Rights Commission. 'Has [Mbeki] not learned', she asked, 'that when one uses race as a political rallying point, racial conflict gains a momentum of its own that is often difficult to reverse in times of crisis? Has ethnic conflict in Bosnia, Rwanda, Burundi and Serbia not taught him anything?' (*Mail & Guardian*, 1–7 September 2000). For another commentator, the tendency was 'potentially fascist' and reminded him of the Nazis, who set an 'allegedly united *volk* against an allegedly alien minority, the Jews. In both cases', he went on, 'the rhetorically alienated minority was thus denied its legitimate claim to the same nationality' (*Sunday Independent*, 17 September 2000). In somewhat similar vein, leading newspaper editor John Battersby warned of the real danger that these trends could lead to 'greater and greater racial polarisation and, ultimately, to an explosion of racial hatred which, given our history, has the potential to be the worst the world has ever seen' (*Sunday Independent*, 17 December 2000).

For many observers, the first serious consequence of the politics of re-racialisation is that whites seem to be denied a birthright. Writers have noted, for example, that 'on the simple argument that every white is a crypto or blatant racist, nearly five million people have been illegitimised' (*Sunday Independent*, 10 September 2000); that, if a recent ANC document was to be believed, whites 'are incapable of a non-racist and, so, a constructive contribution to the future' (*Mail & Guardian*, 14–19 April 2000); and that 'if we continue to stereotype whites, we effectively silence their right to democratic citizenship' (*Mail & Guardian*, 5–11 January 2000). There are also the more personal responses: such as one published as a 'letter to the editor'. 'I also want to feel part of the future', its author wrote. 'A continued reference to colour . . . perpetuates a sense of hopelessness in me . . . Gather us, rather than separate us' (*Mail & Guardian*, 20–26 October 2000). And in a statement that doubtless also arose from personal conviction, Mandela himself has attacked what he termed 'an arrogant black elite', blaming them for breeding insecurity among South Africa's minority groups (*Sunday Times*, 22 April 2001).

For yet other observers, the deeply uncomfortable analogy is with apartheid itself. 'I'm a South African coloured', wrote one. 'Currently, though, all the messages one gets from government is that we are all different. . . . [A] new social cancer is the fact that these differences are being highlighted as unbreachable. New walls are being built. Ironically that is exactly what apartheid did' (*Mail & Guardian*, 9–15 March 2000). Similarly, leading columnist and editor Howard Barrell noted that '[t]oday, . . . six years into ANC rule, a person's racial identity is – as it was under apartheid – again often a vital determinant of his or her job prospects or life chances' (*Mail & Guardian*, 24–30 March 2000). He also noted that '[i]t's a long time since I've heard anything along the lines of: "We are all South Africans, we have to assert our nationhood and not think of ourselves as black or white, but rather work towards making a better future for all" ' (*Mail & Guardian*, 27 October–2 November 2000). And in an impassioned editorial, that same newspaper commented that '[w]hereas apartheid sought to make blacks feel unwelcome in the land of their birth, we are in danger of making white South Africans feel unwelcome' (*Mail & Guardian*, 23–29 March 2001). Indeed, a prominent judge and former anti-apartheid lawyer, Dennis Davis, had made a similar point some months earlier. Recalling the exclusion of an eminent colleague from a position in the Constitutional Court, apparently on the grounds that he was white, Davis protested that 'his rejection sends a clear message to whites that race has indeed become the only factor. That is not the inclusive society that we had hoped for' (van Rooyen 2000, p. 112).

In such a climate, many white South Africans have opted for exile. They have done so in one of two ways: literally, by emigrating – polls indicate that 63 per cent of young whites expect to emigrate (*Spectator*, 31 March 2001) – or metaphorically, by withdrawing from the forums of civil society. These trends have themselves been the subject of considerable discussion. The *Mail & Guardian* put the matter crisply: 'Many whites caricatured as racists in these attacks felt unable just to shrug off the insult; they concluded there was no place for them in South Africa and packed for Perth, Plymouth or Winnipeg – taking with them desperately needed financial and human capital' (*Mail & Guardian*, 22 December–4 January 2001). And one of that paper's own correspondents spelled out this point with particular attention to the economic implications:

Significant sections of the white population, the main owners of the economy, have been demoralised, in some senses destabilised, as a result. Repeated criticism of whites by President Thabo Mbeki and the ruling party have had direct economic costs, and have contributed to the fragility of sentiment both inside the country and abroad about the prospects for South Africa and its economy. Moreover, while many whites continue to emigrate – notably the young in possession of sought-after skills – others are 'semigrating', as the business leaders put it. That is, they are . . . 'withdrawing, opting out of being citizens' . . . convinced . . . that they can never be anything other than second-class citizens in the present government's eyes. (Nawaal Deane, *Mail & Guardian*, 20–26 October 2000)

Recent 'white' South African popular music deepens and extends our understanding of such responses.[14] It gives subjective substance to what we might think of as 'fugitive' identities. The Honeymoon Suites, for example, are one of a number of bands whose music, lyrics and stage performance make play on the idea of identities as concealed, or in hiding. Here *dressing* is a central image: 'If you could go what would you wear?', ask the Honeymoon Suites ('glamorous gals', after all, 'ain't what they seem'). Unfashionably, what they desire is just 'luminous anonymity' (1999). Using a different figure, several bands project the idea of a journey, or flight – undefined in route, indefinite in length and of ambiguous destination. Sons of Trout, for example, sing: 'I don't care, I don't mind/I just want to leave it all behind/Break new ground' (1997). Valiant Swart often writes songs dealing with restlessness, homelessness, a sense of being uprooted, moving into the unknown. His songs offer bleak stories of loss and spoliation, of finding oneself in a strange place – a metaphorical foreign country where identity is no longer secure and where, in a revealing phrase, you have to '*gaan vra vir die mense in die strate/waar kom jou nuwe naam vandaan*' (go ask the people in the streets/where your new name comes from) (1999). In one of his most popular songs, 'Die Mystic Boer' (1996), the very notion of Afrikaner identity itself comes into question. For forty days and nights the protagonist searches for the 'Afrikaner', figured here as a kind of mystic – '*maar soos die swart perd van middernag gedagtes/bly hy op sy hoede en loer oor sy skouer*' (but like a black horse of midnight thoughts/he stays on his guard and peeks over his shoulder); finally he vanishes without trace.

Other white groups have placed identity in question without making 'fugitive' identities a central concern. Though anti-white sentiment and the politics of re-racialisation remain an inescapable backdrop to their work, it seems impossible to decide whether their work should be thought of as being *determined by* this climate, or occurring *in spite of* it. What characterises this work is a sense of intense creativity, in which open-ended self-reinvention becomes the most compelling feature. For these groups, remarkably, the subjective structure of identity radically resists fixity or closure. Here, musical styles are ironic and unpredictable, assume self-conscious postures, resist genre definitions, are often difficult to classify. For this very reason, the identities configured in the songs are explorative, shifting and inconclusive: they often place performativity itself at the centre. Lyrics may turn around issues of self-definition; or as Boo! seem to ponder in one of their biggest hits ('Gud 2 b tru', Oppikoppi 1998): Who am I, what am I worth, and who are you? The group Not My Dog (2000) are a compelling instance. The name itself is a negation; their music is challenging, adventurous, chaotic; and at one moment of surprise they suddenly incorporate the 'coloured' South African rap group Brasse vannie Kaap. The music is vested in multiplicity and disjuncture. As each chosen style is 'unsettled', space is opened for the importation of other – extraneous – musical sources: what is thus conjured into audibility, in the most striking way, is the sound of the group searching for other and different identities. As stylistic distinctions start to collapse, categories such as 'us' and 'them' begin to merge, or at least to draw closer together. If not yet quite transformed, identity appears as unsettled and changing: the music takes to heart the potential diversity of contemporary South African experience and revels in the confusion and potential of this multifarious, multilingual, multicultural and multimusical dystopia.

Related claims could be made about some of the songs written and performed by Sons of Trout. 'Luscious lipstick lady' (1998), for example, is a satirical, humorously mocking song that once again interrogates and unsettles identity – the identity of the familiar, the established. It 'plays at' a song of seduction, without ever 'being' one, as though the conventional roles are no longer credible or coherent. An important aspect of this is the song's self-conscious parody, in different sections, of three different idioms. The first is a jazzy section using close-harmony vocalisations, a scratchy '78 r.p.m' surface, the quiet hubbub of bar talk and, as melodrama, a strange, unreal dialogue between a white South African man and a woman who replies only in German. The second is a rock-like guitar-and-close-harmony ballad with

126   *Christopher Ballantine*

mock-seductive lyrics ('Luscious lipstick lady, can I tempt you with my love? You're my kitty kat, fancy that, on a platter of cheese. Come into my bathroom, won't you drive my limousine?'). And the third, quite incongruously, is a Latin dance section. Ingeniously, the song switches restlessly back and forth between these, unable to settle on – to identify with – any.

One could make exactly the same sort of case about the work of the award-winning, chart-topping Springbok Nude Girls, the country's leading rock group for several years before their disbanding in 2001. The most immediately striking feature of their 1997 album, *Afterlifesatisfaction*, for example, is the sheer disparity of the musical material – both across the album's duration and within each of its eighteen songs. Nothing here turns out as we might expect it to: not the musical implications of the wayward material, and certainly not the meanings to which these give rise. So what is going on here? As much as anything, this CD seems to be about invention (riotously so), about the transcendence of reified barriers, about imagining the unimaginable, bridging the incommensurable, realising the impossible. What enables this is an attitude of playfulness: more precisely, of playing at, of posturing: a ludic stance that creates ironic distance from the real. And the postures are not 'merely' musical; they also play at, or with, ways of being. Coming from a white band addressed in the main to a white audience, these postures seek also to liberate: to re-invent ways of being white and South African. These are musical images that represent identity as malleable, and as a quest – even if this sometimes puts coherence itself at risk.

The song 'Spaceman', for instance, playfully sets in motion an exhilarating feeling of controlled wildness. Rhythmically, melodically and texturally it keeps changing tack, discovering as it does so a range of original and memorable new timbres, while the lyrics hover on the edge of sense or nonsense, seeming to conjure myriad new meanings:

Jeri won Jeri Bom Bom
Beware I'll be talking about
ya feel one square
we a cold a we on fire
I'm up be setting on I feel entwined
I'm a feeling on my feel one square
If a feeling this getting more square
I'm coming again, I'm coming again
Yeah, Yeah, Yeah

Oooh, I rather tell a spaceman
Oooh, I rather tell a spaceman
Oooh, I rather tell a spaceman

Another song, 'Genie', transgresses from the familiar to the unexpected, and from the gently seductive strains of the beginning to those of burning intensity at the end. It opens with a warmly lyrical vocal part that moves in a very contained range; but a quite unexpected trumpet obbligato introduces a freer, more ecstatic sensibility ('uh oh, a little bit of money,/yeah yeah, from a little bit of hurry') and liberates the passion that in retrospect seems to have been there from the beginning. Tension builds; the timbre of the voice changes as the music grows more unsettled; and during the song's unpredictable course, untapped potential seems to be set free. In the song 'Rabbit', the incommensurable – or rather, its surpassing – is the central concern. The music is again unsettled, constantly shifting, full of contrasts of style, idiom, groove, rhythm, texture, melody and mood (including, at one moment, an egregious parody of a church organ-like cadential passage); and its lyrics are bizarre. The very question of coherence itself seems at issue: will this piece make sense? And yet it does: as the illicit and the utterly extraordinary come playfully into the range of the audible, our sense of a new expressive order, of new subjective possibilities, begins to take shape:

We must try and live together
Cause the rabbit is a carrot
And I am the rabbit
Out of time I get no

Babies fall out of the rabbit's bum
When I come, when I come
And the little boy run, and the little girl run
But she's the only one, she's the only one

I can't go, I must stay
A visible future's not my way
I'm coming back man
Hand over the jack fan
I'm the rabbit head man
Myth of an old school

Giggling I'm so happy I'm giggling
Cause the children are fighting
And the weakling bleeding
In a shaded corner Mama sits
In great despair of her sixty kids

No, no, no

In common with many other groups – though perhaps more luminously than most – the Springbok Nude Girls quite simply seek transcendence. And for a group that sings predominantly in English, this is nowhere more striking than in their invocation of an Afrikaans idiom typically associated with white conservatism: *boeremusiek*. Signifying the idiom principally by means of the piano accordion, 'Beautiful Girl' (1997) is a parody that so extends the idiom's boundaries through interaction with rock that it is quite recast, re-emerging as a hybrid. More dramatically still, 'Pappa ek wil 'n popster word' (1996) is hard 'white' (and Afrikaans) rock – rock premised upon *boeremusiek*, signalled here most directly by a metrically off-beat piano-accordion-and-guitar style. 'Daddy I want to be a pop star': the desire expressed in the title puts on the agenda nothing less than performativity itself, and the idea of identity-as-performance. Articulated as if to a traditional Afrikaans elder, the song's desire is also a scandalous challenge which the music itself *performs*, stretching *boeremusiek* beyond its conventional idiomatic limits so as to display the outlines of a new style of 'white' music, and to present, therefore, the sonic image of an emergent social identity.

V

To return to my graffito writer: None of this may yet answer the demand to 're-release Mandela – the disco version' . . . or any version, for that matter. But post-apartheid white South African music, as I've tried to suggest, is full of surprises: for instance, not

128   *Christopher Ballantine*

only an articulate sense that the new state has in some important ways turned its back on its own people, but also – and perhaps more strikingly – a sense of a radical, questing, openness. In its deep playfulness (doing after all what popular music does best), in its creativity, its self-invention, and above all its resistance to premature closure, much of this music suggests to me that the future of white South African identity is open to inscription, busy reinventing itself, and impossible to predict.[15]

Endnotes

1. An early version of this article was given as a paper at the 11th Biannual Conference of the International Association for the Study of Popular Music, in Turku, Finland, 6–10 July 2001. I gratefully acknowledge the help I have received from my research assistants, Chantel Oosthuizen, Astrid Treffrey-Goatley and Kathryn Olsen – all recent graduates of the University of Natal. I also thank the University of Natal and the National Research Foundation for their financial support for this project. I am also indebted to the relevant publishers for permission to quote lyrics. In the case of two copyright holders, however, all my assistant's efforts to obtain a reply failed: her repeated written and telephonic requests were left unanswered. Should these copyright holders see this article and desire a formal resolution of the matter, they are invited to contact this journal.

2. 'Madiba' is Nelson Mandela's affectionate clan name.

3. Among the other influential white 'protest' musicians of the apartheid era were the youthful Afrikaans *alternatief* singer-songwriters who challenged hegemonic Afrikaans culture during the late 1980s – for example, Johannes Kerkorrel, Koos Kombuis, and Bernoldus Niemand (James Phillips by another name). Various English-speaking rock musicians and rock groups also made an impression – among them Bright Blue with, for example, their moving hit 'Weeping' (1988), voted the South African 'song of the century' in a 1999 Internet poll held by the *SA Rock Digest* and *Amuzine* (www.sarockdigest.com); and Trevor Rabin, whose powerful 'Sorrow (your heart)' (1989) fuses rock with the cyclical guitar licks, rolling bass line, electric organ and backing vocals of *mbaqanga*, includes a black female quartet, and has lyrics that refer to the harsh life of a migrant worker. For more on the social and political significance of the work of white musicians – whether English or Afrikaans speaking – during the apartheid era, see, for instance, Andersson (1981), Kitchen (1995), van der Meulen (1995), Byerly (1996), Jury (1996) and Muller (2000).

4. In the racial ontology of apartheid South Africa, the classification 'coloured' was applied predominantly to those people deemed to be of 'mixed-race' (white-and-black) heritage. Far from withering away, this term – like many others – has enjoyed a new lease of life as a 'race' category in post-apartheid South Africa. Because it continues to be pertinent to South Africans (including popular musicians) and the choices they make, I use the term in this article – but in scare quotes. (That a specific 'coloured' identity has developed over time is incidental to the point at issue here.)

5. Many clubs remain racially exclusive. Suzy Bell, a journalist who writes on popular culture, has noted this:

Bully tactics and blatant abuse of a club's right to admission are reasons why we still have 'black clubs' (Heat, Obsession, the clubbing concept of Vibe 2000), 'coloured clubs' (XTC, Xanadu, Exodus), 'Indian clubs' (Angelo's Cantina, Destiny, Palladium) and 'white clubs' (3–30, Joe Kool's, Eighties, Absolute Chaos, Billy the BUMS cocktail bar) . . . [I]f you're not gay and you're black, Indian or coloured in Durban, you know there are certain no-go club zones. . . . Young clubber Ms Ravina Maharaj said there were not many clubs in Durban where she felt comfortable. . . . Maharaj said the problem lay with bouncers or club owners who 'don't want to be invaded by Indians, coloureds or blacks' (*Sunday Independent*, 26 March 2000).

6. A point once made by Albert Luthuli, ANC President-General in the 1950s, is also relevant here: 'The task is not finished: somewhere ahead there beckons a civilisation, a culture. It will not necessarily be all black, but it will be African' (cited by Charles Villa–Vicencio, *Mail & Guardian*, 15–21 September 2000).

7. Brendan Jury's (1996, p. 101) précis of the hegemonic ideology propagated by white Afrikaans-language popular music during the late apartheid era sketches a relevant background:

[The] standard formula is in the main the urbanised volkslied (*lit.* Afrikaner traditional folksong) pop ballad form set in a disco or country and Western aesthetic. Lyrics conform predominantly to stylised sentimental romantic themes (liefdesliedjies, *lit.* Afrikaans love songs). To a lesser extent national sentiment, flora and fauna of South Africa, significant symbols of Afrikaner culture such as rugby and national service, religious themes or translations of European folk songs generate the lyrics of the popular mainstream. The liefdesliedjie, the most popular genre, is characterised by its propagation of rigid gender stereotypes. In the lyric content, women are idealised as passive, acquiescent, and the victims of unrequited love. Conversely, men are portrayed as active manipulators of space and time, usually as farmers, soldiers or men of courage who engage in heroic struggles and quests. The patriarchal nature of Afrikaner culture is faithfully reflected in these gender stereotypes.

Typifying this perversion is Bles Bridges, currently the most successful white singer in South Africa. By 1990, Bridges had sold more than 1 million units and had released twelve albums. Bridges combines disco and some of the vastrap (*lit.* 'two-step') rhythmic style of boere musiek (*lit.* traditional Afrikaans folk music) with a Las Vegas-like kitsch packaging of glitter, sequined tuxedo and cowboy boots. Bridges states explicitly: 'Love is the only thing worth singing about. To sing about politics has never done anybody any good' (Jury 1996, p. 101).

8. The research for that study was funded by South Africa's Department of Labour and the Norwegian Development Agency.
9. As a result of a series of legal challenges motivated by an intense and sustained public outcry, the government partially backed down in October 2002 by agreeing in principle to make anti-retrovirals available to the approximately six million South Africans living with HIV/Aids.
10. Among whites, according to this Norwegian report, the income ratio for these same strata is 12 to 1.
11. The fraudulence of this strategy is demonstrated by, for example, those social tendencies that move in the opposite direction. One of these is the growing number of white workers who are moving away from historically white trade unions and signing up for membership of predominantly black unions and federations, such as Cosatu, the National Council of Trade Unions (Nactu) and the Federation of Unions of South Africa (Fedusa). Nactu has hailed this as 'good for the country, for racial harmony and reconciliation' (*Mail & Guardian*, 9–15 March 2001). In similar vein, Zwelinzima Vavi, the general secretary of Cosatu, has said:

I think the development is part of the normalising of society, towards non-racialism. Members of the working class are beginning to realise they belong together. Their futures are intertwined, they are dependent on each other. Whereas in the past white members were not happy to carry a placard to toyi-toyi outside an

employer's office, we are now seeing this happening. In fact, more whites are becoming shop stewards in Cosatu. (*ibid.*)
12. Masterbond' is a reference to a huge investment scheme that was undermined by massive fraud and that left many people destitute in one of the country's biggest financial scandals of the 1990s. The 'Matie-rector' is a nickname for the rector of the University of Stellenbosch, the oldest and most prestigious Afrikaans-language university. 'De Klerk' is F.W. de Klerk, the white South African president at the time of the transition to democracy.
13. The title punningly misspells the colloquial Afrikaans word *gatvol* ('fed up'). Here spelt *Gautvol*, the word alludes to Gauteng, South Africa's richest province, dominated by Johannesburg and Pretoria; but since Gauteng was one of the provinces created in the democratic era, the misspelt word also alludes to the new South Africa. The title (*Gautvol in Paradise*) is therefore deeply ironic: one possible gloss would be 'A belly-ache in the new South African "paradise"'.
14. Taste cultures – shaped by apartheid along racial lines – are changing, as this article suggests. But changing slowly: the recent music referred to here is 'white' in the sense that it is still largely made and consumed by whites – via mediations that include CDs, radio, television, festivals and clubs.
15. Writing an honours thesis in 2001 at the University of Natal, Durban, on the topic of white identities in post-apartheid South African literature, a young, white, Jewish woman made a not dissimilar observation:

[I]n recent years, I have begun to reflect on my own position as a white South African. This has led me to critically engage with my own identity. In addition, I have become attuned to the attempts of broader white South African society at large to materially re-negotiate identities for themselves in the new South Africa. I have been a part of and witness to this re-negotiation of identity. This project is thus important to me in laying bare the fraught and difficult nature of post-apartheid white identities in which I am implicated by virtue of the history of my country, where so much was invested in racialised identities. This thesis has led me on a journey of self-discovery and investigation into the attitudes and beliefs of my friends, associates and myself. (Bass 2001, pp. 4–5)

References

Andersson, M. 1981. *Music in the Mix: The Story of South African Popular Music* (Johannesburg)

Back, L. 1996. *New Ethnicities and Urban Culture: Racisms and Multiculture in Young Lives* (London)

Ballantine, C. 1993. *Marabi Nights: Early South African Jazz and Vaudeville* (Johannesburg)

Bass, O. 2001. 'Imagining white identities in post-apartheid South African literary fiction', B.A. (Hons.) thesis, University of Natal

Byerly, I. 1996. 'The music indaba: music as mirror, mediator and prophet in the South African transition from apartheid to democracy', Ph.D. thesis, Duke University

130   *Christopher Ballantine*

Coetzee, J. 1988. *White Writing* (Johannesburg)

Erasmus, Z. 2001. 'Re-imagining coloured identities in post-apartheid South Africa', in *Coloured by History, Shaped by Place: New Perspectives on Coloured Identities in Cape Town*, ed. Z. Erasmus (Cape Town), pp. 13–28

Fanon, F. 1986. *Black Skin, White Masks* (London)

Gilroy, P. 1993. *The Black Atlantic: Modernity and Double Consciousness* (London)

Hall, S. 1997. 'Random thoughts provoked by the conference "Identities, democracy, culture and communication in Southern Africa" ', *Critical Arts*, 11/1–2, pp. 1–16

Hesmondhalgh, D. 2000. 'International times: fusions, exoticism and antiracism in electronic dance music', in *Western Music and its Others*, ed. G. Born and D. Hesmondhalgh (Berkeley and Los Angeles), pp. 280–304

Hollinger, D. 2000. 'The end of a marriage of convenience: multiculturalism and affirmative action in the United States', *Perspektiven: Internationale StudentInnenzeitung*, 36/June, pp. 22–6

Jury, B. 1996. 'Boys to men: Afrikaans alternative popular music 1986–1990', *African Languages and Cultures*, 9/2, pp. 99–109

Keil, C., and Feld, S. 1994. *Music Grooves* (Chicago and London)

Kitchen, S. 1997. 'Where have all the flowers gone? The shifting position of folk music within white South African popular music culture from 1960 to the present', B.A. (Hons.) thesis, University of Natal

Lipsitz, G. 1994. *Dangerous Crossroads: Popular Music, Postmodernism and the Poetics of Place* (London)

Maré, G. 2003. ' "Non-racialsim" in the struggle against apartheid', *Society in Transition*, 34/1, pp. 1–25

Muller, S. 2000. 'Sounding margins: musical representations of white South Africa', Ph.D. thesis, University of Oxford

Ndebele, N. 2000. 'Iph' indlela? Finding our way into the future', Steve Biko Memorial Lecture, University of Cape Town, unpublished

Norwegian Insitute for Applied Social Science. 2002. *Metsebetsi Labour Force Survey*

Said, E. 1994. *Culture and Imperialism* (London)

Saul, J. 2001. 'Cry for the beloved country: the post-apartheid denouement', *Monthly Review*, 52/8, pp. 1–51

Schlemmer, L. 2002. 'A better life for all? Poverty trends in South Africa', *Focus*, 26, pp. 20–3

Touraine, A. 2000. *Can We Live Together? Equality and Difference* (Oxford)

van der Meulen, L. 1995. 'From rock 'n' roll to hard core punk: an introduction to rock music in Durban, 1963–85', M.Mus. thesis, University of Natal

van Rooyen, J. 2000. *The New Great Trek: The Story of South Africa's White Exodus* (Pretoria)

Select discography

Amersham, *Upside Down*. BMG CDCLL(SB) 7023. 1998
    12 Songs. BMG CDCLL(LF) 7038. 2000
Arapaho, *Wicked Wonder*. Teal MMTCD 1924. 1995
Battery 9, *Wrok*. Tic Tic Bang Bang BANGCD 038. 1998
Janjie Blom en die Bushrockbandvriende, 'Ek sal jou 'n leeu gee', *Om to Breyten*. GWVCD 24. 2000
Boo!, *Monki Punk*. Muce Music BOOCD 1. 1999
Bright Blue, *The Rising Tide*. EMI EMCJ (L) 4063771. 1988
Buckfever Underground, *Jou Medemens is Dood*. Janus JNSD 78. 1998/99
Johnny Clegg, *Johnny Clegg Anthology*. Connisseur VSOP CD 266. 1999
Coleske, *Faith in Love*. Gallo GWVCD 27. 2000
Tony Cox, *Matabele Ants*. Sheer SSCD 051, 1999
Danny De Wet and the Lowveld Garage Band, *Hypocrites Unite*. Polygram TRIP 007. 1998/99
Egyptian Nursery, *New Anthem*. Fresh CD 100. 1998
Eugenie, *Storm in Eden*. EUG 01. 2000
Anton Goosen, *Danzer*. Gallo CDHUL 40288. 1992
    Bushrock (of a White Kaffir of Africa). Gallo CDGMP 40693. 1996
Honeymoon Suites, *Where in the World Would You Rather Be?* HMS 555. 1999
Just Jinger, *Something for Now*. BMG CDCLL(SB) 7020. 1998
Johannes Kerkorrel, *Bloudruk*. Tusk TUCD 21. 1992
    Cyanide in the Beefcake. Tusk TUCD 33. 1994
    Ge-trans-for-meer. Tusk WOND 142. 1996
    Die Ander Kant. Gallo GWVCD 28. 2000
Syd Kitchen, *AmaKoologik*. Universal WIMAX 004. 1999
    Africa's not for Sissies. No Budget NOBUD 001. 2001
Koos Kombuis en die Warmblankes, *Blameer Dit op Apartheid*. Wildebeest WILDE 001. 1997
    Greatest Hits. Gallo GWVCD 30. 2000
David Ledbetter, 'Nteselle', *Spashy Fen: Celebrating 10 Years of Music under the Mountains*. 3rd Ear Music 3eZSF 001/2. 1999
Marimba!, *Die Kind is nie Dood nie*. JNS Musiek JNSD 73. 1999

Not My Dog, *Dogumentary*. Wolmer INT 009. 2000
Wendy Oldfield, *On a Pale Blue Dot*. Scorpio Music SMSPCD 819. 1999
Oppikoppi, *Bushveld Blast*. Oppikoppi KOPPi 001. 1998
James Phillips and The Lurchers, *Sunny Skies*. Shifty Music CDSHIFT(WL) 54. 1993
Point Sirens, *Point Sirens*. PS 011. 1999
P. J Powers, *Thandeka: Woman of Africa*. Mike Fuller Music PJCD 3002. 1995
Qcumba Zoo, *Wake Up & Dream*. Gresham Records CDDGR 1350. 1996
Trevor Rabin, *Can't Look Away*. Elektra 9 60781–2. 1989
Laurika Rauch, *Hot Gates*. Tusk WOND 131. 1995
Rustler's Valley, *Sound Journey*. RV 001. c. 1999
Leon Schuster, *Gautvol in Paradise*. EMI (South Africa) CDGAUT (WR) 1. 1997
Sons of Trout, 'Kombi', *Oppikoppi Live*. Wildebeest Records WILD 006. 1997
    Ticks on George. Gallo GWVCD 5. 1998
Springbok Nude Girls, 'Pappa ek wil 'n popster word', Wingerd Rock 1, *Songs uit die Bos*. Polygram TRIP 001. 1996
    Afterlifesatisfaction. Sony Music CDEPC 5287. 1997
Squeal, *Man and Woman*. Tusk WOND 145. 1997
Sugardrive, *Sand Man Sky*. Gallo CDNIC 001. 1997
Valiant Swart, *Die Mystic Boer*. Wildebeest Records SWART 001. 1996
    Deur die Donker Vallei. Wildebeest Records SWART 004. 1999
Tananas, *Unamunacua*. Gallo CDGMP 40684. 1996
Trans.Sky, *Killing Time*. Tic Tic Bang Bang BANGCD 039. 1998
Tree, *63*. EMI LUSCD (WI) 003. 1999
Matthew van der Want and Chris Letcher, *E. P. Tombi*. Tic Tic Bang Bang BANGCD 028. 1997
    Low Riding. Tic Tic Bang Bang BANGCD 033. 1999
Watershed, *In the Meantime*. EMI CDEMCJ (WI) 5848. 2000
White Trash, *Homegrown*. Trippy Grape Records TRIP 005. 1997

[8]

Borderland Pop: Arab Jewish Musicians and the Politics of Performance

Galit Saada-Ophir
Hebrew University of Jerusalem

"You're Gone" (2002), a song sung in both Hebrew and in a Moroccan dialect of Arabic by the Jewish Moroccan singer Amir Benaaiun, was aired on an Israeli current affairs radio program on August 2002. At that time, political debate centered on the incursion of the Israel Defense Force (IDF) into areas under the control of the Palestinian Authority, including the city of Tulkarem. Tommy Lapid, the head of the liberal Eurocentric–Zionist political party Shinui (Change), was interviewed shortly after the song was broadcast.[1] Lapid, who was of Jewish Yugoslavian origin, commented: "I heard this song and I reached the conclusion that it was not us [the state of Israel] that conquered Tulkarem, it was Tulkarem that conquered us." What aroused public outrage about this statement was the connection that it made between the culture of Jewish Moroccan Israelis with Christians and Muslim Palestinians who had previously been depicted as enemies of the State of Israel.

This reaction reflected the contentious public sentiment regarding the cultural proximity of Israeli Jews who originated from Arab and Muslim countries and Christians and Muslim Arabs. Arab Jews who immigrated to the state of Israel, mostly after its establishment in 1948, are known as Mizrahim (Easterners).[2] Not only have they suffered economic and social subordination in Israeli society, but Mizrahim have also been forced to erase their cultural origins and adopt the dominant quasi-Western Israeli culture constituted by Ashkenazi Zionists. Ashkenazim are Jews who immigrated to Israel–Palestine from Europe (mainly Eastern Europe) and North America, and they have become the dominant ethnic group in Israeli state and society through Zionist practices of land colonization and the delimitation of state boundaries.

Within dominant discourse, the discussion of Ashkenazi–Mizrahi relations is considered an internal Israeli Jewish debate, isolated from the Israeli–Arab Palestinian conflict. However, this artificial division masks the cultural proximity between Mizrahim and Christian and Muslim Arabs, including Palestinians.

Moreover, it creates a dichotomy of "Arabs" and "Jews" as two antagonistic groups locked in endless conflict. This discourse has been challenged by subversive political and cultural practices as well as by the practice of some scholars (Alcalay 1993; Lavie 1996; Shenhav 2003; Shohat 1999a, 1999b, 2003) by using the term *Arab Jews* to abolish the delimitations that the term *Mizrahim* attempts to preserve. The pioneering work of these scholars focuses on the dominance maintained by Ashkenazi Zionists—and the Arab Jewish resistance to it—in a way that stresses the location of the latter in a space that lies in between Arab and Jewish entities. This article follows their lead, emphasizing not merely Arab Jewish agency but also the power struggles that occur within this in-between space. In addition, it questions the ways in which Arab Jewish agency both undermines and reinforces musical, ideological, and national boundaries in the Middle East.

This perspective reflects my position as a researcher of Arab Libyan Jewish origin born in Israel. For me, this topic is not merely academic but a means of examining my relationship with the dominant Israeli identity, the Arab Jewish community, and my Libyan cultural roots. This study, therefore, simultaneously marks a path back to my homeland in the Arab Jewish slums scattered across Israel and an escape route for me as an anthropologist to reflect critically on the silencing of certain Arab Jewish identities. In this article, I present an Arab Jewish borderland in the field of popular music that has emerged in the space between Israeli Jewish culture and the diverse Arab and Muslim cultures that lie in close proximity.[3] As there is not space to present the full range of musical practices along this borderland, my focus will be on how the borderland can be a site of empowerment for some Arab Jews, mostly Yemenites, while simultaneously being an area that encompasses multiple ethnic conflicts. This multiplicity has led to the paradoxical nature of the borderland, in which the frequent crossing of musical borders not only fails to breach national boundaries but also serves to sustain them.

The Borderland and Subaltern Agency

Academic debates focusing on the demarcation between states, societies, and cultures often do not grasp the border as a dynamic space in which people work and live. Earlier work describes the border as "frozen in time" (Alvarez 1995:453) or as the place of "people without culture" (Rosaldo 1989:197). Contemporary scholars, especially those who grew up in borderlands, have begun examining it as a dynamic space in which varied cultural practices take place. In the wake of this new perspective, the name of this space has changed to *borderland*. A number of breakthrough studies have looked at the activity of subaltern groups in different borderlands (see Alvarez and Collier 1994; Anzaldúa 1987; Behar 1993; Fusco 1989; Lavie 1996; Rosaldo 1989; Saldivar 1997; Torstrick 1993). Contrary to earlier discourse that located the border in a specific place and presented it as a fixed boundary, this new perspective presents the borderland as an evasive space of interwoven entities, emerging through ongoing negotiations between state policies, such as border patrols, checkpoints, and containment walls, and the agency of those residing there.

Although the state establishes and maintains borders, the culture molded out of the daily practices and historical fragments in this geographical domain is not entirely disciplined by these demarcations (Lavie and Swedenburg 1996). The transnational flow of people, ideologies, styles, and technologies that cross borders creates the borderland's culture "as a hyphenated rather than as a fixed entity, thereby refusing to settle down in one (tubicolous) world or another" (Trinh 1991:159). Subaltern identities, in such spaces, thereby transcend the dichotomous discourse of identity as essence and identity as conjuncture (Lavie and Swedenburg 1996:11–13), because they are based not only on past identifications but also on the simultaneous re-creation and utilization of these in the weaving of a modern identity. Although the marginal location of subaltern groups along the borderlands might, in some cases, render them powerless in political, social, and cultural fields, subaltern marginality may, in other cases, facilitate the accumulation of power. As Paul Gilroy states, "Their special power derives from doubleness, their unsteady location simultaneously inside and outside the conventions, assumptions, and aesthetic rules" (1993:73).

This scholarly focus on processes in the borderland has reinforced the use of the term, contributing to its emergence as a vague and universal concept in a postmodern celebration of the unrestricted flow of cultural components from different social groups free from relations of social control. Roger Rouse (1991) describes the borderland created by the migration of rural Mexicans to and from the United States as a postmodern social space. In a similar vein, Akhil Gupta and James Ferguson (1992) portray the crystallization of a postmodern borderland disconnected from a specific time and space. These descriptions risk the neutralization of the unique political aspects that exist in different borderlands and the creation of an apolitical perspective that does not discern between oppressors and oppressed (Heyman 1994).

In the following passages, I recontextualize the borderland and "return" it to sociopolitical time and space by presenting a case study of the Middle Eastern borderland constituted by the establishment of the State of Israel. The first two scholars to use the notion of the "borderland" in their discussions of Israeli identity are Rebecca Lee Torstrick (1993) and Smadar Lavie (1996). Torstrick deals with the ways in which the residents of the mixed Jewish and Palestinian city of Acre work amid Israeli-state policies, and Lavie presents the proliferation of a literary borderland by Arab Jewish and Palestinian authors who blast Israeli nationalism. I use these groundbreaking works and apply them to the field of popular music to explore a popular Arab Jewish musical borderland. In so doing, I follow the work of Amy Horowitz, who focuses on this musical style, using its popular designation: Musica Yisraelit Yam Tikonit (Israeli Mediterranean music). In her earlier work (1994, 1999), Horowitz placed the style in between Israeli nationalism and Mizrahi ethnicity, describing it as both a social mediator and a disputed territory; more recently (2005), however, she places the style more squarely within the Israeli–Palestinian conflict, focusing on its potential to deterritorialize this border. In contrast to other studies in the field, I emphasize how the borders that demarcate ethnic and national entities in the Middle East have not only been established by the practices of the nation states (or their dominant groups) but also by the subversive practices of Arab Jewish subalterns trapped within these interstices.

As with other borderlands, the Arab Jewish borderland is invisible, evasive, and indefinable. This vagueness traps researchers in an everlasting paradox, as every attempt to study the borderland becomes, in effect, a powerful means to define and control it (Alvarez 1995). To minimize this risk, it is important to trace Arab Jewish musical practices that do not comply with the category of the Arab Jewish musical borderland. Such practices flow between different musical categories, and this fluidity makes it impossible to attribute these practices to a specific musical genre. Although appearing to weaken the conceptual robustness of the term borderland, these flows illustrate the power of the subaltern agent to upset the categories dominating social life.

Popular Musical Borderlands

Popular music currently serves as a central means of demarcating national borders (Stokes 1994). The recent cooperation between the global music industry and nation states legitimizes the musical genres of dominant groups, a process that reinforces the imaginary cultural boundaries of the nation state.[4] The emergence of a musical Arab Jewish borderland on the edge of different musical genres is not a unique phenomenon. Subaltern groups who find that the sanctified musical genre of the nation does not fully represent them tend to create new musical hybrids from the margins. Two examples of contemporary musical borderlands are African American rap and Algerian raï.

Rap music emerged in the United States in the early 1970s out of elements of Jamaican music and the Bronx subculture. It hybridized African American oral and musical traditions with Western technological innovations to articulate the problems and desires of subaltern African Americans who were trapped between their African past (both real and imagined) and current U.S. life. The gradually increasing popularity of rap among Anglo-American youth in the 1990s has granted it central status in Western pop music, and this has reinforced its commercialization worldwide (Hager 1984; Krims 2000; Perkins 1996; Rose 1994).

Raï emerged in the 1920s in the Algerian town of Oran through the fusion of the music of Algerian rural migrants with Moroccan Sufi music and cabaret musical genres. In the late 1970s, raï saw a resurgence in Oran through the addition of Western pop music components, and in the 1980s, it gradually gained popularity and became the dominant musical style in Algeria. With the movement of Algerian migrant workers to France in the 1990s, the style became familiar there as well and later moved to the United States. It has become representative of contemporary

Franco-Maghrebi identities, situated between the dominant cultures of Algeria and France (Gross 1996; Marranci 2003; Schade-Poulsen 1999; Swedenburg 2001). Although nation-states will often attempt to conceal the syncretic character of the dominant musical style, subaltern groups tend to celebrate the mixtures and the border crossings of their fusions. The mixture of "old" and "new" and the sampling of components from different spaces are viewed as representing their distinct identity and their ambivalent attitudes toward their in-between way of life.

The crystallization of the Arab Jewish musical borderland exemplifies the processes described above. The uniqueness of this genre is its positioning in the gaps between Israeli identity and Arab identity, which have been situated in continuous conflict. Although the borderlands of rap and raï empower the community by returning to previously forgotten cultures, the sampling of Arab components from the Arabic Jewish past or from current global Arab culture is perceived in the Zionist context as forming an affinity with the enemy. This sociopolitical complexity casts a shadow on the fusion of this borderland and enhances the double consciousness of its creators and consumers.

Demarcating Zionist Borders through Popular Music

The establishment of the State of Israel changed the Middle East dramatically and shaped the conflict between Arabs and Jews. Fundamental to the creation of society and culture in Israel (Kimmerling 1998, 2001), this conflict also influenced the evolution of the two dominant Israeli musical genres: Shirei Eretz Yisrael (Songs of the Land of Israel), commonly referred to as SEY, and Rock Yisraeli (Israeli Rock). The shaping of these genres by Ashkenazi musicians was accomplished via the subordination of Middle Eastern indigenous music cultures.

SEY

As a part of the Zionist establishment in Europe and Israel–Palestine at the beginning of the 20th century, SEY was the first national musical genre of Israel (Hirshberg 1995). Through a process of incorporating Arab Jewish musicians (especially Yemenite women) while also marginalizing them by defining them as folklore carriers, the Ashkenazi creators of the genre were crowned the local musical elite. SEY reflected the values of the Sabra who were the crystallization of the ideal type of Israeli nationalism. In comparison to the Diaspora Jew, who was described within Zionist discourse as passive and weak, the "new" Jew was depicted as a fighter and a tiller of the soil who had returned to settle the desert land of his ancestors (Almog 2000; Lavie 1996:59; Raz-Krakotzkin 1993). This "negation of exile" by Zionist Ashkenazi Jews took shape through molding SEY from a fusion of central European ingredients (representing "enlightened culture") with Middle Eastern ingredients to imbue the hybrid with local authenticity. This musical fusion jettisoned most of the traditional components of Yiddish or Ashkenazi culture developed in Eastern Europe.

The lyrics of SEY recount Jewish immigration to Israel–Palestine and describe the landscape while glorifying the Sabra. The melodies based on European classical structures are interwoven with Middle Eastern elements (Hirshberg 1995; Lavie with Hajj and Rouse 1993:380; Regev and Seroussi 2004:49–70). Because non-Jewish Arabic music was considered the music of the enemy, the Zionist establishment made few references to it and focused on Arab Jewish music. Thus, Arab Jews, especially Yemenites, were presented as the exotic community that has preserved ancient Jewish customs and aesthetics, which the Zionist movement wished to revive.[5] The musicologist Oded Asaf recalls the constitution of this hybrid:

> From the homes of the *Ashkenazi* fathers, you could borrow the cantillational notes; the new trends in Europe supported the abandonment of Major and Minor harmonies in favor of ancient modes; and here, in the land, the musicians anticipated an exciting encounter with Arab music and Eastern Jewish ethnic groups, especially the Yemenites. Out of these materials (after a selection!), the folk singing and artistic creation with the taste and color of the new Israel will be assembled. [1988:8, my translation]

The process of shaping SEY involved the promotion of Arab Jewish female singers, especially those of Yemeni origin, who were perceived as giving birth to the nation in their songs.[6] They introduced European composers and score writers to Arab Jewish musical styles by collaborating with them in performing SEY. Bracha Zphira, the first female Yemenite singer to sing these songs, became famous in the 1930s after collaborating with the Ashkenazi composer and pianist Nahum Nardi. Her appearance on stage, barefoot and with long flowing hair, produced the image of a wild and exotic young Yemenite girl, which became a central figure in the development of a "native" Middle Eastern Zionist culture.[7]

In 1948, a new arena for SEY was established with the creation of *lehakot tzevaiyot* (army ensembles) within the IDF. The army ensembles represented combat units, and its members were young Ashkenazi soldiers performing in uniform. They were directed by well-known Ashkenazi civilian composers and performed in front of soldiers in military camps and civilian audiences across the country. Most of their songs and comic sketches praised Zionist colonialism and depicted military life. Popular throughout the 1950s and 1960s, this performance genre blurred the boundaries that separated Israeli society from the culture of military forces, reinforcing a connection to militarism among civilians (Regev and Seroussi 2004:90–112; Seroussi 1996:10–11).

The creation of SEY as the first Zionist musical genre was accomplished via the crowning of Ashkenazi musicians as the Israeli musical elite. They were not considered as merely one of a number of Israeli ethnic groups but as the Israeli ideal type. The decline of SEY dominance and the adoption of rock music, at first mostly by young Arab Jewish musicians, did not abolish this dominance but presented yet another strategy for marginalizing Arab Jews.

From Lehakot Ketzev to Rock Yisraeli

Until recently, the historiography of Israeli music moved directly from SEY to Rock Yisraeli by emphasizing the activity of Ashkenazi musicians who started with SEY but later absorbed global rock music (see Regev 1992, 2000). This history disregards the role of the *lehakot ketzev* (beat groups) and Arab Jewish musicians in this transition.[8] Not only has this history been concealed but this musical genre has been pushed to the Israeli margins.[9]

As part of the resocialization process required of Arab Jews by the Israeli state, they were asked to adopt SEY and abandon their Arab Jewish music and culture. As in other resocialization projects, they exhibited ambivalent responses to this demand. They may have listened to SEY, but they did not desert their Jewish Arabic and Arabic music of origin. As a result of this cultural confusion, they were able to absorb an additional musical style reflecting their ruptured identity. Starting at the end of the 1960s, Arab Jewish youth began to associate with Western rock, and through this style, they articulated their disidentification with the dominant Ashkenazi culture.[10]

Throughout the country, lehakot ketzev were established. They performed covers of U.S. rock music and rock songs in English and in Hebrew and played Western musical instruments such as electric guitar and drums. Performances took place primarily in discotheques and night clubs located in industrial zones near the slums of south Tel Aviv and in the cities of Ramla and Bat Yam.[11] Well-known lehakot ketzev were Chocolate, The Churchills, The Goldfingers, Ha'zarim (The Strangers), and Ha'kokhavim Ha'keulim (The Blue Stars). These names were unusual in the Israeli musical landscape as they were devoid of Zionist associations. The names of mainstream civilian groups that sang SEY were customarily taken from the culturally glorified field of agriculture, such as Batzal Yarok (Green Onion) and Ha'Tarnegolim (The Roosters). In an attempt to establish themselves as part of Western pop and rock culture, the lehakot ketzev preferred English names or names associated with the U.S. glamour world.

Avner Gadassi, a Yemenite musician and a key member in the lehakot ketzev, recalled his success as a rock musician among Arab Jewish youth:

> After I became known as a singer in the clubs in Rechov Hamasger [a street in South Tel Aviv], I was introduced to the beat groups in Ramla. With one or two hits, I was a star there. I used to come to the clubs with shining shirts and Bordeaux pants with white stripes on the sides. We dressed differently from the other youngsters in Israel. I straightened my hair, at first with the help of my sisters. I wanted to be like the Beatles; they had straight hair. There was a long queue of fans at my shows, I felt like Elvis Presley. I had bags full of fan mail; I was a real king. A king without the approval of the media . . . . The lehakot tzevaiyot dominated the media, but we broke up their conventions, the way you can create music. It took them [the Ashkenazi public] ten years to "digest" it. [Interview with author, December 2, 2004]

The rock music of the lehakot ketzev was classified by the Ashkenazi public as a cheap imitation *(chikui zol)* of Western rock, and it was kept on the margins of the Israeli musical field. It was only after a coincidental collaboration between Arik Einstein, a successful Ashkenazi singer who graduated from the lehaka tzevait (military ensembles), and a lehakot ketzev, The Churchills, that rock music became successful in creating a genre known as Rock Yisraeli, and Einstein became an Israeli icon. Rock Yisraeli hybridized SEY with the ideology and aesthetics of rock music (Regev 1992), thus weakening the powerful hold that the lehakot ketzev enjoyed. In contrast to SEY, the lyrics of Rock Yisraeli generally dealt with everyday life and romantic relationships.

The cultural elite's appropriation of rock music facilitated the reproduction of the musical elite as Ashkenazi. Most of the Arab Jewish musicians who played in lehakot ketzev remained on the margins because their style was not classified as representative of Israeli nationalism. During the 1970s and 1980s, Rock Yisraeli became the dominant national genre, referred to as Musica Yisraelit [Israeli music] (Regev 1992; Regev and Seroussi 2004:137–160). This style offered an up-to-date dominant Israeli identity that sought to be part of global Western culture (Regev 2000). The Westernization of Israeli music was intensified with the creation of a local music industry that functioned as a branch of the Western popular music industry. For example, Hed Arzi is the local representative of Warner and BMG, NMC represents Sony and EMI, and Helicon represents Polygram (Regev 1997:121). This local industry has served as a gatekeeper to the national musical field by marginalizing the hybrid music of subaltern musicians.

The delimitation of the boundaries of Israeli culture in the production of SEY and later Rock Yisraeli facilitated the image of Israel as a quasi-Western society, disconnected from the Middle Eastern Arabic states and societies yet related to Middle Eastern geography. The absorption of different Arab Jewish musical styles and the marginalization of its musicians strengthened the place of the Arab Jews within Middle Eastern borders and led to the production of the Arab Jewish musical borderland.

The Emergence of the Arab Jewish Borderland

The Arab Jewish musical borderland is a dynamic field that has been a site of cooperation and empowerment for some Arab Jews, mainly Yemenites, while simultaneously fragmented by multiple conflicts. The conflicts emerged not merely between the borderland and the dominant Israeli musical genre, but through internal struggles between different Arab Jewish styles competing for cultural visibility. In spite of the partial recognition that the Israeli Turkish and Israeli Moroccan styles have gained, the borderland has not allowed all of its inhabitants to feel a sense of belonging. This is particularly the case with the Libyan Jews.

The Dominance of the Israeli Yemenite Style

The Arab Jewish musical borderland was formed at the end of the 1960s through the collaboration of Arab Jewish youths performing in lehakot ketzev and another group of youths from Kerem Hatemanim (The Yemenite Vineyard), a proletariat neighborhood in south Tel Aviv. This collaboration resulted in the formation of a Yemenite elite in the borderland.

The Israeli Yemenites' success in the popular musical field was not coincidental. A unique dynamic evolved between Yemenite Jews and the Ashkenazi Zionist leadership who regarded the Yemenites as subordinate associates in the Zionist project, and therefore, their music was allowed to have a partial presence in the national culture. The initial intersection between these two groups occurred in 1882, when the first Zionist immigrants from Eastern Europe came to Israel–Palestine and encountered Yemenite Jews. According to Yehuda Nini (1982), between the years 1881–1908, Israel–Palestine absorbed about 3,000 Jewish immigrants from Yemen, the largest number of Jewish immigrants to arrive from Arab or Islamic countries during this period. This immigration was one of a number of waves of immigration of families and small communities from the Ottoman Empire. However, the leaders of the Zionist movement who encountered Yemenite Jews for the first time allowed for the constitution of a narrative of "national resurrection" to take place simultaneously in Europe and in the Islamic world.

Until the early 20th century most Yemenite immigrants settled in traditionalist Jewish communities, separated from Zionist Ashkenazi immigrants who started to arrive in Israel–Palestine. Following the employment of Yemenite Jews in 1909 and 1910 in agricultural Zionist settlements (Shafir 1989:193), the Zionist leadership sent a special delegate, Shmuel Yavnieli, to Yemen in search of healthy young Jewish workers to provide a cheap labor force that could compete with Palestinian workers. The Yavnieli mission encouraged the emigration of Yemenite Jews who would occupy a lower social position than Zionist Ashkenazi workers but higher than Palestinian workers in the labor market. Yemenite men, women, and occasionally children worked primarily as agricultural laborers while women also worked as domestic laborers. Because of their lower wages, this group suffered from poor health, and premature death was commonplace (Druyan 1979; Shafir 1989; Shohat 1988:13–16).

As in other colonial relationships,[12] the relation of the Yemenite Jews to the dominant group that subordinated them was ambivalent. This ambivalence was intensely expressed in the musical activity in the Kerem Hatemanim neighborhood. During the 1960s, musicians spontaneously organized *haflât*—an Arabic word meaning a party that entails the playing of music, singing, eating, and sometimes dancing. In Kerem Hatemanim, like other Arab Jewish neighborhoods, haflât took place at night in people's homes, backyards, and on sidewalks. These parties inverted the dominant Zionist musical practice that had adapted Middle Eastern tunes to classical European models. Although Arab Jews had adopted SEY in response to the demands of the national culture, they were not fully committed to it. In performing SEY, they interwove it with Yemenite Jewish traditional musical practices and played the music in an Arab Jewish style.[13] By the end of the 1960s, after a spontaneous recording of a wedding in Kerem Hatemanim and the sale of the tapes in the groom's electric products store, the haflât became more com-mercialized (Horowitz 1994:172–175; Regev and Seroussi 2004:204–205). Music from these parties was recorded on tape and sold in street markets, especially in the nearby Tel Aviv central bus station. In addition, some musicians started per-forming for a fee at Arab Jewish family events (like weddings and Bar Mitzvahs) and in nightclubs.

The marginal location of the Yemenites led them to increase their friendly mu-sical relations with the musicians of the lehakot ketzev who performed in similar surroundings in Tel Aviv. As a result of composing and performing songs to-gether in the early 1970s, they crystallized the Arab Jewish musical borderland by hybridizing several musical styles and blurring the musical differences between them. This new hybrid form included SEY, Yemenite music, Western pop and rock music, Arab music, Jewish religious chants and prayers, Greek pop music, and Latin music. The texts of these songs often dealt with romantic relationships and described the conditions of Arab Jews in Israeli society. They played mod-ern Western instruments, such as the electric guitar and the keyboard, in addition to Middle Eastern instruments, such as the *darbukka* (hand drum), the *bouzouki* (Greek guitar), the *'ud* (an Arab lute), and melodic instruments such as the violin.[14]

Through the use of an essential concept in the Israeli cultural field—*aicuti* (quality) and *lo aicuti* (low quality)—the Arab Jewish new hybrid was classified as low quality because of its disassociation from dominant Israeli styles, and it was accordingly located at the bottom of the Israeli musical hierarchy. For example, Ahuva Ozeri's hit song, "Where is my Soldier" (1975), which deals with the disappearance of a soldier on a battlefield, was perceived as low quality because its theme was considered demoralizing to Israeli Jewish society, and the Israeli media was forbidden from playing it on the air.[15] Similarly, Nissim Saroussi's love song written in a military prison, "I Can't Any More" (1973), was classified as a poor imitation of Western pop music.[16] Zohar Argov's song, "I Went to the Employment Bureau" (1990) described the discrimination against Arab Jews in seeking employment and their recruitment to the IDF. Despite his Yemenite origin, Argov sang this song in Hebrew along with a mix of Libyan and Moroccan dialects of Arabic. In this instance, Argov's song was marginalized as representing an unjustified complaint.[17]

Over the years, the Israeli Yemenite style has gradually gained legitimacy in the Israeli musical field in a way that has not been possible for other Arab Jewish peoples, especially Jews from Morocco and Iraq whose performance venues were limited to family events and nightclubs in Arab Jewish slums across the country.[18] The uniqueness of the Yemenite community that resulted in their musical success has stemmed from three main factors. The first, as mentioned above, is the unique relationship between Ashkenazi Zionist and Yemenite Jews that led to a mutual sampling of musical components and gave the Yemenites room to maneuver within Israeli culture in a manner that has not challenged Israeli nationalism and Ashkenazi hegemony. The second is the new blend of ingredients from Arab Jewish music and modern pop and rock that reflected the identity split of Arab Jews in Israeli society and captivated Arab Jewish youth. The third is the commercialization process that enlarged the potential audience for this style.

As a result, some of the Yemenite musicians consolidated their position and became the elite of the musical borderland. They possessed production and distribution facilities and became the spokespersons for the Arab Jewish borderland. Starting in the mid 1980s, some of these performers became increasingly famous through occasional appearances on TV and radio programs that dedicated a few short hours a day to this genre.[19] Their struggle for media representation and album production in mainstream record companies became more public (see also Regev and Seroussi 2004:213–235). In spite of the marginalized location of musicians of the lehakot ketzev and from the Kerem Hatemanim neighborhood, their musical collaborations eventually resulted in the creation of a Yemenite borderland elite. However, this has also facilitated the marginalization of the musical styles of other Arab Jewish ethnic groups.

The Struggles of the Turkish and Moroccan Israeli Styles

Two additional musical styles emerging in the borderland during the 1980s were the Israeli Turkish style and the Israeli Moroccan style. They contributed to the transfer of musical components across the borderland not only through cooperative practices but also through inner struggles.

The Israeli Turkish style was shaped during the 1980s by adapting Turkish *arabesk* songs to the Hebrew dialect.[20] Although Turkey is not an Arabic country, the fact that Israeli Arab Jews have adopted Turkish music validates the placement of this style within the borderland. Through this style, Arab Jews have asserted their "Arabness" by adopting a Middle Eastern music that, despite its name, is not perceived as Arabic. Contrary to the case of Israeli Yemenite musicians who are mostly Yemenite and the Israeli Moroccan musicians who are mostly Moroccan, most of the musicians of the Israeli Turkish style are not Turkish but hail from diverse countries, such as Iraq, Libya, and Morocco. This musical style, therefore, unites musicians from different countries of origin through their social and cultural marginalization while blurring their internal ethnic diversity.[21]

The texts of Israeli Turkish songs deal mainly with romantic relationships, the betrayal of friends and spouses, loneliness, and financial difficulties. This musical style is a fusion of Western instruments, such as electric guitar and keyboard, with Middle Eastern instruments, such as the darbukka and the 'ud, but with the addition of the *bağlama* (a Turkish string instrument). The absence of significant musical and financial networks with Ashkenazi and Yemenite musical elites as well as the prevalence of Arabic quarter tones nonexistent in Western music has doomed the Israeli Turkish style to a marginal position. Consequently, it is regarded by both Ashkenazi and Yemenite musicians as being low quality. Despite millions of cassette tapes and disks sold and nightclub performances before audiences of passionate fans, the genre has almost never been broadcast in the mainstream Israeli media, other than a brief and partial success in the mid 1990s.[22]

For example, a central figure in the Israeli Yemenite style derided the style: "The Turkish style is exaggerated; it can spoil the youth. Part of them sings songs about joints, about smoking drugs. It is not cultural music; it is delinquency. But I don't include all of them—those who write at a high standard become popular" (interview with author, December 2, 2004). For musicians performing in the Israeli Turkish style, success would only be possible by abandoning Turkish tunes and adapting Israeli Yemenite elements. Some individuals who have crossed the borders of the genre into the dominant Yemenite milieu to become Israeli superstars are Zehava Ben, Sarit Hadad, Moshik Aafia, and Lior Narkis. These musicians have attained the derogatory title Mishtakenez (becoming an Ashkenazi) within the Israeli Turkish milieu. Yossi Eden, a key proponent of the Israeli Turkish style, who refuses to adopt Israeli Yemenite elements into his music, responded to the undervaluation of this style:

> These are songs from my soul, I do not write for money . . . . I am not a Mishtakenez. I write because I want to make songs that will help the people. If I were a Mishtakenez, I would make songs that would only cause them to dance . . . . My fans are children and adults living in hostels, in slums; they are attached to this kind of music, and they live the life I sing about. [interview with author, December 20, 2004]

The Israeli Moroccan style was consolidated by the band Sfataim (Lips), which was formed by Moroccan Jews from Sderot in southern Israel. Throughout the 1970s, members of the band collaborated with one another as amateurs to form lehakot ketzev in their town. As adults, they set up Sfataim and played pop and rock songs in Hebrew and English at family celebrations. Having received a positive response to their translation of a well-known Israeli pop song into the Moroccan dialect of Arabic, the band was encouraged to perform more songs in this way.[23]

Sfataim built up a repertoire of songs, some in Hebrew and the rest in Moroccan Arabic; some were old Moroccan songs, familiar to them from their homes, and others were pop songs, such as raï, originally played by contemporary North African musicians. The sound was a blend of electric guitar and keyboard with the percussive elements of the darbukka and Cuban bongos underneath melodies played on the accordion and violin. When Sfataim became successful toward the end of the 1980s, they began to assert the value of reviving their Jewish Moroccan past and representing their distinct Moroccan Israeli identity. Haim Uliel, the leader of the band, affirmed the need for this revival:

> It irritated me that there are cultural products that people are not familiar with. We are the largest ethnic group in Israel, and people are not familiar with our cultural products. Everybody knows the stories about the Cossacks in Eastern Europe, the stories being taught in schools, and other stories of different ethnic groups are left out. Our culture is disappearing. [interview with author, November 17, 1995]

The success of the band was made possible because of the unexpected cooperation between the band and the local branch of Fonokol, a mainstream recording
company that was able to utilize the assistance of a successful Israeli Moroccan producer. On the one hand, this cooperative venture allowed the band to bypass the cassette industry, the dominant medium of the other two Arab Jewish styles, and it also
brought the band artistic recognition. On the other hand, this very success weakened the band's ability to empower additional Moroccan musicians by producing
their albums. Nonetheless, because of their success within the Israeli musical
field, the members of Sfataim were able to distinguish themselves from other Arab
Jewish styles operating in the borderland by being able to classify themselves as
a more professional band.

Following the success of Sfataim, additional bands like Renaissance and
Sahara adopted the Israeli Moroccan style. The band Renaissance, also from the
town of Sderot, was founded by the nephews of one of Sfataim's founders and
mostly performs at family celebrations. The members of the band Sahara, playing in
a similar style, grew up in Netivot,[24] a town of mostly Moroccan Jews located near
Sderot. A distinctive Israeli Moroccan subgenre was developed by the musicians
Sushan and Amir Benaaiun, each of whom added unique elements to the Israeli
Moroccan style: Sushan, through the creation of dance music in the Moroccan
dialect of Arabic, and Benaaiun, through the addition of melancholic compositions
and impressive vocal qualities.

In sum, the crystallization of the musical borderland out of the Israeli
Yemenite style has, to a certain extent, created a site of resistance and empowerment for additional Arab Jewish ethnic groups. Although the Turkish and
Moroccan styles have gained this limited success, other Arab Jewish ethnic groups,
such as Libyan Jews, have not been able to produce an alternative musical style
recognizable within the borderland.

The Nonappearance of a Libyan Style

Despite the similarities of oppression experienced by people of Arab Jewish origin and their common existence at the Israeli margins (Alcalay 1993;
Bernstein and Swirsky 1982; Dahan-Kalev 2001; Khazzom 2003; Lavie 1996;
Motzafi-Haller 2001; Saporta and Yonah 2004; Shohat 1988, 1999a, 1999b, 2003),
the ethnic differences between various groups of Arab Jews have not disappeared
completely and a sense of "homelessness" is felt by some of the ethnic groups who
inhabit the borderland. Such is the case of the Libyan Jews, whose unique musical
style has remained largely invisible.

As a researcher and as an Arab Jew of Libyan origin, my interest in the activity
of popular Israeli musicians from Libya is an attempt to understand the position
of Arab Jewish ethnic groups that have not been able to produce an independent
musical style. As with most Arab Jews born in Israel, the socialization process
of becoming Israeli caused me to distance myself from the family culture of my

youth, and as an adult, I still have ambivalent feelings regarding such a search. Listening to Arab Jewish music in Hebrew or in Yemenite, Turkish, or Moroccan dialects is easier and more enjoyable for me, but when I hear music in the Libyan dialect, I feel somehow uneasy. At the same time, despite my delight in listening to these other Arabic dialects, I do not feel that they fully represent my Arab Jewish identity. In my search for popular Israeli Libyan musicians, I found David D'Or, Eli Luzon, and Tamir Gal, each of whom has a different strategy for molding a contemporary Israeli Libyan identity.

David D'Or, famous for his falsetto voice, is a well-known Israeli musician who blends the disparate genres of pop and dance, "classical," baroque, and Arab Jewish music. He started his musical career in the mid 1980s in lehaka tzevait, singing the music of SEY and light Israeli rock. During the 1990s, D'Or became successful in the Israeli musical field, and in 2004, he represented Israel in the Eurovision song contest. As a countertenor, he performs with symphony orchestras around the world, and in 1995, he performed for the late Pope John Paul II. His musical activity located him almost entirely outside the Arab Jewish borderland and connected him to the "world music" scene. By performing in local and global pop and Western classical musical fields, D'Or presents a strategy of an Arab Jewish musician who has shaped a quasi-Western identity.

In contrast with D'Or, Eli Luzon, an albino musician, has performed on the border of the Israeli Turkish and Israeli Yemenite styles from the beginning of his career. He has composed music according to Israeli Turkish stylistic criteria, but most of his albums have been produced by the Israeli Yemenite industry. Over the years, Luzon has gradually gained renown in the Israeli-pop and Arab Jewish borderland. His musical style oscillates between Arabic and Turkish tunes to Israeli pop tunes but with no direct references to his Libyan origin. His fifth album included Arabic songs in different dialects (Egyptian, Lebanese, Jordanian, and Palestinian), but with the notable absence of his mother tongue. Luzon shapes his Arab Jewish identity to communicate with the dominant Ashkenazi identity by interweaving Israeli pop and rock and Israeli Yemenite styles.

Tamir Gal grew up in a Jewish environment as the son of a Libyan Jewish mother and an Arab Druze father.[25] He is a key member of the Israeli Turkish style but is almost unknown to Ashkenazi audiences. Gal became famous by starring in independent films based on his life story, including one recounting the death of his younger sister from drug addiction. These films have attained a certain "cult" status in the slums. He sings mainly in Hebrew and Turkish, but not in the Libyan or Druze dialects. Gal seeks to create a pan-Arab–Jewish identity formed on the basis of shared social marginalization but with no direct connection to his exclusive ethnic origin.

These musicians represent the split of the Libyan community among three different models of articulating a current Arab Jewish identity: a quasi-Western identity almost entirely concealing one's Arab Jewish origin, an Arab Jewish hybrid that corresponds with the dominant Israeli identity; and a pan-Arab–Jewish identity that conceals the national differences among Arab Jews. The absence of Libyan ingredients in these strategies reflects an inability to define that specific Arab Jewish community through music.

This inability to articulate an Arab Libyan identity musically has strengthened my perception that my discomfort with the Libyan dialect is not been idiosyncratic—there is no place for the Israeli Libyan community and its musical practices within the borderland. This absence reveals, as well, the difficulty of other ethnic groups, such as Iraqis and Tunisians, to fully present themselves. Although recordings of Israeli Libyan music do not exist, some traces of Israeli Iraqi and Israeli Tunisian music can be found. For example, there is a recorded performance of "classical" music in the Iraqi dialect of Arabic by Yair Dalal, a muscian of Iraqi origin.[26] Another recording includes a rendition of two songs in the Tunisian dialect of Arabic by Etti Ankri, a musician of Tunisian origin.[27] These fragments suggest a limited presence of Iraqi and Tunisian musical styles but, given their continued erasure in the musical hierarchy, this presence is one that is almost impossible to reconstruct.

The Borderland Gains Power

In spite of the marginal location of the borderland and its partial representation of the diversity of Arab Jewish ethnic groups, it has, nonetheless, amassed extensive power in the Israeli musical field over the years. Arab Jewish musicians engage in three practices that may be described as "the politics of ploys" (de Certeau 1984:xxiv). These are: the commodification of the borderland through the creation of an alternative cassette and movie industry; collaborations between successful Arab Jewish musicians and unknown musicians to facilitate the latter's entry into the Israeli mainstream; and the tactical appropriation of Israeli parodies of Arab Jewish performers as a way of becoming recognizable to mainstream audiences. Although these ploys, in some ways, reinforce the dominance of Israeli Yemenite tunes and the internal hierarchy of ethnic styles, they also challenge the exclusive position of Yemenite musicians in Israeli public culture and thereby empower the expression of diversity within the Arab Jewish borderland.

Commodification of the Borderland

The exclusion of Arab Jewish musicians from producing albums in the dominant Israeli musical industry and the high demand for musical style among Arab Jewish audiences led to the constitution of an alternative industry controlled by Yemenite musicians in the mid 1970s. Although other music industries have developed in the borderland from the mid 1980s, which are for the most part connected to the Israeli Turkish style, they have not succeeded in challenging the dominance of the Israeli Yemenite style.

Despite limited funding, new recording industries, public relations, marketing and distributing, and filmmaking have all been established in the borderland. This revolution was made possible by new low-cost DIY technologies that have enabled the transformation of Arab Jews from passive consumers of music to creators of cultural products. This revolution began among Israeli Yemenite musicians who used domestic tape recorders to record haflât in Kerem Hatemanim and then distributed copies of these performances at a low cost.[28] The first cassette of this genre was made in 1974 at a wedding celebration of Asher Reuveni, the owner of a small record and electronic shop. In response to a growing demand, Reuveni began to sell cassette recordings of the live performance at his wedding and also began to produce others. He later founded A'achim Reuveni (Reuveni Brothers), one of the largest musical production companies of the borderland (Horowitz 1994:172–175; Regev and Seroussi 2004:204–205).

Through the 1980s, A'achim Reuveni and A'achim Ben-Mush (another large production company producing the Israeli Yemenite style) prospered as family businesses operating on the margins of the Israeli musical industry. They controlled the Arab Jewish market and promoted mostly Israeli Yemenite singers. Paradoxically, in recent years, in spite of the increasing legitimacy of the Yemenite style, these companies have suffered financially and the production of an album by a new artist has become a rare event for them. The reason for this financial decline stems largely from the growth of new production companies connected to the Israeli Turkish style and from an increase in pirating and forgery.[29]

The activities of these newer production companies working primarily with young and unknown musicians can be divided into two parts. Initially, the company gave new musicians exposure to Arab Jewish audiences by booking performances at family events and nightclubs and having them sing songs primarily in the Israeli Turkish and Israeli Yemenite styles. The second step was gaining the status of an Israeli superstar for these musicians by having them perform music that downplays Turkish influences while also increasing elements of Israeli Yemenite and pop music. Avi Gwetta's production company is a good example of this strategy in its promotion of Sarit Hadad, a daughter of Jewish immigrants from the mountainous district of East Caucasus. Their joint work initially afforded Hadad success as an Israeli Turkish singer, and later, it facilitated her entry into the Israeli mainstream to become one of Israel's most successful female pop stars. This strategy has given Gwetta's company a central position in the borderland industry, enabling him to work with more mainstream musicians.

At the end of the 1980s, an independent film industry emerged alongside the music industry affiliated mostly with the Israeli Turkish style. Key players in this genre were Yamin Mesika, a film producer, and Yirmi Kadoshi, a film producer and an actor who established a movie corporation together called Hafakot ha-Mizrach (The East Productions). Despite severe financial difficulties, they produced films set in the slums of Israeli society that depicted everyday Arab Jewish life. The stars of these productions were mostly singers of the Israeli Turkish style whose songs appeared on film soundtracks. The movies were screened infrequently in theaters and on major television channels; however, video copies were also sold at open markets or were available for rent at a limited number of video stores. Despite their limited distribution, the movies became a major hit among Arab Jewish audiences, and tens of thousands of copies were sold. Importantly, none of the musicians who participated in these movies crossed from the Turkish to the Yemenite style but perform in the borderland margins.

The movie *Kerem Hatikva* [The Vineyard of Hope] (Kadoshi and Sugbaker 1997) is one example of an exceptional cooperation between Hafakot ha-Mizrach and Israeli Yemenite musicians. The movie was filmed in Kerem Hatemanim during the mid 1990s and it refers to "the Yemenite children affair" from the 1950s.[30] The story begins with a young adopted girl arriving in the neighborhood from the United States to search for her biological parents of Yemenite origins. She rents a room in a house that belongs to a young man who broadcasts from a neighborhood pirate radio station. He presents her story over the radio, thereby raising a public debate concerning the missing Yemenite children. In the film, a revolt breaks out in the neighborhood against the Israeli establishment that is blamed for participating in the kidnapping of the babies. It ends tragically with the police killing an innocent neighbor and arresting the radio operators.

Although the music industry that gave the Israeli Yemenite style a central place has been challenged by these more recent commercial initiatives, this expansion has not reduced the dominance of Israeli Yemenite tunes. This dominance has been further reinforced by Arab Jewish efforts to place younger musicians in the Israeli mainstream through adopting the Yemenite style.

Musical Collaboration as an Empowering Practice

Throughout the 1990s, collaborations between successful Arab Jewish musicians and unknown musicians have facilitated the latter's entry into the Israeli mainstream. The figures who have led this movement include Shlomi Shabat, Ze-ev Nehama, and Kobi Oz. Their promotion of young musicians not only has been a means of empowerment but also a tool for training them to fit into the mainstream music scene that had initially been monopolized by Yemenite musicians.

Shlomi Shabat began his career on the margins of the Israeli musical field in the 1980s as a rock musician. He won artistic acknowledgement in the mid 1990s when he hybridized rock, arabesk, and South American music and became engaged in a musical collaboration with Arkadi Duchin, a respected Israeli rock musician of Ashkenazi origin. In spite of his Turkish origin, Shabat was not attached to the Israeli Turkish milieu but to the Yemenite elite. After he became successful, he began to tutor young Arab Jewish musicians by performing with them. The most recognizable example of this would be his relationship with Lior Narkis, a former singer of the Israeli Turkish style who began to diminish the Arabic and Turkish influence in his music while working with Shabat. A song that Shabat composed and performed with Narkis became a major hit in 2001, and this success transformed Narkis into a popular artist even among Ashkenazi audiences. Narkis represented

Israel in 2003 at the Eurovision song contest, which ensured his entrance into the Israeli mainstream.

Ze-ev Nehama, of mixed Ashkenazi and Arab Jewish origins, and Tamir Kalinski, of Ashkenazi origin, are from the band Ethnix, one of the most successful bands in Israel throughout the 1990s. By combining Eastern and Western components, this band located themselves on a fine line between Rock Yisraeli and the Arab Jewish borderland. They also assisted in bringing other Arab Jewish singers into the mainstream by having them downplay the Arabic elements in their music. In 1991, Ethnix invited Zehava Ben, a female musician of Moroccan origin who had been associated with the Israeli Turkish style, to perform the song "Keturne Masala" with them. Tremendously successful, this helped Ben to enter the Israeli mainstream as well as boosting the status of the band. Eyal Golan, an Israeli Yemenite singer, also cooperated with Ethnix after having already achieved some success in the Israeli Yemenite style. By the end of the 1990s, he started to record albums with the band and performed with them for several years to become an Israeli superstar.

The Tunisian Israeli singer Kobi Oz was brought up in the town of Sderot, the cradle of the Israeli Moroccan style, and he later became one of the central figures in the town's musical scene as the lead singer in the successful pop band Tipex. Although not associated with the Israeli Yemenite elite, he has become a central figure in the Israeli popular musical field because of his unique fusion of Arab Jewish elements with pop music. His use of colorful clothing, flamboyant jewelry, and comic behavior create a "carnival" atmosphere that has allowed him to claim a place in the Israeli musical mainstream. The song "Why Have You Gone from Him?" performed by Oz in 1997 with Sarit Hadad, under the supervision of Gwetta's production company, also helped Hadad move from the Israeli Turkish style to the Israeli mainstream. In an effort to help other young Arab Jewish musicians become mainstream singers, Oz has founded a musical label named Levantiny (Levantine, a derogatory term in Israel) in 1998 and thereby established himself as a musical producer.

The ongoing collaboration between established musicians and unknown newcomers has transformed the borderland into a creative force in the Israeli musical field. Although this success has challenged the exclusive position of Yemenite musicians and reinforced Arab Jewish ethnic diversity within the borderland's elite, Arab Jewish musicians who do not conform to this trend continue to remain outside the mainstream.

Appropriation of Israeli Parodies by Arab Jewish Performers

Despite the increasing popularity of the Arab Jewish musical borderland and its commercial success in Israel, it still is not classified as high quality. One of the current means of subordinating this music has been to parody it by emphasizing its syncretism. In its infancy, the Zionist movement labeled Arab Jewish music as "folklore," thereby making it representative of Middle Eastern authenticity. Because of the use of electronic instruments and Western methods of production and distribution, the new borderland hybrids could not be classified as folk music. Instead, the mainstream began to parody these musical styles as a demonstration of its low quality. A parody performed by the comic duo Guri Alfi and Asi Cohen for their television show Shidurei H'amaapecha (Revolutionary Broadcasts) in the summer of 2002 is a prominent example of this practice of subordination. The comedy makes fun of a fictitious Arab Jewish singer named Koko, who bears an unmistakable resemblance to Koko from Eilat, an Arab Jewish performer in the Israeli Turkish style who was famous mostly in the Israeli southern resort city of Eilat. In the show, Koko is dressed in a gaudy suit, speckled shirt, and gold chains. His attire clearly depicts a stereotypical representation of the Arab Jewish male, derogatively named in Israel as *ars* (an Arabic word meaning a pimp). In the Israeli mainstream, the figure of the ars is presented as "the opposite of political correctness, he switches very swiftly to verbal or physical violence, he sees women as his personal property or accessory . . . [and he is] ridiculously dand[ified]" (Livne 2002). In the skit, Koko's character sang short songs that parodied the musical styles of the borderland. The hit from the show was a song that quoted from notes left on windshields by truck drivers and movers who were illegally parked and hoped to avoid a ticket. The chorus was as follows: "Traffic cop, I'm unloading merchandise, I will be back, traffic cop I'm unloading merchandise, do not give me a parking ticket, be a man bro, I am Mizrahi too."

Koko has a sidekick named Steve, who accompanies him on the keyboard. Steve's silence is pronounced, making it difficult to determine his ethnic origin. He is dressed like an ars, but his name and skills on the electronic keyboard create doubts about his Arab Jewish origins. This scene of an ars singing ridiculous songs with a keyboard player at his side embodies a critique of the Arab Jewish musical borderland: linguistic shallowness and an unreasonable blend of East (Koko) and West (Steve) creating a musical hybrid lacking aesthetic value.

The presentation of the hybrid practices of subalterns as amusing is not at all unusual (Lavie and Swedenburg 1996:8). However, the response of Koko from Eilat, the musician who had been the butt of this joke, challenged the power of this parody. He began performing the song "Traffic Cop, I'm Unloading Merchandise" to gain access to the Ashkenazi audience, resulting in exposure in the Israeli media. Therefore, the allegedly linguistic shallowness and technological "wretchedness" of the Israeli Turkish genre was neutralized by his imitation of the mainstream. In this way, he disrupted the prevailing codes that legitimized ridicule of Arab Jews performers.

The counterparody of Koko is but one of many instances in which Arab Jews have tried to gain national exposure through presenting themselves as ludicrous. Although this may have helped Koko gain media exposure only for a short time, other musicians have been more successful in penetrating the mainstream to challenge its aesthetic codes. This is the case of Kobi Oz, who used self-parody to become a celebrated Israeli musician. His use in performance of Arab Jewish slang and bodily styles enable him to succeed in both the Israeli core and its fringes. For example, one of his latest hits, the cheerful disco song "Sami Ve-Somo" (Sami and Somo), describes the life of two Arab Jewish criminals who are fond of disco music. By laughing at Arab Jewish culture, Oz blurs the boundaries that separate the Israeli musical mainstream and Arab Jewish borderland.

The strategies presented above have empowered the borderland and strengthened the dominance of the Israeli Yemenite style through the positioning of this style as a signifier of diversity within the national community. Selective recognition of the borderland as a popular Israeli style raises questions regarding the power of musical border crossings to affect the demarcation of national borders and influence the Israeli–Arab Palestinian conflict.

Musical Borderland and National Boundaries in the Middle East

Since the outbreak of the second Palestinian Intifada in October 2000 and during the endless bloodbath that has ensued, the Arab Jewish musical practice of nationalizing the borderland has intensified dramatically. Numerous Arab Jewish musicians, especially from the Israeli Yemenite style, perform old SEY songs with a prominent "Middle Eastern" flavor. The extensive popularity of this practice within Israeli Jewish society demonstrates the complex relationship between musical border crossings and the demarcation of national borders.

As previously mentioned, Zionist culture molded by Ashkenazi Zionists hybridized Western culture with "Middle Eastern" components, thus granting legitimacy to the Israeli nation-building process. After the establishment of the Israeli state and with increasing pressure from people within the Arab Jewish musical borderland for recognition, the borderland began to function as an "authentic" Middle Eastern national practice, enabling Ashkenazim to shape a quasi-Western identity. With the current escalation of the Israeli–Palestinian conflict, the liminal location of Arab Jews caught between Israeli nationality and the diverse Arab community has become unbearable for them. Their need for national identification finds expression in a return to SEY, the genre that had previously marginalized them as carriers of folklore, and this has paradoxically reinforced Israeli national boundaries through their use of musical components that are associated with the Arab "enemy."

The practice of nationalizing the borderland reflects the complex location of musicians of the Israeli Yemenite style whose agency is recognizable only as a means of reinforcing Zionism. This suggests that the demarcation of Israeli national boundaries is not promoted by the state and its dominant group alone but is produced paradoxically by numerous Arab Jewish agents who have been located within these gaps. However, their taking up this Zionist mission has not ensured their inclusion within the Israeli mainstream. Ashkenazi demands to suppress the rebellious elements in Arab Jewish music combined with the need of Arab Jews to express their Otherness have doomed them to an everlasting uneasiness within Israeli society. Styles that have not adopted the national practice of the Israeli Yemenite style but struggle for cultural legitimacy, such as Israeli Turkish and Israeli Moroccan music, continue to occupy an uncertain position. They perform from the margins with no obvious commitment to Israeli nationalism in their move toward Arabic and Middle Eastern musical practices.

These contradictory outcomes establish the borderland as a field that allows movements across musical borders within the Middle East but in a way that does not challenge the ideological, national, and military practices defining national borders. It has not yet actualized its potential to become a creative presence in the Middle East that could challenge state policies by presenting a space in which Arabs and Jews do not exist in endless conflict. The marginal location of Arab Jews may fortify their efforts as creators of an alternative musical field, but at the same time it prevents them from challenging the very terms of the Israeli–Arab Palestinian divide.

Notes

Acknowledgments.   I wish to thank Yoram Bilu, Tamar El-Or, Carol Kidron, Smadar Lavie, Moshe Ophir, Tamar Rapoport, Dalia Markovich, and Yehouda Shenhav for their valuable comments, and Eli Bareket and Marko Martziano for the long discussions on the topic of Arab Jewish music. I would also like to express my deep gratitude to Ann Anagnost and to the three anonymous reviewers of *Cultural Anthropology* for helping me clarify my arguments.

1. The party Shinui, under Lapid, succeeded in the Israeli political field from the end of the 1990s, especially among the Zionist bourgeoisie, through formulating itself in opposition to the Shas party. Shas gathers together religious, "traditional," and secular Arab Jews to produce a separate ultraorthodox identity by reinventing its Arabic Jewish past. Shinui's campaign against Shas aimed at ending the governmental budget transfers to Shas's religious institutions and the recruitment of Arab Jewish young ultraorthodox students to the IDF.

2. Over the years, a number of terms have been used to portray this collective. The central terms were *Bnei Edot Ha-Mizrach* (ethnic groups of eastern origin), *Sefaradim* (Jews expelled from Spain in 1492, most of whom moved to Muslim countries), *yisrael ha-Shniya* (second Israel), and *Mizrahim* (Easterners). The contemporary term among radical scholars, which I have also chosen to use in this article, is *Yehudim Aravim* (Arab Jews). This term does not neglect the Arab components that exist within the collective, and it simultaneously contains and reflects the borderline location of this group.

3. This musical borderland is called by many names: Musicat Cassetot (cassette music) refers to its proliferation through the taping and distribution of cassette recordings; Musicat Ha'Thana Ha'Merkazit (central bus station music) refers to the stands located across Tel Aviv's central bus station where it was often sold; Musica Mizrahit (Mizrahi music) reflects the ethnic origin of its producers and consumers (see Regev and Seroussi 2004); and Musica Yisraelit Yam Tikonit (Israeli Mediterranean music) alludes to its Mediterranean origin (see Horowitz 1994, 1999). In this article, I present an alternative term, the Arab Jewish musical borderland that locates the production of this style on the border that separates Arabs from Jews. Because the article focuses on popular music, I do not refer to Arab Jewish musicians

identified with "World Music," such as Shlomo Bar (the bandleader of Ha'breira Ha'tivhit [Natural Choice]), Yair Dalal, and Ilana Elia.

4. On shaping national musical styles through the engagement of the global pop and rock music industry and aesthetics, see, for example, Frith 1987:74, Malm and Wallis 1992, Regev 1994, Wallis and Malm 1984.

5. On the issue of labeling Yemenite music folklore, see Horowitz 1994:34–35, 192–193; Regev and Seroussi 2004:196–199.

6. Important SEY female singers include Bracha Zphira, Esther Gamlielit, Shoshana Damari, and Yaffa Yarkoni. Apart from Yarkoni, who is of Caucasian origin, all the other singers are of Yemenite origin.

7. For more on Arab Jewish female musicians and especially Zphira, see Flam 1986, Hirshberg 1995:187–198, Regev and Seroussi 2004:196–197.

8. The term *lehakot ketzev* was borrowed from the British beat groups and was connected to the beatnik youth culture of the 1960s. For the origin of the term in Britain, see Wicke 1991:xi–xii. The activity of lehakot ketzev was first described in Regev and Seroussi 2004:138–144.

9. It is important to mention the television series *Yam Sel Dmaot* [Sea of Tears] (Kachlili 1998), which was named from one of Zoar Argov's greatest hits. The series was broadcast on Israeli television at the end of the 1990s and documents the crystallization of the Israeli Yemenite style.

10. The central figures were Avner Gadassi, Nissim Saroussi, Gabi Shooshan, and Shimi Tavori, all of whom are well-known Arab Jewish singers today. Two compilations of lehakot ketzev were published by the leading Israeli recording company Hed Arzi: *Israeli Rock of the 1960s* (1989) and *Israeli Beat Festival* (2003).

11. Ramla and Bat Yam are cities populated mainly by Arab Jewish working class people. Ramla is a city with a mixed population of Jews and Palestinians.

12. For postcolonial studies literature that focuses on the schizophrenic identity of subaltern groups, see, for example, Anzaldúa 1987; Ashcroft with Griffiths and Tiffin 1989; Bhabha 1984; Fanon 1967; Gilroy 1991, 1993; Trinh 1991; Guha and Spivak 1988.

13. The central figures were Moshe Ben-Mush, Yossi Levi (Daklon), Rami Danuch, Shlomo Mor (Doval'e), Ahuva Ozeri, and Shalom Shuvali. Over the years, only Ben-Mush, Daklon, and Ozeri have gained some success as Israeli musicians.

14. Regarding this fusion, see Halper with Seroussi and Squires-Kidron 1989; Horowitz 1994, 1999, 2005; Regev 1986, 1996, 2000; Regev and Seroussi 2004:191–212; Seroussi 1996, 2003; Shiloah and Cohen 1983.

15. The first stanzas of Ozeri's song are as follows: "Where is my soldier? / Where is my soldier? / When will I run towards him? / When will I feel his hand? / Where is my soldier? // Letters he did not send / Best regards he did not deliver / Please help, help me my friends / Letters he did not send / Best regards he did not deliver / Please help, help me my friends // Where is my soldier? / Where is my soldier? // Why is everybody so silent? / Why are they not speaking? / Is he not, is he not alive?" (1975).

16. The first stanzas of Saroussi's song are as follows: "I cannot suffer any more / to see them walking hand in hand / While she left me here alone // I cannot suffer any more / to see them walking across the street / While her heart is so close to him // Oh, why did you go from me? / Even though they warn me from you / I thought you gave me your heart" (1973).

17. The song of Argov is as follows: "I went to the employment bureau; he asked me: 'where are you from?' / ... I told him: 'from Morocco', he told me: 'go away' ... [in Hebrew] / We trusted the people [Zionist establishment] that separated us from our parents / We arrived [in Israel] and did not find any attention / Oh God, please have mercy on us

[in a mixed Libyan and Moroccan dialect of Arabic] // 'I went to the employment bureau'; he asked me: 'where are you from?' / . . . I told him: 'from Poland', he told me: 'please enter' . . . [in Hebrew] // . . . Seven days we depart by ship / We arrived to Haifa (a harbor town in the north of Israel) and took a rest / . . . From Haifa to Beit Lid [a military base], they are teaching us right and left [a military march] . . . [in a mixed Libyan and Moroccan dialect of Arabic]" (1990).

18. They did not succeed in becoming an acknowledged Israeli phenomenon. Prominent Moroccan musicians were Reimond Abexasis, Jo Amar, and Zoara el-Fasia. Iraqi musicians included Albert Chetrit (known as Filfel al-Masri), Salim and Daud al-Kuwati, Yossef Sem-Tov (known as Yossef al-A'awad), Salim al-Nur, and Suzan Saarabani (known as Iman).

19. The central figures are Margalit Tzanani, Zohar Argov, Haim Moshe, and the brothers Yishai and Nati Levy.

20. Arabesk music is a popular style in Turkey defined by local intelligentsia as a lowly style belonging to labor migrants who moved from the southeast of the country to urban areas of western Turkey. The name *arabesk* indicates the Arabic origin of the style, which is a hybrid of Arabic and Western pop music elements, and it is dominated by the playing of the bağlama. Through the mid-1980s, the style was co-opted by the Turkish state in its efforts to present itself as a European Muslim state connected to its Ottoman past (Stokes 1992, 2000).

21. The central figures of this style are Avi Biter, Siko Chaik, Yossi Eden, Offer Levy, and Linet. In addition, some non-Jewish singers from Turkey, such as the young singers Mugda and Agar, immigrated to the state of Israel for a short time and became well known from the end of the 1980s until the mid 1990s.

22. The marginalization of this style has not prevented it from gaining popularity in Turkey. A good example is a female singer named Linet, an Israeli singer who moved to Turkey in the mid 1990s only to become quite famous "in exile."

23. The Hebrew name of the song is "Nachlieli" (Wagtail), sung by Mati Caspi and written by Ehud Manor; the name of the Moroccan version is "Lala Haisa" (The old woman named Haisa) with lyrics by Haim Uliel.

24. The town of Netivot presents a unique case of producing an Israeli Moroccan Jewish identity by creating saints' shrines. See Ben-Ari and Bilu 1997.

25. Another singer of Israeli Druze descent is Sharif, who began as a child to sing in Hebrew and Arabic dialects in haflât in Israel for Arab Jewish and Palestinian audiences. The production of his albums within the Israeli Yemenite industry paved the way for him to attract an Arab Jewish audience base to become a central performer of the borderland by the 1990s.

26. Yair Dalal is a composer, violinist, and a prominent Jewish proponent of the 'ud. He is located outside the pop musical field in the "World Music" scene. Some of Dalal's prominent albums are: *Samar* (1997), *Al Ol* (1995), *Azazme* (1999), and *Perfume Road* (1999).

27. The two songs that the Israeli pop star Etti Ankri sings in the Tunisian dialect of Arabic are "Eshebo" (1998) of Cheb Khaled and "Tull Umri" [All My Life] (2001), which is her own composition.

28. For more on the development of a global "cassette culture," see Abu-Lughod 1989, El-Shawan 1987, Manuel 1993, Wong 1989–1990.

29. New production companies include Avi Gwetta, Moshe Gwetta, Roni Rotem, and Matana Yifrach.

30. This terrible episode, which occurred during the immigration wave of Jews from Yemen after the establishment of the state of Israel, refers to the disappearance of

228 CULTURAL ANTHROPOLOGY

hundreds or even thousands of babies (most of them Yemenite and others of different Arab and Muslim descent) from immigrant absorption centers and hospitals. According to Yemenite activists, these babies were kidnapped by Ashkenazi doctors and nurses, who sold them for adoption to Ashkenazi couples for a small payment. Parents were told that their children had died, but bodies or graves were never shown to them. Commissions appointed by the state to investigate these cases over the years, as a result of pressure from families and activists, have been inconclusive (Madmoni-Gerber 2003:237–239; Shohat 2003: 65–66).

References Cited

Abu-Lughod, Lila
    1989   Bedouins, Cassettes and Technologies of Public Culture. Middle East Report and Information 19(4):7–12.
Alcalay, Ammiel
    1993   After Jews and Arabs: Remaking Levantine Culture. Minneapolis: University of Minnesota Press.
Almog, Oz
    2000   The Sabra: The Creation of the New Jew. Berkeley: University of California Press.
Alvarez, Robert R.
    1995   The Mexican–US Border: The Making of an Anthropology of Borderlands. Annual Review of Anthropology 24:447–470.
Alvarez, Robert R., and George A. Collier
    1994   The Long Haul in Mexican Trucking: Traversing the Borderlands of the North and the South. American Ethnologist 21(3):606–627.
Ankri, Etti
    1998   Eshebo. *From* The Show: Etti Ankri and David D'Or. Tel Aviv: Hed Arzi.
    2001   Tul Umri. *From* Yam. Tel Aviv: NMC.
Anzaldúa, Gloria
    1987   Borderlands/La Frontera: The New Mestiza. San Francisco: Spinsters/Aunt Lute Foundation.
Argov, Zoar
    1990   I Went to the Employment Bureau. *From* Yam Sel Dmaot and To be a Human Being. Tel Aviv: Ben Moosh Production.
Asaf, Oded
    1988   The Song and the Artistic Music. Musica 12:6–11. [Hebrew]
Ashcroft, Bill, with Gareth Griffiths and Helen Tiffin, eds.
    1989   The Empire Writes Back. London: Routledge.
Benaaiun, Amir
    2002   You're Gone (an adaptation of *Now You're Gone* by Jeff Lynne). *From* Fall. Holon: Helicon.
Behar, Ruth
    1993   Translated Women: Crossing the Border with Esperanza's Story. Boston: Beacon Press.
Ben-Ari, Eyal, and Yoram Bilu
    1997   Saints' Sanctuaries in Israeli Development Towns: On a Mechanism of Urban Transformation. *In* Grasping Land: Space and Place in Contemporary Israeli Discourse and Experience. Eyal Ben-Ari and Bilu Yoram, eds. Pp. 61–68. Albany: State University of New York Press.

Bernstein, Debora, and Swirsky Shlomo
  1982   The Rapid Economic Development of Israel and the Emergence of the Ethnic Division of Labor. British Journal of Sociology 33(1):64–85.
Bhabha, Homi K.
  1984   Of Mimicry and Man: The Ambivalence of Colonial Discourse. October 28(Spring):125–133.
de Certeau, Michel
  1984   The Practice of Everyday Life. Steven Rendall, trans. Berkeley: University of California Press.
Dahan-Kalev, Henriette
  2001   You Are So Pretty, You Don't Look Moroccan. Israeli Studies 6(1):1–14.
Dalal, Yair
  1995   Al Ol. Saint-Hubert: Magada.
  1997   Samar. Saint-Hubert: Magada.
  1999   Azazme. Saint-Hubert: Magada.
  1999   Perfume Road. Saint-Hubert: Magada.
Druyan, Nitza
  1979   The Growth and the Development of the Yemenite Jewish Community in Eretz Yisrael in the Years 1881–1914. Ph.D. dissertation, Department of Jewish History, Bar-Ilan University.
El-Shawan, Castelo-Branco Salwa
  1987   Some Aspects of the Cassette Industry in Egypt. World of Music 29(2):3–45.
Fanon, Franz
  1967[1952]   Black Skin, White Masks. London: Pluto Press.
Flam, Gila
  1986   Bracha Zefira: A Case Study of Acculturation in Israeli Song. Asian Music 17(2):108–125.
Frith, Simon
  1987   The Industrialization of Popular Music. In Popular Music and Communication. James Lull, ed. Pp. 53–77. Newbury Park, CA: Sage.
Fusco, Coco
  1989   The Border Art Workshop/Taller de Artfronterizo: Interview with Guillermo Gomez-Pena and Emily Hicks. Third Text 7(Summer):53–76.
Gilroy, Paul
  1991[1987]   "There Ain't No Black in the Union Jack": The Cultural Politics of Race and Nation. Chicago: University of Chicago Press.
  1993   The Black Atlantic: Modernity and Double Consciousness. London: Verso Books.
Gross, Joan, David McMurray, and Ted Swedenburg
  1996   Arab Noise and Ramadan Nights: Rai, Rap and Franco-Maghrebi Identities. In Displacement, Diaspora, and Geographies of Identity. Smadar Lavie and Ted Swedenburg, eds. Pp. 119–155. Durham, NC: Duke University Press.
Guha, Ranajit, and Gayatri Charavorty Spivak, eds.
  1988   Selected Subaltern Studies. Foreword by Edward W. Said. New York: Oxford University Press.
Gupta, Akhil, and James Ferguson
  1992   Beyond "Culture": Space, Identity, and the Politics of Difference. Cultural Anthropology 7(1):6–23.
Hagar, Steven
  1984   Hip Hop: The Illustrated History of Break Dancing, Rap Music, and Graffiti. New York: St. Martin's Press.

230   CULTURAL ANTHROPOLOGY

Halper, Jeff, with Edwin Seroussi and Pamela Squires-Kidron
    1989   Musica Mizrakhit: Ethnicity and Class Culture in Israel. Popular Music 8(2):131–
    141.
Heyman, Josiah McC.
    1994   The Mexico-United States Border in Anthropology: A Critique and Reformula-
    tion. Journal of Political Ecology 1(1):43–65.
Hirshberg, Yehoash
    1995   Music in the Jewish Community of Palestine 1880–1948. Oxford: Clarendon
    Press.
Horowitz, Amy
    1994   Musica Yam Tikhonit (Israeli Mediterranean Music): Cultural Boundaries and
    Disputed Territories. Ph.D. dissertation, Department of Folklore and Israeli Studies,
    University of Pennsylvania.
    1999   Israeli Mediterranean Music: Straddling Disputed Territories. Journal of American
    Folklore 112:450–463.
    2005   Dueling Nativities: Zehava Ben Sings Umm Kulthum. *In* Palestine, Israel, and the
    Politics of Popular Culture. Rebecca L. Stein and Ted Swedenburg, eds. Pp. 202–230.
    Durham, NC: Duke University Press.
Israeli Beat Festival
    2003[1969]   Yoav Kutner, ed. Tel Aviv: Hed Arzi.
Israeli Rock of the 1960s
    1989   Yoav Gra, ed. Tel Aviv: Hed Arzi.
Kachlili, Ron, dir.
    1998   Yam Sel Dmaot (Sea of Tears). 50 min × 4. Herzliyya: United Studios of
    Herzliyya. [Hebrew]
Kadoshi, Yirmi, and Ilana Sugbaker, dirs.
    1997   Kerem Hatikva (The Vineyard of Hope). 60 min. Kefar Sabba: Hafakot
    ha-Mizrach. [Hebrew]
Khazzom, Aziza
    2003   The Great Chain of Orientalism: Jewish Identity, Stigma Management, and Ethnic
    Exclusion in Israel. American Sociological Review 68(4):481–510.
Kimmerling, Baruch
    1998   Political Subcultures and Civilian Militarism in a Settler-Immigrant Soci-
    ety. *In* Security Concerns: Insights from the Israeli Experience. Daniel Bar-
    Tal, Dan Jacobson, and Aharon Klieman, eds. Pp. 395–415. Stanford: JAI
    Press.
    2001   The Invention and Decline of Israeliness: State, Society, and the Military. Berkeley:
    University of California Press.
Krims, Adam
    2000   Rap Music and the Poetics of Identity. Cambridge: Cambridge University Press.
Lavie, Smadar with A. Hajj and Forest Rouse
    1993   Notes on the Fantastic Journey of the Hajj, His Anthropologist, and Her American
    Passport. American Ethnologist 20(2):363–384.
    1996   Blow-Ups in the Borderzones: Third World Israeli Authors' Groupings for Home.
    In Displacement, Diaspora, and Geographies of Identity. Smadar Lavie and Ted
    Swedenburg, eds. Pp. 55–96. Durham, NC: Duke University Press.
Lavie, Smadar, and Ted Swedenburg
    1996   Introduction: Displacement, Diaspora, and Geographies of Identity. *In* Displace-
    ment, Diaspora, and Geographies of Identity. Smadar Lavie and Ted Swedenburg, eds.
    Pp. 1–25. Durham, NC: Duke University Press.

Livne, Nery
  2002   The New A'arsim. Haaretz, June 9. [Hebrew]
Madmoni-Gerber, Shoshana
  2003   Orientalism Reconsidered: Israeli Media and the Articulation of Resistance. Cultural Studies 17(2):230–249.
Malm, Krister, and Roger Wallis
  1992   Media Policy and Music Activity. London: Routledge.
Manuel, Peter Lamarche
  1993   Cassette Culture: Popular Music and Technology in North India. Chicago: University of Chicago Press.
Marranci, Gabriele
  2003   Pop-Raï: from Local Tradition to Globalization. *In* Mediterranean Mosaic: Popular Music and Global Sounds. Goffredo Plastino, ed. Pp. 101–120. London: Routledge.
Motzafi-Haller, Pnina
  2001   Scholarship, Identity and Power: Mizrahi Women in Israel. Signs: Journal of Women in Culture and Society 26(3):697–734.
Nini, Yehuda
  1982   Yemen and Zion: The Jews of Yemen, 1800–1914. Hassifriya Haziyonit: Jerusalem. [Hebrew]
Ozeri, Ahuva
  1975   Where is my Soldier. *From* Where is my Soldier. Tel Aviv: Achim Reuveni.
Perkins, William E.
  1996   The Rap Attack: An Introduction. *In* Droppin' Science: Critical Essays on Rap Music and Hip Hop. Pp. 1–45. Philadelphia, PA: Temple University Press.
Raz-Krakotzkin, Amnon
  1993   Exile within Sovereignty: Toward a Critique of the "Negation of Exile" in Israeli Culture. Teoria Ve-biqoret 4:23–55. [Hebrew]
Regev, Motti
  1986   The Musical Soundscape as a Contest Area: "Oriental Music" and Israeli Popular Music. Media, Culture and Society 8(3):343–356.
  1992   Israeli Rock, or a Study in the Politics of "Local Authenticity." Popular Music 11(1):1–14.
  1994   Producing Artistic Value: The Case of Rock Music. Sociological Quarterly 35(1):85–102.
  1996   Musica Mizrahit, Israeli Rock and National Culture in Israel. Popular Music 15(3):275–284.
  1997   Organization Fluency, Organizational Blocks, Cultural Relevance: The Case of the Music Industry in Israel. Teoria Ve-biqoret 10:115–132. [Hebrew]
  2000   To Have a Culture of our Own: On Israeliness and its Variants. Ethnic and Racial Studies 23(2):223–247.
Regev, Motti, and Edwin Seroussi
  2004   Popular Music and National Culture in Israel. Berkeley: University of California Press.
Rosaldo, Renato
  1989   Culture and Truth: The Remaking of Social Analysis. Boston: Beacon Press.
Rose, Tricia
  1994   Black Noise: Rap Music and Black Culture in Contemporary America. Hanover, NH: Wesleyan University Press.
Rouse, Roger
  1991   Mexican Migration and the Social Space of Postmodernism. Diaspora 1(1):8–23.

232 CULTURAL ANTHROPOLOGY

Saldivar, Jose D.
    1997 Border Matters: Remapping American Cultural Studies. Berkeley: University of California Press.
Saporta, Ishak, and Yossi Yonah
    2004 Pre-Vocational Education: The Making of Israel's Ethno-Working Class. Race, Ethnicity and Education 7(3):251–275.
Saroussi, Nissim
    1973 I Can't Any More. *From* The Hit Parade of Nissom Saroussi. Tel Aviv: Israeli Artists.
Schade-Poulsen, Marc
    1999 Men and Popular Music in Algeria. Austin: University of Texas Press.
Seroussi, Edwin
    1996 Popular Music in Israel: The First Fifty Years. Cambridge, MA: Harvard College Library.
    2003 Yam Tikhoniyut: Transformations of the Mediterranean in Israeli Music. *In* Mediterranean Mosaic: Popular Music and Global Sounds. Goffredo Plastino, ed. 179–198. New York: Routledge.
Shafir, Gershon
    1989 Land, Labor and the Origins of the Israeli–Palestinian Conflict, 1882–1914. Cambridge: Cambridge University Press.
Shenhav, Yehouda
    2003 The Clock, the Cage and the Fog of Sanctity: The Zionist Mission and the Role of Religion among Arab-Jews. Nations and Nationalism 9(4):511–531.
Shiloah, Amnon, and Eric Cohen
    1983 The Dynamics of Change in Jewish Oriental Ethnic Music in Israel. Ethnomusicology 279(2):227–251.
Shohat, Ella
    1988 Sephardim in Israel: Zionism from the Point of View of its Jewish Victims. Social Text 19–20:1–35.
    1999a The Invention of the Mizrahim. Journal of Palestine Studies XXIX(1):5–20.
    1999b Taboo Memories, Diasporic Visions: Columbus, Palestine, and Arab-Jews. *In* Performing Hybridity. May Joseph and Jennifer Fink, eds. Pp. 31–156. Minnesota: University of Minnesota Press.
    2003 Rupture and Return: Zionist Discourse and the Study of Arab Jews. Social Text 21(2):49–74.
Stokes, Martin
    1992 The Arabesk Debate: Music and Musicians in Modern Turkey. Oxford: Clarendon Press.
    1994 Introduction. *In* Ethnicity, Identity and Music. Pp. 1–27. Oxford: Berg.
    2000 East, West, and the Arabesk. *In* Western Music and its Others. Georgina Born and David Hesmondhalgh, eds. Pp. 213–233. Berkeley: University of California Press.
Swedenburg, Ted
    2001 Arab "World Music" in the US. Middle East Report 31(Summer):34–41.
Torstrick, Rebecca L.
    1993 Raising and Rupturing Boundaries: The Politics of Identity in Acre, Israel. Ph.D. dissertation, Department of Anthropology, Washington University.
Trinh, Minh-ha T.
    1991 When The Moon Waxes Red: Representation, Gender and Cultural Politics. New York: Routledge.

Wallis, Roger, and Krister Malm
  1984   Big Sounds from Small Peoples. London: Constable.
Wicke, Peter
  1991   Rock Music: Culture, Aesthetics and Sociology. Cambridge: Cambridge University Press.
Wong, Deborah
  1989–1990   Thai Cassettes and Their Covers: Two Case Histories. Asian Music 21(1):78–104.

ABSTRACT   *This article deals with the emergence of a popular musical field as an Arab Jewish borderland on the margins of the Middle East conflict. This borderland has crystallized as a site of empowerment for some Arab Jews, mostly Yemenites, and has simultaneously encompassed multiple ethnic conflicts. The conflicts have emerged between the borderland itself and the dominant Israeli musical style and concurrently through the inner struggles between different Arab Jewish styles competing for cultural supremacy. This study demonstrates the paradoxical nature of the Arab Jewish musical borderland, in which frequent crossings of musical borders not only fail to breach national boundaries but also serve to sustain them.* [borderland, Israel, Middle East, Arab Jews, popular music]

Part II
Global Perspectives

[9]

Are we global yet? Globalist discourse, cultural formations and the study of Zimbabwean popular music[1]

THOMAS TURINO

As a cultural category "global" is at once too all-encompassing and vague, and too deeply, indexically, tied to the contemporary discourse naturalizing increased capitalist expansion and control throughout the world – a discourse referred to here as "globalism". The article suggests a different framework for thinking about trans-state cultural processes involving three ideal-type social formations: immigrant communities, diasporas and cosmopolitan formations. A discussion of popular music in Zimbabwe forms the final part of the paper and is intended to illustrate the usefulness of this framework. Following the work of many, the author recognizes the imperialist processes of capitalist globalization but suggests that ethnomusicologists avoid naturalizing the processes by eschewing terms and premises embedded in globalist discourse except in cases where the phenomenon in question affects everyone everywhere – that is, where it is actually global in the literal sense.

In step with scholars in many disciplines, attention to globalization as a process, and the use of "global" as a cultural category, exploded in ethnomusicology during the 1990s and continues to gather steam in the new century. Since the 1990s, granting agencies have created special funding initiatives for the study of "global" processes.[2] Over the last five years the administration of my university, seemingly one among many, has been pushing special initiatives for the

[1] Partial versions of this paper were delivered at Northwestern University and the University of California–Santa Barbara in 2002 and 2003. I thank the participants of those colloquia for their helpful comments and criticism. I would also like to thank Tom Bassett, Tony Perman, Charles Capwell, Bruno Nettl, Gabriel Solis and my anonymous readers for their comments and criticism of earlier drafts. Special thanks goes to Jennifer Munroe for her careful reading of various drafts. I am grateful to the Centre for Advanced Study at the University of Illinois for the fellowship that allowed me to undertake this work.

[2] Throughout this paper, I use quotation marks to indicate the use of a term in relation to its "home" discourse – for example, "global" when used within the discourse of globalism, or "national" when used within the discourse of nationalism, or "traditional" and "modern" when used in the sense projected by the discourse of modernity.

52   BRITISH JOURNAL OF ETHNOMUSICOLOGY VOL.12/ıı 2003

interdisciplinary study of "global culture" as if it were a new objective reality, an already established fact. The word *global* is used widely in the mass media and is becoming common in cosmopolitan conversation. In these contexts, as in much ethnomusicological work, the meaning of the term is varied, and the thrust behind *globalism* as a discourse is still too often left unexamined or forgotten. Processes once conceptualized as "international" relations, specified types of economic-power relations, and cultural interchanges between specific sites and groups of people, are now glossed as "global cultural flows", "local–global relations", the "global economy", and "global culture". Why this shift in focus and terminology specifically in the 1990s?

In the first part of this essay, I summarize problems with globalism as a discourse and as an analytical approach. The second part of the paper provides an alternative to the concept of *global culture* for studying trans-state cultural and musical processes. The framework involves three different ideal-type cultural formations: *immigrant communities*, *diasporas* and *cosmopolitan formations*. In contrast to recent approaches that emphasize trans-local cultural *flows* and Appadurai's celebrated notion of *scapes*, the approach advocated here is an old-fashioned one fundamentally grounded in individual and group subjectivities and socialization. I find the concepts of flows and scapes too abstract and believe that the actual site of social and cultural dynamism resides in specific people's lives and experiences. The grounding of analysis in *personhoods* is especially important when dealing with ideas, products, practices and processes that are geographically diffuse. The third portion of the paper is devoted to a specific case study of popular music in Zimbabwe, especially as it involves middle-class artists and audience members who are part of the capitalist–cosmopolitan cultural formation. The case study is intended to illustrate why the concept of cosmopolitanism is more useful than globalist approaches for understanding cultural dynamics in this and other similar instances.

Terminology

Nowadays, the word *global* is sometimes used as a synonym for "transnational" or "international" (e.g., Jones 2001:58; Perrone and Dunn 2001:7), or simply "foreign" (*Time,* 8 December 2002: Y9). *Global* is also commonly used to designate the spread of something to a number of non-contiguous sites in different parts of the world, without indicating who and how many people are involved in these different places (e.g., Waxer 2002:17). The term sometimes simply implies "not local," and this usage is both a product and illustration of the growing acceptance of a "local–global" dichotomy that enlists the terms as cultural categories. Roland Robertson locates the meaning of the term *global* "in primary reference to the dual aspects of the intensifying connectivity (Tomlinson 2000) and the spreading and deepening consciousness of the world-as-a-whole" (Robertson 1992, 2001a; quote from 2002b:6254) – indicating the ground of both objective relations and subjective recognition.

Following the *Oxford English Dictionary*, I want to reserve the term *global* to describe phenomena that literally encompass the geography and populations of the globe.[3] By this definition, the holes in the 0-zone, the potential of nuclear war, and global warming are, indeed, global problems because they affect everyone everywhere. The events of childbirth and sunrise are global; radio may, by now, be almost global. E-mail, the web, CD players, "global investing", "world music", and salsa are not yet global phenomena because there are numerous places and populations that cannot afford to invest or to have these machines and that are not involved with these musical styles. By the literal definition, the state system is global whereas nation-states are not (see Hobsbawm 1990). As a descriptive category, then, *global* refers to objective conditions and is thus distinct from Robertson's idea of *globality*, based in a subjective consciousness of "the world-as-a-whole". If radical world-wide climate changes affect people everywhere, the changes are global in scale regardless of whether their effects are conceptualized only in relation to one's own locale or through a consciousness of the world-as-a-whole.

Geographers such as Tom Bassett (pers. comm.) and Philip Kelly (1999) argue that categories such as *local, regional, state, trans-state, global* are social concepts referring to the geographical scale or reach of a given phenomenon or process. These categories are not oppositional, but rather are nested, the larger scales necessarily including the smaller. As summarized by Kelly (1999:388), conceptualizing *the global* also becomes a problem of whether one is thinking merely in terms of reach – e.g., involving a smattering of people in a good number of non-contiguous countries – or in terms of depth, that is, phenomena that affect whole populations of all countries. To rescue the term from its current discursive use of naturalizing capitalist expansion, it is important to emphasize the effects of a given phenomenon on whole populations in *all* regions of the world. In this regard Kelly notes that "whole world regions and enclaves (both spatial and social) are not a part of globalization processes" and that, "for academics and other elites with access to travel, email, the World Wide Web, etc., the idea of globalization is altogether more real than for those about whom many of us write" (1999:388).

While Kelly seems to associate *globalization* directly with capitalist expansion and cosmopolitan connectivity, the term could be used analytically to describe the process or intent of achieving global reach (in the literal breadth–depth sense), be it for imperialist or economic purposes, religious conversion, or for programmes of ecological survival or social justice. That is, the term could be used to describe any programme or phenomenon that affects or is intended to affect the world-as-a-whole (Robertson 1990, 2001b). The problem is that the terms *global* and *globalization* are increasingly being indexically tied to one particular programme – the expansion of capitalist cosmopolitanism.

I use the term *globalism* specifically to refer to the contemporary discourse that indexically equates "global" and "globalization" with free market capitalism and its technologies, ideologies, institutions and products. Let me be

---

[3] Tracing the term back to 1892, the *OED* defines *global* as "Pertaining to or embracing the totality of a number of items, categories, etc.; comprehensive, all-inclusive, unified; total; pertaining to or involving the whole world; world-wide; universal".

54   BRITISH JOURNAL OF ETHNOMUSICOLOGY VOL.12/ıı 2003

clear on this point. Whereas *global* and *globalization* could be used simply to describe scale and universalist projects, respectively, without denoting a particular phenomenon or the project's success, they are increasingly being appropriated as terms to *naturalize* the spread of a particular economic–political–cultural complex.

The manner in which a given discourse *naturalizes* a set of ideas (i.e., makes them common sense, unnoticed; constructs them as reality) is easily observed in relation to globalism because of the recent emergence of this discourse. The first stage involves the highly redundant juxtaposition of a particular set of terms (e.g., global/capitalist, global economy/free market economy) within public discourse across a variety of fields. Through redundant juxtaposition, gradually strong indexical relations are established between the paired terms such that one can come to replace the other, i.e., they become synonyms (global = capitalist). Indexicality within the discourse is key to making the substitutions seem actual and natural; that is, we have heard the terms together so frequently in our actual experience that we often do not even notice when one starts to replace the other. Through this process, the objects of the original signs become fused and a new conception of reality emerges: global culture = capitalist cosmopolitan culture. "We are the world."

1. Globalism

It is not a coincidence that the discourse of globalism came into academic vogue in the United States during the 1990s, in step with the "defeat of communism" in the Soviet Union and the fall of the Berlin Wall in 1989 (see Robertson 1990:16). During the cold war, Soviet/Chinese communism and American/European/Japanese capitalism were the two leading contenders for creating trans-state social orders. With one contender severely weakened, the contemporary discourse of globalism emerged in the political, corporate, journalistic and academic spheres both as a victory song and, dialectically, to ideologically naturalize the increasing reach of cosmopolitan capitalism.

Although the *discourse* of globalism is new, imperialist projects connecting different parts of the world in the interest of economic control and gain are not. Wallerstein and Kurth identify European colonialism of the sixteenth century, under the hegemon of the Habsburg Empire and culminating in the Thirty Years War, as the first period comparable to, and in some senses undergirding, the present one. Kurth points to European and American expansionism in the nineteenth century as a second period of globalization under the hegemon of the British Empire and culminating in World Wars I and II, "which some historians have called a second thirty years war (1914–45)". Kurth identifies the beginning of the third period of globalization with the collapse of the Soviet Union, and sees the United States as the successor to the Habsburg and British Empires for this third phase.

> Its leadership is facilitated and legitimated by the three great international, now global economic institutions, the International Monetary Fund (IMF),

the World Bank, and the World Trade Organization (WTO).

(Kurth 2001:6285–6)[4]

Against this backdrop, colonialism, anti-colonial nationalist movements and globalization should not be understood in opposition to each other but rather should be seen as three interwoven processes within the same trajectory of modernist-capitalist expansion throughout the world (see especially Hobsbawm 1990:37–38, 40). One clear effect of nationalist movements in the colonized regions of the world was to open new minds to "modern" thinking and desires, and thus new markets for industrial commodities, much as European colonists had done previously. The vanguards of most twentieth-century post-colonial nationalist movements operated from the basis of the discourse of modernity (e.g., see Gellner 1983; Chatterjee 1986), and cultural nationalism typically involved the "reform" of indigenous (so-called 'traditional') practices and art forms in light of "modern" cosmopolitan features, contexts, ethics and aesthetics (Turino 2000). Nationalists from China to Zimbabwe to Bulgaria to Brazil used the "traditional–modern" dichotomy to define cultural practices and, with state education and resources, to usher people towards "the modern" (Turino 2004a).[5] Nationalism in the twentieth century was a modernist project, and its functionaries served as key conduits between indigenous villages, states, and interstate relations and knowledge.

While local middle-class and elite nationalists played a central role in "modernizing" people the world over, and organizing larger "rational" bureaucratic units for other states and corporations to work with, by the end of the twentieth century, post-colonial states that tried to assert independence were seen as impediments to trans-state corporations – for example in the form of tariffs, "nationalized" industries and legislation to protect "national" workers and resources. Thus at one stage, nationalist movements were important for diffusing and organizing modernist-capitalist ideas and relations in many parts of the world, but by the second half of the twentieth century, nationalist tenets of state independence and sovereignty in the "third world" were seen as an impediment to the progression of trans-state corporations" growth and control.

Under the banner of globalism, liberal democracy and economic liberalism are now backed by the "relatively monolithic … 'Washington consensus,' in whose terms the market oriented development model is the only feasible model for a new global regime of accumulation and, accordingly, the structural adjustment it calls for must be carried out worldwide" (de Sousa Santos 2001:6284). Over the last several decades, the US state has redefined liberal democracy and economic liberalism as universal human rights, and the US government has used these ideas to legitimate expansionist war. The unprovoked attack on Iraq

---

[4] One could also argue that competition between emerging blocs of capitalist power – the US, the EU and in Asia – is key to contemporary dynamics and globalist discourse, with capitalist relations, institutions and competition being more important engines than any given state or regional bloc.

[5] Citing a 1964 article by Parsons, Robertson notes that "Communism" and "democratic capitalism" have constituted alternative forms of acceptance of modernity (1990:17).

for regime change, marketed as "Operation Freedom Iraq", is the most obvious recent example. In addition to direct military intervention to further the
"Washington consensus", the sovereignty of weaker states is also more commonly threatened by trans-state funding agencies and multinational corporations in the form of structural adjustment programmes and other arrangements.

Economic structural adjustment programmes (ESAPs) were instituted in
countries in Africa, Asia and Latin America during the last decades of the
twentieth century. These programmes required post-colonial states to reduce
government spending on health, education, social programmes and development
projects (which would make them more independent) and halt economic protec-
tionism; IMF/WB loans were contingent on governments falling in line. State
and business leaders in many places benefited from the influx of foreign aid and
loans and so took the bait; probably in many cases the loans were seen as temporary. Kenneth Kaunda, former president of Zambia, commented to me after
a lecture that IMF/WB loan programmes represented a form of neocolonialism
(pers. comm. May 2003).[6] Robert Mugabe expressed the same sentiments in
his Independence Day speech in 1993: "The World Bank and the IMF are the
new colonisers" (*The Sunday Mail*, 18 April 1993), yet Mugabe's government
adopted an ESAP in Zimbabwe in the early 1990s. The Zimbabwe case provides
merely one of many examples of the economic hardships and decline that result
from such programmes (e.g., Kanji and Jazdowska 1993; MacGarry 1993).
Measures of this type, and trans-state economic agreements that allow major
corporations access to cheap labour, natural resources and expanding markets
the world over are the basis of what is discursively framed as "the global economy". Similarly, *global culture* is discursively constructed in relation to capitalist products and technologies within the context of expanding markets.

Global culture in advertising and academia

Roland Robertson notes that since the 1980s the increased attention on *the
global* "within intellectual discourse has proceeded in tandem with the ever
more conspicuous invocation of the adjectival form in promotional and advertising contexts" (2001b:6254). "Global" and "global culture" are now commonly employed to describe and advertise capitalist institutions, products,
practices and technologies – McDonald's, computers, Coca-Cola, Visa cards,
the "World-Wide Web", "global investing", the "World Bank", "world music",
Nike running shoes – by corporations and scholars alike. In their academic
article "Globalization and World Culture", Boli and Lechner write: "Popular
culture increasingly creates *global tastes*." "In Beijing, meanwhile, McDonald's
American origins can be attractive to upwardly mobile Chinese as a symbol
of participation in *global society*..." Referring to the "worldbeat" or "world
music" market, they write: "Adapting indigenous instruments or rhythms,
African musicians participate in a *global musical movement*" (all quotes, 2001:
6263, emphasis added). In all these instances and many like them, it is difficult

---

[6] This statement was made to me in conversation after his talk.

to discern the meaning of global. How many companies and investors in how many countries have to be involved in "global investing" to make it pertain to the world-as-a-whole? Are relatively small groups of "world music" fans in a dozen countries enough to designate this a global musical movement?

Robert Burnett notes that the "big five" music companies stress their global reach with slogans such as: "The world is our audience" (Time Warner); "Think globally – act locally" (Sony); "A truly global organization" (Thorn-EMI); "A European based global recording company" (Polygram); and "Globalize local repertoire" (BMG) (1996:8). His study of the complexities of penetrating music markets in specific places and marketing particular styles beyond their sites of origin makes it clear that such slogans are partially expressions of corporate desire and intent, partially advertising to help realize the desire, and partially descriptions of what is occurring to the extent that their marketing intentions have been realized. It is important to separate these three different aspects in relation to the discourse of globalism in advertising and scholarship more generally.

Critical voices such as Anthony D. Smith argue that "the idea of a 'global culture' is a practical impossibility, except in interplanetary terms" (1990: 171) and, like many, he ties the idea to a new type of capitalist imperialism and Americanization (Smith 1995:16–17). Others such as Robertson, Boli and Lechner, Erlmann, Taylor, and many ethnomusicologists see capitalism as a prominent engine but seem to accept the idea of a "global culture" as fact (e.g., Erlmann 1999:6; Taylor 1997:xv, 198). By the end of the 1990s, the notions that "we *now* live in a global era" and that a *global culture* exists simply seemed to be assumed by ever-growing numbers of people in cosmopolitan circles. The ubiquity of phrases like "we *now* live in a *global world*" (world-world? global-globe?) suggests new clusters of meaning attached to the term, as well as buzz-word excesses that have inspired creative responses: "globologna!"

Like advertising and political statements, academic work is an important node of discourse production that shapes and guides emerging conceptions of reality within a given cultural formation. The terms we use and the way we use them matter – both for the acuity of thought and politically. At the present time, the terms *global* and *global culture* seem so deeply entrenched in the discourse naturalizing capitalist expansion that their very use by academics may contribute to the process. Redundancy of terminology across fields (advertising, academia, journalism, corporate and political statements) is crucial to the process of making given conceptions common sense. Without careful definition, the continuing use of a politically loaded terminology helps to naturalize and actualize the conceptions through an iconicity with their uncritical and even blatantly self-serving use in other fields such as advertising and political discourse. Thus book titles including the phrases *Global Pop* (Taylor 1997), *Global Jukebox* (Burnett 1996), *Global Imagination* (Erlmann 1999), *Excursions in World Music* (Nettl et al. 1997), help lend reality to the concept of a global culture even if the books' contents make its problematic nature plain. What emerges is a kind of critical belief rather than an inquiry into the status of the phenomenon or problem from an initial position of doubt or disbelief (global culture? world music? where?

58 BRITISH JOURNAL OF ETHNOMUSICOLOGY VOL.12/ii 2003

when? among whom?). As ideas and terms become more widely diffused and increasingly taken for granted across fields, it becomes simultaneously more difficult and more important to begin from a position of critical disbelief regarding the premises of the discursive practice.

Of time and space

The framework developed in my book on Zimbabwean popular music (2000) was meant as an alternative to globalism. An argument in that book is that the discourse of globalism is to space what the discourse of modernity is to time. As Fabian suggested in *Time and the Other* (1983), the discourse of modernity assigns peoples and practices designated as "traditional" to the past and a kind of timelessness; those designated as "modern" are the present and future, "our time". While certain types of modernist movements and occupations have use for "the traditional" and the past (e.g., nationalists, historians, ethnomusicologists), in the main this discourse woos people to join the modernist cultural formation. I believe this is clearly documented in the Zimbabwe case (see Turino 2000, chapters 4 and 5). The discourse of modernity hijacks contemporary time to universalize a particular sociocultural formation. In similar fashion, the discourse of globalism hijacks the totalized space of the Earth for a particular cultural formation – "leaving people with alternative life ways no place to be and no place to go" (Turino 2000:6).

Just as the traditional–modern dichotomy was a paradigmatic substitution for the earlier social evolutionist primitive–civilized diad, the local–global contrast is the new paradigmatic substitution for the traditional and the modern. As a discourse becomes discredited or outmoded, its terms and premises come to be recognized as problematic (most people don't say *primitive* any more), and the discourse is thereby weakened as a determiner of world view or truth. But the older discourses do not disappear completely – iconic layers of meaning remain among the paradigmatic terms. The discourse of modernity is still underpinned by social evolutionism, just as globalism is underpinned by the discourse of modernity. All three paradigmatic pairs use the economic and technological developments and the cultural style of one particular socio-cultural formation – modernist-capitalist cosmopolitanism – as the pinnacle of development and the valued point of arrival. The will to actualization of all three, simply put, is that everyone should join and be like "us".

2. Trans-state cultural formations

In place of the way that the concept of *global culture* is often used nowadays, I propose that we think in terms of at least three more specific types of trans-state cultural formation: immigrant communities, diasporas and cosmopolitan formations. These three categories share certain dynamics but are also distinct in fundamental ways. Here I sketch only a brief outline of the three types, but hope that the comparison will suggest their usefulness and inspire further development of this kind of approach.

Immigrant communities

The first type of trans-state cultural formation is *immigrant communities*, and here I am concerned with *communities* rather than isolated immigrants who do not find each other in their new home. If an immigrant group is to emerge as a new cultural formation in the "host" country, it will involve a relatively stable settlement and recognition and relations among the immigrants that are typically based around common origin. Distinct from diasporas and cosmopolitans, immigrant communities are defined by *bilateral* relations and movement between the new and the original home environments and, prominently, by a combination of practices, ideas and objects from the two locations.

Specific immigrant communities come, and stay, together for a variety of reasons. Initially they often form around a core of early immigrants who provide assistance such as lodging, employment and orientation for later arrivals. This is particularly pertinent for lower-class immigrants who are economically vulnerable. Immigrant and diasporic groups also come and stay together for a host of other reasons, religion prominent among them. Cultural and religious separatism is sometimes internally generated because people regard their own life ways and ethics as more positive for themselves and their children than those of the "host" country. Formal immigrant cultural associations and religious institutions are common phenomena that provide on-going practical, social and emotional support. Immigrant communities and diasporic groups often emphasize cultural practices and styles from the original home as indices and activities that unite and maintain the group in the new location. Group activities that are distinctive of "home" are particularly powerful in this regard, making music, dance and festivals common unifiers.

Conditions in the host country influence the formation and dynamics of immigrant communities and diasporas in important ways. In places where prejudice against foreigners is pronounced, immigrants who can "pass" as locals may attempt to assimilate as quickly as possible and eschew markers, and relations with people, of the original home. Those who cannot assimilate easily for physical, cultural or economic reasons may be particularly apt to join with others from the original home, inspiring strong community bonds. Legislation in the "host" state – the ease of gaining citizenship; ease of obtaining, and length of, visas; work permits, etc. – is another fundamental variable.

As is well documented, immigrant communities often operate according to a particular generational logic whereby the ties to, and influences of, the original homeland are most pronounced in the first generation, are often rejected by the second, and may be rediscovered and used emblematically by subsequent generations in particular contexts. Certain ideas and practices of the original society may be passed on unselfconsciously through early socialization in the home, and these habits may linger for generations.

The tendency in immigrant communities, when possible (i.e., when a factor like racism is not in play), however, is gradual assimilation into the new home society and the disappearance of the group as a distinct cultural formation.

Diasporas

Diasporas are a second type of trans-state cultural formation. Unlike immigrant communities, diasporas are not bilateral but, rather, involve multiple sites in a number of states, both synchronically and diachronically. Like immigrant communities they symbolically, if not pragmatically, emphasize the original homeland and a historical heritage that originates there (see Safran 1991; Tölölyan 1996). Whereas immigrant communities tend to assimilate and fade within a few generations, diasporic cultural formations tend towards longevity and recognition of social continuities across space and time. Longevity is often crucial for the creation of complex diasporic cultural forms, such as the Yiddish language, or klezmer, that draw from a relatively long, multi-sited history. Senses of history are crucial to both diasporic and immigrant groups, not so in cosmopolitan formations.

For both immigrant communities and diasporas, icons and indices of the original homeland are often used in a more pronounced, conscious or manneristic way (Turino 2004b). In my study of Aymara migrants in Lima, Peru (1993), I showed how the fashioning of their pan-pipe performance in the city emphasized "exact copies" of hometown style through the strict imitation of cassette tapes, tightly organized musical parts and a hierarchical ensemble organization, including an authoritarian director. These practices were meant to ensure musical iconicity with the homeland as the basis for their regional identity as migrants and as the basis of their community in the city. The emphasis on "exact copy" at the level of sound, however, required fundamentally different musical practices and values because many of the migrant club members had not been interested in music before leaving the highlands and had lived in the urban soundscape of Lima for at least half their lives. The resulting innovations ultimately generated a different, more mannered, sound by comparison with the hometown where non-hierarchical ensembles perform in a much looser fashion and eschew imitation of other groups in favour of originality. The dynamic resulting from a discourse about the "sameness" with the homeland, necessarily realized through new innovations because of differing conditions in the "host-land", is fundamental to the nature of immigrant communities and diasporas as cultural formations. This is clearly demonstrated in a variety of case studies of different diasporic groups (see Turino and Lea 2004).

As in immigrant communities, the incorporation of cultural resources from the "home" and "host" societies is basic to diasporic cultural dynamics. In diasporas, however, the sources for ideas, practices and styles are drawn from a number of sites as well as from the new and old homelands. In fact, another diasporic site may be a more important source for cultural resources than the original homeland, although "home" tends to remain primary at the symbolic level. As Greg Diethrich describes for *desi* music in Chicago, Indian film music (an index of "home") is combined with sound elements from *bhangara* (or *bhangra*, an Indo-British pop music form) and African-American popular music, especially *house* (an index of "here") to make sense of self among Indian-American youth. Diethrich's example illustrates how *desi* music can simultaneously model Indian *diasporic* youth by indexing India, Indian youth in England, and also Chicago in particular, within a single artistic form (Diethrich 2004).

Diasporic consciousness, i.e., subjective recognition of membership, is fundamental to cultural creativity in that it is this recognition that attracts members in one site to the practices and forms of other sites of the diaspora. For example, Afro-Blocs of Bahia, Brazil fashioned *samba-reggae* and other musical forms and Carnival themes drawing from many sites in the African diaspora and Africa only after the idea of diaspora emerged in Brazil. For both immigrant communities and diasporas, feelings and activities of belonging to the formation – circumscribed by the symbol of the homeland and by selected practices, objects, ideas and styles from there – are key to the formation's very existence. In contrast, subjective feelings of belonging and senses of history as a group are *not* a basis of cosmopolitan formations, oddly enough because cosmopolitans do not perceive themselves as belonging to a specific cultural formation.

Cosmopolitanism

Like all cultural groups, cosmopolitan formations are defined by constellations of conceptions, ethics, aesthetics, practices, technologies, objects and social style – habits and resources for living. Like all cultural formations, specific cosmopolitan formations come into being through basic processes of socialization: in a given family and in particular social networks. Membership is a subjective condition formed through on-going relations to particular environments and external conditions. The conceptualization of cosmopolitanism as a *type of cultural formation*, i.e., involving processes of socialization and comprising *shared* internalized dispositions, is fundamental to its usefulness as an analytical term.

It is not difficult for people to recognize that there are different diasporas (Jewish, Armenian, African, etc.) with distinct social make-ups, histories and cultural characteristics co-existing at any one time. But I have found that people have a harder time thinking of cosmopolitanism as a type of cultural formation and conceptualizing the fact that various cosmopolitan formations may coexist in the world. The reason for this difficulty is that cosmopolitan discourse itself stresses individuality, placelessness, universalism and a pan-historicism that results in ahistoricity. The discourse projects cosmopolitans as "above" and independent of parochial times, places and social groups. When most people use the term *cosmopolitan* they are speaking from within the discourse of cosmopolitanism itself, whether these traits are seen as negative, e.g. Nazi castigation of Jews as [not-national] cosmopolitans, or positive, as in "sophisticated citizen of the world". Despite this problem, the term is closest to the type of trans-state formation that I am concerned with, and hence, rather than making up a new word, I prefer to elaborate it from outside its own discourse. That is, moving outside our own views of ourselves, cosmopolitan groups parallel immigrant communities and diasporas as a *type* of trans-state cultural formation.

Like diasporas, cosmopolitan formations exist across multiple sites in a number of states, and a cosmopolitan group may represent a small minority within a given country. Cosmopolitan formations may have far-flung diffusion, but often do not have deep penetration within whole populations in many locations. This point differentiates cosmopolitan and global phenomena if *global* is understood to mean "everyone everywhere". Yet it is the broad diffusion of certain forms of cosmopolitanism, especially among elites in different countries, that erroneously leads to the perception of their global status – especially among elites of other sites of the same formation. This point recalls Kelly's statement that "for academics and other elites with access to travel, email, the World Wide Web, etc., the idea of globalization is altogether more real than for those about whom many of us write" (1999:388). Both cosmopolitanism and globalism are universalizing discourses, and this facet has to be continually deconstructed if the terms are to have any analytical utility.

Like diasporas, a number of cosmopolitan formations may exist simultaneously in time. For example, during the second half of the twentieth century we might identify the *modernist-socialist, modernist-capitalist*, and *fundamentalist-Islamic* cosmopolitan formations as prominent. Several formations may also co-exist within the same state: e.g., the latter two in Saudi Arabia, the former two in the United States during the 1930s (e.g., Lieberman 1989; Fried 1997). As with diasporas, members of the same cosmopolitan formation are attracted and related to members in the same and other sites around the world through a substantial degree of cultural similarity as well as travel, institutions and concrete communication loops. As with diasporas, each local site in the formation is also socially and culturally distinct because of unique local conditions. The Zimbabwe case elaborated below illustrates that the distinctiveness of a local cosmopolitan site increases with time.

One thing that distinguishes cosmopolitan formations from diasporas is the absence of an original homeland as a key symbol, if not an actual ground for the formation. This distinction is difficult from two points of view. First, it plays into the aims of cosmopolitan discourse itself. Cosmopolitans project universalism, a common humanity unfettered by localized identities and locations, as basic to who they are. That is, cosmopolitan discourse denies the fact that it is a type of local and simultaneously trans-local subject position and sociocultural network. The second problem is that cosmopolitan formations *do* often have power centres – particular sites that have more influence within the formation than others. The United States, Western Europe and Japan are currently power centres within the modernist-capitalist formation. The Soviet Union and China were/are power centres of the modernist-socialist formation.

Whereas members of a diaspora trace their lineage to an elsewhere, cosmopolitans may well be native to their own location. Diasporic formations travel with actual groups of immigrants. Cosmopolitan formations may also travel in this way, e.g., with British, French and Dutch colonialists in Africa, but *membership in the cosmopolitan formation is not dependent on immigrant status or heritage*. The ideas, practices and technologies of a given cosmopolitan formation travel through communication loops independently binding people culturally who are not, otherwise, related by location or heritage. It is this feature that makes cosmopolitanism unique as a type of cultural formation, and particularly important as a specific analytical concept. It is this feature that makes cosmo-politanism closest to what is typically referred to as "global culture".

Cosmopolitans are more thoroughly local, in that they and their ances-tors often grow up and live in their heritage home, while also being culturally trans-local – belonging to the trans-state cultural formation – at the same time. Cosmopolitan subjectivities are a crucial site of the local–trans-local dialectics that are of such concern to contemporary scholars. The study of specific cosmo-politan formations in specific places and individuals' lives grounds the study of trans-state cultural flows in concrete ways.

3. Class, popular music and cosmopolitanism in Zimbabwe

My notion of cosmopolitanism developed out of a conceptual need in my empirical work on Zimbabwean popular music, on the African middle class, and on the concrete links between colonialism, nationalism and state actions in the post-independence period in that country. Africanist cultural and ethno-musicological analysis along with nationalist discourse itself, has too often used overly simple black–white, African–European, traditional–modern, and now local–global, dichotomies to think about cultural positions, artistic aesthetics and issues of authenticity. Early in my fieldwork I was struck by the fact that my Shona colleagues at the University of Zimbabwe seemed to have as much or more in common with me than they did with rural Shona peasants. I was also struck by the fact that my middle-class neighbours in Mabelreign suburb knew less about rural Shona music and indigenous ceremony than I did and some-times more about jazz and US country music than I did. In spite of the African cultural-insider status granted to these friends by the discourses of race, ethni-city and nationalism, they were culturally quite distinct from the majority of their countrymen. Yet they were certainly genuinely Africans and locals. They were not pretending to be "Black Europeans" and were not "traitors to their own culture" or other such nonsense suggested by a variety of essentialist discourses. They were *authentically* Zimbabwean cosmopolitans, and belonged to the local variant of the same modernist-capitalist formation that I did. Their authenticity was based in the fact that they were socialized within this cultural formation; this was simply who they were. This realization opened new vistas to under-standing the cultural policies of the Mugabe state, directed by cosmopolitans, and the developments of urban popular music in Zimbabwe.

The African middle class

By the 1930s an African middle class began to emerge in Zimbabwe, largely through the process of missionary education. Especially on mission-station lands, in cities and, after 1930, in African purchase areas, a distinctive cultural group of black Zimbabweans began to emerge. This small group was socialized within the Christian religion and modernist-capitalist discourse that affected economic practices and goals, the preferred style of weddings, monogamy, and the proper behaviour for women as homemakers, as well as aesthetics of dress, music, dance and entertainment, among other aspects of life. Missionary women's clubs, for example, taught women how to keep a clean home and cook food in a "modern" hygienic fashion, as well as how to sing in a "well-organized" manner. Men learned the value of personal capital accumulation that could lead to having a small business or cash-crop farming in African purchase areas. This situation contrasted with indigenous Shona customs of redistributing wealth among family members, and it certainly changed extended-family dynamics (see Cheater 1984). As historian Michael West has noted (1990), differences of wealth among black Zimbabweans was never very pronounced; education levels, occupation, and social and cultural style were the primary determiners of class and status.

From around 1910 to the 1940s, Zimbabwe had only an incipient black cosmopolitan group, since these aspects of socialization were only one, or at most two, generations deep at the level of the family and neighbourhoods. The *imitation* of Europeans for social acceptance and advancement within the colonial order was probably still common. By the 1960s and 1970s, however, the modernist-capitalist formation had enough generational time depth such that children in cosmopolitan households and communities were socialized within this cultural formation through the imitation of other black Zimbabweans – their parents, siblings, neighbours, teachers, local musicians, and so on. At this point the local site of the formation became self-generating as well as influenced by the people, institutions and happenings in other sites.

While the modernist-capitalist-Christian formation has the greatest time depth in Zimbabwe, during the nationalist period of the 1960–80s, modernist-socialist discourse and practice became influential among the nationalists and within the post-1980 government. During the war years, the two leading nationalist parties turned to Russia (ZAPU) and China (ZANU) for direct support, training and ideas, and the socialist formation was seen as an important alternative to, and rejection of, the capitalist Rhodesian state. These two forms of modernist-cosmopolitanism co-existed in Zimbabwe during this period. During the 1980s, however, socialist programmes and intentions gradually faded, and capitalism emerged as predominant in the early 1990s with ESAP. This shift was due both to external pressures (e.g., trans-state financial institutions) and to internal pressures, that is, within the hearts and minds of the leadership itself.

The leaders of the post-Independence state were originally socialized within the capitalist-Christian formation and many were involved in personal capital accumulation and investment, even during the years of socialist rhetoric and programmes. Because of the personal experiences and alliances of the leadership who fought the "Liberation War" and went on to control the state, both socialist and capitalist currents mingled within the same individuals. In his Independence Day speech of 1993, for example, Mugabe appealed to his revolutionary comrades and the grassroots masses, he branded the IMF/WB as a neocolonialist force, yet he laid the groundwork for the black elite to gain control of privatized parastatal organizations (see Turino 2000:214–15). In the end, capitalist ethics and class-based relations rose to the top; they were always close beneath the surface.

Recognition of these two co-existing, in fact competing, cosmopolitan formations is important for understanding dynamics in Zimbabwe since the 1960s. In general, however, capitalist, Christian and modernist ethics and practices are the dominant components of middle-class Zimbabwean cosmopolitanism. For the sake of brevity, in what follows when I use the term without qualifiers it should be understood that I am referring to this particular formation and not reverting to the idea that there is only one type of cosmopolitanism. It was the cosmopolitan formation with power centres in the United States, Western Europe, and England, rather than Russia and China, which had the greatest influence on Zimbabwean popular music, with the brief exception of war songs of the 1970s and in the early 1980s.

Indigenous music and the school song tradition

Middle-class cosmopolitans represent a cultural minority, numerically, in Zimbabwe. People socialized with indigenous Shona ethics, practices and life ways are the majority, with other indigenous groups – especially the Ndebele – comprising additional minorities. The dance-drumming genre known as *dandanda* is one of many that is vitally performed in indigenous Shona villages and in the townships in the contemporary period. *Dandanda* is used to bring ancestors into their mediums in Shona spirit possession ceremonies in rural Murehwa district some eighty miles northeast of Harare. It is a participatory tradition: anyone present is able to join in with singing, dancing, *hosho* (shaker) playing, and clapping. The drumming is more specialized than these other roles. The aesthetics and performance practices exhibited are common to indigenous Shona music generally. The form is cyclical, repetitive and open-ended, with beginnings, endings and internal dynamic shifts being fluid according to the needs of participants in the moment. Dynamic intensity will mount to help bring on possession. The length of performances will vary according to whether the given song is working to inspire continued participation. The parts are interlocked at the micro level, for example in the *hosho* parts, and at the level of the overall call-and-response organization. The texture is extremely dense, with much overlapping and individual variation creating an aura of sound surrounding the main melodic parts.

In all the ways described, indigenous Shona musical aesthetics, practices and style contrast with those in modernist-cosmopolitan formations. Modernist cosmopolitanism was initially learned in mission schools, so it should come as no surprise that cosmopolitan musical aesthetics, practices and style were learned in these contexts, as part-and-parcel of the same ways of being. From the Umtali Teachers Training College Choir's recording of "Shortend Bread" (recorded by the radio, circa 1958) we get a glimpse of the style that was diffused in mission and government schools. Here the parts are well ordered within set arrangements, the textures extremely clear, the enunciation precise, and the harmony European. The piece "Shortend Bread", copyrighted in 1899, comes from nineteenth-century US popular culture, known at the time as a "coon song" – a white, professionally penned, or at least arranged, imitation of supposed Southern black music.[7]

In the school song tradition, the attitudes about what performance is, and the very conception of what a piece is, differ fundamentally from indigenous Shona ceremonies. In indigenous contexts "a song" or "a piece" is a loose aggregate of resources used for sonic and kinesic social interaction. In the capitalist-cosmopolitan conception, a song is an artistic item with a fully controlled form, a set beginning and end, created by one group, the artists, for the edification of another, the audience. A participatory ethic underlies indigenous performance and evaluation. In the modernist-capitalist cosmopolitan formation, the major transformation involves the favouring of presentational, and ultimately recorded, modes of performance and a higher value placed on distinction and specialization. Control and rational order are ethical features of modernist discourse. The desire for artistic distinction and specialization, and the objectification of a piece as an item, may have a variety of impetuses in different cultural formations,[8] but these features are part of capitalist ethics in a particular way; if a song is not a set item it cannot be copyrighted and sold as property. If it were perceived that anyone could sing a song equally well, there would be no star system and no reason to pay good money for concert tickets. The ethical dispositions underlying the differences between indigenous style and this choir's performance of "Shortend Bread" are not random, nor are they isolated from the broader ethical differences between the two cultural formations.

Concert

The first style of Zimbabwean urban-popular music to emerge in the incipient cosmopolitan formation grew out of the school song tradition in the very direct sense that its practitioners, style and repertory came out of the school choirs. Primarily performed before silent, well-dressed black middle-class audiences in township recreation halls, I have labelled this style *concert*. Important *concert* groups like Kenneth Mattaka's Bantu Actors, founded in 1937, and De Black Evening Follies, formed in 1943, were primarily male vocal quartets, quintets and sextets backed by African-jazz musicians who were trained in military bands. Female vocalists were also sometimes incorporated into these and other *concert* ensembles. Some *concert* groups like De Black Evening Follies were variety acts. Recordings and filmed performances of De Black Evening Follies illustrate that they were most influenced by the African-American group, the Mills Brothers, which was tremendously popular among cosmopolitans in a number of countries during the 1940s.

---

[7] "Shortend Bread" was "arranged and composed" by Carl Lexhoizt, and copyrighted in 1899 as part of "Georgia Jubilee". My thanks to Lawrence Gushee for bringing this collection to my attention.

[8] For example, artistic distinction may be the product of individual ambition to excel in a given field, and it might also function in different status systems that do not have capital accumulation as their basis.

Ernest Brown (1994) and, more recently, Isaac Kalumbu (2002) have emphasized the pan-African, or African-diasporic nature of foreign popular music influences in Zimbabwe. I interpret the paramount influence of the Mills Brothers model in *concert*, however, as being based in cosmopolitanism rather a diasporic consciousness. Out of all the African-American artists and styles available, middle-class *concert* performers did not imitate Charlie Patton, Robert Johnson, the Mississippi Sheiks, or even Bessie Smith, artists who appealed widely to working-class, sometimes more localized, African-American audiences.[9] That is, it was not simply African-Americanness that attracted *concert* performers. Rather, they chose an African-American group that was already popular with cosmopolitan audiences in the US and Europe because its performances were deeply grounded in cosmopolitan style and aesthetics in the first place.

The Mills Brothers were part of the same cultural formation as Zimbabwean *concert* artists. The fact that they were black may have been attractive, but interviews with Mattaka and others suggest that the smooth, controlled, sophisticated style of sound, dress and choreography that the Mills Brothers presented was the more important lure. It was this imagery that black middle-class Zimbabwean audiences either aspired to or, in the case of someone like Kenneth Mattaka, already deeply identified with because of his own socialization.

Concert groups also imitated many others who were not black. In 1961, De Black Evening Follies, with Joyce Ndoro, were filmed doing an imitation of a Carmen Miranda-styled act. Here we see another clear example of the workings of cosmopolitanism. Miranda was born in Portugal, first became popular in Brazil, and then entered US popular culture in the context of the Good Neighbour Policy, and the US culture industry's interest in selling exoticism. Genres and styles from a variety of places were adopted by Zimbabwean groups once they had been incorporated into cosmopolitan popular culture – in the Miranda case through US films, but also through "Latin" ballroom dance crazes. *Concert* artists stayed current with cosmopolitan popular music trends elsewhere in the formation. Indicating the speed of communication of these trends, De Black Evening Follies recorded a version of Little Richard's "Long Tall Sally" in 1960, and an *African Parade* photograph from 1959 shows the Follies performing an Elvis imitation – the lead singer's hold on the mic stand, his stance with knees turned inwards are unmistakable. White singers such as Elvis, and later the Beatles, were as important as black performers such as Little Richard, and later Otis Redding. The claim that an African-diasporic consciousness was the impetus for selecting foreign artistic models seems a partial reading at best.

The diffusion of Mills Brothers records and Carmen Miranda films to places like Zimbabwe is a phenomenon that nowadays would be labelled as, and be

---

[9] It is significant that a working class/peasant style of acoustic guitar playing emerged in Zimbabwe that was much closer to these African-American artists and to US country performers like Jimmie Rodgers than to the style presented by the Mills Brothers and *concert* groups. Middle-class standing, as it articulated with cosmopolitanism, was the key variable for selecting the Mills Brothers model. For a discussion of the working-class acoustic guitarists, see Turino 2000, chapter 7.

used as evidence of, "global culture". During the 1940s through the 1960s when these products were popular and influential, they were explicitly conceptualized as "modern" in Zimbabwe and were specifically used as indices of the black middle class.[10] That is, they were not then (and similar products like rap recordings and videos are not now) *global* in the sense of being deeply incorporated into the lives of the total population of Zimbabwe – especially among the peasant majority, but also among adults in the monolingual-indigenous-languages segment of the urban working and lower classes.[11] These cultural products pertain to specific minority groups in Zimbabwe – those socialized within the cosmopolitan formation and those, especially among urban youth, aspiring to "modern" life. The diffusion of popular culture products in electronic form from the power centres of a cosmopolitan formation is not a new process. What has changed is the paradigmatic substitution of terms among outside observers to refer to the phenomenon – "global" instead of "modern" – a discursive shift that most Zimbabweans, even many cosmopolitans, have not yet adopted.

Cosmopolitanism and local originality

Both Mattaka and Moses Mpahlo, leader of De Black Evening Follies, emphasized that original composition and style were not highly valued in the *concert* tradition. Rather, they adopted or combined popular songs from North America, England, South Africa and elsewhere, and often translated them into various African languages. Between the late 1930s and the early 1960s, careful imitation was a prominent value. Nonetheless, recordings and film clips indicate that *concert* artists still infused their performances with local aspects that made them distinct from the originals – language, timbral and rhythmic accents and movement style among other features. The given sites of a cosmopolitan formation will always exhibit these signs of local distinction because the people in that site were socialized with the multiple influences of that place, some of which, more or less depending on the site, originate outside the cosmopolitan formation.

Art is related to the representation of identity in two basic ways. First, artists can consciously choose and manipulate elements for a desired representation. For example, the conscious imitation by Zimbabweans of other sophisticated cosmopolitans creates an iconicity that signals similarity and belonging. Second, however, the total life experiences of artists and audience members, their own socialized habits, will also influence art and reception in more unselfconscious ways. *Dicent* signs of identity are those that are directly affected by the same socialization and subject position that the signs are interpreted as represent-

---

[10] For example, *concert* groups were featured at mass nationalist rallies and were described by local black journalists as "modern" and "new". At the rallies, these groups alternated with "tribal" dance groups doing their "old", "traditional" dances. One journalist made the explicit observation that the nationalist party (ZAPU) was "endeavoring to blend the old and the new". (*African Parade* May 8, 1962: 8.)

[11] This assertion is based on interview data and observation specifically regarding musical preferences among different segments of the Zimbabwean population during my fieldwork, 1991, 1992–93, 1996 (see Turino 2000).

ing.[12] Speech accent, ways of moving, body language, senses of rhythm and intonation, preferences about the organization and density of musical textures and forms, senses of colour, light and space all tend to be deeply socialized elements hardly noticed. Yet these dispositions, often outside of focal awareness, influence the production of signs of identity in art in fundamental ways, and thus signify subject positions as much, if not more, than those consciously manipulated to represent identity. As the cosmopolitan formation developed and gained time depth in Zimbabwe, there was a movement from conscious imitation and manipulation to a type of self-expression and regimes of taste and etiquette that simply emerged from being socialized largely within the modernist-capitalist cosmopolitan formation.

By the 1950s, middle-class concerts could not have been more aesthetically different from the boisterous participatory atmosphere of religious ceremonies or beerhall performances attended by Shona peasants and members of the black working class. In concerts, artist–audience distinctions were emphasized, formal dress required, and the seated audiences were so quiet, performers commented, that "you could hear a pin drop". The members of this cultural formation were not simply imitating Europeans by this time but were rather acting out of their own deep-seated senses of propriety and taste, and the members of this generation still express dismay at both indigenous styles of performance and the less-polite popular club scene that emerged after the 1960s.

Popular music of the 1960s

Concert began to fade in the early 1960s. By the second half of the 1960s two fundamental aspects changed in the production of popular music within the Zimbabwean cosmopolitan formation. First, there was a growing emphasis on originality; and second, musical performance began to be conceived as a viable full-time profession by a substantial number of young people for the first time. Before the 1960s, popular artists largely modelled themselves on groups and styles from cosmopolitan sites outside Zimbabwe; here, as in indigenous Shona music making, originality of compositions and style was not a primary value.[13] With the main exception of Police Band members who moonlighted as jazz musicians, full-time professional performers were a rarity; *concert* performers thought of themselves as specialized amateurs who held *real* day jobs. By the

---

[12] A weathervane indicating wind direction is a classic Peircian example of a dicent sign. The wind direction (object of the sign) actually influences the weathervane direction (sign). For a fuller discussion of Peircian sign types, see Turino 1999.

[13] Especially in spirit possession ceremonies, adherence to repertories and styles of performance that the ancestors, several generations back, would recognize, feel comfortable with and be attracted by is key to drawing spirits into the ceremony. This supports cultural conservatism and limits innovation. In recreational music and dancing there is more room for individual creativity and innovation, but this usually happens within the aesthetic limits of a given genre or style. New genres and styles have certainly come into existence in MaShonaland, but there isn't a primary value placed on creating them, in contrast to the popular music field of the 1960s and 1970s.

1970s, originality had become a key criterion for artistic status, and the desire to become a full-time professional musician had become common. These two revolutionary developments are linked to capitalist cosmopolitanism, and to each other, in a variety of ways.

In contrast to the early *concert* performers, the new generation of artists coming up in the early 1960s could use local groups like De Black Evening Follies as models as well as directly as teachers. Thomas Mapfumo, among other prominent artists, recounted how as a young boy he would attend performances by local *concert* and jazz groups and then go home and practise the music he heard which, by 1959, included rock 'n' roll. In the early 1960s, Mapfumo actually worked with and learned directly from Kenneth Mattaka. Sufficient time depth allowed aspiring artists to model themselves on cosmopolitan elders within the same site; local cosmopolitan artistic production became substantially self-generating. By the late 1980s, successful members of the 1960s generation, such as Mapfumo, had become models for the next generation of popular artists in Zimbabwe who aspired to capturing cosmopolitan audiences both at home and abroad. Like the members of any cultural formation, modernist-cosmopolitan youth in Zimbabwe were attracted to other cosmopolitans there because of similarities in ethics, aesthetics, aspirations and social style. Mattaka's manner of performance attracted Mapfumo, just as Mapfumo's success at home and abroad attracted a new generation of musicians working in the early 1990s.

This shift to local models represents a key moment in the development of a given cosmopolitan site. *Concert* and local jazz groups always had their own Zimbabwean *tint* due to dicent elements. Local accents became organically compounded when subsequent generations began learning from local cosmopolitans as primary models – local tints became part of the model to which subsequent generations added their own dicent elements. Thus, as the local cosmopolitan formation matured and became self-generating it produced increasingly original local art that still fitted within cosmopolitan aesthetics and ethics because these were the aesthetics of the artists socialized within this formation.

The move towards originality in Zimbabwean popular music during the 1960s and 1970s had two additional sources beyond the basic generational accruing of local accents and elements. The mid-1960s saw the rise of a separate youth culture with teen-time dances and TV programmes. By 1968, cosmopolitan youth culture – the Beatles, hippiedom, soul music and the black power movement – provided central models for urban Zimbabwean youth, both black and white. Interracial rock bands and festivals sprung up in the early 1970s as black and white adults were preparing their children to go to war with each other. Soul groups were formed, Afro hairstyles and hippie clothing became common among youth within the formation.

As part of the aesthetic discourse of cosmopolitan youth culture – modelled on the Beatles, the Stones and singer-songwriters like Bob Dylan – the Zimbabwean black press began to emphasize artistic originality. Music writers praised local groups that wrote their own songs and developed their own styles, yet criticized acts that simply imitated other groups. These critics primarily had influence among the readerships of newspapers and magazines directed at the black middle class, such as the *Bantu Mirror* and *African Parade*. That is, the discourse stressing artistic originality was not *global* (i.e., universal) in Zimbabwe but pertained primarily to the urban middle class and artists attempting to attract this segment of the population. This value was internalized, however, by cosmopolitan artists of the 1960s generation, and they began to experiment with ways to produce original music. Mapfumo told me that this was his first impetus for trying to play indigenous Shona music within a rock-band format – in order "to come up with his own sound". Other groups of the time did very much the same thing as well as experimented in other directions.

Cosmopolitan images of wealthy rock stars inspired increasing numbers of young people to think about music as an occupation for the first time. It also inspired entrepreneurs to create a Zimbabwean recording industry during the 1960s and 1970s. These two developments along with a recent liquor-law change that allowed Africans to drink hard alcohol,[14] in turn made African nightclubs profitable and created an environment in which musical professionalism seemed possible and attractive. The desire to "make it" commercially was directly coupled with the need for originality as the valued means for distinguishing oneself and attracting a record-buying, club-going audience. It is through these combined and complementary processes that songs became redefined as capitalist products, and musical performance as a professional occupation – specifically within and due to the maturing of the modernist-capitalist formation in that site.

African nationalism was the third, and best-known, impetus for creating distinctive Zimbabwean art within a cosmopolitan aesthetic and ethical frame. Mass cultural nationalism developed during the 1960s and 1970s, parallel in time to the other developments discussed. Nationalism was, itself, a modernist-cosmopolitanism ideology and project and was directed by a cosmopolitan leadership.[15] Zimbabwean nationalists designed events and underwrote artistic creations that blended images of indigenous uniqueness, "the traditional", with emblems of "the modern". Mass nationalism slowly created an audience for art of this type, and young musicians with professional aspirations, such as Thomas Mapfumo, Oliver M'tukudzi and Zexie Manatsa among many others, created such fusions to attract and sell to this audience during the 1970s. Modernist-socialist cosmopolitanism, introduced by the two leading nationalist parties, also influenced the imagery in popular song texts during this time – e.g., mention of Mao and other socialist African leaders as well as socialist principles (Turino 2000, chapter 6).

---

[14] Formerly black Zimbabweans had been restricted to local millet beer. The liquor-law change occurred in 1957, allowing Africans to legally consume "European" types of alcoholic beverages.

[15] The basic ideas of nationalism were part of both the modernist-capitalist and modernist-socialist formations during the 1960s and 1970s. Zimbabwean nationalist leaders modelled their movement on ideas taken from Russia, China, Ghana, the United States, England and elsewhere. Zimbabwean leaders had grown up in the capitalist formation but aligned themselves with the socialist formation during the war years and the early 1980s, opening up wider spheres of influence, and aid, across two different formations.

From local sites to trans-state circuits

Basic to my idea of cosmopolitanism is that it comprises cultural elements and products drawn from any site within a given formation. For something to be attractive to cosmopolitans elsewhere, however, it has to have marks of local distinctiveness or at least some type of novelty; otherwise, it will be indistinguishable from what is already available within the formation. Saxophonist August Musarurwa's 1950s classic "Skokiaan", later recorded by Louis Armstrong and by groups as far away as the Dominican Republic, represents an early example of this process. By the 1950s, jazz was a cosmopolitan tradition within modernist – both socialist and capitalist – formations (e.g., see Erlmann 1991; Atkins 2001; Jones 2001).[16] Based on Zimbabwean and South African urban-popular rhythms, harmony and melodic gestures, Musarurwa's piece was certainly distinctive for cosmopolitan jazz fans in the US, Europe and Latin America. And, in fact, in the process of incorporating it into the cosmopolitan formation it was actually exoticized with words penned by South African, Tom Glazer, who, in tin-pan alley style, created images of sensuous natives and tropical bungalows, where one could live like a king "right in the jungle-ungleo" (see Turino 2000:142).

The music of Thomas Mapfumo and the Bhundu Boys, with its clear marks of Zimbabwean originality, especially through the use of *mbira* elements and/or fast 12/8 *hosho*-like rhythms, represents the next wave of exports, this time within the context of the worldbeat phenomenon during the 1980s.[17] Although less garish, exoticism also underpins the success of artists within the worldbeat market.

While artists sold within the "worldbeat" or "world music" commercial categories are often considered to be part of a "global musical movement" (e.g., Boli and Lechner 2001:6263), the audiences for artists such as Mapfumo, Ladysmith Black Mambazo, King Sunny Ade, and other worldbeat stars, outside their countries of origin, tend to be relatively small and specialized. For example, regarding the marketing of Bob Marley early on in the worldbeat phenomenon, Island Records' Chris Blackwell remarked: "I felt that reggae was the white liberal market. I always hoped that it would sell to black America, but it never did because the music was too ethnic-ish … The only people who really related to it were white liberal, college oriented-type people …"(interview in Fox 1986:306). Like jazz, "world music" pertains to specialized fan groups within modernist cosmopolitan formations. Members of immigrant and diaspora communities, Africans in London, Paris, Chicago, New York, Champaign may also attend shows and buy recordings of African artists marketed as "world music". Detailed research is necessary to assess the size and nature of this portion of the world music audience in different locales and to understand the distinc-

---

[16] It has never been *global* in that jazz did not penetrate the entire populations of the countries where it was performed, not even in its country of origin.

[17] Mapfumo was the only Zimbabwean musician listed on *Billboard*'s "World Music" charts (see Taylor 1997:7–8)

tive meanings the music must have for them. For African music shows I have attended in the United States – in Austin, Chicago and central Illinois – Africans represented a fairly small minority. In the few shows I attended in London in the mid-1980s, Africans comprised a larger portion than in the US but were still in the minority.[18] Thus, while "world music" artists reach these specialized audiences in a variety of countries, with the exception of a few recordings such as Simon's *Graceland* they do not penetrate the majority music markets even in those countries and so can hardly be considered *global*.

As Paul Simon expressed it regarding his choice of South African styles incorporated on his *Graceland* album, worldbeat success is dependent on balancing the "familiar and foreign-sounding at the same time" (*Graceland* liner notes, 1986). "Familiar" here refers to what is already known and appreciated within a given cosmopolitan formation. "Foreign-sounding", however, no longer simply refers to being of another country or locale. Rather, *it signifies difference from what is already common in the cosmopolitan formation regardless of location*. Thus, on *Graceland*, styles (and social groups) on the margins of the cosmopolitan centre in the US – *zydeco* and Los Lobos – are included as "roots" sources commensurate with South African performers. Zimbabwean artists who perform soul music, rap, country or gospel, and who do not sound distinctively African enough, will not easily find a place in cosmopolitan world music markets. For example, a member of the Bhundu Boys told me that during the late 1980s they had wanted to experiment with county and western, but their British fans rejected them when they tried this.[19] For this market, authenticity is defined by being external (exotic) to the cosmopolitan, but the crucial differences must also be largely couched within *familiar* cosmopolitan ethics, aesthetics and style.

In general, as Ajun Appadurai and Veit Erlmann have noted, capitalism trades on difference, i.e., the continual need to sell new products that are distinct in some way. Exoticism is simply one source of distinction and novelty, and the short shelf life of worldbeat artists illustrates this point. At the same time, differences of all types are incorporated within frameworks of similarity: of forms, ethics, aesthetics, practices and contexts that comprise the given cultural formation.

---

[18] Here, under the rubric of "world music" shows, I am not including specialized African music performances within African diasporic and immigrant associations, such as *fontomfrom* drumming among the Akan community in Toronto, or Ewe ritual drumming at Ewe celebrations in New York.

[19] There are some indications that this situation is changing as the worldbeat or "world music" phenomenon matures. For example, Oliver M'tukudzi, one of the most popular singers in Zimbabwe, developed a unique style that is not easy to locate geographically. Even six years ago my American students reacted negatively to his music, commenting that "it sounded too much like pop" and that it was not African enough. In 2002, M'tukudzi is finally enjoying major success among US world music audiences. One interpretation here is that with growing sophistication and knowledge, African music fans in the USA no longer need the clear markers of Africanness, and are more able to enjoy a performer for his or her individual merits.

Earlier I stated that while cosmopolitan formations don't have homelands, they do have power centres. The "exotic" products inserted into cosmopolitan loops usually do not come from outside the formation but rather are typically produced by cosmopolitans themselves, albeit in marginalized sites in the so-called "Third World", and by marginalized groups in the cosmopolitan power centres. Both Musarurwa and Mapfumo were socialized within Zimbabwe's modernist-capitalist formation, although at different points in its development (see Turino 2000 for biographies). This socialization was an important basis for their relative successes within the broader formation outside Zimbabwe; they already knew how to walk the walk, talk the talk and perform the notes of this formation, yet with the distinctive Zimbabwean tints that allowed them to sell difference – a value functionally specific to the modernist-capitalist formation. Parallel cases could be outlined for Carmen Miranda, Ravi Shankar, Salif Keita or, David Byrne's Afro-Peruvian discovery, Susana Baca. Essentialist racial and national discourses aside, it is typically cosmopolitans who contribute to cosmopolitanism and who are able to succeed within their formation more broadly.

Conclusions

The processes, people and events sketched here are not global. They are local to Zimbabwe and are part of a specific trans-local cultural formation – modernist-capitalist cosmopolitanism. The modernist-socialist formation had real influence in the political sphere and had some influence on cultural production in the 1970s and 1980s in Zimbabwe, but it was short lived because both the politicians and the musicians were socialized largely within the capitalist formation – and socialization within a given cultural formation is the key point. Despite Mugabe's repetition of Marxist–Leninist slogans from time to time, it is the capitalist formation with its structural adjustments and drive for personal accumulation that serves as the basis for the leadership's positions and thus is the key to understanding current events in that country. Yet the concept of co-existing cosmopolitan formations (the modernist capitalist *and* socialist) is necessary for a detailed understanding of the different political and artistic movements.

The terminology and premises of globalism are too all-encompassing to aid understanding of specific people, places and processes, even in the very best of recent ethnomusicological work. Lise Waxer, for example, is careful to differentiate terms. For her, "transnational" means "cutting across national boundaries" and "global" means "truly worldwide". From this basis she suggests that "Although salsa's spread to different countries within Latin America might be best classified as trans-national, its adoption in Europe, Japan, and Africa certainly approaches global proportions." Here she reverts to the conception of *global* as involving several non-contiguous sites. She goes on to say, "The dozens of salsa-related Web sites that have emerged on the Internet also speak to increasing globalization in this medium" (2002:16–17).

The framework suggested here – including different immigrant, diaspora, and cosmopolitan cultural formations – allows us to probe and delineate salsa's spread to Japan, Europe and Africa in a different way. In each location, who, and how large, is the audience for salsa? In Japan and Africa, cosmopolitans are probably involved and probably represent a relatively small group of fans (one "taste-subculture" among many) rather than comprising the entire populations in those countries. The European case may be different, at least as suggested by processes in the United States. The spread of salsa to towns and cities throughout the United States involves at least two distinct groups and processes. Middle-class (often "Anglo" and Asian-American) cosmopolitans with former interests in ballroom and/or "world music" are involved in one trajectory. Salsa, however, also has become a central emblem and activity for Latin American immigrant communities in North America. The dynamics here – involving claims of ownership, authenticity and distinct (sometimes country-specific) performance styles – differ and intersect with the non-Latino salseros in interesting ways, often within the same club scenes.[20]

As with *nueva canción* and Andean "folkloric" music formerly, the situation with salsa in Europe may similarly involve different trajectories. It would be interesting to investigate if Latin Americans in Europe use the consciousness of diaspora to connect with Latinos in North America *and* "the homeland" vis-à-vis salsa, or simply operate bilaterally as immigrant communities; it would also be interesting to know what European cosmopolitans" investment in the style involved and whether it was connected, for example, to earlier waves of Latin dance and music crazes on the continent. In relation to the spread of salsa via the Internet (see also Perrone and Dunn 2001:7–8), it becomes important to ask: Who has access to computers and computer literacy and who does not? Who is being included in "global culture" on this basis and who is being excluded through lack of interest, or economic ability, or the specific types of cultural knowledge needed to be involved with computers?

The delineation of different types of trans-state cultural formations provides a platform to begin these and other inquiries that would shed crucial light on the different meanings and effects of trans-local musical styles and practices in different places, and among different cultural groups in the same locales. In spite of academic concern with "local–global" interchange and refinements such as "glocalization" (Robertson 1995), the term *global* does not provide sufficient handles to distinguish different types of trans-state cultural processes and subjectivities. *Outside the discourse of globalism*, global culture includes everybody. The phenomena that affect this social scale are limited and consequently the term has limited utility except to refer to phenomena that really affect everyone everywhere. *As part of the discourse of globalism*, the idea of "global culture" is a component of the sales pitch intended to naturalize the spread of capitalist culture, commodities, and control. The term *global* has become so strongly tied to this project within political, corporate, journalistic, and popular discourses that any use of the term may contribute to this naturalization process regardless of the meaning intended by the speaker or writer, i.e., the term will increasingly be "read" within the discourse as the discourse fans out more broadly.

---

[20] Joanna Bosse is currently completing her dissertation at the University of Illinois documenting this process.

Globalism has a direct parallel in the way that social evolutionism supported colonialism in its heyday, as now, a century later, has become widely recognized. It also parallels and piggybacks on the way the discourse of modernity helped to attract different cultural groups to the capitalist, or at least the industrial–bureaucratic–nationalist, fold. The importance of discourses for supporting asymmetrical power relations is now understood in some detail. Echoing others, Veit Erlmann writes: "I see the power of imperial conquest and colonial hegemony residing as much in the forms, discourses, and commodities it created *to colonize other people's minds* as in the violence with which it subjected their bodies" (1999:36, my emphasis). Insights of this kind have given us a vantage point to consider the political effects of the language and premises we use *before* we contribute to the naturalization of discourses that are detrimental to ourselves and the people we work with.

References and sources

Appadurai, Arjun (1996) *Modernity at large: cultural dimensions of globalization*. Minneapolis: University of Minnesota Press.

Atkins, Taylor E. (2001) *Blue Nippon: authenticating jazz in Japan*. Durham: Duke University Press.

Bhabha, Homi (1992) "The world and the home." *Social Text* 31–32:141–53.

Boli, J., and Lechner, F. J. (2001) "Globalization: political aspects." In Neil J. Smelser and Paul Baltes (eds), *International encyclopedia of the social and behavioral sciences, vol. 9*, pp. 6261–6. Oxford: Elsevier Science Ltd..

Brown, Ernest (1994) "The guitar and the Mbira: resilience, assimilation, and Pan-Africanism in Zimbabwean music." *The World of Music* 36.2:73–117.

Burnett, Robert (1996) *The global jukebox: the international music industry*. London: Routledge.

Chatterjee, Partha (1986) *Nationalist thought and the colonial world*. Minneapolis: University of Minnesota Press.

Cheater, Angela (1984) *Idioms of accumulation: rural development and class formation among freeholders in Zimbabwe*. Gweru: Mambo Press.

de Sousa Santos, B. (2001) "Globalization: legal aspects." In Neil J. Smelser and Paul Baltes (eds), *International Encyclopedia of the social and biological sciences*. Oxford: Elsevier Science Ltd., pp. 6277–84.

Diethrich, Gregory (2004) "Dancing the diaspora: *Desi* music in Chicago." In Thomas Turino and James Lea (eds), *Identity and the Arts in Diaspora Communities*. Warren, MI: Harmonie Park Press, in press.

Erlmann, Veit (1991) *African Stars: studies in Black South African performance*. Chicago: Chicago University Press.

—— (1993) "The politics and aesthetics of transnational musics." *The World of Music* 35.2:3–15.

—— (1999) *Music, Modernity, and the Global Imagination: South Africa and the West*. New York: Oxford University Press.

Fabian, Johannes (1983) *Time and the other: how anthropology makes its object*. New York: Columbia University Press.

Featherstone, Mike, ed. (1990) *Global culture: nationalism, globalization, and modernity*. London: Sage Publications.

Featherstone, Mike, Lash, Scott, and Robertson, Roland, eds (1995) *Global modernities*. London: Sage.

Fox, Ted (1986) *In the groove: the people behind the music*. New York: St. Martin's Press.

Fried, Albert (1997) *Communism in America: a history in documents*, New York: Columbia University Press.

Frith, Simon (1989) *World music, politics, and social change*. Manchester: Manchester University Press.

Gellner, Ernest (1983) *Nations and nationalism*. Oxford: Basil Blackwell.

Gilroy, Paul (1987) *"There ain't no black in the Union Jack": the cultural politics of race and nation*. Chicago: Chicago University Press.

Guilbault, Jocelyne (1993) "On redefining the "local" through world music." *The World of Music* 35.2:33–47.

Hall, Stuart (1991) "The local and the global: globalization and ethnicity." In Anthony B. King, ed. *Globalization and the World System*, pp. 19–39. Binghamton: State University of New York Press

Hobsbawm, Eric (1990) *Nations and nationalism since 1780: programme, myth, reality*. Cambridge: Cambridge University Press.

Jameson, Fredric (1991) *Postmodernism or, the cultural logic of late capitalism*. Durham: Duke University Press.

Jones, Andrew (2001) *Yellow music: media culture and colonial modernity in the Chinese jazz age*. Durham: Duke University Press.

Kalumbu, Isaac G. (2002) "Pan-African connections in the popular music of Zimbabwe, 1930s to the Early 2000's." Paper delivered at the 47th Annual Meeting of the Society for Ethnomusicology, October 26.

Kanji, Nazneen, and Jazdowska, Kiki (1993) "Structural adjustment and women in Zimbabwe." *Review of African Political Economy* 56:11–26

Kelly, P. F. (1999) The geographies and politics of globalization. progress in human geography, 23.3:379–400.

Kurth, J. (2001) "Globalization: political aspects." In Neil J. Smelser and Paul Baltes (eds), *International encyclopedia of the social and behavioral sciences, vol. 9*, pp. 6284–7. Oxford: Elsevier Science Ltd..

Lieberman, Robbie (1989) *My song is my weapon: people's songs, American Communism, and the politics of culture, 1930–1950*, Urbana: University of Illinois Press.

MacGarry, Brian (1993) *Growth? Without equity? The Zimbabwean economy and the economic structural adjustment programme*. Gweru: Mambo Press.

Muller, Carol (2002) "Disembodying the voice of South African jazz." Paper delivered at the 47th Annual Meeting of the Society for Ethnomusicology, October 25.

Nettl, Bruno, Capwell, Charles, Bohlman, Philip, Wong, Isabel, and Turino, Thomas (1997) *Excursions in world music*. Upper Saddle River, N.J: Prentice Hall.

Peirce, Charles Sanders (1955) *Philosophical writings of Peirce*. Edited by

Justus Buchler. New York: Dover Books.

Perrone, Charles A. and Dunn, Christopher, eds (2001) *Brazilian popular music and globalization*. Gainesville: University Press of Florida.

Ritter, Jonathan (2002) "Terror and the global village: September 11th in Ayacuchan song." Paper delivered at the 47th Annual Meeting of the Society for Ethnomusicology, Estes Park, CO., October 26.

Robertson, Roland (1990) "Mapping the global condition: globalization as the central concept." In Mike Featherstone (ed.), *Global culture: nationalism, globalization, and modernity*, pp. 15–29. London: Sage.

—— (1992) *Globalization: social theory and global culture*. London: Sage.

—— (1995) "Glocalization: time–space and homogeneity–heterogeneity." In Mike Featherstone, Scott Lash and Roland Robertson (eds), *Global modernities*, pp. 25–44. London: Sage.

—— (2001a) "Globalization theory 2000+: Major problematics." In G. Ritzer and B. Smart (eds), *Handbook of social theory*, pp. 458–71. London: Sage.

—— (2001b) "Globality." In Neil J. Smelser and Paul Baltes (eds), *International encyclopedia of the social and behavioral sciences, vol. 9*, pp. 6254–8. Oxford: Elsevier Science Ltd.

Safran, William (1991) "Diasporas in modern societies: myths of homeland and return." *Diaspora* 1.1:83–99.

Slobin, Mark (1992) "Micromusics of the West: a comparative approach." *Ethnomusicology* 36.1:1–88.

Smith, Anthony D. (1990) "Towards a Global Culture?" In Mike Featherstone (ed.), *Global culture: nationalism, globalization, and modernity*. London: Sage.

—— (1995) *Nations and nationalism in a global era*. Cambridge, England: Polity Press.

Taylor, Timothy D. (1997) *Global pop: world music, world markets*. New York: Routledge.

Tölölyan, Khachig (1996) "Rethinking diaspora(s): stateless power in the transnational moment." *Diaspora* 5.1:3–36.

Tomlinson, J. (2000) *Globalization and culture*. Chicago: University of Chicago Press.

Turino, Thomas (1993) *Moving away from silence: music of the Peruvian Altiplano and the experience of urban migration*. Chicago: University of Chicago Press.

—— (1999) "Signs of identity, imagination, and experience: a Peircian semiotic theory for music." *Ethnomusicology* 43.2:221–55.

—— (2000) *Nationalists, cosmopolitans, and popular music in Zimbabwe*. Chicago: University of Chicago Press.

—— (2004a) "Musical nationalism in Latin America: Theoretical Considerations and Selected Case Studies." *Latin American Music Review* 24.2, in press.

—— (2004b) "Introduction: identity and the arts in diaspora communities." in Thomas Turino and James Lea (eds), *Identity and the arts in diaspora communities*, Warren, MI: Harmonie Park Press, in press.

Turino, Thomas and Lea, James, eds. (2004) *Identity and the arts in diaspora communities*, Warren, MI: Harmonie Park Press, in press.

Wallerstein, Immanuel (1974) *The modern world system.* 3 vols. New York: Academic Press.

Waxer, Lise (2002) *The city of musical memory: salsa, record grooves, and popular culture in Cali, Colombia.* Middletown: Wesleyan University Press.

West, Michael (1990) "African middle class formation in colonial Zimbabwe, 1890–1965." Ph.D. dissertation, Harvard University.

Young, Crawford (1976) *The politics of cultural pluralism*, Madison: University of Wisconsin Press.

Note on the author

Thomas Turino is Professor of Musicology and Anthropology at the University of Illinois at Urbana-Champaign. He is author of the books *Moving away from silence: music of the Peruvian Altiplano and the experience of urban migration* (University of Chicago Press, 1993), and *Nationalists, cosmopolitans, and popular music in Zimbabwe* (University of Chicago Press, 2000). He has published various articles on Andean and Zimbabwean music, the semiotics of music and the use of music within political movements.

[10]

Interpreting world music: a challenge in theory and practice[1]

JOCELYNE GUILBAULT

This article focuses on the issue of meanings in 'world music'[2] practices. The main questions addressed are how such musical cultures take on meanings, and what meanings are constructed by such cultures. As Deborah Pacini has indicated, the term 'world music' in this case does not refer to a musical genre. It is used, rather, '[as] a marketing term describing the products of musical cross-fertilisation between the north – the US and Western Europe – and south – primarily Africa and the Caribbean Basin, which began appearing on the popular music landscape in the early 1980s' (1993, p. 48). From 1985, the expanding 'world music' umbrella has come to include practically any musics of cultures of non-European origin.[3]

These musics include those embodying a hybrid character that embrace attentiveness to musical, social or political change occurring elsewhere. They are marketed as 'world music'; they are industrialised; they fuse capital, technical and musical elements from diverse origins; and they are frequently accompanied by an ethnographic and educational discourse visible

in such innovations as extensive liner notes, well-annotated catalogues, and, in the case of the mass media, articles and programs featuring not only current releases, hits and stars, but including as well in-depth features on such topics as the origins of the various styles, or on the cultural (and sometimes political) contexts characterising the 'home' countries of the various musics. (Pacini 1993, p. 55)[4]

From such a definition, world music cultures must be conceived as both transnational and translational, to use Homi Bhabha's terms to describe Third World cultures in general. They must be conceived as transnational in the sense that such musical cultures are, for the most part,

rooted in specific histories of cultural displacement, whether they are the 'middle passage' of slavery and indenture, the 'voyage out' of the civilising mission, the fraught accommodation of Third World migration to the West after the Second World War, or the traffic of economic and political refugees within and outside the Third World. (Bhabha 1994, p. 172)

World cultures must be conceived also as translational but, I would argue, for reasons different from those offered by Bhabha. In his view, world cultures are translational insofar as 'such displacements – now accompanied by the territorial ambitions of "global" media technologies, make the question of how culture signifies, or what is signfied by *culture*, a rather complex issue' (Bhabha 1994, p. 172). I believe that all cultures, not just those with global ambitions, require the work of cultural translation and that all of them, by embodying multi-layered, crisscrossing webs of meanings, are complex to interpret. The reason for stressing that world cultures (in our case, world *music* cultures) are translational is to signal that they present a specific type of configuration which is different from other types of cultures. Because they are 'packaged' as being outside the mainstream, world musics are marketed within specific categories. They are played on specific broadcasts, often organised in compilations with carefully selected line-ups, and, as mentioned above, accompanied in many instances with extensive liner notes, etc. so that they can be 'translatable' (that is, accessible) and have worldwide appeal. From this perspective, to conceptualise world musics as 'transnational' becomes useful through emphasising the specificity and particular challenges these musics present, most particularly in relation to the ways by which they are musically constructed and positioned on world markets.

The label 'world music' could be understood as just another 'plot', a commercial scam to develop new markets and to find new material, sounds and ideas in an area once referred to as 'ethnic music'. While this may be the case, one can also look at world music from another viewpoint and see this new labelling as a site 'from which something *begins its presencing*'.[5] In other words, from the moment phenomena or people are categorised, the very categories that are used to refer to them become the signal of a new presence. My reason for looking at world music from this angle is influenced by post-colonial and post-modern perspectives as conceived by Bhabha. As he explains:

if the jargon of our times – postmodernity, postcoloniality, postfeminism – has any meaning at all, it does not lie in the popular use of the 'post' to indicate sequentiality – *after*-feminism; or polarity – *anti*-modernism. These terms that insistently gesture to the beyond, only embody its 'restless and revisionary energy if they transform the present into an expanded and ex-centric site of experience and empowerment'. (Bhabha 1994, p. 4)

My point of departure in this examination of meanings in world music is to posit that world music allows us to see more clearly than do many other more subtle phenomena the epistemological limits of the ethnocentric and colonial ideas that underpin several of the theoretical assumptions and models that have informed the work of ethnomusicologists. At the same time, I wish to argue that the specificity and processes engaged in the construction of world music have the benefit of inviting us to move beyond the quest for narratives of originary and initial subjectivities, and to address new questions that acknowledge the complexity and fluidity of meanings involved in the act of constructing and rearticulating identities through music.

Rethinking some theories

Some of these questions can best be addressed by referring to *zouk* as one example of world music. *Zouk* is a popular music of the French West Indies and is known as a world music that emerged in the early 1980s. It is usually sung in French-based Creole and is identified as a hybrid music *par excellence* by its music-makers as well as by journalists in the local and international communications media. It is recorded in two stages: the percussion and vocal sections are recorded in the West Indies and the brass section in Paris. The mixing and pressing are done in Paris and then the recordings are shipped to the West Indies and other countries. Most of the artists are constantly flying between both places and touring takes them even futher afield.

As is typical of artists in the French West Indies, most *zouk* musicians have been exposed to and participated in a wide range of musical genres all their lives. These range from local drumming song-dance music, *quadrille*, *biguine*, and *mazurka*, to Haiti's *compas direct*, Dominica's *cadence-lypso*, the Dominican Republic's *merengue*, French-Africa's *soukous*, Latin America's salsa, Jamaica's reggae and dub, the United States's soul, funk music and rap – and other genres with which Antillean musicians are also familiar. *Zouk* music today, in different ways, at different times and for different reasons, draws on many of these musics and as a result has come to encompass an extremely wide range of musical practices. French West-Indian musicians, incidentally, often do not confine themselves to playing only *zouk*. They also play, record and feature on stage other types of music, as exemplified by the keyboard player Jean-Claude Naimro of the leading *zouk* group, Kassav, who frequently performs with Peter Gabriel.

Ethnicity, identity and music

The complexity of the *zouk* phenomenon, typical of many world musics, raises many issues. The first concerns the no longer obvious (if it ever was) relation between ethnicity and music. Indeed, in ethnomusicology, as in many other fields, the belief has persisted that a musical genre could stand for the group with which it is associated – in other words, that a so-called ethnic music reflects the group's ethnicity, its identity. The problem here, it must be stressed, is not the fact that specific musics are associated with specific groups – these relations are not only commonly made but are essential to situate the musics at issue – but rather that only *one* given music is used to define an ethnic group and its identity.

In his article 'Ethnic music traditions in the USA (black music; country music; others; all)', Charles Keil remarks that his research on Gypsy music has led him to recognise that people are in fact 'less mono-ethnic and much more complicated musically, historically, culturally than we think' (1994, p. 176). In the same way as *zouk* artists usually speak of identifying themselves with at least three or four musical genres, the older Gypsy musicians whom Keil interviewed could relate to as many musical genres, if not more. These cases of multiple or overlapping identities, Keil suspects, more often than not represent the norm. From an ethnographic perspective, the question of ethnicity becomes rather problematic and can hardly be defined through the sole examination of the musical genre with which the group is most strongly associated. As Keil puts it, the question is:

Should analysts, both humanist and social scientist, continue to draw tight circles around people and call them members of a culture or subculture? We have just published a book about Polish-American polka music (Keil *et al.* 1992) but only two or three per cent of the Polish-Americans in western New York are enthusiastic enough about polka dances to go to one every so often; have we falsely characterised this community by putting polka music in an emblematic pose, the soul music of an ethnic working class community? (1994, p. 177)[6]

Even though the low percentage of participation Keil is talking about in his case-study on polka does not relate to that observed in the French West Indies for *zouk*, the problem remains essentially the same. His assessment that 'reifying culture and simplifying the identities of people has been standard practice in the American academy for a long time now' (Keil 1994, p. 177) is equally applicable to ethnomusicological research.

Such 'interpretive moves', to use Feld's expression (1984), that made a musical genre stand as the unproblematic emblem of a particular population group – and, by implication, of its musicians – are challenged more than ever by the visible, multiple allegiances that musicians of world music display in their musical practices. What is the relation between musics, a population group's identities, and the issue of ethnicities? Confronting these complex realities calls not only for a redefinition of culture but also for a redefinition of bonds, boundaries and borders.

Bonds, boundaries, and borders: points of articulation and rearticulation

As many authors have stated (for example, Clifford 1992; Slobin 1992; Pacini 1993; Chow 1993; Cohen 1994;), national boundaries are becoming increasingly irrelevant to locate cultures, 'as commodities of all sorts – including music – are being produced and consumed in multiple international contexts rather than one culturally-specific location' (Pacini 1993, p. 48). As Bhabha explains, 'the very concepts of homogenous national cultures, the consensual or contiguous transmission of historical traditions, or "organic" ethnic communities – *as the ground of cultural comparativism* – are in a profound process of redefinition' (1994, p. 5). In this context, Keil has made the recommendation of going acoustic or going through the process of 'retribalisation, planting the seeds for new ethnicities' in order to fight the trend that he sees as 'the universalising, the globalisation of culture and the trend toward a single civilisation'; he also suggests starting new local music groups to lift his scepticism about 'the global economy eroding the old nation-state identities and leaving space for local communities to reassert themselves' (1994, p. 177-8). Even though the two recommendations may be worthwhile enterprises in themselves, they do not represent, in my mind, a solution to locating cultures and doing ethnographic or documentary work today. World musics are proliferating and are, so to speak, here to stay. What is needed, I believe, is a new focus, one that shifts away from trying to identify and document already formed and stabilised cultures towards examining the *processes* by which these are constituted and continually reformulating and realigning themselves. This new focus should be on what have been called *points of articulation and rearticulation*.

Several authors (see Mouffe 1979; Middleton 1990; Shepherd 1993) have already noted the importance of looking at points of articulation, but the notion of what this involves has varied tremendously from one writer to another. The idea to which I refer has little to do with a politics of subversion that is purportedly engaged in reassigning meanings in received musical symbols through the process of consumption or reproduction. Rather, following Will Straw's definition, it concerns the making and remaking of alliances between communities as the crucial processes within popular music (Straw 1991, p. 370). Following Grossberg, points of articulation refer not only to what establishes productive links between, say, political or musical practices but also to how two or more practices are being shaped by and through each other (Grossberg 1992, p. 50). As Grossberg reminds us,

Pointing out that these two practices are articulated together, that the pieces 'fit' together, is not the same as defining the mode of that articulation, the nature of that fit . . . Nor is arguing that a particular articulation is taken up the same as describing the way it is taken up. Without this dimension, the analyst's stories can only be stories of our historical losses. They can only tell how a context has already been articulated. They cannot identify the form of that articulation nor, in more social terms, the investment that has been made in it. (1992, p. 56)

In practice, the focus on how, at which levels, and why *bonds* or cleavages are created requires that we pay attention to the strategies involved in music-making at different times, for different spaces and for particular interests in relation to specific markets and the various musical scenes in which the music is performed (Straw 1991). By doing so, the advantage of focusing on points of articulation and rearticu- lation is twofold: it allows us not only to examine the processes involved in the construction of identity but also to acknowledge the performative aspect of iden- tity[7] and thereby its relational character. In addition, it helps researchers to avoid totalising experiences and 'fixing' cultures as well as subjects.

The syncretism characteristic of world musics such as *zouk* has allowed these musics to develop 'affective alliances' (Grossberg 1984) that are, as Will Straw points out, 'just as powerful as those normally observed within practices which appear to be more organically grounded in local circumstances' (1991, p. 374). From a symbolic perspective, we also need to look at points of articulation to see how *boundaries*, erected under the banner of 'we' and 'they', signify different things at different times and in different contexts. For example, the affective alliances developed through *zouk* take on different meanings for French West Indian musi- cians, depending on, for instance, whether they perform *zouk* in France, Mar- tinique or Guadeloupe. In the first case, Martinicans and Guadeloupeans, notwith- standing their rivalry back home, form a 'we' in relation to those whom they identify as non-West Indians. When *zouk* is performed or heard in Martinique or Guadeloupe, it is at times perceived as a unifying force, a means of overcoming the rivalry historically cultivated by France.[8] At other times, it becomes a contested terrain where Martinicans and Guadeloupeans see themselves as opponents in local markets, with one form of Creole vying with the other and so on.

The process of creolisation

The performative aspect of identity is an issue not only in relation to the making and remaking of affective alliances but also in the *process of creolisation*[9] that charac- terises most world musics, including *zouk*. The new attention to creolisation that is put into relief in a music such as *zouk* is not, as Pacini makes clear, a consequence

of the musical exchange itself – which has been taking place between northern colonial metropolises and their former African and Caribbean colonies for decades – but rather the emergence – practically simultaneously around 1982 – of new, interlocking commercial infrastructures established specifically to cultivate and nurture the appetites of First World listeners for exotic new sounds from the Third World. (1993, p. 49-50)

In this context, what is different is that creolisation has acquired a new status: it used to be looked down upon and ascribed pejorative connotations as a result of the legacy of colonialism, but now it is considered – at least by a large portion of the local Caribbean populations – as positive, a sign of health and growth, and an openness to the world. From an analytical point of view, the new status and attention given to creolisation, as Martinican political scientist Fred Reno remarks, have 'the benefits of bringing into focus specific histories and cultures and oppos- ing polarising generalisations' (1994, p. 13).[10] Furthermore, examination of the process of creolisation in world music has shown how musicians often act as *cultural brokers*, to use Chris Waterman's expression (1990). In *zouk*, the leading group, Kassav, has been telling Guadeloupeans and Martinicans what it means to be French West Indian. By making the conscious move of using musicians from both islands in their group and by promoting the explicit *métissage* of their music – to mention only these two instances – Kassav has greatly helped (according to local observers, journalists and fans alike) to build a sense of pan-French West Indian identity, even though this is at times contested among Martinicans and Guadeloupeans.

The issue of creolisation, taken up most prominently in discourses about world music, has permitted, in my view, a productive questioning of the theory that there must be some degree of compatibility, determined on the basis of immanent qualities, to allow musics to intermingle (see Kartomi 1981; Middleton 1990; Shepherd 1993). The discussion of world music makes it clear that the question of compatibility cannot be addressed in terms of the immanent or essentialist characteristics of a music. Rather, it must be seen in terms of people's conceptions of, and agreement upon, which musical elements are compatible and which are not. The amazing juxtaposition of rhythms, instruments, sounds and melodic lines embodied in world musics such as *zouk*, *bhangra* and *rai*, to name only these better known musical genres, have surprised some listeners by the daring, novel combinations hitherto never imagined or thought possible.[11]

Structural homology

In the same vein, the complexities involved in world music make us more suspicious of many of the assumptions underpinning the theory of structural homology, a theory which has been widely used in ethnomusicology – even if the concept has seldom, if ever, been called homology (Morrison 1993, p. 1). Even though the theory has been criticised by many in this field, especially in relation to its chief exponent, Alan Lomax (1968), the insistence on structural resonances, or more precisely, on homologous relationships between music and social structures, definitely persists.[12]

However, as Val Morrison argues, the concept of structural homology 'is increasingly problematic when applied to the contemporary study of culture' (1993, p. 12), as is well illustrated by the case of world music. If the establishment of a correspondence between the structure of an activity in a village and that of a musical practice in the same village has often found some easy acceptance in the past – even though, as will be explained below, it was problematic nonetheless – the specificity of world music by its characteristic combination of several musical elements makes such a correspondence appear, as noted earlier, more suspicious. The problem, initially, presents itself this way: by appropriating various musical so-called 'structures', do world musics not suggest through their creolisation that the meanings of such structures are in fact reinscribed? that a 'structure' placed in a different context, precisely by taking on other meanings, can no longer be related or be made to correspond to another structure, simply because the two structures look similar? This type of argument is normally what incites some researchers to re-examine the assumptions underpinning the theory of structural homology. Viewing world music from this perspective raises, perhaps more forcefully than heretofore, the need to reconsider this theory. But it should be made clear, it is not in its application to world music that the theory of structural homology is problematic: the flaw is an epistemological one.[13]

As many authors have explained elsewhere (Archer 1988; Appadurai 1990; Middleton 1990; Shepherd 1991, 1992, 1993; Morrison 1993), the theory of structural homology can be challenged because it identifies relations from characteristics found in one practice, A, and another practice, B, and from that basis derives the meanings of the two. As Line Grenier explains, this model implies: first, that the characteristics of the two practices are taken as given; secondly, that they are fixed; thirdly, that the structures on which these practices apparently rest are given a status of something seemingly pre-existing; and, fourthly, that these structures, in and of themselves, are given the highest importance in understanding the meanings of the practices in question – at the expense of everything else, that is, all the other aspects that are also constitutive of practices.[14] In such a model, the specificity of each practice is erased and the characteristics of these ahistorical *structures* define the practice.

This questioning of the premises underpinning the theory of structural homology does not mean that structures no longer have any meaning or that they are not important. What it stresses, however, is that instead of looking at 'structures' as pre-existing things, we must look at how they have been formed. Within this perspective, we may more appropriately use the term 'configurations' to highlight how, through mediations, some patterns seem to have been crystallised and attributed a semblance of fixity. Unlike that of structure, the notion of configuration emphasises the conjunctural and the singular and, by implication, signals that some of the configurations that inform the practices in question may have more weight than others – at certain times for different reasons and for different people. The benefit of such an approach, I believe, is that it permits us to avoid privileging a priori some elements as being, by definition, more significant than others. Moreover, it allows us to understand how some of the canons in music in particular have been constructed.

Music and space

At another level, a music such as *zouk* that is conceived in different localities and circulated widely raises the issue of *borders*, the relation between music and space. A world music such as *zouk* permits us to see how geographical references are rearticulated in the process of their enactment (or placement) and circulation. It is not that the geographic reference disappears but that its status in the analysis is changed. In other words, when one hears *zouk*, one can, and often does, associate this music with Guadeloupe and Martinique. As Morrison observes,[15] the symbolic construction of community through space remains as strong as ever, but the symbol of that space or, more precisely, the meanings invested in that space, is what changes – not only over time but also within the group constructing that space.

World music provides a privileged site from which to observe the interrelation of spaces and the importance such networks have in how spaces are defined. In practice, this means that the association of Guadeloupe or Martinique with *zouk*, for example, leads us to conceive Guadeloupe or Martinique less as isolated or fixed entities than in relational terms, in connection with the various other spaces with which these countries interact. More specifically, this means that, depending on the context in which *zouk* is played, the symbolic status granted to Guadeloupe and Martinique may be thought of more in: political terms, *zouk* played in France places Guadeloupe and Martinique as French Departments; cultural terms, *zouk* played in Africa suggests Guadeloupe and Martinique as spaces strongly influenced by African-derived traditions; or social terms, *zouk* played in African or Caribbean nightclubs in Montreal places Guadeloupe and Martinique as Third World countries, minority-status places. The list could continue, in racial, linguistic, religious terms, etc. Within this perspective, one can conclude that the symbolism of spaces (such as Guadeloupe and Martinique) in connection with the wider circulation of a world music (such as *zouk*) takes on different meanings for different people depending on the various social, political and economic positions these people occupy in relation to the country and the music.

Rethinking methodologies

In ethnographic work, the challenge posed by the constant, ever-changing creolisation of various elements in world musics and the multiple allegiances and senses of belonging that such musics create have led several researchers of world music and, more generally, of popular music to focus less on the experience of a given 'community' and more on the experience of individual subjects. Several studies are prominent (Collins 1985; Erlmann 1989, 1991; Davis and Simon 1992; Crafts, Cavicchi and Keil 1993; Loza 1993), but the one that stands out is that of Sara Cohen. In her article 'Ethnography and popular music studies' (1993) for example, she shows how a focus on subjects in their specific and multiple social, cultural, political and economic networks allows us to re-examine many of the assumptions made about popular music practices and processes by investigating, as Frith suggests, 'how commercial decisions are reached . . . how musicians make their musical choices, how they define their social role, how they handle its contradictions' (as quoted by Cohen 1993, p. 127). While detailed ethnographic studies have yielded much information on the complexities involved in subjective experience and the flexible and dynamic character of that experience, the interpretation of such experiences, however, has represented a real challenge for many researchers. In practice, this has led many of them to re-examine the traditional modes of explanation used in the social sciences. The perspective of Antoine Hennion is most useful in this respect. In his book *La Passion Musicale* (1993, pp. 221–67), he summarises the main traditional modes of explanation used in the social sciences in two categories: the linear and the circular models.

The linear model makes music an artefact of the society or of the subject, which means that the characteristics of a society or of a subject are used to explain a musical practice. In other words, music is explained in terms of other orders of things, namely, society and subject. The circular model, on the other hand, attempts to correlate the characteristics (taken as given) of any activity, object or phenomenon in a society with those of a musical practice in that same society. In the first model, as Hennion explains (1993, p. 232), what is seen as the *cause*, namely, the society or the subject, is too strong and substitutes itself for realities that are in fact heterogeneous, and it furthermore reduces the object, in our case, music, to the social or, vice versa, the social to music (for a similar argument, see Williams 1961, p. 45). In the second model, the correlation of the characteristics of an activity, object or phenomenon with those of music is also problematic, as it becomes simply an exercise of rationalisation, an attempt to prove coherence. This then leaves aside any contradictions or what are then considered marginal occurrences, and at the same time erases the specificity of the music in question.[16] This is where, I believe, a focus on *mediations* becomes useful.

Mediations and agency

The term 'mediation' has been given several meanings by different authors.[17] The definition I am proposing for my purposes is as follows: mediations, which may be construed as a subject, an event, a technology, a musical field, or a historical narrative, are where the social materialisation, the cultural expression of music, and the construction of its meanings are delimited and configured. What makes the identification of mediations extremely important is that it points out what, at a particular time, comes into play in the ways people conceive and perceive things. As I have explained elsewhere,

[T]he term 'mediation' is here chosen over what is often loosely referred to as 'context' by ethnographers, because what is described as 'context' too frequently takes the form of an amorphous element that is simply there, part of the scene where a given phenomenon is enacted. By choosing the term 'mediation', I want to stress the agency and the transformative effect of specific events, experiences, and sets of circumstances involved in shaping the experience of *zouk* in the islands. (Guilbault 1992, pp. 132–3)

The advantage of the studies that take mediations into account, as Hennion explains (1993, p. 225), is that they show not only how mediations help to shape and orient meanings in musical practices but also how they act as a screen between a musical practice and its interpreters. In other words, by taking into account the work of mediations, researchers are less tempted to rush into either attributing too much authority to the subject and too many attributes to the object or to reducing object and subject into the arbitrary explanation of 'the group' (Hennion 1993, p. 225). In the first instance, I am referring to ethnographic accounts that would read, for example: 'Pierre-Edouard Décimus, the founder of Kassav, advised that, to succeed internationally, Antillean musicians needed to produce more technically sophisticated music.' To simply say this would be to overstate the authority of Edouard Décimus and attribute too many properties to the music Antillean musicians used to play. To appreciate how Décimus came to give such advice, one would have to be told about all the mediations at work here – the comments of tourists, his tours in Europe and the particular circumstances, time and place in which he operated. One would also have to understand how he was what he was at the time, how he came to define the Antillean music scene as he did, and how he attributed to Antillean music certain characteristics and to musicians certain talents and skills. Only then could one make sense of his advice on what needed to be done to penetrate the international market.

In other words, a focus on mediations allows us to see how certain events, people, technology, etc., are defined through specific mediations and how they, in turn, mediate specific social, political, cultural or economic practices. This, in my opinion, is precisely what makes a focus on mediations so important: it allows us to view realities as being always in process and, by so doing, to conceive of 'agency' as well as 'agents' in ways which are less restrictive than has usually been the case. If we accept that realities are always in process, agency cannot be about change, but rather about qualifying the process(es) by and through which realities are enacted. In other words, agency calls attention to *how* projects are put into place. *What*, at the material level, puts these projects into motion is what will be referred to as 'agents'.[18] Agents, in this case, are no longer the exclusive attribute of human beings, as has been often proposed.[19] For example, the publicity about the University of Ottawa's bilingual official mandate (discourse), the proximity of the University campus to one's home (physical location), as well as its faculty members (human beings), could all be identified as the 'agents' which have allowed a group of students to continue their higher education at the University of Ottawa (material realisation of their project).[20] At a practical level, a focus on mediations as defined above becomes a crucial analytical tool which allows us to understand the means by which authority is produced, how the systems of power/ knowledge are defined and how the politics of representation (who speaks for whom by playing such and such a music, and why focus on this musical event rather than another one) are articulated.

A focus on both mediations and agency[21] has direct implications for ethnographic work. In practice, this means that attention should be paid not only to the more stable and visible forces such as those associated with the long-established institutions that help to orient and shape musical practices and meanings. It should also take into account the less visible, informal contacts and unofficial, but otherwise extremely powerful, polylateral markets and exchanges that may not only inform the ways in which these practices are conceived (Guilbault 1993a) but also help to put them into motion. It should be noted that to pay attention to agency should not be taken to mean that each instance of musical change or synthesis should be read, as Straw warns us, 'as unproblematic evidence of a reordering of social relations' (1991, p. 375).[22] Rather, what a focus on agency stresses is how agents are engaged in the 'dialogic, performative "community" of [a musical culture]' (Gilroy referred to in Bhabha 1994, p. 178) – with all the paradoxes this usually entails. For example, while Antillean musicians foreground their difference through *zouk*, and while this difference is celebrated in France, this same difference is used in France to make it easier to ghettoise the very musicians who have put it forward (see Guilbault 1994).

Conclusion

My initial questions on the issue of meanings in 'world music' practices stemmed from my experience with the study of *zouk* (Guilbault 1993b). In common with several authors of ethnographic studies on popular music, I have tried to provide a sense of the multiple possible constructions and interpretations involved in such phenomena. However, each of the perspectives put forward ended up being presented as 'fixed'. What has been missing in my account has been to show how, through music, people position themselves differently according to specific spaces, times, and interests and, by so doing, mobilise different politics of identity.

The aim of this article has been to explore ways by which ethnographers can theoretically and methodologically address the issue of fluidity of meanings in musical practices. To do so, I chose to focus on so-called 'world musics', not because this question is unique to them – such a question could be addressed in relation to any type of music – but because, as previously explained, they are conceived as transnational and translational and, from this perspective, can be said to best dramatise the issue of meanings in relation to many questions central to ethnomusicology. In particular, I concentrated on precisely those questions which world musics seem to problematise: the relation of music and ethnicity/identity, and that of music and space. The multiple allegiances the musicians of many world musics have exhibited through their music practices and the various positionings they have adopted in various international markets all point to the fact that cultures or people's identities are not 'lodged' somewhere or in something but rather, as I have argued, emerge from points of articulation. What has been at issue, here, has been to show how, by focusing on points of articulation in terms of the making and remaking of alliances between communities as the crucial processes within popular music, one can acknowledge the relational and perform-ative aspect of identity through music.

In this article, I have drawn on the fact that many of the so-called world musics are intentionally (re)presented and celebrated as hybrid musics,[23] as emer-ging from the process of creolisation in order to make two arguments. In the first case, using as my point of departure the fact that world musics commonly appropriate to themselves various musical structures and, within this different context, assign them new meanings, I have examined critically the premises on which the theory of structural homology is based. I have argued principally that, instead of looking at 'structures' as pre-existing entities with fixed correspond-ences, we must look at how they have been formed. Related to this argument, my second point has gone a little further by suggesting that the term 'configurations' may be more apt than structures at describing how some patterns have acquired more weight than others and how, in some cases, they have become musical canons.

My attempt to acknowledge the fluidity of meanings in world musics has led me to rethink the basis from which ethnographers make their interpretations. If we accept that the making and remaking of alliances play a crucial role in the construction of identity, then as Grossberg pointed out, the next question to be asked was: what has made these alliances possible and meaningful? I proposed here to focus on mediations and agency as our points of entry to understanding what, at a particular time, comes into play in the ways people conceive and per-ceive things (mediations) and what, at the material level, puts alliances into motion (agency/agents). It is with this focus in mind that, I hope, we may be in a better position to meet the challenge in theory and practice of developing a better under-standing of the multiple and ever-changing meanings of world musics.

Endnotes

1. I would like to thank the Social Sciences and Humanities Research Council of Canada for its financial assistance, without which this art-icle could not have been written. I am most grateful to Ramon Pelinski for inviting me to give a series of lectures in his graduate sem-inar on popular music at the Université de Montréal and giving me the opportunity to test my ideas. My sincere thanks to all the participants for their helpful questions and comments. I am especially indebted to Line Grenier and Val Morrison for sharing their insights with me. An earlier version of this article was presented at a colloquium on Re-Theorizing Music organised by P. Brett and J. Pasler at the UC Humanities Research Insti-tute at the University of California, Irvine, December, 1994.

2. In the United States, 'world beat' is a widely used expression. See Deborah Pacini's article 'A view from the South: Spanish Caribbean perspectives on world beat' (1993, p. 58) for her explanation of why the label 'world beat' is preferred in the United States.

3. The description that follows was formulated with the collaboration of Line Grenier and Val Morrison (November 1994).

4. Steven Feld's own definition of 'world music' emphasises its essential characteristic of 'wide circulation'. He states, 'as a marketing label, the term has come to refer to any commercially available music of non-Western origin and circulation, as well as to musics of dominated ethnic minorities within the Western world: music *of* the world to be sold *around* the world' (1994, p. 266). Feld's problematisation of the concomitant label of 'world beat', used at times interchangeably with the term 'world music', is most important but goes beyond the scope of this article.

5. This way of conceiving labelling is inspired by a passage from Homi K. Bhabha's book *The Location of Culture* (1994, pp. 4–5) on the meanings of the demography of the new internationalism.

6. For a similar argument on the relation between cultural identity and musical practices, see Slobin (1992, p. 2).

7. This new attention to the performative aspect of identity is tellingly illustrated by the list of daily themes at the Glasgow 1995 International Conference of IASPM (International Association for the Study of Popular Music), which include *'Performing History'*, *'Performing Technology'* and *'Performing Texts'* (my emphasis).

8. For further information on the legacy of French colonialism in Martinique and Guadeloupe, see Guilbault (1996, pp. 26–7).

9. The term 'creolisation' refers here to a mixture of elements and should not be confused with the terms 'Westernisation' and 'acculturation'. Whereas the term 'Westernisation' refers exclusively to the adoption of Western elements by a given culture, the term 'acculturation' refers to the transfer of an element from a culture (not necessarily Western) to another culture. The term 'creolisation' does not imply any of these definitions. It here refers to the process whereby several influences or traditions come into contact to give birth to a new, distinctive entity. It does not suggest a priori the predominance of one tradition over another, or the existence of a given tradition before various elements come into contact. Rather, closer to the meaning given to the term 'syncretism', it invokes the merging into one of two or more unique influences or traditions (Wester's definition of the term 'syncretism'). For a critical review of many of these terms, see Kartomi (1981).

10. This quotation has been translated from French.

11. For further information on the remarkable combination of most contrasting musical elements in such musics, see Guilbault (1993b) on *zouk*, Burton and Awan (1994) on *bhangra*, and Morgan (1994) on *rai*.

12. It would be easy here to name several authors, but this would not be fair. I feel that most of us have had recourse to this analytical model at some point or another.

13. I warmly thank Val Morrison and Line Grenier for guiding me through my argument here.

14. This analysis is based on Line Grenier's insights shared with me in an informal conversation, November 1994.

15. I thank Val Morrison for sharing this insight with me.

16. Note the similarity between the circular model as described by Hennion and the theory of homology discussed earlier.

17. See, for example, Theodor Adorno's well known, if contested, theory of mediation (1976); Ian Chambers' insistence on the importance of taking into account the complex density of mediations involved in the production and reproduction of pop music (1982); Antoine Hennion's call to look at mediation rather than media (1983, 1986, 1993); Richard Middleton's comments on the various definitions and uses of mediation (1990); and Jesus Martin–Barbero's emphasis on mediations to highlight 'agency' (1993). For my use of 'agency', see below.

18. This way of conceiving agency and agents is inspired by Grenier's own translation of Foucault's approach to discourses. For further information on this subject, see Grenier (in press).

19. Anthony Giddens defines agency as 'the stream of actual or contemplated casual interventions of *corporeal beings* in the ongoing process of events-in-the-world'. This definition, as Giddens explains, assumes that the notion of agency is connected directly to *'human practices*, as an ongoing series of "practical activities"'; that a *person* could have acted otherwise; and that the world as constituted by a stream of events-in-process independent of the agent does not hold out a pre-determined future' (1993, p. 81, my emphasis).

20. Agents, it should be specified, cannot be taken as 'givens'; they are always identified at the analytical level insofar as what is said to put projects into motion may be associated with different things, people or institu-

tions by different interpreters whose views may vary in relation to a multitude of factors, including among others time, place, gender, profession, location as well as the relative investment the interpreters have in the project(s) in question.

21. The two terms, albeit conceptually interrelated, should not be confused. Whereas mediations point to the various forces that orient

the ways in which experiences are conceived and perceived, agency refers to the processes by and through which these experiences take place.

22. See also Erlmann (1993, p. 5) on the subject.

23. Ironically so, since hybrid musics in general have been for so long denigrated for this very reason. For further information on this subject, see Guilbault (1991).

References

Adorno, T.W. 1976. *Introduction to the Sociology of Music* (New York, first printed in German in 1962)

Appadurai, A. 1990. 'Disjuncture and difference in the global cultural economy, in *Global Culture*, ed. M. Featherstone (London), pp. 295–310.

Archer, M.S. 1988. *Culture and Agency* (Cambridge)

Bhabha, H.K. 1994. *The Location of Culture* (London)

Burton, K. and Awan, S. 1994. 'Bhangra bandwagon: Asian music in Britain', in *World Music: The Rough Guide*, ed. Simon Broughton *et al.* (London), pp. 228–32

Chambers, I. 1982. 'Some critical tracks', *Popular Music*, 2, pp. 19–36

Chow, R. 1993. *Writing Diaspora: Tactics of Intervention in Contemporary Cultural Studies* (Bloomington)

Clifford, J. 1992. 'Traveling cultures', in *Cultural Studies*, ed. L. Grossberg *et al.* (New York), pp. 96–116

Cohen, S. 1993. 'Ethnography and popular music studies', *Popular Music*, 12/2, pp. 123–38

1994. 'Identity, place and the "Liverpool sound" ', in *Ethnicity and Music: The Musical Construction of Place*, ed. M. Stokes (Oxford), pp. 117–34

Collins, J. 1985. *African Pop Roots: The Inside Rhythms of Africa* (London)

Crafts, S., Cavicchi, D. and Keil, C. (eds) 1993. *My Music* (Hanover and London)

Davis, St. and Simon, P. 1992. *Reggae Bloodlines: In Search of the Music and Culture of Jamaica* (New York)

Erlmann, V. 1989. 'A conversation with Joseph Shabalala of Ladysmith Black Mambazo: aspects of African performers' lifestories', *The World of Music*, 31, pp. 31–58

1991. *African Stars: Studies in Black South African Performance* (Chicago)

1993. 'The politics and aesthetics of transnational musics', *The World of Music*, 35, pp. 3–15

Feld, S. 1984. 'Communication, music, and speech about music', *Yearbook for Traditional Music*, 16, pp. 1–18

1994. 'From schizophrenia to schismogenesis: on the discourses and commodification practices of "World Music" and "World Beat" ', in *Music Grooves* by C. Keil and S. Feld (Chicago), pp. 257–89

Giddens, A. 1993. *New Rules of Sociological Method* (Stanford)

Grenier, L. (in press) " 'Cultural exemptionalism' revisited: Quebec music industries in the face of free trade', in *Media, Culture and Free Trade: NAFTA's Impact on Cultural Industries in Canada, Mexico and the United States*, ed. E. McAnamy (Austin)

Grossberg, L. 1984. 'Another boring day in paradise: rock'n'roll and the empowerment of everyday life', *Popular Music*, 4, pp. 225–58

1991. 'Rock, territorialization and power', *Cultural Studies*, 5/3, pp. 358–67

1992. *We Gotta Get Out Of This Place: Popular Conservatism and Postmodern Culture* (London)

Guilbault, J. 1991. 'Ethnomusicology and the study of music in the Caribbean', *Studies in Third World Societies*, 45, pp. 117–40

1992. 'A world music back home: the power of mediations', *Popular Music Perspectives*, 3, pp. 131–40

1993a. 'On redefining the local through world music', *The World of Music*, 35, pp. 33–47

1993b. *Zouk: World Music in the West Indies* (Chicago)

1994. 'Musique et développement: le rôle du *zouk* en Guadeloupe', paper presented at a colloquium 'Musiques et Société', Festival de Fort-de-France, Martinique, 24 July

Hennion, A. 1983. 'The production of success: an anti–musicology of the pop song', *Popular Music*, 3, pp. 159–94

1993. *La Passion Musicale* (Paris)

Hennion, A. And Meadel, C. 1986. 'Programming music: radio as mediator', *Media, Culture and Society*, 8, pp. 281–303

44   *Jocelyne Guilbault*

Kartomi, Margaret J. 1981 'The processes and results of musical culture contact: a discussion of terminology and concepts', *Ethnomusicology*, 25, pp. 227–50

Keil, A., Keil, C. and Blau, R. 1992. *Polka Happiness* (Philadelphia)

Keil, C. 1994. ' "Ethnic" music traditions in the USA (black music; country music; others; all)', *Popular Music*, 13/2, pp. 175–8

Lomax, A. 1968. *Folk Song Style and Culture* (New Jersey)

Loza, S. 1993. *Barrio Rhythm: Mexican American Music in Los Angeles* (Urbana)

Martín-Barbero, J. 1993. *Communication, Culture and Hegemony: From the Media to Mediations* (London)

Middleton, R. 1990. *Studying Popular Music* (Philadelphia)

Morgan, A. 1994. 'Thursday night fever: Algerian Rai', in *World Music: The Rough Guide*, ed. S. Broughton *et al.* (London), pp. 126–34

Morrison, V. 1993. 'The structural homology and its discontents: accounting for contemporary popular music', unpublished manuscript

Mouffe, C. 1979. *Gramsci and Marxist Theory* (London)

Pacini, D.H. 1993. 'A view from the south: Spanish Caribbean perspectives on world beat', *The World of Music*, 35, pp. 48–69

Reno, F. 1994. 'Introduction', in *Les Antilles–Guyanne au Rendez–Vous de L'Europe: Le Grand Tournant?*, ed. R. Burton and F. Reno (Paris), pp. 5–18

Shepherd, J. 1991. *Music as Social Text* (Cambridge)

    1992. 'Music as Cultural Text', in *Companion to Contemporary Musical Thought*, ed. Paynter et al. (London), pp. 128–55

    1993. 'Value and power in music: an English Canadian perspective', in *Relocating Cultural Studies*, eds V. Blundel, J. Shepherd, and I. Taylor (London)

Slobin, M. 1992. 'Micromusics of the West: a comparative approach', *Ethnomusicology*, 36, pp. 1–88

Straw, W. 1991. 'Systems of articulations, logics of change: communities and scenes in popular music', *Cultural Studies*, 5/3, pp. 368–88

Waterman, C. 1990. 'Our tradition is a very modern tradition: popular music and the construction of a Pañ-Yoruba identity', *Ethnomusicology*, 34, pp. 367–79

Williams, R. 1961. *The Long Revolution* (London)

[11]

Between globalisation and localisation: a study of Hong Kong popular music

WAI-CHUNG HO

Abstract

Popular music in Hong Kong is the production of a multi-faceted dynamic of international and local factors. Although there has been much attention to its growth from different perspectives, there has been no single study that systematically addresses the complicated interplay of the two interrelated processes of globalisation and localisation that lie behind its development. The main aim of this paper is to explore how social circumstances mediate musical communication among Hong Kong popular artists and audiences, and contribute to its growing sense of cultural identity – how locality emerges in the context of a global culture and how global facts take local form. Firstly, I propose a conceptual framework for understanding the cultural dynamics of popular music in terms of the discourse of globalisation and localisation. Secondly, I consider local practices of musical consumption and production. Thirdly, this paper discusses the impact of the global entertainment business on local popular music. I conclude with a summary of the effects of the interaction between globalisation and localisation on Hong Kong popular music.

A framework of analysis: globalisation and localisation

Globalisation, which generally implies westernisation and the Asianisation of Asia, is often posited to be a culturally, economically, technologically and socially homogenising force in the distribution of music, whilst localisation refers to the empowerment of local forces and the (re)emergence of local music cultures. These two notions of globalisation and localisation seem to be mutually contradictory, posing a fundamental dilemma for the understanding of the transformation of popular cultures into global forms. As argued by Law (forthcoming), the debate between globality and locality, or between homogeneity and heterogeneity in globalisation discourse, could be regarded as a product of similar antagonisms in the literature of development concerning theories of modernisation, dependency and world systems. Although there is no clear definition or model of globalisation (Hirst and Thompson 1996), its discourse attempts to theorise the phenomenon in terms of the temporal and spatial compression of human activities on the globe, to recognise, explore and explain the interaction and interdependence of economics, politics and cultures beyond local, regional and national boundaries, and to predict possible influences on human activities (Law, forthcoming, also see, for example, Featherstone 1995; Comeliau 1997; Poisson 1998; Jones 1999; Crawford 2000; Croteau and Hoynes 2000). Cohen (1995) suggests that locality could be most usefully used in popular music studies 'to discuss networks of social relationships, practices, and

processes extending across particular places', and to draw attention to interconnections and interdependencies between, for example, space and time, the contextual and the conceptual, the individual and the collective, the self and the other (p.
65). In this respect the local is defined by reference not only to a community, but
also to a shared sense of place within global culture. Globalisation promotes the
meeting of musical cultures, whilst simultaneously encouraging regional differences.

Local popular industries perceive their potential audience in international
terms, and 'local' pop markets are now awash with global sounds, since, as Wallis
and Malm (1984) maintain, globalisation encourages popular musical practices to
look towards global styles for possible inspiration, whilst also looking inwards to
(re)create national music styles and forms. For decades, critics have depicted the
international circulation of American and British pop as cultural imperialism. Yet
US-American and British youth have increasingly been shaped by Asian cultural
imports, such as 'Sweet and Sour Chicken', 'Spring rolls', 'Ginger Beef', and 'Peking
Duck' in their local Chinese restaurants, to the point at which 'Chicken Masala' has
now replaced fish and chips as the most popular take-away meal in the UK. On the
other hand, variations also exist in the interpretation of East-West food and the
fusion of flavours and cooking styles may make the dishes more exciting, such as
East-west combinations like 'Peking Duck and Chips' and 'Chicken Tikka Masala'.
These dishes are not only the creation of Asian-Western food combinations, but are
also symptomatic of processes of cultural assimilation. Similarly, there is widespread recognition of the willingness amongst popular musicians 'to create novel
forms that express a widespread experience of dislocation' (Jenkins 2001, p. 89).
For example, contemporary Afro-pop sometimes combines the 'electric guitars of
Western rock and roll with melodies and rhythms of traditional African music',
whilst Western rock drummers have long adopted 'a tradition from Africa whereby
the sounds of different drums are combined' (Croteau and Hoynes 2000, p. 333).
Jenkins (2001) describes such musical eclecticism as the product of 'third-culture'
youths, who fuse elements from mixed racial, national or linguistic backgrounds.
Although the big international music companies affect local production, their markets are also influenced by particular local cultures. So, globalisation signifies more
than environmental interconnectedness, and the meaning of musical products with
global features strikes at the heart of the major social and political issues of our
time. This is how Bennett (1999) represents the attempts to rework hip hop as a
localised mode of expression by Turkish and Moroccan youth in Frankfurt.

Economic globalisation is often considered to undermine the local foundations
of the popular culture industry. The flow of capital through transnational monetary
systems and multinational companies means that words, ideas, images and sounds
of different cultures are made available to vast networks of people through the
transmission of electronic media. Among the most prominent multinational electronic media companies are two Internet partnerships – MusicNet, involving AOL,
RealNetworks, EMI, BMG and Warner; and Duet, incorporating Yahoo!, Universal
and Sony. The two most recognised online music providers so far, Napster and
MP3.com, have also linked up with record companies (Source: http://www.
grayzone.com/ifpi61201.htm). Furthermore, the international division of labour and
the global circulation of commodities have ensured that processes of production
and consumption are no longer confined to a geographically bounded territory.
Consequently, economic globalisation has been characterised as the 'deterritorialisa-

tion' (Appadurai 1996) or 'denationalisation' (Sassen 1996) of nation-states. Global economic forces 'reside in global networks that link different nations and cultures in profit-maximising webs of production', leading to the transformation of all sectors of all state economies and their mutual accommodation in the global context (Crawford 2000, pp. 71–2). Negus (1999) maintains that the 'global market' is a concept that has to be constructed in a particular way to target 'the most profitable categories of music within the recording industry' (p. 156). However, as we have seen, the (re)emergence of local cultures competes with global factors in a process that Morley and Robins (1995) refer to as the 'new dynamics of re-localisation' in the attempt to achieve 'a new global-local nexus, about new and intricate relations between global space and local space' (p. 116). Levitt (1983) explains that localisation is practised by multinational companies insofar as they must have a committed operating presence in the markets of other nations. For example, when Chang Huei-mei (also named as A-mei) sang the Taiwanese national anthem at President Chen Shui-bian's inauguration party on 20 May 2000, it was seen as a major political *faux pas* by the mainland Chinese authorities, since China regards Taiwan as a rebel province that must be reunited with the mainland. Following China's consequent ban on a national radio and television advertisement for Sprite, along with other video and audio products involving Chang Hui-mei, Coca-Cola, who produce the drink, dropped Chang from its multi-million dollar advertising campaign (see *Taipei Times*, 3 June 2000; *Communications Law in Transition Newsletter*, 1/6, 10 June 2000; Guy 2002), thereby revealing the political constraints on economic globalisation.

However, electronic communications have also enabled the global broadcasting of messages of universal peace and love, and, in the case of www.indymedia.org, have even served as anti-capitalist noticeboards. Anderson (1983) suggested that the nation depends for its existence upon a sense of social-psychological affiliation to an 'imagined community', which was facilitated by the emergence of the mechanical printing press and consequent capital investment (Negus and Roman-Velazquez, 2000, p. 330). Similarly nowadays, global electronic communications can evoke a sense of a trans-national 'imagined community'. In music, an example can be well illustrated by the 11 September 2001 tragedies in New York and Washington D.C. The US-American national anthem was thundered not only all over the States but also in other countries, such as at St Paul's Cathedral in London. Whitney Houston's record company intends to re-release her version of the US-American national anthem that was produced ten years ago during the Gulf War. International popular artists such as U2, Britney Spears, Limp Bizkit and Destiny's Child, worked together for the album *What's Going On*, the market profits from which will be donated to funds for the relief of the families of victims of the tragedies of September 11. John Lennon's 'Imagine', which evokes a world free from all state boundaries, has now become popular even in some non-English speaking regions, and was sung by all the artists involved in the Carlsberg's Rock Music Concert held in Hong Kong on 24 September 2001, who also prayed for those who died in the disaster two weeks earlier.

Gobalisation and localisation are in a dynamic dialectic. Globalisation is a process of local hybridisation that determines a great number of processes that change and even transcend the regional and national characteristics of popular music. Current debates about globalisation in popular music show that local actors become increasingly involved in global flows of meanings, images, sounds, capital, people, etc. Through the technology of global networks, new affinity group formations emerge, centring on particular musical styles and ways of expression. Economic globalisation always has cultural effects on the localisation of popular music.

The author will describe Hong Kong popular music within the framework of globalisation and localisation. In what follows, whilst I intend 'Hong Kong singers' to imply those who sing in Cantonese and/or Mandarin (though most of their albums are produced only in Cantonese), I intend 'Canto-pop singers' to imply those who sing entirely in Cantonese.

Localisation and Hong Kong popular music

The localisation of Hong Kong popular music involves a struggle for Cantopop to build a sense of its own authenticity in order to supersede English pop and Mandarin pop. The music referred to as 'Cantopop' needs to be heard as not merely commercial, but driven by some shared creative urge on the part of the people who produce and consume it: it needs to be heard as both *deriving from and contributing to* the cultures that listen to it. As early as the end of the 1960s, Taiwanese pop songs, sung in Mandarin, became the mainstream of local pop music. Taiwanese 'campus folk songs', such as 'Olive Tree' (Ganlan Shu), were particularly popular in Hong Kong during the late 1960s and 1970s (for details, see Huang 1990). During the 1960s and 1970s, Western popular songs dominated the local music market and the Beatles, the Bee Gees, Olivia Newton John, the Rolling Stones and Simon and Garfunkel were the idols of Hong Kong youth (for details, see Cui 1984; Liu 1984). Western pop began to fade in Hong Kong as disco was eclipsed by punk in the West in the late 1970s.

Cantopop has developed since the early 1970s with a demand from Hong Kong audiences for popular music in their own dialect, Cantonese. Cantonese is one of the most widely known and influential forms of Chinese, and is spoken in the southern provinces of Guangdong and Guangxi and throughout South-East Asian countries such as Singapore, Malaysia and Thailand. Furthermore, owing to the migration of Cantonese speakers from the Guangdong area and Hong Kong, Cantonese is one of the major dialects of Chinese communities in the United States, Canada, England and elsewhere. The influence of Cantonese and its culture on China as well as other Chinese populated areas has increased in recent years due to the popularity of films, television programmes and popular songs from Hong Kong. Cantonese became the most influential popular music in Hong Kong and is regarded as an authentic part of its culture. This section traces the significance of locality as a mark of cultural identity in Hong Kong Canto-pop, which has set the scene for Hong Kong youth since the 1970s. In particular, it focuses on the role of the mass media in at least five respects: (i) the promotion of Canto-pop by local musicians; (ii) the allocation of time slots for Canto-pop in music programmes; (iii) the recognition of Canto-pop by various music awards; (iv) effective concert management for local popular musicians; and (v) the flourishing state of the music business (see also Ho 1996).

Britain and the United States, in particular, dominated the production and distribution of popular music in Hong Kong for a few decades, when, to use Wallis and Malm's term (1990), Hong Kong was experiencing a period of 'cultural imperialism'. But since the 1970s, popular musicians have gradually relinquished their repertoire of English and Taiwanese songs in Mandarin, as Hong Kong became conscious of its own 'non-Chinese consumer culture', embracing films, TV dramas and popular songs (see Choi 1990A, B; Chan 1994). Sam Hui is viewed as one of the most important pioneers to promote Canto-pop when he started to promote it on his TV programme for Television Broadcast Limited's (TVB) 'Two Stars Reporting Good News' (Shuang-xing Bao-xi). Chan (1990) asserts that the monopoly of Cantonese television by the TVB has played a vital role 'in the birth and consolidation of Hong Kong's indigenous culture' (p. 510). Owing to the popularity of TV drama songs, Canto-pop came to be 'an independent cultural product in its own right' (Choi 1990B, p. 543). Sandra's 'A Marriage of Laughters and Tears' was the first popular Cantonese TV drama theme song in Hong Kong in the early 1970s, since which time local songwriters such as Joseph Koo and Martin Lai wrote many TV drama theme songs that all served to promote the localisation of Hong Kong popular music.

Many Canto-pop singers such as Paula Tsui, Roman Tam, Alan Tam, Leslie Cheung and Kenny Bee changed from singing Mandarin or English songs to Cantonese ones. Although George Lam draws from Western influences, he has written songs in the local dialect, which he delivered with style and charisma. Other 1980s songwriters such as Lam Man-yee, Anthony Lun, James Wong and Lowell Lo began to compose popular music for local singers, demonstrating that Canto-pop no longer depended on copying foreign tunes. Three local bands – Beyond, Taiji and Tat Ming Pair – lead the Cantopop scene in the late 1980s, and in the 1990s singer-songwriters such as Eason Chan, Nicholas Tse and Faye Wong, have been promoted as cult idols.

Radio broadcasts of Cantopop and the presentation of Cantopop music awards have made a major contribution to the recognition of local popular music. The government sponsored Radio Television Hong Kong (RTHK) first began promoting broadcasting Cantopop in 1974 on RTHK2, the popular music channel, during a programme called 'New World Sun' (Sun Tin Dei). RTHK later instigated a weekly chart of top Cantopop songs, and the annual 'Top Ten Chinese Gold Songs Awards' from 1978, which is for composers and text writers as well as singers, and has played an important role in stimulating standards of local music production. At the turn of the 1980s, a similar trend of localisation was furthered by Commercial Radio (CR). Its popular music channel, CR2, was once described as the English song channel, but when Winnie Yu was appointed General Manager in the mid-1980s, she implemented a policy of promoting local Cantopop for twenty-four hours a day, as a result of which it accounted for about 90 per cent of the music programmes by December 1988 (see Choi 1990B, pp. 537–64; Chao 1995, p. 12). Metro Broadcast Hong Kong, which is another commercial radio station, has also been broadcasting Canto-pop since 1991. Like RTHK, these two commercial stations present annual awards for home-produced songs, as does the Composers and Authors Society of Hong Kong Ltd (CASH), which has awarded 'Winners of the CASH Song Writers Quest', 'Best Chinese (Pop) Melody and Lyrics Awards' and 'Most Performed Cantonese Pop Work on Radio and TV' since the 1980s.

Since the 1980s the local popular music concert business in Hong Kong has blossomed. The Hong Kong Coliseum, which has a seating capacity of 12,500, opened in 1983 and has been an important popular venue for Canto-pop artists such as Sam Hui, who was the first such performer there on 7 May 1983 (Huang 1990). During 1989, Leslie Cheung gave thirty-three concert performances, Anita Mui gave twenty-eight, Paula Tsui gave thirty-two, whilst Alan Tam was recorded as giving the highest number of performances at thirty-eight. In 1989 the Hong

Kong Coliseum sold 1,350,271 tickets, to the value of HK$168 million, which was about half the value of the total record sales for local songs (Choi 1990B, p. 543). These concerts provide good business for local artists. For example, each of Leslie Cheung's 2001 concerts was estimated to earn about US$103,800 (*Next Magazine*, 18 October 2001). Though the concert attendances for each individual singer at the Coliseum can never compete with the 1980s, the overall number seems to be increasing. According to Carmen Choi, editor of new indie-music monthly *15-Tracks*, there were one to three alternative concerts a year in 1999, and about four a month in 2001 (Mok 2001).

Other venues for Canto-pop include the Queen Elizabeth Stadium, the Hong Kong Cultural Centre, and the Hong Kong Convention and Exhibition Centre. These local concerts are characterised as 'show business', rather than as 'concert performances', since 'music becomes a mere pretext, and singers, instead of performing with the voice, must excel more in their inventiveness with costumes, dancing and acrobatics' (Chow 1993, p. 392). The emphasis of this type of 'show business' is on 'buying' the visual enjoyment of the entertainers' stage performance. This, and the way that fans uphold the notion of local sounds and scenes, indicates the growth of popular music as a presentation of image. During her 1996 concert, Sammi Cheng, with the help of eight dressers, changed into thirteen different outfits, one with a cone-bra top, in a matter of minutes. In his recent Passion tour, Leslie Cheung, whose skirts and translucent stage costumes have brought storms of criticism, wore eight Jean-Paul Gaultier outfits, showing off shaved legs and undergarments and wearing a long wig. Nicholas Tse, on the other hand, who regards his concerts to be more explosive and unusual than other Canto-pop ones, declares that he does not need pretty clothes for his performances, for which just jeans and pants suffice (Drake 2001).

Cantonese popular music has flourished as a consumer product promoted by international and local music companies. Following the success in promoting local songs and artists enjoyed by Capital Artists (TVB's music recording arm), various record companies, especially the international ones, changed to marketing foreign repertoires (Choi 1990B). In the early 1990s, the five major international record companies – Germany's Bertelsmann, Dutch Polydor, Japan's Sony, Warner of the US and Britain's EMI – explored Asian markets and established offices in most Asian cities (Balfour 1993, p. 52). Local record companies like the Emperor Entertainment Group (EEG) Limited (symbolising 'Energy', 'Exhilaration' and 'Globalisation'), which, since January 1999, has committed itself to focusing on four themes of the entertainment business: music production and distribution, film production, shows management and artist management (source: information obtained from EEG's official Website). During recent years, the EEG has successfully promoted a few young popular singers such as Eason Chan, Edison Chen, Nicholas Tse and Joey Yung, who have become idols among Hong Kong youth. Edison Chen and Nicholas Tse, in particular, are described as 'character Canto-pop', meaning musicians working in an atypical style (Mok 2001). Recently, the EEG has been successfully promoting two local girls, called Twins, and they recently scored a platinum disk by selling 50,000 copies in three weeks (Chow 2001B). Twins' Canto-pop 'The Boy in the Girls' School' scored high on the RTHK's Chinese pop chart, Commercial Radio Top 20 and Metro Radio Pop Chart. Adults as well as young people welcome Twin's songs, since, according to Metro's DJ Wayne Kwok, who is in charge of the station's Hong Kong Hit Chart, Twin's school songs remind adults of their teenage years – the sweetest and happiest days with the least pressure (Chow 2001B). The high sales of Twins' albums seem to be the story of the Hong Kong music business, which has not responded to the worsening economy of the city, even after September 11.

Nonetheless, Cantopop is not known for originality or innovation; rather its songs have subsumed a range of influences from the USA, Britain, Japan and Taiwan, whilst continually readjusting to shifting local markets and socio-cultural climates. Many well-known songs in Hong Kong are Cantonese-language 'cover versions' of Japanese or Western songs. The struggle for authenticity is manifest in the use of Cantonese rather than English lyrics or Japanese lyrics in popular songs. For example, five cover versions of Wham's 'Careless Whisper' were released simultaneously, each with different Cantonese lyrics (Zhou 1990, p. 156). Hacken Lee sang the Television Broadcasts Limited's 2002 World Cup theme song 'Victory', which was based on the song of the same title by the London string quartet, Bond. There have also been many Cantonese cover versions of Japanese songs by Anita Mui, Faye Wong (also known in an earlier incarnation as 'Shirley'), and other top Hong Kong artists. For example, Faye Wong's cover of Nakajima Miyuki's 'Easily Hurt Woman' (1994) went gold in Hong Kong, mainland China and Taiwan simultaneously. As will be explained further in the next section, any readily identifiable local popular music is a manifestation of multiculturalism.

Globalisation and Hong Kong popular music

Hong Kong, as a multi-cultural metropolis that combines Chinese with Western cultures, has been called the crossroads between East and West. Global culture in Hong Kong can be seen in every walk of life including eating, clothing, the entertainment business and music. Pacific Coffee Company entered the Hong Kong market in 1993, followed by the Seattle-based Starbucks, and more recently McDonald's has also joined the caffeine war (Schwartz 2001). Besides watching local TV dramas, US dramas such as 'The X-Files', 'ER' and 'Friends' have drawn Hong Kong people's attention. If you take a walk through Madame Tussaud's Hong Kong, located at Level 2, the Peak Tower, you will find the musical legends of Michael Hutchence (lead singer of the Australian Band 'INXS'), Madonna, Michael Jackson, Elvis Presley, Jimi Hendrix, Kylie Minogue, Tina Turner, Mick Jagger, Jon Bon Jovi and Freddie Mercury (lead singer of 'Queen'). Hong Kong is not only 'the world capital of Canto-pop', but has also been a stage for international pop and rock artists, such as Air Supply, Boyzone, Celine Dion, Oasis, Suede, Westlife, Ricky Martin, Kinki Kids (Japan), Dragon Ash (Japan), Primal Scream, B'z, Corrs, Robbie Williams and Elton John, who have all played there in recent years. However, owing to not having a suitable large concert venue, major stars like Michael Jackson, the Rolling Stones and Bruce Springteen have bypassed Hong Kong on their Asian tours.

Furthermore, Cantopop stars are mobbed in Beijing and Taipei, and also in London, Singapore, Melbourne, Toronto and Las Vegas, where Jacky Cheung sang in the Rod Laver Arena in March 2002 and Sammi Cheng had a sell-out show at the Crown Palladium. There are five key features of globalisation influencing Hong Kong popular music today: (i) the establishment of Hong Kong popular artists as international stars; (ii) Canto-pop superstars experimenting with different sounds; (iii) the presentation of music awards for Chinese popular music in the wider Chinese community; (iv) the exchange of musical culture between Hong Kong and Japan; and (v) advances in technology speeding the consumption and reception of Hong Kong popular music.

Hong Kong culture has been exposed to large audiences in Southeast Asia and other Western countries through its movies and record albums, and popular artists now perceive their potential audience in international terms. Hong Kong's popular music and film industry provide a significant part of the dynamic of 'globalisation' in the Chinese and Hong Kong worlds. Like MacDonald's and Coca-Cola, Disney movie soundtracks spotted a yawning demand. This demand was quickly satisfied by soundtracks from *Beauty & the Beast* and *Aladdin*, which reached at least gold-record status in every Asian market, pushing music sales there up by 660 per cent between 1990 and 1994 (*Billboard*, 27 August 1994, 106/35). Since *Beauty and the Beast*, Disney has released soundtracks in seven languages, using Hong Kong artists like Jacky Chan and Sara Chan to cover songs so that Cantonese children can understand them (*Billboard*, 27 August 1994, 106/35). CoCo Lee, born in Hong Kong but raised in San Francisco, provided not only the voice for the main character in the Mandarin-language version of Disney's animated adventure *Mulan*, but also sang the film's theme song as well. She was the first Asian to ever win the Best International Female Award for MTV Music in 2000. Coco Lee sings the closing song, 'A Love Before Time', in *Crouching Tiger, Hidden Dragon*, which she performed for the Academy Awards on 25 March 2001. In April 2001, Lee was named Chinese cultural ambassador by a group called the Global Foundation of Distinguished Chinese. Other Hong Kong popular artists such as Jacky Cheung, Andy Lau and Faye Wong have also gained international fame. Faye Wong, a singer from Beijing who is now based in Hong Kong, was featured as a Cantonese pop princess by *Time* in October 1996.

In order to increase business, most Hong Kong popular artists produce their albums in both Cantonese and Mandarin, and during the past few years there have been more Putonghua releases by local singers (see Witzleben 1999; Ho 2000), thereby widening markets to include mainland China, Taiwan and other Chinese communities of Asia, America and Europe. For example, Faye Wong started out singing Cantonese pop in Hong Kong, and in 1994 her first Mandarin album *Mi* (Riddles; Enigma) shot up to number one on Taiwan's top-ten chart and remained there for months. According to Tam (2000), Mandarin pop has made 'a big splash in the U.S. music scene' (p. B1), with Andy Lau and Jacky Cheung becoming the Chinese equivalent of Latin heart-throb Ricky Martin, whilst CoCo Lee is viewed as the Chinese Mariah Carey (Tam 2000). According to figures released by the International Federation of Phonographic Industries (Asia) (IFPI) at the Midem Asia '97 fair, the market share for Putonghua products in Hong Kong and the region rose by 5 per cent to 70 per cent over the five years from 1992 to 1997 (Chung 1997). According to Sandy Yang, YesAsia's (a San Francisco-based site) marketing manager, U.S. sales of Mandarin pop and other Asian music accounted for 85 per cent of the company's total sales in 1999 (Tam 2000).

Music awards have been set up to bring Chinese popular music to a higher level of popularity in the greater Chinese communities. Since 1995 the prestigious World Music Awards and the Billboard Music Awards have included categories for Chinese singers. The former named Jacky Cheung as the world's best selling Chinese artist between 1995–7, whilst Billboard honoured Andy Lau for similar achievement. The first Asia Chinese Music Awards, held at the Arena of Stars,

Genting – City of Entertainment on 11 November 2000, provided greater communications between Chinese artists from Hong Kong, Taiwan, China, Malaysia, Singapore and Thailand. The top fifteen hits included songs by Wang Lee-Hom, Sammi Cheng, Daniel Chan, Kelly Chan, Faye Wong, Sandy Lam, Michael & Victor, China Doll, Ah Liang and Chang Yu (Source: http://www.genting.com.my/en/live—ent/2000/acma/). The RTHK's 2001 'Top Ten Chinese Gold Songs Awards', held at the Hong Kong Coliseum on 19 January, leapt beyond customary geographic boundaries by extending the selection of nominated songs to mainland China. Apart from presenting the fourteen local awards, the concert added new categories including the 'Most Popular Singer Award (Mainland)' and 'Song of the Year (Mainland)'. The public voted by means of forms or on the Internet, and professional adjudication was conducted by the Research and Survey Programme of Hong Kong Lingnan University, and overseas by Chinese radio stations and the mainland China radio stations (source: the official Website for Hong Kong Radio Television). The '12th International Pop Poll' Award Presentation, which was also organised by RTHK, pooled together local and overseas showbiz mega-stars on 30 March 2001. Among a total of eighteen awards, fourteen went to English and Japanese songs.

Hong Kong popular artists have needed to cross conventional style and genre boundaries, and to become all-round artists. During the 1980s, Canto-pop attracted a wide audience throughout Asia, with famous pop stars like Leslie Cheung selling 200,000 copies of an album, but today he sells no more than 50,000 (Mok 2001). Overall Canto-pop sales plunged from 9.2 million albums in 1996 to 4.9 million in 1998 (Mok 2001). In response to criticisms of Canto-pop's formulaic romantic ballads and brain-dead dance tunes, Hong Kong popular singers are changing their acts. Though the idol market still prevails in Hong Kong, there is room for Canto-pop to expand into other music genres. In 1996, the Hong Kong Philharmonic Society invited Jacky Cheung to perform two concerts with them in Hong Kong, and in the following year he performed in a fully-fledged Canto-pop stage musical – *Shuet Long Wu* ('Snow Wolf Lake') – which ran for forty-three nights. Cheung produced *Shuet Long Wu* with the Taiwan-based, Singaporean artist Kit Chan, and six composers, though most of the songs were by Dick Lee. All the songs were arranged by Iskanda Ismail, who is a renowned composer, arranger, music producer and music director in Hong Kong and Taiwan. Cheung and Chen sang some thirty new tunes in the show and ten were issued as an album by Polygram. Roman Tam (Lo Man), who was popular in Hong Kong in the 1980s, invited the Russian Voronezh State Symphony Orchestra to run his concerts at the Hong Kong Convention and Exhibition Centre in March 1999. Eason Chan has experimented with different genres, ranging from folk-pop to synth-dance and even stadium rock, and his 1997 release on a rock taster album, which is an uncommon form in Hong Kong, broke into the circle of major singers. Two local stage performances, namely *The Labyrinth of Mirror and Flower* and *A Brave New World of Suzie Wong*, were the highlight of the 2001 Hong Kong Arts Festival. They starred the leading popular singers Candy Lo and Eason Chan, and 'broke new frontiers in the realm of art' (*CASH*, No. 34, May 2001, p. 13). *The Labyrinth of Mirror and Flower* was a multimedia stage performance headlined by Candy Lo and combined dance, music, video, 2D graphics and lighting. Sammi Cheng, once known as the queen of ballads, recently included techno tracks and new-wave rock on her albums (Mok 2001). Alan Tam gave a rave-style concert at the Hong Kong Convention and Exhibition Centre in June 2001. LMF (i.e.

Lazy Muthafucka) have established themselves as the spokespersons of Hong Kong Hip-hop, and are viewed as a local cultural expression. LMF released their self-financed debut record 'Housing Estate Boys' in February 1999. Seven months later, the band joined Warner Music's alterative DNA label. When their second album *Lazy Clan* was released in 2000, it sold more than 80,000 copies in Hong Kong (Bennett 2001). Even in Malaysia and Singapore, where LMF's explicit lyrics provoked government bans, they are also popular among youths and street vendors, who reportedly sold some 70,000 illicit discs (see Chung 2001). Their music expresses anti-social feelings and sub-cultural differentiation. MC Yan, who is a member of LMF, distinguishes Canto-rap from the hardcore U.S. brand in terms of their lyrics, which focus not on racial oppression but on the division between rich and poor that concerns so many Hong Kong people (Chung 2001).

Besides Western influences on its popular culture, Hong Kong has been inclined towards Japanese youth culture, setting up Japanese music sections, as in Taiwan and elsewhere. Japanese popular culture including comics, in particular those for young girls, has been attracting Hong Kong young people since the 1990s, since when several publishing companies have imported more, such as *Tokyo Love Story*, *Black Jack*, and Tezuka Osamu's comic series. Japanese animation songs are very popular in Hong Kong, such as: Eason Chan's Cantonese version of the title song of the Japanese comic *Ultraman Tiga*; *Chibimaruko's* ending theme, 'Let's Dance'; *Miyuki's* ending theme, 'Full of Memories'; *Cat's Eye's* opening song, 'Cat's Eye'; *Candy's* opening theme 'Candy Candy'; and *Heidi's* opening theme song, 'Please tell me!'. Other Japanese TV drama theme songs such as *Love Generation*, *With Love* and *Long Vacation* are also popular among Hong Kong youths. Performers like Yumi Matsutoya, a pop music pioneer in Japan, were also extremely influential in the development of the extravagant stage shows with multiple costume changes that characterise contemporary Hong Kong performances. The Hong Kong popular music industry also employs musical elements of Japanese songs, such as adaptations of Japanese language and other cultural elements. For example, Kwok's recent popular song 'Para Para Sukura' uses a mixture of three languages – Cantonese, Japanese and English – and includes lyrics like 'Ah Come Come Come Come Nan Desuka Sakura, Ah Come Come Come Come Nan Desuka Sakura', sung against MTV's backdrop of ParaPara dancing and Sakura flowers. Lee (2000) argued that the overall style and production of Hong Kong popular music is highly derivative of Japanese pop. Singing and film megastars like Andy Lau, Leon Lai, Aaron Kwok and Jacky Cheung – the four 'heavenly kings' of Chinese pop – contribute to the success of Pacific Asia's own version of Hollywood and Bollywood. Andy Lau's recent hit film *A Fighter's Blues* co-starred Japanese actress Takka Tokiwa, and Aaron Kwok starred with Norika Fujiwara in *China Strike Force*, which obtained a good box office rating during the New Year of 2001. Canto-stars, such as Kelly Chan, who have recorded in Mandarin and English, more recently have begun to sing in Japanese in order to woo a huge additional music market. Faye Wong recorded a new series of commercials for the Japanese cellular phone company J-Phone, and was also the lead actor in a prime time Japanese television drama series on Fuji TV, for which she sang the theme song. EMI has released a Japanese version of her album *Fable* with two bonus tracks, 'Eyes on Me' and Faye's first Japanese song, a cover of 'Chanel'.

Besides its interaction with Japanese popular culture, Hong Kong has also been influenced, along with Taiwan and China, by Korean popular culture, particularly TV dramas in the late 1990s. Korean popular music has also been sweeping Hong Kong, as Korean stars expanded their markets throughout Asia, by means of concert tours and albums translated into various languages. For instance, Korea's platinum dance group H.O.T. have become teenage idols in China, and others, such as Shinhwa and Baby Vox, are attracting teenagers in Hong Kong. Although the Korean International Superstars Show, which was held at the Hong Kong Convention and Exhibition Centre in August 2001, was in celebration of the ninth anniversary of Korea's establishment of diplomatic relations with China, it seemed more like a celebration of newly found Korean pop culture on the part of Chinese youth.

Hong Kong has entered a fully computerised era in terms of its emerging potential to use karaoke, satellite broadcasting and cable television to spread popular music. Karaoke technology was developed in Japan, and the 'culture' of karaoke clubs emerged in Hong Kong in the 1990s. Star-TV is one of the most prominent regional satellite and cable television operations in the world, reaching from the Arab world to Asian countries. In December 1990, a licence was granted to Hutchison Whampoa's satellite broadcasting company, HutchVision, to begin a Direct Broadcast Satellite (DBS) service via AsiaSat (Source: http://www.mbcnet.org/ETV/S/htmlS/startvhong/starvhong.htm). By this means, and by Cable TV networks, songs of Hong Kong singers have been transmitted over a wide area of the globe. Several Chinese record labels have used the Internet to attract overseas audiences. The Rock Entertainment Group, one of the largest Chinese-language music labels in Taiwan, together with the Hong Kong-based division of Sony Corp's music arm, has established several sites for Asian music (Tam 2000). RTHK on Internet – The Cyber Station started to provide synchronous Webcast versions of prime time RTHK programmes – has been on stream since April 2000. Hong Kong is among the fastest growing markets in the world in terms of the number of households connected to the Internet. According to Pastore (2001), NetValue's examination of ten Internet markets in the first half of 2001 found that Hong Kong leads the list with 27.9 per cent growth from January to June 2001. The other nine countries are Spain, Korea, France, Singapore, U.K., Germany, Demark, Taiwan and the U.S.A., with percentage growth of 25.3, 15.0, 14.1, 12.9, 9.3, 5.6, 3.5, 1.7 and -0.2, respectively. The growth of online households may also be an indicator of more e-audiences for local radio broadcasts as well as other music programmes.

Changes in economics and technology resulting from globalisation have reformed the patterns of production and reception of Hong Kong popular music. Hong Kong has become a leading centre of high technology in Asia, with its employment of synthesizers, sampling, MIDI sequencing, digital recording, digital sound effect processing, audio-visual synchronisation, and digital mixing/mastering for music production, and new technological tools for the transmission and reception of Hong Kong popular music. Mobile phone companies adopt popular tunes to promote their business. Ringtone King is the first company to trade solely in tunes for ringtone downloading onto mobile phones (Chow 2001A). Users only have to dial a computer-operated IDD hotline and enter a code to receive Canto-pop hits by Sammi Cheng, Kelly Chen and Aaron Kwok. Chan Fai-hung, managing director of I-Content Technology, which launched Ringtone King, has been trying to expand Ringtone King's repertoire with foreign music, but so far has only been able to offer The Beatles (*ibid.*). Hutchison Telecommunications (Hong Kong) Limited also allows their users to personalise their phone ringing tones with unique three-chord compact MIDI format music clips from popular Canto-pop, versions of

Japanese popular drama theme songs, festive music and traditional folk songs (Source: http://www.openwave.com/newsroom/2001/20010503_huchison_ 0503.html). PlanetMG.com, the first music portal in Asia Pacific to offer song downloads from international chart-topping artists, opened in Hong Kong in October 2000 (Source: http://www.sony.com.hk/Electronics/pr_t/pr/planetmg_ eng.htm). However, a global attack on music piracy has been launched against individuals and companies uploading illegal MP3 files, and Internet service providers hosting illegal MP3 sites. Threatened by the ease of digital duplication, the music industry has paired with electronics companies to develop technologies that put digital locks on songs and limit how often they can be played or copied and on which devices (*South China Morning Post*, 5 September 2001).

To sum up, the economic and cultural dimensions of globalisation have become determining factors on developments in Hong Kong popular music, especially the establishment of international Hong Kong popular artists, the internationalisation of musical styles, and the instantaneous communication and interaction by means of electronic media. The globalisation of Hong Kong popular music has now extended its original dominance by the West to embrace other Asian domains, as is exemplified by local popular artists widening their interests to include Mandarin pop. Currently, technological developments, driven by a liberal, free market ideology, work together to create a global economic culture.

Conclusion

This article has reflected on the changes wrought on Hong Kong popular music by the dialectic between media globalisation and resurgent localism. It has explored the complexities of global-local dynamics involved in the process of cultural globalisation and localisation in the industry of Hong Kong popular music. The story of Hong Kong pop in its global-local interaction is not only a case of cultural (Western) imperialism and the Asianisation of Asian, but also involves a process of negotiated cultural identities, as expressed in the language of Cantonese and other representational means. Hong Kong popular music is an expression of the locality but in line with a productive framework which ensures that the globe is already in the local as a global discourse. An overview of key popular artists, together with the growth of the mass media and the music business between the 1970s and the twenty-first century, has demonstrated that the cultural dynamics of globalisation include developments of information technology and the integration of Western and Eastern music businesses. One major characteristic of local popular music is the high degree of cross-fertilisation between various musical cultures and idioms and the consequent emergence of hybrid styles. Nowadays, the global sounds of Hong Kong popular music, in terms of the inclusion of various genres, technologies and multi-media expressions, are already serving as local means towards new creative fusions.

Despite movements of popular artists, capital and technologies across national boundaries, nation-states still constitute the nexus of global-local exchange. Global localisation involves the adaptation of global products to suit the local Hong Kong conditions. Whilst the development of Hong Kong pop has been enabled by the development of multinational media industries such as EMI, Warner and Sony, the growth of the local Emperor Entertainment group (EEG) Limited has injected new energy to the Hong Kong music business. Nonetheless, the 'international success' of Hong Kong artists is still almost exclusively within the Chinese diaspora in Southeast Asia, Canada and the USA, and the UK, with more modest success in Japan, and very little inroad into mainstream English-speaking markets in the West (although top local popular artists have performed there). Owing to the lack of a large concert venue, some famous international pop artists will not perform in Hong Kong. If there were such a venue it would also provide a platform of equal significance for local, and other Asian artists, which in turn would stimulate local songwriters.

The implication of globalisation for the future of international capitalism is that economic prosperity will come to reside in global networks that link local popular and international artists, or even local and multi-national music businesses, in profit-maximising webs of production and distribution. During a dynamic process of change, it is the interaction of global and local factors that brings about endless possibilities for the development of pop music and other popular forms such as fashion. So far, neither the mainstream discourses of cultural studies nor the social sciences have sufficiently addressed the key problems of the present era: globalisation and localisation. Discussions of local and international repertoires, global locality in music production and reception, and commercial interests in constructing local pop for the global music market would all help to make clearer the formation of local music industries in the era of globalisation, and thereby to identify appropriate measures for regulating and promoting the future cultural, economic and political development of the popular music industry. It is problematic to draw sweeping generalisations from any single case, and further research into the tensions of localisation and globalisation is obviously needed to substantiate an inclusive analysis of popular music in Hong Kong and other Asian countries.

Acknowledgement

I would like to express my gratitude and deepest appreciation to the Editor, Dr. Keith Negus and two anonymous reviewers for their insightful and constructive comments on my manuscript.

References

Anderson, B. 1983. *Imagined Communities: Reflections on the Origin and Spread of Nationalism* (New York)

Appadurai, A. 1996. *Modernity at Large* (Minneapolis)

Balfour, F. 1993. 'Faster tempo: western pop-music publishers set their sights on Asia', *Far Eastern Economic Review*, 6 May, pp. 52–3

Bennett, A. 1999. 'Hip hop am main: the localization of rap music and hip hop culture', *Media Culture & Society*, 21/1, pp. 77–91

Bennett, B. 2001. 'Hip-hop goes canto', *Time Asia*, 158/15, available at: <TIMEasia.com>

Billboard, 27 August 1994, 106/35

CASH, No. 34, May 2001

Chan, H.M. 1994. 'Culture and identity', in *Hong Kong Report: 1994*, ed. D.H. McMillen and S.W. Man (Hong Kong), pp. 443–68

Chan, K.C. 1990. 'The media and telecommunication', in *The Other Hong Kong Report: 1990*, ed. R.Y.C. Wong and J.Y.S. Cheng (Hong Kong), pp. 507–35

Chao, B. 1995. 'Golden days of local music', *South China Morning Post: Young Post*, 3 March, p. 12

Choi, P.K. 1990A. 'From "slavery culture" and "cultural desert" to the birth of local culture: the connection between the development of Hong Kong culture and its relationship with Chinese revolution' (Comg nuhua jiaoyu ji wenhua shamo dao bentu de taitou: xianggong de fazhan yu zhongguo jindai geming de zhuanzhe), *CUHK Education Journal*, 18/2, pp. 153–64

156   *Wai-chung Ho*

1990b. 'Popular culture', in *The Other Hong Kong Report: 1990*, ed. R. Wong and J. Cheng (Hong Kong), pp. 537–64

Chow, R. 1993. *Writing Diaspora: Tactics of Intervention in Contemporary Cultural Studies* (Bloomington and Indianapolis)

Chow, V. 2001a. 'Tone of the future', *South China Morning Post*, 27 September, available at: <http://www.asiamedia.ucla.edu/Weekly2001/09.25.2001/HongKong7.htm>

2001b. 'Double bubble', *South China Morning Post*, 28 September, available at: <http://www.totallyhk.com/TimeOff/Entertainment/Features/Article/FullText_asp_ArticleID-20010928002622300.asp>

Chung, W. 1997. 'Pop stars can rock in any language', *South China Morning Post*, 1 July, available at: <http://www.hongkong97.com.hk/newera/life/stagescreen/Article19970629175602264.html>

2001. 'Who's an LMF?' *Asiaweek*, 16 March, 27/10, available at: <Asiaweek.com>

Cohen, S. 1995. 'Localizing sound', in *Popular Music – Style and Identity*, ed. W. Straw *et al.* (Montreal), pp. 61–7

Comeliau, C. 1997. 'The challenge of globalization', *Prospects*, 27/1, pp. 29–34

Communications Law in Transition Newsletter, 10 June 2000, 1/6, available at: <http://pcmlp.socleg.ox.ac.uk/transition/issue06/china.htm>

Crawford, D. 2000. 'Chinese capitalism: cultures, the southeast Asian region and economic globalization', *Third World Quarterly*, February, pp. 69–86

Croteau, D., and Hoynes, W. 2000. *Media Society: Industries, Images, and Audiences*, Second Edition (London)

Cui, S.M. 1984. 'Can the new music hit have a breakthrough from the Beatles?' (Xing yuechao neng yado pitousi ma?), *The Seventies* (Qishi Niandai), No. 170, March, pp. 36–8

Drake, K. 2001. 'People don't really take us seriously as musicians', *Time Asia*, 21 October, available at: < http://www.time.com/time/asia/arts/column/0,9754,170514,00.html>

Featherstone, M. 1995. *Undoing Culture: Globalization, Postmodernism and Identity* (London)

Guy, N. 2002. ' "Republic of China National Anthem" on Taiwan: one anthem, one performance, multiple realities', *Ethnomusicology*, 46/1, pp. 96–119

Hirst, P., and Thompson, G. 1996. *Globalization in Question: The International Economy and the Possibilities of Governance* (Cambridge, MA)

Ho, W.C. 1996. *Hong Kong Secondary Music Education: A Sociological Enquiry*. Unpublished Ph.D. Degree Thesis (Institute of Education, University of London)

2000. 'The political meaning of Hong Kong popular music: a review of socio-political relations between Hong Kong and the People's Republic of China since the 1980s', *Popular Music*, 19/3, pp. 341–53

Huang, Z.H. 1990. *Yueyu Liuxingqu Sishi* (Cantonese Popular Songs for These Forty Years), Forwarded by T. Liang (Hong Kong)

Jenkins, H. 2001. 'Culture goes global', *Technology Review*, July/August, 104/6, p. 89

Jones, P.W. 1999. 'Globalization and the UNESCO mandate: multilateral prospects for educational development', *International Journal of Educational Development*, 19, pp. 17–25

Law, W.W. Forthcoming. 'Globalization, localization and education reform in a new democracy: Taiwan's experience', in *Globalization and Educational Restructuring in the Asia-Pacific Region*, ed. K.H. Mok and A. Welch (London), pp. 79–127

Lee, J. 2000. 'China – pop/rock: Cantopop and protest singers', in *The Rough Guide to World Music: Latin & North America, Caribbean, India, Asia and Pacific* (Vol. 2), ed. S. Broughton and M. Ellingham with J. McConnachie and O. Duane, pp. 49–55

Levitt, T. 1983. 'The globalization of markets', *Harvard Business Review*, 61 (May–June), pp. 92–102

Liu, Y.T. 1984. 'Can the American-British popular music become a strong force?' (Yingme Xinyin Chaochui Yaohan Xianggong Ma?), *The Seventies* (Qishi Niandai), No. 170, March, pp. 38–40

Mok, D. 2001. 'Getting in the grove', *Asiaweek*, 10 August, available at: <Asiaweek.com>

Morley, D., and Robins, K. 1995. *Spaces of Identity: Global Media, Electronic Landscapes and Cultural Boundaries* (London)

Negus, K. 1999. *Music Genres and Corporate Cultures* (London & New York).

Negus, K., and Roman-Velazquez, P. 2000. 'Globalization and cultural identities', in *Mass Media and Society*, ed. J. Curran and M. Gurevutch (London), pp. 329–45

Next Magazine, 18 October 2001 (Hong Kong)

Poisson, M. 1998. 'Education and globalization', *IIEP Newsletter*, 16/2, pp. 1–2, 6

Pastore, M. 2001. 'Asian internet markets grow in 2001', available at: < http://www.isp-planet.com/research/2001/asia_grows.html>

Sassen, S. 1996. *Losing Control?* (New York)

Schwartz, S. 2001. 'McDonald's wakes up to coffee culture', *South China Morning Post*, 4 October, available at: <http://hongkong.scmp.com/ZZZ5EXEP1SC.html>

South China Morning Post, various issues (Hong Kong)

Tam, P.W. 2000. 'Here come Asia's Ricky and Mariah – not just for karaoke anymore, Mandarin pop could be the next crossover sensation', *Wall Street Journal* (New York) (Eastern Edition), 31 March, p. B.1

Taipei Times, 3 June 2000 (Taipei)

Wallis, R., and Malm, K. 1984. *Big Sounds from Small Peoples: The Music Industry in Small Countries* (London)

    1990. 'Patterns of change', in *On Record: Rock, Pop, and the Written Word*, ed. S. Frith and A. Goodwin (London), pp. 160–80

Witzleben, J.L. 1999. 'Cantopop and Mandapop in pre-postcolonial Hong Kong: identity negotiation in the performances of Anita Mui Yim-Fong', *Popular Music*, 18/2, pp. 241–57

Zhou, H.S. 1990. *Xiaofei Wenhua: Yingxiang Wenzi Yinyue* (Consuming Culture: Image, Words and Music) (Hong Kong)

Web resources

<http://www.grayzone.com/ifpi61201.htm>

<http://www.genting.com.my/en/live_ent/2000/acma/>

<http://www.openwave.com/newsroom/2001/20010503_huchison_0503.html>

<http://www.sony.com.hk/Electronics/pr_t/pr/planetmg_eng.htm>

<http://www.mbcnet.org/ETV/S/htmlS/startvhong/starvhong.htm>

The official websites for the Hong Kong Radio Television (RTHK) and local Emperor Entertainment group (EEG) Limited

[12]

¡Hip Hop, Revolución!
Nationalizing Rap in Cuba

GEOFFREY BAKER / University of London

In August 2004, shortly before the opening date of the 10th Havana Hip Hop Festival, I spoke to Alpidio Alonso Grau, president of the Asociación Hermanos Saíz, the cultural wing of the Union of Young Communists and the primary force behind the organization of the festival. Alonso told me with pride about the association's efforts to promote rap, and he enthused about the dialogue between rappers and their audiences and the "authenticity of their discourse." He emphasized the importance of the debates stimulated by rappers on a national and international level, portraying Cuba not simply as a country which offers a space for such debates, but as a global leader. Rap originated in the United States, Alonso said, as a form of resistance to the dominant culture, in other words, as a revolutionary social message. Here he echoed his own words at an earlier press conference when he had described the aim of the festival: "to project a revolutionary message from Cuba, a commitment to the cause of the downtrodden in the world." Rap in Cuba, he told me, embodied a struggle to change the world through ideas and music, and so "it's very symbolic that this event takes place in Cuba, with rappers who come mainly from Latin America, from countries that are subject to this imperialist pseudo-cultural invasion."

It was striking to hear the head of a Cuban state organization promoting rap, a musical form that is widely perceived as profoundly North American and either a potent expression of protest or a celebration of individualism and hedonism, depending on one's historical and geographical perspective. Yet his comments about rap as a "revolutionary message" and a "struggle to change the world," and his characterization of Cuba as a place of critical debate and the festival as a symbolic event, shed light on the intriguing question of how a musical form recently imported from Cuba's ideological arch-enemy, and frequently voicing a high degree of social protest, has not only been assimilated into Cuban national culture but has come to be positively promoted by the state within little over a decade of its emergence. The Cuban government not only organizes and finances the annual hip hop festival but supports two institutions which promote rap groups, the Asociación Hermanos Saíz (AHS) and the Agencia Cubana de Rap (Cuban Rap Agency, ACR). My intention here is to examine how and why the state has become so deeply involved with rap music in Cuba, a situation that is surely unique in global terms, focusing in particular on the discursive strategies of leading figures in the Cuban rap movement and of officials like Alpidio Alonso, the Cuban functionary who talked so fluently and positively about hip hop.

The importance of examining how people talk and write about music in understanding constructions of national culture and identity is underlined by Peter Wade in his study of Colombian popular music: "the success of Costeño music lay in great part in its multivocality, which meant it could be talked about productively by different people in many different ways ... When I say productively, I mean that the music could be harnessed effectively to the constitution of identity" (Wade 2000:238). In Cuba, I was frequently struck by the ways that people talked about rap, though in this case it was the *similarity* between discourses which caught my attention. When I read interviews with, or spoke to, certain key figures in Cuban hip hop, or attended public events like the colloquium during the rap festival—an event which lasts up to three days, illustrating the extent to which talking about rap is central to official conceptions of the festival—I noticed a marked consistency in discussions of the relationship of hip hop to notions of national culture and state ideology. Leading "spokespeople" and commentators had seemingly taken a position on the subject, and I was drawn to explore what lay behind this "party line" on Cuban rap.

Rap Cubano: An Introduction

Cuban rap emerged in the early 1990s, a response to the rapid socio-economic changes resulting from the end of Soviet subsidies and the subsequent crisis known euphemistically as the "Special Period in a Time of Peace." By 1995 there were enough rap groups in Havana to merit the organization of a festival by an East Havana collective called "Grupo Uno," led by the cultural promoter Rodolfo Rensoli. The festival organizers soon realized the advantages of seeking logistical help from the state youth cultural organization, the AHS, and the festival became an annual event. As the rap movement grew and attracted increasing attention from Cuban youth as well as from foreign artists and journalists, the Cuban state began to engage further with the genre. In 1999 Abel Prieto, the progressive Minister of Culture, declared rap to be "an authentic expression of Cuban culture" (Robinson 2004:119) and added: "It's time we nationalize rock and rap" (Pacini Hernández and Garofalo

1999–2000:42). 1999 was also a key year for Cuban rap on the international scene: it saw the launch of the hugely successful first album by the Cuban rappers Orishas, formerly Amenaza, who had emigrated to and recorded in France,[1] and it was also the year that the first compilation of Cuban rap for overseas distribution, *The Cuban Hip Hop All Stars Vol. 1*, was recorded in Havana.[2] The following three years were a boom time for Cuban rap both on the island and abroad, and the state responded by injecting more funds into the annual hip hop festival, making more venues available for regular performances and, in 2002, creating the Agencia Cubana de Rap (ACR) and launching a magazine entitled *Movimiento: La Revista Cubana de Hip Hop* (Movement: The Cuban Hip Hop Magazine). There were reputedly two to three hundred rap groups in Havana at this peak, with perhaps several dozen given regular performance opportunities by the AHS, and a select group of eight to ten directly employed by the ACR. Until 2002 there was a relatively unified rap scene, generally described as "underground"; but since that year, a divide has emerged between the leading AHS groups, which tend to maintain this "underground" aesthetic, and other artists—including a number of the most established rappers, now members of the ACR—who have been attracted by the commercial possibilities of *reggaetón*, the Spanish-language style of Jamaican dancehall that had become the music of choice for many young Cubans by 2004.[3]

This booming music scene attracted the interest of many foreign journalists, documentary-makers, and academic researchers. Pacini Hernández and Garofalo published a path-breaking study of the formative years of the rap movement (Pacini Hernández and Garofalo 1999–2000), while West-Durán has examined questions of race and identity in rap lyrics (West-Durán 2004). These articles pay little attention, however, to the institutionalization of rap, arguably one of the features most unique to hip hop in a Cuban context. Pacini Hernández and Garofalo completed their research in 1999, shortly before state involvement increased markedly, though they did note that a "major development" was likely in this area (Pacini Hernández and Garofalo 1999–2000:42). West-Durán, meanwhile, focuses on rap lyrics and the history of race relations, and while his textual analysis and contextualization are insightful, his description of the interaction between the state and rappers is brief and debatable: he writes of the Cuban rap movement in terms of "a politicization and mobilization that is not tied to the state or party ideology, even if many Cubans share the ideals expressed by these two official institutions. Cuban rappers are functioning as a countervailing voice and the government knows this, which is why since 1999 it has 'recognized' and tried to co-opt their activities and concerts" (West-Durán 2004:8). This analysis fails to account for the complexity of the relations between rappers and the state, and is symptomatic of a widespread view of rap as a "resistant" musical form which has been a target for "co-optation" by state institutions.

Sujatha Fernandes has considered the role of the state in the develop-ment of Cuban rap in considerably more depth (Fernandes 2003). For all the considerable virtues of her study, however, it is weakened by a tendency to refer to an undifferentiated "state" and therefore to gloss over the nuances and inconsistencies of policies with regard to rap. The Cuban state cannot be regarded as a monolithic entity (Kapcia 2000); it incorporates divergent ideological tendencies, and this lack of uniformity is reflected in cultural policy. Whereas Fernandes sees an evolution in state policy from support for "commercial" rap to "underground" rap, in reality fractures in the cul-tural politics of the Cuban state have been exposed by the differing policies towards rap pursued simultaneously by the two organizations charged with promoting the genre, the AHS and ACR, as well as the contradictory and per-plexing resistance to rap from the state-run media. Furthermore, Fernandes' account elides the individuals involved and thus glosses over many of the detailed and often contradictory workings of the process of institutionaliza-tion, and I would argue that it is only through close examination that it is possible to move beyond abstract and often misleading generalizations such as "appropriation."

Processes of cultural "nationalization" are carried out by human agents, not some kind of actorless hegemony. As Wade (2000:11) argues, much of the "appropriation" of Colombian coastal music was in fact done by work-ing- or middle-class musicians and businessmen, including many from the coastal region itself, and we must therefore beware of a polarized view of "appropriators" and "appropriated." To take a Cuban example, any account of the struggle for acceptance of *nueva trova* ("new song") which omitted the role played by the Revolutionary leader Haydée Santamaría in creating a haven for this music at the Casa de las Américas (Moore 2003:14)—even in the late 1960s, a time of maximum ideological conservatism and uniformity of cultural policy—would paint an overly simplistic picture of "musicians versus the state." The situation in the 1990s has arguably been more com-plex. The state/rappers dichotomy employed by Fernandes and West-Durán ignores the crucial role of cultural intermediaries who are neither govern-ment functionaries nor rappers in the assimilation of rap into national culture. Pacini Hernández and Garofalo (1999–2000:37–38) noted the influence of "mentors" on young Cuban rappers. I would argue, however, that these same figures had an equally important influence on relations with the state and that, in direct contrast to West-Durán's portrayal, the rap movement *has been* tied to state or party ideology through the mediation of these interme-diaries—whose aim is to stimulate the development of the rap movement, not to co-opt it—even if some rappers do not share their ideals.

State involvement cannot simply be reduced to "co-opting" rap. The process of *rapprochement* between rappers and state representatives was initiated by these articulate leaders of the rap community who have consistently underlined the history of Cuban assimilation of foreign culture. They have further drawn attention to elements of "conscious" rap that are shared by Cuban national ideology in order to shape a discourse that is acceptable or even attractive to government officials, Cuban rappers, and foreign observers alike. The motivation for such a strategy was to avoid the problems that had plagued rock, another musical import from Cuba's ideological enemies, and to open the door to state support. In addition, the development of Cuban rap has outstripped that of other countries in the region, and the state must be given some credit for this. Many of the groups and fans that I spoke to in 2004 saw AHS involvement at least partially in positive terms, and most appreciated the efforts of the AHS rap promoter, William Figuerero. Figuerero is a popular figure among the rap community who is also a rapper himself (and who had a tendency to break into verse while I was interviewing him). Through the AHS, the state provides free concert space, lighting, audio, and limited publicity for groups; Figuerero would try to persuade the directors of radio shows to announce forthcoming concerts, to play a song, and perhaps to interview the group—something that the artists clearly regarded as vital promotion. Figuerero's open preference for critical, "underground" rap could be seen in his support for some of the most "hardcore" groups, like Explosión Suprema, Los Paisanos, Hermanos de Causa, and Los Aldeanos. Although a state employee, he could hardly be regarded as a controlling influence on the rap scene.

An examination of the proactive role of certain key intermediary figures will therefore encourage a reconsideration not only of the institutionalization of rap in Cuba, but also of accepted notions of "global" rap as a "resistant" music (as portrayed in many of the contributions to Mitchell 2001 and Whiteley et al. 2004),[4] and of state involvement in popular music as a purely negative, controlling influence. Studies of music in socialist countries tend to paint a polarized picture, drawing a sharp distinction between "official" and "unofficial" rock groups (e.g., Ramet 1994). Soviet and Eastern European musicians who received substantial state backing usually made significant artistic compromises and were not taken seriously by "real" rock fans. However, the generalized anti-authoritarianism of rock, which makes its assimilation by state organizations problematic, cannot be mapped directly onto rap, which tends to articulate protest against marginalization and inequality rather than against authority *per se.*

At the root of my argument is the contention that the progressive philosophy of "conscious" hip hop overlaps in many respects with the discursive framework of Cuban Revolutionary ideology. Further, this overlap has allowed a considerable degree of accommodation between state institutions and rap artists without seriously affecting perceptions of their artistic integrity. In this respect there is a stark contrast between rap and Cuban *timba* or rock. Many timba musicians have embraced a conspicuous materialism and hedonism that runs counter to official socialist ideologies and that has often set them at odds with the Cuban authorities (Perna 2005), though they have continued to flourish because of their importance in generating revenues for the state. Rock has provoked official disapproval for a variety of reasons, including its lack of any clear artistic philosophy, and for the first twenty-five years of the Revolution it was variously censored or denied institutional support as it was considered "the mouthpiece of global imperialism" (Manduley López 1997:137). Rap, however, does not carry the same association with U.S. cultural imperialism as rock because of its African American origins (Pacini Hernández 2003:27), and in its more politicized forms, it can be presented as part of a coherent vision of progressive social action, something which makes it more comprehensible to Cuban state officials than rock or timba.

While the "domestication" of Afro-diasporic musics in Latin America has been widespread—for example, reggae and rap have taken root across the region (Pacini Hernández 2003:27–28), and funk made significant inroads in Brazil (Sansone 2001)—the involvement of the state lends a distinctive character to the case of Cuban rap. Given the almost total absence of a domestic recording market, the only way for groups outside the ACR to make money through music is to sell their self-produced CDs to foreigners at concerts; the concerts themselves can only take place in venues accessible to tourists due to the collaboration of certain branches of the state, in particular the AHS. Only two rap groups had a commercial recording contract at the time of writing, and both these—Eddy-K and Cubanos en la Red—were in fact releasing reggaetón rather than rap (despite their inclusion in the ACR). There are many important artists outside the ACR who have never received a dollar in professional payment. They have been able to continue for years partly because the state provides them with regular performing opportunities, and partly because of the dual economy which means that a rapper can make the equivalent of a month's salary in pesos by selling one CD in hard currency to a foreigner. So for all the suspicions raised by state involvement in popular music, it must be recognized that the concentration of rap activity in Havana, and the longevity of many leading groups, are closely linked to government support.

In other parts of Latin America, there is a much closer correlation between success and commercial viability, since the establishment of "non-national" musics has depended primarily on audience demand and the music industry. Looking at the assimilation of reggae in Puerto Rico (Giovannetti 2003) or in Carnival in Salvador, Bahia (dos Santos Godi 2001), it is clear that record companies, large commercial sponsors, and the media have played leading roles, as have popular reactions to new styles. Musical developments are thus largely media- and market-driven. In Cuba, however, the virtual absence of a domestic market has led to quite different dynamics. Reggaetón, for example, has swept the island on a wave of bootleg recordings of Puerto Rican stars and, to a lesser extent, artists from eastern Cuba such as Candyman; the accessibility of recording technology allowed this boom to take place before significant local production began.[5] I repeatedly heard the suggestion that reggaetón caught on in Havana thanks to its popularity among bicycle-taxi drivers, who often have loud stereos mounted on their vehicles and who therefore act as a conduit for the latest popular songs and styles. Be that as it may, the spread of reggaetón from eastern Cuba to the rest of the island may be considered a form of "nationalization from below," driven by the copying and collective use of CDs rather than by record companies or commercial sponsors, though it is increasingly finding a space in the media. The "nationalization" of rap in Cuba, however, is quite a distinct case, in that it has been a process of engagement between artists and audiences mediated by the state, rather than by the music industry or by recording technology.[6]

For this reason, questions of national identity have been foregrounded much more noticeably in the case of Cuban rap. The establishment of rap depended on live performance and therefore government support, which in turn depended not on the commercial viability of rap, but the extent to which it could be incorporated into dominant visions of national identity. In the other cases mentioned above, arguments over the relationship between foreign music and national identity, though commonplace, tend to be somewhat extraneous to the actual musical developments and make little impact on popular practices.[7] But as the high profile of Cuban rap relied on state involvement, a greater degree of accommodation and negotiation was necessary. The relationship between rap and Cuban identity continues to be explored explicitly at the time of writing: the official announcement of the 2005 festival states that "the central objective of the competition will be the search for a national identity for the movement."[8]

Because I focus on the negotiations involved in the "nationalization" of rap, my study is restricted to Havana. This focus is not to suggest that rap is only a phenomenon of the capital; in fact, it has taken root in most Cuban cities, regional festivals have been organized, a handful of groups from the provinces are invited to the Havana festival, and the AHS organized a national tour in early 2004 to assess the health of rap around the island and to try to stimulate its development. Havana, however, has by far the greatest concentration of groups and, more importantly for my purposes, it is where the key figures in my account reside—figures who have no counterparts in other cities. If the Havana-centrism of much academic writing on Cuban music has been rightly criticized,[9] such a focus is in fact an integral part of my story, in that I argue that the "nationalization" of rap has not simply been a process of adoption by artists and audiences across the island, as in the case of reggaetón, but has taken its particular (and unique) course largely due to the strategies and negotiations pursued by a small number of Havana-based figures.

The Intermediaries

Rodolfo Rensoli, the founder of Grupo Uno who had organized the first rap festival in 1995, took the first step in the institutionalization of rap in 1997 when he approached Roberto Zurbano, then vice-president of the AHS, and proposed that the AHS collaborate in the organization of the festival. Rensoli already had experience of promoting rock and alternative music in East Havana, an interest he shared with Fernando Rojas, president of the AHS, who was trying to create a space for rock at this time. As Zurbano recalls, he and Rojas were "working in parallel, questioning, in different fields, solidified concepts of nation, national culture and cultural politics"; they mediated between artists, the upper levels of state bureaucracy, concert producers, and the press, explaining, pleading, even insulting, "glimpsing a utopian horizon, believing in the construction of a new culture" (Zurbano Torres 2004:7). There are three key points to note here: firstly, that a leading figure in the nascent rap movement approached a state organization for help, rather than the other way around; secondly, that this first institutional step depended on a shared predisposition towards alternative, "foreign" culture among the three figures involved; and thirdly, that Zurbano and Rojas were state cultural officers who ran the AHS, yet who had to struggle against the preconceptions of other, less forward-thinking branches of the state apparatus in order to create a legitimate, visible space for rap. From the outset, then, we are forced to reconsider both the idea of "state appropriation" of rap and the notion of a unified policy towards the genre.

Pablo Herrera is Cuba's longest established and most prolific rap producer; Ariel Fernández is the editor of the hip hop magazine *Movimiento,* having previously worked as rap promoter for the AHS, and he presents a weekly half-hour rap show on Havana's Radio Progreso. Cuba's foremost producer and DJ respectively, they have also taken an intellectual interest in hip hop. Fernández's article, "Rap cubano: ¿Poesía urbana? O la nueva trova de los noventa" ("Cuban Rap: Urban Poetry, or the Nueva Trova of the '90s?") (Fernández 2000), was a landmark attempt to promote hip hop among intellectual and government circles as a significant cultural phenomenon that could not be ignored by the state, while Herrera has contributed to the academic canon on Cuban rap (Herrera and Selier 2003). Herrera and Fernández are figures of authority within the rap scene who have played a fundamental role in mediating between the expectations of the state, rappers, and foreign observers, their fluent English playing an important part in this last respect. They are both highly articulate and confident figures who have forged links with senior figures in the AHS and the Ministry of Culture and have attended many of the most important meetings in which state support of hip hop has been discussed, working with both the AHS and the ACR. They have used their knowledge of Cuban cultural politics and of the global rap movement to shape a discourse which manages to "stay true" to both the aims of the Cuban Revolution and to perceived core values of "underground" hip hop. Crucially, they have taken their ideas to government officials, aiming to legitimize the movement in the eyes of the state.

Protest Music: Rap and Nueva Trova

One of the prime issues faced by members of the rap movement has been the need to justify the inclusion of "protest music" within Cuban culture and society. A key strategy of these rap "spokespeople" has been to highlight elements of constructive criticism and positivity, which they claim as central to both "old-school" U.S. hip hop and its Cuban counterpart. The constructive nature of criticism is crucial to gaining acceptance from the Cuban state, a notion that dates back to Castro's statement in 1961: "Inside the Revolution, everything; outside the Revolution, nothing."[10] By emphasizing that rap works *within* the Revolution in order to try to improve the realization of Revolutionary goals, these intermediaries have sought a space for rap that is legitimated by the state. Herrera told the author Stephen Foehr:

> Hip-hop artists are a major challenge to the social and cultural structures, so as to make them better. What they are implementing is the evolution of the 1959 Revolution. It's almost the same ideological agenda as Castro's Revolution, but the next step ... I'm talking about black youth as a social group, to create a space where we as black youth can participate constructively and positively in the development of our society and our nation, "positively" and "constructively" meaning that, if the Revolution is in place and has given us proof that it's valid and worthwhile, then we should devote ourselves to making it better, to making it greater. Not to make it die, but to make it flourish. Not that the mainstream discourse doesn't have that talk; it's just that mainstream is the officials, the State. (Foehr 2001:13-16)

Herrera has made similar statements in many interviews (e.g., Pacini Hernández and Garofalo 1999-2000:38; Robinson 2004:121). He seeks to resignify the critical aspect of hip hop as popular participation in improving, not challenging, the Revolutionary process. This line is echoed by other members of the rap movement. Fernández told Robinson: "This is a cultural movement that focuses its message on improving the nation's social health. The rappers are not trying to escape from society's problems, they're trying to solve them" (Robinson 2004:118). Fernández, like Herrera, is consistent on this point (e.g., Fernández 2002), and Pacini Hernández and Garofalo (1999–2000:31–32) noted that "Cuban rappers were quick to point out that it [criticism] was always done 'in a positive way.'"[11]

Gaining a space for rap, then, did not involve curbing its protest aspect. In her classic study of U.S. rap, Tricia Rose writes: "Rap music, more than any other contemporary form of black cultural expression, articulates the chasm between black urban lived experience and dominant, 'legitimate' (e.g., neoliberal) ideology regarding equal opportunity and racial inequality" (Rose 1994:102). Cuban rappers, too, expose the gap between official discourses and lived experience: broadly speaking, this criticism is acceptable as long as it is the *gap* that is criticized rather than the discourses themselves. Many interpret "constructive criticism" as the right to demand that state representatives strive towards the goals of the Revolution. This appears to be the accepted way to frame social critique in contemporary Cuba. Thus, the Afro-Cubans interviewed by Pérez Sarduy and Stubbs in the mid-1990s were individuals who "all remain committed to the aims and ideals of the Cuban Revolution, while critical of aspects of policy and practice" (Pérez Sarduy and Stubbs 2000:xiii). With the radical changes that have affected Cuba since the early 1990s, there is plenty of room to be critical of the Revolution from within for failing to live up to its billing. The most radical group in Havana in 2004, Los Aldeanos, displayed a kind of "Revolutionary fundamentalism" in its attacks on inequalities, special privileges, materialism, and a decline in solidarity. As James Scott notes in his study of the "arts of resistance," elites are vulnerable precisely in the areas in which they make the rules. Accordingly, an examination of the most "hardcore" Cuban rap groups illustrates his contention that "many radical attacks originate in critiques within the hegemony—in taking the values of ruling elites seriously, while claiming that they (the elites) do not" (Scott 1990:105–06).

As any criticism which can be presented as aiming to improve the Revolution is theoretically acceptable, a distinction cannot be made between those who criticize and those who support the state and its policies; publicly, at least, most "underground" rappers do both. Rather, there is a very blurred dividing line between "constructive" and "negative" criticism, a line which can move from moment to moment, from place to place; what is acceptable at the AHS venue, La Madriguera, is often beyond the pale on the radio or TV, for example. But some degree of criticism is permitted, even expected. Alpidio Alonso explicitly allows space for criticism: "The preoccupations that the rappers demonstrate are in line with the sense of justice of the Revolution. The Revolution was born to eliminate racial discrimination and it's important that the rappers are concerned about these kinds of prejudices which still continue ...The Revolution provides this kind of space [for expression]" (quoted in Henríquez Lagarde 2002). Rather than ruling out criticism, Alonso inscribes it within the Revolutionary project. This approach allows the government to take credit for the development of Cuban rap—something that Alonso does regularly—and to draw rappers' fire by describing them as the vanguard of the Revolutionary process, instead of suppressing dissent and facing consequent accusations of censorship.

Critical rap may be seen as an example of a recent "revival of moralism," a "back to basics" ethos recapturing the committed political rhetoric of the 1960s (Kapcia 2000:241). Rather than simply criticizing state representatives like the police, rappers also attack increasing individualism and materialism among the general population. This critique of the Revolution from within can also be seen in the revived interest in Che Guevara among young people. Che is a hallowed, state-sanctioned figure, yet also a symbol of an early, idealistic stage of the Revolution, untarnished by the difficulties of the Special Period. Identifying with his image or words is thus a means of articulating both commitment and dissent, a kind of "safe radicalism," allowing critics to take up a discordant position within the ideological framework of the state (Kapcia 2000:212). This clearly overlaps with the "constructive criticism" of rappers who demand the equality promised by the Revolution. Indeed, the figure of Che is ubiquitous in the rap movement, worn on T-shirts and praised in the lyrics of even the most "underground" rappers. Los Paisanos include Che's slogan "Hasta la victoria siempre" (Forever onward toward victory) in the chorus of their song "Hip hop";[12] a poster of Che with the word "guerrillero" (guerrilla) was prominently displayed on stage at one concert that I attended; and both members of the leading group Anónimo Consejo have Che's image tattooed on their shoulders. By aligning themselves with Che and describing Cuban rap in terms of constructive radicalism—also a defining feature of "conscious" U.S. hip hop, as we shall see below—rappers and intermediaries succeed in framing their music with the discourses of state ideology, youthful dissent, and global hip hop.

In forging a space for protest music, rap's spokespeople were able to draw on lessons learned nearly three decades earlier by the musicians of the Cuban nueva trova movement. Initially there had been considerable official suspicion of this music, a local manifestation of the Latin American *nueva canción* which started out as an underground movement in the late 1960s—just as did rap in the early 1990s—and musicians had to thrash out the relationship between protest song and the Revolution. The turning point came when nueva trova received the backing of the Union of Young Communists, which recognized its appeal to youth and invested in equipment and organized festivals (Foehr 2001:48–50); this change in status offers many parallels with the involvement of the AHS in the development of rap a quarter of a century later. The history of nueva trova provided the rap movement with an important model for the incorporation of protest music within the Revolution. Herrera comments: "The hip-hop generation could be the second wave of the Revolution that was started rolling by the nueva trova movement in the early 1970s" (Foehr 2001:22). Fernández claimed that the founders of nueva trova "showed the direction for how to make revolution with the music ... Those musicians explored how, as a revolutionary, you talk about the things that are bad within the Revolution" (Foehr 2001:35). This parallel was, of course, the bedrock of Fernández's groundbreaking article, "Cuban Rap: Urban Poetry or the Nueva Trova of the Nineties?" (Fernández 2000). The rap–nueva trova parallel is also articulated by rappers in interviews and songs (e.g., Fernández n.d.:8). This analogy clearly provides a useful tool for discussing the place of rap in national culture. By emphasizing continuities within the cultural politics of the Revolution, these members of the rap movement claim a legitimate place for their music while defending their right to voice criticisms.

Aside from the question of protest music, other issues which raised suspicions about rap in Cuba were its North American roots and the ostentatious commercialism and materialism of the current U.S. rap scene. With respect to materialism, rap's spokespeople have characterized the Cuban scene as an "old-school," "underground" movement harking back to the early days of rap before it became a global business. They explicitly distance Cuban rap from the material impulses that are so dominant in its U.S. counterpart today. Both Herrera and Fernández have claimed that Cuban rappers would rather forgo commercial success than sell out (Foehr 2001:21, 41). It is interesting to note how certain features of the Cuban rap scene that could be regarded negatively—such as a paucity of commercial opportunities and a lack of material resources—are thus resignified as indicators of "authenticity," of an "old-school vibe," and often of the moral superiority of the Cuban offspring to its North American parent.

As far as the issue of North American roots is concerned, there are two main discursive strategies, both employed by Fernández. The first is to downplay the American roots of rap in favor of the African, emphasizing rap as a music of the African diaspora (Fernández 2000:5). The second places rap within the broader context of twentieth-century Cuban culture, underlining Cuba's historical capacity for incorporating and transforming North American cultural forms. Fernández describes transculturation as an inherently Cuban process:

> The mestizo, emancipatory character which is at the root of Cuban culture, together with our position as an island, means that everything that reaches our shores ends up being appropriated, recreated, transculturated, as Fernando Ortíz would have wisely put it. This is what is happening right now, in Cuba, with hip hop culture ... It happened before with baseball, jazz and rock, and now it's the turn of hip hop. (Editorial, *Movimiento* 1, inside front cover)

Fernández thus claims that the music may not be Cuban but the way of processing it is, and that assimilating cultural elements of foreign origin is itself an integral part of Cuban national culture. Elsewhere, he stresses U.S.-Cuban musical interaction as a two-way process with deep historical roots, drawing on the example of the huge influence of Cuban musicians in New York throughout the twentieth century as well as the impact of American jazz on the iconic figure Beny Moré (Fernández 2000:4). Fernández's involvement in "nationalizing" rap—simply the latest stage in a century-long process of assimilation, as he presents it—is clear.

"¡Hip Hop, Revolución!"

If the efforts of key intermediaries in the rap movement to attract support from the state have revolved around stressing continuities within national culture, it has been equally important to ground the idea of rap as a positive force for change and as "Revolutionary culture" among the rappers themselves. Intermediaries did not simply formulate strategies for talking about rap to state officials, but also played a role in shaping the rap movement itself. For Cuban rap did not start out as a beacon of "conscious" rap on the global scene, as it is portrayed today. Rather, observers recall the early days of Cuban hip hop as slavishly imitating the lyrics and style of U.S. gangsta rap—down to the heavy coats and hats, even in the tropical summer—, and Fernández frequently refers to an evolution from this early "mimetic" period to an "authentically Cuban rap" (e.g., Fernández 2002). It is important to note, therefore, that the Cuban rap scene was deliberately channelled by figures who saw that "conscious" hip hop held the key to peaceful co-existence with the state. "Nationalization" was thus something that they sought, rather than being simply something imposed from outside. As Cuba's leading rap producer, Pablo Herrera has been in a prime position to bring his influence to bear on the local scene. He says that while he was teaching about hip hop at the University of Havana, he started working with artists, "trying to push them to higher levels, telling them, 'You need to read this book about this and write songs about it'" (Smith n.d.). This influence is openly acknowledged by the emblematic group Anónimo Consejo, who said of Herrera: "He advises us on everything from production to how we should express ourselves onstage. He gives us ideas for lyrics, and he also writes the choruses if necessary" (Fernández n.d.:9).

Anónimo Consejo have played a key role in putting Herrera's ideas into practice, and their philosophy, summed up by their slogan "Hip hop, Revolución," shows the influence of his blend of conscious hip hop and Revolutionary thought.[13] The journalist Annalise Wunderlich paints a revealing picture of Herrera working with the duo:

In a T-shirt with the words "God is a DJ," Herrera shuffles through a stack of CDs and smokes a cigarette while Yosmel and Kokino sit on his couch, intently studying every page of an old Vibe magazine. "Yo, check this out," Herrera finds what he's looking for. "*En la revolucion, cada quien hace su parte.*" In the Revolution, everyone must do his part. Fidel's unmistakable voice loops back and repeats the phrase again and again over a hard-driving beat. Herrera nods to Yosmel, who takes his cue: "The solution is not leaving/New days will be here soon/We deserve and want to always go forward/Solving problems is important work." (Wunderlich 2001)

Another characteristic Anónimo Consejo chorus drives home the Revolutionary message:[14]

Despierta pueblo, Revolución, compadre,	Wake up, people, Revolution, my friend,
Es momento de justicia, Revolución, compadre,	It's time for justice, Revolution, my friend,
Anónimo Consejo, Revolución, compadre,	Anónimo Consejo, Revolution, my friend,
Hip hop Revolución, Revolución, compadre.	Hip hop Revolution, Revolution, my friend.

The slogan "Hip hop, Revolución" in many ways encapsulates a "formula for success" within Cuban hip hop, in that it appeals in equal measures to government officials and to foreign hip hop aficionados. Anónimo Consejo are one of the eight groups selected for inclusion in the state-run ACR, but they also feature prominently in many of the foreign documentaries about Cuban rap, one of which, *ANC Hip Hop Revolution,* is devoted entirely to the duo.[15] This rhetorical strategy has been adopted by a number of Cuban groups and has provoked occasional scepticism precisely because of its success. One leading figure privately described this kind of politicized rap to me as a tactic for accruing benefits such as overseas travel, and Los Aldeanos made the following acerbic observations in one of their songs during the 2004 festival:

> *Aquí no todo es "hip hop, revolución" como parece*
> *Con los MCs que se creen duros que están más flojos que SBS*
> *[...]*
> *Muchos son los que sin razón gritan "revolución"*
> *En cada canción, ignoran su profesión verdadera*
>
> Here it's not all "hip hop, revolution" like it seems
> With those MCs who think they're tough but who're limper than SBS[16]
> [...]
> There are many who for no reason cry "revolution"
> In every song, but they don't know their true profession

In an interview, Ariel Fernández and Anónimo Consejo discussed how other groups have jumped on the bandwagon of "Revolutionary rap." Fernández claimed that "we have seen opportunists ... who use it to gain a space for themselves, so as not to remain outside of what's going on." Adeyeme replied that "many of them today keep saying 'Hip hop, Revolution!' yet they can't read a book by Che or Malcolm X" (Fernández n.d.:6).

Yet however we may view it, "Revolutionary rap" has been a distinguishing feature of the Cuban scene, and the scepticism of some must be balanced by a recognition that the idea of revolution is central to the discourses of the U.S. rap groups most admired by Cuban fans, such as Public Enemy, The Roots, or Dead Prez. Public Enemy's most recent album is entitled "Revolver-lution," Dead Prez released "Revolutionary but Gangsta," and Boston rappers The Foundation describe themselves as "sons of revolution" in an unreleased collaboration with Los Paisanos. Revolutionary rhetoric cannot therefore be regarded simply as a diplomatic line. This is undoubtedly why Herrera's comments struck Robinson as "delivered with obvious sincerity but also with the polish of a high-priced public relations consultant" (Robinson 2004:212). Herrera is highly educated and is at ease with a range of discourses. His rhetorical strategies are clearly self-conscious, but this does not make them insincere. I am arguing that rap was allowed to prosper in Cuba because it could be talked about "productively." From this perspective, whether or not all artists employed, or believed in, certain rhetorical strategies is less important than the fact that a sufficient number did and that they were sufficiently credible, not just to state officials but also to many fans (due to the overlap with politicized U.S. rap), in a way that official Soviet Bloc rockers, for example, generally were not. In the final analysis, this is a study of public discourses about rap and of coherence in explicit artistic philosophy (rather than output or beliefs). The achievement of Herrera, Fernández, and others has been to shape this philosophy around a multiplicity of artistic responses.

Havana: The New Home of "Old-School" Hip Hop

A key part of legitimating "Revolutionary rap" among artists and fans has been to emphasize the continuities between this discourse and that of "old-school" or conscious rap, in other words, to construct Cuban hip hop as an "authentic" movement harking back to the genre's original spirit. Without this, Revolutionary rap might well have gone down the same path as "official" Soviet rock and lost all credibility as it gained state support. Ariel Fernández has played a pivotal role in underlining connections between old-school U.S. and Cuban rap, and thus influencing the direction of the movement, by educating the rap community about the roots of hip hop both as a DJ and as editor of Movimiento magazine. All three editions of Movimiento that have appeared to date begin with articles about the history of rap, focusing on the birth of the genre in the 1970s and its politicization in the 1980s;

conspicuously lacking are any references to the 1990s, when rap became a huge commercial success. Articles concentrate on "old-school" or conscious U.S. rappers like KRS-One, The Roots, and Dead Prez. Characterizing recent American developments as a descent into crass commercialism and a thus betrayal of the genre, a number of Cuban commentators have concluded that Cuba's rap movement is not merely "authentic," but has become the guardian of the "original spirit" of hip hop which U.S. rappers have largely abandoned (e.g., del Río 2002).

In order for this imaginative reversal to take on full legitimacy in the eyes of the Cuban rap community, another important element was necessary: the acceptance by foreign rappers and observers of the characterization of Havana as the new home of "old-school" hip hop, as the new South Bronx. This consent was duly given, thanks in great measure to the efforts of Nehanda Abiodun, a U.S. citizen and former black liberation fighter living in exile in Havana, who has played a key role in influencing the Cuban rap scene and increasing its legitimacy in the eyes of both rap fans and state officials. Abiodun is often described as a "godmother" to the Cuban hip hop movement, teaching young rappers about black history and politics. Like Herrera and Fernández, she has mediated between the rap community and government officials, using her authority as a revolutionary exile to argue the case for rap as a tool in the service of the Revolution. She has also helped to shape the Cuban rap movement by forging links with conscious rappers and activists in the U.S. In 1998, an organization called the Black August Collective was formed out of conversations between Abiodun, the Malcolm X Grassroots Movement, and various hip hop journalists and activists in New York (Asho 2004). Black August sought to bring revolutionary politics back into hip hop, to draw attention to "political" prisoners in U.S. jails, and to support the burgeoning Cuban rap scene. Thanks to the efforts of Abiodun and Black August, radical U.S. artists such as Dead Prez, Common, The Roots, and Black Star were invited to perform at Cuban festivals, making a big impression on local rappers and audiences, and they enthusiastically endorsed the local scene. These concerts provided a unique opportunity for Cuban artists and fans to connect with the outside hip hop world, and played a key role in raising the profile of conscious, politicized rap within Cuba. Thus the development of Cuba's "Revolutionary" rap discourse was shaped to a considerable degree by an exiled American in Havana, a transnational collective, and by visiting U.S. conscious rappers. While this development undoubtedly emerged with one eye on acceptance by the state, it cannot be described in terms of state appropriation.

Along with U.S. artists came foreign observers and writers who started to talk the "old-school talk." Journalist Brett Sokol wrote of rap in Havana: "it was hard not to be reminded of the beginnings of American hip-hop. Not unlike the American groups that gave birth to rap in the South Bronx in the late 70's and early 80's" (Sokol 2000). U.S. rapper Fab 5 Freddy talked about his visit to the city in 1997: "It reminded me of the spirit of hip-hop here in the early days when it was really raw, in the parks, with guys literally hooking up to the light posts for electricity" (quoted in Smith n.d.). The CD sleeve notes of *The Cuban Hip Hop All Stars Vol. 1* begin: "Habana, Cuba in the 21st century: Crumbling architectural relics, stray dogs and proud people. With a powerful vibrant culture. Not much different from the South Bronx in the '70s and '80s."

The crucial point here is that these positive foreign perceptions of Cuba as retaining a link to the "original spirit of hip hop," now lost in the over-commercialized popular music industry of developed countries, have fed back into the Cuban scene, both legitimating local artists and reinforcing the discourses that were being formed around their music. Fab 5 Freddy, for example, subsequently became a founder member of the Black August Collective; his initial perceptions of Havana as a throwback to New York in the 1970s led to his involvement in a transnational organization which sent "old-school" rappers to Havana, in turn influencing the direction of Cuban hip hop. Danny Hoch and Kofi Taha, two other founder members of Black August, both went on to publish articles on the Cuban scene back in the U.S., thus stimulating a steady flow of foreign producers, journalists, researchers, and documentary-makers to check out Cuban "underground" rap. Partly as a result, an "underground" direction—or at least a stated orientation—was adopted by the majority of Cuban rap groups.

The "nationalization" of rap, then, emerges as a markedly transnational process. Indeed, the sheer volume of foreign production on Cuban hip hop—undergraduate theses at U.S. and Canadian universities, doctoral dissertations completed or in progress, scores of magazine and newspaper articles around the world, and more than a dozen documentary films (Zurbano Torres 2004:10)—illustrates that the "multivocality" (Wade 2000) of Cuban rap, so important to its success, goes far beyond its usefulness to Cuban rappers and government officials; further, this coverage has clearly impacted the Cuban movement. The notion, validated by overseas visitors, that the Cuban scene is of extraordinary interest, perhaps unique today, a reminder of hip hop "back in the day," has raised Cubans' sense of pride in local hip hop. Fernández suggests that the Cuban rap movement is "one of the most critical in the world, perhaps, because of the influence of the social and political system that it has developed in" ("Encuentro entre amigos" 2004:22). Adeyeme of Anónimo Consejo speaks of the high level of Cuban lyrics in comparison with other Latin American countries, claiming that "nobody can compare with us." He goes on:

> Cuba is one of the Spanish-speaking countries with the highest cultural level and
> the richest language. Many Latin American rappers are just copying the Ameri-
> cans, with their lyrics about drugs, violence, material things. You've really got
> to search to find a positive lyric in Latin American hip hop. I think that, because
> Cuba is a country of revolution and struggle, you can see positive messages re-
> flected in our lyrics. It's because of that that many people see us as the roots of
> hip hop that have been lost in the United States. (quoted in Fernández n.d.:9)

This sense of pride and even superiority has been voiced by other rappers,
Cuban journalists and cultural authorities (e.g., "Encuentro entre amigos"
2004:20; Zamora Céspedes 2004:56; Henríquez Lagarde 2002). It is interesting to compare the Cuban rap movement with others, such as the Australian
or British scenes (Maxwell 2003; Hesmondhalgh and Melville 2001), which
have struggled against (self-)perceptions as little more than pale imitations
of U.S. rap. Looking at Cuba, we can see just how effectively rap has been
harnessed to the construction of national identity, by artists as well as by
state representatives.

While the effect of this foreign interest on the direction and self-percep-
tions of the rap movement should not be underestimated, it also affected
relations between rappers and the state. International interest in Cuban rap
increased not only through the efforts of the Black August Collective but
especially after the worldwide success of Orishas' first album, released by EMI
France in 1999. The world's press started attending the annual rap festival
in increasing numbers from 2000 onwards (Robinson 2004:208). State support for the festival also increased markedly in this year. Cuban elites have a
history of accepting their country's popular music only after approval from
abroad. As Robin Moore points out, transnational links and exchanges with
the Chilean protest song movement in late 1960s undoubtedly contributed
to the acceptance of nueva trova within Cuba (Moore 2003:21), and this kind
of reaction to positive foreign perceptions of Cuban popular music dates
back to the 1920s (Moore 1997:104–05). A concrete example of foreign
influence on the state's attitude to rap is the involvement of the American
singer, actor, and social activist Harry Belafonte, who visited Cuba in the
pivotal year of 1999 ("Encuentro entre amigos" 2004). Belafonte, who has
a long-standing interest in hip hop as a force for social change, met with
leading representatives of the rap community and then went straight on to
a meeting with Fidel Castro. Belafonte related that he had an eleven-hour
meeting with the Cuban leader, of which perhaps half was spent talking
about hip hop around the globe, and he noted Castro's great interest in the
subject ("Encuentro entre amigos" 2004:19). The Minister of Culture, Abel
Prieto, had already expressed interest in rap earlier that year, and Belafonte's
intervention at this important juncture may well have helped to consolidate

the government's involvement. Rapper Magia from Obsesión reflected on these key meetings in a round-table discussion in 2002:"After that meeting there were some very positive changes for us.And many others came out of that meeting that Harry had with Fidel.We know that and it will go down in the history of Cuban hip hop" ("Encuentro entre amigos" 2004:19).

It is widely assumed that state support for hip hop must have Castro's personal approval,and for that reason it is worth noting not only his meeting with Belafonte, but also an incident from the earliest days of the Revolution, when Castro was visiting New York in 1960. Unhappy with his treatment at his midtown hotel, he was invited by Malcolm X to move to Harlem to stay at the Hotel Theresa. Castro decided to accept, regarding Harlem as the place where his "best friends" were (Young 2003:31).This marked the beginning of a long history of Cuban solidarity with African American causes, and Castro revisited Harlem in 2000 to speak before largely appreciative audiences.We might regard this early alliance with radical black politics and sympathy for minority struggle in the U.S.—in particular, the personal connection with Malcolm X, an iconic figure for "conscious" rappers—as sowing the seed of Cuban state involvement with radical hip hop nearly four decades later; it certainly points towards a number of shared concerns.

Figure 1. Los Paisanos.

Cuba and Hip Hop: Two Revolutions, One Idiom

Underpinning the efforts of cultural intermediaries to create a space for hip hop in Cuba was the crucial realization that conscious rap and the Cuban Revolution share a number of discursive tropes and moral positions centered on the concept of "revolution," and therefore that rap could be presented to cultural officials in familiar, comprehensible terms. To put it another way, the revolutionary discourses of conscious rap have proved eminently compatible with the Revolutionary ideology of the Cuban state. As Fernández has said, "hip hop is a completely revolutionary culture, in the broadest possible meaning of the word" (Robinson 2004:120). By focusing on rap's origins as a music of resistance against the U.S. state and dominant classes, cultural intermediaries and Cuban officials interpret rap as revolutionary music, as the global protest music of all those oppressed and marginalized by U.S. power. Rap therefore sits easily with the ideology of a Revolutionary "protest state" at loggerheads with the U.S. Both conscious hip hop and the Cuban government give a prominent role to critiques of dominant U.S. ideologies, and the critical stances of U.S. rappers like The Roots or Dead Prez are therefore music to the ears of Cuban officials. Cuban rap is lauded by the international hip hop community for its rejection of materialism and its critical focus, for providing a voice for the marginalized and a critique of imperialism and globalization. These are all features that are perceived as close to the "original essence" of hip hop, yet they are also ideas that underpin Cuban state ideology.

To take another example, the idea of hip hop as an arena for ideological debate in which Cuba is prevailing over the U.S. dovetails with the political vision of Cuba as a country which outscores the U.S. primarily on an ideological level. A large sign outside the U.S. interests section on the Malecón in Havana proclaims: "Batalla de ideas, un combate de nuestro tiempo" (Battle of ideas, a struggle for our times), a message echoed by a sign by the bridge over the Río Almendares which quotes Fidel: "Las ideas pueden más que las armas" (Ideas are more powerful than weapons). This clear preference for doing battle on an ideological, rather than material, level is a logical step for a small and economically overstretched country like Cuba, yet it meshes with the philosophy of conscious hip hop. The editorial of the first edition of *Movimiento* is subtitled "moviendo ideas" (moving ideas) while the group Los Paisanos claim in one of their songs that hip hop "es una religión sin Dios, pero es verdadera/no se adoran imágenes, se adoran ideas" (it's a religion without God, but it's real/we don't worship images, we worship ideas).[17] Cuban commentators contrast the ideological rigor of these local rap artists with the degenerate commercialism of U.S. stars. Critical rap thus serves both elite and popular constructions of national identity, while also marking out the rap scene as a distinct, progressive cultural movement within Cuban society.

In examining the parallels between conscious hip hop and Revolutionary ideology, it is instructive to examine the "codes" which the political historian Antoni Kapcia regards as underpinning Cuban national ideology throughout the twentieth century and as having received a renewed boost in the 1990s (Kapcia 2000:85–91, 237–43). If we ignore the first, agrarianism, the remainder—collectivism, moralism, activism, culturalism, revolutionism, and internationalism—all have clear links with the philosophies of conscious hip hop groups.[18] It is instructive to examine first "the Black August Hip Hop Collective Statement of Purpose," given the influence that this organization has had on Cuban rap ideology:

> The Black August Hip Hop Collective strives to support the global development of hip hop culture by facilitating exchanges between international communities where hip hop is a vital part of youth culture, and by promoting awareness about the social and political issues that effect [*sic*] these youth communities. Our goal is to bring culture and politics together and to allow them to naturally evolve into a unique hip hop consciousness that informs our collective struggle for a more just, equitable and human world …Through an effective merging of hip hop culture and political information, The Black August Hip Hop Collective promotes our own hip hop aesthetic, which emphasizes sincere self-expression, creativity, and community responsibility.[19]

The parallels between this expression of "hip hop ideology," the Cuban scene, and Kapcia's "codes" are numerous and striking. *Collectivism* is evident in the very title, "The Black August Collective," the rhetoric of "collective struggle," equality and "community responsibility," and the insistence of Cuban commentators on referring to rap as a "movement." *Moralism* underpins "conscious" hip hop: Black August envisions "a more just, equitable and human world," and much "underground" Cuban rap is based around a series of moral judgments about racial discrimination, abuse of authority by policemen and Party officials, the perceived moral laxity of young women, materialism, the deterioration of bonds of friendship, and "*doble moral*"—a view of a society in moral decline under the pressure of tourism and dollarization. Similarly, the Black August Collective stresses the link between U.S. conscious hip hop and community *activism*, underlining their "collective struggle" against racial oppression; the word "struggle" also permeates the rhetoric of Cuban rappers, who are regarded by many observers as among the most politically active members of Cuban society.

Culturalism, or faith in education, culture, and in the intellectual's political role, grew as a reaction against philistinism, the pursuit of wealth, corruption, brothels, and gambling (Kapcia 2000:89). Cuban "underground" rappers consistently promote education and reflection, and react against mindlessness, materialism, corruption, and frivolity. The negative feelings about reggaetón that currently dominate the rap scene center on a perceived distinction between rap, as a serious activity and stimulus for reflection, and reggaetón, which is rejected by many rappers as mere diversion, idle partying, and dancing. The leading Cuban rap collective La FabriK (consisting of Obsesión and Doble Filo) combines culture and education in their community projects with children and prisoners (Borges-Triana 2004:8–9). *Revolutionism* underpins both U.S. and Cuban underground rap as well as Cuban state ideology, as we have seen repeatedly. This amalgam is perfectly expressed in one of Black August's press releases:

> Black August holds these elements—hip-hop, U.S. political prisoners, and Cuba— together with the common theme of revolution: Hip-hop was and is a revolutionary cultural art form. Cuba, with all its faults and attributes, is defined by its revolutionary history. And U.S. political prisoners and exiles, many of whom have been given asylum in Cuba, are products of revolutionary movements within the United States. (Talking Drum Collective 2003)

Finally, Kapcia illustrates his code of *internationalism* with early twentieth-century examples of Cuban efforts towards Latin American solidarity. It will be remembered that Alpidio Alonso told me, with regard to the rap festival: "I think it's very symbolic that this event takes place in Cuba, with rappers who come mainly from Latin America, from countries that are subject to this imperialist pseudo-cultural invasion." For the cultural leadership, then, the festival represents not just a series of concerts but a chance to bring together Latin American rappers in condemnation of U.S. imperialism, symbolically uniting their countries under a Cuban banner against U.S. hegemony in the hemisphere. Black August, meanwhile, is a transnational organization, its aims including "facilitating exchanges between international communities" and "artist-to-artist contact and collaboration across international borders," while Latin American-centered internationalism is expressed clearly by Hermanos de Causa in their song "Latinoamérica," a collaboration with Argentinean rapper Malena, with its chorus:

Adelante, Latino, rompe dictadura,	Onwards, Latino, bring down dictatorship,
América es la casa, tu raza sólo una,	America is your home, you are one race,
Cuba los convoca, alzen la cabeza,	Cuba summons you, raise your heads,
En la unión radica nuestra fortaleza.	Our strength lies in unity.[20]

This comparison reveals a remarkable degree of overlap between Cuban national ideology and the philosophical underpinnings of conscious hip hop, a compatibility that was underlined by key figures in order to facilitate the assimilation of rap into national culture. Although I am arguing against a simple model of appropriation by the state, it is clear that state representatives have exploited the overlap between hip hop and national ideology for political purposes. The lead-up to the 2004 Havana Hip Hop Festival provided one of the most explicit demonstrations of the strategic merging of hip hop and Revolutionary discourses by officials of the AHS in a website that they created as part of the 2004 festival. The website, the address of which re-appropriates Anónimo Consejo's slogan "Hip hop, Revolución," was intended as an internet discussion forum on hip hop and introduces nine themes for discussion:[21]

> (1) Hip hop is a universal socio-cultural phenomenon that embodies struggle and resistance against the fascist, belligerent, and marginalizing politics of imperialism.
>
> (2) Hip hop is a cultural manifestation of rebellion by minorities who are oppressed and excluded by the political and economic power-centers of capitalism.
>
> (3) Rap has arisen in Cuba as the new voice of an island that is besieged and assailed by the U.S. empire. It is also the sound of the Revolution, expressing the problems and hopes of young rappers.
>
> (4) An avant-garde, belligerent, critical rap can be an alternative to the pseudo-cultural products of the musical market.
>
> (5) How can the Latin American hip hop movement unite further and create new spaces for cultural and ethical exchange and debate?
>
> (6) Can rap now be considered a genre or a style?
>
> (7) Hip hop, with its special characteristics, can be considered part of the national culture of a country. Is that happening in the various scenes where hip hop is developing today?
>
> (8) Latin(o)s have played a very important part since the birth of hip hop. Very few of the books that supposedly relate the history of this culture refer to this. What is your opinion of this?
>
> (9) Rap is considered a belligerent response to the phenomena of social exclusion and marginalization and an opportunity for expression on the part of the oppressed masses. Should its cultivators focus on the transnational music market? Should they change this perspective and pursue other avenues of promotion and commercialization without abandoning the aesthetic and ethical premises of the movement? Is there an alternative which responds to these particular promotional needs?

The language and themes of these questions for discussion provide a fascinating insight into the uses of rap to the current AHS leadership, encapsulating many of the points made so far. Rap is interpreted as the resistance of the marginalized against oppression and exclusion by the forces of capitalism and imperialism as embodied by the U.S. state, an interpretation which is close to classic analyses of U.S. rap (e.g., Rose 1994). More specifically, Cuban rap is perceived as a voice of resistance to the pressure exerted on the island by its powerful neighbor. Whereas writers on global rap have tended to de-essentialize the genre in order to legitimize local scenes (e.g., Mitchell 2001:1–12), the AHS discourse stresses the perceived essence or origins of rap in order to keep the focus of critique on the U.S. government and its policies, rather than adapting to local circumstances, where the Cuban state might then become the object of criticism. At the same time, however, there is no mention of the U.S. as the originator of genre. Instead, rap is a "universal phenomenon" and the role of Latinos in its gestation is underlined, and thus the use of this critical tool in Cuban hands is validated. Interestingly, although Latinos are mentioned, the Afro-diasporic roots of rap are not, and the question of race is at least partially replaced by that of class ("the oppressed masses"). Other themes are already familiar, such as the incorporation of rap into national culture (point seven), pan-Latin solidarity (points five and eight), and anti-commercialism (points four and nine).

From this list of questions, it can be seen that hip hop has provided an appropriate discursive framework within which to restate long-standing ideological positions of the Cuban state such as critiques of U.S. power, the defense of the oppressed, Latin American unity, and anti-capitalism. As Alpidio Alonso told me, the rap festival provides an opportunity "to project a revolutionary message from Cuba." The attractiveness of rap to the state is thus clear, and it is interesting to see how this "foreign" music has been bound so quickly to the construction of national identity. Global recognition of the Cuban rap movement is also useful to the government, as praise from foreign observers for Cuban rap is seen as reflecting positively on the Revolutionary social project. Cuban commentators and officials such as Alonso seize upon international validation of Cuban rap as evidence of the virtues of the political system in which it thrives (e.g., Henríquez Lagarde 2002). Foreign perceptions of Cuba as a key node in a global conscious rap movement, even "deposing" the United States as its leading force, have considerable appeal to government officials (as well as to rappers). Hence Alonso's description of the festival as a "symbolic" event, uniting Latin American countries against U.S. imperialism under a Cuban banner. The possibilities for expressing national ideologies through the language of hip hop, and for reflecting positive judgements onto the nation, certainly go some way towards explaining state promotion of rap.

Reggaetón: A Common Enemy

While both state representatives and "underground" rappers have made the most of the common ground between their ideologies, a shared attitude to reggaetón illustrates an overlap in interests which suggests that their relationship cannot be reduced even to mutual appropriations. While live reggaetón performances were less frequent than those of timba or rap in Havana in 2004, the recorded music was everywhere, and it was overwhelmingly the most popular music among young listeners (Castro Medel 2005). It was also the favored target of critical barbs by rappers, derided for being trite and mindless, and for promoting pointless diversion and dancing over social consciousness. It came up in virtually every conversation that I heard, public or private, about the state of the rap scene. A song by Los Aldeanos begins with a parody of a famous reggaetón track by Cubanitos 20–02, "Mátame," and then makes the rap/reggaetón distinction clear:

Mátanos, mátanos, mátanos la gana de rapear . . .	The urge to rap is killing us . . .
Repartición de bienes, reggaetón pa' mover culo,	Distribution of assets, reggaetón for shaking your ass,
O rap pa' poner madura la mente del imaduro.	Or rap for maturing the mind of the immature.

By the end of 2004, reggaetón had come to the attention of party officials at the 8th Congress of the Union of Young Communists, where it was criticized by none other than Alpidio Alonso of the AHS. In fact, the voices of a number of cultural commentators were starting to be raised against the perceived dangers of reggaetón (Castro Medel 2005). This coincidence between the viewpoint of the president of the AHS and the "underground" rap community illustrates another side to the ideological overlap that has been so important to the "nationalization" of rap, and counters any suggestion that this coincidence of interests is entirely manufactured. Indeed, what is shared here, I would argue, is a fundamental privileging of male eloquence over female bodily expression. Both the Cuban political elite and the Cuban rap scene are masculine worlds focused on the power of the spoken word, and both share an ideological preference for text- or intellect-centered musics—rap, nueva trova—over body-centered genres such as reggaetón, timba, or Afro-Cuban folkloric music. There are clear parallels with Susan McClary's remarks about the tensions between political song and disco in the 1960s and 1970s: "The political folk song is the Left's version of the Calvinist hymn: words foregrounded to control 'the meaning,' music effaced to the status of vehicle, all untoward appeals to the body eliminated" (McClary 1994:31–32). In rappers' and politicians' reactions to reggaetón, there is the same dismissal of a dance genre designed to maximize physical engagement that McClary describes in relation to disco, and the same "fear of the feminine, the body and the sensual." Reggaetón puts female dancers center-stage, whereas male rappers keep the focus on their words with repeated exhortations like "this is music for listening, not for dancing." Their derisive comments about reggaetón often focus on its sexualized dance moves. What we see here, I believe, is a shared understanding between state representatives and "underground" rappers about the relative value of masculine utterances and feminine movements.

Fractures in State Policy

For all that rappers and the AHS found a common language which allowed them to work together, there have been many inconsistencies within state policy which undermine the relatively harmonious picture painted so far. The very term "state policy" must in fact be questioned, given the wide range of state employees who have regularly taken contradictory decisions relating to rap. Some of these internal contradictions were externalized in 2002, a crossroads year in Cuban rap. With the formation of the Agencia Cubana de Rap (ACR), an elite group of rappers were taken on as professional state employees, thereby dividing the scene into amateur members of the AHS and professional members of the ACR. While there has been much talk about the ACR as an institution created to "control" Cuban rap, it is important to point out that the idea of the Agency grew out of discussions between rappers, the AHS, and officials at the Ministry of Culture, and that its stated aim is to promote and commercialize the groups under its aegis. In other words, it was the outcome of negotiations in which leading rap groups, in many cases frustrated at their lack of commercial success, played a key role. As the founder of Primera Base, Rubén Marín, put it recently: "The Agency was something that we, the rappers, always wanted, a dream come true" (quoted in Cordero 2004:23). Nevertheless, it must be acknowledged that the ACR is widely unpopular outside the small circle who benefit from it, and a more negative view of institutionalization has developed in the wake of its inception. But, for all the grumbling that I heard about the Agency, the worst accusations that were laid at its door did not concern concrete cases of control or manipulation, but rather a failure to live up to expectations in terms of organization and promotion, a perceived lack of democracy in the selection process which left several well-known groups on the outside, and above all, the division of a previously united rap scene.

Fractures thus started to emerge more clearly in 2002. A strong discourse, flexible enough to be attractive to most of the parties concerned, had been constructed around the idea of Cuban rap as harking back to the days when hip hop was about changing the world, not making money. Nevertheless, some of the best-known rap groups were making a bid for greater commercial exposure under the aegis of a state agency, and several even began trading in conscious rap for reggaetón. This turning-point was exemplified by Cubanitos 20–02, a Havana-based reggaetón group formed that year by ex-members of pioneering "underground" rap group Primera Base, which went on to become the biggest-selling band in Cuba. By the time that I went to Cuba in 2004, there were signs of serious dissent, not just among AHS rap groups who felt excluded, but from a range of figures of authority and cultural commentators close to the scene. One senior AHS figure involved with rap who spoke to me, who was committed to the anti-commercial, amateur ethos of his organization, was utterly dismissive of the ACR, refusing even to discuss one of the Agency's most successful groups due to its commercial orientation. The point is not simply that a gulf was emerging between rap's "underground" rhetoric and the practice of some of its leading exponents, but also that it is impossible to talk about a homogenized "state" in relation to rap music, since two state-funded organizations began pursuing diverging policies in relation to rap and considerable tensions emerged between the two. The ACR is committed to making its groups more commercially success-ful, whereas the AHS promotes critical reflection on Cuban social reality, an important aspect of which is a critique of increasing materialism and com-mercialism in Cuban society. The contradiction is evident in the fact that in 2001, Abel Prieto, the Minister of Culture, praised leading rap groups for "the seriousness and rigor with which they take on real problems, at the same time rejecting commercialism" (quoted in Fernandes 2003:594). Yet within a year, the Ministry of Culture had incorporated the same groups into the ACR, the stated aims of which include "to commercialize the groups in its catalogue" (*Movimiento* 1, inside back cover).

The issue becomes more complicated when we consider the role of the state-backed media. TV and radio program directors have their own cultural-political agendas, and complaints have been rife for years that they have given rap only a fraction of the airtime of other genres. This inconsistency in attitudes to new music, especially by the media, was also apparent in the early 1970s with the rise of nueva trova: "Each different cultural institution or area of culture had its own cultural line and logic. The radio and television, and each program director, had their own ideas about culture. One radio station might play a song and another station would ban it" (Foehr 2001:50). Even when conditions improved for the *trovadores,* media resistance persisted (Moore 2003:20), revealing radio and especially TV to be some of the most conservative branches of the state apparatus, something which is abundantly clear with regard to rap. There were one or two directors who showed inter-est in rap in 2004, but the majority seemed unwilling to become involved, despite the fact that rap concerts were taking place in Havana under the auspices of state organizations at least once a week. The gulf between the attitudes of the AHS and the media was illustrated vividly to me when I ac-companied the group Los Paisanos and William Figuerero, the AHS promoter (and therefore a state employee), to a radio broadcast to promote a forthcom-ing concert organized by the AHS. After a short interview, the group played one of their tracks—"Negro," a song about race relations—and although it had featured regularly in concerts at AHS venues, the program director was extremely unhappy when he heard it and ejected the artists from the build-ing, telling them not to come back.

Sekuo of Anónimo Consejo, a group which, as we have seen, epitomizes "politically correct" Revolutionary rap and which is employed by the state ACR, expressed his bewilderment at the gulf between the state's supportive rhetoric and the limited promotion of conscious rap in the media: "It's difficult to understand how in Cuba, a country that is synonymous with revolution in every sense, we don't hear Anónimo Consejo or Hermanos de Causa, yet on every radio station we hear Eminem, an American rapper who is obscene, foul-mouthed and one of the most violent examples of this culture" (quoted in Fernández n.d.:8). The director of an anti-drugs music video by ACR groups Primera Base and Alto Voltaje spoke at the colloquium during the 2004 festival and expressed his disappointment that the video, recorded by artists in the employ of the state, with its positive message for Cuban youth, had never been shown on TV. The failure to show film footage from previous rap festivals on national TV was also roundly criticized at both the colloquium and a meeting between rappers and the AHS leadership at La Madriguera. Nor is it just members of the rap movement who criticize the media for its shallow musical content: an article in the official newspaper *Juventud Rebelde,* condemning the pervasive influence of reggaetón, referred to "the poor quality of some programs in the media" (Castro Medel 2005). Thus any attempt to understand the relations between the "state" and the "rap movement" must take into account the fact that different branches of the state have been pursuing contradictory policies since 2002, leading to a corresponding fragmentation of the rap community.

Conclusions

Cuban rap has gone from a street subculture to an official, sponsored part of national culture in the space of a decade. An examination of this development reveals the extent to which the formation of national culture is negotiated on a variety of levels rather than being imposed from above, constituting not a top-down process but a consensus forged through discussions among practitioners, key cultural intermediaries, and state officials (Askew 2002; Wade 2000). For all that the aim to "nationalize rap" was articulated by the Minister of Culture, this process has not simply been one of "state appropriation" or any other such abstraction which denies the active participation of non-elite sectors; rather, it reflects how rap could be talked about fruitfully by different sectors of Cuban society. Non-Cubans have also played a significant part in the assimilation of rap in Cuba, both on a practical level but also by contributing to the production of rap discourses. There is a palpable sense of self-belief about the Cuban rap movement which comes as much from the approval of foreign observers as it does from acceptance by the state or popularity among audiences, and which has nothing to do with commercial success. Much of the writing about global hip hop has focused on the local uses of globalized cultural tools, but what is notable in the Cuban context is the involvement of foreigners at every stage of the process. Ian Condry writes of the arrival of hip hop in Japan as "a flying spark that traveled from the Bronx across the ocean to light a fire. This image of a flying spark is important, for it reminds us that although popular music styles travel on the winds of global capitalism, they ultimately burn or die out on local fuel" (Condry 2001:222). Though there is clearly plenty of fuel in Cuba, it was not just the spark of rap that flew across the ocean but a host of U.S. rappers, journalists, activists, academics, and documentary-makers in its wake to fan the flames, revealing that Cuban hip hop continued to be transnational in a very concrete sense long after it had taken root. Non-Cubans, too, found that they could talk productively about Cuban rap, and they profoundly influenced its "nationalization."

It is important to uncover the complex, negotiated nature of the assimilation of rap in order to form a considered response to state involvement. When I went to a screening of the Cuban hip hop documentary *Inventos* in London, I was struck that the audience laughed when Pablo Herrera mentioned Abel Prieto's statement in 1999 that it was time to nationalize rap.[22] This brought home to me that most non-Cubans and Cuban emigrés tend to assume that nationalization and rap are incompatible, or that nationalization is a negative concept with respect to popular music. However, I suspect that many Cuban audiences, or indeed rappers, would not have found this remark particularly strange; after all, it was the leading rap groups who clamored for their own agency, and many AHS artists, aware that they lack the resources to put on their own concerts, would like to see more involvement from this state organization. Most culture is nationalized in Cuba, and as people like Rensoli and Fernández were well aware, nationalization is vital to expansion and greater visibility. Unlike their nueva trova predecessors, they could look back on thirty-five years of the institutionalization of culture and see that this process, if not always problem-free, had nevertheless allowed space and eventual popularity for such important artists as Pablo Milanés, Silvio Rodríguez, and Carlos Varela.

The other leading actors in my account, progressive or revolutionary African Americans like Nehanda Abiodun or Dead Prez, generally have a positive view of the Cuban Revolution. For such radical African Americans, it is often perceived as a success and as the ideal towards which they are striving in the U.S. (Fernandes 2003:583). Abiodun, for example, has said that she supported the Revolution since the age of ten, when Castro met Malcolm X in 1960, and she shows a continued belief in and willingness to engage with the Cuban state (Talking Drum Collective 2003). These African American activists who have been influential in Cuban hip hop do not, as a whole, share the scepticism of my fellow London audience-members about the Cuban state. There are parallels with Moore's contention that "the most consistent support for first-generation *trovadores* [nueva trova singers] is now among non-Cubans abroad rather than at home. For the politically conscious youth of the 1970s and 1980s who grew up in Latin America and Spain, the Cuban Revolution became a symbol of their aspirations; it demonstrated that grassroots action could accomplish significant change" (Moore 2003:32). Similarly, Cuban rap has flourished in part through a continued interest on the part of idealistic non-Cubans for whom the Revolution has kept its appeal and for whom politically committed Cuban music therefore occupies a special position.

Accounts of the nationalization of rap thus depend on their ideological starting point. Those who take a negative view of state intervention, like West-Durán, see "co-optation"; or, as one Cuban exile put it, the state has two methods—censorship or assimilation (quoted in Moore 2003:24). However, having seen a group perform at the opening concert of the postponed rap festival in November 2004 and criticize both Alpidio Alonso and Susana García, the head of the ACR, by name, concluding that the postponement of the festival was evidence that "the institutions are full of shit," I would suggest that such a polarized view is untenable with relation to contemporary Cuban rap, however relevant it may have been at earlier stages of the Revolution. Certainly both censorship and assimilation continue, and there are many artists active in the AHS rap scene who are vocal in their criticism of state institutions, above all of the ACR.[23] On the other hand, the very fact that such criticism is voiced openly is significant, and I also heard positive views expressed about the AHS. It says a lot about Cuba today that the biggest threat that rap has faced in its ten years of "official" existence is not censorship or co-optation but the current boom in popularity of the rival genre of reggaetón, which has tempted both audiences and some leading groups away from the fold. The AHS has been cast in the role of protecting rap from the "market forces" which threaten to swamp it, and can therefore hardly be accused of simple "appropriation."

It is interesting to note Alpidio Alonso's public concerns about reggaetón in light of the AHS/ACR split discussed above. While Alonso, the president of the AHS, criticizes reggaetón, his opposite number at the ACR oversees eight "rap" groups, half of which are in fact busy churning out reggaetón hits. In the light of Alonso's attempts to champion "conscious" rap over reggaetón, I would suggest that it is unhelpful to start from the idea that any state involvement is necessarily "a bad thing." As Moore has argued, a starkly negative characterization of the institutionalization of popular music in studies of the Soviet Union is inappropriate in the case of Cuban nueva trova (Moore 2003:33), and I would extend this argument to rap. We have seen that a number of state officials have been at least partially supportive, while the change in direction on the part of a number of rap groups has been largely a response to the commercial possibilities opened up by the boom of reggaetón, rather than to any political pressure. This consideration harks back to Wade's contention that the "appropriation" or commercialization of Colombian coastal music was led largely by coastal musicians themselves.

That is not to suggest that state involvement has always been positive, by any means. Robinson talks of a "constant, low-level struggle" between rappers and the authorities throughout the 1990s (Robinson 2004:114), and I witnessed signs that for all the recent history of state support, this struggle continues. In the aftermath of the cancellation of the rap festival in August 2004 due to hurricane damage, a concert by ACR groups was also cancelled—so late that the audience was already present—but this time without any explanation being given to the audience or to the artists, who are of course state employees. Hastily-organized replacement concerts in the patio of the Teatro Mella in Vedado were interrupted on several occasions when the venue director pulled the plug on the sound system with rappers in mid-sentence. He reacted nervously to lyrics that were commonplace in more typical rap venues such as the AHS-run La Madriguera. Yet when the festival was finally put on in November, Los Aldeanos, arguably the most radical group in Havana, was allowed to perform a full, typically critical set at the giant La Tropical venue. The "nationalization" of rap, then, has never been straightforward, and contradictions between policy and practice abound, usually being met with the typical shrug and "es Cuba"—"That's Cuba."

Behind the issue of evaluating state involvement there also lies the question of agency. I would argue that not enough attention has been paid to the role played by Cuban rappers and their spokespeople. Fernandes does mention "the agency of local actors who comply with official narratives in strategic and self-conscious ways" (Fernandes 2003:596), but her account is still overwhelmingly of the state "harnessing," "relating to," or "appropriating" the rap movement. She unquestionably provides the most valuable account of state involvement to date, but she still puts the state largely in the driving seat. In reality, the state was reactive rather than pro-active: AHS involvement was a response to Rensoli's demands, while the formation of the ACR was a reaction to rappers' requests for their own music agency. In late 2004, the ACR groups seemed to be largely setting their own agendas—going "commercial" or, in the case of Obsesión and Doble Filo, pursuing their own independent projects as "La FabriK"—leaving the Agency staff to do the explaining (sometimes to hostile audiences of excluded "underground" rappers). Looking at the complex engagement between artists, intermediaries, and state institutions, we can see at different times appropriation, support, conflict, and the co-existence of genuine shared beliefs, hence a resistance/appropriation model is far too simplistic.

An examination of Cuban hip hop is also an opportunity to question the characterization of rap as "oppositional music," something of an orthodoxy in studies of global rap. Our case demonstrates that globalized tools are available not just for constructing "resistant identities" but also for bolstering dominant or state ideologies, and indeed that "resistant identity" and state ideology are not necessarily at opposite poles in an ideologically progressive society. Rappers reinforce ideological positions of the state, while the state provides spaces that rappers use to criticize government institutions and representatives, a notable example of "entanglements of power" (Sharp et al. 2000). In Cuba, the nationalization of protest music has not entailed the purging of resistant elements, but instead the highlighting and exploiting of facets that correlate to the ideology of what may be considered a "protest state." I am brought back again to Peter Wade's remark that the success of Costeño music in Colombia depended on its "multivocality" (Wade 2000:238). Cuban rap has been talked and written about extensively by Cubans and non-Cubans, incorporated into constructions of national identity and of both local and global progressive cultural movements. Rap flourished in Cuba due to the crystallization of a Revolutionary discourse which facilitated the constitution of collective identity among rappers as a much-admired "underground" hip hop movement while simultaneously reinforcing prominent features of national identity. Cuban rappers and state representatives, by drawing on a shared rhetoric of revolution and resistance to U.S. hegemony, bring a transnational dimension to hip hop's characterization as oppositional music.

Acknowledgments

This article is based on fieldwork carried out in Havana in 2004. An earlier version was presented at the Centre of Latin American Studies, University of Cambridge. I am grateful to all those who helped me in Havana, but special thanks are due to Miguelito, Huevo, Randéee, Yari, Aldo, Humbertico, Alexis de Boy and L3 y 8, Explosión Suprema, El Novato, Ariel Fernández, William Figuerero, and Rodolfo Rensoli. I also thank Robin Moore and T.M. Scruggs for their helpful suggestions. Comments are welcome: geoff.baker@rhul.ac.uk.

Notes

1. Orishas, *A Lo Cubano* (EMI France, 1999).

2. Papaya Records, 2001.

3. At the time of writing, five of the eight groups employed by the ACR were focusing on reggaetón, and two—Cubanos en la Red and Eddy-K —had achieved commercial success with the genre.

4. The supposed resistance of U.S. commercial rap has been critiqued quite widely (e.g., Krims 2000), but there has been much less questioning of rap outside the USA as "resistant" music; Fernandes 2003 is, however, a rare (and valuable) example.

5. I noticed a preference for Puerto Rican reggaetón in Havana. This preference may reflect an urge for cosmopolitan identity, the greater availability of copies of foreign CDs, or a Havana-Santiago rivalry (since Cuban reggaetón is associated largely with Oriente). But reg-

gaetón production was increasing markedly in Havana by late 2004, not least in the hands of ACR groups, all of which are based in the capital.

6. This is not to say that the state has not been involved in other countries. Gilberto Gil, the Brazilian Minister of Culture, has promoted rap as positive social action and has argued for its incorporation into national culture (http://observer.guardian.co.uk/omm/story/0,13887,1066318,00.html [accessed 29 March 2005]). State involvement in Puerto Rican rap has been much more focused on repression rather than support (Giovannetti 2003:86–87). But it would be hard to argue that the development of Brazilian or Puerto Rican rap was substantially affected by such state initiatives, which pale by comparison with the influence of the media.

7. See Castro Medel 2005 for negative responses to reggaetón in Cuba, which show little sign of having any impact on the popularity of the genre.

8. Personal email received from the AHS.

9. E.g., "Not such a *Buena Vista*: Nostalgia, Myopia and the B.V. Social Club Phenomenon outside and inside Cuba," paper delivered by T.M. Scruggs at the "Caribbean Soundscapes" conference at Tulane University, 13 March 2004.

10. This phrase is still in use: I attended a meeting between rappers and AHS officers at La Madriguera in November 2004 at which a senior party official, a member of the Central Committee, used this expression to explain the need for responsibility to rappers who were to perform at the forthcoming rap festival.

11. Robinson, like Pacini Hernández and Garofalo, noted the use of "politically correct" language: "[Fernández] framed the whole thing in impeccable official rhetoric, at times quoting Fidel himself" (Robinson 2004:118).

12. Los Paisanos, *Paisanología* (demo CD), track 2.

13. Anónimo Consejo explain their philosophy in detail in Fernández n.d.

14. Track 4 of the unreleased compilation, *Cuban Hip Hop All Stars, Vol. 2.*

15. Melina Fotiadi, *ANC Hip Hop Revolution,* Cuba/France, 2003.

16. SBS was a pioneering salsa-rap group in the 1990s which achieved considerable success but was much derided by "real" hip hop fans.

17. Los Paisanos, *Paisanología,* track 3.

18. For an overview of the discourses of Cuban rappers, I have relied largely on interviews published in the first three editions of *Movimiento,* supplemented by my own conversations with members of the rap movement.

19. The full statement can be found at http://www.afrocubaweb.com/rap/blackaugust00.html (accessed 5 October 2004).

20. Hermanos de Causa, *La Causa Nostra* (demo CD), track 5.

21. http://www.cubava.cu/hiphoprevolucion/foros/index.htm (accessed 20 August 2004). The forum never took place due to the postponement of the festival.

22. Eli Jacobs-Fantauzzi, *Inventos: Hip-Hop Cubano,* USA, 2003.

23. Groups such as Los Paisanos, Los Aldeanos, and La Prosa Oscura repeatedly criticize the ACR in their songs, at concerts, and at public meetings. El Huevo of Los Paisanos raps in a song with El Cartel: "Para más información, esto es hip hop real/Sin estar en una empresa o una mierda similar/Hay que pertenecer para ser profesional/Tantos pertenecen y no son profesional" (For more information, this is real hip hop/Without being in an agency or any shit like that/You've got to belong to be a professional/But so many belong yet they're not professional).

References

Asho, DJ. 2004. "Black August/Agosto Negro: Apuntes para la historia de un proyecto integracionista y solidario." *Movimiento* 3:40–3.

Askew, Kelly. 2002. *Performing the Nation: Swahili Music and Cultural Politics in Tanzania.* Chicago: University of Chicago Press.

Borges-Triana, Joaquín. 2004. "La fabriK: Obreros de la construcción y embajadores de la creación." *Movimiento* 2:5-9.

Castro Medel, Osviel. 2005. "¿Prohibido el reguetón?" http://www.jrebelde.cubaweb.cu/2005/enero-marzo/feb-13/print/prohibido.htm (accessed 29 March 2005).

Condry, Ian. 2001. "A History of Japanese Hip-Hop." In *Global Noise: Rap and Hip-Hop outside the USA,* edited by Tony Mitchell, 222-47. Middletown, CT: Wesleyan University Press.

Cordero, Tania. 2004. "Persistir en Primera Base." *Movimiento* 3:21-3.

del Río, Joel. 2002. "Amulatao, aplatanao, cubaneao." *La Jiribilla* 67(August). http://www.lajiribilla.cu/2002/n67 agosto/1607 67.html (accessed 23 November 2004).

dos Santos Godi, Antonio. 2001. "Reggae and *Samba-Reggae* in Bahia: A Case of Long-Distance Belonging." In *Brazilian Popular Music and Globalization,* edited by Charles A. Perrone and Christopher Dunn, 207-19. Gainesville: University Press of Florida.

"Encuentro entre amigos." 2004. *Movimiento* 2:18-23.

Fernandes, Sujatha. 2003. "Fear of a Black Nation: Local Rappers, Transnational Crossings, and State Power in Contemporary Cuba." *Anthropological Quarterly* 76(4):575-608.

Fernández, Ariel. 2000. "Rap cubano: ¿Poesía urbana? O la nueva trova de los noventa." *El Caiman Barbudo* 296:4-14.

———. 2002. "Los futuros inmediatos del hip hop cubano." *Juventud Rebelde-La Ventana,* 13 November. http://www.lafogata.org/elpueblova/educacion/hip.htm (accessed 23 November 2004).

———. n.d. "Identidades e interiores de ciertos consejos anónimos." *Movimiento* 1:5-10.

Foehr, Stephen. 2001. *Waking Up in Cuba.* London: Sanctuary Publishing Limited.

Giovannetti, Jorge. 2003. "Popular Music and Culture in Puerto Rico: Jamaican and Rap Music as Cross-Cultural Symbols." In *Musical Migrations: Transnationalism and Cultural Hybridity in Latin/o America, Vol. 1,* edited by Frances R. Aparicio and Cándida Jáquez, 81-98. New York: Palgrave MacMillan.

Henríquez Lagarde, Manuel. 2002. "Rap cubano: Con la manga hasta el codo." *La Jiribilla* 68(August). http://www.lajiribilla.cu/2002/n68_agosto/1629_68.html (accessed 23 November 2004).

Herrera, Pablo, and Yesenia Selier. 2003. "Rap cubano: Nuevas posibilidades estéticas para la canción cubana." *Boletín Música* 11-12:96-101.

Hesmondhalgh, David, and Caspar Melville. 2001. "Urban Breakbeat Culture: Repercussions of Hip-Hop in the United Kingdom." In *Global Noise: Rap and Hip-Hop outside the USA,* edited by Tony Mitchell, 86-110. Middletown, CT: Wesleyan University Press.

Kapcia, Antoni. 2000. *Cuba: Island of Dreams.* Oxford: Berg.

Krims, Adam. 2000. *Rap Music and the Poetics of Identity.* Cambridge: Cambridge University Press.

Manduley López, Humberto. 1997. "Rock in Cuba: History of a Wayward Son." *South Atlantic Quarterly* 96(1):135-41.

Maxwell, Ian. 2003. *Phat Beats, Dope Rhymes: Hip Hop Down Under Coming Upper.* Middletown, CT: Wesleyan University Press.

McClary, Susan. 1994. "Same As It Ever Was: Youth Culture and Music." In *Microphone Fiends: Youth Music and Youth Culture,* edited by Andrew Ross and Tricia Rose, 29-40. Routledge: London.

Mitchell, Tony, ed. 2001. *Global Noise: Rap and Hip-Hop outside the USA.* Middletown, CT: Wesleyan University Press.

Moore, Robin. 1997. *Nationalizing Blackness: Afrocubanismo and Artistic Revolution in Havana, 1920-1940.* Pittsburgh: University of Pittsburgh Press.

———. 2003. "Transformations in Cuban *nueva trova,* 1965-95." *Ethnomusicology* 47(1):1-41.

Pacini Hernández, Deborah. 2003. "Amalgamating Musics: Popular Music and Cultural Hybridity in the Americas." In *Musical Migrations: Transnationalism and Cultural Hybridity in Latin/o America, Vol. 1,* edited by Frances R. Aparicio and Cándida Jáquez, 13-32. New York: Palgrave MacMillan.

402   Ethnomusicology, Fall 2005

————, and Reebee Garofalo. 1999–2000. "Hip Hop in Havana: Rap, Race and National Identity in Contemporary Cuba." *Journal of Popular Music Studies* 11–12:18–47.

Pérez Sarduy, Pedro, and Jean Stubbs, eds. 2000. *Afro-Cuban Voices: On Race and Identity in Contemporary Cuba.* Gainesville: University Press of Florida.

Perna, Vincenzo. 2005. *Timba: The Sound of the Cuban Crisis.* London: School of Oriental and African Studies.

Ramet, Sabrina Petra. 1994. *Rocking the State: Rock Music and Politics in Eastern Europe and Russia.* Boulder: Westview Press.

Robinson, Eugene. 2004. *Last Dance in Havana: The Final Days of Fidel and the Start of the New Cuban Revolution.* New York: Free Press.

Rose, Tricia. 1994. *Black Noise: Rap Music and Black Culture in Contemporary America.* Hanover, NH: Wesleyan University Press.

Sansone, Livio. 2001. "The Localization of Global Funk in Bahia and Rio." In *Brazilian Popular Music and Globalization,* edited by Charles A. Perrone and Christopher Dunn, 136–60. Gainesville: University Press of Florida.

Scott, James C. 1990. *Domination and the Arts of Resistance: Hidden Transcripts.* New Haven: Yale University Press.

Sharp, Joanne, Paul Routledge, Chris Philo, and Ronan Paddison, eds. 2000. *Entanglements of Power: Geographies of Domination/Resistance.* London: Routledge.

Smith, Shawnee. n.d. "Hip hop a la Cubano." http://www.afrocubaweb.com/rap/pabloherrera. htm (accessed 23 November 2004).

Sokol, Brett. 2000. "Rap Takes Root where Free Expression is Risky." 3 September. http://www. afrocubaweb.com/rap/pabloherrera.htm (accessed 23 November 2004).

Talking Drum Collective, The. 2003. "Nehanda Abiodun." http://www.thetalkingdrum.com/neh. html (accessed 23 November 2004).

Wade, Peter. 2000. *Music, Race and Nation: Música Tropical in Colombia.* Chicago: University of Chicago Press.

West-Durán, Alan. 2004. "Rap's Diasporic Dialogues: Cuba's Redefinition of Blackness." *Journal of Popular Music Studies* 16(1):4–39.

Whiteley, Sheila, Andy Bennett, and Stan Hawkins, eds. 2004. *Music, Space and Place: Popular Music and Cultural Identity.* Aldershot: Ashgate.

Wunderlich, Annelise. 2001. "Cuban Hip-Hop, Underground Revolution." http://journalism. berkeley.edu/projects/cubans2001/story-hiphop.html (accessed 23 November 2004).

Young, Robert. 2003. *Postcolonialism.* Oxford: Oxford University Press.

Zamora Céspedes, Bladimir. 2004. "El hip hop en la isla de las utopias." *Movimiento* 3:55–56.

Zurbano Torres, Roberto. 2004. "Se buscan: Textos urgentes para sonidos hambrientos." *Movimiento* 3:6–12.

[13]

Bandiri Music, Globalization and Urban Experience in Nigeria*

Brian Larkin

Beside Kofar Nassarawa, a gate to the mud wall that once ringed the Muslim heart of Kano, northern Nigeria, there is a *mai gyara*, a mechanic who repairs scooters and motorbikes. On this atrophying wall in the 1990s there was a poster of Ibrahim El-Zakzaky, a radical Islamic leader, and next to him one of Ayatollah Khomeini, the Shi'a leader Zakzaky championed. No doubt the mechanic or one of his assistants was a fan of Zakzaky, a figure of some charisma among the Muslim youth of the North, but the fact that someone else had tried to tear off the poster of Khomeini registered the wider suspicion that Hausa Sunnis have for Shi'a worship. Once, while my vespa was in a line waiting to be repaired, one of the assistants switched cassettes on an old tape player and started playing a *bandiri* tape. As he did so one of the customers started to hum along, recognizing the Indian film tune on which the song was based, but not knowing the words of this Hausa variation. Bandiri singers are Hausa musicians who take Indian film tunes and change the words to sing songs praising the prophet Mohammed. This action sparked an immediate response from two customers who looked with distaste—clearly uncomfortable at being subjected to this music while waiting for their bikes to be repaired. Their discomfort provoked a mild but clear debate splitting the mechanics and customers—all from the old city of Kano—into three discrete groups: those who wanted to hear the bandiri music; those, who included the man humming along, who did not care one way or another, and the last two customers asking for the music to be stopped.

Knowing the controversy around bandiri music because of my research on Indian film in Nigeria I found it interesting that the two customers

* Acknowledgements: the research for this article was provided by the Wenner-Gren foundation. Lawan 'Dan Yaro Magashi, Alh.; Alh. Rabi'u B.K.; Yusufu Hamid introduced me into the world of bandiri music. Translations were provided by Usman Aliyu Abdulmalik and Alhaji Abdulkadir. Presentations of this work at the University of Iowa, Columbia University seminar in South Asian Studies provided me with valuable feedback as did the comments of numerous people: Meg McLagan; Teja Ganti; Birgit Meyer; Rafael Sanchez and Sudeep Dasgupta. I thank them all.

reacted, not with anger but with a palpable sense of distaste, a sort of weary disappointment, as if the music like cigarette smoke in a restaurant was a repugnant physical presence being forced on them. It emphasised the ambivalent quality of a musical form such as bandiri which, with roots in a secular realm of entertainment, is also religious. It partakes of the elaborate Sufi tradition in which recitation of praises to the Prophet carry with them spiritual and sometimes magical benefits and sound has tangible properties beyond the aural. The distaste against bandiri may well have been motivated by a dislike of the migration of Indian films into Hausa popular culture. But while one may not like Indian music it does not make the same claims on one's spiritual well-being and mode of honouring God. It was the ability of bandiri to compromise its orthodox religious listeners by creating an unorthodox, Sufi environment that generated unease. This is an anecdote about the everyday reproduction of music and while a marginal, fleeting, moment it captures in that evanescence three themes that govern the production and circulation of bandiri music: the flow of Indian films to Nigeria, providing the raw symbolic material from which bandiri is fashioned; deep rooted practices of Sufism which have marked West African Islam for hundreds of years; and the recent spread of an anti-Sufi Wahhabi movement generating the contested religious space in which bandiri operates.

Singing live at public ceremonies such as weddings, or selling cassettes through local markets, when bandiri[1] singers sing Hausa praise songs to Indian tunes they are effecting a transformation from the profane to the sacred. The popularity of the genre rests, however, on the common cultural competence of listeners who recognise their favourite Hindi film songs. By doing so these listeners see through the mask, so to speak, as the profane original haunts the sacred copy. As suggested above this is a contested phenomenon in a Muslim society undergoing an Islamist revival. Is it really Islamic, many Hausa Muslims ask, to use songs taken from sensual, un-Islamic origins for religious purposes? Moreover, the controversy over bandiri music is not just about Indian love songs. Bandiri is named after the drum—the *bandir*—used in ritual practice by Sufis to enter into trance. Is it really Islamic, many Hausa Muslims ask, to enter into trance, or to use drums inside the mosque, indeed to be Sufi in a world where Wahhabi belief moves provocatively across the Muslim world? Bandiri sits at the nexus of these very different sorts of transnational flows, Islamist revival and Indian popular culture that meet and make sense in Northern Nigeria, in the context of a spatial configuration of culture, media and religion.

My aim in this paper is first to analyse the workings of a cultural form like bandiri with its complex intertwining of sacred and profane, remembering and repressing. Second, I wish to use the example of bandiri, and of the three networks or sets that it exemplifies: the history of Sufi adherence,

---

1.   Bandiri is also known as *mandiri* in Hausa.

the flow of Indian film to Nigeria and the recent rise of a new legalistic Islamic movement to make a larger argument about the construction of urban space in Africa. Focussing on Kano, Nigeria the city where bandiri began I argue, following Lefebvre (1991), that space is produced and organized over time by the penetration and transformations in capital which insert any particular place into wider networks of exchange that facilitate the flow of cultural and religious forms. Urban areas such as Kano are made up of congeries of overlapping networks. When new cultural and religious forms emerge they do so in an urban crucible that is already overdetermined according to the particular structure of those networks as they exist in a city like Kano. These networks provide the structural precondition that shapes the symbolic form and social meaning of a phenomenon like bandiri and it is the articulation of these networks together that creates the raw material from which urban experience might be fashioned.

Producing Urban Space in Africa

Recent analyses of urban space in African studies and anthropology have stressed urban space as a crucible for the flow of cultural forms across borders (see for example: Appadurai 1997; Gaonkar 1999; Inda & Rosaldo 2002). The theoretical move here has been to argue that the West and non-West have mutually constituted each other in a structurally uneven, but nevertheless two sided, process. This is clearly aimed at asserting the agency of African or Asian societies, that while the traffic in culture from the West is prominent in African societies, as Jean-Francois Bayart remarks this is always an act of reinvention and appropriation rather than simply domination (Barber 1997; Barber & Waterman 1995; Bayart 1993; Hannerz 1992). Ferguson has recently made a persuasive argument that we ought to examine the nature of urban (and rural) identities in Africa as modes of cultural style: poles of signification that people can move between depending on wealth, education and cultural competence. Ferguson is mobilising an idea of urban space as defined by a syntagmatic chain of difference. To be "rural" or "urban" or "local" or "cosmopolitan" are not temporally distinct states of being where one evolves into another, but rather are produced in relation to each other within the same social field. Urban life, as represented here, is the matter of choosing between differing stylistic modes: whether to speak a European language or an African one; whether to dress in traditional clothes, in the bureaucratic attire of suits and ties, in baggy jeans and football shirts or in the hijab. The danger here is that the urban is defined as an arena in which a free flow of symbolic forms clash and compete without stepping back to address the issue of how these forms arrived in the first place.

Ferguson is well aware of this danger and warns against it[2] though his central aim is not to analyse how cultural forms emerge from specific political-economic contexts. Rather, for the Copperbelt urban dwellers he examines, Western clothing, Congolese rumba, South African theatre and West Indian reggae comprise the established forms of urban space out of which cultural style is fashioned. By probing into the background of this space—how it comes to be organised in the way that it does—my aim is to unite this concern for hybrid cultural exchanges with a sense of the material underpinnings that make those exchanges possible.

Kano, northern Nigeria is a large, sprawling city on the edge of the Sahelian desert. If the city is an event, as Simmel has argued, and urban experience the outcome of a ceaseless series of encounters then those encounters in this city are constituted within the limits of the networks that bump up against each other there. Sufi religious brotherhoods, Lebanese businessmen, Ibo traders, and Hausa politicians are based in Kano but embedded in their own discrete networks that extend in different directions over the world. Space in this account is not something that is simply there but, as Lefebvre (1991) argues, is something that is the outcome of capitalist relations of exchange and those relations create the peculiar sets of networks that exist in any particular urban place. For the movement of cultural goods to occur—be they Indian films, hip-hop from the U.S. or high fashion from Europe and Japan—a formal and informal infrastructure has to be established creating the material channels that allow transnational cultural flows to move. These infrastructures connect certain points in a network, ranking and separating one place from another, enabling the possibility of certain connections while foreclosing other linkages. "Flows" for all their seemingly disembodied nature (see Tsing's critique 2000) require material conduits and they appear because a place—in this case urban Kano—is embedded in precise networks of social relations built over time.

Infrastructures are the material forms that bind and knit urban spaces into wider sets—forcing us to think of space not in terms of discrete buildings or isolated moments on a landscape but as networked amalgams of built space connected physically by railways, shipping lanes, and air routes. As capital depends on infrastructure that facilitates the circulation of goods, successive regimes of capital build the infrastructures necessary for that mode of exchange in the process making over urban space in their own image (Harvey 2000; Lefebvre 1991; Graham & Marvin 1996, 2001). The

---

2. Ferguson derives his concept of cultural style from performance theory and specifically the work of Judith Butler but he argues that this work can suffer from lack of attention to wider fields of political-economic structures. He cites Kath Weston's work as a corrective to the tendency in performance studies to construe identity as in part of play of signification without due concern to the material constraints the shape the possibility of performance (FERGUSON 1999: 98-101). Ethnographically he supports this with a keen sense of the political-economic contexts in which Zambian migrants (and return migrants) operate.

location of markets; the siting of districts for business and residence; the layout of roads, railways stations, airports, are all fundamentally affected by waxing and waning of different infrastructural forms. Related to this is the fact that the physical links created by infrastructures—which places get connected into a network—has huge effect on the cultural life of a city. It shapes which migrants arrive there, which languages become commonly used, and which cultural forms become part of an urban arena.

Lefebvre argues that as space is continually reformed by the necessities of capital newly developed networks do not eradicate earlier ones but are superimposed on top of them creating an historical layering over time. As he memorably put it, this makes space seem like the flakiness of a *mille-feuille* pastry rather than homogenous and discrete (Lefebvre 1991: 86). At any one point, then, urban space is made up of the historical layering of networks connected by infrastructures. These are the conduits that dictate which flow of religious and cultural ideas move and therefore which social relations get mobilised in their wake. Their historical layering helps explain why dormant cultural, religious and economic forms can suddenly gain purchase again, be reawakened and re-energised in a new situation.

Urban spaces such as Kano can be seen as assemblage of different sets that connect Hausa to other networks. By set I am loosely using the mathematical definition of a set as the combination of different elements interlinked to form a totality. Infrastructures—both material and immaterial—are the connecting tissues that bind these elements to the whole. They are material in the obvious sense of the construction of air routes, railways and so on that join one place to another. They are immaterial in that they require linguistic competencies, professional expertise, educational styles and cultural philosophies that facilitate the exchange of information and goods across cultural boundaries. Islam, for instance, is one such set integrating Kano Muslims into a wider totality of the Muslim *umma* by means of shared religious practice, pilgrimages, education, Sufi adherence and so on. Islam itself can be broken down into multiple sub-sets only some of which Hausa are involved in. When we refer to the "urban experience" partly what we are referring to is the particular assemblage of sets that forms the unique configuration of a city. These are layered over time and the introduction of new layers interacts with previous existing ones, re-energising some, closing off others but creating the unique configuration of a city. This evolution orients Kano internally toward Southern Nigeria but also across the Sahara to North Africa and the Middle East, across the Atlantic and increasingly over the Indian ocean to Asia (Bayart *et al.* 1999). Northerners chase modernity through Muslim connections to Saudi Arabia, Dubai and other Islamic centres, as well as through connections to the West. All this makes Kano integrated yet distinct from its sister cities in the south and it is out of this Kano based configuration of Islamic and Western modernity, that the unlikely synthesis of bandiri music, with its roots in Sufi worship and Hindi lovemaking, is possible.

Set One: the Lovers of the Prophet

In 1996 I was taken by the bandiri singer Lawan 'Dan Yaro Magashi to a
bandiri performance in Magashi quarters of the Kano *birni*. Magashi is an
area in the old city of Kano, for Muslims the traditional moral heart where
Islamic values and lifestyles are maintained (Barkindo 1993; Larkin 2002;
Tahir 1975). It is an overwhelmingly Sufi area, predominantly Tijaniyya
but with a large and powerful minority of Qadiriyya followers (Paden 1973;
Anwar 1989). Outside a house where a naming ceremony was being performed the group had tied loudspeakers to the walls across the narrow alley-
way. The singer held the microphone and sang Hausa words to Indian film
tunes and behind him four youths sang back in response each of them beating the bandir, the large black tambourine-like drum from North Africa.
In front of them all were another seven or so youths dancing a Sufi dance,
punching their arms back and forth in time to the music. In the doorways
young girls listened, laughing, their bodies covered in brightly coloured
prints and their heads encased by large scarves while the alleys around were
packed with a mob of boys listening, shouting and sometimes singing to
the song being played. Older men looked on, somewhat sceptically, from
a distance. As the song finished another youth took the place of the singer
pitting his skill at lyric writing and singing against the one who came before
(and who would come after).

   In a way, bandiri could only have emerged in areas like this in Kano,
or similar areas in sister Sufi[3] cities in the north such as Sokoto and Zaria.
Kano was one of the urban areas where Indian films first emerged in the
1950s and today it remains the distribution centre for pirate video cassettes
of Indian films (the main way they circulate in the north). In the second
half of the twentieth century it has been a font for the introduction of new
modes of Islamic education paving the way for the emergence of a cadre
of modernist religious scholars that have gone on to lead new anti-Sufi
Islamist movements. But most famously for nearly a century has been
known as a dominant centre of Tijaniyya Sufi affiliation and learning.

---

3. Sufism is based around the charismatic authority of a founding saint whose
    knowledge, is passed down in a direct line of descent from sheikh to disciple.
    As orders mature over time they extend over space generating dispersed networks
    linked by common ritual practices, pilgrimage, and education. As Kano was an
    economic center of pre-colonial trade, there has been a long connection between
    Sufism and dominant Kano trading families. These families are associated with
    important Sufi Sheikhs and many have produced their own lineages of distin-
    guished religious scholars. Many scholars have pointed out that the common
    religious affiliation of particular Sufi orders has been key to the creation of non-
    kin based trading networks that rely heavily on credit and trust and that the
    success of Sufism is an example of the clouding of religious and economic activi-
    ties (PADEN 1973; TAHIR 1975). In Kano the success of the Sufi order Tijaniyya
    is strongly linked to its role in producing patron-client networks that are seen
    as central to the order's reputation for economic success. It is this crucible of
    Sufi affiliation that lies behind the success of bandiri.

Bandiri music developed from the religious use of the *bandir* drum by Qadiriyya Sufi adepts. Every evening in Kano, Qadirriyya Sufis gather at certain mosques for the public performance of the *dhikr* the ritual that uses the bandir drum to regulate the speed of chanting litanies (Loimeier 1997). Loimeier (1997: 60) highlights the importance of repetition "where through the constant chanting of a short phrase like Allah Allah [...] the participants breathe in or against the rhythm of their chanting." leading to the invoking of trancelike states (Buba & Furniss 1999). This is a public phenomenon and arose in the late 1950s as part of the effort by a Qadirriyya Sheikh, Nasir Kabara, to turn Sufi practice from an elite, secret movement into a mass movement. As Loimeier observes, the regular public ritual of bandir drumming has become a public spectacle of Qadiriyya affiliation in that "the presence of the tariqâ [Sufi order] in the city is underlined not only visually but also acoustically from day to day and night to night." (*ibid.* See also Paden 1973).

As a musical practice, bandiri derives significance from this ritual use but is different in key ways. For the most part it is played at events such as wedding parties and naming ceremonies which have both a religious and a non-religious dimension (see also Buba & Furniss 1999). Often times different singers will gather with the same backing group. They will take a particular Indian film, such as *Khabhi Kabhie*[5](Dir. Yash Chopra) and divide up the songs between them, each one responsible for translating a different song from the film into a Hausa praise song. Then during the performance the singers will take turns, each competing with one another for the best performance. There is a tremendous excitement to this, in the energy of the dancing, the sound of the drums, and the reaction of the crowd gathered around. While the audience is mostly young, certain songs are chosen from 1950s and 1960s Indian films to directly appeal to older people in the audience. Bandiri is seen by both performers and audience as a religious form but it clearly borders many of the activities and genres of secular music.

Bandiri orginated in the practice of youths studying at Islamiyya schools, the new schools in Nigeria that teach Islamic subjects in a Western pedagogic framework. Students at these schools got together to sing songs in Hausa on how to obey parents, or translated short *hadith* (the record of the sayings and deeds of the Prophet Mohammed) and turned them into songs, or simply sang praises to the Prophet Mohammed. The first songs were religious versions of popular songs by Hausa musicians such as Mamman Shata or 'Dan Kwairo and after a while youths began to adapt Indian films songs (it was and remains common for Hausa youth to sings Indian film songs in school). Their aim was revivalist, to introduce a more religious dimension to popular activities such as wedding parties and naming ceremonies and to attract youth back to religious contemplation through the form of popular mass culture.

In the late eighties as bandiri began to take off in popularity societies such as *Kungiyar Yabon Manzon Allah* (Society for Praising the Messenger of God) and *Kunigiyar Ushaq'u Indiya* (Society for the Lovers of India) were created to formalize the coming together of young Hausa singers performing bandiri music. *Ushaq'u* is an Arabic word meaning a passionate or ardent lover and is derived from *'Ishq*—passion or yearning. In Hausa (as opposed to Arabic) the word is associated with a religious register in contrast to the more familiar term for romantic love *so*. As one singer explained to me *'ishq*, in the Hausa usage at least, refers to the deepest possible love[4]. While singers do sell cassettes that are sold generally on the market bandiri is still primarily a live performance genre. Groups are sponsored by individuals to perform at specific ceremonies and they often try to translate their prestige from bandiri performance into a patron client relation with prominent Sufi *malams*[5] (religious teachers) (Buba & Furniss 1999). As bandiri gained in popularity singers started to sell cassettes through specialist dealers at the market. The first tapes were compilations of different bandiri singers and grouped under the heading of the Society of Ushaq'u singers[6] and labelled *Ushaq'u Indiya 1, Ushaq'u Indiya 2* and so on. The tapes themselves contain an opening prayer and a brief introduction to the singers. Some tapes address the audience as "My brothers, Lovers of the Messenger of Allah (S.A.W.)" implicitly constructing the audience as fellow Sufi members (likely to be the case) and reasserting the religious intention to the music.

Set Two: the Rise of Anti-Sufism

Bandiri music grew and developed in an arena of overt conflict. Those who perform bandiri realise that this is a controversial activity. As one

4. *Ishq* is an Arabic word and consequently has become common in several languages not the least of which is Hindi where it is used as a much more everyday term for love—witness the 1999 film, *Ishq* (Dir. Indra Kuma) starring Aamir Khan.
5. Singers do attempt to make money through the commodification of bandiri by selling cassettes but for the most part the material benefit of bandiri comes through prestige which can be used within the Sufi network itself. The most prestigious activity, for instance, is to be invited by an important Sheikh to perform at *maulud* celebrations that celebrate the brithday of the Prophet Mohammed or of important Sufi saints. These celebrations are deeply controversial in Hausa society. Many Wahhabis attack these acts of commemoration as un-Islamic. Despite that they remain central rituals in the Sufi calendar.
6. Each tape has a brief introduction which reaffirms the religious intent of the cassette and introduces the society and particular singers. I quote here from the opening to the cassette *Ushaq'u Indiya na sha biyu* (Ushaq'u India number 12). In the name of Allah the most gracious and most merciful, may peace be upon the Prophet Muhammad and may God bless him and his family. My relatives, lovers of the Messenger of Allah, we are now going to introduce Ushaq'u India cassette number 12. The singers are: Muhammad Lawan Yaro Magashi, Muhammad Abubakar Baffajo, Marmara Auwalu Iguda Takasai, Balarabe Musa Kabada, Sani Garba S/K Dan/Dago. Mallam Inuwa Bala is the person to beat the drum.

told me, "You know religion in our country. One man's meat is another man's poison" and that while many people are against bandiri music many more find it hugely attractive. This conflict does not just derive from the software of bandiri—the songs and their borrowing from Indian films—but the hardware itself—using the *bandir* drum—and the drum's significance as a symbol of Sufi adherence. The identification of bandiri with Sufism has made it deeply controversial in Nigeria piggy backing onto the wider religious conflict that has pitted established Sufi orders against the rise of a new Wahhabi oriented movement—Izala (*Jama'at Izalatil Bid'a wa Iqamatus Sunna* - The Movement Against Innovation and for a Return to the Sunna)—and its intellectual leader Abubakar Gumi (Barkindo 1993; Gumi 1972, 1992; Loimeier 1997; Umar 1993).

The rise of Abubakar Gumi is significant because his figure represents the shift to a new configuration of Hausa economy, politics and society. Gumi was one of the first Islamic scholars to be educated by the British within the colonial education system and certainly the first major religious leader to come to prominence through his participation in the colonial and postcolonial bureaucracy. Before him Sufi scholars were linked to aristocratic elites and to old trading families who were deeply suspicious of Western education and the *boko* (Western) lifestyle. Gumi's support network was different, it relied on his alliances within the postcolonial bureaucracy and his close relations with elected politicians, military figures and bureaucrats. And for Gumi it was precisely his bureaucratic colonial links—as a scholarship student to the Sudan, and as Nigerian Pilgrims Officer to Saudi Arabia—that Gumi began to travel widely within the Muslim world. Gumi was especially known for his close relationship with Saudi Arabia, one that began with his stint as Pilgrim's Officer but was cemented by his role as religious leader to the Sardauna of Sokoto, the Premier of the Northern Region of Nigeria at independence. Gumi adopted the legalistic, anti-Sufi brand of Islamic belief prominent in Saudi Wahhabism and it was this which he brought back to Nigeria.

In the early 1970s Gumi began to outline a critique of Sufism in a variety of fora from tafsir at the mosque, to newspaper articles, to radio broadcasts. This critique followed orthodox Wahhabi lines: he attacked Sufism as an innovation *(bid'a)* in Islamic practice in a religion where innovation in matters of faith was not allowed; he criticised the veneration of Sufi saints and the practice of Sufi orders, in its stead he argued for a return to the key texts of Islam—the Qur'an and the hadith—texts which were available to everyone through education and reason. In 1972 his critique was centralised into a book *The Right Belief is Based on the Sharia* which caused uproar in Nigeria. Gumi's strategy was to take central ritual symbols of the prominent Sufi orders in Nigeria—the Tijaniyya and Qadiriyya—and to argue that they ran contrary to the teachings of the Qur'an. In the case of Qadiriyya the tactic was to take on one of the central ritual of the order—the use of the bandir drum in the mosque—and to argue that it was an illegal innovation. Most shockingly he did so in sharp, inflammatory language claiming that "those who combine drumming with religion [...] reduce their religion to a plaything [...]. They will taste the punishment which they disbelieve" (Gumi 1972: 43).

The effect of this attack was electric. The history of Islam in Nigeria has been rent with religious conflict but to this point this had always been conflict within and between Sufi orders. Gumi was now claiming that they were all "imposters in islam" (1992: 142) sparking an intense backlash that spilled over into armed conflict between followers of the different camps. The use of the bandir was defended by Nasiru Kabara the Qadiriyya sheikh[7] with which the practice was most identified but Gumi's attack, and Kabara's defence meant that the use of the bandir drum came to be a defining symbol of Sufi belief or deviance. It became a dense symbol of the conflict between Sufis and anti-Sufis, something to be championed or rejected but never ignored.

It is no accident that the use of bandiri music, with its evangelical goal of using popular Hausa songs and Indian film tunes to bring youths back to religious practice arose at a time when Sufi practice itself was under unprecedented assault from a Wahhabi inspired anti-Sufi movement. The activity of singing praise songs, even of calling the singers "lovers of the prophet" is an implicit attack on the condemnation of praise singing by the transnational spread of orthodox Wahhabi ideas to Nigeria. These themes are often explicitly dealt with in the songs themselves when singers assert their right to praise the Prophet despite "whoever is against him"[8], a dark warning neatly conflating non-Muslims with followers of Izala, the movement led by Abubakar Gumi. The background of Sufi-Izala conflict provides the cultural and religious reason why Indian film music was taken up—in this way and at this time. By drawing on the massive popularity of the film style and already existing practices of singing Hindi films songs, Sufi followers managed to establish a powerful and popular new music genre the significance of which lies in the layering of social relations and space: the position of Kano as the node of two very different circuits of cultural and religious flows: one reaching out across the Sahara and the other across the Indian ocean.

---

7. For an account see LOIMEIER (1997).
8. Take this example: a version of a song by Sidi Musa from the Indian film *Ham Dono*.
S : Praising Mustapha is necessary for us, whoever is against Him, the Prophet is ours....
S : In the name of God I intend to long.....
    I going to praise my Mustapha.....
    If they like it or if they don't like it.....
    Our Messenger is in front.....
    Because he is the one that we love my Mustapha.....
A : Praising Mustapha is necessary for us, whoever is against Him, the Prophet is ours.
S : I swear I love you O Sayyadi.....
    O my life, O my Mohammad.....

Set Three: Indian Films in Kano

Indian music saturates the popular culture of northern Nigeria creating a landscape of desire and spectacle and a field for nostalgia and memory. This nostalgia derives from the long historical popularity of Indian films among Nigerian audiences dating back to the 1950s which has imprinted generations of Hausa with the songs, narratives and stars of Indian film (1997). Bandiri taps into these emotions, creating an intertextual play with romance and devotion; charisma and stardom; traditional culture and modernity. It is a form of mimicking whereby the "copy" draws from the power and symbolic richness of the original but only at the cost of raising questions of cultural authenticity, and cultural erosion. The tunes that bandiri singers borrow bring with them memories and tastes of the original context of reception. A song about the love of followers for the Prophet Mohammed is shadowed by an image of the actor Salman Khan doing press-ups in the film *Maine Pyar Kiya*, and other songs are haunted by the actors and actresses symbolically superimposed over every song of praise. Nigerian Sufi followers resignify this music into devotional songs, syphoning and transforming charisma from one context to another. Bandiri thus relies upon a dialectic of similarity and difference. The copy has to be similar enough to the original be recognized, to recoup the profits of mimesis, but yet it has to be transformed, religiously and culturally. Its original context must be obliterated at the same time as it is invoked, in order to take on sacred meaning. This is the aura that local Hausa singers bring to a devotional tradition of praise singing with a long, elaborate history. At the same time as redefining Indian films in a Hausa context, then, they are redefining Sufi praise music in terms of its association with the glamorous modernity of Indian films. And they project, through mimicry, Hausa popular culture into the prestigious and alluring world of global cultural flows.

One of the interesting features of the popularity of Indian films in northern Nigeria is the dialectic of similarity and dissimilarity and the ways that cultural borrowing involves elaborate acts of remembering and repressing. For instance, I have previously discussed the complicated way in which Hausa people see Indian culture as "just like" Hausa culture: in its depiction of relations between the genders; in the negotiation between a reified "traditional" culture and an equally reified "Westernisation"; and in the mise-en-scène and iconography of everyday life *(ibid.)*. This is one aspect of the ways in which Indian films benefit from a perceived similarity and a strong identification between the two cultures, one based on cultural practice, moral ethics and linguistic similarity. Many Hausa, for instance, argue that Hausa and Hindi are descended from the same language—an argument also voiced to me by an Indian importer of films in accounting for their popularity. While "wrong" in terms of linguistic evolution this argument takes

into account the substantial presence of Arabic and English loan words in
both languages, a key factor in creating this perceived sense of similarity.
Hausa and Indians have also been linked through the common denominator
of the British Empire and it is interesting to speculate on the mediating
presence that empire had in creating a sense of commonality that helps
account for the popularity of Indian films[9]. All this feeds in to the cultural
background of the Indian postcolony and explains part of the identification
of Hausa audiences with Indian culture in the common historical experience
of British Empire and the perceived tension between traditional culture and
a modernising western one.

The powerful sense of identification between the two cultures is also
explained in terms of Bollywood's alterity from American and British film
and television and its depiction of moral problems that are simply absent
from most Western media *(ibid.)*. This was brought over to me in a discussion about the film *Maine Pyar Kiya* starring Salman Khan, a hit in
Nigeria as elsewhere. My male friend identified hugely with the central
tension of the films—Salman Khan's father forbidding his son permission
to marry a poor girl and attempting to force him to marry the rich daughter
of a business friend. The overt sentimentality was not seen in terms of
fantasy but as something that emerges out of the historical experience
of common people—an historical experience common to Nigeria and
India: the power of elders over youth and the corruption of traditional relations by the pursuit of money. As my friend commented: "So the film is
educative in fact. I have never watched an Indian film very interesting
like this one. Because I shed tears, tears in watching the film [...] though
knowing the film is fiction but I still shed tears, because it just showed a
real dedication to what is happening in the world"[10]. This comment is
common in northern Nigeria where people see Indian films as representing
real, everyday problems and not in the terms of kitsch fantasy with which
they are greeted in the West. This is what makes them educative. Bashir
made this explicit: "American films are based mainly on [...] its either
action, war or just a show, like documentaries, so that is it. But Indian

---

9.   In many ways the British Empire can be regarded as a set that placed diverse
     societies into articulation via the historical experience of colonisation. When
     the British took over northern Nigeria they brought with them principles of Empire
     that had been first elaborated in the crucible of South Asia. Certainly there was a
     traffic in administrative personnel, in modes of bureaucracy, in language (English)
     in educational principles, in cultural styles, fashions, food and even in forms of
     ritual such as the famous Hausa durbar *(sallah)*—now seen as a "traditional"
     Hausa festival occurring after the Eid festival but imported to Nigeria directly
     from India by the British. It is interesting to speculate whether this common
     historical experience may help account for the Hausa sense of similarities with
     Indian society.
10. Interview, Sani Bashir, November 1996.

films on the other side, they base their films on their problems and on the problems of the masses, their masses. Anyway I don't watch much American films..."[11].

When Hausa refer to Indian films being "just like" Hausa culture—a sentiment echoed here by Bashir—they actually mean the films are *more like* Hausa culture than the other two dominant mass cultural fields Hausa engage in—southern Nigerian and American media. Indian films are more sexually demure than American films but they are far more transgressive than everyday Hausa culture and as much as reflecting problems inherent to that society they are potentially threatening and destabilising of it. This tension between like and unlike, similarity and distance is key to the appeal of transnational cultural forms as it allows imaginative play which is tolerated *precisely because it is different.* Hausa can watch Indian films and appreciate their similarities while the differences can be easily downplayed. This has been recently dramatised by the rise of a Hausa video film industry in the late 1990s. Unlike their southern counterparts Hausa filmmakers have explicitly borrowed from Indian films moving away from themes of magic, witchcraft, corruption and money that mark southern Nigerian videos and emphasising instead the theme of love. The alterity of Hausa videos from southern Nigerian ones and their similarity to Indian films is most marked by the song and dance sequences between the actor and actress which heavily borrow from Indian films. These sequences follow the generic conventions of Indian films: songs stand as a proxy for physical love and for intense emotions that cannot be expressed in everyday language; they take place outside of the diagetic space of the story in areas of picturesque natural beauty; and this fantastic, extra-real environment is accentuated by frequent costume changes within the same song sequence. While massively popular these sequences have caused huge controversy in Hausa society for initiating what is seen as an un-Islamic, and un-Hausa mode of courtship into Hausa film. In the wake of the introduction of shari'a law in 2001 and in response to the public outcry the making of these Hausa videos were banned in Kano state (the prime site of production). Later the ban was eased so that filmmaking could continue as long the song sequences did not include sexual intermixing. Interestingly enough, during this controversy the new Islamic state saw no need to ban Indian films and nor does the new censorship board censor Indian films which continue to be popular. The tension arose when styles of love and sexual interaction from Indian films were dramatised in a Hausa context. What could be tolerated while safely confined to the practices of another culture however "like" Hausa culture was simply too controversial when the necessary gap for cultural borrowing was collapsed. Indian films are more demure than Hollywood ones, less explicit than recent southern Nigerian videos, but they are still sexually transgressive for an orthodox Islamic society and like

---

11. *Ibid.*

all cultural flows the popularity of Indian film depends on the maintenance of a safe distance, a stable alterity the lack of which can be powerfully threatening.

Bandiri

Emerging out of the long Sufi tradition of singing praise songs to the Prophet, bandiri partakes of that tradition in using a language of erotics whereby mystical arousal is linked to emotional arousal. In ritual use, trance can be used to provoke mystical love culminating in ecstasy whereby the person possessed can mystically communicate with God or the Prophet (Qureshi 1995). In bandiri, Mohammed is often the focus of intense love and longing and bandiri singers (and Sufi adepts) refer to themselves as "lovers of the prophet" the emotional excessive realm of secular love being used to convey to quite different but equally emotional parameters of religious love. Take this example sung by Sidi Musa and adapted from the film *Geet Gata Chal* (1975 Dir. Hiren Nag):

S : My heart is longing for you, my soul loves you, me, I am longing for my messenger, the Prophet of God
A : My messenger the Prophet of God
S : My heart is longing for you, my soul loves you, me, I am longing for my messenger, the Prophet of God
A : My messenger the Prophet of God
S : Owo You are the one I am longing for Mustapha na Sayyadi. You are the one longing for Habibi, Prophet of God.
A : Habibi, Prophet of God.
S : I am longing... O... I am continuously longing for you. I am longing more and more.
A : O Mohammad Prophet of God, O my lover[12].

(S = singer; A = *Amshi* or reply).

In this Hausa song the vaulting strings of Indian film songs are absent as is the western and Indian instrumentation leaving only the beating of the drum. Where the original film song is based around a duet between a man and a woman each singing verses in turn Sidi Musa uses the more familiar African form of call and response played out between him and his backing singers. What is shared between Musa's song and the original is the melody and the sense of emotional excess, with Sufi followers using the ecstatic enactments of love in Indian films and stripping them of their secular trappings. Bandiri creates a play of similarity and difference, like and dislike, profane and sacred. We can see this process at work better by examining a Hausa song, *Zumar zuma bege*, by the bandiri singer Lawan 'Dan yaro Magashi. *Zumar zuma* is an adaptation of a famous song *Jumma chumma*

---

12. See also BUBA & FURNISS (1999: 39).

de de (Jumma give me a kiss) performed by Amitabh Bachchan in the film *Hum* (1991 Dir. Mukul Anand).

The song sequence from which *Jumma chumma* is taken is set in an Indian shipyard warehouse where a petty rogue, Tiger, dances with his docker friends singing to his girlfriend demanding that she give him a kiss. Jumma refuses as she sashays across a platform above them, raising her long red flamenco dress and revealing her black stockinged legs while her breast heaves in and out. Tiger and his friends dance in choreographed ecstasy, their pelvises thrusting back and forth. Finally, Tiger, impatient with her denials, picks up a hose large enough to represent the symbolic ejaculation of the dockers and drenches Jumma, tearing off her dress, knocking her from her platform into the midst of the gyrating men below. The distance between them collapsed, she dances with the men, her body wet and uncovered. Still she refuses to kiss her lover maintaining the teasing distance between them until finally she and Tiger are engulfed by the dancing men and when Tiger emerges his face is covered with the bright red marks of her lipstick.

'Dan Yaro Magashi took the song from this sequence and wrote a Hausa version in honour of the prophet Mohammed. In this version the Tiger's song to Jumma is transformed into an African call and response between 'Dan Yao Magashi and the bandiri drummers providing accompaniment. The skill here lies not just in copying the Indian tune or the quality of the singing, but also in the cleverness with which 'Dan Yaro chooses Hausa words which closely mirror the original Hindi.

Jumma chumma de de		**Zuma zumar bege**
Jumma chumma de de	S :	Zuma zumar bege
jummaa chumma de de, jumma		zuma zumar bege mu sha
jumma chumma de de	A :	*Zuma zumar bege*
	S :	Bege bege
	A :	*Zuma zumar bege mu sha*
Jumma chumma de de jummaa	S :	Zuma zumar bege........bege
		zuma zumar bege mu sha
	A :	*Zuma zumar bege*
	S :	Bege bege
	A :	*Zuma zumar bege mu sha*
Jumma ke din kiyaa chumma	S :	Zumar yabo ta gurin
kaa vaadaa		dan Amina,
Jumma ko to diyaa chumme		manzo masoyi masoyina
kaa vaadaa		na raina
le aa gayaa re phir jummaa-chummaa	ko yar kadan ni ina so na kurba in sha...
Jumma chumma de de	A :	*Zumar zuma bege*

(S = singer; A = *Amshi* or, reply).

"Jumma chumma de de jumma" (Jumma—a girl's name—give me, give me a kiss) becomes "zuma zumar bege mu sha" (honey, honey we are longing to drink). Similarly, the verse line "Jumma ke din kiyaa chumma kaa vaadaa" is transformed into "Zumar yabo ta gurin dan Amina". The purpose of bandiri music is to strip the Indian song of its original lyrics, thus symbolically divorcing it from its original filmic context. Here that context is a song sequence famous within Indian films for its raunchiness[13]. Bachchan plays a docker and Katkar the object of his desire. The sequence opens with Katkar parading down a runway above a band of seething dockers alternately raising and lowering her red flamenco dress. The wide shots of the group are intercut with medium close up of Tiger (Bachchan) and his cronies thrusting their pelvises in and out. Here the Indian films plays with the boundaries of the gendered moral universe of Indian films. As Sunita Mukhi points out Katkar repeatedly says "no no" to Bachchan while her actions mime "yes yes". It is striking that a song with such a sexualised, origin could be seen as fodder for religious meditation but this is part of the ambiguous place Indian films play in the landscape of Northern Nigerian culture.

Remembering and Repressing

As much as bandiri rests upon the dialectic of similarity and difference it intimately engages emotions of remembering and repressing. For copying to be successful the original tune has to be recognised and the Hausa lyrics are tied physically to the Hindi originals. But every moment of copying carries with it the anxiety produced by the immoral origins of the song. This immorality is heightened when we consider the ambivalent place of cinema within the conservative social arena of northern Nigeria. There cinemas used to be largely all male places, the few women who did attend were seen as prostitutes and sexual desire was to be found both on and off the screen (Larkin 2002). Since the introduction of Islamic law in 2001 women have been formally banned from these arenas and strict sexual segregation enforced. It is in this context that Indian films, the aura of relative sexual freedom they display and the teasing independence of actresses (shown well in Kimi Katkar's flirtation with Bachchan) gain sexual and moral purchase. Indian actresses are often seen as quintessential prostitutes not because they are immoral but because their deportment and relative freedom in interacting with men, their sexual freedom and their glamour are all attributes associated with *karuwai* (prostitutes) in Nigeria. It is not uncommon that important female and male homosexual prostitutes in Kano name themselves after favourite film actresses, playing with these identities and borrowing from the aura of Indian stardom in a way that is analogous to bandiri music but morally inverting its use. In the context of Hausa society then, Indian films can be sexually transgressive, their erotic display, their sexual

---

13. The song sequence by Laximant won the 1991 Filmfare award for best song sequence.

intermixing and the use of music for carnal and not religious purposes combine to keep them beyond the pale of orthodox Islam. For bandiri singers these origins must be repressed at the moment they are invoked, forgotten (so to speak) just at the time they are remembered for the transformation from secular to sacred to occur. This action is often addressed in the songs themselves as in this example from Sidi Musa's song from *Geet Gata Chal* cited above:

S : My heart is longing for you my soul loves you. I am longing for my messenger the Prophet of God
A : My messenger the Prophet of God...
S : Oh whenever I start translating an Indian song leave me this work and I shall finish it.
A : Ai you are the one to finish it...
S : Those who are longing for women should stop it. They should long for my Messenger the Prophet of God.
A : My Messenger the prophet of God
S : Those who are longing for women should stop it. They should long for my Messenger the Prophet of God.
A : My Messenger the prophet of God.
S : We should forget about Indian songs, they are useless.
A : They are useless
S : I am saying, in Indian songs I heard them singing Geet Gata Chal, but I am singing the Prophet of God.
A : The Greatest
A : O Mohammed, Prophet of God, O my lover.
S : Sidi Musa, son of Sidi, I am the one who composed this Praising of the Prophet of God.

Here you get a prime instance of the ways in which the original context is repressed in the moment of its mimesis. The association of songs and longing for women sets up the unIslamic nature of Indian song—*ba shi da amfani*—it is useless. But at the same time the song carries the intense emotions familiar from Indian films. As in Western musicals, songs in Indian films are often timed to appear as proxies for powerful feelings characters cannot convey in everyday conversation. Bandiri singers wish to maintain that intensity of emotion, to copy it, but then to divorce it from its original context leaving only a heightened state of being.

Mimicry then, lies at the heart of the social meaning of bandiri music. Taussig (1993: xiii) argues that "the power of mimesis lies in the copy drawing on the character and power of the original, to the point whereby the representation may even assume that character and power". What is occurring her is a siphoning of charisma, as Sufis are harnessing the glamour and transnational prestige associated with Indian films to the quite different charisma of religious devotion[14]. But in this case, bandiri can only be

14. Meg McLagan provides an interesting discussion of the tension between religious charisma and media celebrity in her discussion of the resignification of the Dalai Lama in the Tibet movement. See MCLAGAN (2002).

successful if the meanings generated through mimicry can be limited. Whether this can be completely achieved is an open question. Certainly older Hausa and non-Sufis who look down on bandiri music and some who criticise it fiercely believe that the shadow of its original filmic performance haunts the reproduction, undermining it and making it either detrimental to Hausa culture (because of foreign borrowing) or unIslamic, depending on your point of view. Peter Manuel (1993) observes the same tension operates in the performance of parodies in the Indian context, especially devotional ones where "the borrowed melodies may remind listeners of the specific cinematic scenes in which they were picturized" and that these "extra-musical" associations can never be divorced, and perhaps threaten to overwhelm, the transformed meaning of the copy.

This suggests the difficulty, mentioned above, of being able to "repress" the filmic origins of particular songs to the degree necessary to make them sacred and no longer profane. The singer Lawan 'dan Yaro Magashi explained to me that he always sings "classic" songs from older films because it takes the older generation by surprise when they recognise a song from their youth. He talked of how old people would come up and reminisce about seeing the film from which the original song was taken, suggesting that he explicitly aimed to evoke the original moment of reception in order to draw upon it to give the Sufi version emotional resonance and meaning. Sudhir Kakar (1989) has written about the important ways that the common cultural competence of youths immersed in Indian films (or any other sort of films) such as my Hausa friend above, creates a common memory that provides a field of nostalgia later in life. Writing of himself, Kakar recalled his early childhood sexual pleasure at watching wet saree scenes. When he saw such a scene recently, "I felt grateful to the world of Hindi movies for providing continuity in an unstable and changing world [...] When I was a child, the movies brought the vistas of a desirable adulthood tantalizingly close; as an adult, I find they help to keep the road to childhood open" (1989: 26). Remembering and repressing, mimesis and alterity are the oppositions that provide the productive tensions making bandiri work.

Indian Songs, Copies, Originals, and Copies again

If Bandiri music is a copy it brings up the question of what is the original of which it is a copy? This can be a significant question in the case of Indian film songs which, as many observers point out, are nothing if not rapacious in culling melodies and rhythms from religious, folk and popular musics of the world. One famous source of Hindi film songs, for instance, are qawwalis, the rhythmic chanting, drumming and clapping performed by Sufi followers in India and Pakistan, intended to stimulate intense emotions (Qureshi 1995; Manuel 1993). From the inception of Indian cinema qawwali was subsumed to the secular needs of the new medium. Instrumentation was made more diverse, emotional intensity was retained, but the focus was shifted to include romance as well as religion. Qureshi points out that over time there has been a feedback loop between live qawwali performances and filmic qawwalis. Film music has borrowed heavily from the religious genre, but then the transformations it has introduced have fed back into live qawwali performances. Moving across space to Northern Nigeria, Hausa Sufi followers, unaware of the Sufi roots to some of the songs they listen to nevertheless recognise the emotional intensity (that first attracted music directors to qawwali) and re-resignify that emotional ecstasy back into an "original" Sufi context. Which one is the copy? In the case of *Jumma Chumma* this is all the more byzantine in that, unknown to Lawan 'Dan Yaro Magashi the Hausa singer of *Zuma zumar bege*, *Jumma Chumma* is itself an adaptation of *Yeke Yeke* a west African song by the Malian singer Mory Kante.

*

When, between 1970 and 1983, the Nigerian government banked $140 billion from the boom in oil revenues the surge of these oil monies through the urban networks of cities such as Lagos, Port Harcourt, Onitsha and Kano had similar and dissimilar effects. On the one hand all of them experienced the 'fast capitalism' of oil wealth: rapid urban growth, a flood of consumer goods, and a shift toward a consumption based economy (Watts 1992). But in many ways these monies set in motion different effects. The south's long-standing interaction with the West led to an increased penetration of evangelical Protestantism into southern Christianity and meant that more people than ever before began to travel, work and be educated in Europe and the United States. In the north of Nigeria, the arrival of oil monies hugely intensified Hausa interaction with the wider Islamic world. Oil enabled Hausa to invigorate pre-colonial and colonial participation in Sufi networks. It facilitated mass participation in the hajj intensifying the educational, financial and political links between Nigeria and Saudi Arabia that were crucial to the rise of Wahhabi ideas and movements.

In this way the structural reorganization brought about by the oil boom set in motion both similar and dissimilar effects in Nigerian cities. The reason for this lies in the historical residue of social practices, the layering of social spaces, which accumulate in any particular place. Transformations in capital energize the historical layers embedded in a city, facilitating the intensification of some, initiating others while closing down still more. It helps explain why dormant cultural, religious and economic forms can suddenly gain purchase again, be reawakened and re-energised in a new situation. As Lefebvre (1991: 73) argues, "itself the outcome of past actions, social space is what permits fresh actions to occur, while suggesting others and prohibiting yet others".

Bandiri emerges out of the urban crucible of Kano, northern Nigeria and the specific historical configuration that creates the conditions for Kano urban experience. In Kano, air routes link the metropolis to Beirut, Jeddah, Lagos and London. Stickers of Sufi preachers contest with Osama Bin Laden, Sani Abacha, Shah Rukh Khan, Tupac Shakur, and Ali Nuhu for space on Kano buses and taxis[15]. The recent revival of Shari'a law is contemporaneous with the jump in popularity of gangsta rap and hip hop available on vcd and satellite television. As an urban centre Kano is the node of overlapping sets of cultural, religious and economic networks that provide the skeleton around which Kano urban life is built. They provide the raw material that cultural actors use to express identity. Cultural and economic ties to the West are countered by the increasing orientation of Nigerian traders toward the Middle East and Asia and the pilgrimage to Mecca has become the context for legal and illegal trade as well as for religious observance.

The bricolage of culture inherent in a phenomenon such as bandiri is not a free-floating event. It is the fashioning of cultural performance from the availability of cultural forms in a particular given space—urban Kano, Nigeria. Media generate urban form by activating connections in a network, placing Kano Hausawa (Hausa people) into material and immaterial connection with movements and ideas from over the world making the urban arena "a multiplicity of spaces crosscutting intersecting or aligning with one another, or existing in relations of paradox or antagonism" (Massey 1994: 3). In this way bandiri can be seen as an epiphenomenon of an historical trajectory that brings certain social sets into articulation in the crucible of Kano bringing about the historical conditions of possibility from which something like bandiri might emerge. Urban possibilities are formed out of the unintended juxtapositions of different sets present in urban space. Bandiri music highlights how much Hausa audiences are avid and longtime consumers of a transnational circulation of Indian images and music for which they are the unintended recipients. For forty years an information flow has been persistently diverted off the mainstream of its distribution circuit to other places south of the Sahelian desert. It is there that in rubs up against an Islamic society in the midst of religious revival and out of that experience a new form of music—bandiri—emerges.

Barnard College, Columbia University.

---

15. Osama Bin Laden is the Islamic terrorist; Sani Abacha is a former dictator of Nigeria; Shah Rukh Khan is a famous Indian film star; Tupac Shakur is the late African-American rap artist and Ali Nuhu is a star of Hausa video films.

BIBLIOGRAPHY

ANWAR, A.

1989 *The Struggle for Influence and Identity: The Ulama in Kano, 1937-1987.* M. A. Thesis (Maiduguri, Nigeria: University of Maiduguri).

APPADURAI, A.

1997 *Modernity at Large. Cultural Dimensions of Globalization* (Minneapolis: University of Minnesota Press).

BARBER, K. (ed.)

1997 *Readings in African Popular Culture* (Bloomington: Indiana University Press).

BARBER, K. & WATERMAN, C.

1995 "Traversing the Global and Local: Fùjí Music and Praise Poetry in the Production of Contemporary Yoruba Popular Culture", in D. MILLER (ed.), *Worlds Apart. Modernity through the Prism of the Local* (London: Routledge): 240-262.

BARKINDO, B. M.

1993 "Growing Islamism in Kano City Since 1970: Causes, Forms and Implications", in Louis BRENNER (ed.), *Muslim Identity and Social Change in Sub-Saharan Africa* (Bloomington: Indiana University Press): 91-105.

BAYART, J.-F.

1993 *The State in Africa. The Politics of the Belly* (London: Longman).

BAYART, J.-F., ELLIS, S. & HIBOU, B.

1999 *The Criminalization of the State in Africa* (Oxford: James Currey).

BUBA, M. & FURNISS, G.

1999 "Youth Culture, *Bandiri* and the Continuing Legitimacy Debate in Sokoto Town" *Journal of African Cultural Studies,* 12 (1): 27-46.

FERGUSON, J.

1999 *Expectations of Modernity. Myths and Meanings of Urban Life on the Zambian Copperbelt* (Berkeley: University of California Press).

GAONKAR, D. P. (ed.)

1999 "Alter/Native Modernities" *Public Culture,* 11 (1).

GRAHAM, S. & MARVIN, S.

1996 *Telecommunications and the City. Electronic Spaces, Urban Places* (London: Routledge).

760   BRIAN LARKIN

2001   *Splintering Urbanism: Networked Infrastructures, Technological Mobilities
       and the Urban Condition* (London: Routledge).

GUMI, A. M.

1972   *'Aqidah Al-Sahihah Bi Muwafiqah Al-Shari'ah.* The Right Belief is Based
       on the Shari'ah (Ankara: Hilal Publishing).

1992   *Where I Stand* (Ibadan: Spectrum Books).

HANNERZ, U.

1992   *Cultural Complexity: Studies in the Social Organization of Meaning* (New
       York: Columbia University Press).

HARVEY, D.

2000   *Spaces of Hope* (Berkeley: University of California Press).

INDA, J. X. & ROSALDO, R.

2002   *The Anthropology Of Globalization: A Reader* (Oxford: Blackwell).

KAKAR, S.

1989   *Intimate Relations: Exploring Indian Sexuality* (Chicago: University of Chicago
       Press).

KOOLHAS, R., HARVARD PROJECT ON THE CITY, BOERI, S., MULTIPLICITY PROJECT,
KWINTER, S., TAZI, N., OBRIST, H. U.

2000   *Mutations* (Bordeaux: Aetar).

LARKIN, B.

1997   "Indian Films and Nigerian Lovers. Media and the Creation of Parallel
       Modernities" *Africa* 67 (3): 406-440.

2002   "Materializing Culture: Cinema and the Creation of Social Space", in
       F. GINSBURG, L. ABU-LUGHOD & B. LARKIN (eds), *Media Worlds: Anthropol-
       ogy on New Terrain* (Berkeley: University of California Press): 319-336.

LEFEBVRE, H.

1991   The Production of Space. Translation by D. N. SMITH (Oxford-Cambridge,
       Mass.: Blackwell).

LOIMEIER, R.

1997   *Islamic Reform and Political Change in Northern Nigeria* (Evanston: North-
       western University Press).

MANUEL, P.

1993   *Cassette Culture. Popular Music and Technology in South India* (Chicago:
       University of Chicago Press).

MASSEY, D. B.

1994   *Space, Place and Gender* (Minneapolis: University of Minnesota Press).

MUSICAL "MÉTISSAGE" IN NIGERIA   761

MATTELART, A.

1996   *The Invention of Communication.* Translation by S. EMANUEL (Minneapolis: University of Minnesota Press).

2000   *Networking the World, 1794-2000* (Minneapolis: University of Minnesota Press).

MCLAGAN, M.

2002   "Spectacles of Difference. Cultural Activism and the Mass Mediation of Tibet", in F. GINSBURG, L. ABU-LUGHOD & B. LARKIN (eds), *Media Worlds: Anthropology on New Terrain* (Berkeley: University of California Press).

PADEN, J. N.

1973   *Religion and Political Culture in Kano* (Berkeley: University of California Press).

QURESHI, R. B.

1995   "Recorded Sound and Religious Music: The Case of Qawwali", in L. A. BABB & S. S. WADLEY (eds), *Media and the Transformation of Religion in South Asia* (Philadelphia: University of Pennsylvania Press): 139-166.

RAJADHYAKSHA, A. & WILLEMEN, P.

1994   *Encyclopaedia of Indian Cinema* (London: BFI Publishing; New Delhi: Oxford University Press).

TAHIR, I. A.

1975   *Scholars, Saints, and Capitalists in Kano, 1904-1974. The Pattern of Bourgeois Revolution in an Islamic Society.* Ph. D. (Cambridge University).

TAUSSIG, M.

1993   *Mimesis and Alterity: A Particular History of the Senses* (New York: Routledge).

TSING, A.

2000   "The Global Situation" *Cultural Anthropology* 15 (3): 327-360.

UMAR, M. S.

1993   "Changing Islamic Identity in Nigeria from the 1960s to the 1980s: From Sufism to Anti-Sufism", in L. BRENNER (ed.), *Muslim Identity and Social Change in Sub-Saharan Africa* (Bloomington: Indiana University Press): 154-178.

WATTS, M.

1992   "The Shock of Modernity: Petroleum, Protest and Fast Capitalism in an Industrializing Society", in A. PRED & M. WATTS (eds), *Reworking Modernity: Capitalisms and Symbolic Discontent* (New Brunswick: Rutgers University Press).

WATTS, M. & SHENTON, R.

1984   "State and Agrarian Transformation in Nigeria", in J. BARKER (ed.), *The Politics of Agriculture in Tropical Africa* (Beverley Hills: Sage Publications).

762   BRIAN LARKIN

ABSTRACT

This paper provides an analysis of the working of a musical form: bandiri. Bandiri is a musical genre performed by Sufi adepts in northern Nigeria who take popular Hindi film songs and change the words to sing praises to the Prophet Mohammed. In doing so they are involved in a complicated process of taking a profane genre and sacralizing it. I argue that bandiri is the result of the convergence in Kano, northern Nigeria of three very different sorts of transnational cultural and religious networks: the long presence of Sufi brotherhoods in the north, the recent emergence of an anti-Sufi Islamist movement; and the continuing popularity of Indian films and songs. As an urban centre Kano is made up of overlapping sets of cultural, religious and economic networks that constitute its particular configuration. These networks create structural preconditions that provide the raw material from which urban experience might be fashioned.

RÉSUMÉ

La musique bandiri, globalisation et expérience urbaine au Nigeria. — Cet article offre une analyse du façonnement d'une forme musicale : le bandiri. Le bandiri est un genre musical pratiqué par les Sufi du nord du Nigeria qui se servent des chansons des films indiens et en modifient les paroles pour chanter les louanges du prophète Mohammed. Ils sont ainsi engagés dans un processus compliqué qui consiste à s'emparer d'un genre profane pour le sacraliser. Dans cet article, on soutient que le bandiri est le résultat de la rencontre, qui s'est produite à Kano au nord du Nigeria, de trois différentes traditions culturelles et religieuses transnationales : celle des confréries sufi du nord de ce pays, celle du mouvement anti-sufi qui y a récemment vu le jour et enfin celle des films et des chansons indiens. En tant que centre urbain, Kano se compose de réseaux culturels, religieux et économiques qui lui donnent une configuration singulière. Ces réseaux constituent la matière première sur laquelle s'édifie l'expérience urbaine.

Keywords/*Mots-clés:* Nigeria, globalization, popular culture, urban space, Indian film/ *Nigeria, globalisation, culture populaire, espace urbain, films indiens.*

Part III
Music Industries

[14]

The cassette industry and popular music in North India

PETER MANUEL

Since the early 1970s the advent of cassette technology has had a profound effect on music industries worldwide. This influence has been particularly marked in the developing world, where cassettes have largely replaced vinyl records and have extended their impact into regions, classes and genres previously uninfluenced by the mass media. Cassettes have served to decentralise and democratise both production and consumption, thereby counterbalancing the previous tendency toward oligopolisation of international commercial recording industries.

While the cassette boom started later in India than in areas such as the Middle East and Indonesia, its influence since the early 1980s has been no less significant. In other publications, including a previous article in this journal, I have referred briefly to the ramifications of the cassette vogue in India and other countries (Manuel 1988a, pp. 173–5, 1988b, pp. 6–7, 214). This article attempts to summarise, in somewhat greater depth, albeit still superficially, the salient effects of cassette technology upon the production, dissemination, stylistic development and general cultural meaning of North Indian popular music, by which I mean to comprehend all those genres, including commercialised folk music, which are marketed as mass commodities and have been stylistically affected by their association with the mass media.

Popular music in India before 1980

In the aforementioned publications I have summarised the development and major styles of North Indian popular musics since the advent of recording technology around 1900. At this point it will suffice to reiterate a few of the most basic and relevant characteristics of the popular music scene during this period. The most salient of these features was the relatively undemocratic structure of the music industry, control of whose production was concentrated in a tiny and unrepresentative sector of the Indian population. From the mid-1930s until the advent of cassettes, commercial film music accounted, by informed estimates, for at least 90 per cent of record output.[1] The dominant entity throughout was the Hindi film industry, whose production itself lay in the hands of a small number of firms, producers, actors and actresses, and music producers. Given the vast output of film songs, a certain amount of stylistic and regional variety was naturally evident, as has been stressed, for example, by Arnold (1988). Nevertheless, the stylistic homogeneity of the vast majority of film songs was far more remarkable, and was most conspicuous in the overwhelming hegemony, for over thirty years, of five singers – Asha Bhosle, Kishore Kumar, Mohammad Rafi, Mukesh, and above all,

Lata Mangeshkar. Since vocal style in music is such an essential and basic aesthetic identity marker, the stylistic uniformity of these singers – especially of Lata's several thousand songs – stands in dramatic contrast to the wide diversity of folk music and singing styles throughout North India.[2] Further, while regional folk musics did contribute to many film songs, most film composers and musicians avoided recognisable folk elements in an attempt to appeal to a pan-regional market (Chandravarkar 1987, p. 8). As a result, the overwhelming majority of songs adhered to a distinctive mainstream style, which, although itself eclectic (Arnold 1988), was hardly representative of the variety of North Indian folk musics.

Song texts were equally limited in subject matter, dealing almost exclusively with sentimental love, again in contrast to regional folksong. In this respect, however, they were suited to the romantic and fundamentally escapist nature of Indian movies themselves, which studiously avoided realistic portrayals of the grinding poverty and class antagonisms so basic to Indian society.

Popular music was apprehended largely through cinema and the radio; only the urban middle and upper classes had extensive access to records, due to the expense and power requirements of record players. His Master's Voice (of EMI) enjoyed a virtually complete monopoly in the record industry, having absorbed or eliminated regional rivals in the early decades of its appearance in India.

While charming melodies, moving lyrics and professional production standards were not lacking in Indian popular music, what was remarkably deficient was any sort of affirmation of a sense of community, whether on the level of region, caste, class, gender or ethnicity. It is such a sense of community that may be said to be the most vital and essential aspect of folk songs, which celebrate collective community values through shared, albeit specific performance norms and contexts, musical style, textual references and language. Insofar as film music succeeded in appealing to, if not creating, a homogeneous mass market, it did so only at the expense of this affirmation of community, thereby, it could be argued, becoming as ultimately alienating as the escapist cinematic fantasies it was embedded in.

The advent of cassettes: alternatives to His Master's Voice

While commercial Indian music cassettes began appearing in the early 1970s, it was not until a decade later that they appeared in such quantities as to restructure the entire music industry. In India as elsewhere, cassettes and players were naturally preferable to records due to their portability, durability, low cost and simple power requirements. Aside from these advantages, the timing of their spread in India was attributable to another set of factors. First, the number of Indian guest workers bringing 'two-in-ones' (radio-cassette players) from the Gulf states had by that point reached such a level that luxuries of this kind had become familiar throughout the country. More importantly, in accordance with the contemporary economic liberalisation policies pursued by the ruling Congress Party from around 1978, many of the import restrictions which had inhibited the acquisition of cassette technology in the 1970s were rescinded, thereby permitting the import of players and, more importantly, facilitating the local manufacture of cassettes and players with some foreign components. Thirdly, indigenous industry itself, after decades of infant-industry protection, had improved to the point that Indian manufacturers were now able to produce presentable cassettes and players, whether using some imported components or not.[3] Finally, the aforementioned economic liberalisation policies, while of questionable benefit to the lower class majority, considerably enhanced the purchasing power and general consumerism of the middle classes and even some sectors of the lower-middle classes, in the countryside as well as the cities. This development, among other things, has greatly contributed to the proliferation of televisions and cassettes in slums and villages throughout the country.[4]

The advent of cassette technology effectively restructured the music industry in India. By the mid-1980s, cassettes had come to account for 95 per cent of the recorded music market, with records being purchased only by wealthy audiophiles, radio stations and cassette pirates (who prefer using them as masters).[5] The recording industry monopoly formerly enjoyed by HMV (now Gramophone Co. of India, or 'GramCo') dwindled to less than 15 per cent of the market as over 300 competitors entered the recording field. While sales of film music remained strong, the market expanded so exponentially – from $1.2 million in 1980 to over $12 million in 1986[6] – that film music came to constitute only about half of the market, the remainder consisting of regional folk and devotional music, and other forms of 'non-filmi', or in industry parlance, 'basic' pop music.

In effect, the cassette revolution had definitively ended the unchallenged hegemony of GramCo, of the corporate music industry in general, of film music, of the Lata-Mukesh vocal style and of the uniform aesthetic of the Bombay film music producers which had been superimposed on a few hundred million music listeners over the preceding forty years. The crucial factors were the relatively low expense of the cassette technology, and especially its lowered production costs which enabled small, 'cottage' cassette companies to proliferate throughout the country. The small labels tend to have local, specialised, regional markets to whose diverse musical interests they are able and willing to respond in a manner quite uncharacteristic of the monopolistic major recording companies, which, as we have seen, prefer to address and, as much as possible, to *create* a mass homogeneous market. In the process, the backyard cassette companies have been energetically recording and marketing all manner of regional 'little traditions' which were previously ignored by HMV and the film music producers. Rather than being oriented toward undifferentiated film-goers, most of the new cassette-based musics are aimed at a bewildering variety of specific target audiences, in terms of class, age, gender, ethnicity, region and, in some cases, even occupation (e.g. Punjabi truck drivers' songs). The smaller producers themselves are varied in terms of their region, religion and, insofar as many are lower-middle class, their class backgrounds as well. Ownership of the means of musical production is thus incomparably more diverse than before the cassette era. As a result, the average, non-elite Indian is now, as never before, offered the voices of his own community as mass-mediated alternatives to His Master's Voice.

The cassette producers now vary greatly in size, orientation, operating practices and other parameters. On the one hand are the handful of major firms, *viz*, GramCo, which, hampered by inefficiency and inability to compete, relies primarily on its back catalogue of film music; CBS and a break-away firm, Magnasound, which specialise in releases of Western music; Polygram's Music India Ltd. (MIL, formerly Polydor); T-Series/Super Cassette Industries (SCI), a newer business founded by the ruthless entrepreneur Gulshan Arora, with a

diverse catalogue now including most current film music; Venus, a Bombay-based
concern with a similarly diverse repertoire; and TIPS, which specialises in cover
versions of pop songs. On the other hand are the smaller regional producers,
which probably number between 250 and 500 nationally.[7] These themselves range
in size from regional folk/pop producers like Delhi's Max, Sonotone and Yuki, with
over a thousand releases each, to operations like Chandrabani Garhwal Series,
whose series, as of 1989, consisted of a single cassette. Beyond this level are
numerous provincial entrepreneurial individuals who record music and sell copies
upon request out of their residences, dubbing them with simple one-to-one setups.

Technology, financing and piracy

The expenses and technical resources of the cassette producers naturally vary in
accordance with their size, audience orientation and other factors. Both large and
small companies may have their own recording studios and dubbing facilities, and/
or they may rely on rented studios and other duplicators. While a few of the better
studios have such features as sixteen-track recorders, most professional studios
have only four-track technology. Recorders are almost all imported; dubbing
machinery may be either imported, or may consist of one-to-four duplicators made
for around $6,000 by indigenous and generally unlicensed companies. Similarly,
blank tape and cassette shells may either be imported, acquired from indigenous
makers, or, in the case of larger companies like T-Series, manufactured by the firm
itself; smaller producers assemble the cassettes by hand.[8] Cassette recorders themselves range from high-fidelity products of Japanese-Indian 'tie-ins' (e.g. Bush-
Akai and Orson-Sony) to locally made players, in which only the heads and micro-
motors are imported, and which sell for around $18.

Recording expenses vary widely. With studio charges and fees for engineers
and musicians, production of a 60-minute tape of mass-market film songs and
Hindi pop music may on occasion cost up to Rs. 200,000 ($12,000). While the
average recording expenses are closer to $1000,[9] many recordings of folk music are
produced for as little as $75. Cassette duplication then proceeds in accordance with
demand, with retailers often being able to return unsold tapes to the manufacturer
for re-recording (hence the absence of labels on many regional cassette shells).
Most cassettes sell for around Rs. 18, or slightly more than a dollar; HMV's tapes
range from Rs. 24 to Rs. 36. Tape fidelity ranges from acceptable to worse, with
poorer cassettes leaving oxide deposits on tape heads and wearing out after a few
listenings; customers learn to request to listen to tapes before purchase to ensure
that they are not already defective.

Piracy, or the sale of unauthorised duplications of recordings, has plagued
the cassette industry from its inception. The first half of the 1980s was the worst
period in this respect. Extant copyright laws were unequipped to deal with cassette
piracy, while the government showed little interest in prosecuting offenders.
HMV's inability to reissue its old film hits provided the pirate producers with
ample repertoire to market. New companies faced onerous bureaucratic obstacles
in legitimately obtaining licences, including absurd export requirements. Due to
high government taxes on blank tape, and the myopic pricing policies of the large
cassette companies (especially HMV), legitimate tapes cost nearly twice as much as
pirate versions. Further, while most pirate cassettes were of inferior quality, some,
such as the tapes of Goanese music produced and purchased in the Gulf states by

guest workers, were actually superior to the legitimate cassettes. By 1985, pirate cassettes were generally estimated to account for 90 per cent of all tape sales.[10] While most of the piracy was perpetrated by small producers, the fledgling T-Series was widely accused of being a major culprit. Meanwhile, cassette stores and dubbing kiosks proliferated throughout the country, recording favourite songs selected by individual customers.

In the latter half of the decade, the situation improved somewhat. Most legitimate producers lowered their prices, making pirate tapes less competitive. The government, under increasing pressure from the industry, reduced its various taxes and bureaucratic hindrances to registration of new companies; more importantly, realising the extent of its tax losses, it enacted a more effective copyright act in 1984 and intensified attempts at enforcement. Legal cover versions of the classic hits became widely marketed. Consumers gradually became aware of the advantages of buying legitimate tapes. As a result of these changes, piracy, although still open and widespread, diminished considerably, at least in relation to the market as a whole. In the absence of accurate figures, I would estimate its share at roughly one third of the market.

The impact of cassettes on musical trends

The cassette vogue has played a central role in the flowering of a number of commercial music styles of North India, especially the 'non-filmi' genres which have come to rival, if not surpass the popularity of film music. Film music, of course, continues to be the single most dominant North Indian genre, and cassettes have naturally served to disseminate it considerably more widely than before. Nevertheless, as I have suggested, by making possible more diverse ownership of the means of musical production, cassettes have served as vehicles for a set of heterogeneous genres which provide, on an unprecedented level, stylistic alternatives to film music, and to which listeners have responded to the tune of some $60 million annually. In the process, relatively new genres of stylised, commercial popular musics have arisen in close association with cassettes. The following discussion, rather than attempting a descriptive survey of these styles, endeavours to outline the connection between their emergence and cassette technology.

Ghazal

The Urdu *ghazal* has played an important part in North Indian culture since the early eighteenth century. As a literary genre (consisting of rhymed and metered couplets employing a standardised symbology and aesthetic), it has been and remains widely cultivated among educated and even many illiterate North Indians, especially Muslims. As a musical genre, it emerged as a rich semi-classical style, popularised by courtesans and, in the twentieth century, by light-classical singers of 'respectable' backgrounds. With the advent of film music, a 'filmi' style of *ghazal* emerged, distinguished from its semi-classical antecedent by characteristics typical of film song in general, *viz.* orchestral interludes between verses, occasional use of Western instruments and harmony, absence of improvisation, and a standardised vocal style epitomised by its main exponents, Talat Mehmood and a handful of other singers, including, of course, Lata Mangeshkar.[11]

While the film *ghazal* had declined after Mehmood's heyday in the 1950s, in the late 1970s a new style of *ghazal*-song flowered which was at once commercially popular, distinct from the earlier film and light-classical styles, and lacking direct association with cinema. Indeed, the new crossover *ghazal*, as popularised first by Pakistanis Mehdi Hasan and Ghulam Ali, was the first widely successful popular music in South Asia which was independent of cinema or, for that matter, radio. With its leisurely, languorous tempo, its vaguely aristocratic ethos, its sentimental lyrics and soothing, unhurried melodies, the new *ghazal*, though disparaged by purists as yuppie relaxation music, came to acquire an audience far wider than *ghazal* had ever had before. Much of the new *ghazal*'s audience consisted of devotees of the formerly melodious film songs who were dismayed by the recent film music trend toward disco-oriented styles more appropriate to the action-oriented *masālā* ('spice') films of the 1980s. In the hands of the subsequent *ghazal* stars – Pankaj Udhas, Anup Jalota, Jagjit and Chitra Singh, and others – the crossover *ghazal* style has become even more distinct, with its diluted Urdu, often shallow and trite poetry, general absence or mediocrity of improvisation, and a silky, non-percussive accompaniment and vocal style which render it immediately recognisable. As the genre became ever more remote from its semi-classical ante-cedent, 'pop goes the *ghazal*' soon became a journalistic cliché.

What is significant for the present study is the role that cassettes played in the popularisation of the crossover *ghazal*. The *ghazal* vogue had gathered momentum by the late 1970s, but reached its apogee in the first half of the next decade, in tandem with the cassette boom. The two trends, indeed, reinforced each other, at the expense of vinyl records and film music in general. Cassette producers in the firms most closely associated with the *ghazal* vogue – GramCo and MIL – saw themselves as not merely responding to popular demand, but actively promoting, if not creating the trend. Thus, MIL vigorously pushed *ghazal* tapes partly in order to outflank cassette pirates by creating a market for a genre distinguished by relatively high fidelity and an affluent, yet mass audience (unlike pirate cassettes, most of which consist of poor-fidelity tapes of film hits aimed at lower-class buyers).[12] Similarly, a GramCo executive related:

What became necessary [after the decline of melody-oriented film music] was to take *ghazals* and *bhajans* to a wider market, thus simplifying them and making them more universally accepted . . . Many such trends can be created.[13]

While our informant is no doubt overstating the ability of the music industry to create trends outright, it is clear that the deliberate promotion of *ghazal* cassettes by the larger recording companies actively helped popularise both the medium and the music. In the wake of these developments, commercial cassettes were established as the most dynamic sector of the music industry by the early 1980s, such that future developments in the realm of Indian popular music were closely allied to the new medium.

Devotional music

If the crossover *ghazal* boom confirmed the transition from vinyl to cassette record-ing, it was the unprecedented vogue of commercial versions of devotional music that accompanied and fed the extension of the cassette market beyond the urban middle classes. The devotional music trend did not, of course, emerge from a vacuum. India, with its vast, diverse and intensely religious population, continues to host an extraordinarily rich variety of devotional music traditions. The most widespread of these have been the various, often collectively performed songs associated with the Hindu *bhakti* traditions, which celebrate personal devotion rather than karma, caste or formalistic ritual. Commercial film versions of *bhakti git* (song) had been familiar for decades, and several film *bhajans* (Hindu religious songs) and *ārtis* (prayer chants) had acquired the status of hits, being subsequently sequently sung by devotees throughout the country (such as the *ārti* 'Om jay Jagdish Hari' from the film *Purab aur Paschim*). Filmi versions of Muslim *qawwāli* had also become a common feature of Bombay movies (Manuel 1988a, pp. 167–8). Further, record companies (primarily, of course, GramCo) had traditionally come to time new releases with the main Hindu festivals (especially the simultaneous Bengali Durga Puja, Gujerati Navratri, and Maharashtrian Ganesh Puja), when the public went on gift-buying sprees. Nevertheless, the extent of the commercial *bhakti* vogue in the early 1980s was quite unprecedented.

The immediate forerunner to the trend was the widely successful series of recordings by Mukesh consisting of tasteful musical settings of Tulsidas' version of the *Ramayan* epic (Manuel 1988a, p. 175). Although first released on LP format, it was not until it was issued on cassette in the late 1970s that this series achieved mass sales. The phenomenal popularity of subsequent television serials of the *Mahabharat* and *Ramayan* epics played an even more important role in promoting mass-mediated realisations of religious works, including cassette recordings of devotional musics. As with *ghazals*, however, the cassette medium itself played the crucial role in popularising commercial *bhakti git*. Cassette producers recognised that a successful devotional cassette may enjoy a considerably longer 'shelf life' than most other pop music releases, whose sales generally dwindle after a few months.[14] Further, producers saw that the country's extant devotional music traditions constituted a relatively untapped gold mine of inestimable commercial potential. Accordingly, several commentators have opined that the vogue of pop *bhakti* music was due primarily to the advent of cassettes rather than to any resurgence of religious fervour in the country. Thus, for example, veteran *bhajan* singer Purshottam Das stated:

Bhajans have always been popular in certain segments of our society. But now the catchy tunes have been successful in attracting the youth. Essentially, it is the cassette medium which is responsible for the growing sales rather than growing interest (Upadhyay 1985, p. 15).

Similarly, a music journalist argued, 'Perhaps the real reason for this manic following of *bhajans* was the spectacular rise of audio-visual electronic consumer goods and the rise of the *ghazal*' (Lalitha 1988).

The variety of commercially marketed devotional musics in North India is remarkable. The most conspicuous genre is what may be described as a 'mainstream' *bhajan* style, sung by a solo vocalist with light instrumental accompaniment. It was this genre that started the *bhakti* boom, in the wake of Mukesh's *Ramayan* and, more importantly, the *ghazal* vogue. Hence it is not surprising that in style, instrumentation and leading performers (Jalota, Udhas), the mainstream pop *bhajan* had marked affinities with the crossover *ghazal*. While this sort of *bhajan* continues to enjoy mass appeal, cassette producers have since marketed an extraordinary variety of religious musics, which, needless to say, come incomparably closer to representing the rich diversity of Indian devotional musics than film musics ever attempted to do. Predominant in the field, naturally, are sub-genres of Hindu devotional music, including musical settings of traditional prayers (e.g. *Hanuman chalisa,* or the epics), *bhajans* devoted to various cult leaders (e.g. Sai Baba), or to deities (e.g. Santoshi Ma), *bhajans* sung in light-classical style by classical vocalists like Kumar Gandharva, and all manner of old and new songs in regional languages. Musics of other religions are also well represented. *Qawwāli* cassettes continue to sell, as do tapes of semi-melodic discourses by Muslim religious leaders. Sikh devotional songs – especially *shabd gurbāni* – enjoy a large market (and are remarkable for their avoidance of the stylistic commercialisation typical of many other devotional musics). Christian hymns, Jain *bhajans,* and even Marathi Buddhist songs also have their own customers.

While most cassettes, including the mainstream *bhajans,* are essentially for recreational listening, others are more functional in intent and usage. Housewives, for example, may routinely play a cassette of the *Satyanarayan kathā* during their occasional ritual fasting, in place of inviting a *pandit* to chant the story, or reciting it themselves. The important thing, in terms of spiritual benefit, is that the story be heard, regardless of whether one recites it oneself or listens to it while doing housework.

Smaller cassette companies frequently produce tapes for specific festivals celebrated annually at shrines or temples. A fledgling company in Lucknow, for example, produced a tape of songs connected with the annual festival in nearby Deva Sharif, and has been selling some $600 worth at the event every year since. Such profits, of course, may be too small to interest the larger recording companies, but suffice to keep many smaller producers in the market. Indeed, aside from the appeal of *bhajan* superstars like Anup Jalota and Hari Om Sharan, it is the ability of cassette producers to represent the innumerable 'little traditions' that accounts in large part for the extent of the devotional music vogue. Perhaps due to the virtually inexhaustible nature of these traditions, the commercial *bhakti* boom, unlike that of the *ghazal,* shows no signs of abating at present.

'Versions' and parodies: recycling the classics

A third important genre in the contemporary cassette-based popular music scene comprises cover versions of prior hit songs. Such recordings can be grouped into two broad categories: in one case – that of the cover version proper, or in modern Indian parlance, a 'version' recording – an extant song is re-recorded, generally by a different label, with different vocalists; the second category consists of cases where a new release uses the melody of an extant hit, but set to a new text. The latter instance, of course, constitutes parody (and is commonly referred to as such in India). Parodies substituting new texts in the same language – a common practice in modern film music – are generally not classified in the 'version' category, and lacking direct association with cassettes, will not be discussed in this article. Of greater relevance here are those parodies substituting a new or translated text in a different language from the original.

Like *ghazal* and devotional songs, cover versions and cross-language parodies are neither new nor unique to Indian commercial music; for that matter, the use of stock tunes is basic to folk music in India and many other countries.[15] Furthermore, for several decades, Indian folk musicians throughout the country have freely borrowed and adapted film melodies. Nevertheless, the extent of the current popularity of commercial versions and parodies is quite unprecedented in India and, to my own knowledge, unparalleled in any other country (with the possible exception of Indonesia, for which see Yampolsky 1989). The deluge of 'version' recordings covering classic film hits now constitutes a separate market category that occupies a sizeable niche in most urban cassette stores. Further, every major hit song of recent years, regardless of its original language, has spawned several parody versions in regional languages.

Rather than being a fortuitous fad, the boom of versions and parodies can be attributed to specific conditions obtaining in the Indian musical environment. The wide use of stock and borrowed tunes in Indian folk, light-classical and even classical music constitutes an initial precedent. In the realm of popular music, a more immediate precondition has been the relatively lax Indian Copyright Act (of 1956–7, section 52), which allows any party to make records of an existing work by filing a notice of intent and paying a nominal royalty. Added to this legal tolerance is the unwillingness or inability of the government to prosecute the innumerable small cassette producers who release recordings, typically of folk or devotional music, which employ melodies borrowed from films or other pop music.

Beyond these factors, the primary impetus for the vogue of cover versions has been the inability of GramCo to meet the demand for releases of its vast catalogue of past film songs. GramCo, by virtue of its longstanding virtual monopoly, held the rights to essentially all film songs recorded until the early 1970s. While many of these were forgettable and forgotten, many others were still in demand, but were not being re-issued, largely due to the company's monopoly-bred inefficiency. The advent of cassettes and the subsequent emergence of competing producers provided, for the first time, a means of meeting this demand. T-Series founder Gulshan Arora was the first to capitalise upon this situation; since the original recordings were copyrighted by GramCo, he set out to produce 'versions' of the most popular classic film hits. As the original vocalists were either prohibitively expensive (Lata), deceased (Kishore, Talat, Mukesh), or bound by contract obligations to GramCo, Arora scouted college talent shows for clone singers, coming up with a stable of inexpensive, undiscovered vocalists. He then released an ongoing series of 'version' tapes entitled *Yaaden* ('Memories'), whose labels acknowledge, in small print, that the singers are not those of the original recordings. The versions are recorded in stereo, using modern technology, and thus offer considerably better fidelity than the originals. Other labels followed suit, and the category of 'version' recordings boomed. Most of these have been based on Hindi-Urdu film songs, but some labels have specialised in offering regional-language versions of non-Hindi songs (such as Sargam's version series of past Marathi hits[16]). While GramCo belatedly began reissuing some of its back catalogue, its cassettes, as noted above, remain considerably more expensive than those of other labels, including versions.

Critics and aficionados often complain that the version singers are inferior to their models. Nevertheless, the wide sales of these recordings suggest that the public, when given an alternative, is not as exclusively fixated on Lata and Kishore as film producers have been. The vogue of versions also illustrate how cassettes can contribute to the decentralisation of the music industry even where ownership of the repertoire remains monopolised.

The boom of parody songs in regional languages is another development intrinsically tied to cassettes and the diversification of music industry ownership. Of course, Bombay film music producers had often borrowed melodies from regional folk music and given them new or translated texts, generally in Hindi. But the advent of cassettes and the decentralisation of the music scene enabled this process to occur on an unprecedented scale, and in reverse. First of all, the new parody recordings were marketed independently of cinema, whether the borrowed hit melodies originated in film music or not. Secondly, the parody songs generally contain new texts in regional languages, rather than mainstream Hindi-Urdu; thus, they have been aimed at regional markets (Punjabi, Bengali, Marathi, etc) and in that sense serve to promote linguistic diversity rather than the hegemony of Hindi-Urdu in pop culture.

For example, the three top hit songs of 1988–9, 'Hawa hawa', 'Tirchi topi-wala' and 'Ek do tin', have all appeared in versions in various North Indian regional languages. They have also, for that matter, been relentlessly parodied and plagiarised, with new texts in Hindi, by film composers like Bappi Lahiri. Usually the regional parodies are marketed in the form of cassettes parodying several top songs. (Both for market purposes and in public conceptions, such tapes are classified separately from folk music cassettes which occasionally use borrowed film tunes.) T-Series, Venus and, above all, the TIPS labels have been the most aggressive in tapping, if not creating the lucrative market for regional-language parodies. Some current hit cassettes – both filmi and non-filmi – borrow Western tunes, such as Alisha Chinai's 'Madonna' tape, consisting of Hindi-language versions of her idol's songs, with a cover depicting Alisha dressed, appropriately, in a gaudy brassiere and no shirt. Interestingly, two of the most successful parody tapes (TIPS' 'Love me' and 'Follow me') have consisted of settings of current Indian pop tunes, including those mentioned above, with English-language texts, thereby exploiting, and again, helping create an entirely new market for Anglophone, Indian-style pop music. Although English is not a 'regional' Indian language, the vogue of such songs is another illustration of the ability of the cassette industry to target diverse, specialised markets – in this case, a certain sector of educated, middle-class Indian pop music fans.

The ideological and aesthetic implications of the vogue for regional-language parody songs are too complex and contradictory to be treated in depth in this article. As Yampolsky (1989) has noted in reference to Indonesian inter-language parodies, such songs could be seen as revitalising and empowering regional cultures, since hit songs are now available in various languages aside from the dominant one (Bhasa-Indonesia in Indonesia, Hindi-Urdu in North India). However, as Yampolsky also observes, it may be more accurate to regard such songs as extending a hegemonic mainstream *style* into regional markets. In that sense, it could be argued that such regional parodies are better seen as reinforcing the dominant class/region/corporate aesthetic rather than constituting commercialisations of the practice of tune-borrowing in regional 'little traditions'.

Regional folk-pop musics

While pop *ghazals*, *bhajans* and version songs have come to form new and important components of the Indian popular music scene, it is the commercial recordings of regional folk musics that constitute the most significant development within the music industry. Regional folk musics, or stylised versions thereof, now appear to account for around 40 to 50 per cent of all cassette sales in North India.[17] Moreover, it is the emergence of regional commercial musics which most clearly illustrates and derives from the decentralisation and democratisation of the music industry at the expense of Hindi-Urdu, corporate-produced film music.

As with the other genres discussed above, commercial recordings of non-filmi regional folk-pop musics had been extant for several decades before the cassette boom, but they were limited in quantity and variety, and their audience was largely restricted to urban middle-class consumers who could afford record-players. Mostly they consisted of short, stylised settings of lively folk songs, or new songs in folk style, accompanied by instrumental ensembles playing pre-composed interludes between verses. With the advent of cassettes, modernised versions of such songs continue to sell, but now compete with an unprecedented variety of other genres. Styles popular primarily among the lower classes, previously largely ignored by the record industry, are now represented on cheap cassettes. Further, unrestricted by the time limits of 78 or 45 rpm records, cassettes now offer a wide diversity of genres which require longer time to present, and are in many cases more representative folk music genres than the short songs formerly marketed on records. Thus, for example, western Uttar Pradesh residents can purchase dozens of cassettes of their cherished *kathās*, or narrative song-stories (especially '*Alha*' and '*Dhola*'), representing different episodes sung by different performers. Meanwhile, Rajasthani and Haryanvi listeners can choose from a few hundred cassettes of old and new *kathās* in their own dialects. Extended, sequential genres like Bhojpuri *birhā* are also widely marketed, along with shorter song forms like the Braj-bhasha *rasiya*, which had previously been represented by fewer than a dozen records.

Even more dramatic is the vogue of commercial cassettes in regional languages which had been essentially ignored by the record and film industries. For instance, Garhwal, Haryana and the Braj region, all within 150 miles of Delhi, have come to constitute lively markets for cassettes in their own languages, with several producers, large and small, issuing new releases each month. Most of these tapes consist of either traditional folk songs, or more often, new compositions in more or less traditional style.

Needless to say, while film music sought to homogenise its audience's aesthetics, the cassette-based regional musics are able to celebrate regional cultures and affirm a local sense of community. Unlike film songs dealing exclusively with amorphous sentimental love, regional song texts abound with references to local customs, lore, mores and even contemporary socio-political events or issues.

Much of the new cassette-based regional music resists easy classification into 'folk' or 'popular' categories. Many cassettes consist of traditional genres recorded in straightforward traditional style. Others are 'modernised' or 'improved' (as producers put it) by the addition of untraditional instrumental accompaniments. Once marketed, even traditional songs can sometimes be 'discovered' and enjoy the ephemeral mass popularity of pop hits; for instance, the Punjabi nonsense song 'Tutuk Tutuk', as recorded by the UK-based Malkit Singh, sold over 500,000 copies.[18]

Such sales, however, are highly unusual for regional folk music, and the indefinite continuance of the commercial market for folk music is uncertain. Several producers of regional folk cassettes told me that the majority of their customers were of the older generations, who were less interested in film music than the young. To the extent that such is indeed the case, the present abundance of folk music cassettes may constitute a unique and relatively brief moment in recording history.

Cassettes, style and film music aesthetics

Thus far, this article has emphasised the ways in which the cassette-based music industry differs from the film music industry in offering a much greater diversity of musics and styles, which more faithfully represent the variety of North Indian genres and aesthetics. Nevertheless, the effects of cassette technology are complex and contradictory, and in some respects can be seen to reinforce, rather than negate, tendencies manifest within the earlier, corporate-dominated Indian music industry. Cassettes, after all, are commercial commodities whose production is subject, in varying degrees, to the same constraints and incentives of capitalist enterprises in general, such as goals of maximisation of profit and economies of scale. Accordingly, if film music can be accused of distorting consumers' aesthetics by superimposing values deriving from the inherent structure of the music industry, cassette-based musics can be seen to perpetuate some of the same tendencies.

An initial constraint is that cassette producers, whether small or large, will only market those genres which prove profitable. Thus, for example, because a market must have a certain minimum size, within a given region it may be only certain genres, or certain styles of a given genre that are marketed on cassette. A case in point is the commercial music scene in the Braj area, around Mathura. Most cassettes here consist of *rasiya*, the single most popular folk music genre. *Rasiya* itself is rendered in a variety of styles, including village women singing informally in the evening, a dozen or more devotees singing responsorially in a temple, a *dangal* ('competition') between two professional groups, a chorus singing in the *Hathrasi* style influenced by *nautanki* theatre, or a solo professional accompanied by drum and harmonium. *Rasiya* commercial cassettes, with a very few exceptions, present only the latter kind of format. Further, while many traditional *rasiyas* are devotional portrayals of Krishna and Radha, the vast majority of *rasiya* cassettes are secular, spicy (*masāledar*) erotica. Some of the best singers continue to go unrecorded because they sing in styles other than that favoured by cassette companies. Producers also tend to avoid vocalists who perform in peripheral, lesser dialects (e.g. Mevati) with smaller potential markets. Thus, while cassettes are able to offer incomparably‧ greater regional and stylistic variety than did film music, there are limits to the degree of diversity they represent.

A particularly conspicuous characteristic of Indian cassette-based popular musics is the tendency to eliminate improvisation. This trend is especially apparent in *ghazal*, whose traditional light-classical style was based on *bol banāo*, or improvised textual-melodic interpretation. While several cassettes of Mehdi Hasan, Ghulam Ali and others do feature some improvisation, the majority, like earlier film *ghazals*, consist of purely pre-composed renditions whose appeal lies in the fixed tune, rather than in the singer's skill at improvisation. Similar trends can be observed in other commercialised North Indian genres, suggesting that the more a genre becomes dependent on the mass media, the less improvisation will be tolerated.[19]

Similarly, cassettes have tended to perpetuate the aforementioned practice of 'improving' or 'decorating' songs with instrumental interludes and accompaniments (frequently including chordal instruments). Of course, many cassettes employ purely traditional instrumentation, in cases where producers think their more traditional-minded listeners would disapprove, or when they are disinclined or unable to pay for extra musicians, arrangers and rehearsal time. But the trend toward non-traditional instrumental accompaniments, already established in film music and radio broadcasts of folk music, is clearly being spread by cassettes.

Another tendency of Indian popular musics which is being reinforced by cassettes is the promotion of short songs. While as mentioned above, lengthy narrative song genres are widely marketed on cassette, other more flexible genres (e.g. *qawwāli*, *rasiya*, *bhangra*, *ghazal* and *bhajan*) tend to be compressed into four- to six-minute formats. One producer of *qawwāli* cassettes told me that in his experience, this format was the first thing customers looked for in a cassette. Whether deriving from the influence of record format, or from the desire to acquire several tunes in a single purchase (the favourites of which can always be replayed), the perpetuation of this custom on cassettes reinforces the 'sound bite' aesthetic in popular musics and extends it to genres previously uninfluenced by the mass media.

While reinforcing a degree of stylistic and formal standardisation, cassettes have provided a remarkable stimulus for the creation of new texts and, in some cases, melodies. Many cassette companies, from T-Series to several smaller producers interviewed, insist that their performers, regardless of genre, sing primarily new material, that is, material with new lyrics. In the case of regional folk genres like *rasiya*, a considerable amount of the familiar traditional repertoire may have been exhausted in the first years of the cassette boom, such that the producers' demand for new material keeps several lyricists occupied (while generating much verse that aficionados find forgettable). Insofar as novelty is a virtue in itself, this aspect of cassette impact should not be regarded as unwelcome.

Similarly, certain genres appear to have acquired markedly greater melodic variety in recent decades, although it is difficult to attribute this development solely to the cassette boom, or, for that matter, to any other specific factor. Modern renditions of Rajasthani *kathā*s and the Braj-bhasha *Dhola* are both said to be considerably more sophisticated and varied in their styles and melodic content than a generation ago.[20] While professionalism and mass media influence in general appear to have contributed to this development, the cassette-based commercialisation of these genres may well have accelerated the process. Another factor related to this phenomenon has been the aforementioned borrowing of film tunes, which, of course, had also become a common practice in North Indian folk music well before the advent of cassettes. Cassettes have not only served as vehicles for such parody tunes, but may have intensified the practice by increasing demand for new material.

In discussing how cassette technology may reinforce, rather than oppose certain features of film music and other related tendencies within the Indian music industry, we may also reiterate that cassettes are vehicles not only for the spread of filmi aesthetics and borrowed film tunes, but also of film music itself. Film music still accounts for at least one third, and possibly as much as sixty per cent of cassette sales. Even in stores in provincial towns, roughly half the shelf space is often devoted to film music. While cassette technology has enabled other competing genres to flourish, some of the same virtues which enabled this development to occur – low cost, portability, etc. – have also promoted the increase of film music sales, especially among the lower-middle classes and rural dwellers. Thus, while film music's share of cassette sales as a whole has dropped significantly, film music sales themselves do not appear to have declined, as the entire market for recorded music has expanded so dramatically. In this sense, the impact of cassettes has been contradictory.

Cassettes and live performance

A further factor to be considered in evaluating the impact of cassette technology on musical life in North India is the influence cassettes have had on live performance and the general vitality of traditional music genres. It has been a commonplace observation that the mass media often flourish at the expense of live performance, and that they have contributed significantly to the decline of many traditional musics worldwide, if not to the decrease of communal social life in general. In North India, several scholars have attributed the well-documented decline of various folk music genres to the influence of the mass media, and particularly cinema (e.g. Tewari 1974, p. 18). Given the remarkable spread of the cassette industry, it would be logical to suspect that, sooner or later, it may have a similarly detrimental impact on live performance traditions.

At this point, however, it is difficult to verify such trends with certainty, due to the fact that they tend to be overdetermined by a wide variety of social factors, and also due to the relative novelty of cassettes and the fact that significant changes in performance traditions generally take more than a decade to become apparent. Evidence does suggest, however, that in certain cases, cassettes have exacerbated the media's tendency to discourage live performance. One particularly common example is the aforementioned widespread practice of housewives playing cassettes of ritual *vrats* (prayers) or *kathās* rather than personally chanting them or hiring a *pandit* to do so. Rajasthani folklorist Komal Kothari has also suggested to me that the professional standards of proliferating cassettes may intimidate lesser skilled amateurs from taking part in collective genres where participation was traditionally valued over vocal expertise (or even basic competence). In the realm of professional performance, several of my informants, including a few village former concert-goers, opined that the spread of cassettes constituted a disincentive to attend live performances (of genres like *rasiya* or Bengali *adhunik gān*), and that the frequency of such programmes was diminishing accordingly. Similarly, one *Dhola* singer told me that he had resisted offers to record out of fear that his present audiences would subsequently simply listen to his tapes rather than book him for a programme.

However, in the case of many genres, both participatory and professional, there is little evidence that the cassette vogue, or the mass media in general have decreased live performance. I have noticed that some housewives may play a cassette at a household ritual in order to sing along with it, rather than to replace their own singing. Similarly, my urban Punjabi acquaintances insisted that despite the sales of wedding-song cassettes, and their occasional usage at marriages, there was little tendency for such tapes to replace live singing by women at weddings. As for professional genres, several performers and producers insisted to me that renown via cassettes boosts rather than lessens a performer's fees and concert bookings, and, when told of the aforementioned *Dhola* singer's fears, they invariably scoffed at his 'backward' attitude. Contemporary scholars have also noted that some genres which are now widely marketed on cassette, such as Rajasthani *kathā* and Bhojpuri *birhā*, today appear to be performed live more than ever before within memory.[21] Accordingly, it is clear that aside from studio accompanists, very few, if any, performers rely on recording fees for more than a small fraction of their livelihood; rather, cassettes are seen as useful for publicity, and for the flat payment received, which is often no more than the standard fee for a live programme.

Conclusions

Popular music has been well described as a site of negotiation, where diverse and often contradictory social ideologies and aesthetics are mediated, dramatised and contested (e.g. Middleton 1985). The mass media themselves, including cassettes in North India, can be seen to embody this process. On the one hand, cassettes have perpetuated, if not exacerbated, many features of corporate music industries in general, and of the film-dominated Indian music industry in particular; such tendencies include the discouragement of improvisation, the replacement of live performance by passive listening, and various other features associated with the commercialisation of genres which were previously relatively free of market and media influence.

On the other hand, cassettes have decentralised and diversified the music industry, challenging the alienating hegemony of the escapist, corporate-controlled film music industry. By offering a greater variety of products and drawing extensively from the rich 'little traditions' of regional musics, cassettes are able to affirm a sense of local community and revitalise traditions, rather than obliterating them with musics superimposed by a mass-market, lowest common denominator pop music.

At the same time, the affirmation of aesthetic and ideological diversity is not without its costs. While negating some of the alienation promoted by a hegemonic culture industry, a decentralising music technology naturally may promote certain 'community values' which are controversial, if not reactionary or even destructive. Hence, in India one finds tapes of Rajasthani *kathās* glorifying *sati* (widow-burning), as well as all manner of political campaign songs and speeches, from Punjabi paeans to Beant Singh (an assassin of Indira Gandhi), to Hindu chauvinist calls for the expulsion or murder of Muslims. Further, one might question whether even the innocent celebration of regional and sectarian difference is desirable when India is being wracked by the most vicious ethnic and religious violence. For an optimist faithful in the ability of individuals and groups to work out their differences rather than having heavy-handed ideologies imposed on them, a decentralised, if provocative music industry should seem preferable to one consisting of a tiny corporate elite mass-producing bubble-gum music for a captive audience. Unfortunately, in the context of Indian capitalism, it is difficult to imagine any alternatives to these two scenarios.

Acknowledgements

Research for this article was conducted in 1989–90 under a grant from the American Insitute of Indian Studies. I am indebted to the informants cited above, and many others too numerous to mention here. Special thanks are also due to Shubha Chaudhuri and the staff at the Archive and Research Centre for Ethnomusicology in New Delhi.

204   *Peter Manuel*

Endnotes

1 Music critic and record archivist V.A.K. Ranga Rao, interviewed in 1989.

2 Thus, while Lata may have recorded in over a dozen languages, she cannot really be argued to have sung in more than one style.

3 Anil Chopra, editor of *Playback and Fast Forward* (a music industry trade journal), interviewed in March 1990.

4 See, e.g., 'Rural consumerism', *India Today*, 15 March 1990.

5 See Vijay Lazarus, interviewed in *Playback*, June 1986, p. 30.

6 *Ibid.*, p. 30.

7 Anil Chopra, interviewed in March 1990, estimates the number of cassette companies at 500. A 1987 survey (cited in *Playback*, July 1987, p. 27) listed 256 producers. I myself enumerated about 200 in selected regions of North India. Note that the record industry distinction between 'majors', who own production and distribution as well as recording facilities, and 'indies', who generally only record, is not meaningful in reference to most cassette producers.

8 India, indeed, is now the world's second largest manufacturer of blank tapes.

9 Biswanath Chatterjee, interviewed by Anil Chopra in *Playback*, July 1986, pp. 36–7.

10 See, e.g., Dubashi 1986, and Vijay Lazarus, interviewed in *Playback*, June 1986, pp. 30–1.

11 For further discussion of the *ghazal* in Indian popular music, see Manuel 1988a, p. 167, 1988–9.

12 See, e.g., Vijay Lazarus, interviewed in *Playback*, June 1986, p, 30,

13 GramCo manager Sanjeev Kohli, interviewed by Anil Chopra in *Playback*, August 1986, p. 31.

14 This aspect of devotional music cassettes, initially pointed out to me by Scott Marcus, was corroborated by cassette producers in India.

15 See articles by music journalist and archivist V.A.K. Ranga Rao (1986) for a sketch of the history of version recordings in Indian film music.

16 See 'Marathi versions booming', in *Playback*, January–March 1990, p. 11.

17 Anil Chopra, interviewed in March 1990, estimates 50 per cent. Accurate figures are unavailable due to piracy, the unreliability of sales reports from the major companies, and the absence of data from the smaller ones.

18 'HMV fights back', in *Playback*, November–December 1989, p. 7. Folk songs in the West, like 'La Bamba', can also acquire 'hit' status.

19 Contrast, for example, the improvised guitar solos on many 1960s acid-rock records, with the carefully-crafted, over-dubbed, pre-composed solos of today's heavy metal guitarists.

20 Personal communications with Komal Kothari and Susan Wadley, respectively.

21 Personal communications with Komal Kothari and Scott Marcus, respectively.

References

Arnold, A. 1988. 'Popular film song in India: a case of mass-market musical eclecticism', *Popular Music*, 7/2, pp. 177–88

Chandravarkar, B. 1987. 'Tradition of music in Indian cinema', *Cinema in India* (March), pp. 8–11

Dubashi, J. 1986. 'Cassette piracy: high stakes', *India Today*, 31 March

Lalitha, S. 1988. 'The business of Bhajans', *The Times of India*, Oct. 1: II, p. 1

Manuel, P. 1988a. 'Popular music in India: 1901–86', *Popular Music*, 7/2, pp. 157–76

1988b. *Popular Musics of the Non-Western World: An Introductory Survey* (New York)

1988–9. 'A historical survey of the Urdu ghazal-song in India', *Asian Music* (Fall/Winter)

Middleton, R. 1985. 'Popular music, class conflict, and the music-historical field', in *Popular Music Perspectives*, 2, ed. D. Horn (Gothenburg and Exeter)

Ranga Roa, V.A.K. 1986. 'Version recordings: new controversy, old issue', *Playback and Fast Forward*, August, pp. 26–27, and September, p. 29

Tewari, L. 1974. *Folk Music of India*, Ph.D. dissertation, Wesleyan University

Upadhyay, M. 1985. 'The bhajan samrat' (interview with Purshottam Das), *Playback and Fast Forward*, July, p. 15

Yampolsky, P. 1989. 'Hati Yang Luka, an Indonesian Hit', *Indonesia*, 47, pp. 1–18

[15]

RECYCLING INDIAN FILM-SONGS:
POPULAR MUSIC AS A SOURCE OF MELODIES FOR
NORTH INDIAN FOLK MUSICIANS
by
Scott Marcus

In a large number of the folk music traditions across northern India, there is no melodic composition. Musicians who perform the music do not make up new melodies; similarly, composers who create new songs do not compose new melodies. In short, in many genres of North Indian folk music, no one is creating new melodies. That is not to say there there are no new songs. In fact, for many of these same genres, especially entertainment genres, there is a constant need for new songs. A professional singer must begin the new year with a least six to eight new songs so that he can stand in front of last year's audiences with new material.

If a music culture has ruled out new melodies, then what form do all the new songs take? As it is, they are all new texts, set to pre-existing melodies. This approach is often called parody, an English term known to a small but significant number of Indians. In Hindi, in addition to the occasional use of the term "parody," people refer to the phenomenon using the words *tarz* or *dhun* for melody, and *bol* for words, e.g., *usī tarz ko lekar ham durse bol lagāte hain* -- "Using this melody, we set new words to it." In these musics, the composing of new texts is done by local poets. These local poets are considered to be the *gurū*s or *ustad*s of the singers who perform their songs. The singers are their "disciples" (*celā*s).

Why would folk cultures value pre-existing melodies to the extent that they disallow (or feel no need for) new compositions? The answer to this question is a complex one, requiring us to consider a wide range of religious, philosophical, and cultural data, which we can only but mention here. Indian culture has continually emphasized the importance of orality. Knowledge and truth exist most profoundly in oral/aural rather than written realms. (The Vedas, for example, existed for centuries in oral rather than written form. Music education is also based on oral rather than written communication.) Sound and its sub-branch, music, have always been understood to have special creative, generative, and associative power. (Note the goddess Saraswatī, and the concepts *nāda brahma, mantra, rasa,* and *bhāva.*)

In the realm of Indian folk music, individual melodies have often had specific roles and identities. In the Gangetic plain area, for example, there is a special melody associated with singing the *Rāmāyaṇa* (called *Rāmdhun*). There are special women's melodies for specific life-cycle rituals, for example, for childbirth (*sohar*). Still other tunes are reserved for specific seasons (e.g., *kajalī* for the rainy season, *holī* for the time of Holī, *caitī* for the month of *cait*). Many of the regional epic traditions have their own particular melodies, so that a given epic might be minimally defined as a specific story with its own specific melody (*Ālhā, Canainī, Ḍholā*, etc). Still other melodies are associated with specific castes: in the Banaras region, cowherders, washermen (*dhobīs*), and boatmen all have their own melodies (*birahā* and *kharī birahā, dhobī gīt*, and *mallāh gīt*, respectively). In Banaras, even the act of "calling up to a friend from outside his house" has its own specific (albeit rudimentary) melody.

Thus, in traditional society, when walking up to a music event, you would know the exact nature of the event as soon as you heard the specific lilt of the melodic line. Melody would identify the genre; the words would provide additional detail. Traditional melodies, then, each had a socio-cultural significance which made them major markers within the society. Melodies played important roles by both reflecting *and* generating major aspects of society. Melodies helped reflect and reinforce the caste system, the calendric cycle, life-cycle rituals, gender roles, and communal and regional identity.

We know that this phenomenon of "no melodic composition" is a long-standing tradition. In 1886, for example, George Grierson, an official in the British civil service and an avid researcher of North Indian folk music culture, wrote, "In the country districts, I have never heard of a new tune being invented. There seems to be a certain stock of melodies ready made, to which the words of every new song must be fitted" (in Marcus 1989:98-99).

The introduction of the motion picture industry, and especially films with sound in 1931 (Manuel 1988:176) was to have major consequences in the world of North Indian folk music. For the first time, it seems, Indian folk musicians were confronted with an unending source of new melodies. Because of the nature and tremendous popularity of the new film medium, and also of its supporting sister medium, the radio, film songs entered the intimate

Symposium. Marcus: *Popular Music in North Indian Folk Music 103*

worlds of North Indian folk musicians. It was as if the world's most prolific composer had just moved in next door.

For folk musicians used to parodying specific traditional melodies, the appearance of this unending stock of new melodies presented contradictory emotions and reactions. From one perspective, the new melodies clearly should not be used, for they were devoid of the traditional associations which were such an important part of traditional melodies. From another viewpoint, many of the new melodies were catchy, refreshing, and occasionally even beautiful. Moreover, they were exceedingly popular. Many were major hits among the urban population, enjoying "top-40s"-type popularity. Folk musicians could partake of this popularity by parodying the film melodies in their performances. Singers active in the 1940s and '50s tell of approaching their poets and requesting that specific film melodies be incorporated into both new and old songs.

Film melodies were generally incorporated in one of two ways. In some genres (such as *nauṭaṅkī*, Hindu *bhajans, kajalī,* and Muslim *n'at* and *qawwali*), entire songs were often set to a single film melody.[1] Alternately, a given film melody could be used as a temporary mid-song substitution, as in the Banaras-based Bhojpuri genre called *birahā* (discussed in greater depth in Marcus 1989). *Birahā* is a narrative genre. A given performance typically consists of 10 to 15 songs and may last through the night. Individual songs have several dozen text lines and commonly take up to 45 minutes to perform. Traditionally, *birahā* was sung to a single melody. In the 1940s, singers and poets introduced a new feature. After singing a substantial portion of a given song in the traditional tune, a singer would announce a change in the melody: "OK, friends, here we're changing the tune." The singer would then present three or four lines using a film melody, after which he would return to the traditional *birahā* tune. Thus, in a given song, the singer might incorporate one or two film melodies. At the same time, *birahā* singers started incorporating passages of other traditional, but non-*birahā* melodies in their songs. They would occasionally include melodies associated with specific castes (other than their own), or perhaps the melody used in a local epic genre.

The fact that the film melodies were devoid of traditional associations *was* controversial for some, who regarded their usage as too marked a break from tradition, and as simply inappropriate. But while the film songs were usually devoid of traditional associations, they were not devoid of associations altogether. Quite to the contrary, they came with a brand new set of associations, for they were trendy, urban, and modern, and as such, they offered associations with modernity, and with contemporary popular culture.

In the early years when film melodies were first used in *biraha*, a number of other changes were occurring in the genre itself. These changes had a direct bearing on the incorporation of film melodies. Initially, *biraha* was performed by two to three singers, who played metallic idiophones called *kartal*. The 1940s and '50s witnessed a growth of the traditional performance ensemble to include, first, a drummer (on *dholak*), and then after some time, a harmonium player. The growth of the ensemble brought a need for a new sense of professionalism. Prior to this point, musicians were paid only in the form of tips from the audience. Little money ever changed hands. Now, to assure that the larger five-member ensemble (singers, drummer, and harmonium player) showed up for an engagement, pre-established fees became necessary. The genre moved from the realm of avocation to vocation.

As mentioned above, the non-professional *birahā* ensemble had performed using the main *birahā* melody as the sole or, at least, predominant melody. As such, performing was not a demanding task from a melodic point of view. Now, with an ensemble of professional performers, it was possible to require the musicians to learn a succession of new tunes. Folk tunes which these musicians had heard all their lives were obviously not hard to incorporate. However, the task of keeping up with the latest film tunes was somewhat more demanding -- although not inappropriate (or beyond the skills) of what were now professional musicians. The addition of the harmonium was an important facilitator, keeping the singers "on track" in new and sometimes challenging melodies. Thus, changes in the nature and makeup of the performing ensemble served to facilitate the incorporation of film tunes.

As the new professional ensemble emerged, *birahā* musicians came to seek a greater urban presence for their art form. They sought and increasingly gained performance opportunities in the main urban centers, especially in the city of Banaras. Once exclusively based in rural areas, *birahā* became an urban genre as well. Significantly, the urban audience was substantially more preoccupied

Symposium. Marcus: *Popular Music in North Indian Folk Music 105*

with film music than were village audiences. Thus, the incorporation of film meldies made good marketing sense.

With this new mix of elements (a new type of ensemble, a new professionalism, and a new type of urban, trendy, and fashion-conscious audience), film tunes became a highly desirable feature. Speaking of their performances in the 1950s, a few prominent *birahā* singers recalled with pride that their songs had become "back-to-back film melodies." Four lines in this film *tarz*, the next four lines in another film *tarz*, and so on. Meanwhile, traditional regional melodies were still also included, never completely fading from use.

There has been considerable experimentation in *birahā* from the 1940s and '50s to the present, with poets and singers trying to determine the ideal mix of the original *birahā* melody, other traditional folk tunes, and Bombay film melodies. After initial experimentation with extreme doses of film tunes, poets and singers alike realized that they did not want to rely exclusively on film songs. Able to appear modern, urban, and trendy by appropriating Bombay film tunes, folk musicians realized that there was more to their sense of self-identity than being modern and urban. Regional, rural, and caste affiliations were equally important. With this realization, traditional folk melodies gained a renewed importance. Thus, *birahā* musicians began to consciously manipulate a variety of melodies. A singer would parody one or two film songs, and thus assert his "modernity." Then he would turn to a traditional folk melody, preceding his use of this tune with a somewhat lengthy prologue, saying, "We come from the Bhojpuri region, a region where there is an endless supply of traditional folk tunes. Now I'd like to use a melody that our people have been singing for countless generations." This melody might be one traditionally associated with a neighboring caste, a regional epic, or it might be a women's melody. Whatever, by explicitly stating the associations of the various melodies, *biraha* musicians have been able to consciously shape the identity of their genre. In doing so, they are able both to reflect and help generate the identity of Bhojpuri culture as a whole.[2]

Birahā is primarily a narrative entertainment genre. Initially, when new melodies were introduced into it, the singers might typically announce in mid-song that the next four or so lines would be set to a new *tarz*. They would then continue the song, returning after four lines to the original melody. Melodic interest was increased, but there was no break in the narrative process. Then, in the interests of entertainment, singers started experimenting with a new idea. After announcing a change in melody, they would sing a small portion of the borrowed melody's original text. This was a complete digression in terms of the story that was being told, but it proved to be an entertaining diversion. In time it became the norm that singers would stop their story midstream, announce a change in the melody, sing a portion of the new melody's original text, and then finally return to the story they were singing by presenting the new tune with story-related text.

The following examples, excerpts from performances recorded in Banaras in 1983, illustrate this process. Here we see singers introduce a film song, a *qawwāli*, and a women's wheat grinding song into their *birahā* songs. In the first example, Amarnath Yadav begins a song of prayer and entreaty (a *bandanā*) to Lord Shiva by saying, "A devotee requests fromhis god . . . " Then, interrupting his own sentence, he continues, "These days, there is a really popular film in town; the name of the film is *Nadiyā ke Pār*. It is from this film that the melody *(tarz)* has been taken." He then sings one-and-a-half lines of this film song with vocal and instrumental accompaniment by his ensemble members. Again stopping mid-line, he says, "So this is the *tarz*; now its parody. Yes, a devotee is requesting . . . [now singing] 'O Shiva, when will you ask about your devotee.' " The song continues with entreaties to Lord Shiva not to forget his devotees.

Example 1: excerpt of a Shiv *badanā* performed by Amarnath Yadav. Text in lower case letters is spoken: text in upper case letters is sung.[3]

> bhakt apne bhagawan se prārthanā kah rahā hai . . . Ā
> j-kal, film baṛā jor-shor men calal ho; film kā nām bā
> 'Nadiyā ke Pār.' Wahī film se i tarz lehal gayal ho.
>
> KAUNE DISHĀ MEN LEKE CALA RE BATOHIYĀ,
> ṬHAHARA ṬHAHAR, YE SOHANĪ-SĪ DAGAR . . .
>
> Ye to rahā tarz, ab ekar parodī. Hān, bhakt kah rahā
> hai:
>
> BHAGATAN KE, BHOLĀ, HAB LEBA HO KHABARIYĀ

Symposium. Marcus: *Popular Music in North Indian Folk Music 107*

In the second example, Mangal Yadav interrupts a song about the birth of Lord Krishna, saying "Now you'll hear this *tarz* . . . [then singing] 'Fulfill my wishes, O Muhammad, I will not leave your door empty handed.' " This is the refrain from a well-known *qawwāli* by the Sabri Brothers. After singing this line a number of times with his ensemble, Mangal stops and says, "But, the words of (our) song, my friends, . . . [then singing] 'O Krishna, all the gods came running to see your sweet beauty. ' "

Example 2: excerpt of the song "Shiv se Kṛṣṇa Darshan" by Mangal Yadav.

Lekin, tarz milegī:

BHAR DO JHOLĪ MERĪ, YĀ MOHAMMAD, TERE DAR SE NA JAŪṄGĀ KHĀLĪ [a Sabri Brothers *qawwali*]

Lekin gānī kā bol, premiyon:

SHAYĀM TERĪ KSHAṬĀ MĀDHURĪ KĀ, KARNE DARSHAN SABHĪ DEV DĀYE

In the third example, hira Lal Yadav is performing a song based on a story from a local epic, when he stops and says, "But here the *tarz* changes. It's that *tarz*: when our mothers and sisters used to get up early in the morning to grind the wheat, what would they sing?" He then sings with his ensemble, "O my betrothed, it's time for our wedding: instead you've gone off to live in a distant city." After repeating this line a few times, Hira Lal says, "This is the *tarz*, " and returning to his original storyline, he sings, "Phulawa dressed as an ascetic, and left the city of Mahoba . . . "

Example 3: excerpt of "Amarjīt haraṇ" performed by Hira Lal Yadav.

Lekin tarz badal gayal. U tarz ho, kī bhor men, mātā-bahan log, jab jātā pisat rahalin pahale, to gāweñ kā?

HARE, GAUNĀ KARĀWLA E HARĪ-JĪ, APNE VIDESH MEN GAYALA HO CHĀE

Yehī tarz bai.

BANALĪ JOGINIYĀ HO PHULAWĀ, MAHOBĀ
NAGARIYĀ GAYALĪ HO CHŪṬ

To conclude, we might ask again what is happening with the introduction of mass-media-produced film melodies into folk traditions. The use of these melodies is clearly a break with the past, as is widely recognized by folk musicians themselves. Indeed, musicians tell of opposition to the use of film melodies from within their own ranks immediately after the practice began in the 1940s. New opposition occurred when singers started including portions of the borrowed melodies' original texts. But I would argue that, by incorporating Bombay film melodies into their performances, *biraha* musicians succeeded in an act of empowerment, rather than an act of subjugation. The singers themselves become modern and up-to-date. They are not rural peasants singing quaint rustic songs. They are in sync with the latest trends and fashions. At the same time, they are able to stress their rural and regional roots by the self-conscious use of traditional folk melodies.

Far from simply "covering" Bombay film songs, *biraha* singers have continued to perform their own poets' lyrics -- lyrics that reflect the concerns and aspirations of present day Banaras-region folk. *Biraha* is performed by local musicians, and is produced and staged by local, neighborhood-based groups. These groups commonly carry on door-to-door solicitation of funds in the days prior to a performance. Two rupees are collected from individual donors, with shopkeepers contributing five, eleven rupees or more. The performances are thus important neighborhood events and sources of neighborhood pride. Using local musicians, local poets, local organizers, and local contributions, these events serve to promote local community ties and roots. In the end, Bombay film melodies serve as vehicles for the affirmation of regional identity. Musicians help mold the region's self-image as a dynamic North Indian subculture that is both modern and yet intimately linked to its traditional and ancestral roots.

University of California, Santa Barbara

Symposium. Marcus: *Popular Music in North Indian Folk Music 109*

Notes

[1]Henry (1991:236-239) gives an insightful discussion of this phenomenon with respect to *nirgun bhajans* and even women's ritual music. See also Slawek (1986) discussed in Henry (ibid.). Booth writes that Indian brass bands use Indian film music "almost exclusively" in their performances (1991:65; see also Booth 1990). In the case of these bands, however, there is no attempt to create new songs by adding new texts to the film melodies. Rather, the bands' goal is to "cover" the pre-existing songs.

[2] In his study of a Newar neighborhood in Nepal, Grandin recognizes similar forces at work. People's sense of identity is built upon an understanding of <u>self</u> and of the <u>other</u>. "Both these aspects of identity-buliding . . . are articulated in the music practice of the neighborhood, and both have helped shape . . . the pattern in which media-related resources have been taken up by local people" (Grandir 1989:209). In thank Mark Slobin for pointing out this work to me.

[3] Research in India during 1983-84 was funded by a Fulbright-Hays research grant. Copies of all recordings made in India are housed at the Archives and Research Center for Ethnomusicology in New Delh and at the UCLA Ethnomusicology Archive. The three excerpts cited in this article are from songs catalogued as MAR COLL 114, MAI COLL 88, and MAR COLL 122, respectively.

110   Asian Music, Fall/Winter 1992/1993

References   Cited

Booth, Gregory
   1990   "Brass Bands: Tradition, Change, and the Mass
                   Media in Indian Wedding Music." *Ethnomusicology*
                   34 (2):245-262.

   1991   "Disco *Laggī*:   Modern Repertoire and Traditional
                   Performance Practice in North Indian Popular
                   Music." *Asian Music* 23(1):61-83

Grandin, Ingemar
   1989   *Music and Media in Local Life: Music Practice in a
                   Newar Neighbourhood in Nepal.* Linkoping, Sweden:
                   Linkoping University.

Henry, Edward O.
   1991   "*Jogī*s and *Nirgun Bhajan*s in Bhojpuri-Speaking
                   India: Intra-Genre Heterogeneity, Adaptation, and
                   Functional Shift." *Ethnomusicology* 35(2):221-242.

Manuel, Peter
   1988   *Popular Musics of the Non-Western World: An
                   Introductory Survey.* New York: Oxford University
                   Press.

Marcus, Scott
   1989   The Rise of a Folk Music Genre, *Biraha.* In *Culture
                   and Power in Banaras,* ed. Sandra Freitag. Berkeley:
                   University of California Press, pp. 93-113.

[16]

CHARISMA'S REALM: FANDOM IN JAPAN[1]

Christine Yano
Harvard University

Most studies of Japanese social organization focus upon structural elements of duty and obligation. This study of Japanese fan clubs uses the concept of charisma to analyze the voluntary bonds that connect individuals to one another. The concept of charisma recognizes individual choice, transcendental affect, and the role of the exceptional. Moreover, this study examines charisma within the context of popular music. Charisma here becomes not a mystical enigma, but a manipulable tool of big industry and fan alike. (Japan, consumption, popular culture, charisma)

Weber (1968:xviii) defines charisma as "a certain quality of an individual personality by virtue of which he is set apart from ordinary men and treated as endowed with supernatural, superhuman, or at least specifically exceptional qualities." Charisma, however, only exists within a particular set of relationships between a leader and those for whom that leader's magnetism finds resonance. One cannot, therefore, speak of charisma without referring to an intrinsically social relationship founded upon ties of transcendent appeal. Most studies of charisma focus on religious movements and political leadership. This article, however, explores the relationship between charismatic performer and audience, which is cultivated on stage and screen and ritualized in fan clubs. The ways in which an ordinary listener becomes an ardent fan strikes at the core of charisma-based human interaction and the formation of resultant social groups.

This essay explores that core in the context of fan clubs for popular singers of *enka*, a sentimental musical genre in Japan that appeals primarily to older adults. As a genre which reputedly sings of and from "the heart/soul of the Japanese," enka not only expresses what are considered traditional values, but also exemplifies them in its patterning of fandom. The organization of fandom by and around commercial industries in Japan does not lessen the emotional grip among members or invalidate its community of ardent fans. The charisma of a popular singer may (or may not) be individually derived, but its maintenance by a profit-seeking music industry forms the basis of fandom in Japan. The questions addressed here are: 1) What is the patterning of fandom in Japan? 2) How is the charisma-based relationship between performer and audience cultivated by the music industry? and 3) What is the nature of the community created by fan clubs?

Most studies of Japanese social organization focus on structural elements of duty and obligation. This study of fan clubs uses the concept of charisma to analyze the voluntary bonds that connect individuals to one another. The concept of charisma recognizes individual choice, transcendental affect, and the role of the exceptional. These elements have been long neglected within anthropological studies of Japan. Moreover, this study examines charisma within the context of popular music (clearly charisma for profit); that is, charisma which is industrially produced, culturally sanctioned, and economically deployed. Charisma here becomes not a mystical enigma, but a manipulable tool of big industry and fan alike.

THE CULTURAL PATTERNING OF FANDOM IN JAPAN

Fandom in the United States is often denigrated as social pathology, as "a psychological symptom of a presumed social dysfunction" (Jenson 1992:10). Fans are negatively viewed as passive victims of manipulation who have easily fallen prey to the seductive powers of mass media. Fandom is perceived as symptomatic of a lack in people's lives, as action which rests upon filling an emotional void with a fantasized "parasocial" relationship (cf. Horton and Wohl 1956). Indeed, Weber (1968:333) describes charismatic relationships as those born "in times of psychic, physical, economic, ethical, religious, political distress." A fan is someone lacking the individuality to stand on his or her own. To be a fan is to be a follower, without independent ideas or an inner core of one's own, without control over one's actions. These all carry negative stereotypes in Western theorizing of charisma-based group relationships (Le Bon 1952; Freud 1959; Bion 1961).

However, in Japan, to be a fan is to be part of a culturally affirmed dyad of dependency (*amae*), constituted by one who seeks indulgence (*amaeru*) and complementarily one who provides that indulgence (*amayakasu*) (Lebra 1976:54-55). Whereas the most fundamental relationship of dependency may be structured upon the child (amaeru) and mother (amayakasu), here the public figure seeks the indulgence of his or her fans. In fact, the dependency works in both directions. The fans support the public figure directly through economic means; the public figure supports the fans indirectly through symbolic means. The very charisma of the public figure becomes defined by the devotion of the followers. Fans make a person into a public, charismatic figure. Likewise, fans themselves become identified as particularized followers through the object of their adulation. One only exists within the context of the other.

Not only is the position of the fan culturally affirmed in Japan, it is culturally lauded. To be a fan is to exemplify cultural values of loyalty and dedication, service to one's public superior, and empathetic support. A fan is one who embarks upon a permanent relationship of servitude. The hierarchical nature of that relationship is taken for granted and may even be part of the attraction. A fan is one eager for the opportunity to serve, because in serving rests consummation of the relationship, binding the two together.

This cultural niche for fandom in Japan may be seen in various kinds of relationships, including that of husband and wife, child and mother, master and servant, sumo wrestler and *tsukebito* (attendant). These dyads consist of a figure (often public) and an attendant whose duty is to provide total "around the body" (*mi no mawari*) care (Lebra 1984:131). The same cultural niche has also been institutionalized in the form of the *kōenkai* (support group) common to the worlds of politics, sports, and entertainment.

In fan clubs of enka singers, this kind of support translates directly into economic activity. Fan clubs organized by record companies become effective extensions of a public relations department, promoting the star singer in various ways: buying his recordings and other products, populating promotional events, attending stage and broadcast performances, requesting his latest songs on radio and television, and singing his songs to karaoke. A well-run company-based fan club does the work of not merely one promoter, but a myriad of small promoters, each an advocate within her local sphere.[2]

Whereas in the United States fans are castigated for having succumbed to the persuasions of mass media (Jenson 1992:14), in Japan the attitude toward such manipulation is different. In accordance with a cultural belief in *tsukutta mono* (things made), emotions, opinions, feelings, and desires are more easily accepted as things wrought. The molding of desire by mass media is not so different from shaping a tree by pruning. Through pruning one acquires greater harmony with one's surroundings, and thereby greater beauty. Through the purported teachings of the mass media, one presumably acquires information on the needs, wants, and pleasures of the greatest number of people, or at the least on what these should be. Adopting those needs, wants, and pleasures, then, promotes greater harmony with one's social surroundings. Acceptance of the processes of molding and manipulation is a matter of course and even part of a cultural definition of maturity. Within this system, the threshold for acceptable limits of manipulation runs relatively high. This is not to say that the threshold is limitless, nor that consumers respond uniformly to manipulation. Skov and Moeran's (1995) edited volume makes the point through various examples that Japanese consumers may well be objects of manipulation, but they are also manipulators of consumption.

Fandom in Japan may also be considered a function of surrogacy (cf. Lebra 1992). The fan becomes a private surrogate for the star, singing his or her songs, sharing vicariously in his or her fame and triumphs. Here too, however, the degree of surrogacy as well as the cultural attitude toward it differs. In the United States surrogacy is limited in scope and derided as mere (though necessary) substitution. A surrogate in the U.S. may also be derided for his or her vain attempt at matching the original, which is deemed peerless. In Japan, on the other hand, surrogacy is a function of *omoiyari* (empathy), the basis for human interaction structured on the mother-child bond. Lebra (1976:38) discusses omoiyari as "among the virtues considered indispensable for one to be really human, morally mature, and deserving of respect." One becomes a surrogate through internalizing the other, through empathy. The empathetic internalization is complete. In Japan a fan is she who publicly takes on the responsibilities and obligations of the star, upholding the star's image, anticipating the star's needs. Through the created bonds of surrogacy, a fan takes on the burdens (and glory) of stardom. Surrogacy becomes the greatest form of intimacy (cf. Kasulis 1990). Again, the various conflations (star singer with record company with fan club member) and their frankly commercial implications do not in any way threaten the integrity of the intimacy, nor the resultant sense of charismatic community. However, this is community which for the most part remains dis-embodied, never fully present. The community of enka fans constitutes itself as an affectively wrought imaginary community, shaped through individual consumption of songs and celebrity.

CASE STUDY: THE MORI SHIN'ICHI KŌENKAI

Singer Mori Shin'ichi (b. 1947) epitomizes the well-groomed, tuxedoed male enka singer. Debuting in 1966 with the song *"Onna no Tameiki"* (The Sigh of a Woman), he has since reached the top of the profession by singing women's songs; either directly from the point of view of a woman, or indirectly with songs about the most important woman in many Japanese men's lives, mother (cf. Allison 1996). He is considered a "woman's man," sensitive, serious, and vulnerable.

Analyzing Mori's popularity, ethnomusicologist Koizumi (1984:32-38) has come up with four elements: 1) Mori expresses women's feelings (*"onna no kimochi"*); 2) he sings in an older nineteenth-century narrative style called *shinnai* (type of ballad drama) which Koizumi feels present-day Japanese still appreciate; 3) his songs combine both Japanese pentatonic scale and Western blues; and 4) he is handsome, yet looks like he could be easily hurt (*hansamu de nan to naku kitsuki-yasui*). Mori also fulfills Weber's requirement that charismatic figures have "a unique and innate capacity to display highly colored emotions . . . more vivid than ordinary mortals . . . more potent than ordinary emotional life" (Lindholm 1990:26). Charismatic individuals display a "connection with . . . some very central feature of man's existence and the cosmos in which he lives. The centrality, coupled with intensity, makes it extraordinary" (Shils quoted in Dyer 1991:57). I argue that what defines Mori's charisma, following both Weber and Shils, is his perpetual suffering. More than actual suffering, it is his image as having the capacity to suffer, and the intensity with which he seems to expose that capacity, which make him a magnet for those who seek to protect him. Biographies of Mori focus on his early life of hardship and privation, and particularly on his close relationship with his mother, who committed suicide during Mori's adult life. One television program on Mori includes a taped telephone call to his mother, in which she gives him ordinary motherly advice (*Mori Shin'ichi: Kandō no Kiseki* 1991). During the program, the audience watches as Mori listens to the tape, now morbidly heart-wrenching in light of her ensuing death. Wiping the tears from his eyes, he launches into his 1971 signature song, *"Ofukuro-san"* (Mother Dear), a paean to his mother.

Mori's voice, which is unusually husky to the point of hoarseness, presents another dimension of his charismatic appeal. Japanese sound aesthetic is one which relies heavily on texture and timbre for expression. Even within this aesthetic, Mori's voice may be considered more of a liability than an asset. According to a biography of Mori, his first efforts as a singer were continually rebuffed by record companies because of his voice: "That voice is no good [*Dame da yo, ano koe wa*]" (Asahi Shimbun Nishi-bu Honsha 1992:285). But, according to his fans and critics, therein lies his strength. Mori himself says, "People continue to say I've got this terrible voice, but life is strange, isn't it? It's a good thing that I did not give up" (Asahi Shimbun Nishi-bu Honsha 1992:285). In effect, he has had to overcome the hardship of his improbably hoarse voice. A listener gets the sense that he must constantly exert greater effort than most, even to be heard. The effort itself becomes precious. As a commentator writes, "The mystery of Mori's husky voice is that it is able to impart strong emotions in Japanese people's hearts" (Asahi Shimbun Nishi-bu Honsha 1992:285). The fact that he has done so, and with such success, expressing emotions with even greater intensity in part because of the inborn hardship of his voice, becomes cause for deep admiration among his fans.

When confronted with Mori in person, all female fans I have spoken with comment on how handsome he is. Interestingly, the word they often use is "*kawaii*" (cute, endearing), a term more often applied to babies, girls, certain types of women, and baby animals than men (Kinsella 1995). "Kawaii" emphasizes Mori's vulnerability rather than his virility. At 46 years (in 1993), he seems to evoke as many maternal feelings in his fans as sexual ones. When Mori's fans were polled in 1987 as to what place Mori holds in their life (*dō iu sonzai ka*), over 10 per cent of respondents answered, "as a son" (Mori Shin'ichi Kōenkai 1987).

He presents, in effect, the image of the perfect Japanese son; handsome, well-groomed, serious rather than frivolous, and above all devoted to mother. Moreover, unlike real sons who may leave home, he is always there via broadcast media, cassette tape, or videotape. As the mood strikes, a fan can call up a Mori which will make her cry because of his longing for mother or from a broken heart. This kind of neediness is part of what draws Mori's female fans to him.

Fans comment that he is intelligent (*atama ga ii*) and serious (*majime*). Mori is known as a man of few words. Watching him for the first time, Americans are surprised by his lack of showmanship; e.g., informal chatting between numbers, dramatic gestures, and playing to the crowd. Instead, he stands woodenly, with little movement or facial expression, singing song after song. This stage manner alternates with periods of mingling with the audience during particular songs at prescribed points in a concert. Each type of action (formal and staid, or informal and expansive) is patterned, prescribed, and ritualized. Mori is by turns the serious, statue-like, unsmiling singer, and the friendly, roving, smiling handshaker. Fans say that his performance shows just how sincere he is. Instead of gussying up his songs with empty chatter or needless smiles, he typically sings in a direct, unpretentious manner. But to assuage his fans' great desire to touch him, he generously allots a certain amount of time during a performance when he can reach out and touch them.

In the aforementioned 1987 poll of fans, the other most frequently occurring responses to the question of what kind of place Mori holds in fans' lives were as follows: gives my life meaning (*ikigai*; 18.4 per cent);[3] soothes me (*yasuragi*; 12.2 per cent); supports my heart/soul (*kokoro no sasae*; 8.2 per cent); and pleasure (*tanoshimi*; 6.1 per cent). For these fans, Mori fills particular needs, giving them a sense of purpose. That purpose is created out of his own neediness: he sings songs of loneliness and heartbreak with great conviction, which evokes an empathetic response in his listeners. Through empathy, his fans want to simultaneously comfort him and commiserate with him. The commiseration becomes the soothing of a fellow sufferer, who in turn becomes a fellow supporter. These kinds of psychological explanations of a star's appeal ignore manipulations by the music industry of a singer's image. Nonetheless, they form a kind of public discourse aimed at rationalizing charisma.

A Mori Shin'ichi Kōenkai has been in existence since Mori's debut over 25 years ago; however, the Mori Shin'ichi Kōenkai in its present form was organized in 1979 when Mori went "independent" and set up his own production company. In 1992, there were over 10,000 members of the kōenkai from all over Japan and a few from foreign countries. According to the organization's 1987 survey, women outnumber men by approximately four to one, but my informal survey of those attending events in 1992-93 (including concerts, parties, and info-meetings) suggests that among the organization's more active members, the female-to-male ratio is closer to nine to one. The age range of members is from the twenties to the nineties, with the majority in their forties or fifties.

Like other enka singers' kōenkai, Mori's is run by the production company under which he sings (his own) in conjunction with the record company to which he is contracted. Workers at the kōenkai, therefore, are not necessarily fans of Mori, but employees of a production or record company. According to one worker, although she herself is not a fan, she must give the impression of being one, or at least of never favoring another singer over Mori. In subtle ways such as this, the kōenkai presents itself as a fan-generated organization of routinized charisma, although it is admittedly a company-derived one.

The organization does not hold meetings per se, nor does it have officers. But approximately two to three times a year it holds a *rikuesto shūkai* (request gathering; info-meeting) in the middle of a weekday in both Tokyo and Osaka. The use of the English word "request" suggests that the gathering has been generated at the request of fans. In reality, it is a creation of the production and record companies that form and control the kōenkai. During these gatherings, fans listen attentively while representatives of the production and record companies and the club head (a paid employee) talk about Mori's upcoming appearances and activities. At the two that I attended, between 30 and 60 members were present at each, almost all women in their fifties or sixties. Each person attending was given a promotional packet containing a list of television and radio stations, program times, station addresses, and twenty prepaid postcards to be mailed to the stations in order to request Mori's latest single.

The role of the kōenkai as an arm of the publicity department of a production or record company is not insignificant. At the info-meeting, fans were asked by Mori's manager not only to keep requesting Mori's songs by phone or postcard, but also to sing Mori's songs in karaoke; to spread the song, as it were, into the ears of the listening public. One meeting strongly encouraged fans to attend a publicity event, a crowd-generating rally scheduled for the following week. This patterning of fandom makes a perfect fit of fans and singers (or their production companies and record companies): Mori needs support to be a success, fans want to support Mori, and their support is best shown by promoting his records. The following fan letter expresses the personal pleasure a fan derives from seeing Mori's song (and thereby Mori) do well.

When Mori's latest song became a big hit this autumn, my heart beat fast. I can hear it a lot on the radio, and seeing it lined up with the "Best 10" when I enter a record store makes me so happy. Fellow fans, let us all try our best to spread [*shintō suru*] the melody of "Warui Hito" throughout Japan. (Mori Shin'ichi Kōenkai 1993 169:3)

Fans therefore take it upon themselves to ensure Mori's success. Through omoiyari, the fan assumes Mori's goals as her own.

One worker at Mori's kōenkai office relates several ways in which avid fans treat Mori as a kind of *kamisama* (god). The kōenkai sells *zabuton* (cushions) with Mori's signature; often members who buy these zabuton would never think of defiling them by actually sitting on them. Packs of Mori facial tissues are also sold. These same members never use the tissue, but merely collect the packs (or give them as presents to friends) as but another item in a stockpile of mounting Mori treasure. This same kind of buying to collect rather than use goes for telephone cards, towels, hand-kerchiefs, chopstick holders, and other items. By collecting these bits of Mori *kyaarakutaa gudzu* (character goods; items for sale bearing a likeness, signature, and/or emblem of a well-known figure), fans dotingly accumulate bits of symbolic Mori, in much the same way religious fanatics surround themselves with icons of devotion.

The kōenkai issues a *kaihō* (newsletter) every month, *The Shin'ichi Mori News,* and typically the front of the newsletter carries a color photograph of Mori. Measuring approximately ten by fifteen inches, the newsletter is folded into sixths to fit into an envelope for mailing purposes. According to a kōenkai worker, one month the fold of the newsletter resulted in the photo of Mori's face being folded lengthwise in half. Several upset fans called the office to complain—an idol should not be seen cut in half. Since then, newsletter designers have been careful to place the front cover photograph strategically, framing his face beautifully and symmetrically, even when folded in sixths.

Expressions of fandom are often motherly. When Mori appears on television and does not look well, the kōenkai office is flooded with calls the next morning inquiring after his health. At a concert, devoted fans bring *bentō* (lunch; boxed meal) to kōenkai workers who are busy selling items at a booth in the theater lobby. After the concert, some members busy themselves picking up rubbish and cleaning up the theater. According to a member, a messy theater after a Mori concert reflects badly on Mori himself. A fan expressed her concern for other fans' behavior at concerts, doing such things as leaving rubbish under seats and taking flowers from the lobby: "In these kinds of ways, Mori's fans' manners are called into question. After a while it will be regrettable when it becomes an impediment [*shishō*] to Mori['s image]" (Mori Shin'ichi Kōenkai 1993 169:3). As Japanese mothers to their children, fans like these regard Mori as extensions of themselves. Again, omoiyari links fans to singer.

For an entrance fee of ¥1000 and a monthly fee of ¥500,[4] members receive: 1) seasonal greetings at midsummer and New Year's in the form of a photo postcard of Mori; 2) the opportunity to prepurchase concert tickets for the best seats; 3) notice of free activities such as the info-meeting; 4) *The Shin'ichi Mori News*; 5) an invitation to purchase a ticket for the annual *fuan tsudoi* (fan gathering, party);[5] and 6) notice of special events, such as members-only concerts and tours with Mori himself. A more detailed examination of the last three sheds some light on the ways in which the kōenkai becomes an effective interface between the singer, the singer's image, and fans.

The Shin'ichi Mori News monthly is the most frequent and regular point of contact between the kōenkai and its members. The format of each issue is similar: a front page with a large color photo of Mori and formulaic seasonal greetings;[6] a second page with a philosophical "talk essay" by Mori, a *haato tsūshin* (heart communication) greeting by a person in some way connected to Mori's current work and a response by Mori, and concert information; a third page with *fuan no hiroba* (fan's section, including fan letters), a display of Mori "character goods" for sale, a letter from the kōenkai office staff, and a two-month schedule of Mori's activities; and a fourth page filled with glossy color photos of Mori in his recent concert and television appearances.

What is most important for members is that the newsletter becomes a charismatic carrier, giving the impression of intimate communication between Mori and themselves. Greetings on the front page are written in the form of a personal letter. Coupled with a blown-up photograph of Mori staring out from the page, the effect is one of Mori looking directly at the fan and speaking with her. An example translated from the November 1993 issue follows:

We are well into autumn by now, so how is everyone?

I thank you for the great cheers of support [*ōkina go-seien*] I have received everywhere on my nationwide Min'on[7] concert tour which began in October. Thankfully, I feel very happy that the concerts have been well received.

With cheering from all of you [*minnasama no go-seien ni yotte*], my song "Warui Hito" [Bad Person] has been able to ride the crest of popularity, and I wholeheartedly [*kokoro o komete*] face the challenge of making this a song which many people hear and can sing to themselves [*kuchi-zusamu*].

From now on this is the time of year in which it gets colder by the day, so everyone, please take good care of yourselves.

[Signed,] Mori Shin'ichi (Mori 1993 171:1)

The language of the letter is respectful, written from the point of view of an inferior to a superior. The first and last paragraphs are formulaic greetings, appropriate to the month of November. Mori continually emphasizes the cheering (*seien*) he receives from his fans, and his resultant gratitude. Never resting on his laurels, he works hard, "wholeheartedly facing the challenge" to make his newest song a success. That success is indicated by its having penetrated the bodies of a great number of people, embedded in their ears and on the tips of their tongues. One gets the impression of an earnest, hard-working singer who strives to please his fans. The relationship is embedded in a dual dependency, a kind of rebounded amae—the singer depends on his fans for support; fans depend on the singer for emotional sustenance (cf. Doi 1973; Lebra 1976:54-55; Johnson 1993). Each serves the other.

In the talk essay portion of the newsletter, the image of Mori subtly switches from Mori the servant to Mori the sage. Each essay is supposed to impart a bit of wisdom, a bit of a lesson for life. In one example Mori talks of losing his voice at a concert and the resultant lesson is never to take things for granted (Mori 1992 156:2). In another he talks of evaluating personal happiness not from one's daily fluctuations, but from a lifelong perspective (Mori 1993 164:2).

One of the most valuable sections of the newsletter is the fuan no hiroba, a compilation of fan letters and Mori's responses. Reading the letters imparts a sense of community among kōenkai members, many of whom share the sentiments expressed by the letter-writers. Each letter is only partially anonymous; the writer's initials and city or prefecture are given. Some of the most common expressions found in these letters include the following phrases, all of which focus on *kokoro* (heart): *kokoro ni hibiku* (resonate in one's heart); *kokoro ni nokoru* (remain in one's heart); *kokoro o tsunagu* (connect to one's heart). It is heart that lies at the center of Mori's charisma, binding fans to him and to each other through him.

Mori's interdependent relationship with his fans is cultivated, as in the following example:

T. H. from Yamaguchi prefecture: I went to your April 18 concert in Hiroshima. Your wonderfully appealing singing voice—your humorous comments during the concert—your gentle smiling face [*yasashii egao*]. On that red stage wearing a red suit, you looked like such a young person.[8] When I see you on stage, I lose all track of time passing [*toki no tatsu no o wasurete shimaimasu*]. . . . That night after my family had gone to bed, I was alone, so I took out the fan club bulletin with the lyrics to your latest song in it, and quietly sang the song to myself. I think I would like to master the song and sing it at karaoke places. I look forward to seeing you again in your June concert.

Mori: . . . Thank you for your support at the Hiroshima concert. During my June concert, I will certainly sing my new song again. I feel that I would like my fans to sing along with me (in a quiet voice!?) at the concert. (Mori Shin'ichi Kōenkai 1992 153:3)

Mori responds to another fan letter by saying, "I have long been conscious of my responsibility as a singer to my fans who have supported me, and from now on I will persist in meeting the expectations of my fans" (Mori 1992 153:3). Yet another Mori response reiterates his indebtedness to his fans: "Without forgetting my indebtedness to you my fans, I will persevere" (Mori 1992 160:3).

The letters are often intimate, expressing the flush of excitement of a fan in the presence of Mori, as well as, at times, Mori's official mutual appreciation.

Y. E. from Kanagawa prefecture: [During the concert I attended], I got to shake your hand, and I forgot my age, and it became a wonderful memory. Your hand was amazingly soft, a hand which had the warmth which moves people's hearts [*hito no kokoro o ugokasu*]. I think that I would like to make the emotion of that day live on in my daily life as nourishment for my heart [*kokoro no kate*]. (Mori Shin'ichi Kōenkai 1992 154:3)

H. F. from Hyōgo prefecture: [During the concert I attended], I got to shake hands with you, and I grasped your soft hand with both of mine. I was greatly moved, and it was a night which transported me out of the fatigue of the day. . . .

Mori: Thank you. I feel that your appreciation of my recital also lifts me out of any fatigue that I might have. From now on, I will strive to please you all. (Mori Shin'ichi Kōenkai 1992 159:3)

M. K. from Osaka: I was thrilled to have a commemorative photo with Mori. . . . Some time later on the train home from the fan club party, I would look at my photo [of the two of us together] and remember the warmth of Mori's cheek on mine and feel so happy. I hold the warmth of Mori in my heart/breast [*mune*] and promise to support him all the more from now on.

Mori: Thank you. I, too, hold my fans' warmth in my heart. (Mori Shin'ichi Kōenkai 1992 160:3)

Some letters specifically talk of tears, of crying while listening to Mori's songs, especially those about mother, such as "Ofukurosan" and "*Usagi*" (Rabbit).

T. H. from Tokyo: I was moved to tears [by your singing in concert], but if they are tears with such fine aftertaste, then it would be fine for them to flow any number of times [*konna ni atoaji no ii namida nara nando nagashite mo ii*]. (Mori Shin'ichi Kōenkai 1993 161:3)

H. T. from Kanagawa: [At the concert I attended,] without thinking, I found myself singing along with Mori, softly to myself. And upon hearing Mori's heartfelt rendition of "Usagi," tears came to my eyes and I was enraptured [*kiki-horemashita*]. (Mori Shin'ichi Kōenkai 1993 162:3)

K. from Tokyo: My mother was shot by a gunman and hospitalized. On the days when I went to visit her in the hospital, there was the television program "*Omoide no Merodii*" (Melodies of Memories). I knew of the program through the kōenkai newsletter, so I switched the television on and waited for Mori's appearance. My mother seemed to be living by drops on a truly meager liquid diet, but at that time she opened her eyes. Taking my mother's hand and stroking her face, I listened, crying, to "Ofukurosan." With those tears in my eyes, I couldn't see Mori's face, but I listened with feelings that I hadn't felt before. My mother could hear clearly, too. Now my mother's life is just about over, but for me her life was the greatest gift. I will listen to Mori from now on treasuring her. I am eternally grateful to Mori's singing.

Mori: Thank you for your story. For me, too, when I sing "Ofukurosan," I remember in my heart various aspects of my own mother. From now on, I would like to sing the song with all my heart as a song well loved by everyone. (Mori Shin'ichi Kōenkai 1993 170:3)

Some letters express ways in which Mori has made their lives better. In one, for example, a mother writes that she and her twenty-year-old daughter happily attend

Mori's concerts together. "Through Mori's songs, this mother and daughter have no discord" (Mori Shin'ichi Kōenkai 1992 157:3). Another letter praises his talk essays, claiming that she is improved by reading them. "I feel in my heart that because Mori's singing is born of such wisdom, he has an appeal altogether different from other singers" (Mori Shin'ichi Kōenkai 1992 156:3).

The primary benefit of membership in Mori's kōenkai is the opportunity to get closer (physically and emotionally) to the star. One example is the annual fuan no tsudoi (fan get-together) held in the fall. Many fans regard this event with great anticipation because it is the physically closest many can get to Mori. Approximately 450 fans (around 90 per cent of whom were female) were at the one in November 1992 at the Shin Takanawa Prince Hotel in Shinagawa, Tokyo. Mori entered the room singing, greeted by murmurs of excitement by fans. He walked through every aisle, singing, having his picture taken, shaking some hands.

Among the activities of the evening was a quiz game about Mori. Fans were asked mundane questions about Mori; the two who answered the most correctly were given prizes. The questions included: 1) What kind of tree does Mori like? a. *sakura*, or b. cedar (answer: *sakura*); 2) What kind of quiet place does Mori like? a. ocean, or b. mountain (answer: ocean); 3) When Mori catches a cold, what does he do? a. go see a doctor, or b. go to bed right away (answer: go see a doctor); 4) If Mori buys a cute puppy, what does he call it? a. Mori-chan, or b. Shin-chan (answer: Mori-chan). Clearly, the game rewarded those who knew the most about Mori or could second-guess him.

The fan party also featured a *karaoke taikai* (karaoke contest) restricted to Mori's songs. Before the party, 42 contestants were prescreened, leaving ten to perform at the party. These ten competed for three prizes ranging from a Mori CD or cassette to a choice of one of Mori's stage jackets. The contest rewarded those who could most closely approximate Mori in performance.

For many fans, the most important part of the event is the opportunity to have their photos taken with Mori. This occurs at the end of the evening, when fans line up with their tickets which entitle them to one photo. A professional photographer takes the picture with an on-the-spot-developing camera, so that the fan can take home the treasured record of the evening she spent with Mori. Some fans carry in their purses photos from previous years.

Another example of this kind of feigned intimacy as a special event of the kōenkai was the opportunity to speak with Mori individually by phone in a "telephone date" held in July 1993. Here Mori's relationship with fans emulated a "real" (hetero)sexual one; however, participation in the date was contingent upon the fan buying Mori's latest single release. In other words, the telephone date was a thinly veiled promotional tactic to boost record sales. The prize was Mori himself, or at least a few minutes of his time by telephone. In order to apply, kōenkai members were required to submit their name, address, phone number, available times, subject for discussion, and the record company insignia and product number cut from the CD or cassette label of "Warui Hito," Mori's newest single. From these applicants, three were selected. The August 1993 issue of *The Shin'ichi Mori News* included transcripts of all three conversations. The topics of conversation tended to be mundane (diet tips, golf, songs) and each woman expressed her excitement, not unlike that of a young girl on a date, with phrases such as, "This is like a dream!" and "Oh, dear, what shall I do? This is the real thing, isn't it? Oh, my heart is pounding!" One date confessed that she had intended to take a tranquilizer for the momentous occasion, but accidentally took some fever medicine, making her feel even more intoxicated. In each case, Mori chatted a while, but invariably got to the point of asking his date what she thought of his newest song.

A final example of the kōenkai as a form of patterned intimacy between singer and fans is the occasional tour offered to fans, an opportunity to travel with the star. In March 1994, approximately 70 fans travelled to Honolulu, Hawaii, with Mori. During that trip, Mori took great care to make himself accessible to his fans, conscientiously working through the schedule of patterned interaction set up by his staff. Mori greeted each of his fans from Japan with a flower lei. Both fans from Japan and Hawaii attended a luncheon, during which a karaoke taikai of Mori's songs was held. After lunch came the opportunity to take a picture with him. Mori went on a dinner cruise with fans from Japan, during which he danced the hula with fans, greeted everyone at each table, and took photos with each fan. Before the end of the four-day tour, Mori took the time to visit each of the fans' hotel rooms, chatting with each person briefly. Most important for Mori's image was that all these activities were photographed and publicized in the following month's newsletter.

The mutual dependency of singer and fans becomes a kind of ritualized reciprocity. Mori generates maternal and sexual emotions that impel his fans to support him and do whatever they can to help him. At the same time, his efforts help them in their lives and support their emotional needs. These kinds of interactive processes form the basis of a charismatic relationship generated in part by a commercial organization, but no less real or important to Mori's thousands of fans.

Beyond the relationship between Mori and his fans, a relationship among fans also develops through the kōenkai. Devotion to Mori in some cases creates common bonds of friendship. Fans see each other at concerts, seated together through tickets bought by mail from the kōenkai office. They also see each other at meetings and parties, and sometimes on tours. Inevitably fans come to recognize each other's faces and, sharing a passion, they have plenty to discuss: Mori's latest television appearance, Mori's newest song, Mori's photo in last week's magazine. Catching a train after a Mori concert, a stranger recognized me as a fellow member and made room for me in the seat next to hers. The subsequent conversation revolved around Mori, of course. One woman mentioned that she had traveled alone for two hours by train to attend Mori's annual dinner party, which was worth the trouble because once at the party she was surrounded by people with whom she could feel comfortable, even if she did not know them well. The degree to which members who do not otherwise know each other socialize outside of club activities varies from not at all to occasionally. However, concerts, meetings, and parties which occur approximately eight to ten times a year become occasions for renewing friendships.

CONCLUSION

The ritualization of charisma structured in organizations such as the Mori Shin'ichi Kōenkai revolves around an ideal of mutual dependency and support. Mori reaches out to fans in patterned ways, patterned settings, patterned expressions of song. His reaching is institutionalized within the kōenkai through newsletters, preprinted seasonal cards sent to members, and pre-set activities at parties. In each case, Mori (as well as his staff) takes the humble position of a servant working hard to please his fans. Like all good servants, his skill presumably rests upon the ability to anticipate his fans' needs through omoiyari. This image of the striving servant is essential to his charismatic appeal.

Fans also reach out to Mori in ritualized ways, giving him flowers and gifts at certain times in concerts, waving penlights in unison during the performance of particular songs, and becoming members of his kōenkai. As members, they write letters, show up at promotional info-meetings, attend parties, request his songs, sing his songs. Most important, they reach out by reaching within, adopting an attitude of omoiyari which makes his needs their own. Servanthood gets stood on its head—they want to serve the servant. Their very recognition of Mori as a charismatic figure establishes the relationship upon which both fandom and stardom rest.

Omoiyari works on both sides of the charisma equation. Mori's omoiyari is well planned and intentional, a product of an office staff concerned with record sales. There is no way that Mori could empathize with every one of his fans. Yet his expressions must convey his personal, individualized concern for each fan's needs. What is convenient is that those needs may be generalized under a larger umbrella. That umbrella is part of the efficacy of charismatic ritual; one pattern may apply to a variety of needs because the needs themselves have become generalized. Fans, on the other hand, generate expressions of omoiyari on their own, as well as with the help of the kōenkai organization. Their phone calls, flowers, gifts, gestures are both individual and group expressions of Mori's concerns. Harnessed by the production and record companies, and fueled by their profit-seeking strategies, the kōenkai becomes an efficiently patterned empathizer.

This commercially created, ritually maintained community is held together by charisma, but not charisma as Weber would have it, left to the vagaries of extraordinary times, places, and people. Rather, this is charisma industrially generated and managed. Never constituted in any one place or time, this community may persist with more affective force and greater coherence in the collective imagination of fans. Yet, what is even more important for the fan than the collective is the individual, personal relationship with the star. For ardent fans, tied by patterned processes of surrogacy, empathy, and dependency, membership in this

348   ETHNOLOGY

charismatic (albeit commercially based) community gives shared meaning to their lives.

NOTES

1.   Fieldwork for this article, conducted from 1991-93 in Tokyo and Yokohama, was generously funded by a Japan Foundation Dissertation Fellowship, the Crown Prince Akihito Scholarship Foundation, and the Center for Japanese Studies at the University of Hawaii, for which I am very grateful. My thanks also go to Takie Sugiyama Lebra for her valuable support and suggestions. A version of this article was presented at the 94th Annual Meeting of the American Anthropological Association, Washington, D.C., November 1995.
2.   I have genderized the pronouns here to suggest that female fans run in far greater numbers in fan clubs than male fans. This holds true for both male and female star singers, but more so for male singers.
3.   This finding corroborates Mathews's (1996) study of ikigai over the lifecourse, since Mori's fans are typically older women whose child-rearing responsibilities (apart from grandchildren) have diminished.
4.   Exchange rates averaged ¥110 to U.S.$1.00 during most of my fieldwork in Japan.
5.   Two fan parties, one in Osaka and one in Tokyo, are held annually in the fall within a few weeks of each other.
6.   Letter-writing in Japan is highly formulaic. One can construct an appropriate letter using patterns found in letter-writing manuals. In general, Mori's letters follow these patterns closely.
7.   Min'on is one of Japan's largest music organizations, sponsoring concerts, publications, and archives.
8.   Red is the color of youth. Red coupled with white is also the color of festivals and celebration.

BIBLIOGRAPHY

Allison, A. 1996. Permitted and Prohibited Desires. Boulder.
Asahi Shimbu Nishi-bu Honsha. 1992. Hana ga Aru: Gendai o Utsushi-dasu Hitobito (There are Blossoms: People Who Cast Light upon Our Times). Tokyo.
Bion, W. 1961. Experiences in Groups. New York.
Doi T. 1973. The Anatomy of Dependence. Tokyo.
Dyer, R. 1991. Charisma. Stardom: Industry of Desire, ed. C. Gledhill, pp. 57-59. London.
Freud, S. 1959. Group Psychology and the Analysis of the Ego. New York.
Horton, D., and R. R. Wohl. 1956. Mass Communication and Parasocial Interaction: Observation on Intimacy at a Distance. Psychiatry 19(3):188-211.
Jenson, J. 1992. Fandom as Pathology: The Consequences of Characterization. The Adoring Audience, ed. L. Lewis, pp. 9-29. London.
Johnson, F. A. 1993. Dependency and Japanese Socialization. New York.
Kasulis, T. P. 1990. Intimacy: A General Orientation in Japanese Religious Values. Philosophy East and West 40(4):433-49.
Kinsella, S. 1995. Cuties in Japan. Women, Media and Consumption in Japan, eds. L. Skov and B. Moeran, pp. 220-54. Honolulu.
Koizumi F. 1984. Kayōkyoku no Kōzō (The Structure of Popular Songs). Tokyo.
Le Bon, G. 1952. The Crowd: A Study of the Popular Mind. London.
Lebra, T. S. 1976. Japanese Patterns of Behavior. Honolulu.
———— 1984. Japanese Women; Constraint and Fulfillment. Honolulu.
———— 1992. Migawari: The Cultural Idiom of Self-Other Exchange in Japan. Self as Person in Asian Theory and Practice, eds. R. Ames, W. Dissanayake, and R. Kasulis, pp. 107-23. Albany.

Lindholm, C. 1990. Charisma. Cambridge MA.

Mathews, G. 1996. What Makes Life Worth Living? How Japanese and Americans Make Sense of Their Worlds. Berkeley.

Mori S. 1992. The Shin'ichi Mori News.

———— 1993. The Shin'ichi Mori News.

Mori Shin'ichi: Kandō no Kiseki (Mori Shin'ichi: The Locus of Emotions). 1991. Victor VIVL-30. Videotape.

Mori Shin'ichi Kōenkai. 1987. Unpublished poll.

———— 1992. Fuan no Hiroba (Fans' Corner). The Shin'ichi Mori News.

———— 1993. Fuan no Hiroba (Fans' Corner). The Shin'ichi Mori News.

Skov, L., and B. Moeran (eds.). 1995. Women, Media and Consumption in Japan. Honolulu.

Weber, M. 1968. Max Weber on Charisma and Institution Building. Chicago.

[17]

Cross-cultural perspectives in popular music: the case of Afghanistan

by JOHN BAILY

The problem of definition

It is inevitable that the first issue of this yearbook will raise questions about the use of the term 'popular music'. I do not believe that this question is going to be easy to answer and, as a precaution, I think we should regard quick and seemingly clearcut solutions with suspicion. In fact, we may eventually have to operate with intuitive, poorly defined and rather elastic definitions of popular music. Before we resort to that expedient, however, the problem of definition must be considered and discussed from various points of view.

The editors have offered the following two definitions (the numbering is mine):

(1)   From one point of view 'popular music' exists in any stratified society. It is seen as the music of the mass of the people . . . as against that of an élite.

(2)   From another point of view there is at the very least a significant qualitative change, both in the meaning which is felt to attach to the term and in the processes to which the music owes its life, when a society undergoes industrialisation. From this point of view popular music is typical of societies with a relatively highly developed division of labour and a clear distinction between producers and consumers, in which cultural products are created largely by professionals, sold in a mass market and reproduced through mass media. (P. 1 above)

The first of these definitions is very general, the second very specific. Within the Western world they are perhaps appropriate. But are they valid at a cross-cultural level? Consideration of varieties of world music suggests that 'popular music' is a transcultural phenomenon. In this wider context the definitions seem more questionable. The first is too loose, too unspecific, and does not distinguish between the possibly separate analytical categories of 'popular' and 'folk' music. The second definition is too tight because it implies that 'popular music' is characteristic only of industrialised societies. We shall return to this matter later.

In this paper I shall describe in some detail a kind of music typical of the cities of Afghanistan that I believe can be legitimately labelled

106   *John Baily*

'popular music'. Beyond the ethnographic data I am also concerned with the theoretical issue of the basis on which we label a genre of music as 'popular music'. In justifying the use of this label cross-culturally one is in effect having to define the characteristics of popular music.

Two points should be made in relation to this theoretical issue. Firstly, the ethnomusicological approach suggests that labels such as 'art music', 'folk music' and 'popular music' can be used with justification in a cross-cultural context *only* when the society concerned makes such distinctions itself. Otherwise we are in danger of distorting the data to fit preconceived analytical concepts and definitions that may be totally inappropriate. We must try to understand a music system from the inside, from the point of view of the people who create and use the music. For example, in the case of the term 'art music' it seems perfectly justified to use this term for those musics of Asia that are considered to be 'art' by the people themselves. Use of the term 'art music' implies that the society concerned distinguishes at least two kinds of music: 'art' and something else that is not 'art'. The music of an hypothetical society that has only one kind of music could not be analytically labelled as 'art', 'folk' or anything else, for there is no contrast, it is simply 'music' as opposed to 'non-music'.

Secondly, even if we agree that we should only use the term 'popular music' when it corresponds to a native category in the folk view,* we are still left with a definitional problem. We have to put forward some criteria in order to test whether what *appears* on the surface to be a 'popular music' category in another music system really does correspond to our own analytical concept of 'popular music'. Some possible criteria for identifying 'popular music' will be suggested later in the paper. These criteria amount to a partial definition of 'popular music'.

Major categories of music in the thinking of Heratis

The ethnographic data to be described were collected in Herat Province in western Afghanistan during two years' ethnomusicological fieldwork in the mid-1970s.† Most of my fieldwork was carried out in the city of Herat, the third largest city in Afghanistan, eighty miles

---

* By 'folk view' I refer to the perceptions and cognitions of the people themselves. The important distinction between native and analytical evaluations is discussed in Merriam 1964, pp. 31–2. Where Merriam uses the term 'folk-evaluation', I prefer 'folk view'.

† This research was funded by the Social Science Research Council of the United Kingdom, whose generous support is gratefully acknowledged. Fieldwork was carried out in 1973–4, when I was an SSRC Post-Doctoral Research Fellow, and again in 1976–7 under an SSRC Conversion Fellowship Scheme.

Cross-cultural perspectives in popular music: Afghanistan   107

from the Iranian border. Reference is also made to Radio Afghanistan, broadcasting from Kabul, the capital (in eastern Afghanistan), but extensive research has not been carried out at the radio station.*

Any musical ethnography must go into the question of how the people classify the different kinds of music that they use. This matter is of crucial importance, for, as already explained, we can only talk about a genre of music as 'popular music' if it corresponds to an equivalent native concept. For various reasons the folk classification used by a people is often difficult to elucidate. Distinctions that may appear obvious to the outsider may not be apparent to the people (suggesting that the outsider has failed to understand the folk view), or a category may be found to exist in their thinking but to have no generally agreed label.

A faithful representation of the ways that Heratis distinguish and label different genres of music would be rather complex and beyond the scope of this paper. As a simplification let us accept that amongst their categories the four shown in Figure 1 are of major importance. In Figure 1 the four categories are represented as being at the same level of a system of classification.

Musiqi-ye klasik refers to Hindustani vocal music of the *khayal* and *tarana* genres, which is widely known in Afghanistan and is performed by some Afghan† musicians. In Afghanistan this genre is regarded as 'art music'. The word *klasik* is the English word 'classical', probably derived from India, where Hindustani music is often referred to as 'Indian classical music'.

Ghazalkhani refers to the singing of serious Persian poetry in the *ghazal* form. Some of the poetry used comes from the great poets of the past, such as Hafez and Sa'di; some is of more recent provenance, penned by Afghan and Indian-born poets writing in Persian. Similar *ghazals* (in Urdu rather than Persian) are performed in India and Pakistan. In certain contexts this is also regarded as 'art music' by Heratis.

Musiqi-ye mahali refers to 'local music'. In Herat, this label refers to those kinds of music that the people identify as Herati. Certain kinds of *mahali* could be regarded as 'folk music', being handed down through oral tradition over the generations and being performed by non-

---

* In writing about the use of music in Afghanistan, I have adopted the convention known as the 'ethnographic present', in which a state of affairs that existed in the past is described in the present tense. Political events in Afghanistan since 1978 make it highly unlikely that the situation I describe persists unchanged.

† I use the term 'Afghan' here to refer to inhabitants of Afghanistan irrespective of ethnic origins. The two main ethnic groups are Pashtuns and Tajiks; most inhabitants of Herat are the latter. The two official languages are Pashtu and Persian. Persian is the language of Herat.

108   *John Baily*

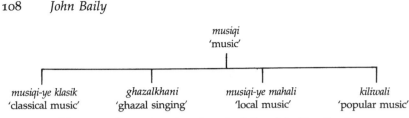

Figure 1.   Four categories of music distinguished by Heratis

specialists. 'Local music' from other regions is often identified by Heratis in ethnic or geographical terms, viz. *Uzbeki* (Uzbek, an ethnic group) or *shomali* (northern).

Kiliwali is tentatively labelled in Figure 1 as 'popular music'. The major characteristics of this genre will be described in the remainder of this paper. Essentially, the term refers to a kind of urban music broadcast from the radio station and copied over the rest of the country, especially in the towns and cities.

A few words of qualification are needed about my use of the term *kiliwali*. This Pashtu word means 'of the village', and when used in Pashtu properly refers to Pashtun regional music, the 'ethnic' music of the Pashtuns. In Herat, which is Persian-speaking, the term *kiliwali* is used by some people, especially by musicians, to refer to those genres of music which are discussed below, and which have been tentatively labelled 'popular music'. They probably use this label because the main formal and structural characteristics of the music were originally derived from Pashtun regional music. I use the term for simplicity of expression, and because it is used by some Heratis.

Main features of *kiliwali* music

Musical aspects

Kiliwali has a distinct musical style: two of its most dominant features are the constant alternation of vocal and instrumental sections, and the frequent use of rhythmic cadential devices. As with other genres of Afghan music, *kiliwali* is monophonic in concept (i.e. linear melody with no vertical harmonic or polyphonic component) and heterophonic in execution (because the instruments that accompany the singer each play the melodic line slightly differently). There is no consistent use of continuous drones. *Kiliwali* uses a series of modes which can, for convenience, be thought of as corresponding to certain Hindustani modes (*ragas*). Most *kiliwali* music is in one of three modes: *Bairami*, *Pari* and *Kesturi*.

Kiliwali music has both vocal and instrumental aspects. Most of the

Cross-cultural perspectives in popular music: Afghanistan 109

items in the repertory are songs, each with its own text and melody and associated instrumental piece. In most performances of *kiliwali* the singer is accompanied by melodic and rhythmic musical instruments. The song itself is usually divided into sections that we might label 'verse' and 'refrain' (*beit* and *pazarb*) and these are usually sung to different, but often related, melodies, known as the *antara* and the *astai*.

After the refrain has been sung the instruments may continue playing the melody of the *astai* as an instrumental refrain, coming to an end with a pronounced rhythmic cadence and a slight pause ('*istad*, the stop). This instrumental section is called the *duni*, and it generally shows some degree of acceleration in tempo before the rhythmic cadence. After the *duni* it is usual to insert another instrumental section, the *naghme*, which has a quite different melody from the *astai* and *antara*. This is played several times and again comes to a rest with a rhythmic cadence before the singer starts the next verse. Each song has its own *naghme* associated with it. It is also possible to add other instrumental sections.

It is acceptable for song melodies with attendant *naghmes* to be played as instrumental pieces, either solo or by a group of instruments. This is especially characteristic of amateur musicians, where there are more competent instrumentalists than singers. There are also a few purely instrumental pieces in the *kiliwali* repertory, some of them played as dance music.

It is not possible to go into the matter of song texts here. The songs deal with a variety of topics. The bulk of them are love-songs, either of a romantic kind, such as those describing the physical attributes of the beloved, or on the unrequited love theme. These texts are not considered to be 'good poetry' in comparison with the texts used for *ghazalkhani*. The performance of a song takes five to ten minutes, though performances on the radio are usually shorter (and often omit the *duni* section).

Although song is such an important element of *kiliwali* and there can be no doubt that the inner structure of the music shows the influence of linguistic and poetic constraints, the music is conceived of as something apart from song, as conforming to its own set of *musical* rules. It is a system of organised sounds having two essential elements: *sor* (pitch modulation) and *lai* (metred rhythm).

Occurrence and use

It is necessary to distinguish between the centre and the periphery of the *kiliwali* phenomenon. The periphery consists of the cities and towns of Afghanistan that support their own local *kiliwali* music-making. Here we look at the periphery only from the point of view of Herat. Centre and periphery together form a two-way communication system, from the centre to the periphery and from the periphery to the centre. There is also some communication directly between different parts of the periphery. These relationships are represented in Figure 2.

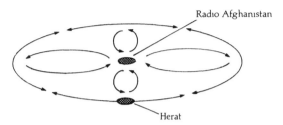

Figure 2.   Centre and periphery of the *kiliwali* network

The radio station as the centre

The only radio station in Afghanistan is that in Kabul, known orig-inally as Radio Kabul, later called Radio Afghanistan. The radio station is located in a modern complex of buildings in a suburb of Kabul, near the airport, and was built with Soviet aid. The large staff is engaged in planning and making all sorts of programmes: news; educational pro-grammes for select groups such as women, farmers and children; re-ligious programmes; plays; panel games; and music. Some of the pro-gramming staff have received training abroad. Most broadcasting is in Persian and Pashtu, with a few programmes in the languages of ethnic minorities. Some English language programmes are also broadcast.

The radio station broadcasts many kinds of music including the four types mentioned in Figure 1. Here we refer only to the *kiliwali* category. For the making of music programmes the station employs both in-strumentalists and singers. The instrumentalists are all men. Many of them are from hereditary musician families living in the musicians' quarter in the old city. Instrumentalists are full-time employees of the radio station; some have worked there for many years. A few of them are famous masters (*ustads*) who sometimes perform solo instrumental music, but most of the time the instrumentalists work together in various orchestras.

For example, the *Orkestra Bozorg* (the Big Orchestra), as I observed it rehearsing for a song on 3 October 1976, consisted of: two *rubabs* (short-necked plucked Afghan lutes), two *tanburs* (long-necked plucked Afghan lutes), mandoline, Spanish guitar, *tulak* (cross-blown wooden Afghan flute), Boehm flute, piccolo, two tenor saxophones,

Cross-cultural perspectives in popular music: Afghanistan 111

clarinet, piano, string bass (plucked, not bowed), *tabla* (Indian drum pair), *sitar* (long-necked plucked Indian lute), *delruba* (bowed Indian lute). This orchestra shows a mixture of Afghan, Indian and Western instruments. The precise instrumentation of the big orchestra probably varies from day to day.

In the smaller ensembles the instruments are more usually those associated with Afghan urban music as played in the provinces. Some of these are regarded as Afghan instruments: *rubab, tanbur,* fourteen-stringed *dutar, sarinda/sarang* (bowed lute), *ghichak* (bowed lute) and drums such as *dhol* and *zirbaghali*. Others have come originally from India but have been used in Afghanistan for long enough to have become fully assimilated: *'armonia* (hand-blown harmonium), *tabla, delruba, sarangi* (bowed lute). It is striking how many kinds of lutes are used by the Afghans.

Both male and female singers work at Radio Afghanistan, and they are of both amateur and hereditary professional origins. Few, if any, are employed full time simply as singers. A few of the amateur singers who are from the educated middle class are employed as production and administrative staff and also make some broadcasts as singers. A very few are employed as song-writer–singers, with contracts to compose and record a fixed number of songs per month. There are many other singers who regularly perform for the radio and who are paid on a per recording basis.

The radio station is also ready to record almost any musician from the provinces who is visiting Kabul. It is a matter of considerable prestige for a singer or instrumentalist, amateur or professional, to have made a tape at the *esteshan* ('station', another English word). This is one way in which the periphery feeds back on to the centre. A brief survey of the holdings of the radio archives in 1977 showed that sixty-three Heratis (nearly all of them singers) had made tapes at the radio station. Most of them were residents of Herat; a few had moved to Kabul. Tape recording at Radio Afghanistan only started in the 1960s; before then, all music broadcasts were live.

Some of the best-known radio singers of *kiliwali* have a special social status as 'stars' (see Slobin 1974, pp. 245–6). Particular songs are identified with known artists and are viewed with reference to the total body of that individual's creative work (as composer and/or performer). There is keen interest in the latest work of the individual. The private lives of these singers are of considerable interest to music 'buffs' and there is much gossip about them in these circles. Familiarity with a 'star system' has come about in part through the Indian films that play in Afghan cinemas, the sale of postcard portraits of famous Indian actors and actresses and magazine articles about them.

Figure 3. A well-known Kabuli radio singer, Zaland, educated, of amateur origin, employed (formerly) as singer and song-writer by the Ministry for Information and Culture. Performing at a Ramazan concert in a modern hotel in Herat. Note his suit and tie, symbols of his urbanity, the standing position while he plays the *'armonia*, the accompanying *dhol* (traditional Afghan drum), radio-cassette machines with microphones mounted on the aerials (*delruba*- and flute-players in accompanying ensemble not visible).

Cross-cultural perspectives in popular music: Afghanistan 113

We turn now to the important matter of the origins of the songs in the *kiliwali* repertory. There is a steady turnover of the repertory, with new songs continually being created and older ones falling into disuse. Many new songs are written by those Kabuli singers who are regularly associated with the radio, a few of whom have contracts to supply new songs. Amongst these compositions various styles within the *kiliwali* genre can be distinguished.

Local songs (*mahali*) from different regions of Afghanistan also form an important input to the repertory. Some singers have made trips to the provinces to learn *mahali* songs, or such songs may have been recorded at the station by provincial musicians, broadcast, and taken over by a radio singer. In either case the songs are reworked into the *kiliwali* mould, a *naghme* is composed and they are broadcast with orchestral accompaniment, often provided by a large orchestra like that already described. In this way a *mahali* song enters the *kiliwali* repertory. Though it may still be recognised as a local song, especially by the people from whose region it has come, it has been transformed into a *kiliwali* song, a new song in the radio repertory.

Another source of new songs is provided by the films from India and Pakistan which are shown in the cinemas of Kabul and other cities and large towns and are well attended by Afghan audiences. Most Indian films rely heavily on music and dance. Film (*filmi*) song texts are usually in Hindi or Urdu (very occasionally a song in Persian is found) and are not really comprehensible to most Afghans. This does not seem to detract from the audience's appreciation of them. This music has had an important influence in Kabul and other cities. In some cases radio singers have adopted such songs, making up a new text in Persian, or fitting a pre-existing text to the tune. *Filmi* songs are sometimes sung with nonsense words that approximate the sounds of the original. Again, some Kabuli song-writers copy the style of Indian film songs in their new works.

A further source of new songs is Iran. In the 1970s Iran was undergoing a period of strong interest in music, with regular radio and television broadcasts and thriving record and tape companies (see Nettl 1972, who has no hesitation in calling this 'popular music'). Some Iranian songs, transmitted by radio or cassette, are adopted by Afghans, especially in Herat, and adapted to the *kiliwali* style. Some such songs have reached Radio Afghanistan (usually via Herat) to be performed by the radio station's regular singers. It is likely that Pakistan and possibly Tajikistan (a republic of Soviet Central Asia) also contribute in some measure to the *kiliwali* repertory.

114   *John Baily*

Herat as the periphery

We come now to examine the periphery of the *kiliwali* network as illustrated by the example of Herat. Although there are bound to be local variations, Herat can be considered representative of the periphery as a whole. The music-making at Radio Afghanistan would be of little interest to us if it did not also stimulate, support and provide a model for music-making in the provinces.

Despite the existence of a long-standing prejudice against music from an orthodox Islamic viewpoint, weaker now than in the past but still operative, Herat city is the scene of many sorts of musical activity. Music is an indispensable part of a variety of social situations. Live music is played at wedding parties, in the theatre, at visiting circuses, at concerts during the month of fasting (*Ramazan*), at tea-booths set up at the frequent springtime country fairs (*meles*), at dancing-boy parties (*bache bazi*), at *mehmanis* (dinner served to guests at a private house), *shau nishinis* ('sitting together' till late at night) and *shauqs* (get-togethers of amateur musicians) and on various other occasions.

With certain exceptions (such as female singers in the male patronised theatre) there is separate music-making for men and women, with male and female musicians playing exclusively to male and female audiences respectively. This makes for a social division between male and female musicians. A second important distinction made by Heratis is between professional and amateur musicians (see Baily 1979 for a discussion of this as it applies to men). Analytically, we can distinguish four types of performer (male professional, male amateur, female professional and female amateur), though this is something of a simplification of the over-all situation, for other categories of performer occur too.

The four kinds of musician perform in rather different social contexts, they use different musical instruments to accompany their singing and they utilise different genres of music. Table 1 attempts to summarise these data.

Each of the four categories of musician performs at least some *kiliwali*. The sound of *kiliwali* as produced by Heratis is inevitably different from the 'radio sound'. In part this arises from the fact that in Herat music is performed 'in context', in dynamic social situations which inevitably operate to control the performance. More interesting from the point of view of ethnomusicological analysis are the large differences that exist *between* the four categories of Herati performer in terms of the sounds they produce. Ultimately these differences must be related to variations in the social organisation of the groups of people who perform and use the music. These underlying social factors are manifest in more obvious factors affecting sound production,

Cross-cultural perspectives in popular music: Afghanistan   115

Table 1. *Comparison of four types of musician. (Instruments given in parentheses have some but not frequent use.)*

Category	Social contexts	Instruments	Genres
male professional*	weddings theatre circuses *Ramazan* concerts *meles* dancing-boy parties	*'armonia* *tabla* *rubab* *dutar* *zirbaghali* (*delruba*)	*klasik* *ghazal* *kiliwali*
male amateur	small private parties	*'armonia* *rubab* *dutar(s)* *zirbaghali* *tanbur* (*chahartar*†) (flutes) (*daire*‡)	*kiliwali* (*mahali*)
female professional	weddings	*'armonia* *tabla* *daire*	*kiliwali* *mahali*
female amateur	small private parties domestic entertainment for children	*daire* (*'armonia*)	*mahali* *kiliwali*

* Baily 1979 distinguishes between two kinds of male professional musician on the basis of recruitment: *kesbi*, hereditary professional; and *shauqi-kesbi*, amateur who becomes a professional musician. To avoid unnecessary technicalities, these two groups are treated as a single category here.
† *Chahartar*: long-necked Iranian plucked lute.
‡ *Daire*: frame drum.

such as knowledge of a folk theory of music, the musical instruments used and development of instrumental skills.

Becoming familiar with the repertory and learning the newest songs involves several processes. Musicians themselves are always on the lookout for the emergence of new songs. Initially these are learned direct from the radio. Professional musicians can usually learn the melodies of the song and instrumental section after one or two hearings but they are learned more laboriously, and often incorrectly, by amateurs. The ability to learn quickly by ear is an essential skill for a professional musician in Afghanistan. Learning is made easier by the predictability of many Afghan melodies once the rules governing their organisation have been assimilated. Song texts may be written down; some singers even carry notebooks of texts with them, but never the

Figure 4. The periphery. A group of Herati musicians performing in a tent during one of the spring fairs, with singer–*armonia*-player, 2 *dutar*-players and *zirbaghali* (drum). The musicians are seated on a wooden bed and wear traditional dress. Re-creation of radio music.

Cross-cultural perspectives in popular music: Afghanistan 117

music in notated form. Sometimes musicians learn new songs from cassettes rather than direct from the radio. Once one singer is performing a new song others will begin learning it from him. If the audience likes it too, then it will probably enter the local repertory and be performed frequently for some months or even a year or two.

Rather little interest is expressed by Heratis in old items of the *kiliwali* repertory. It surprised me when I first discovered that songs described as *qadimi* ('ancient') or *kohne* ('worn out') were songs that had been common only five to ten years before. The attention of the Heratis is focussed on the latest songs, the *ahang-e mod* ('fashionable tunes') or *khandan-e mod* ('fashionable songs'). The word *mod* is derived from the French *mode* ('fashion'). Of an old song one may say *az mod rafte* ('out of fashion'). Amongst men, at least, there is little interest in Herati *mahali* songs unless they have been revitalised through radio broadcasting and so transformed into *kiliwali*.

One clear indicator of the transient popularity of songs is their usage by children. Apart from lullabies there are very few distinct children's songs in Herat, a fact that is possibly related to religious prejudice against music in the past. Children sing and dance during their games, and the songs they sing are adults' songs from the *kiliwali* repertory. At any one time the children seem to have a rather small repertory, perhaps no more than five or six songs, and they are usually songs that have been popular with adults a few months earlier and are perhaps already out of fashion.

The choice of songs sung at a performance event is to some extent controlled by the audience through a request system. At more formal public events such as large wedding receptions, *Ramazan* concerts and theatre performances, requests are written on the backs of postcards, usually showing Indian film stars or Iranian singers, and presented to the singer. In the theatre in Herat the names of the requesters are read out by the compère to the audience before each song is performed.

Professional musicians are well aware of the way the audience dictates what they play. Hereditary professional musicians in particular do not esteem *kiliwali*, which they regard as easy to play, with texts that are lacking in profound meaning, unlike *ghazals*, which are highly valued as poetry and considered a more difficult type of music to perform. Such musicians consider themselves servants of the public; their livelihood depends upon meeting the requirements of their audience. At their own occasional gatherings – for example, at the wedding of a musician, when the hereditary musicians take turns to perform – little or no *kiliwali* is played. Although such musicians perceive a discrepancy between the music they choose to play and the music the public wants, this does not lead to alienation of the kind described by Becker (1951) for jazz musicians.

There is no record industry in Afghanistan. In Herat the cassette tape-recorder had come to occupy quite an important role in the 1970s. Ownership of radio–cassette machines was widespread amongst all strata of society. Thousands of Heratis who went to work as migrant labourers in Iran for a few months returned with these machines, or the money to buy them. Many Heratis make their own recordings of all the kinds of musical performance to which men have access. This has greatly increased the exposure of Herati musicians to their public. Members of the audience are considered to have the right to make recordings without charge and only at *Ramazan* concerts of visiting Kabuli singers have I seen people paying to record.

There are also small tape businesses, run from shops in the main bazaars of Herat, that sell recordings of local musicians, made either live or in specially set up recording sessions. They also sell tapes made by similar businesses in Kabul and other cities. Herati musicians seem content that their music reaches a wider public and secures them more engagements, and do not expect to make significant income from making recordings for sale in the bazaar.

Social aspects

The origin of *kiliwali* music is closely linked with the history of radio broadcasting in Afghanistan. The following facts are derived from Gregorian (1969). Radio broadcasting in Afghanistan was initiated in 1925, in the time of the progressive King Amanullah (1919–29), who was deposed by a religious-based reaction to his attempt to modernise Afghanistan. During this time, radio achieved a small breakthrough, with an estimated 1,000 receiving-sets in Kabul in 1928. After the chaos that followed Amanullah's departure, there was no serious move to resume broadcasts until 1936. Radio Kabul began experimental broadcasts in 1939 and was officially inaugurated the following year. The stated aims of the radio were (a) to spread the message of the Koran, (b) to reflect the national spirit, (c) to perpetuate the treasures of Afghan folklore and (d) to contribute to public education.

Broadcasting was seriously hampered during the Second World War by difficulties in obtaining new equipment or spares. Not until the late 1940s was an effective broadcasting service established that could be received in most parts of the country. In the early days, ownership of radio receivers was uncommon and the problem of reception was aggravated by the varying voltage of the electricity supply even in the largest cities. To assist with the dissemination of radio broadcasts,

Cross-cultural perspectives in popular music: Afghanistan 119

receiver apparatus linked to loudspeaker systems in the main streets were set up in various cities, and they broadcast the news, music and popular programmes.

Kiliwali music seems to have originated in response to the need to create a music suitable for radio broadcasting. In the absence of accounts from the actual architects of the new music, only the broad outlines of the process can be discerned. It would seem that the new music was created through a mixing of elements already present in Afghanistan. The over-all form and style of *kiliwali* appears to have been drawn from Pashtun regional music. This connection is apparent in the use of instrumental sections, rhythmic cadences, certain modes and musical instruments. The Pashtun roots of the radio style may explain why the music as a whole is termed *kiliwali* (see remarks on page 108 above). Certain other elements may have come from a type of 'Persian music' formerly found in Kabul and Herat that had links with the 'art music' of Iran. Persian became the language of most *kiliwali* texts.

The creation of *kiliwali* involved both professional and amateur musicians but hereditary musicians whose fathers and grandfathers had been brought to Kabul from India as court musicians in the late nineteenth century seem to have played a crucial role. Ustad Qasem, who lived from 1882 to 1955, is celebrated as the 'Father of Music in Afghanistan'. In this connection it is interesting to note that a number of Indian 'art' musicians have been actively involved in making music for the Bombay film studios.

The broadcasting of this new kind of music has had other important social implications. These have been studied in Herat in connection with the invention of a new musical instrument, the fourteen-stringed Herati *dutar*, and are described by Baily (1976). In summary, the coming of radio music (in Herat) has been accompanied by an over-all increase in music-making and a decrease in religious prejudice against music. There has been an improvement in the social status of musicians, and an increase in the number of amateur musicians who turn professional. It is difficult not to interpret these changes as being directly linked with the decreasing power, political and social, of the religious establishment of orthodox *mullahs* and *'ulema* (legists), and the gradual secularisation of Afghan society. It seems unlikely that the architects of *kiliwali* music were unaware that orthodox Islam would condemn their activities, and they may well have intended to use radio music to help change traditional values and undermine the authority of the religious establishment.

The identification of *kiliwali* as popular music

Up to this point we have considered some of the features of the Afghan *kiliwali* genre. The question that now has to be faced is whether or not this should be considered a type of popular music.

According to the second definition quoted above, 'popular music is typical of societies with a relatively highly developed division of labour and a clear distinction between producers and consumers, in which cultural products are created largely by professionals, sold in a mass market and reproduced through mass media'. It is also clear from this definition that these conditions typically come into being when a society undergoes industrialisation.

On some of these criteria *kiliwali* could be described as a type of popular music. Afghan urban society does have a relatively highly developed division of labour. There is a system of social stratification based mainly on wealth, consisting of three classes: landowners; merchants and shopkeepers; craftsmen, artisans and labourers. Afghan cities are important centres of commerce and manufacture, supporting a wide variety of professions and trades. There are certainly large differences between producers and consumers, and this applies to music as to other things: the professional musician is a highly differentiated economic specialist.

But although an Afghan city like Herat has a high degree of division of labour, it cannot be said to have undergone industrialisation in the Western sense of the word. There are a number of modern trades and skills but these are not apparently linked with a significant change in social organisation. If urban society has not changed *fundamentally* for a long time, and there has been no significant move towards industrialisation, then it is hard to explain the recent origin of *kiliwali* in terms of an industrialisation process. On this criterion it appears that *kiliwali* is not popular music.

However, I do not believe that the factor of industrialisation is crucial. There are other important features that allow us positively to identify *kiliwali* as popular music. It conforms to the following criteria, which are, I believe, characteristic of popular music as a transcultural category.

(1) The people themselves distinguish the genre in question as a distinct category, and contrast it with other kinds of music that they use.

(2) In contrast with the other kinds of music used by the society, popular music has a rapid turnover of repertory. The recognition of this fact by the people is an important part of their perception and appreciation of the music. Continual change in the repertory is not

simply accepted as an inevitable part of using the music, it is made into an issue of central interest.

(3) Popular music is closely associated with the sound recording and broadcasting media, which form an indispensable element in the network of communication between the users of the music – the creators, performers and audience.

The sound media are especially important in the process of creation of new music, but such music will later be recreated at the local level, where music becomes a medium of social interaction, part of a dynamic social process.

(4) Popular music involves the 'cult of personalities', with leading exponents elevated to a special social status.

Of the factors mentioned above, the one that seems to be of greatest importance is the involvement of the sound media. In one sense popular music *is* the music of the media, specifically, those kinds of music that have been created for the media, or in whose creation communication within a media network is important. The characteristics of popular music are to some extent the outcome of constraints inherent in the nature of the media. Identification of those constraints should be the focus of further research.

It follows that when mass sound media are set up in any society it is likely that a genre of popular music will come into being. The technology of the media is the product of industrialisation, but the media can be freely deployed in non-industrialised societies, with this as one probable result.

References

Baily, John, 'Recent changes in the Dutār of Herat', *Asian Music*, 8:1 (1976), pp. 29–64.

'Professional and amateur musicians in Afghanistan', *The World of Music*, 21:2 (1979), pp. 46–64.

Becker, Howard S., 'The professional dance musician and his audience', *American Journal of Sociology*, 57 (1951), pp. 136–44.

Gregorian, Vartan, *The Emergence of Modern Afghanistan. Politics of Reform and Modernism, 1880–1946* (Stanford, 1969).

Merriam, Alan P., *The Anthropology of Music* (Northwestern University Press, 1964).

Nettl, Bruno, 'Persian popular music in 1969', *Ethnomusicology*, 16 (1972), pp. 218–39.

Slobin, Mark, 'Music in contemporary Afghan society', in *Afghanistan in the 1970s*, ed. Louis Dupree and Albert Linette (Praeger, 1974), pp. 239–48.

122   *John Baily*

Discography

Examples of *kiliwali* music performed by singers and musicians at Radio Afghanistan can be found on the following two discs:

Music of Afghanistan, Folkways F E 4361. Recorded by Radio Kabul.

Afghanistan: Music from the Crossroads of Asia, Nonesuch H–72053 (Explorer series). Recording and commentary by Peter Ten Hoopen.

Critical comments on the second disc are given in two reviews by Lorraine Sakata, in *Asian Music*, 5:2 (1974), pp. 61–3, and *Ethnomusicology*, 18 (1974), pp. 468–9. Sakata also refers to the Folkways disc and mentions other recordings of *mahali* materials performed by singers and musicians at the radio station that are of interest.

[18]

Trends and taste in Japanese popular music: a case-study of the 1982 Yamaha World Popular Music Festival*

by JUDITH ANN HERD

Music is the common language of all mankind. Disdaining political and economic boundaries, the joys of music form an instantly communicated bond between men everywhere, and this international festival is dedicated to that spirit.

Kawakami Genichi, President, Yamaha Music Foundation†

Introduction

The contemporary popular music audience in Japan is exposed to a large variety of music, both domestic and imported; tastes are well defined. In particular, such factors as: the singer's 'image', what I call maintaining a standard formula, ambiguity and sentimentalism can be pinpointed as important to the music's appeal. In spite of this, the similarities of Japanese popular music to Western musical styles can suggest that a conventional musical analysis will be sufficient for understanding this music. Thus, many critics who evaluate Japanese popular music usually consider it merely a parody of the 'correct' styles that they are accustomed to hearing. Concentrating merely on the musical analysis, however, underestimates the cultural factors that give Japanese popular music distinctive characteristics which are highly valued in Japan. To offset the shortcomings of such analysis, this article is an attempt to examine Japanese popular music in terms of those cultural factors most important to popular music genres. The first section is a general review of current trends in popular music in Japan, paying particular attention to the characteristics that make the music uniquely 'Japanese'.

I will then develop my observations through an actual case-study. The 1982 Yamaha World Popular Music Festival, where I served as a judge, was chosen because this is an international music contest where prizes are awarded according to Japanese standards. This festival

* I am grateful to the Fulbright Commission and the Japan Foundation for financial support during the period when the research for this article was undertaken, and to Dr Tokumaru Yoshihiko for his valuable advice and support.

† I have followed Japanese practice in writing Japanese names (family name first, followed by given name) except for names quoted from Yamaha literature, where they were 'westernised'.

76   *Judith Ann Herd*

provided me, a foreign participant, with a unique setting for contrasting my own tastes with those of the other judges, Japanese and foreign, as well as those of the audience.

The Yamaha festival is only one of the many types of popular music contest continually shown on Japanese television. If we are to believe a 1982 Japanese Broadcasting Company survey, which states 93 per cent of the Japanese public enjoys listening to music on television, rather than in any other media form*, these contests must have a great deal of impact on popular music. Certainly, the musical styles that are broadcast on television and promoted by the music industry are representative of the mainstream of popular music in Japan. Several winners of previous Yamaha World Popular Music Festivals – Kosaka Akiko, Komuro Hitoshi, Nakajima Miyuki, Sera Masanori and Twist – have become famous and have been promoted by the Yamaha company as a result of the contest.

Another reason for my choice of case-study was that since the Yamaha festival promotes *new* singers and songwriters (unlike the majority of festivals, which feature top stars who have already achieved fame), this study can be used as one way of observing how the music industry discovers what will sell and why, in order to understand and encourage the trends that will benefit the company in the future. Whether or not the industry actually controls the audience's taste or vice versa is a question that is nearly impossible to answer. However, what is clear is that the Yamaha festival and others like it are not held merely for goodwill, but follow and reflect the mainstream of popular music in Japan for economic reasons.

The pressures to conform to existing popular styles, accepted by the Japanese audience and entertainment industry, are great. Perhaps the reasons for this homogeneity are due to the centralisation of the music and communication industry in Tokyo and the intense competition for a primarily domestic market. Even the Yellow Magic Orchestra, stalwart rebels against the mainstream, have recently returned to the fold with their 1983 album *Uwakina bokura* (Naughty Boys). The musical styles that I describe in this article are the most representative of Japanese popular music and reflect the tastes of the majority of the

* *Types of media preferred for listening to music*

	Almost every day	Often	Occasionally	Total
Television	28%	37%	28%	93%
Radio	21%	22%	27%	70%
Tape	15%	22%	26%	63%
Records	4%	20%	35%	59%

Source: NHK 1982, p. 38.

Japanese audience. By juxtaposing the dominant themes found in popular music in general and those of the Yamaha Music Festival, we can get a better understanding of the trends and tastes in Japanese popular music.

Current trends in Japanese popular music

The most popular stars in Japanese popular music, and perhaps the longest lived in the music world, are those from *kayōkyoku*.* Broadly defined, *kayōkyoku* is the music heard most often on television, radio and film, and it encompasses several subdivisions such as folk, New Music, *enka* and *kawaiko-chan* styles. With the exception of *enka* and some folk songs, most of the *kayōkyoku* are written like Western popular music, using heptatonic major and minor scales and standard triadic harmony. There are usually no outstanding audible differences between songs in this genre and popular music in the West. However, there are some striking differences in the way the music is presented. I will discuss the factors listed above (p. 75).

Image. Projecting the correct or acceptable image is essential to the *kayōkyoku* singer's success. This image varies according to the performer's style, but within each classification the images are fairly standard and rarely deviate from those associated with the customary characters.

To anyone who watches Japanese television, the most easily recognised image type is the *kawaiko-chan* or 'cute girls and boys't who, for many viewers, are the true representatives of Japanese youth. Often, these teenage idols are not chosen for their outstanding vocal or physical attributes, but instead it is the singer's character that holds the viewers' attention. Kuroyanagi Tetsuko, the mistress of ceremonies for a popular television music programme, *The Best Ten*,

---

* In a 1982 survey conducted by the Japan Broadcasting Corporation (NHK 1982, p. 629), the respondents were asked to list the styles of music that they enjoyed listening to. The ten most popular musical styles, rated by percentages, were:

66%   *Kayōkyoku*
51%   *Enka*
40%   *Nihon minyō* (traditional Japanese folksongs)
33%   Film music
27%   Western-style folksongs
21%   Current popular hits
20%   *Rōkyoku* (narrative songs with *shamisen* accompaniment)
16%   Rock
16%   Easy listening/pops

† Strictly speaking, *Kawaiko-chan* is a term used only when referring to girl singers, aged between about fifteen and twenty, although there are exceptions to this age limit. However, when seen as a type, the boys in this age group have the same image.

believes that Japanese people love *kawaiko-chan* for their sweetness and purity which should be protected carefully (Booth 1983, p. 5). If the singer is above average in appearance, ability and charm – not too much to alienate or offend the audience, but just enough to give the illusion that 'you can also be a star if you try hard enough' – he or she can have a secure career simply by being a cute, nice, average teenager with no special talent.

Rather than adhering to the strict stereotypes of the teenage idol, the heroes and heroines of the other styles found in *kayōkyoku* are allowed more individuality by the music producers, but their success usually depends upon how well they can relate to their audience rather than on a unique, and therefore possibly alienating, style.

One prescribed image was set in the mid-1960s with the emergence of the 'Group Sounds' movement, led by such singers as Sawada Kenji, who became one of the most popular stars in the business. When he started singing with The Tigers, who were the leaders of the 'Group Sounds', Sawada's image was that of the rebel. His long hair identified him as a nonconformist, though nearly all his admirers rushed to copy him and 'Group Sounds' nonconformity became everyday fashion. Today, Sawada is one of the most adventurous popular music performers and says that he will do almost anything to increase his record sales. However, this does not apply to his songs or lyrics. In spite of his recent attempt to include new wave elements and modernise his material, his music has not changed significantly in twenty years. Musically, there are few differences between Sawada and his peers, who intentionally perpetuate the styles that have been successful because they are the guaranteed routes to stardom.

Image is also important in folk and New Music* genres. Folk singers usually have a relaxed manner, compose many of their own songs and accompany themselves during performance. Generally they begin their careers in small clubs, and even when they achieve fame these performers retain the image of authentic 'downhome folks'. Their links to tradition are often emphasised by using pentatonic melodies, harmony with minor chords and a singing style influenced by older Japanese models. Performers of New Music, a style that became popular among young adults in the mid-1970s, communicate with their audience through lyrics that intimately express the difficulties of growing up, without being too direct.

Enka, another subdivision of *kayōkyoku*, is noticeably different from

---

* New Music is a style that is popular among young adults, between about fifteen and twenty-nine. It has an easy listening/pops character; the lyrics are less ambiguous than in other forms of *kayōkyoku*, although not too direct or outspoken. Performers of this genre are usually singer–songwriters.

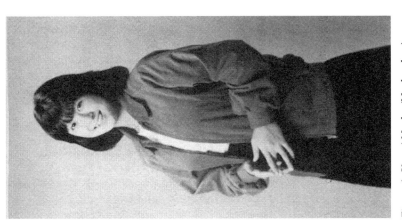

Figure 1. Kawai Naoko (Naoko-chan), now age twenty, is one of the oldest *kawaiko-chan* who still has a large following. Ever conscious of her age, she is currently trying to change her image from a cute girl to a more sophisticated and feminine young woman.

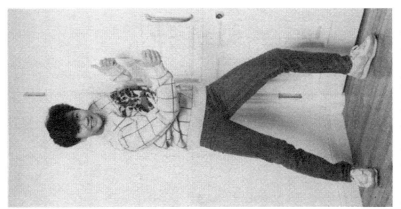

Figure 2. Kondō Masahiko (Matchy), a member of the Tanokin Trio, won seventeen New Singer awards in 1981 and broke a record for the most songs sold (over seven million) in two years. He has consistently released No. 1 hits since his debut in 1979, and currently there are over 170,000 girls and boys in the 'Matchy Fan Club'.

Figure 3. Yakushimaru Hiroko (Hiroko-chan) is the star of *Satomi Hakkenden*, one of 1984's biggest movie hits in Japan. She enjoys her stardom as one of the most popular *kawaiko-chan* singers and actresses, a young idol who is the most popular pin-up girl of promotional photos.

80   *Judith Ann Herd*

Figure 4. Yashiro Aki has for several years been consistently voted one of the top female *enka* performers. Recently, she changed record companies in order to concentrate more on a pure *enka* style. (Photo courtesy of Mr Tanaka Hideo, Century Records)

Western popular music. Its musical characteristics, such as simple strophic form, a quasi-linear texture and melodies based on the *yonanuki* and minor scales (the former omits the fourth and seventh degrees of the diatonic scale), are borrowed from traditional music. From as early as the middle of the Meiji Era (*c.* 1890), the lyrics of *enka* have dealt with love, social events and other aspects of daily life.

Like other *kayōkyoku* performers, *enka* stars have certain images, although these are slightly more complicated. Rarely loved for who they are but adored for what they represent, they take advantage of this by portraying popular personalities, usually the heroes of *chanbara* (*samurai*-sword) or police television dramas. On the other hand, popular personalities sometimes expand their roles and become *enka* vocalists; for example, Kotokaze, a famous *sumō* wrestler, recently became an *enka* singer. It is common for male *enka* vocalists to wear a traditional *kimono*, often gaping open to the waist, and to carry a sword when they portray *samurai*. They speak in low, masculine voices and

Trends and taste in Japanese popular music 81

Figure 5. Kitajima Saburō, an *enka* singer who is the archetype of Japanese masculinity, is one of the most popular stars with the greatest longevity in the entertainment world. (Photo courtesy of Crown Records)

suggest a fantasy of the 'ultimate masculine hero'. These singers are aware that if they deviate too far from the characters they represent and cease to deliver the vicarious pleasure their fans crave, their careers will be jeopardised.

Female performers will often present themselves as women who have experienced all there is to life, while they simultaneously smile coquettishly and crinkle their noses like young girls. This dual role is one of the most important parts of a female *enka* performer's image. The facets of her personality which are slightly hidden from the audience but which could surface at any moment are the part of the star's image that sells the most records. Like other *kayōkyoku* singers, *enka* performers appeal to many different types of people for many different reasons, and therefore have a wide range of admirers.*

* The 1982 NHK survey shows that *enka* ranks as one of the five music genres most

82   *Judith Ann Herd*

Formula. Certain types of standardisation are apparent in the way popular music is presented on television. In 1982, 93 per cent of the respondents in a Japan Broadcasting Company survey said they listen to music on television rather than on any other medium (NHK 1982, p. 38). If the public is expected to enjoy and sponsor this music, it needs to be designed for the layman. Therefore, the bulk of popular music that is broadcast is structurally uncomplicated, has a melody that can be recalled easily, has simple harmonic progressions so that the amateur can play along and has lyrics of a familiar type which express the concerns of the ordinary Japanese citizen. In addition, because there is a tendency to copy popular hits, certain song types are perpetuated and create types of 'forme fixe' of *kayōkyoku*.

Maintaining a standard formula is not limited to the music but also applies to a singer's image. It is difficult for the audience to identify with a popular singer whose image is unapproachable or unfamiliar to the general public, and it is economic suicide for a star not to realise that the fans enjoy watching reflections of their own ideals in the mirror of television. Production companies have an active role in maintaining these formulae, particularly in the case of teenage idols. Nearly everything is decided for the star, from how they must dress to what they must say to their admirers. Arrogance is never tolerated, and if the singer is asked about his or her talent, the standard reply is that they will try to do better in the future or that they owe their success to their fans. When singers transgress, and additional coaching does not help, they are reprimanded or dropped from the payroll; blacklists are circulated among music management companies to eliminate the troublemakers (Booth 1983, p. 5).*

Perhaps the greatest contributor to maintaining formulae is the '*karaoke* boom', which began in the mid-1970s. *Karaoke* (literally 'empty orchestra') is a new form of entertainment in which popular songs are pre-recorded on tape, omitting the original singer's voice. The performer sings into a microphone while the tape is playing, and for the duration of one song, he or she can be a star. As support, in case the

popular with people between thirty and sixty-nine. When respondents were classified according to profession, the survey shows that *enka* ranks in the top five favourite music styles of every profession except white collar professional workers (NHK 1982, pp. 70–1, 78).

* In summer 1983, a rejected boyfriend of Takabe Tomoko, a budding *kawaiko-chan*, sent photographs of Miss Takabe in various immodest poses to a gossip magazine and subsequently ruined her career. Ken Naoko, a popular singer and television personality, was arrested at a party in September 1977 on suspicion of possession of marijuana. Her television commitments were immediately cancelled until the following January. After making a public apology, Ken was able to return to her career, although some other stars affected by the affair were permanently banned. Her return was unusual, and many observers claim that it was her amiable, easygoing personality that saved her.

Trends and taste in Japanese popular music   83

singer forgets the melody, the vocal line is usually doubled by an instrument such as a clarinet, saxophone or guitar.

Karaoke has had a profound effect on the manner in which people experience popular music. Approximately 80 per cent of men over thirty who answered NHK's survey said they sing their favourite songs in bars or at parties using *karaoke* machines (NHK 1982, p. 23). Recently, *karaoke* video has become popular among devotees of this new art form (Nagashima 1982). As the singer stands before a videotaped landscape, designed to set a particular mood, the lyrics of the song appear at the bottom of the video screen. The performer can tape himself or herself against this background and instantly appear on television.

Singing along with pre-recorded tapes and dubbing your voice on to the original soundtrack requires some concentration, especially on style, on the atmosphere the performer wants to project through the song and on the original star's image which the *karaoke* singer wishes to imitate. This image, as explained previously, is important, although the focus of a *karaoke* performance is less on mere imitation of the star's personality than on the image expressed in the lyrics. To recreate the best rendition of the song, the words must be studied carefully and coordinated with body movements and expressions which enhance the song's meaning. Conveying the image and interpreting the lyrics seem to be even more important in *karaoke* than the singing itself.

Sentimentalism. Sentimentalism in the lyrics can take many forms, ranging from ecstasy to resignation and lifelong sorrow. Most often, the choice of songs in *karaoke* bars is *enka* with its melancholy themes that can move the listener to tears. Unrequited love, sadness, happiness, desire and indignation are common subjects (Tokumaru 1969, p. 18), and the wailing tones of the voice as well as the pain or joy on the singer's face invite others to commiserate and release their deepest feelings through the song.

Ambiguity. Anger and dissatisfaction with the present conditions of life are not as a rule expressed openly in Japanese society, but if this is done through channels that disguise it by distracting attention from the individual, protest becomes acceptable. To express it openly might mean unemployment or divorce, but it is safe and comforting to release tensions and remorse through music. Group identification, especially in a drinking place, is clearly part of this experience, but the capacity of the lyrics to express the individual's repressed thoughts and to provide a release is one of the biggest attractions of *enka* and other forms of *kayōkyoku*.

Suggestion, rather than explicit description of the facts, is important in popular lyrics. The words must be flexible enough to allow for

84   *Judith Ann Herd*

individual interpretation, as demonstrated by one of the most famous *enka*, 'Kanashii sake' (Melancholy *Sake*).

Melancholy *Sake*

Alone at the bar, the *sake* I'm drinking
Is flavoured by the tears I shed when we parted.
As I drink, your reflection that I long to forget
Still floats in my glass.

If there's a soul in this *sake*,
Let it stop this lovesick pain in my breast.
Although I know that liquor will only make me worse,
I can do nothing but drink and cry because of love.

I say I'm truly happy being single
But I'm crying inside.
I'm bitter towards a world that keeps lovers like us apart.
The night lingers on.

Kanashii sake

Hitori sakaba de nomu sake wa
Wakare namida no aji ga suru
Nonde sutetai omokage ga
Nomeba gurasu ni mata ukabu.

Sake yo kokoro ga aru naraba
Mune no nayami wo keshite kure
Yoeba kanashiku naru sake wo
Nonde naku no mo koi no tame.

Hitoribocchi ga suki da yo to
Itta kokoro no ura de naku
Suki de soenai hito no yo wo
Naite urande yo ga fukeru.

(*Nihon Kayō dai zenshū* 1980, p. 292)

In this song, the gender of the spurned lover and the whole story of the love affair are unclear. The only fact we know is that someone is unhappy with his or her life, with an aloneness resulting from some unknown events. The ambiguity of these lyrics, as in much popular music in Japan, is valued highly because it allows for a freer, individual interpretation and gives everyone a chance to empathise with the rejected lover.

As in popular music everywhere, appreciation and taste are collective experiences that are determined by both the fans and the promoters. No matter how hard the company tries to force its music on the public, the star's success is determined by the tastes of the Japanese audience. A way to see the importance of these tastes and how they correspond to the dominant themes in Japanese popular music is to evaluate the judging procedure and audience reactions at a music festival that awards prizes according to Japanese standards.

The Thirteenth Annual World Popular Music Festival

Every October since 1970, the Yamaha World Popular Music Festival has been held at the Nippon Budōkan, a building constructed for the martial arts competitions of the 1964 Tokyo Olympic Games, and one of the largest festival halls in Japan. The 1982 festival, held on October 29–31, was supported by the Ministry of Foreign Affairs, the Agency for Cultural Affairs, the Tokyo Metropolitan Government, Japan Air Lines, Fuji Television, Nippon Broadcasting, Yamaha Motors and Nippon Gakki, in addition to minor sponsors who cooperated in various ways. In the festival's fourteen-year history, singers from nearly every country in the world have applied for entry (*Dai-jūsan-kai sekai kayōsai* 1982, introduction), and in 1973 and 1978, the festival was cited by the International Federation of Festival Organizations as the most outstanding worldwide music festival (*Creating Music for Tomorrow* 1982, p. 21). Elton John, Dionne Warwick, George Chakiris and Glen Campbell are only a few of the famous singers who have been featured in previous competitions.

After a careful screening by the Yamaha Music Foundation of a total of approximately 2,000 applicants, the following thirty vocalists representing twenty-one countries including Japan competed for the grand prizes in the 1982 event.*

Peter Lundblad	Sweden
#†Harvey Malaeholo and the Geronimo Singers	Indonesia
Carlene Davis	Jamaica
#†Asuka	Japan
#†Céline Dion	France
Bryan Adams	Canada
#†Mio Honda	Japan
#†Yoshio	Mexico
Stella	Belgium

* The prizes offered in 1982 were the Grand Prize – US $10,000, a gold medallion and certificate of honour; Most Outstanding Performance Award – US $3,000, a gold medallion and certificate of honour; Best Song Award – US $3,000, a silver medallion and certificate of honour; Outstanding Song Award – US $1,000, a silver medallion and certificate of honour; and the Kawakami Prize – award not specified. In all, ten prizes were awarded – see Table 1, p. 93.

86   *Judith Ann Herd*

Takashi Tono'oka and Channel 2	Japan
Dollar	United Kingdom
†Taffy McElroy	United States
#†John Rowles	New Zealand
†Maneenuch Smerasut	Thailand
Jonathan Gregg	Ireland
†Braulio	Spain
Yayoi Satō	Japan
#†Anne Bertucci	United States
#†Piero Cassano	Italy
#†Ronen Bahunker	Israel
Sheeba	Holland
#†Mikiyoshi Iwakiri	Japan
†Sarah Chen	Taiwan
Tony Helos	Australia
Cristóbal	Chile
Richard Dewitte	France
Jade	United Kingdom
†Sumiko Toyohiro	Japan
†B. J. Thomas	United States
Diana Pequeno	Brazil

†*Finalists*
#*Prize winners*

The six Japanese singers were selected at the nationwide 'Pop-Con' popular song contests sponsored by Yamaha that are held every year for the purpose of discovering new talent for Pony/Canyon Records, a Yamaha subsidiary. Similarly, popular music contests sponsored by Yamaha were held on a national level in many of the participating countries, and the grand prize winners were invited to Tokyo to compete at an international level.

Of a total of twenty-three judges, thirteen were from a cross-section of the Japanese public while three were official representatives of the Yamaha Music Foundation. To add credibility to this international event, the remaining seven judges were foreign, representing Canada, England, Indonesia, Ireland, Switzerland, Taiwan and the United States. All judges passed a qualifying examination which screened their opinions of the featured songs in the 1982 festival.* Except for the

---

* The examination for foreign judges, held over two days, was administered to sixty people who were selected from their applications according to their nationality, age and occupation. Everyone taking the test listened to fifteen (one half) of the songs that were to be featured in the 1982 contest and gave their opinions of the presentation, content and orchestration, and their general impressions, of each song, on a prepared ballot paper. Seven finalists were selected for their answers and assembled on the

three official representatives from the Yamaha Music Foundation, all panel members were amateurs; this is because the company believes that the choices of these music lovers, who represent a wide variety of people, will indicate how well the contestants' records will sell on the market.

Creating an image

During the three-day event, it seemed that the singers who failed to project the preferred images were disqualified. Although there was no obvious premeditated bias in selecting the winners, the contestants whose images fitted the expectations of the audience and the judges were the ones who won prizes. (The judges, surrounded by the audience, could hardly help being influenced by their reactions; indeed, we were told to bear audience response in mind.)

Two teenage entrants, Ronen Bahunker (aged thirteen) from Israel and Céline Dion (aged fourteen) from France fitted the teenage idol stereotype very well. Their youth and talent were emphasised several times by the MCs as the audience cheered loudly. In spite of their youth, their voices were powerful and their performances were relatively sophisticated, although they both continued to project sweetness and naiveté. Dion's song was dedicated to her mother and thanked her for her unselfish love. Wearing a white lace dress with ribbons in her long, wavy hair, she looked like a Japanese *kawaiko-chan*. Ronen's song was also about love, but the lyrics were ambiguous, asexual and aimed at a general audience. His youthfulness infatuated his new fans who gave him a tribute reserved only for the most popular teenage idols by chanting his name each time he walked onstage.

The young American contestant, Taffy McElroy, did not do as well. An aspiring country & western singer from Tennessee, she was too mature for the image of Japanese young talent. Furthermore, the lyrics of McElroy's song encouraged rebelliousness.

Just one chance to be free.
Just one chance to be truly young.
And it's so easy being me
And not what they want me to be.

(Copyright 1982 Fred Mollin Music. Rights for Japan and Fareast Asian Countries assigned to Yamaha Music Foundation)

McElroy obviously tried to create the atmosphere of the Grand Old Opry for her act, complete with its earthy songs and flashy costumes,

weekend before the festival to listen to the remaining fifteen contest songs and take a practice examination to ensure that the judging procedure would go smoothly during the official festival days.

88   *Judith Ann Herd*

but the audience who expected cuteness showed their lack of appreciation.

The three prizewinners from Japan, who were excellent representatives of *kayōkyoku*, knew that to take their performances out of their normal contexts or to fail to conform to Japanese expectations were not the best routes to success. Asuka, the Grand Prix winner, sang a love ballad with lyrics inspired by a *kyōgen** play. Following the New Music style, she composed her own song, 'Hana nusubito' (Flower Thief), and accompanied herself on the piano. Honda Mio danced to a lively song, using all the props of the *kawaiko-chan*, such as routine dance movements and mini-skirts. In spite of the differences between the two girls, their publicity briefs described them both as nice college students, in order to point out their similarities and close relationship to their potential admirers, also nice college students. Iwakiri Mikiyoshi followed the formula of the popular folk-rock duo, *Fuki no tō* (similar to Simon and Garfunkel) and borrowed an Israeli folk song for his music, adding original expressive poetry, just as *Fuki no tō* had done with Latin American folk songs since the 1970s.

Some contestants did not attempt to cross cultural barriers in their performances and were disqualified. Expecting a rousing samba or bossa nova, the audience applauded Diana Pequeno from Brazil when she walked on to the stage barefoot, wearing a beautiful, aqua-blue gown trimmed with sequins. A native of Bahia, Pequeno emphasised her mixed heritage with a type of folksong-ballad that described her birthplace, but many of the words could not be translated into Japanese or English, and the audience could not relate to the descriptions of nature and wildlife that are indigenous to Brazilian jungles. Moreover, to those accustomed to the routine movements and the stiff, erect carriage of most Japanese popular singers, Pequeno's excessive body movements were interpreted as being too sexy and bordering on the grotesque. In contrast to her original reception, the applause at the end of her performance was muffled and reserved.

The contestant to use an image most cleverly and to her greatest advantage was Anne Bertucci, the Grand Prix winner from the United States. Originally a hard rock performer who sang with Ted Nugent, Alice Cooper and Cheap Trick, she changed her image from that of a scantily clad singer on Japanese television commercials to one of a sweet young woman dressed in black lace,† cradling a teddy bear in her

---

* *Kyōgen* (literally 'crazy words') is a traditional drama style that reflects social conditions and daily life through the use of comical situations and mime. *Kyōgen* is often performed with *Nō* plays.

† Black does not necessarily suggest sexiness, but is a colour commonly chosen by young female singers in the New Music style and considered attractive and sophisticated for a Japanese woman.

arms for good luck. Before her performance, Bertucci told the MCs and reporters that she 'cannot sing her song without shedding tears since it recalls so many painful memories'. Her sentimentalism and complete change of image are indications that she carefully studied Japanese tastes and used them to her advantage.

Maintaining the standard formulae

Consistency is not limited only to the star's image but extends to all aspects of the way music should be presented and produced. As one Tokyo critic remarked, the preference for standardisation of material in the 1982 festival was striking (Gold 1982). Every song in the contest was a lyrical ballad, had the 'verse-refrain' form commonly found in Western-style popular music and was short and simple. In addition to thematic similarities between texts, the harmonic progressions did not venture too far beyond I–IV–V–I arrangements.

The preference for standard song types was not the only indication of the importance of maintaining the norms. Often 'standard' in Japanese popular music is synonymous with 'average', and in line with this, the judging procedure used in the festival was designed to find the mean and to eliminate the extremes. Each ballot sheet listed the singer's name, country, song title, the composer and/or arranger of the song, and three columns marked 'yes', 'no' and 'Best Singer'. Before the contest, the only instructions the judges received were to concentrate solely on the good points of each performance and to consider how well the songs rated, under the headings of musical arrangements and characteristics, the vocalist's performance, the lyrics and their relationship to the song and movements on stage.

Instead of the point system that is used for most international contests, each judge was asked to vote either 'yes' or 'no', indicating whether or not they liked the song, and to place a circle in the respective boxes on the ballot sheets. From a total of thirty songs, the judges were requested to mark approximately sixteen 'yes' votes, and if adjustments were necessary, they could draw a line through the circle to negate a 'yes' or 'no' vote and add additional circles, as shown in Figure 6. If the judges especially liked a performance, the 'Best Singer' square was marked with a circle. In this case, selections were limited to five and the procedure was similar to the one described above. When the total number of votes was tallied on the second night of the festival, the sixteen entrants with the greatest number of 'yes' votes qualified as finalists and had a chance to perform again on the last night for the Grand Prix and other prizes. Additionally, the 'Best

90

Figure 6. Festival Ballot

SONG TITLE	COUNTRY	SINGER	COMPOSER	YES	NO	BEST SINGER	BEST SINGER ADDITION*
1. 'Dancing in Madness'	Sweden	Peter Lundblad	Tim Norell	⌀	○		
2. 'Lady'	Indonesia	Harvey Malaeholo and the Geronimo Singers	Anton Issoedibyo	○			○
3. 'Quicksand'	Jamaica	Carlene Davis	Carlene Davis	○	⌀		
4. 'Hana nusubito' (Flower Thief)	Japan	Asuka	Minako Suga	○		⌀	

* This column was for 'second thoughts' nomination for the Best Singer award, at the end of the judging period.

Singer' award was given to the contestant with the most circles in the Best Singer columns.

The most interesting element of the decision-making process was its preference for the ordinary. In a society that values compromise and agreement over strong, individual tastes, the Yamaha system helped the judges to reach a consensus vote, and, in many cases, eliminate those songs that were either outstanding or very poor in favour of those that were the least offensive and best understood by the majority. With this systematic process, the winners were not necessarily the most interesting musically or visually, but they were the least unpleasant, the ones well received by most of the audience and the judges.

Ambiguity

Sometimes being too explicit and demonstrative was a problem. One example of this was 'Escucha y calla!' sung by a popular Chilean vocalist, Cristóbal. In a song expressing strong passion and indignation, he sang:

Spanish	English
Escucha y calla!	Listen and be quiet!
Ya no queda nada –	There is nothing left –
Solo un vaso de ron	Only a glass of rum
Para olvidar, olvidar,	To forget, forget,
Mis tristezas olvidar.	To forget my sorrows.

Japanese
Damatte okiki
Mō nani mo nokotte inai
Tada ippai no ramushu de
Wasureru dake, wasureru dake,
Boku no kanashimi wo wasureru dake.*

(Text translated by Yamaha Music Foundation)

As his face contorted with emotion, Cristóbal's gestures on stage were exaggerated. Many judges wondered what his movements represented as his face grew red and his arms waved in the air when he sang 'Calla!' (which would be more satisfactorily translated as 'Shut up!' or 'Urusē!'). Unable to understand the full meaning of the emotional Spanish text, the judges followed the Japanese translation word for

* A more accurate translation of the Spar   would be: Listen and shut up!/There's nothing left between us/But a glass of rum, To forget, forget,/Forget my sorrows.
   The Japanese text provided by Yamaha could be translated: Be quiet and please listen./Now nothing remains –/Only one glass of rum to/Merely forget, merely forget,/Merely forget my unhappiness.

92   *Judith Ann Herd*

word. Rather than using suggestion, Cristóbal's performance presented an explicit physical expression of what appeared to be a relatively simple text, and he was omitted from the final contest.

The only Japanese finalist who did not win a prize was Toyohiro Sumiko who sang an example of *enka* entitled 'Tawamure no koi no mama ni' (Just a Passing Love). Toyohiro offered an almost perfect image of a female *enka* star, with her sapphire-blue satin gown and sultry voice, but the lyrics of her song did not follow this style:

Just a Passing Love	**Tawamure no koi no mama ni**
All alone in my room at dusk	Tasogare no heya ni hitorikiri
I crawl between crisp white sheets	Shawā no shizuku nugui mo sezu
Not bothering to wipe the dampness	Shiwa no nai shiroi shītsu
That still clings from my shower.	Omoide to nemuru
I'll sleep with my memories.	Yakusoku no toki ni otozureta
Darkness comes to embrace me	Yūyami ga kata wo dakiyosete
At the promised time.	Mune no botan kakeru yubi ni
My finger, playing with the button	Namida ga atsui, Love me
on my chest,	Dakishimete mō ichido
Is bathed in hot tears. Love me.	Tawamure no koi no mama ni.
Embrace me one more time.	
It's just a passing love.	

In contrast to the typical female *enka* singer with her dual image (see p. 81 above), Toyohiro appeared to be a young woman who had lost her innocence and had no intention of repenting. She disqualified herself by eliminating the ambiguity that is necessary in the genre she represented.

Sentimentalism

All of the songs in the contest were similar in many respects, but strikingly so in lyric content (*Dai-jūsan-kai sekai kayōsai* 1982). In a total of thirty songs, twenty-six (or 87 per cent) were about love, while freedom was the subject of two (Jamaica and the United States) and the remaining two songs were descriptive ballads (Brazil and France). All six of the songs performed by Japanese entrants concentrated on affection and devotion, and of those, five focused on unrequited love, a favourite theme of *enka*, New Music and other forms of *kayōkyoku*. Overall, unrequited love was the subject of 40 per cent of the songs, although 47 per cent were about the happiness that love can bring. The prize-winning songs clearly showed a tendency towards themes expressing indignation or to do with unhappy love affairs, as seen in Table 1. All the songs, particularly those that won prizes, dealt with

Table 1 *Prize-winning contestants and songs*

Prize	Singer	Title (first the original title, then the translation)	Topic
Grand Prix	Anne Bertucci United States	'Where Did We Go Wrong?' (Kodoku no tobira)	Unrequited love
Grand Prix	Asuka Japan	'Hana nusubito' (Flower Thief)	Unrequited love
Best Singer	Yoshio Mexico	'Enseñame a Querer' (Teach Me to Love)	Love fulfilled
Outstanding Song	Céline Dion France	'Tellement J'ai D'amour Pour Toi' (I Have So Much Love For You)	Parental love
Outstanding Song	Mio Honda Japan	'Ai Dansa' (Sad Dancer)	Unrequited love
Best Song	John Rowles New Zealand	'Holiday in Mexico' (Horidei in Mekishiko)	Love and adventure
Best Song	Mikiyoshi Iwakiri Japan	'Haru ni nareba' (Come Home in the Spring)	Unrequited love
Best Song	Ronen Bahunker Israel	'Mikol Shirey A'havati' (Of All My Love Songs)	Love fulfilled
Best Song	Piero Cassano Italy	'Donna Blu' (Blue Lady)	Unrequited love
Kawakami Prize	Harvey Malaeholo and the Geronimo Singers Indunesia	'Lady' (Itoshi no reidi)	Unrequited love
Kawakami Prize			Unrequited love

pleasure or pain in a way that offered the vicarious enjoyment which is important in Japanese popular music.

A common topic is admiration for someone who has struggled for a long time and finally conquered the obstacle that blocked the way to success. Perhaps this is the reason why the headlines announcing Anne Bertucci as a Grand Prix winner stated 'Bijin kashu kusetsu jūnen' (After ten years of hardship, the beautiful woman finally is a star vocalist!) (*Focus*, 12 November 1982, p. 13). The article goes on to explain how she suffered in the United States before she was discovered in Japan and that with luck she will be the first female American singer 'imported' back to her home country.

Similarly, Yoshio first captured the hearts of the Japanese audience when he was featured on a Japan Broadcasting Company television programme in April 1982. Of Mexican–Japanese extraction, Gustavo Nakatani Avila (alias Yoshio) is a popular *ranchero* singer in Mexico, and was invited to attend this year's international festival with his entire family. With tears in his eyes after his son's first performance, Yoshio's father told the audience in Japanese that 'after fifty years, it is nice to be back home'. The audience and the majority of the judges seemed to be more impressed with Yoshio's family members and his bi-cultural background than with his talent. When Yoshio won the Best Singer and Outstanding Song awards, he accepted them on behalf of his parents.

At times, translations into Japanese became even more romantic than the original. Although it was evident to everyone that 'love' was a central theme of the festival, the Japanese titles made sure this was clear. 'Lady' sung by Harvey Malaeholo and the Geronimo Singers became 'Itoshi no reidi' (Beloved Lady), 'Where Did We Go Wrong?' sung by Anne Bertucci became 'Kodoku no tobira' (The Door to Solitude) and 'Tellement j'ai d'amour' (I Have So Much Love For You) sung by Céline Dion became 'Mama ni okuru uta' (Song for My Mother), just in case someone overlooked the fact that Dion was a young, innocent girl who was grateful for her mother's love. Cristóbal's song 'Escucha y calla!' (Listen and Shut Up!) was changed completely to 'Kanashimi no kaisō' (Remembering My Sadness). A preference for the sentimental and romantic, a dominant quality in popular Japanese music, was a conspicuous theme in the 1982 contest.

Conclusion

Popular music in Japan is deeply rooted in the culture. While the musical elements such as harmony or orchestration are usually 'international' and can be evaluated musically in the same way as with singers or groups in other countries who have similar styles, the preferences of the Japanese public reveal much about what is Japanese in this music.

For example, singers in many Western countries are often popular because of their distinct appearance, talent or personality. However, in Japan, stars must appear to be like everyone else and are idolised because they are not so different or outstanding. Lyrics in American or British popular music can contain precise description while Japanese lyrics are usually ambiguous or vague. The ideas presented in certain genres of popular music in the United States and the United Kingdom, particularly in punk rock, reggae or the protest music of the 1960s, are controversial, and often the politics are a strong selling point. Japanese popular music, on the other hand, is apolitical, and any hint of controversial ideas will detract from the song's popularity. Female singers in many Western countries emphasise their sexuality, but *kawaiko-chan* cannot even hint at it or their singing career will be ruined.

In order to understand Japanese popular music fully, we must understand the criteria and values of the audience for which the music was intended. It is easy to make mistakes of interpretation or overlook significant factors in Japanese popular music genres if we judge this music from an inappropriate perspective. Unless we broaden our analysis, we will be hopelessly culture-bound and even further away from Yamaha's 'international' ideal than we can imagine.

Bibliography

'Bertucci, Asuka win Grand Prix awards in World Song Festival', *The Japan Times*, 1 November 1982

'Bijin kashu kusetsu jūnen: Sekai kayōsai yūshō no Anne Bertucci' (After ten years of hardship, the beautiful woman finally is a star vocalist: the World Song Festival award winner, Anne Bertucci), *Focus*, 12 November 1982, pp. 12–13

Booth, W. 1983. 'I touched Matsuda Seiko's boots', *Tokyo Journal*, 1 February 1983, p. 5

Creating Music for Tomorrow: Yamaha's Music Activities. 1982. (Tokyo)

Dai-jūsan-kai sekai kayōsai (*The Thirteenth World Popular Song Festival*). 1982. (Tokyo)

Gold, S. 'Yamaha's 'non-rock' song festival', in 'Music beat: raves and waves', *Mainichi Daily News*, 6 November 1982

Kayōkyoku (Tokyo). This is a monthly magazine concerning popular music in Japan

Komota N., Shimada H., Yazawa T. and Yokozawa C. 1980. *Nihon ryūkōka-shi* (*Sengo-hen*) (A History of Japanese Popular Songs: Post-war) (Tokyo)

Mita M. 1967. *Kindai Nihon no shinjō no rekishi: Ryūkōka no shakai shinri-shi* (A History of Sentiment in Modern Japan: the Social Psychology of Popular Songs) (Tokyo)

96   *Judith Ann Herd*

Nagashima H. 1982. 'Karaoke sounds good, to manufacturers at least', *The Japan Times*, 11 July 1982

NHK hōsō seron chōsa shohen (The Public Opinion Survey Committee of the Japan Broadcasting Corporation). 1982. *Gendai-jin to ongaku* (Modern Man and Music) (Tokyo)

Nihon kayō dai zenshū (A Complete Collection of Japanese Popular Songs). 1980. (Tokyo)

Okada M. 1982. 'Kayōkyoku', in *Ongaku dai-jiten* II (Tokyo), pp. 621–4

'Popular song fest grand prix dominated by two songstresses', *The Japan Times*, 7 November 1982

Sakamoto R. 1983. 'Nihon no rokku-shi wo saikentō suru' (A re-examination of the history of rock in Japan), *Marquee Moon* (April), pp. 52–3

Sonobe S., Yazawa T. and Shigeshita K. 1980. *Nihon no ryūkōka: Sono miryoku to ryūkō no shikumi* (Japanese Popular Songs: Their Appeal and the Structure of Their Popularity) (Tokyo)

Tokumaru Y. 1969. 'Kayōkyoku no sho-mondai' (A minor problem of Japanese popular songs), *Ongaku geijutsu*, 27: 7 (July) pp. 18–23

World Popular Song Festival in Tokyo '82, the performances of the prizewinners of the Thirteenth World Popular Song Festival, Tokyo, Yamaha Music Foundation, STEREO 19–249/YL–8213

Yoi-ko no kayōkyoku (The Popular Songs of 'Good Kids') (Tokyo). This is a monthly magazine concerning the popular songs of Japanese teenage idols

[19]

POPULAR MUSIC IN INDONESIA SINCE 1998, IN PARTICULAR FUSION, INDIE AND ISLAMIC MUSIC ON VIDEO COMPACT DISCS AND THE INTERNET

By Bart Barendregt and Wim van Zanten

Abstract

In this article we analyse some developments in the popular music of Indonesia, especially those that have occurred during the last five years. The concept of "popular music" in present-day Indonesia is discussed briefly along with an analysis of how it is used in the negotiation of the identity of particular communities, playing a vital role in a dialogue of power at local, national and global levels. We ask how the different pop scenes comment on and act to change society in an age of shifting identities and sensibilities. At the beginning of the twenty-first century, issues of copyright and intellectual property rights seem to have become even more important than they were in the 1990s.

Examples are taken from both the national and regional pop musics with attention being paid particularly to the emergence of "world music" or "fusion", Islamic music and the *Indie* music scene. The question of how these different types of pop music are represented in and shaped by the new forms of mass mediation, in particular the video compact discs and the Internet, is raised and discussed. With the demand for political change (*Reformasi*) and fall of President Suharto, the figurehead of the "New Order" regime, in 1998, these developments seem to have accelerated more than ever before.

Introduction[1]

The notion of "popular" (*rakyat, populer*) music is important in Indonesia, although it is defined there in ways that are distinct from the ones familiar to observers of popular music in, for instance, Europe or the United States. Our focus is on dominant and emergent musical forms created by Indonesian artists, mostly within living memory, which are "clearly commercial, rooted in the music industry (including production and distribution) and a clientele able and willing to purchase the commodity" (Lockard 1998:19). "Rooted" does not mean entirely embedded; live concerts, *karaoke* renditions, popular songs sung in folk drama and social dance, and impromptu rehearsals while taking a bath are understood to

---

[1] In this article we make use of some sections of a research plan written by the authors in 1999 together with Saini Kosim M., Paula Bos, Matthew I. Cohen and Kees Epskamp. We are grateful for their contributions. Together with Paula Bos, the authors presented a panel on popular music in Indonesia at the ICTM conference in Rio de Janeiro, July 2001, concentrating on three regions (West Sumatra, West Java and East Flores), and the role of the World Wide Web and video-CDs. We thank Tuti Hasanah for checking our translations of Sundanese song texts. Last but not least, we thank the two anonymous reviewers of this article for their valuable suggestions for its improvement.

68   2002 YEARBOOK FOR TRADITIONAL MUSIC

be selected moments in a circuit of production and consumption that incorporates music videos, television variety show performances, audiocassettes and (video) compact discs.

Relatively little research has focussed on Indonesian popular music. Overviews of Indonesian popular music are presented in Manuel (1988), Yamashita (1988), Hatch (1989), Lockard (1996, 1998), and Wong and Lysloff (1998) while some general information on recordings may be found in Broughton et al. (1994:425-32). Scholars have paid attention to certain aspects of *kroncong* (Becker 1975; Heins 1975; Abdurachman 1977; Kornhauser 1978; Kartomi 1998), *dangdut* (Frederick 1982; Mona Lohanda 1983; Murray 1991; Pioquinto 1995; Browne 2000), and selected other "national" genres (Remy Sylado 1983; Yampolsky 1989; Arps 1996; Sutton 2000), but about regional popular music much less has been written. That of West Java has been studied to a reasonable extent (Manuel and Baier 1986; Wright 1988; Subagio 1989; Williams 1989; Hellwig 1989, 1993, 1996; Cohen 1999; Jurriëns 2001) and recently one of the present authors published an article about Minangkabau popular music (Barendregt 2002). The popular music of central and East Java, or the other islands, however, is far less represented in the literature.

Hence, there is a need for mapping the topography of Indonesian popular music in more detail. Indonesia's music industry, centred in Jakarta, defines Indonesian popular music as either "national" or "regional". National genres, including rock, hardcore, rap, country, jazz, disco, house, Hawaiian, *pop Indonesia, kroncong, dangdut, qasidah,*[2] generally feature lyrics in Indonesian (though sometimes in English) and are marketed primarily in urban regions throughout the archipelago, both as audiocassette and compact discs (mainly in video-CD, less in audio-CD form). The music trend, both on the national and regional levels, is shifting towards popular music, which is almost entirely a product of the recording studios, live performances being rare.

A regional popular music is targeted at consumers who are the residents of a specific region, or the members of specific ethnic groups, rather than at Indonesians in general (Yampolsky 1989:12-13). Lyrics tend to be in "local" or "ethnic" languages and dialects such as, for instance, Sundanese or Ambon Malay. Instrumentation and the musical idiom used are also likely to be related to residual local traditions of music making. The relatively lower volume of consumption by and the lower economic class of most purchasers of regional popular music mean that few audio compact disc (CD) recordings are made: the regional popular music industry since circa 1970 has been almost exclusively an audiocassette industry (Sutton 1985; Yampolsky 1987). Since 1997-1998 the video compact discs (VCDs), which are cheaper than audio CDs (see below), have gradually been taking over the role of the audiocassettes.

Generic definitions and meta-generic clusters are responsive to market demands; the name for a musical form may shift depending on how well it sells, while new popular genres are constantly being invented by audiocassette

---

[2] Also written *quasidah.*

producers and enterprising performers.[3] More than one regional-popular musical genre can be found in many regions of Indonesia. Sometimes, though not always, these genres are grouped together and classified as *pop daerah* (regional pop). *Pop Jawa*, *pop Sunda*, and *pop Minang* are particularly well known, and refer respectively to the Javanese in central and East Java, the Sundanese in West Java, and the Minangkabau in West Sumatra.

Traditional Indonesian art often aids in consolidating a collective identity by stressing a group's historical tradition and thereby invoking a shared past. For instance, many song texts in *tembang Sunda Cianjuran* accentuate a shared tradition going back to the semi-legendary, pre-Islamic kingdom of Pajajaran, which evokes a cultural participation in an imagined Sundanese homeland in West Java (Van Zanten 1989:70-1, 75-9). Below we will give examples of how Sundanese pop music still employs texts and music that evoke such a shared past which, by being contrasted to other realities, reshapes Sundanese identity.

Many devices have been employed for determining the character of *pop Minang* (West Sumatra), including the use of emblematic instruments. Images iconic of Minang-ness are also widely used on cassette covers and posters, while song texts refer to popular folktales and proverbs. However, three components stand out in the current discourse on how to shape a genuine Minang music, which can withstand the challenge of the twenty-first century: the politics of language, the representation of the motherland and the musical expression of longing for home (Barendregt 2002). *Pop Minang* addresses an overall Minang community, and is, in an era of scale increase, technological innovations and the growing need for re-localisation of this Minang identity, one of the fastest and most direct ways to react to these developments.

Indonesia's hundreds of regional language groups do *not* have equal representation in the recording studios. The policies of Indonesia's media tycoons, mainly ethnic Chinese, are likely to not always correspond with the wishes of the majority. At the same time, mass media are quickly responsive to changing world circumstances. Although music industries that record and distribute popular music genres in local languages have been emerging since the early 1970s, not all of these have been equally successful. As Jabatin Bangun (2001:13) points out, so far only a few cities can claim to have accommodated

---

[3] Take, for instance, *gamad* or *gamat* music from west Sumatra, which features solo singing accompanied by accordion and/or violin, guitar and drums (Rizaldi 1997:93). Audiocassettes of "pure" *gamad* music without synthesiser are released under labels like *gamad asli* (original, authentic *gamad*). If the audiocassette or VCD just mentions *gamad*, *joged gamad* (or *joget*, that is, the faster and danceable songs of the *gamad* repertoire), or *top hits gamad*, the singing is very likely to be accompanied by just a synthesiser with a drum-pattern. Further, there is *gamad Cha Cha Cha*, etc. Similarly, the singing with bamboo flute (*saluang*) accompaniment in west Sumatra may be called *saluang klasik* (classical *saluang*) to indicate the "original" music, in contrast to *saluang modern* (modern *saluang*) and *saluang dangdut* (after *dangdut*, Indonesian pop music; see also Yampolsky 1989:16). Labels like "Reformasi" usually mean nothing in a musical sense, but rather indicate novelty; see also Figure 1.

successful music industries, including Jakarta, Medan, Padang, Palembang, Surabaya and Ujung Pandang. Remarkably, Jabatin Bangun does not mention the large cities of Bandung and Yogyakarta, which we also see as prominent centres of the recording industry.

The boundary between regional music and ethnic music is rather diffuse, both having their roots in the same phenomena. However, whereas regional music tends to be mass-mediated and to possibly be exposed to Western influences in the process, ethnic music is (sometimes proudly) said to be more "pure". Some musics tend to be somewhat more problematic. Chinese language music, for instance, is especially under-represented in present-day popular music, in spite of the fact that citizens of East Asian descent are well represented in the recording industry. In itself this is not surprising, as expressions of Chinese-ness have only recently been tolerated again after being suppressed for thirty-five years. Chinese *lagu mandarin* was a cassette genre that was popular in the 1980s and early 1990s, but that seems to have lost ground in the second half of the 1990s. Sales of Mandarin recordings have been low, partly due to the restrictions on Chinese language materials initiated by president Suharto's New Order regime.[4] In the post-Suharto era, opportunities to listen to and perform Chinese music in public seem to have increased.[5] For instance, *Kompas Cyber Media* (3 March 2002) reports on Chinese music and dances performed at the "China Town Festival" held in Bandung on the occasion of the Chinese New Year Imlek 2553. Similarly, Chinese Song Festivals (Festival Lagu Mandarin) and Chinese language *karaoke* (see below) contests have only recently been allowed, while private radio stations increasingly have special programs devoted to the pop Mandarin genre.

International popular music coming from the United States, Western Europe, India and China is also having a growing impact on Indonesia's music scene. These three related musical domains—the local, the national and the international—lead to discussions about "individual", "ethnic" and "national" identities.

Frederick (1997:62) has suggested interesting parallels between the cultural life in the colonial Netherlands East Indies of the 1930s and that in the

---

[4] Sen and Hill (2000:170) mention an additional Rp.1200 censorship fee levied on Mandarin language materials, which could be responsible for the relatively low volume of sales, although we do not have concrete statistics on these sales. As with regional pop albums, it might be that *pop mandarin* albums sell less well than national pop albums do. On the other hand, they are sold over quite a long period, whereas national pop albums are soon replaced by the latest trend.

[5] Before the Suharto New Order regime, the situation seems to have been more liberal as well. Films made by the Netherlands-Indies information services in the 1920s-1930s, for instance, show examples of Chinese dragon dances during the annual *Cap-goh-meh* processions, performed in the streets of Padang, west Sumatra (*Mahamoelia* 1929). According to Clara van Groenendael (1993:17), popular Chinese hand glove puppet theatre (*po-té-hi*) has not been performed since 1967 (and after the supposed communist coup of 1965 and accusations of Chinese efforts to influence Indonesian politics), when a new measure forbade the public display of Chinese culture.

Indonesia of the early 1990s. Both eras were characterised by the search for a true modern Indonesian culture, which should be spontaneous and not restricted to only some classes or ethnicities, and which should moreover transcend the simple dichotomies of Eastern and Western and traditional and modern. Although in both eras this striving for a unified and more varied modern culture was linked to the emergence of new media, in the 1930s radio and cinema and in the 1990s especially VCDs and the Internet, there are also considerable differences between them, such as a much larger population and thus a much larger audience that has furthermore been increasingly impacted by a plethora of cultural influences. Another considerable difference has been the rise of Indonesian upper and middle classes that have increasingly tried to gain access to a cosmopolitan lifestyle. "Increasingly large numbers of Indonesians of all social and economic classes not only have access to world culture, but are cultural tourists in their own nation, even their own region" (Frederick 1997:77).

Indonesia is now at a critical juncture in its history. In the process of reformation (*Reformasi*) that was put into motion with the resignation of president Suharto and the fall of his New Order regime in 1998, dominant conceptions of *bangsa* (people, nation, race), *suku* (ethnic group) and *daerah* (territory, region)—many originating in Indonesia's colonial past—have lost their mooring. Emergent *and* primordial units of affiliation have come to the fore, associated with inter-ethnic and inter-religious violence throughout the archipelago and with open discussions about regional autonomy, independence for East Timor, federalism, and Indonesia becoming an Islamic state. There are signs that in the post-Suharto and *Reformasi* era popular music will have an even more important role in the formation of identities.

New sounds and the fusion of musical traditions

Musical performances and texts were important sites for signifying opposition to the New Order discourse of order and stability. Sen and Hill (2000:164) describe how in the music industry the line between mainstream-profitable and counter-cultural was a very thin one, and foreign (Western or Westernised) musical codes and icons were frequently indigenised into conscious political opposition to the New Order, although at the same time the New Order government apparatus tried to mobilise musical performances in its own interest. Subversion is thus not a characteristic of music as was proven by Wiranto, the former four-star general and commander-in chief of the Indonesian army at the time of the unrest and killings in East Timor and Aceh. Shortly after he was sacked from parliament in 2000, and with the majority of the nation criticising the armed forces for its violent campaigns, Wiranto released his debut album "For you, my Indonesia" (*Untukmu Indonesiaku*), consisting of ten all-time sentimental Indonesian songs. The money from the CD sales was to go to aid an estimated 900,000 refugees from Aceh, Maluku and East Timor, but while the album sold thousands of

72   2002 YEARBOOK FOR TRADITIONAL MUSIC

copies, human rights groups have denounced it as a gross insult to the people of East Timor.[6]

The call for political reforms (*Reformasi*) was popular for a while, bringing together a variety of interest groups, crosscutting all layers of society. This call was especially prominent in popular culture, and specifically in music. Popular music became a common vehicle of protest during the monetary crisis, and many songs, cassettes and genres were provided with the adjective 'reformasi'; see figure 1.[7] Developments since Suharto's resignation, however, make clear that in many respects *Reformasi* was mostly an empty slogan, largely played out through the mass media and, due to its lack of specific content, able to serve a variety of causes. In the meantime, more subtle and structural developments have been taking place with possibly much greater long-term effects on popular musics.

Figure 1. The Reformasi that started 1997 and lead to the resignation of president Suharto was extensively used as a label to sell music and other commodities, also by the well-known protest singer Iwan Fals. The small piece of paper, attached to the cover on the down-left, shows that the government has given permission for its publication and that sales taxes are being collected.

---

[6] See, for example, *Jakarta Post Online*, 19 October 2000 and *CNN* [E], 2 November 2000 (where necessary, we indicate the electronic—online—journals with the superscript [E]; these articles are mostly also available in printed form).

[7] For an overview of nationalistic and patriotic student songs, but especially of the genre of protest songs that was soon popularly labeled *lagu Reformasi*, and which commented directly on this transitional stage in Indonesian politics, see Van Dijk (1999).

After decades of standardisation and the "folkorisation" of the arts, pop musicians slowly seem to have regained an interest in the traditional arts. The recent relaxation of restrictions on the media and the drive toward reforms that welled up in its wake have led many pop musicians to experiment with "their own musical heritage". As a local newspaper recently wrote, "One form of *Reformasi* in the field of music is to explore our own regional musical traditions and make this into modern music" (*Suara Pembaruan Online*, 5 June 1998). Thus, popular artists like Kahitna and Oppie Andaresta have recently been using Minangkabau traditional music within a pop idiom, while the singer Franky Sahilatua musically quoted Manggarai (Flores) traditional music in the song *E wada*. Another such experiment was undertaken by Nyak Ina Raseuki, a woman from Aceh, who studied ethnomusicology in the USA, and at home recorded an album called *Archipelagongs* (2000), on which she is assisted by musicians and popular singers like Djaduk Ferianto, Oppie and Rita Effendy. All of the songs, including *Remember Maninjau* (Minangkabau), *The Gates of Puya* (Toraja) and *Keumalahayati* (Aceh), are based on regional traditions.

Rock groups like Kantata and Gong 2000 have been involved in experiments with traditional music to a lesser extent. Recently the phenomenon of pop artists seeking inspiration in traditional music received some reinforcement from another trend of the 1990s, known as *campur sari*, but soon called *musik dua warna* (two-colour musics) after a television show aired by the RCTI broadcast station. The two colours refer to the characteristic mix of diatonic and pentatonic tonal systems, in practice leading to all manner of combinations, like gamelan music mixed with piano, or traditional instruments with Latin music. The genre is often associated with the composers Djaduk Ferianto (leader of the *Kua Etnika* ensemble) and Aminoto Kosin (Sutton 2000:44), but especially with Erwin Gutawa. The latter also musically arranged Chrisye's re-mastered version of the classical *Badai pasti berlalu* album (1977), once again turning its 2000 version into one of the most successful Indonesian pop albums ever.

Gideon Momongan (2000:51) wrote in the pop magazine *NewsMusik* that "the aesthetics of our [Indonesian] ethnic music truly has high potential for the market". Indonesian music magazines like this increasingly feature their own world music columns, while at the same time a new genre of radio stations called "ethnic radio" has emerged. These so-called Etnikom (see *Indonesia Radio Directory* [E]) are a growing network of local radio stations, active thus far in Sumatra and Java, that have special programs of (mainly Indonesian) traditional music. Taking Jamaican reggae and Brazilian bossa nova as examples, the Indonesian media, in the midst of a socio-political and economic crisis, hoped that this new approach would bring Indonesia the authentic popular genre many had been waiting for, instead of being doomed to merely copy Western pop music. This echoes the aspirations voiced by President Soekarno in his 1959 speech, where he urged the nation's youth to come up with an authentic but modern Indonesian music (Tambajong 1992:19; Sen and Hill 2000:166).

The Sundanese music of West Java has undergone interesting developments during the last decades of the twentieth century, which were also

74   2002 YEARBOOK FOR TRADITIONAL MUSIC

appreciated in other parts of Indonesia. Hellwig's film *Sundanese popular culture alive!!!* shows how the Sundanese started experimenting with the popular genre *jaipongan* as soon as it was created,[8] creating *breakpong* (combination of break dance and *jaipongan*) and the like (Hellwig 1989).

In the late 1980s, a piano played by the jazz pianist Bubi Chen was added to the traditional Sundanese combination of two zithers and a bamboo flute (*kacapi-suling*). The new combination gave a few concerts, among others in Jakarta, and made the cassette tape *Kedamaian* (1989; Peace of mind). On this tape the *kacapi-suling* musicians play more or less as they would do without the piano while Bubi Chen improvises in a style that is close to the playing style of the small zither (*kacapi-rincik*), with many notes and using syncopations that are a common feature of the bass part of the large zither (*kacapi indung*). In the introduction to the cassette, Harry Roesli, a jazz musician from Bandung, writes that for the last hundred years music from Indonesia has regularly been combined with music from "the West". This recording, however, he considers a masterpiece, and he welcomes the "spiritual child" (*anak kandung batin*) of *maestro* Bubi Chen and the well-known zither player Uking Sukri. This musical form did not achieve popular success but it may nevertheless have had an important influence on later developments.

Pop music, "fusion", as well as "world music", are increasingly created in combination with musicians from other parts of the world. Burhan Sukarma, who was a famous Cianjuran flutist in the 1970s-1980s, left West Java in the late 1980s for the USA, but regularly returns to his homeland Sunda. He made some recordings of "world music", in cooperation with Vidal Paz, like the one on which his Sundanese flute is combined with the Sundanese *kacapi* zither, Sundanese drums, a Balinese mouth harp[9] and *tabla-djembe-congas* from other parts of the world (*Sunda Africa* 1998). On the cover of the CD it says "Sunda Africa is a fusion of cultures that brings the world together", and a quote of the Chinese *I Ching* is given: "Music has power to ease[10] tension within the heart and loosen the grip of obscure emotions". One may wonder whether this should be classified as "popular music". It has many characteristics of Sundanese music though one important element is absent, namely the Sundanese language as this recording is only of instrumental music.

In 2000, the English pop singer and guitarist Sabah Habas Mustapha (alias Colin Bass) made a CD *So la li* with The Jugala All Stars group from

---

[8] Helwig (1989) claims that *jaipongan was* "invented" in 1978, but according to Robert Wessing (personal communication), this music and dance form was both "hot" and popular in the Bandung area when he arrived there to do fieldwork there in June 1970. At the time, Wessing bought a Jugala cassette on which the genre was indeed already called *jaipongan*.

[9] The zither is called a "harp" on the cover. The Balinese mouth harp *genggong* is mentioned, though presumably the Sundanese mouth harp, *karinding*, is what is meant.

[10] On the cover is written "easy".

Bandung.[11] The group uses the Sundanese bamboo flute, drums, zithers and also a violin, acoustic guitar and electric bass guitar. The songs are mostly in Sundanese though some are in English.[12] This band uses a few "classical" song texts as used in Cianjuran music. Sabah told one of the present authors that he was struck by the lyrics, often describing melancholy and living in another country (like in the song *Di nagara deungeun*), themes that he also feels to be present in Sundanese music. The Sundanese vocalist Tati Ani Mogiono sings in Sundanese and very much in the Sundanese style. In translation this text runs as follows:

> Faintly can the sound of the *degung* and bamboo flute be heard. Accompanied by soft singing, they blend very beautifully. Well, this is the song. It is called "Hoisting the sail". The sound of the bamboo flute is melancholy; it makes sad people even sadder. The sound of the *degung* is deep and comforts those who are upset. (Van Zanten 1989:211-2).

In popular Sundanese music, including the new experiments with "world music" or "fusion", almost without exception at least a few Sundanese instruments are used. This is different from, for instance, Indonesian *kroncong* and *dangdut* and the Minangkabau *gamad*. As audiences other than the Sundanese themselves also appreciate, there is still a lot of Sundanese-ness in pop Sunda; for instance, on the CD with *Sambasunda* (1998) music, shaken and beaten bamboos (respectively *angklung* and *saron bambu*), *kacapi* zithers, and instruments of the *gamelan degung* are used, along with a violin and some percussion instruments. Like the CD *Sunda Afrika* (1998) the *Sambasunda* CD includes just instrumental music.[13]

---

[11] The former singer of the cult band 3 Mustaphas 3 actually had an earlier "world music" hit in Indonesia, being the composer of the 1993 hit song *Denpasar Moon*. In an interview, Mustapha told how the song was actually part of a demo-cassette, but that he later found out that in the meantime Sony had heard this song and recorded a version of it in Tokyo with a young lady singer from the Philippines. This was Maribeth, winner of the 1991 Voice of Asia contest, who was enormously successful with this English language reggae song; see also her cassette tape *Alone against the world* (1993). Mustapha: "It sold over half a million cassettes and then many local artists made cover-versions—I now have a collection of over 50 different ones in various music-styles and languages. Later they started a soap opera on the TV with the same name using the song as its theme. Yes, I had inadvertently [sic] written an Indonesian classic."
(*www.insideworldmusic.com/library/weekly/aa070999.htm*)
[12] Even Sabah himself tries to sing in Sundanese, but in June 2001 he told me [WvZ] that some Sundanese had jokingly said that, because of his bad pronunciation, they thought he sang in Spanish!
[13] See also *Kompas Cyber Media* (3 March 2002) where it is reported that the "China Town Festival" featured music that was "mixed with Samba Sunda percussion music". The use of some of this music at a Chinese music and dance festival is not surprising, as some *Sambasunda* (1998) songs like *Berekis* also have a "Chinese flavour" that can mainly be heard in the violin part. However, other items like *Kaligat/Goragarago* very much follow Sundanese conventions for *gamelan degung* music structures.

76 2002 YEARBOOK FOR TRADITIONAL MUSIC

The return of religious music in public life

Although all of the world's major religions are represented within the archipelago, it is only Christian and Islamic music that have had a long tradition as mass-mediated popular music. "Spiritual songs" (*lagu rohani*) is the general Indonesian term for religious songs, although as a marketing label the term has largely been reserved for Christian popular songs. The latter have mostly been recorded within the national language, although the genre has also been associated with Batak and Moluccan musics. Indonesia, a country with more than 200 million people and—like India—with a much larger Muslim population than any Arab country, has various popular Islamic song genres that are likely to become even more popular in the near future. For many decades, contests in which Quranic verses are recited aloud (*pengajian*) have been a popular genre all over Indonesia, and national and international contests have been organised for it. These performances have long been distributed through cassette tapes, which has probably led to their further standardisation. Another well-known format of "religious entertainment" has been that of the recorded monologues of esteemed Islamic leaders (*khotbah*), combining moral teaching with humour and social criticism, often incorporating actual events.

President Suharto's resignation and the following move toward political reform have also triggered reactions from Islamic groups, including student associations and some radical factions. Since 1999 these radical groups have been openly coming to the fore, promoting political Islam and the re-establishment of religious morality as the ultimate form of reformation. In some parts of the archipelago, the advantages and disadvantages of implementing religious *syariah* law are being fiercely debated. VCDs and cassettes of so-called *jihad* groups, showing the holy war in Bosnia, the Moluccas or Afghanistan, circulate in most larger Indonesian cities and, since 11 September 2001, Osama Bin Laden's picture is widely distributed using all forms of popular media (video, cassette tapes and stickers).[14] However, this more radical Islam has thus far hardly found a voice in popular music.[15] Every now and then a controversy arises

---

[14] One particular example of such materials is a VCD that was popularly known as *Osama Bin Laden* (2001). This VCD, showing military exercises in Afghanistan, actually contained material from a CNN documentary that was somehow pirated and released on the VCD format by Haramain Arabic VCD. The VCD soon circulated in most of the larger Indonesian cities and was called a perfect example for the Indonesian Muslim youth by one Islamic teacher (*Pikiran Rakyat Online*, 10 November 2001). See also a list of some 'Islamic & educative' VCDs for rent and sale: *CyberNasyid*.../partner/jundi/index1.shtml.

[15] Platzdasch (2001) talks about the return of Islam in public and especially political life, arguing that at present there is a broadened range of Islamic parties and movements in Indonesia, but that these overwhelmingly support the country's stumbling progress toward democracy. The breakdown of state control since 1998, and especially the weaker position of the state ideology, known as *panca sila*, allowed Muslims to formally adopt Islam as the ideology of political organisations. As a result, many new Islamic parties sprang up and took part in the general elections in 1999. The activities of a relatively small number of these groups go beyond what is legally tolerable.

when Islamic hardliners exhort musicians to adhere to religious standards, which in most cases consists of Muslims criticising Muslim artists for "indecent" behaviour. For example, there was some "to do" when the popular "blues" singer Oppie Andaresta was said to have insulted Islam when she jokingly corrupted a religious formula in one of her songs. This led to her being unofficially boycotted by the media for two or three years, after which the popular singer made a comeback on radio and television.

Almost every region has its own religious musics, like *gambus, salawat* or *indang*, that are based on Islamic traditions. Since the emergence of a national music industry, many of these traditional religious musics have been combined with popular music. New syncretic genres have also emerged.   Frederick (1982:119) described how the *dangdut* genre, which makes use of Western instruments like the electric guitar, emerged in the early 1970s, and how it has been very suitable for conveying Islamic messages. Especially the artist Rhoma Irama may be credited with bringing in a missionary (*dakwah*) element, thus providing Indonesian Islam with a new popular image.[16] Musically, the genre is a mix of Hindustani film music, Malay *joged* dance music, and lately a strong emphasis on reggae-like bass patterns. Since the early 1970s, the genre has become very prominent, eventually even leading to a specialised genre of national *dangdut* films and video clips.

Frederick (1982:119) called Rhoma Irama's 1980 film *Perjuangan dan doa* (*Struggle and prayer*) the world's first Islamic "rock musical motion picture". In the 1980s, the genre somehow lost its Islamic characterisation, and through its explicitly sexual dance style and its overt associations with Western inspired popular culture, it came to be increasingly associated with vulgarity (Browne 2000:24). Initially associated with the Islamic PPP party, many conservative Muslims lost interest in the genre when the *dangdut* star Rhoma Irama decided to join the then ruling Golkar party of President Suharto and when other *dangdut* singers like Evy Tamala openly campaigned for Golkar. The genre thus lost much of its subversive character.[17]

Arps (1996:390) describes how in the same period another syncretic cassette genre emerged that was soon labelled *qasidah modéren*, referring to the classical Arabic poem of the same name. It was a type of popular music that was mainly performed by young women and was targeted at Indonesian Muslim youth. Texts were sung in Indonesian and musically accompanied by an ensemble of synthesisers, piano, flute, several violins, mandolin and electric guitar, producing a sound similar to that of *dangdut* orchestras. Group names were all in Arab, and on the covers of the cassette tapes the performers overtly feature Muslim dress. *Qasidah* is often described as music "breathing Islam", but as Arps (1996:395) argues, Islamic discourse is not identical with Arabic discourse. The use of the adjective *modéren* gave the genre the appearance of being new, while at the same time it was rooted in actuality and was culturally

---

[16] See, for instance, some of Rhoma Irama's songs on the CD *Music of Indonesia 2*.

[17] See, for instance, the article "Lagu dangdut untuk kampanye Golka'" in the newspaper *Suara Pembaruan* (26 January 1997).

and socially relevant. Moreover, by using the Indonesian language, a religious moral is propagated which directly addressed Indonesia's youth. Later new sub-genres emerged, like *qasidah rebana*, which seem to have a more traditionalist approach to Islamic popular music. On the other hand, popular pop bands like Bimbo have recorded *qasidah*.[18] During Ramadhan, the fasting month, national television features "respectable and orderly" *dangdut* artists (Browne 2000:2), like Evy Tamala, Ikke Nurjanah and Iis Dahlia who bring religiously oriented songs, which results in a further blurring of the distinctions between *qasidah* and *dangdut*.

Another Islamic music genre, now widely known as *nasyid*, has recently become increasingly popular in Indonesia.[19] The term *nasyid* comes from the Arab *annasyid* (lecture or reverberation), and means "(singer of a) religious song". Musically, it refers to a song genre that became popular in neighbouring Malaysia in the 1980s and that is used as a vehicle of moral teachings (*dakwah*). In the early 1990s, *nasyid* also became popular in Indonesia, especially in the religious schools (*pesantren*) and mosques, but also in universities and high schools. Bandung, in particular, is the home for many recently founded *nasyid* groups. Many of these groups release cassette tapes on so-called *Indie* (independent) labels and hope for more profitable recording offers. *Nasyid* has only recently been taken up by the Indonesian recording industry and is still in the process of being shaped for mass mediation. At the moment, one can actually speak of three different approaches or sub-genres (*Pikiran Rakyat Online*, 25 November 2001): the first is *nasyid Melayu*, characterised by its typical use of percussion, second is *nasyid acapela* (*a-cappella* singing), and the third is a form that makes prominent use of hymns, and emphasises the defence of one's religion (*jihad*).

Many young people are attracted to the genre, because *nasyid* does not just discuss religious dogmas, but also touches on social issues. In doing this, like *qasidah* and *dangdut*, *nasyid* mostly uses the national language, instead of the more esoteric Arabic used in many sermons. The genre is, moreover, targeted at both the Indonesian and Malaysian markets. With bands like Nada Murni, Raihan and SNada being popular at both sides of the Straits of Malacca and representing one of the world's major religions, the genre is truly trans-national in character.[20]

Well-known *nasyid* groups like Raihan and SNada, are as popular as more Western-oriented popular bands and singers. SNada (*Senandung Nada dan Dakwah*: *Humming a melody* [literally "tone"] *and spreading the message*) has been one of Indonesia's most successful groups thus far. The group, which comes from Jakarta, was started by former students at the Universitas Indonesia and is

---

[18] Cf. Jurriëns 2001:152-60) for more information on this Bandung-based band.

[19] See also the Malaysia-based *CyberNasyid* site: the home to "the e-nasyiders community".

[20] Because the national genres Pop Malaysia and Pop Indonesia, although both sung in Malay, tend to aim only at the national market, few artists have been popular in both countries. Malaysia's Sheila Majid or Siti Nurhaliza are notable exceptions, and are at present still very popular in Indonesia, while especially *dangdut* as a genre is enthusiastically consumed in Malaysia.

regularly featured on Indonesian television. They have released several cassettes and VCDs, among which are *Air Mata Bosnia* (*The tears of Bosnia*, 1996) and, together with pop singer Ita Purnamasari, the album *KepadaMu ya Allah* (*To you, Allah*, 1997) and *Satu dalam damai* (*One in peace*, 1999). After Suharto's resignation, the SNada group teamed up with the Partai Keadilan, a political party that was extremely popular among students in the reformation era, for which they recorded several cassettes and video clips.[21] Their songs, some of which have been recorded in Mandarin, Japanese and English, are overtly religious in character, as may be seen in the English version of the song *Neo Shalawat*:

> Yea Allah please shower your blessing and your salvation/To the Prophet Muhammad, who we all adore/May he always be under your sovereignty/May he forever be under your loving care. (*CyberNasyid*)

In the past ten years, established pop singers have also recorded religious songs. Examples include Rano Karno (*Rumah muslimin dan muslimat*, [*House of the Muslims*, 1995]), singer and actress Novia Kolapaking, who teamed up with her husband Emha Ainun Nadjib to release the cassette *Taubat* (*Repentance*, 1998; see also the cover in figure 2), and recently singer Yuni Shara, who devoted a whole album, *Kembali ke keagunganMu* (*Returning to Your greatness*, 2001) and all-time religious classics previously recorded by other Indonesian singers.[22] The release of such religious albums, or the staging of music shows normally tends to coincide with special annual events like the end of the fasting month of Ramadhan or Christmas.[23]

Emha Ainun Nadjib, who is also a writer, social critic and religious spokesman, released three noteworthy albums with his ensemble Kiai Kanjeng Sepuh, which have been extremely successful among Indonesian youth. These cassette tapes, *Kado Muhammad* (*Muhhamad's gift*, 1998), *Wirid Padang Bulan* (*Padang Bulan recitation*, 1999), and *Maiyah tanah air* (*Togetherness of our country*, 2001), contain an interesting mix of religious sermon (*khotbah*),

---

[21] An example is the cassette *Pemimpin yang membawa kecerahan* (*Leaders that bring clarity*, 1999). See *CyberNasyid*.../infonasyid/profil/snada.shtml.

[22] We should make a distinction between an artist like Ebiet G. Ade, and even the rock group Kantata, who are said to make "spiritual music", and those who overtly make Islamic music. At the beginning of April 2002, the song *Misteri Illahi* (*Divine mystery*) by Ari Lasso scored number two in the national charts (*Tembang*.../*chart*). Although the text is highly spiritual, we do not define such songs as religious songs here. Part of the text runs: "I am still here/Feeling the emptiness in my heart/What haunts me until now/Is the meaning of this life/[...]At the time I was startled/I wanted to shout about those feelings/There is still that remaining love/For my unhappy soul."

[23] Yuni Shara's album appeared in the month of Ramadhan, close to Christmas. In the same week the Jakarta-based Musica company released three other religious albums: *Bintang keabadian* (Eternal Star) by Ronnie Sianturi, *Penyembahanku* (My prayer) by Carlo Saba, and *KepadaMu bersyukur* (Praise to You) by Amat Amigos. In 2001 three Muslim oriented cassettes were among the 40 best-selling albums of the year (*Kompas Cyber Media*, 9 December 2001).

80   2002 YEARBOOK FOR TRADITIONAL MUSIC

Javanese gamelan and more modern instrumental additions (*campur sari*). Emha, who regularly performs with his group throughout Indonesia and comes from a *pesantren*[24] background, considers these performances as either a religious sermon or a form of contemplation (*shalawatan*), and not just a musical show. He hopes that his audience will take home some lessons for life and not just the enjoyment of a live musical performance. Recently, he defined this approach as *maiyah*, togetherness (*Kompas Cyber Media*, 23 November 2001). In a recent interview, he stated that he cannot do much directly about Indonesia's current situation of social injustice and intolerance (*Kompas Cyber Media,* two articles on 9 November 2001). When he presented his latest album *Maiyah tanah air*, he described it as "a form of hope, an invitation to rebuild the huge ship that had been torn to pieces", or as is written on the cover of the album: "Making music for Allah for the sake of Indonesia. For a people and nation that are presently fragmented...".

Figure 2. Cover of the cassette tape *Taubat* with Islamic music and showing female vocalist Novia Kolapaking, wearing a veil (*jilbab*), with her husband Emha Ainun Nadjib.

---

[24] *Pesantren* are boarding schools that give much attention to Islamic religion. In some more traditional *pesantren*, the teaching is only about religious topics, and does not include, for instance, Indonesian, English or mathematics. The more modern *pesantren* are part of the national school system and have to comply with the rules set by the Ministry for Religious Affairs.

Indie: Indonesia's underground goes public

In financial terms, the present-day music industry in Indonesia is small by world standards, but it is the largest in Southeast Asia (Sen and Hill 2000:169). In contrast to the 1950s and 1960s, many studios today are no longer owned solely by producers. Increasingly, artists themselves decide to build a home-based studio, complete with the latest digital equipment from Singapore. Examples of such studios are the well-known *A-System* studio in South Jakarta, where the popular band Portret records, jazz musician Indra Lesmana's *Blue Turtle* studio, or singer Krisdayanti's *Hijau*'s studio. These studios not only specialise in pop music, but simultaneously earn an income by producing advertising jingles or soundtracks for the immensely popular tele-novellas on one of Indonesia's many new television stations. In spite of their size, these studios are therefore part of an often-obscure industry, in which the different media are interrelated and certain conglomerates are still clearly recognisable. Indonesian citizens of East Asian and Indian descent especially continue to be prominent in the business.[25]

In Indonesia, the technological innovations of the 1990s have been further reinforced by the changing political climate since 1998. This has recently resulted in the emergence of a so-called alternative music scene (*musik alternatif*), or Indonesian underground music (*musik di tanah bawah*). Today, this scene is widely known as *Indie*, a collective designation by the music industry for various groups, genres[26] and scenes that prioritise a do-it-yourself attitude and therefore prefer small independent labels. Although some of the bands, genres and labels involved clearly predate former President Suharto's resignation (Hill and Sen 1997; Baulch 1996), most of these subaltern voices have only become public with the loosening of restrictions on media and public life in general.[27] Local radio stations especially have been instrumental in highlighting underground bands by playing demo tapes and organising events. This has even led to special programming of *Indie*-chart shows on the better-known radio stations like *IndieLapan* on the Jakarta-based Radio Prambors, and Radio Arda's *Indie 7*.

In the aftermath of the era of *Reformasi* and the resulting greater freedoms, the *Indie* movement is one of the music industry's largest successes

---

[25]Sen and Hill (2000:169) add that the industry is, moreover, largely based in Java. The Association of Recording Industries in Indonesia (ASIRI) in 1997 had over a hundred members of which the only ones outside of Java were two companies in Bali and one in west Sumatra. It seems, however, that over the past five years the industry has been reorganised, particularly due to the new freedoms of the post-Suharto era.

[26] Although the term *Indie* is internationally used for a genre of popular music, in Indonesia it is comparable to the adjective *Reformasi* (reformation) that briefly was one of the most popularly used designations to promote one's music. Another term that was used for a short time is *progresif*, denoting a music that is more serious and more creative than ordinary pop music (cf. *Kompas Cyber Media*, 7 October 2001). Today the term *Indie* is used for virtually every musical genre ranging from underground hip hop, Indie Jazz, Indie Blues to Indie Rock Country and, of course, *Indie* pop.

[27] See, for example, *MTVAsia*, 13 December 2001.

82   2002 YEARBOOK FOR TRADITIONAL MUSIC

thus far, coinciding with, for example, a movement of *Indie* comic artists, the emergence of numerous new fanzines and magazines, and an Indonesian independent film sector which has had considerable success in the last few years.[28]

Rather than just a musical genre, *Indie* therefore reflects the approach of some Western pop traditions with a similar rebellious image. In recent years punk, metal and ska music have, for example, enjoyed enormous popularity among the youth in places like Jakarta, Medan or Bali. Pickles (2000:9-10) refers to punk as the most theatrical of these youth cultures in Indonesia, which like its Western example is intentionally "in your face" and makes use of a dress code, music and life style that are necessarily cheap, thereby attracting young people from all classes, religions and ethnic backgrounds. Indonesia's youth have indigenised these cultures and given them new meanings. Bandung and Jakarta are particularly known as the home of a large number of punk bands like Out of Control, Fresh Cookies, The Idiots, and Sexy Pig. Some of these groups are politically oriented (for example, the Bandung-based Riotic Collective), although the use of broken English, instead of Indonesian texts, allegedly makes the social criticism voiced in many of the lyrics not always intelligible to its audience. Lyrics deal with rioting, anarchy and the fear of pseudo-reforms and mere empty slogans. An example is the lyrics of Out Of Control's song *Political swindle* as published on their site:

> Flag colours to extends are everywhere/ with slogans aren't efficient/The rhetoric promise a brighter future/then nothing has change 'cos nothing has done.../The citizen don't brave to gave their voices/'cos the justice is done not for the minorities/give them freedom for decided their voices/Don't you talking shit because it won't change.[29]

Indie is not so much characterised by musical aspects as by its emphasis on taking charge of things oneself. With the loosening of the government's grip and increasingly less expensive means of producing and distributing music, it has become the preferred way for many musicians. This is also shown by the English lyrics of The Idiots's song *You are Suck* on the same site *Oi! Indonesia Punks and Skins*:

---

[28] Olle (2000) shows how one of the most striking aspects of the current wave of press freedom has been the growth in the number of new publications. "Since Suharto's resignation, the Ministry of Information has approved almost 1000 new permits. This is in addition to the 200-300 existing ones under the New Order. Much of this press explosion consists of politically oriented tabloids produced weekly, available at a cheap price and with a mass distribution network."

[29] See the site *Oi! Indonesia Punks and Skins*, created by someone called Harry W. Destroy in Depok. Another site is *Medan Underground*, which focuses on the Metal genre. Here one finds reviews of albums and the yearly Medan Underground festival, which this year will be held for the fifth successive time. Popular also is the all-Indonesian Metal website *IndoGrinder*.

> We can prove that we can do without your associated with us/D.I.Y.[30] ethic still
> in our hearts and we never want to joint with you/You are fuckin' bloody
> suck/We never want to coorporate with you/This band was come from to us and
> this band present for the kids/Not for profit and your greed we never want to
> joint with you.

Part of the do-it-yourself mentality of punk, ska and metal fans has been reflected in the enormous increase of low-budget fanzines published by, among others, Gerilya (Jakarta), Megatone Zine (Bali), Post Mangled Zine (Surabaya), Kerkhoff (Solo), or Tigabelas Zine (Bandung), and recently by the increase of Internet sites devoted to these genres. At the same time, underground musicians have sought a public audience through the organisation of local non-commercial concerts, like the Medan Underground Festival in Northern Sumatra, Bali's Sunday Hot Music or Local Gigs at Bandung's Hitam Putih cage, and the Ska festivals at Jakarta's Museum Abri Satria Mandala. As musical styles, punk and ska were short fads in 1999 and 2000. Jun Fan Gung Foo (JFGF) is one of the better-known exponents of this punk and ska craze that gained national fame. In 1997, some high school students founded the group and, although initially a punk band, they soon decided to mix in elements taken from ska and alternative music and later added brass instruments to their soundscape as well. They perform at schools, university campuses and cafes, where they play mostly covers of international ska songs. After winning several contests, they released a first single called *Semua Berantakan* (*Everything is chaos*) that for some weeks was at the top of the *IndieLapan* charts of the popular Jakarta based Radio Prambors. In this way, the popularity of the group increased beyond the capital. In October 1999, the group released the album *NAGA 2000* (*The year of the Dragon, 2000*) for Sony Records, from which the single *Bruce Lee* was taken, emphasising their obsession with Asian martial arts:

> Me and my friends, we all like kung fu/We all like to hang around together, as
> we have a common obsession/Instead of just sitting quietly, you better come
> with us/If you also like kung fu, join with us Jun Fang Gung Foo...[31]

The *Indie* scene has increasingly produced forms that can also be enjoyed by a mainstream audience. Good examples are Slank,[32] one of

---

[30] Do it yourself.

[31] *Aku dan teman—temanku semua suka kungfu/Semua suka nongkrong bareng, semua punya satu obsesi/Daripada kamu berdiam diri, mending gabung sama kami/Kalo kamu juga suka kungfu gabung aja dengan Jun Fan Gung Foo...*

[32] Their cassette tape *Generasi Biru* (*Blue Generation*, 1995) achieved "double platinum" as BASF's largest selling cassette across all musical categories in Indonesia in that year. Slank has diversified to establish a management bureau, a recording studio, a production house and a recording company as autonomous enterprises (Hill and Sen 1997). Market research on the first five Slank albums indicated that 43% of the buyers were between 15 and 19 years old, and 35% between 20 and 24. Fifty-eight percent were males. Although the majority of Slank's fans are in Java, their appeal is national, their sales broadly reflecting population densities.

84   2002 YEARBOOK FOR TRADITIONAL MUSIC

Indonesia's most popular rock bands that carefully cultivated a rebellious image
and built up a huge following among the youth. More recently the band Naif, also
associated with the *Indie* approach, has been very successful. Naif was founded
in 1995 and initially released only cassettes. In 2001, viewers voted their single
Posesif the Most Favourite Video at Penghargaan MTV Indonesia. Avi, the
transvestite in the video, is currently the most famous transvestite in Indonesia,
appearing on several talk shows.[33]

Another example is the compilation album *Indie ten* that was released by
Sony Music Indonesia in 1998, bringing together bands from four of Indonesia's
larger cities that did not yet have a record deal at the time. In the liner notes it
says that "many music groups in the archipelago are talented and have potential,
but that only few have the finances to turn their creations into an album. Sony
Music feels itself therefore responsible to expose their creativity". As in Western
popular music, the *Indie* scene seems increasingly encapsulated by the music
industry. Most of the bands that initially came to public attention through Sony's
compilation album have recorded full albums in the meantime. Bands like Padi,
Wong and Cokelat are presently among the most popular Indonesian groups. The
success of the compilation has recently led to a second volume of *Indie ten*.

Baulch (1996) states that "alternative music has fast become an integral
part of what it is to be an ultimately modern teen" in Indonesia. Ironically,
enough alternative music is associated with a lifestyle that consists of hanging
out in shopping malls, eating at McDonalds and watching MTV; exactly those
things of which alternative music in the West has tried to be the antithesis. More
than protest or social criticism then, the *Indie* scene seems to appeal to the
Western values so often idealised by many young Asians (Lent 1994:2)—a
lifestyle in which modernity, freedom and individuality are emphasised.[34]

Mass media, money, copyright and piracy

Mass media, including the popular press, the recording industry, radio and
television, are not transparent windows onto "what is out there", but as
institutions and communicative vehicles contain their own political and economic
tendencies (Spitulnik 1993). At the same time, mass media are quickly to respond
to changing world circumstances.

The rise of private radio in the early 1990s is clearly related to the
Indonesian policy of "openness" of the late 1980s (Lindsay 1997). The much-

---

[33] Traditionally, transvestites have been prominently present in southeast Asian public life,
as they have been in the world of performing arts. They are generally seen to personify the
philosophical unity of male and female (Kartomi 1976:117, Wilson 1999). Indonesian
television regularly features transvestites, of which Dorce Gamalama is a good example.
[34] This easy-going lifestyle is also portrayed by MTV Indonesia video jockey (VJ),
Shanty. Shanty, a role model for the younger generation and voted the most favourite new
pop singer of 2001 in an MTV poll, was characterised as: "Life is often sweet for
Shanty—thanks to a cool job, and not forgetting, a regular dosage of her favorite drink,
Coke, and occasional indulgences in Cookies & Cream ice cream at Baskin Robbin's"
(*MTV Asia*, …/onair/vjs/ShantyAnnisaa/index.html).

watched multi-lingual musical variety television show *Asia Bagus*, produced in Singapore largely with Japanese money and featuring performers from all over Asia, is linked to emergent notions of Asia as a cultural entity and lines of flow of capital, performers and media products that cross-hatch East and Southeast Asia (Cohen 1998:649). MTV Asia, which regularly plays Indonesian video clips, broadcasts a weekly all-Indonesian chart (*Ampuh*[35] list) and features English-speaking Indonesian video jockeys, marks Indonesia as one node in the global cultural market. The latest developments were plans for an exclusive MTV Indonesia program brought jointly by MTV Networks Asia and Global TV, broadcasting twenty-four hours a day in several large Indonesian cities, as from May 2002.[36] It will feature existing programs such as the *Ampuh* charts, but also a special *dangdut* program and it will cover local events. The idea behind the program is to make television that suits the taste and lifestyle of an Indonesian audience. Employing more Indonesian video jockeys will be one way to provide an Indonesian flavour.[37] Apart from planning an all-Indonesian program, the music multinational has found other ways to reach the Indonesian audience, one of them being a compilation series called *MTV 100% Indonesia* and another being an annual all-Indonesia competition for music videos.

The Asian economic crisis of the late 1990s had a severe impact on the domestic popular music industry in Indonesia, resulting in a drastic drop in the production and sale of cassettes. In 1996 the sales figures were more than eight million cassettes per month, but during 1998 this was reduced to three million per month.[38] It decreased to 2.3 million cassettes per month in 2000, to rise again to 2.8 million cassettes per month at the end of 2001 (*Media Indonesia* [E], 23 December 2001). In the last twenty years or so the price of a cassette tape in Euros or US dollars has hardly changed. However, in rupiahs the price has increased by a factor of ten.

The institutional logic of the media has changed the way music is perceived in Indonesia today. Traditionally, in many parts of Indonesia expressive culture was and is considered to be the outer manifestation of inner, spiritual life (Barendregt 1995:118-9; van Zanten 1994:76). Written and oral texts are perceived as communal property, always available for timely re-writing

---

[35] *Ampuh* is an acronym for Ajang Musik Pribumi Sepuluh, "List of (top) Ten Domestic Music (items)" as produced by MTV Asia (Sutton 2000:39). *Ampuh* also means "possessing magical power" of *krisses* (ceremonial daggers), or "modest and well-controlled" (the ideal voice type for the nobles) (Van Zanten 1989:180).

[36] The station would initially be available in five of the larger cities, including Jakarta, Bandung, Semarang, Surabaya and Medan with an estimated distribution to 15 million households.

[37] The relation between the music industry and MTV tends to be a close one as MTV often employs pop singers. National idol Nadya Hutugalung is a good example of this approach, while VJ Shanty released one of the most successful Indonesian pop albums of 2001. See also the new *MTV Indonesia* website.

[38] *Kompas Online*, 10 January 1999. See also *Detikhot* [E], 4 March 2002. The figures in this section are mostly taken from press reports and are often supplied by the music industry. They are only used to indicate trends.

86   2002 YEARBOOK FOR TRADITIONAL MUSIC

and re-telling. In most traditional musical scenes, it is the social setting as a whole that is important and not just the sound of the music. A musical event is in an intimate environment, made up of related activities—including talking, dancing, flirting, eating—of which playing music is only one (Van Zanten 1997:48). Furthermore, the audience quite often participates in the performance: the borderline between audience and performers is not rigidly defined. Music is a background against which all kinds of social interaction takes place.

All of these aspects of music have come to be disturbed and re-evaluated with the introduction of sound amplification (Sutton 1996), mass-media created super-star performers (Weintraub 1997), and international commodity regulations (Kartomi 1998) in the field of Indonesian performance. Music no longer necessitates a sharing of time and place by performer and public. Recordings produced in studios, without an audience, have re-aligned how people conceive of music. The situation in Indonesia is shifting towards the one Malm (1992:362) describes for reggae in Jamaica, a music that is almost entirely a product of the recording studios:

> Live performances of reggae are rare, since the demands on the equipment are so great and the finances of all but a few top reggae artists so limited. Reggae can be heard live in Jamaica only at major events directed towards tourists.[39]

Indonesia's incorporation into the global economy has also meant involvement in copyright issues. Recently, intellectual property rights (*Hak atas Kekayaan Intelektual*: HaKI) have been much discussed, also in popular music publications. After withdrawing in 1958, in 1997 Indonesia again ratified the Bern Convention for the Protection of Literary and Artistic Works.[40] Critical voices have also been raised in the Indonesian press, claiming that intellectual property rights are only meant to enlarge the profits of multinational companies in the richest parts of the world (*Kompas Cyber Media*, 17 July 2001).[41]

Where presently the international music industry still has a stronghold on distributing and promoting selected artists, the distance between producers and consumers is tending to become smaller, and in the near future the industry might slowly lose its grip as an intermediary. In most countries, the re-configuration of the music industry is in process and indeed tends to focus on issues of copyright, emphasising a shift from a manufacturing industry, in which records and cassettes are sold as commodities, to a rights industry, where the ownership of titles is at stake (Frith 2000:390). In Southeast Asia, and especially Indonesia, where copyrights have traditionally been poorly protected, this configuration might, however, lead to different transformations. Indonesians now

---

[39] The west-Javanese *kacapi-suling* music is a good example of music that is largely a product of recording studios, and also played live for tourists in the larger hotels.
[40] See for an overview, for instance, the statement by the Indonesian director general of intellectual property rights in Geneva, 27 June 2000, *www3.itu.int/MISSIONS/Indonesia/st00627trips.htm*.
[41] For critical comments see also Liebowitz (2002), Garafalo et al. (2001) and Smiers's forthcoming (2003) book, among others.

are in the process of re-negotiating what music as a cultural field means, which is in many cases leading to the individualisation of artistic oral traditions.

A legal initiative concerning royalty payments for the *kroncong* song *Bengawan Solo*, composed by the Javanese songwriter Gesang in 1940 and well-known and often recorded in a number of Asian countries, became a matter of national controversy in 1989-90 and created an awareness of cultural property and heritage that had not been there before (Kartomi 1998). Popular music's capital value (both symbolic and actual) has created new conceptions of what it means to be Indonesian in the global market. Currently, a discussion is underway between the Ministry of Law and the Ministry of Education and Culture on issues surrounding "individual", 'ethnic" and 'national' copyrights. New developments in this field will certainly be forthcoming, and merit close attention.[42]

Although bootleg audiocassettes, recordings by American and European artists re-taped in Asia and sold at a quarter of their original price, had almost disappeared around 1997, at the beginning of 2002 piracy had increased again to previously unknown levels. According to Arnel Affandi, the general manager of the Association of Recording Industries in Indonesia (ASIRI, Asosiasi Industri Rekaman Indonesia) for 2002-2005, it was estimated by the United States Trade Representative that in 1997 only 12% of the CDs and audiocassettes sold were illegal copies (*Media Indonesia* [E], 5 March 2002). In February 2002, 5 out of 6 of the audiocassettes, audio-CDs and video-CDs produced were illegal copies, percentages that seem unsurpassed in the world (*Kompas Cyber Media*, 7 February 2002).[43] Arnel Affandi also expressed concern about possible repercussions from the US government, as the United States Trade Representative had placed Indonesia on the priority watch list for violating copyright laws, especially with respect to VCDs and computer software (*Kompas Cyber Media*, 21 March 2000).

Recent estimated figures show the following production numbers for the year 2001 (*Kompas Cyber Media*, 14 November 2001):

Legal copies of Indonesian audiocassettes:	30-35 million
Illegal copies of Indonesian audiocassettes:	200 million
Illegal copies of Indonesian VCDs (karaoke):	120 million
Illegal copies of foreign audiocassettes:	50 million

It is estimated that because of these illegal copies, the Indonesian government suffered a tax loss of about €60 million (US$54 million) in the year 2000. At the same time the loss for the Indonesian music industry is estimated to be nearly ten times this amount, or €550 million (*Kompas Cyber Media*, 14 November 2001).

---

[42] For general discussions of copyright and music, see Feld 1996; Mills 1996; Seeger 1992, 1996; Zemp 1996.

[43] According to the same source, this was a slight improvement compared to three months earlier, when 7 out of 8 audiocassettes, audio- and video-CDs produced were illegal. The figures in this section are of course rough estimates and usually supplied by the recording industry itself.

88 2002 YEARBOOK FOR TRADITIONAL MUSIC

In 2000, Indonesia seems to have ranked fifth, both on the list of countries violating copyright laws and in terms of lost taxes. It was exceeded only by China, Taiwan, Korea and Malaysia (*Media Indonesia* [E], 20 April 2001).

On 5 June 2002, several parties in the music industry established FOKAP (Forum Komunikasi Anti Pembajakan: Forum for information against piracy) to fight the copying. Its first task would be to inform the general public about the negative effects of piracy and to ask them to buy the original rather than pirated copies. The people involved included composers, makers of song texts, artists and producers. The chairperson of the Indonesian parliament, Amien Rais, was also present at the ceremony in Jakarta (*Media Indonesia* [E], 6 June 2002).

Although cassette tapes are still sold in large quantities, in the five years since 1997 these have been replaced more and more by VCDs. Audio-CDs have never been big sellers, as their price is relatively high. Average prices of the different tapes and CDs with popular music in 2001-2 were:[44]

Legal cassette tape of popular music:	Rp10 000–15 000 (€1.10–1.70)
Legal VCD	Rp16 000–40 000 (€1.80–4.40)
Legal audio-CD	Rp30 000–50 000 (€3.30–5.50)
Pirated Indonesian/Malaysian VCDs	Rp6000–10 000 (€0.70–1.10)

Pirating audiocassettes and VCDs is a booming business in all large cities of Indonesia. Most prominent is the Glodok business area in northern Jakarta where an estimated one million illegal copies a day are produced, worth Rp.3,000,000,000.00 (€330,000.00; *Kompas Cyber Media*, 7 February 2002). Newspaper reports suggest that, in order to keep their financial losses under control, some companies produce illegal copies themselves, right after launching their legal, registered and censored albums.

Apriadi Gunawan, writing in the newspaper *Jakarta Post Online* (1 July 2001) reports about north Sumatra that:

> As far as music is concerned, North Sumatra seems to be in deep slumber, and little or no clamour is heard; but when it comes to piracy in the cassette recording business, it is something else. You will be dumbfounded…Albums of ethnic music are selling like hot cakes; as many as 100,000-300,000 copies are sold each month. In the meantime, sales of national pop music seem to be heading south or dragging at a really slow pace. Seldom can they make a hit but when sales do hit a record high of 100,000 copies a month, there is no doubt that to have achieved that feat, it must have required tremendous effort…In terms of number, pirated cassettes and VCDs of ethnic songs in North Sumatra outnumber or rank level with the sales of albums of Slank or Dewa—two Jakarta music groups that have recently shot to prominence.

---

[44] In March 2002, Rp10.000.-- was equivalent to about € 1.10 or US$1.00. See also *Tempo*, 4 April 2002: the Jakarta police caught thirteen peddlers selling illegal VCDs at the even lower prices of Rp 3000.00-6000.00.

Apriadi Gunawan interviewed H. Sofyan S, the owner of LY Recording Company in Medan, who explained the economics of the cassette industry to him. During the heyday of the industry, this company was able to produce 2-3 albums each month. Sofyan estimated that at present the number of pirated cassette tapes and VCDs sold is twice that of the originals. Producing an album containing twelve songs cost a producer about Rp.12.8 million (US$1100.00)— Rp.4.8 million to pay the singer and Rp.8 million for recording costs. According to Apriadi Gunawan:

> If they could sell 100.000 copies at only Rp.1.000 [€1.10] profit apiece, minus Rp.12.8 million for costs, then they would enjoy a profit of Rp.87 million (US$8000.00)—handsome indeed. The local singers would always come out worst. For singers such as Laila Hasyim and Syaiful Amri, they got Rp.400.000 for each of their songs, but they didn't know about their royalty rights.

These days, however, artists increasingly are members of, PAPPRI (Persatuan Artis Pencipta Lagu dan Penata Musik), the Union of Composers and Performing Artists. In January-February 2001, one of the present authors witnessed the Padang section of PAPPRI dealing with a case of a well-known singer who had used two songs written by another composer on a recording. She had changed the title of one song, and in both cases had put her name on the cover as composer of the song. The case was eventually solved "within the family", with the singer paying Rp.15 million (€1600.00) to the composer, quite a large sum by current Indonesian standards.

Visual aspects on VCDs: relation between image and text

As was discussed in the previous section, the impact of VCDs is rapidly increasing and they may gradually replace cassette tapes. In terms of numbers of consumers, this VCD medium is much more important than the World Wide Web in 2002.[45] In this section, we shall first make some general remarks about the relation between image and text on the VCDs, and then present a few examples, highlighting specific issues.

The covers of the VCDs claim their contents to be *karaoke* music, in which one can turn off the audio-channel with the sound of the vocalist, and just hear the accompaniment and see the images and text. This way one can sing along with the accompaniment, like earlier with the *karaoke* cassette tapes. Previously, a whole album (cassette tape) might contain just one "extra" *karaoke* track. In the early 1980s, tape sets of *karaoke,* which means "empty orchestra", invaded the Japanese domestic sphere (Keil 1984:94), and many Indonesians soon followed suit. After its introduction on cassette tape in Indonesia, the

---

[45] In the years around 1995 and before the VCDs were introduced to the Indonesian consumer market, sound and image were combined on Laser Discs (LDs). However, these never became a success because the discs were expensive (Rp.80,000-90,000, (about €38.00 or US$35.00), as was the apparatus needed to play them. For similar reasons, videocassette tape was never a really popular medium in Indonesia.

90   2002 YEARBOOK FOR TRADITIONAL MUSIC

"empty orchestra" genre continued to play a role in the promotion of the more expensive laser disc around 1995, and eventually the VCD from around 1997. Although the VCDs offer a wealth of visual information together with the music, the various companies producing them emphasise the *karaoke* possibilities, rather than the visual aspects.

In this section we present a first analysis of how the words and the images, and to a certain extent the music, go together. Whereas the early cassette tapes of the 1970s did not always give full information about the performers, songs texts, etc., this was improved in the 1980s and 1990s for both cassette tapes and CDs. The VCDs present the song texts on screen, and also mention the song's composer and the names of the vocalists. However, as with the earlier cassette tapes, information about the performing musicians—except the vocalists—is, remarkably, once again missing on the (legal) VCDs, especially in the regional pop music that we studied. One wonders whether this has to do with copyrights issues and/or protecting the musicians from being sued for doing something illegal. The Cianjuran musician Uking Sukri told one of the present authors that he and the Radio-Bandung instrumentalists were not mentioned on many early cassette recordings of the 1970s. The musicians themselves requested this because they were afraid that their employers, the state radio RRI, would object to these recordings.

The images on VCDs of regional popular music frequently display nature (rivers with waterfalls, mountains, woods, lakes and the sea) or parks in a city. The "sound of longing" is combined with images of the homeland. Furthermore, the artists may appear in several outfits in the same song, from traditional costumes to modern jeans and skirts. Although most images were probably a later addition to the recorded sound, the synchronisation is relatively reasonable. Dancers, for instance four girls, or two boys and two girls, seem to act as stage decor. On some VCDs (for instance, *Doel Sumbang* 1 and 2, *Top hits millennium 2000*) the images of the artists and surroundings alternate with images of a girl, just sitting or standing, brushing away her hair, or doing nothing except "being beautiful" (see figure 3).

Figure 3. Cici Faramida on the backside of the cover of her VCD (*Cici Faramida 1999*)

On VCDs of pop Indonesia, the images are predominantly urban: street life, cars and big houses. However, here too nature is quite often present in the form of gardens with flowers and trees. VCDs are big business, and erotic images are important on almost all of them, as are texts about love. However, the way this is presented is different in that the images on regional pop music VCDs seem to be more restrained than on the national ones. Also, on the regional pop music VCDs the erotic images tend to be produced mainly by actors other than the singers (who "just sing"), whereas on the pop Indonesia VCDs, the singers tend to be more actively involved in producing them.

On almost all VCDs, regional or national, young women and men touch each other, though less closely and more briefly on the regional ones. On some VCDs, the women are filmed very much in close-up, intimately, like on the VCD *Cici Faramida* (1999), where Cici Faramida's mouth is often shown in close-up (see the backside of the cover in figure 3). This is also true of the pop Indonesia VCD *Yuni Shara* (1998). On other VCDs, such as the *Lagu-lagu top klasik Sunda* (2002), in the song *Dikantun tugas* the camera pans the body of the female vocalist Yanti several times from her face to her lap and back. All VCDs have to pass the censor before being released, which is how the government controls both image and text. None of the VCDs we analysed showed a couple kissing although it is suggested a few times, as in the song *Mengapa tidak maaf* on *Yuni Shara* (1998), where the girl touches the head of her beloved and moves as if to kiss him, but then turns away from the camera.[46]

Popular religious songs ask for another approach. Performing religious songs on stage demands a different body language and the singer should be even more convincing in that way his or her message is brought than in secular pop songs. On the covers of cassette tapes the artists are depicted in full religious mufti, which further emphasises this image. Actress Novia Kolopaking went even further, and after her marriage to Emha decided to become a devoted housewife who always wears a veil and devotes most of her time to Islamic charities (*Majalah Suara Hidayatullah* [E], December 2001)

---

[46] The names of pop stars like Yuni Shara and her younger sister Kris Dayanti are also used to attract visitors to pornographic sites on the World Wide Web. One of these sites shows pictures of two nude women that vaguely look like the two stars whose names are written on the pictures. The illegal VCD circuit is definitely also connected to the pornographic industry, as is clear from many newspaper reports. However, pornography has been an obsession for Indonesian authorities for many years. Although VCD players, computer games, the Internet and other emerging technologies prove to be excellent avenues, especially for Indonesian youth, for expressing a desire for modernity and cosmopolitanism at the same time , they have a rather negative image within the national popular press. The VCD format, for example, is primarily associated with piracy, pornography and political violence (Barendregt 2002).

92   2002 YEARBOOK FOR TRADITIONAL MUSIC

Figure 4. Cover of the pirated VCD 'Tertatih' by the *Sheila on 7* group is presumably taken from the cover of the audiocassette with these songs on "Side A" and "Side B".

On pirated VCDs anything may happen. Two pirated VCDs of the well-known Yokyakarta group Sheila on 7 (SO7), *Sheila on 7—Tertatih* and *Sheila on 7—Kisah Klasik*,[47] are remarkable. The first one seems to be taken from an audiocassette (see cover in figure 4) with images added from several regions in China that have nothing to do with the music. On the *Sheila on 7—Kisah Klasik* VCD, #1 and #2 have images of the band Sheila on 7, but are not at all synchronous with the sound: guitars may play on the images while there is no sound, and the singer's mouth does not move in synchrony with the audio. This VCD, furthermore, lacks the subtitling of the song texts while the images with items 3-12 are pictures of insects, fish and African landscapes with lions, giraffes, etc., and presumably North American snow landscapes with buffalos, bears and eagles. Finally, two men fighting, possibly in Hong Kong but definitely not in Indonesia, accompany the song *Lihat, dengar, rasakan*.

After these general remarks we shall now look at some examples in more detail. The first song on the pop Indonesia VCD *Duet legendaris Elvy Sukaesih & Mansyur S.* is *Gadis atau janda* (Maiden or divorcee). Here we see a woman (Elvy Sukaesih) driving a sports car on a beautiful road, presumably in southern Jakarta, and a man (Mansyur) riding a motorbike alongside her. When

---

[47] Duta, one of the singers of the band, declared that the producer of the Sheila on 7 music albums (Sony Music), never released a VCD version (*IndoMedia* [E], 10 Novenber 2000).

the woman stops, he also stops and helps her out of the car. She is fashionably dressed in modern jeans and starts to dance for him, coquettishly moving her hips and her arms, so that her belly can just be seen. He leans against her car, watching. The woman sings, "I've been involved with love several times now". The man continues the sung dialogue: "So is it just me now, your 'elder brother'[48] whom you love?" "Oh, those youths who bother me are all crocodiles!" "You confuse me. Are you unmarried [literally, a virgin], or already divorced [or widow]? Please, tell me, don't be shy."[49] She confesses that she is divorced. That is no problem for him; he still loves her. Then she tells him that she is reluctant because people may hear what she says. But he assures her that no one is around, and then she tells him that she has many children. That, however, is also no problem for him, and together they sing: "Let us just get married!" While they sing images of four to six young women and a young man appear in and around the car, dancing now and then. While singing, the woman and man are also shown driving the car, now with the man at the wheel. Images of cars and beautiful houses keep returning in the other songs on the VCD.

It is interesting to compare Sean Williams's description of a very popular Sundanese *degung kawih* song *Kalangkang* (Shadow, daydream) on audiocassette with a newer version *Kalangkang Bulan* (Shadow of the moon) on VCD. Williams (1989:117) remarks that

> The lyrics of the song are exciting for the Sundanese, because they step further than most Sundanese songs: They actually discuss kissing, embracing, and walking arm-in-arm, urban teenage behavior that, if seen in public at all, only appears on the most fashionable streets in Bandung.

In the song *Kalangkang Bulan* on the VCD *Mega Hits Degung* (2000), Vol.1, the text is rather conventional. Part of the text by Mang Raida[50] is as follows:

> How beautiful is first love/ It cannot be compared to anything/ My heart is enchanted/ Because of our happiness/...It is a pity, it is really a pity/ The beautiful stays only during a flash/ The flower I hoped for disappears/ The shadow of the moon is made.[51]

The images on the VCD show most of the things described in the song text of the earlier *Kalangkang* that was translated by Williams (1989). The images are of the female vocalist with the musicians (*gamelan degung* instruments with *kacapi* zither), and now and then of a boy and girl who do the acting. They walk towards

---

[48]*Abang*, elder brother, is also a commonly used term of address from a wife to her husband.

[49] *Sudah berulang kali aku bermain cinta/ Jadi baru abang yang adik cinta?/ Pemuda yang gangguku semuanya buaya./ Abang jadi ragu pada dirimu./ Kau masih gadis atau sudah janda? Baik katakan saja, jangan malu!*

[50] Also given as Faida.

[51] *Duh éndah cinta munggaran/ Geuning nu taya bandingna/ Duh haté bunga bungangang/ Kabagjaan urang duaan/...Hanjakal, hanjakal teuing/ Éndah sakolébatan/ Léosna kembang harepan/ Kacipta kalangkang bulan.*

each other and embrace (no kissing), and then walk along with his arm around her shoulder. They sit on a garden wall talking hand-in-hand. The boy puts his arms around the girl's neck, and almost kisses her. The girl has her hand on his lap.

    The Sundanese pop musician Doel Sumbang (the stage name of Wahyu Affandie) is mainly interested in texts. Part of his songs is social criticism put in daily language. In fact, his name Sumbang means "out of tune", "incest", "against tradition" or the severe breaking of rules (Van Zanten 1989:194; Jurriëns 2001:142). Thus, with respect to his artistic name he resembles the well-known pop Indonesia singer Iwan Fals (*fals*: out of tune). On the VCDs *Doel Sumbang* 1 and 2 (1999), Doel is only accompanied by a keyboard he plays himself, and by music and texts of his own composition. Doel himself almost without exception just pretends to play his guitar.

    In the love song *Bulan Batu Hiu* (The moon at Batu Hiu), Doel performs playback on a guitar, while keyboard-music is heard. The first images are of the sea, rocks in the sea, and a beach: Batu Hiu (Shark's Rock) lies near Pangandaran on the southeast coast of West Java. In the interlude, a bamboo flute (*suling*) player can be seen, with a real *suling* blending with the keyboard. Further, the picture of a girl is shown now and then, sitting together with Doel who plays the guitar and sings. Now and then four girls are shown, singing short phrases. At one point Doel writes the name "Rina" with a stick in the sand. Part of the text runs:

> The moon is hanging in the sky above Batu Hiu / Only one piece is left/ Left over from yesterday's full moon / The two of us quietly enjoy each other's company/ We are very happy, all our feelings gave in to the temptation/ We declare solemnly the vow for life and death/...The moon is witness during the whole night/ It keeps the secret, it will surely not become known.[52]

Doel Sumbang also addresses social problems. Although he claims he wouldn't like to make "music or songs that filled people's heads with worries", he feels that in songs like *Éma* (The madness of humans) (Édanna Manusia), he really shows who he is (Jurriëns 2001:143, 151). The song *Éma* (Édanna Manusia) on the VCD *Doel Sumbang, Vol. 2* (1999), is about a young boy who trips on ecstasy pills:

> Ema, what are you doing, Ema?/...You are tripping, Ema/...Your life will become a mess/...Everything is gone and nothing left in exchange for ecstasy...Come back soon, Ema![53]

---

[52] *Bulan nu ngangantung di langit Batu Hiu/ Tinggal sapasi sésa purnama kamari/ Urang duaan anteng sosonoan/ Suka bungah, sagala rasa dibedah/ Ikrar janji sahidup samati/...Bulan sapeupeuting nyaksi/ Nyepeng rusiah, moal betus [written is: becus] pasti*
[53] Éma, keur naon silaing Éma?/[...] Silaing triping Éma/[...] Hirup silaing jadi pakusut/ [...] Ludes teu nyésa ditukar actaxy.[...] Geura balik silaing, Éma" See Jurriëns (2001:148-149) for the whole text, which is slightly different from the one on this VCD.

The images are of a boy wearing sunglasses, going home early in the morning, and walking as if he is "high" or drunk. He meets four girls on a road through a tea estate. The girls, who are going to work, look at him in dismay. Then we switch to the boy dancing in a disco with flashing lights. Doel Sumbang watches this all from outside, singing on a bench. Later, the boy is seen at his home, where his father and mother are in despair about his behaviour.

In the song *Nini luar nagri* (Strange grandmother) on VCD *Doel Sumbang*, Vol.2, the images are not at all of the subject of the song, but just show Doel Sumbang singing, alternating with a chorus of girls. The text of *Nini luar nagri* is about an old lady, who still uses lipstick, eye shadow, and a hair ribbon, to attract the attention of young men:

> Wrinkly grandmother, with luxuriant grey hair/ And who does your face with powder and lipstick, with shadow and a hair-ribbon/ Like an evil spirit of the Waru tree/...Walking coquettish like a mannequin/ Laughing all the time with your three remaining teeth/...You sit and watch the bending road/ Teasing the young lads/ Forgetting your age, forgetting your grandchildren/ And imagining you are still beautiful/...Wanting to catch the attention of men more than hostesses[54] do.[55]

Doel Sumbang wants to "sell lyrics" and is less interested in exploiting the possibilities of the music, he told Jurriëns (2001:142-43). The same seems to be true of the images on his VCDs, which are not really erotically daring. It may be that this is generally truer of famous male singers than of female ones, who seem to be in a better position to sell the erotic images.[56] In the present we continue to find traces of the past.

The Internet and popular music: portals, fan cultures and peer-to-peer techniques

In the past decade, the Internet has emerged as a very prominent channel of communication, for instance for e-mail, chatting and file-exchange via the World Wide Web (WWW) or directly from a server (FTP). Much has been written on its supposed economic and political impact as well as that for copyrights, music and ownership.[57] The Internet is likely to have a huge influence on the future of the

---

[54] In the sense of "prostitutes".

[55] *Nini Nini péot Geus gomplok ku huis/ Jeung ngageulis maké bedak maké lipstik/ Maké shadow maké bondu/ Siga jurig tangkal waru/...Ucad-aced hayang siga pragawati/ Surasueri huntu tinggal tilu siki/...Nangkring di jalan tikungan/ Ngaheureuyan budak bujang/ Poho umur poho incu/ Asa aing alah geulis kénéh/...Cumentil leuwih ti hostes.*

[56] Compare, for instance, the pop Minangkabau VCD *Sarunai Aceh* (2000) with male singer Yan Juneid, or *Ucok Sumbara* (2000?) with male singer Ucok Sumbara, and the VCD *Efrinon* (1999) with female singer Efrinon. It would be a serious mistake, however, to conclude that a female artist like Efrinon *only* sells erotic images. By Western standards, furthermore, the pictures are hardly erotic. The idea of the music going with the text remains very important in the Minangkabau.

[57] See, for example, Jones 2000, Dolfsma 2000, and Liebowitz 2002.

music industry. In the future, CDs, cassettes and even VCDs might lose their status as preferred sound carriers, giving way to new formats such as mp3 or divx.[58] Differences between local, national and trans-national markets are further likely to blur as artists now have the possibility of putting their music directly on the Internet (Dolfsma 2000; Kibby 2000: 91).

Until now, little research has focussed on the divergent reactions of local music industries to the introduction of computer-mediated communications, and little is known about how local music practices might be co-opted, eventually leading to "vernacularization or indigenisation of these media" (Appadurai 1996:100).

We can only guess what the impact of the WWW on Indonesian popular music will be in the coming years. In most Internet studies, the term "virtual community" is used in a way vaguely reminiscent of Anderson's (1983) "imagined communities". This conception of communities solely existing in a so-called cyberspace has recently been severely criticised, however (Fornäs 1998, Miller and Slater 2000). The Internet is in no way the "placeless place" that is often suggested and is firmly embedded in off-line realities. Although some research is being done on the use of the Internet in Indonesia, we still know very little about these off-line realities of Indonesian users and the ways the Internet influences musical practice, musical taste or the distribution and experience of popular music. We should, moreover, be really careful not to exaggerate the impact of the Internet on Indonesia and its pop music scene.

In 2002, Indonesia still lacks the necessary infrastructure and many areas are even without such basic facilities as electricity and telephone services, let alone the capacity for computer mediated communications.[59] The WWW remains a community characterised by affluence, and the unequal power balance has already been described as "virtual colonization" (Hall 1999: 40).[60] As in other Southeast Asian countries, the Internet was initially highly elitist in its orientation, available only to technocrats and wealthy entrepreneurs. This has changed with the rapid increase of the number of local Internet Service Providers, the low cost of PCs preceding the economic crisis of 1997-98, and the use of mainly illegal software. The WWW has now become increasingly open to many urban Indonesians. Together with relatively easy-to-use chat software (like ICQ), this has led, within

---

[58] Divx is an illegal version ("crack") of the Mpeg4 format that is becoming increasingly popular on the Internet for the illegal distribution of movies.

[59] "In a country with 210 million people there are only two million PCs and 200.000 Internet dial-up users. If group users and outlet visitors are added to this total, domestic Internet users number only 790.000. Of these, only 72.000 are domestic online shoppers. Of 70 business licenses issued, only 25 have been realized for no more than 5,400 domain names." (Tamara 2000)

[60] At a November 2000 meeting of ASEAN countries in Singapore it was decided to make information technology an important spearhead in the socio-economic development of the region. The e-ASEAN Agreement expressed the need to strive for "digital readiness", develop ASEAN competitiveness, and to "better the lives of their citizens through the application of information and communication technologies [as to] foster the spirit of ASEAN community." (*e-ASEAN agreement* 2000)

a few years, to the enormous success of *kafe siber* (cyber café) in virtually each provincial town in Indonesia.[61] A few years ago, the appearance of Indonesian-language search engines muted the problems of the dominance of English on the WWW. Many local communities in Indonesia now have their own meeting place on the Internet, where local issues can be discussed in a regional language.[62] Furthermore, the number of user lists on all kinds of topics (both national and regional in scope) is rapidly increasing. Quite a few of these sites focus on popular music.

With the wider availability of these computer-mediated communications it seems likely that the discussion, distribution and advertisement of popular music will be strongly affected in the coming years. Fan magazines aimed at the teenage market have dominated Indonesia's printed pop music press. While the Sunday supplements of national newspapers such as *Republika* or *Kompas* sometimes discuss new albums or interview musicians, there are few print forums available for open discussions on the merits of popular music.[63] If an alternative musical press were to develop in Indonesia, it might well be an electronic one; many such discussion sites have appeared over the past few years.

It is important to not see the Internet as the monolithic entity it is sometimes supposed to be. The Internet is an amalgam of interacting, co-existing techniques and practices: e-mail, chatting, e(lectronic)-commerce, e-zines, streaming media, peer-to-peer audio-files sharing-utilities like Napster, KaaZaa, and the like. Locally, these preferences might differ enormously.[64] Below, we shall discuss some of the strategies used by the new electronic media in Indonesia and the ways in which they have shaped and imagined new musical communities. We shall refer to Internet sites, also listed in References Cited, which were available in 2002. Some Internet sites tend to be unstable, and may even disappear entirely within a few years. We therefore tried to restrict ourselves to sites that have seemed reasonably stable.

A first category of Internet sites is that of the so-called fan-sites: homepages dedicated to one group or artist. Many Indonesian bands and singers have their own homepage (often in English), through which commercial orders and bookings can be made.[65] On these sites, the supposed engagement of the artists

---

[61] The participants in these chat-boxes focus on various contents and generally consist of rapidly changing small groups of mainly young urban girls, who preferably communicate in local languages. To most Web watchers, chatting is *the* future of the Internet.

[62] See, for example, the following portals that address the West Sumatran community *Rantau net*, and the recently founded *Minang Net Online*, which is related to a Minang cultural Institute in Jakarta. For West Java, typical examples are *Sunda Net* and *Paris van Java*. An example of a popular Indonesian search engine is *Catcha* (see References Cited).

[63] Here, again, times seem to be changing. There are now electronic magazines together with the printed forms, like *NewsMusik on the net* and *Latitudes*, which focus on all kinds of expressions of popular Indonesian culture.

[64] A good example of the cultural differences in the use of the WWW, and particularly e-commerce can be found in Aoki (2000).

[65] See, for example, the Internet fan-sites of the bands *Slank* and *Naif*, the popular singer *Iwan Fals* and the singer-composer *Melly*, given in References Cited.

98   2002 YEARBOOK FOR TRADITIONAL MUSIC

themselves helps to create the idea of an intimate relationship between the artists and their fans. Music-oriented e-zines[66] is another category that has been rapidly growing. These provide possibilities for artists to comment on new releases, their social life and the latest political developments, thus emphasising the artist as a role model.

A third category is sites from where audio files might be downloaded and listened to (mostly in the mp3 format). These sites are illegal and the addresses tend to change rapidly. Sometimes less public FTP servers are used for this purpose, and one needs special software or even a subscription to use them. Songs in Malay or Indonesian tend to be under-represented in more internationally-oriented peer-to-peer platforms, such as Napster and KaaZaa, indicating that many Indonesians still have problems accessing the Internet.

A fourth category consists of music-related e-commerce: several techniques aimed at the distribution and sale of VCDs and audiocassette tapes, but also related merchandise like stickers, magazines, caps, etc. through the WWW.[67] Although this sector is small and mainly focusses on selling to customers outside Java, it is likely to contribute to the internationalisation of what used to be national or regional Indonesian popular music.[68] There probably is a relation between the emergence of online supermarkets, like *The Indonesian Music Shop* and *YesAsia* (formerly *Asia CD*), and online radio stations on the one hand, and the sudden international fame of singers, like Anggun C. Sasmi on the other hand. Many of these "hot" singers are switching to English or French on their new recordings, always looking for a foreign record deal. Conversely, Western music, other than that selected by the multinational companies, is now also available to the Indonesian market via the Internet.

Polls and charts are a dominant market mechanism in Western Europe and the United States. Until 1998, these were almost unknown in Indonesia, but their number has started to grow tremendously on the Internet. When it comes to actual sales, these charts, often called "song ladders" (*tangga lagu*), may not be trustworthy, but they at least show something about the musical taste of specific audiences. That the charts introduce their own dynamics into the music industry is clear from the fact that many of them are partly or fully sponsored by commercial companies, like the shampoo brand Clear, which has its charts published in the hard-copy *NewsMusik*. Noteworthy also is the rise of an annual contest for Indonesian popular music videos (*Video Music Indonesia*), which has been held since 1999. It underlines the increasing impact of the visual aspects connected with popular music as produced by the industry.

These days, most of these WWW facilities and techniques are combined in so-called music portals (see References Cited). Two of the more popular and

---

[66] See References Cited for some e-zines. These music magazines, for instance, highlight the lives of celebrities and are mostly electronic extensions of already existing magazines.

[67] See References Cited for some e-commerce sites.

[68] For Minangkabau popular music see, for instance, *Minang Record*; for Indonesian pop music see, for instance, *Sony Music Indonesia* that also marketed the popular band Sheila on 7.

daily updated ones are *MusikMu* and *Tembang*. Starting from their home pages one could search the Internet, although the sites themselves have many things to offer, covering short news, album releases and their own charts. These portals also offer other services, like lists with lyrics of both English and Indonesian language pop songs. These "archives" are a new form of making one's own collections of song texts, which was popular among Indonesian youth long before the Internet. Further, screen-savers and e-cards of favourite artists are available. Recently, telephone ring-tones based on popular Indonesian melodies were added and may be downloaded.[69] The sites are accessible to a general public, but most sites aim at frequently returning visitors and offer fashionable e-mail accounts (referring to the site's name), and e-mail based newsletters to registered members. Registered members are also encouraged to engage in so-called chat communities.[70] In short, these sites are home to a community, which only relates on the basis of musical taste and related interests.

The sites seem to be instrumental in counter-balancing the supposed alienation that has followed on the industrialisation of pop music, and the disruption of the line between performers and their audience (Kibby 2000:100). In turn, through such sites the performers and their record companies can learn about the aspirations and wishes of their target group. Daily or weekly polls are a helpful business application through which the taste of a younger generation is determined. Questions can be asked about a variety of topics, such as the popularity of certain artists, genres, producers and songs. Most of the music portals are mainly national in orientation and use the Indonesian language, although they also cover Western popular music. An exception is the trans-national *MTV Asia* site, which uses English and has pages dedicated to the various Asian countries. In March 2002, an Indonesian language MTV chat list was added, in which participants could comment on the coming MTV Indonesia station.[71]

The prohibition of commercial music-file sharing, and in the Indonesian case especially the lack of necessary facilities to do it with,[72] has—like elsewhere—been solved in creative ways. Some years ago, many popular Indonesian tunes were distributed through the Internet in a so-called MIDI format

---

[69] Ring-tones, locally called *nada dering* (see *Ring tones* [E]) are digitally delivered music files that play melodies for up to 30 seconds to alert users to incoming mobile phone calls. Although several Indonesian melodies circulate, interestingly enough the majority of WWW-published tones consist of Western pop song melodies. According to experts, ring-tones are a growing market that represents a potential multibillion dollar industry. Revenues for such services in Japan alone hit an estimated US $300 million (*Business Wire*[E], 6 December 2001).

[70] See, for example, "Forum Musikmu" on the site *MusikMu. eKilat* is the designation of a collection of chat groups; for instance, one of these specialising in Indonesian punk music (.../go-sip/). *Sony Music Indonesia* added a so-called forum to its homepage as well.

[71] In July 2002 this chat list was no longer available, as MTV Indonesia had been established.

[72] Such as a lack of bandwidth and good PCs, making it take too long to download a song from the Internet.

100 2002 YEARBOOK FOR TRADITIONAL MUSIC

(electronically generated music), which only allowed an instrumental version of the songs.[73] One of the more likely solutions for listening to the complete artistic product, including the vocal part and without violating copyright laws, is to turn to so-called "streaming media", through which popular songs can be listened to, but not downloaded into one's own PC. A good example of this strategy is found at the *Tembang* site, where under the header "listen to music" (*denger musik*) approximately 300 recent Indonesian pop songs can be listened to in Macromedia's so-called "flash format".[74] Another way to solve the problem of a lack of bandwidth and other technical facilities is entirely illegal and more local in approach. This is the distribution of so-called "CDs in mp3-format". Since 1997, these "data CDs" are sold in the larger shopping malls in Jakarta and other big cities. Fifteen or more popular music albums may be copied on these pirate CDs, which can be played on a PC with the necessary (simple) software. The price of such pirated data CDs is very low: Rp10 000–15 000 (€1.10–1.60). The price of the legal versions of these fifteen albums (cassette tapes and audio CDs) would be about Rp300 000 (€33).

This and other local transformations should be the focus of the social aspects of popular music studies in the years to come. In doing so, one should be careful not to focus only on the product and the technical possibilities. The Internet is embedded in other social and musical practices, and it is the dialectics of both real-time musical communities and online realities that need to be investigated further. We need answers to the question whether the fast flow of newly introduced techniques structurally alters the ways of communication, and transforms old and new media practices. It might even be that the Internet, as used via the PC, is already a past fad, and that in the near future it may be replaced by new techniques.[75] How will these technologies influence traditional and popular musics, and how will new possibilities interact with, for example, the

---

[73] Although the format was not very successful, it might return in the near future. Illusion Software, a Spanish company, already uses the MIDI-format to distribute their KaraokeKanta player as well as so-called "empty-music" or instrumental *karaoke* files over the Internet, so that people can sing to their favourite tunes. These files are mostly in the MIDI-format.

[74] This approach is likely to be successful in the future because multinational companies like Sony support it. *Sony Music Indonesia* offers musical samples from both Western and Indonesian artist in the real audio format on its site.

[75] At the 2001 ICTM conference in Rio de Janeiro, Janet Sturman presented some thought-provoking materials, arguing that the third generation of mobile phones, for example, might soon be the new frontier, replacing the Internet, as presently approached by PCs. In Japan, there already is a lively exchange of radio, video and audio files via the mobile phone, and in the long term these techniques might be cheaper and more useful for people living in Asia, Africa or the Caribbean. Downloading music to mobile phones, and continuously listening to the music, is one of the much-hyped new services expected from the next generation of high-speed phones (*CNet News* [E], 30 April 2001) Meanwhile, Mp3.com has released a new phone service, dubbed Music and Messaging On-Hold, which allows companies to manage music play-lists and audio advertisements to be heard by phone callers via the Web (*CNet News* [E], 16 February 2001).

increasing popularity of the VCD as the preferable carrier of musical and visual information? Most importantly, how do these practices lend themselves to the representation and re-imaging of (emerging) communities and their ongoing musical aspirations?

Conclusion

Popular music, in live performance or mediated, develops and instils a radically oral awareness of what it means to belong to an ethnic community in contemporary Indonesia. Moreover, on the national level, the dialogues about "East" and "West" and "tradition" and "modernity" are shaped in genres like "fusion", Indie and Islamic popular music. They make use of the new forms of orality made possible by VCDs and the Internet. However, VCDs and the Internet also mediate images, which we have analysed here in a preliminary fashion.

       International popular music coming from the United States, Western Europe, India and China has also made possible new imagined subjectivities. Urban Indonesia has had its fair share of rockers, mods, hippies, disco-queens and Madonna and Michael Jackson "wannabees". Indonesian intellectuals and government authorities have often worried about the detrimental effects of these lifestyles rooted in "foreign" music, even as they are celebrated in popular periodicals.

       The three musical domains—the local, the national and the global—exist in Indonesia today, not in opposition but in tandem, although the national level is losing its position since the downfall of Suharto and the beginning of the "reformation". People live in a world of shifting identities, as they negotiate themselves as members of one or more local communities and a national structure, and are simultaneously linked to people all over the world through the possibilities of the present media-scape.

       At the same time, and this cannot be stressed enough, for most Indonesians today the options available for self-fashioning are restricted by power and money. The bewildering juxtapositions and convolutions of Indonesian popular music are not only interesting as something to be studied by anthropologists and musicologists. Understanding the diverse scenes in which popular music is constructed, consumed and critiqued gives a good view of Indonesia's confrontation with modernity, and its co-option by and resistance to global markets and cultural forces.

REFERENCES CITED

Abdurachman, Paramita R.
1977   Kroncong Moresco, Tanjidor dan Ondel-ondel. *Budaya Jaya*
                109:338-34
Anderson, Benedict R. O'G.
1983   Imagined communities: Reflections on the origin and spread of
                nationalism. London: Verso.

102 2002 YEARBOOK FOR TRADITIONAL MUSIC

Aoki Kumiko
2000   Cultural differences in E-Commerce: A comparison between
                     the U.S. and Japan. *First Monday* 5:11,
                     http://firstmonday.org/issues/issue5_11/aoki/index.html.

Appadurai, Arjun
1996   Modernity at large; Cultural dimension of globalisation.
                     Minneapolis/London: Univ. of Minnesota Press.

Arps, Bernard
1996   To propagate morals through popular music: The Indonesian
                     qasidah modéren. In *Qasida poetry in Islamic Asia and Africa*,
                     eds Stefan Sperl and Christopher Shackle, Volume 1:389-409,
                     Volume 2:320-31, 464-5. Leiden: Brill.

Barendregt, Bart
1995   Written by the hand of Allah: *Pencak silat* of Minangkabau,
                     West Sumatra. In *Oideion; The performing arts world-wide* 2,
                     eds Wim van Zanten and Marjolijn van Roon,113-30. Leiden:
                     Research School CNWS.

2002   The sound of longing for home: Redefining a sense of
                     community through Minang popular musics. *Bijdragen tot de
                     Taal-, Land -en Volkenkunde* 158 (3).411-51.

Baulch, Emma
1996   Punks, rastas and headbangers: Bali's Generation X. *Inside
                     Indonesia* 48 *www.insideindonesia.org/*

Becker, Judith
1975   Kroncong, Indonesian popular music. *Asian Music* 7(1):14-19.

Broughton, Simon, Mark Ellingham, David Muddyman, Richard Trillo and Kim
Burton
1994   *World music: The rough guide*. London: Rough Guides.

Browne, Susan
2000   The gender implications of dangdut kampungan: Indonesian
                     "low-class" popular music. *Monash University, working paper*
                     109.

Clara van Groenendael, Victoria M.
1993   *Po-té-hi*: The Chinese glove-puppet theatre in East Java. In
                     *Performance in Java and Bali: Studies of narrative, theatre,
                     music, and dance*, ed. Bernard Arps, 11-33. London: School of
                     Oriental and African Studies.

Cohen, Matthew I.
1998   Review of "Craig A. Lockard, Dance of Life". *Bijdragen tot de
                     Taal-, Land- en Volkenkunde* 154:649-52.

1999   The incantation of "Semar smiles": A *tarling* musical drama by
                     Pepen Effendi. *Asian Theatre Journal 16* (2):139-93.
                     Also *www.muse.jhu.edu/demo/atj/16.2cohen.html*

Dijk, C. van
1999   The magnetism of songs. Paper for the International Workshop
                 Nationalism and Particularism in present-day South-East Asia,
                 December 1999. Leiden: KITLV.
Dolfsma, W.
2000   How will the music industry weather the globalization storm?
                 First Monday 5:5,
                 www.firstmonday.org/issues/issue5_5/dolfsma/index.html
e-ASEAN agreement
2000   ASEAN leaders adopt e-ASEAN agreement, result of The
                 Fourth ASEAN Informal Summit 22-25 November 2000,
                 Singapore,
                 www.aseansec.org/view.asp?file=/summit/infs4_alag.htm.
Fornäs, Johan
1998   Digital borderlands: Identity and interactivity in culture, media
                 and communications. *Nordicom Review*, 19:27-38.
Frederick, William H.
1982   Rhoma Irama and the Dangdut style: Aspects of contemporary
                 Indonesian popular culture. *Indonesia* 34:102-30.
1997   Dreams of freedom, moments of despair: Armijn Pané and the
                 imagining of modern Indonesian culture. In *Imagining
                 Indonesia: Cultural politics and political culture*, eds Jim
                 Schiller and Barbara Martin-Schiller, 54-89. Athens: Ohio
                 University Center for International Studies.
Frith, S.
2000   Music industry research: Where now? Where next? Notes from
                 Britain. *Popular Music* 19:387-93.
Garafalo, R. et al
2001   A discussion about Napster. *Journal of Popular Music Studies*
                 13:93-102.
Gideon Momongan
2000   Musik kita dalam musik dunia. *NewsMusik* 4:50-51.
Hall, M.
1999   Virtual colonization. *Journal of Material Culture* 4:39-55.
Hatch, Martin
1989   Popular music in Indonesia. In World music, politics and social
                 change: Papers from the International Association for the Study
                 of Popular Music, ed. Simon Frith, 47-67. Manchester:
                 Manchester University.
Heins, Ernst
1975   Kroncong and Tanjidor—Two cases of urban folk music. *Asian
                 Music* 7(1):20-32.
Hellwig, Jean C.
1989   *Sundanese popular culture alive!!!* [A documentary about
                 jaipongan and other performing arts of Sunda.] Video film

104 2002 YEARBOOK FOR TRADITIONAL MUSIC

	VHS 48 minutes; camera: Frank Krom. Amsterdam: Hellwig Productions.
1993	Jaipongan: The making of a new tradition. In *Performance in Java and Bali; studies of narrative, theatre, music, and dance*, ed. Bernard Arps, 47-58. London: School of Oriental and African Studies.
1996	Jaipongan op Java: Populaire traditie of traditionele pop? In *Theater in mondiaal perspectief*, ed. Kees Epskamp, 187-96. Utrecht/Den Haag: Hogeschool voor de Kunsten/ Centrum voor de Studie van het Onderwijs in Ontwikkelingslanden (CESO).

Hill, David T. and Krishna Sen
| 1997 | Rock'n'Roll   radicals.   *Inside   Indonesia   52,   www.insideindonesia.org*. |

Jabatin Bangun
| 2001 | Industri rekaman dan masa depan kultur musik Indonesia: Pendalaman kasus Karo. Paper presented at the symposium *Media Cultures in Indonesia*, 2-7 April 2001. Leiden University: VA/AVMI research project. |

Jones, Steve
| 2000 | Music and the Internet. *Popular Music* 19:217-30. |

Jurriëns, Edwin
| 2001 | Cultural travel and migrancy: The artistic (re)presentation of globalization in the electronic media of West Java. PhD dissertation, University of Leiden. |

Kartomi, Margaret J.
| 1976 | Performance, music and meaning of Reyog Ponorogo. *Indonesia* 22, October 1976. |
| 1998 | The pan-East/Southeast Asian and national Indonesian song Bengawan Solo and its Javanese composer. *Yearbook for Traditional Music* 30:85-101. |

Keil, Charles
| 1984 | Music mediated and live in Japan. *Ethnomusicology* 28:91-6. |

Kibby, Marjorie, D.
| 2000 | Home on the page; A virtual place of music community. *Popular Music* 19:91-100. |

Kornhauser, Bronia
| 1978 | In defence of kroncong. In *Studies in Indonesian music*, ed. Margaret J. Kartomi, 104-83. Clayton, Victoria: Monash University. |

Lent, J.A.
| 1994 | Introduction. In *Asian Popular Culture*, ed. John Lent, 1-28. Oxford: Westview Press. |

Liebowitz, Stan
| 2002 | Policing pirates in the networked age. *Policy Analysis* 438. Internet version, *www.cato.org/pubs/pas/pa-438es.html* |

Lindsay, Jennifer
1997   Making waves: Private radio and local identities in Indonesia. *Indonesia* 64:105-23.

Lockard, Craig A.
1996   Popular musics and politics in modern Southeast Asia: A comparative analysis. *Asian Music* 27(2):149-99.
1998   *Dance of life: Popular music and politics in Southeast Asia.* Honolulu: University of Hawai'i Press.

Malm, Krister
1992   The music industry. In *Ethnomusicology; An introduction*, ed. Helen Myers, 349-64. London: Macmillen.

Manuel, Peter
1988   Southeast Asia. In *Popular musics of the non-Western world: An introductory survey,* ed. Peter Manuel, 198-220. New York: Oxford University Press.

Manuel, Peter and Randall Baier
1986   Jaipongan: Indigenous popular music of West Java. *Asian Music* 18(1):91-110.

Miller, D. and D. Slater
2000   *The Internet: An ethnographic approach.* Berg: Oxford

Mills, Sherylle
1996   Indigenous music and the law: An analysis of national and international legislation. *Yearbook for Traditional Music* 28:57-86.

Mona Lohanda
1983   Dangdut: Sebuah pencarian identitas. In *Seni dalam masyarakat Indonesia: Bunga rampai*, eds Edi Setyawati and Sapardi Djoko Damono, 137-43. Jakarta: Gramedia.

Murray, Alison
1991   Kampung culture and radical chic in Jakarta. *RIMA* 25:1-16.

Olle, John
2000   Sex, money, power: Amidst screaming headlines, the tabloids are recreating political culture. *Inside Indonesia* 61, *www.insideindonesia.org*

Platzdasch, Bernhard
2001   Radical or reformist? How Islamic will the new movements make Indonesia? *Inside Indonesia* 68, *www.insideindonesia.org*

Pickles, J.
2000   Punks for peace: Underground music gives young people back their voice. *Inside Indonesia* 64:9-10 [hard copy.]

Pioquinto, Ceres
1995   Dangdut at Sekaten: Female representations in live performance. *RIMA* 29:59-89.

Remy Sylado
1983   Musik pop Indonesia: Suatu kekebalan sang mengapa. In (), *Seni dalam masyarakat Indonesia: Bunga rampai*, eds Edi

Setyawati and Sapardi Djoko Damono, 144-59. [Originally published 1977]. Jakarta: Gramedia.

Rizaldi
1997 Musik Gamat di kota Padang: Sebuah bentuk akulturasi antara budaya pribumi dan budaya Barat. *Jurnal Seni Budaya ASKI Padangpanjang* 1:92:102.[As from issue 2, the journal is called *Jurnal Palanta Seni Budaya.*]

Seeger, Anthony
1992 Ethnomusicology and music law. *Ethnomusicology* 36:345-59.
1996 Ethnomusicologists, archives, professional organizations, and the shifting ethics of intellectual property. *Yearbook for Traditional Music* 28:87-105.

Sen, K. and D.T. Hill
2000 *Media, culture and politics in Indonesia*. Melbourne [etc.]: Oxford University Press.

Smiers, Joost
Forthcoming *Freedom and protection; The impact of economic globalisation on artistic cultures worldwide.*

Spitulnik, Debra
1993 Anthropology and mass media. *Annual Review of Anthropology* 22:293-315.

Subagio, Gunawan, ed.
1989 *Apa itu lagu pop daerah*. Bandung: Citra Aditya Bakti.

Sutton, R. Anderson
1984 Who is the pesindhèn? Notes on the female singing tradition in Java. *Indonesia* 37:119-33.
1985 Commercial cassette recordings of traditional music in Java: Implications for performers and scholars. *The World of Music* 27(3):23-43.
1996 Interpreting electronic sound technology in the contemporary Javanese soundscape', *Ethnomusicology* 40:249-68.
2000 Global atau lokal? Kemasan musik pada Televisi Indonesia. *Jurnal Seni Pertunjukan Indonesia* X:35-50.

Tamara, Nasir
2000 The opportunities presented by the New Economy. *Kapital* (versi Indonesia), 17 November 2000. *www.kapital.co.id/*

Tambajong, J.
1992 *Ensiklopedi musik*. Jakarta: Cipta Adi Pustaka.

Weintraub, Andrew Noah
1997 Constructing the popular: Superstars, performance, and cultural authority in Sundanese Wayang Golek Purwa of West Java, Indonesia. Unpublished Ph.D. thesis, University of California, Berkeley.

Williams, Sean
1989 Current developments in Sundanese popular music. *Asian Music* 21(1):105-36.

Wilson, Ian
1999   Reog Ponorogo: Spirituality, sexuality, and power in a
               Javanese performance tradition. In *Intersections: Gender,
               history   and   culture   in   the   Asian   context.*
               wwwsshe.murdoch.edu.au/intersections/issue2/Warok.html
Wong, Deborah, and René T.A. Lysloff
1998   Popular music and cultural politics. In *The Garland
               Encyclopedia of World Music, Volume 4: Southeast Asia,* eds
               Terry E. Miller and Sean Williams. 95-112. New York,
               London: Garland.
Wright, Michael R.
1988   Tarling: Modern music from Cirebon. *Balungan* 3(3):21-5.
Yamashita, Shinji
1988   Listening to the city: Popular music of contemporary
               Indonesia. *East Asian Cultural Studies* 7:105-20.
Yampolsky, Philip
1987   *Lokananta: A discography of the national recording company
               of Indonesia 1957-1985.* Madison: Center for Southeast Asian
               Studies, University of Winconsin.
1989   Hati yang luka, an Indonesian hit. *Indonesia* 47:1-18.
Zanten, Wim van
1989   *Sundanese music in the Cianjuaran style: Anthropological and
               musicological   aspects   of   Tembang   Sunda.*   [KITLV,
               Verhandelingen no.140.]. Dordrecht, Providence: Foris.
1994   L'esthétique musicale de Sunda (Java-Ouest). *Cahiers de
               Musiques Traditionelles* 7:75-93.
1997   Inner and outer voices; Hearing and listening in West Java. *The
               World of Music* 39(2):41-9.
Zemp, Hugo
1996   The/an ethnomusicologist and the record business. *Yearbook
               for Traditional Music* 28:36-56.

Internet sites
In the addresses we left the first part 'http://' out. For articles in newspapers we
have given the date, title and site within the general site of the newspaper,
so.../business/news/...means that on the first dots you should include the general
site of the paper, like 'www.kompas.co.id.' As some Internet sites tend to be
unstable, and some sites may disappear entirely within a few years, where not
mentioned, we have only listed the sites that were still available in July 2002.

a. News media
Business Wire: *www.businesswire.com*
6 Dec. 2001   Advisory/experts available to discuss cell phone, music
               industry convergence.
               See www.biz.yahoo.com/bw/011206/62455_1.html
               [page disappeared]

108 2002 YEARBOOK FOR TRADITIONAL MUSIC

CNet News: *news.com.com*
16 Feb. 2001   Cell   phone   music   on   tour   in   Japan.
                    .../2100-1033-256706.html
30 April 2001   MP3.com   to   provide   "on   hold"   phone   music.
                    .../2100-1023-252773.html
CNN: *www.cnn.com*
2 Nov. 2000   Indonesia's ex-military chief sings love songs for nation's
                    refugees.
                    .../2000/ASIANOW/southeast/11/01/indonesia.singing.general/
Detikhot: *www.detikhot.com*
4 March 2002   Pembajakan industri rekaman.
                    .../lifestyle/2002/03/04/20020304-160831.shtml
IndoMedia: *www.indomedia.com*
10 Nov. 2000   Album kedua Sheila on 7 dibajak.
                    .../bernas/2011/10/UTAMA/10hib3.htm
 Jakarta Post Online: *www.thejakartapost.com*
19 Oct. 2000   Former TNI chief Wiranto launches album of love songs.
                    See www.intranet.usc.edu.au/wacana/isn/wiranto_debut.html
1 July 2001   Music in N.Sumatra booms.
                    .../detailfeatures.asp?fileid=20010701.J02&irec=17
Kompas Cyber Media: *www.kompas.co.id*
[formerly Kompas Online: *www.kompas.com*]
21 Mar. 2000   Indonesia masuk daftar utama pelanggar hak intelektual.
                    .../business/news/0003/21/06.htm
17 July 2001   Ornop minta HaKI dikeluarkan dari WTO.
                    .../business/news/0107/17/11.htm
7 Oct. 2001   Rossa, Dewi Yull dan pop progresif.
                    .../kompas-cetak/0110/07/UTAMA/ross01.htm
9 Nov. 2001   Maiyah, album Cak Nun…
                    .../entertainment/news/0111/09/1705.htm
9 Nov. 2001   Emha Ainun Nadjid: "Aku wis tuek, Mas".
                    … /style/people/0111/09/2641.htm
14 Nov. 2001   ASIRI desak presiden bentuk tim baru.
                    .../entertainment/news/0111/14/1723.htm
23 Nov. 2001   Emha Ainun Nadjid: "Saya kambing …".
                    .../berita-terbaru/0111/23/headline/100.htm
9 Dec. 2001   Yuni Shara pun merinding.
                    .../0112/09/UTAMA/yuni01.htm
7 Feb. 2002   Terkait CD bajakan, AS ancam boikot.
                    .../berita-terbaru/0202/07/headline/015.htm
3 Mar. 2002   Seni etnik Cina berbaur dengan Samba Sunda.
                    .../entertainment/news/0203/03/1969.htm
Majalah Suara Hidayatullah: *www.hidayatullah.com*
Dec. 2001   Emha Ainun Nadjib: anak ketiga.
                    .../2001/12/siapa2.shtml

BARENDREGT & ZANTEN   POPULAR MUSIC IN INDONESIA   **109**

Media Indonesia: *www.mediaindo.co.id*
20 April 2001   Pelanggar hak cipta rugikan US$186 juta.
                   .../cetak/berita.asp?ID=200104200036441
23 Dec. 2001   Musik Indonesia bergairah, pembajak.
                   .../cetak/berita.asp?ID=2001122300264826
5 March 2002   Jika pembajakan terus merajalela.
                   .../cetak/berita.asp?ID=2002030501524802
6 June 2002   Jika pembajakan masih tinggi.
                   .../cetak/berita.asp?ID=2002060613040277
MTV Asia: *www.mtvasia.com*
13 Dec. 2001   Going Independent in Indonesia.
                   ...music/features/20011213001 [page disappeared]
MTV Indonesia: *www.mtvasia.com/id.html*
Pikiran Rakyat Online: *www.pikiran-rakyat.com*
10 Nov. 2001   Ásyik nonton Osama.
                   .../prcetak/112001/10/09.htm)
25 Nov. 2001   Menyibak fenomena maraknya nasyid, by Ahmad Furqon.
                   .../prcetak/112001/25/0108.htm
Suara Pembaruan Online: *www.suarapembaruan.com*
5 June 1998   Momentum Reformasi dalam dunia musik kita.
                   .../News/1998/06/050698/Hiburan/hi02/hi02.html
                   [page disappeared]
Tempo: *www.tempo.co.id*
4 April 2002   Polres Jakarta Timur menahan 13 pedagang VCD bajakan.
                   .../news/2002\4\4/1,1,44,id.html

b. Fan-sites
IndoGrinder: *members.tripod.com/indogrinder/indogrinder.html*
Iwan Fals: *www.iwan-fals.com*
Medan Underground: *www.anakmedan.com/mug*
Melly: *www.mellygoeslaw.com*
Naif: *www.naifband.com*
Oi! Indonesia Punks and Skins: *members.fortunecity.com/indonesian1*
Slank: *www.slank.com*

c. E-zines
Latitudes: *www.latitudesmagazine.com*
NewsMusik on the net: *www.newsmusik.net*

d. Portals
General
Catcha: *www.catcha.co.id*
Paris van Java: *www.parisvanjava.net*
Rantau Net: *www.rantaunet.com*

110 2002 YEARBOOK FOR TRADITIONAL MUSIC

<u>Music</u>
CyberNasyid: *www.cybernasyid.com*
Kenada Online: *www.kenadaonline.com*
Musik Kita: *www.musikita.com*
MusikMu: *www.musikmu.com*
  Forum MusikMu.../komunitas/xmb/
  MusikMu Sepuluh (charts).../chart
Tembang (denger musik): *www.tembang.com*
  Tangga lagu (charts).../chart/

e. E-commerce
Minang Record: *www.geocities.com/minang_record*
Musica: *www.diffy.com/musica*
Perdana Disk Info (Video Music Ind.): *www.perdanadisc.info*
Sony Music Indonesia: *www.sonymusic.co.id*
The Indonesian Music Shop: *www.indonesianmusic.com*
YesAsia: *www.us.yesasia.com/*

f. Audiofiles / Radio / Streaming Media / Chatting communities
eKilat: *www.ekilat.com/index.html*
Indonesia Radio Directory: *www.idxc.org/indolocal/*
KaraokeKanta player: *www.karaokekanta.com*
Ring tones: *www.nadadering.tripod.com*
Video Music Indonesia: *www.vmi.rileks.com/menu.html*

Audiovisual recordings

Listed are only the audiovisual sources of which the music and/or images were used for our analysis. Albums just referred to in the article because of the song texts (often also published elsewhere), or because they were discussed in the press, on the Internet, or in other articles, are not listed.

Alone against the world
1993   Cassette tape by Maribeth. Sony Music Entertainemnet Japan C-6820793.
Archipelagongs
2000   Audio CD by Ubiet (alias Nyak Ina Raseuki). Warner Music Indonesia.
Badai pasti berlalu
1977   Cassette tape, by Chrisye. Irma Stereo KA 00291
2000   Cassette tape, re-mastered millenium version of *Badai pasti berlalu* 1977. MusicaMSC 8325.
Cici Faramida
1999   VCD 'Kumpulan terunggul Cici Faramidah' sung by Cici Faramidah. Warner Music Indonesia.

Doel Sumbang, Vol.1
1999   VCD karaoke Sunda 'Doel Sumbang', Volume 1. Vocalists: Doel Sumbang and Dewi Sondari. PolyGram Indonesia/ Blackboard Indonesia.

Doel Sumbang, Vol.2
1999   VCD karaoke Sunda 'Doel Sumbang', Volume 2. Vocalists: Doel Sumbang and Dewi Sondari. PolyGram Indonesia/ Blackboard Indonesia.

Duet legendaris Elvy Sukaesih & Mansyur S.
1999   VCD 'Gadis atau janda', sung by Elvy Sukaesih and Mansyur S. Dian Records/ Dian Dangdut.

Efrinon
1999?   VCD 'Album seleksi pop Minang terpopuler Efrinon', sung by Efrinon. Sinar Padang Record.

Generasi Biru
1995   Cassette tape by group Slank. Virgo Ramayana records / Piss record 001.

Indie Ten
1998   Cassette tape with various artists. Sony Music 491590.4

Kado Muhammad
1998   Cassette tape by Emha Ainun Nadjib with gamelan ensemble Kiai Kanjeng Sepuh. Kali Jogo Kreasi.

Kedamaian
1989   Cassette tape of *kacapi-suling* music (two zithers and bamboo flute) with (acoustic) piano. Performers: Bubi Chen (piano), Uking Sukri (*kacapi indung*), Dede Suparman (*kacapi rincik*), Endang Sukandar (*suling*). Bandung: Hidayat, #8902.

Lagu-lagu Top Klasik Sunda, Vol.1
2002   VCD with Cianjuran music, Degung kawih and Kacapi-suling music. Vocalists Euis Purnama and Yanti. Akurama Records, ARVCD 029.

Mahamoelia
1929   *Mahamoelia, Acte 5, deel III: Door de Padangsche Bovenlanden*. Original: black and white film, 35mm by I.A. Ochse 1925-1928. Production NIFM Polygoon. Documentation Nederlands Audiovisueel Archief [Now under the title *Gordel van Smaragd*, ISBN 90-5679-704-2, see also *www.picarta. pica.nl/DB=3.3/SET=7/TTL=9/SHW?FRST=10>*].

Malam Bainai
1990?   Cassette tape 'Top hits gamad, Volume 3, Malam Bainai', around 1990(?). Performed by Yan Juneid and Rosnida Ys, vocals, and accompanied by Buslidel. Bukittinggi: Tanama Record.

112 2002 YEARBOOK FOR TRADITIONAL MUSIC

Mega Hits Degung
2000   VCD 'Mega hits degung', Volume 1 (Surat Ondangan).
                        Vocalists: Een Ratnaningsih, Iis Fatimah and Aan Suryani.
                        Mega Cipta Pratama MG-068.

Menangis
1997   Cassette tape by Franky Sahilatua. Anggada Irama Melodi.

Music of Indonesia 2
1991   Volume 2: 'Indonesian popular music: kroncong, dangdut and
                        langgam Jawa' in the 20-CD series edited by Philip
                        Yampolsky. Washington DC: Smithsonian/ Folkways.

Osama Bin Laden
2001   Pirated version of CNN documentary. Released by *Haramain
                        Arabic VCD*

Sambasunda
1998   Audio CD 'Sambasunda; Rhythmical in Sundanese people'.
                        CBMW group, lead by Ismet Ruchimat. Jakarta: Gema Nada
                        Pertiwi, #CMNW-005.

Sarunai Aceh
2000   VCD 'Album seleksi lagu-lagu terbaik Yan Juneid; Sarunai
                        Aceh, Bunga Tanjung.' Padang(?): Bundo Record.

Sheila on 7 - Tertatih
2000   VCD, pirated from original audio recordings (1999) of the
                        'Sheila on 7' group. First song 'Tertatih.' On cover: Sony
                        Music Entertainment Indonesia. All files on CD are dated 24
                        June 2000.

Sheila on 7 - Kisah Klasik
2000   VCD 'Kisah klasik untuk masa depan' pirated from original
                        audio recordings (2000) of the 'Sheila on 7' group. On cover
                        only a bar code with number: 713 225 55 81. All files on CD
                        are dated 16 October 2000.

So la li
2000   Audio CD. Sabah Habas Mustapha & The Jugala All Stars
                        group. Berlin, Germany: Kartini Music.

Sunda Africa
1998   Audio CD 'Sunda Africa; No risk no fun (Bamboo flute, harp
                        & drums)' with Burhan [Sukarma], Ismet Ruchimat, Agus
                        Supriawan, Dodong, Vidal Paz. Jakarta: Cakrawala Musik
                        Nusantara.

Taubat
1998   Cassettte tape by Novia Kolapaking and Emha Ainun Nadjib.
                        Musica MSC 8207.

Top hits millenium 2000
2000?   VCD karaoke with pop Batak, performed by several Batak
                        artists. Clara Record.

Ucok Sumbara

2000?   VCD 'Ucok Sumbara – Millenium selection', sung by Ucok
                   Sumbara. Sinar Padang Record.

Wirid Padang Bulan

1999   Cassette tape by Emha Ainun Nadjib with gamelan ensemble
                   Kiai Kanjeng Sepuh. Mundu Nusantara Film.

Yuni Shara

1998   VCD 'Super seleksi Yuni Shara', sung by Yuni Shara. Suara
                   Sentral Sejati VCD-019 B.

[20]

"The World is Made by Talk"

Female Fans, Popular Music, and New Forms of Public Sociality in Urban Mali*

Dorothea E. Schulz

A striking feature of pop music consumption in urban Mali is female adolescents' devotion to women pop stars who, in singing style, lyrics, melody and rhythm, follow the conventions of "griot" (*jeli* in Bamanakan) music, a genre generally associated with Malian tradition and cultural authenticity[1]. In this, female youth sharply contrasts with young men and their

* The article is based on research conducted in the towns of San and Segu in Southern Mali, and in two neighborhoods in the capital Bamako, in the period between 1994 and 2000 (altogether 15 months). I combined qualitative research on different listener segments' reception practices with quantitative data collected in two surveys (1994, 1998) on listeners' reception and on their changing preferences for local radio programs. I thank Bob White and Craig Tower for their thoughtful comments and Tomás Rodriguez for his editorial suggestions. M. Saidou N'Daou helped me think through the material that forms the basis of this article. I feel particularly indebted to friends, neighbors and acquaintances in Bamako, San, and Segu who let me participate in their daily gatherings and graciously responded to my sometimes intrusive questions.
1. The *jeliw* (singular *jeli*) are professional musicians, traditionists and orators who belong to a special category of professional specialists (singular *nyamakala*) who are distinct from "free-born" people (singular *hòròn*) and descendants of serfs (singular *jon*). Until French colonial occupation of the area in the 19th century, *jeli* families lived together with the most wealthy and powerful free- born families of a rural community and passed down their patron family's traditions and histories in exchange for material support. On festive events that were of import to the entire local community, *jeli* women were expected to praise their patron family's prestigious genealogy and heroic origins, and thus to enhance its reputation. Patron families recompensed their *jeli* women's musical performances by giving them occasional gifts in the form of grain, cattle, and captives. To heighten the public renown of their patron families through musical performances and historical recitations was only one of the *jeliw's* tasks. Other important functions were the resolution of conflicts and the restoring of social order and harmony to the local community. In compensation, wealthy patron families provided food and shelter for their *jeli* clients (SCHULZ 2001b: chap. 1).

preferences for diverse, mostly international African musical styles linked to a progressive and "hip" mood and life style. Since Malian independence in 1960, the musical performances by *jeli* women from southern Mali have been extensively broadcast on national radio and, after 1983, television.

While the former institutional context of *jeli* praise changed drastically, the textual properties and performance style of *jeli* singers continued to enjoy such popularity among (mostly female) audiences that more and more singers of non-*jeli* background came to employ central elements of their musical style and turned public flattery on behalf of renowned personalities into a lucrative profession[2]. In this process, *jeli* praise singers, whose performances were broadcast on national radio and, after 1983, on television, became emblematic of "Malian" music and identity. Starting in 1992, however, when the current president Alpha Konaré reached power in the first democratic elections, the politics of communication changed considerably. The broadcasting of *jeli* publicity on behalf of politicians is now prohibited. Also, local radio stations and their national and international music broadcasts introduce greater choice into musical broadcasting formerly dominated by the national radio station.

The pop stars' success, the acclaim they earn in national and international arenas are a function of their resourceful combination of local musical conventions and visual aesthetics with emblems of a cosmopolitan consumer style (Schulz 2001b). A number of authors who work on cultural dimensions of current processes of globalization argue that the spread of media technologies and images does not lead to cultural homogenization but to consumers' selective "appropriation" of globalized cultural forms (Miller 1987; Friedman 1990; Appadurai 1996; Weiss 1996; Piot 1999). The success story of female pop singers in Mali can be read as an illustration of processes of cultural production in which people modify Western consumer styles and thereby leave a local imprint on standardized symbolic forms that circulate at a global scale.

Girls listen to the pop singers' music broadcast on local radio whenever they sit together with friends, relate the most recent social events to each other, and a radio set is available. Even if they lack the opportunity to listen to their favorite singers' music, their conversations quickly turn to the discussion of their favorite stars' personal life, acquisitions, and concerts. References to the lyrics of a song are almost absent. Girls' admiration for the pop singers, their seemingly obsessive talk about their idols' personal lives and success stories is ridiculed by the generation of their parents. The latter hold that many pop stars whom their daughters adore lack the musical and rhetorical skills that former generations of *jeli* singers used to display. Parents decry that to girls, the display of international consumer

---

2. For an account of transformations in the institutional context that changed the social significance of *jeli* performances and moved women as performers to the foreground, see SCHULZ (1998); also see DURAN (1995) and DIAWARA (1997a).

style matters more than musical and textual quality. In their eyes, this proves their daughters' lack of sensibility and taste. At the same time, parents occasionally associate the very pop singers whose lack of skills they deplore with feelings of pride in local musical traditions.

Scholarly evaluations of the pop singers' performances are similarly divided. According to some authors, the pop singers' production of music for a mass mediated market goes hand in hand with the emptying and corruption, of "deep tradition" (Keita 1995; Diawara 1997a; Traoré 2000). This somber depiction of the women singers' musical productions is countered by authors who see the pop stars as "superwomen" (Duran 1995) and representatives of a new generation of women and their emancipation from conventional gender roles (also see Hale 1998)[3].

These equivocal interpretations of the pop stars' significance resonate with similarly contradictory evaluations of mass culture in Western industrial societies and of the role of women, as producers and consumers, in it. Some authors point out that derogatory views of the ephemeral nature of mass culture are often expressed in its feminization. Distinctions between mass culture and "high culture" tend to be linked to the denigration of female consumers, to their "irrational" consumption rituals and bodily expression of consumer "obsessions" (Huyssen 1986). On the other side, there is a tendency in studies on pop culture to celebrate commercial mainstream culture as a site of "resistance through ritual" for groups that are marginal in a patriarchal and capitalist order, such as working class youth subcultures and women (Clarke *et al.* 1976; but see Thornton 1996). More recent studies, in contrast, depart from neatly opposed interpretations and posit a double-edged significance of mass culture productions to consumers' life. They replace previous interpretations of women's consumption in terms of "blind/passive consumerism" versus "creative resistance" with differentiated accounts of the transformational potential and limitations of mass culture products (Radway 1984; Modlesky 1982).

In spite of these efforts, female fan culture remains a field that is considerably less explored than that of male youth. Even if a number of studies followed the initial call for investigation into female "Teeny Bopper" fan culture without assuming that it displays the same features as male subcultures (Mc Robbie & Garner 1976), few studies account for these practices without

---

3. This view does not account for the conservative gender ideology of most of the lyrics which are greatly appreciated as "moral education" by middle-aged women. The latter's emphasis on the "edifying" character of the songs that deplore the degradation of social life under the effects of money seems to contradict women's enthusiasm about the fashionable outfits and wealth that stars display. One reason for the pop singers' popularity among women is that they harmonize in a visually compelling style what otherwise appears as mutually exclusive claims. They mediate between the opposing demands for being a "modern progressive woman" (materialized in certain imported consumer goods) while presenting themselves as being firmly rooted in an "authentic" morality that is associated with the "uncorrupted" life in the countryside (SCHULZ 2001a).

interpreting them as instances of star-centered hysteria or of a "magical obsessive world of fandom" (Cline 1992). Also, because studies on female fan culture focus on cults of male pop idols (Lewis 1992), they leave aside the crucial question as to possible, and essential, differences between male pop idol culture (that revolves around the objectifying of the male star) and the cult of female stars (that allows for admirers' identification with the idol).

This article focuses on female adolescents' fan culture in urban Mali to explore the objective and subjective dimensions of new forms of sociality that emerge at the interface of new media technologies and a commercial music culture in urban Mali. My first concern is to understand what particular, imaginary relationship individual listeners establish with a pop star in the very act of listening to and talking about her. The notion of imagining, as an autonomous mental act (Casey 1976; also see Castoriadis 1975) and as a mimetic practice (Benjamin 1980) may help us understand the particular dynamics at stake in the act of consuming radio broadcasts. In a second step, I assess the implications of local radio stations and their music programs for conventional forms of socializing. I argue that these changes not only make practices related to the consumption of pop music more central to everyday life in town, but give rise to a new kind of public. I explore what is novel about these new forms and how they are constituted. Here too, the act of imagining plays a central role in understanding the dynamics and constitutive features of the new, mass mediated forms of publicness[4].

My interest in the mutually constitutive relationship between practices of imagining and new forms of sociality is inspired by and simultaneously departs from Habermas's account of the bourgeois public in eighteenth century Europe (Habermas 1989). According to Habermas, the latter was constituted by the printed word and its discursive deliberation, and based on shared normative understandings and consensus-oriented argumentation. As Anderson (1983) argues, central to this form of sociality that occasionally spanned over larger distances was the idea of belonging to an "imagined community" created by print capitalism. I take pop music broadcasts and their reception by female youth as a starting point to explore the new realms and forms of publicness created by new electronic media and their normative foundations (Waterman 1994; Barber 1997, 1999).

My approach differs from Habermas's privileging of the political-critical, consensus-oriented dimensions of public debate[5]. Even if the new publics created by local radio stations emerge around debate, the compelling force

---

4. With "publicness" I translate the German term "Öffentlichkeit"; its connotation of openness (in an ideational, not spatial sense) is not conveyed in the terms "public" or "publicity" (HANSEN 1993: footnote1).

5. As CALHOUN (1992) points out, Habermas oscillates between a descriptive statements about the late 17th and 18th century bourgeois public on one side, and normative assertions about its inherently critical nature on the other.

of these debates, and of the performances the stations broadcast, resides not in their critical-rational appeal, but in the "community of sentiment" they create (Appadurai 1990). My perspective also departs from Habermas's focus on one broadcast technology. As I will show, audiences make sense of aural broadcasts by placing them in the larger field of media products, many of which are visual. Media consumption is thus predicated upon the "inter-medial" nature of most commercial culture products and on consumers' *combined* reception of their various (mostly aural and visual) incarnations[6].

The Pop Stars and Their Audiences

Almost all pop stars come from the southern triangle of Mali where people speak two closely related Mande languages, Bamanakan and Maninkakan[7]. Because the women pop stars draw upon the musical repertoire, languages and historical traditions of their home communities, the extensive broadcasting of their songs on national radio, television, video tapes and local radio has rendered them icons of national culture and pride[8]. But they are not equally held in high esteem by people who generally distinguish between them according to their performance skills. At the top of the charts range singers who are mostly of *jeli* birth and started their success story with recordings at the national radio station. Over the past ten years, the position of these *jeli* singers has been increasingly challenged by women of "free birth" who come from the Wasulu, a region south of the capital Bamako[9]. These pop stars are the only ones who are regularly invited to sing in public concerts. Even though older rural and urban listeners often criticize their "venality", they generally hold them in great esteem because of their performances skills that make them emblematic of "local" culture. In contradistinction to these successful women singers, there are numerous women who, to embark on a musical career, try to pass on one of the television music programs. Many of them make up with evocative body movements, a pleasing composure and fashionable dress for their often limited textual knowledge and musical qualities[10].

6. For an interesting parallel, see FABIAN's discussion of the "intertextual" nature of diverse genres of popular culture in Zaire (1997).
7. Some singers whose performances are frequently broadcast on local radio stations are from the Maninkakan speaking areas of Guinea which are part of the same Mande-speaking cultural realm.
8. This dominance of southern languages and traditions in the national Malian arena goes back to the colonial period, when peoples from the south were more willing to be integrated into the colonial administration. The unequal representation of Malian local cultures has been enhanced by the fact that for more than 20 years, international popular press and scholarly publications focused on musicians from the south and their musical traditions (Ali Farka Touré and Boubakar Traoré are being two notable exceptions).
9. The most prominent of these singers is Oumou Sangaré (DURAN 1996).
10. A final category of *jeli* and other nyamakala singers restrict their realm of action to unmediated performance settings. They show up (often uninvited) at family

The pop singers' concerts are literally packed with women of all ages. But evaluations by older married women on one side and younger women and girls on the other reveal significant discrepancies in the importance they attribute to various aspects of a performance[11]. Middle-aged women tend to highlight the "educational" (*"ladili"* in Bamanakan) and moral character of the song text and its consoling effects. Central to girls' conversations, in contrast, is the assessment of the pop stars' outfit and crafty employment of emblems of a cosmopolitan consumer style. Also, middle-aged women have a clear preference for the pop stars whose rhetorical and musical skills, knowledge of the different local musical styles, songs and historical traditions places them in the top ranks of hit charts. In contrast, girls' enthusiasm for a singer's outfit, "air" and elegant body movements makes them admire even singers who are denounced by their parents as performing songs emptied of any deeper meaning[12].

Apart from attending their idols' public concerts, girls and women know about their most recent song releases, outfits and hairstyles from the weekly music programs on television which they await eagerly, follow attentively and debate hotly with their peers[13]. But the number of girls who have an opportunity to watch television is considerably smaller than those who regularly listen to their favorite pop stars on local radio.

The pop stars address women in many songs and deplore their "difficulties" in town where envy rules the relations among relatives and friends, and "money" undermines any sense of moral obligation. They denounce the evils of polygamous marriage, such as back-biting co-wives and husbands who fail to treat their different wives with impartiality. And they laud women for their accomplishments as mothers and spouses and implore them to feel "proud" of their elegance and accomplishment. The following song is characteristic of the mixing of "women's problems" with an appeal to "feel good" about being a woman, in spite of the difficulties she has to put up with. Similar to many popular songs, it represents procreation and motherhood as a central source of women's dignity. The singer, Oumou Dioubaté, comes from the Maninkakan speaking region of Guinea. Her

---

celebrations, such as weddings and baptizing ceremonies, and bestow (and sometimes impose) their praise on hosts and members of the audiences in exchange for money (SCHULZ 1999a).

11. Variations in preferences among women and girls do not clearly correlate with differences in education and socio-economic background. This insight supports Miller's finding that in urban Trinidad, variations in "taste" and "style" do not demarcate and reproduce neat class distinctions (MILLER 1987).

12. Critics employ images of "hollowness" *(kòrò t'a la)* and "distortion" *(donkili karabalèn de do)* to refer to what they experience as the songs' loss in meaning and quality (SCHULZ 2001b: chapter 7).

13. In addition, the second program of the national radio ("Chaîne Deux") created in response to the competition of commercial local radio stations, features their music in special programs.

song, from an audio tape released in 1996, was broadcast on local radio several times a day in 1998 and ranged at the top of the charts.

Oumou Dioubaté: *Women of Africa*

Chorus:
Women are overburdened, women are overburdened, aa
women, aa, women of Africa, you are treated badly
The women are overburdened, the women are overburdened, aa
women, aa, women of Africa, your are badly treated
Oumou Dioubaté:
I say, women are badly treated
women of Lebanon, you are badly treated
women are overburdened, indeed
women of Angola, you are overburdened
women are overburdened
women of Ethiopia, you are overburdened
women are treated badly
women of Liberia
women are treated badly
women of Rwanda are overburdened
their children suffer with them
that's what makes the conflicts even worse
chorus:
repetition lines 1-4
Oumou Dioubaté:
when a woman gets pregnant
when her belly starts hurting
then the truth of the matter becomes evident:
this is the time of women
when her pregnancy reaches its termination
when it is time to give birth to the child
a woman goes into labor
the child's hair is already visible
when she is still in labor
then the real work of giving birth has started
a woman starts doing her real work
the months of pregnancy are over
the times of disquiet are over
the woman's health comes back
the woman comes out of this work with pride
the woman comes out victorious
the woman is noble
your child may turn out to be useless, but you cannot tell
your child may turn out to be a bad spirit, but you cannot tell
your child may turn out to be stupid, but you cannot tell
only God will know it
my belly is hurting hurting hurting me
my belly has started hurting
...
After enumerating further reasons for women's sufferance,
Oumou Dioubaté concludes:
the children of Mali's women are blessed
I say, the time has come

the time of waiting has really come to an end
...
women, come out
women of the world, stand up and work
women, come out and give womanhood its dignity back
women, come out, etc.

Women and girls spontaneous, enthusiastic reactions to the song generally reflect how much they are taken in by the aesthetic force of the
singer's voice, the song's melody and rhythm and the singer's tonal modulation of the text. The text's reduced complexity sets it apart from "traditional" lyrics whose interpretation was predicated upon implicit understandings
of locally determined audiences (Diawara 1997b). But this does not minimize the song's popularity among female urban audiences. One reason for
its appeal is that the singer skillfully combines a compelling rhythm and
melody with a text that "speaks to the heart" of female consumers.

But female adolescents may appreciate the pop stars' performances for
other reasons than their mothers. To understand what renders the pop stars
so attractive to female youth that they devote a major share of their time
to the discussion of their idols professional triumphs and personal trials,
we need to know more about the social setting in which their consumption
takes place.

Youth in Urban Mali: a "Generation-in-Waiting"

The impossibility to clearly demarcate the category of girls and young
unmarried women, whose consumption practices I explore, from women
reflects some of the current predicaments of female youth in Mali[14]. These
predicaments provide the backdrop against which girls' consumption preferences, and the significance they attribute to the pop singers' songs, are to
be understood. Conventional, normative definitions of a female adolescent
by the combination of her unmarried status and the reaching of puberty
(*pògòtigi*[15]) are incongruent with the current situation. Especially in town,
the number of children born out of wedlock, and thus of unmarried mothers,

---

14. Given the historical and cultural variability in notions of adolescence or youth,
    considerable conceptual difficulties are involved in defining "youth" as a (homo-
    genous) category (BAKAN 1972; KETT 1977; GRIFFIN 1993). It seems that this
    task is rendered even more difficult in the current postcolonial world where a
    number of the conditions that allow to set youth apart from the adult world are
    no longer guaranteed, and age no longer serves as a distinctive marker. The
    girls and young, unmarried women whose consumption practices I explore are
    between 12 and 25 years old.
15. The literal meaning of *pògòtigi* is "someone who has (protruding) breasts" that
    is, someone whose breasts have not yet been weighed down as a consequence
    of pregnancy and breastfeeding. This ideal of young female beauty is reflected
    in a variety of visual representations, such as statues, drawings and postcards.

has been skyrocketing over the past fifteen years, to the extent that marriage no longer serves as a marker of female adulthood.

Without assuming homogeneity in consumption preferences or class background, I consider the female adolescents whose consumption practices I explore as a constituency emerging in and around the act of consumption, manifested in girls' informal gatherings[16]. I conceive of "female youth" as a group defined by a common preference for certain consumer styles or, in this case, a particular genre of pop music. My focus is on girls and unmarried young women whose socio-economic background can be roughly described as "middle" and "lower middle class". Only some of their fathers earn a regular income as government officials or teachers, while others try to make a living from activities in the informal sector of the economy[17]. Whenever a father earns a regular salary, this gives his daughter a certain, limited spending power, or at least the possibility to lay claims on her parents' funds. Girls from poorer households regularly visit their better-off neighbors to watch TV music programs. Their actual capacities to spend money is replaced by their constant talk about prices and values of desirable goods which most often they cannot afford to buy.

Marriage constitutes the crucial criterion for "achieving" adulthood and the first step in a life-long endeavor to become and remain a respected member in one's social circle. But the factors that currently impair young people's possibilities of becoming full-grown members of their community are played out differently for male and female adolescents.

The scarcity of income opportunities and employment in the formal economy makes it difficult for most young men to marry and to build an independent homestead, and thus to enjoy an economic and a certain social autonomy from their parents and family. Their on-going economic dependency on their parents keeps men (often until the late 20s) in a status of "adulthood-in-the-waiting" that excludes them from any participation in decision making both at the level of the family and of society at large. Male adolescents' relative exclusion from the tight labor market seriously limits their possibilities of gaining a "name" *("tògò")* and "respect" *("dambe")*, the two markers of individual achievement. Their chances of becoming wealthy both in a social and political way, by attracting a group of followers and friends and having children who contribute to one's affluence and social standing, draw to a close.

Young men's exclusion from the political decision making process constitutes the other face of their marginality (Brenner forthc.). It is one of the most important factors of current political instability in Mali. In

---

16. I am aware of the problematic use of the notion of "female youth consumption" which glosses over differential experiences and consumer preferences. Even though they have to be taken into account, they can not be neatly related to differences in class and educational background (MILLER 1987).

17. In almost all cases, the girls' mothers pursue an income generating activity as well, sometimes as formal employees but most often in the informal economy.

the absence of any hopes for self-sustenance, male adolescents' growing realization of a foreclosed future feeds into their development of clientelist expectations towards both parents and the state, as providers of jobs and a "good life". Frequent conflicts with their parents over allocation of resources, and their constant expression of disappointment with their parents' "stinginess" illustrate an inversion, and even perversion, of earlier conceptions of intergenerational responsibilities (Berry 1985). Prospects for changing one's life situation are small and male adolescents are confined to merely *talking* about the possibility of "venturing out" to the Euro-American West with its promises of employment and a "good life". Their disillusion with the new government to whose ascendancy they contributed substantially[18], is at the basis of an urban oppositional movement. Its destructive force not only poses a threat to the current regime, but nourishes an already existing, widespread disenchantment with the unfulfilled promises of "demokrasi" and the government's incapacity to establish law and order (Schulz 2001b: chapter 3).

Thus, similar to other postcolonial settings (Mbembe 1985; Comaroff & Comaroff 2000a: 306-309) young men's lack of opportunities to become full-blown members of the national community turns them into a "generation in-the-waiting" in a double sense. In urban Mali, they wait not only for achieving a status of adulthood, but for parental support and for the state's creation of the very conditions that would enable them to become full-grown members of the social and political community.

The concerns of girls and young women are manifest in what appears as their obsessive preoccupation with marriage partners. Conversations among them, and the talk radio programs they listen to, center on questions such as how to find a husband, if necessary by occult means, and how to prevent other women from pinching their lovers[19]. Contrary to the conventional terms in which their persistent talk about marriage is framed, it reveals a new, heightened concern that emanates from radically altered conditions for reaching the status of womanhood. Having off-spring and establishing an independent homestead gives a young woman a certain economic autonomy, at least in the long run, when her grown-up children will be able to support

---

18. BRENNER (forthc.) shows convincingly how the "grin", the site of informal gathering (see below), became the most important "cell" of critical political discourse and action. The social basis of this violent opposition was composed primarily of young men without formal education or job opportunities. But the leaders were from a small group of relatively privileged men, unemployed graduates from the national high-schools, whose hopes to find an employment in the public sector were stifled by the reduction of state bureaucracy initiated by the structural adjustment program since the 1980s.

19. Even though girls often state their wish to live in a monogamous marriage (among other things, because this would give them more control over the family income), they prefer a polygamous marriage to not being married at all. This, and the competition over potential husbands, often creates an atmosphere of distrust even among girls who consider each other friends.

her[20]. But the prospects for marriage and procreation, as the socially sanctioned avenues to adulthood for women, are blocked by men's lack of possibilities, and sometimes unwillingness, to marry and assume full financial and social responsibility.

For a man, procreation is only one way of generating wealth and affluence, and not the most prominent way of proving his rightful claim to full membership in the community. For women, by contrast, their capacity to bear children and to contribute through them to family prosperity and repute remains the principal path towards the realization of ideals of femininity. Precisely this capacity to legitimately procreate and augment the family's wealth is seriously impaired under current conditions of economic disparity. Also, the postponement of the socially sanctioned conception of offspring, means to foreclose a woman's (in)famous "power of the bedroom". The latter is based on a woman's abilities to exert influence via informal channels, such as her sons or her capacity to mollify her husband's decisions by withdrawing her affection and sexual attention. Last but not least, only a married status allows a woman to gain full access to social events, such as family ceremonies, in which women perform and thus create themselves as full-blown members of the community.

All of this implies that girls' impaired possibilities to enter the status of adulthood has ramifications that reach beyond the inhibited fulfillment of sexual and emotional desires. The current predicament undercuts a woman's perception of herself as an "accomplished" woman in the double sense: as one who has accomplished what is expected from her (that is, to contribute to the wealth and social standing of the family through procreation) and as one who is a sophisticated and admirable woman.

The conditions that impede or postpone young men's and women's "becoming" a person in the fullest cultural sense (Comaroff & Comaroff 2000b) form part of a recent transformation in which the material and normative foundations of former divisions of labor, of responsibilities and obligations between the generations and between men and women are changing radically. Many men from the lower classes are less and less capable of securing the survival of their family. Their wives are often forced to assume a greater, if not exclusive, economic responsibility. These radical modifications affect middle class households as well. While before, women from many middle class households spent the money they earned on their own consumption, an increasing number of women are forced to come up

---

20. In spite of regional variation in rural areas, marriage generally invests a woman with greater economic independence from her own family because it offers women the access to the means of production, such as a strip of her in-law's land and her husband's labor. Today in urban areas, middle- and upper-middle class women, unless they earn an independent income, are dependent on their husband's financial contributions. Lower-class women, who work for themselves are economically more independent, yet also have to assume a heavier financial responsibility for their family.

for at least part of the family's subsistence. Changes in financial responsibilities engender new conflicts within the field of familial decision-making, a field already ridden with conflicts among co-wives and potential challenges to male elderly control[21]. In a situation where institutions of conflict-mediation that used to stabilize family relations are weakening, these conflicts seriously threaten the stability of conjugal relations. Women's greater economic responsibility gives them more weight in disputes over the use of family resources[22].

Modifications in the relations between men and women are not only manifest in the realm of the economic. Nor are their effects restricted to claims and conflicts over financial contributions. Tensions between gender norms and ideologies, old and new[23], come out most clearly in everyday discussions among men, women, but also in many "folk stories" told on national and local radio. These stories, a modernized form of conventional "human-interest stories", are being framed in the conventional form of story telling. Most stories reflect men's fear of women toppling them in the family and in public settings. These stories, and the fear they convey, have become much more pronounced since 1992, when the party ADEMA took over power and facilitated women's access to leading positions in the state bureaucracy and the governmental apparatus.

Many young men delve in the promises of a greater autonomy from parental control, which in the absence of economic opportunities for its realization remains, by and large, something to talk and daydream about. Girls and young women, on the other hand, nurture very contradictory expectations with regard to marriage and their future husband. These expectations result from a blending of conventional gender roles (such as the expectation of the husband's full economic responsibility for the family income) with ideals of greater female autonomy and decision-making power,

---

21. According to some young men, their incapacity to respond to conventional expectations regarding their role as main providers is exacerbated by the fact that their fathers often hesitate to provide them with the necessary political or/and economic resources to find a job or to start an independent business, because it is in their interest to keep control over their sons.
22. Given the fact that their greater realm of economic maneuver is paired with a greater responsibility, it would be extremely misleading to welcome this development as a sign of women's greater "independence". Women do not necessarily have a greater say in actual decisions but their chances of challenging decisions by the family head are rising.
23. Mass education, substantially improved through reform since 1992, and the growing presence of globalized media images are only two among a number of recent developments that help introduce international conceptions of modern life style and subjecthood to an ever expanding constituency. Caught between donor agencies from the West and the Arab speaking world, Mali straddles between influences from international discourses on Human Rights versus cultural authenticity that provide the basis for a serious challenge to conventional norms about women's appropriate behavior- and for its backlash in the form of a new and markedly patriarchal gender ideology based on "Islamic" values (SCHULZ forthc.).

and the ideal of romantic love. Because many girls do not earn an independent income but work for their mothers, their spending power depends entirely on the gifts that friends, male relatives and lovers make them. This "non-productive" form of income-generation comes close to a "rent" that girls receive in exchange for other favors[24]. Whether they received higher education or not, they show relatively little interest in pursuing a professional career or finding regular employment to gain economic autonomy. Most of them seek to earn money, but only as long as they have not found a husband who, as they hope, will then fully provide for their needs. This expectation stands in stark contrast to economic realities that not only require most women to come up for a share of the family income, but also that their husband's income will hardly give them the spending power they are envisioning.

It is not surprising, then, that the "love" relationships between young men and women constitute a principal site in which changing gender norms and ideologies, and men's and women's ambivalent feelings and expectations towards each other are played out and manipulated[25]. Young men and women talk about short-term liaisons as a kind of "makeshift" solution to the tampered chances for marrying.

The open-ended nature of these current forms of courtship is experienced by many young women and girls as a situation of great emotional and material insecurity. At the same time, the (often vaguely defined) love relations make it possible for them to bend the relationship according to their own interest, be it directed at receiving material favors or at establishing a longer-lasting relationship. Centrally at stake is the access to female sexuality. Beyond the pleasure it entails for both sexes, courtship bears different significances for young men than for women[26]. For the latter, establishing amorous ties is an offshoot or a distorted play-off on the central role that pregnancy plays in their striving for the status of a full-grown woman. Granting or withholding sex to a man becomes a way of attracting

---

24. Male adolescents' expectations towards their future spouses reveal similar ambivalences regarding between partnership ideals, old and new: while they aren't adverse to the idea of women contributing to the family income, they often emphasize that they would prefer their women's full dependence on their own income because this would perpetuate their own control over family decisions.
25. Given that the "love" relationships vary considerably depending, among other factors, on the socio-economic background, the strictness and religiosity of their parents, and the neighborhood, it is difficult to ascertain a clear direction towards which the patterns of interaction between female and male youth evolve. But the urban setting clearly offers new opportunities for less restricted interaction and sexual relations. Parental control, particularly over their daughters, is receding, but there are many families who seek to counter what they perceive as a loss of morals by imposing serious restrictions on their daughters' activities.
26. As I witnessed on numerous occasions, male and female adolescents lay claims on each others' material signs of affection by blurring the distinctions between (sexual) "love making" *("kanu kè")*, feeling attracted to someone *(fè)*, "fooling around" *("tlon kè")* and "true" affection *("jarabi")*.

admirers. As many women admit, sometimes under bursts of laughter, it also serves as a means to obtain some materialized tokens of the lover's affection. Of similar importance is that "being attractive" to a number of lovers helps to show off one's "female qualities" to friends and competitors in the absence of any legitimate possibility to "prove" one's womanly capacities of procreation. Girls are manipulated by as much as they plot against young men. They try to "convince" the latter to marry them by conceiving children or by playing them off against competitors[27]. But these strategies often backfire. Ultimately, the "powerful" position that women seem to have (and that young men often complain about) by granting access to their bodies is of a double-edged nature. Giving sexual favors may inspire in them a temporary feeling of empowerment, but girls' complaints about men's "dishonesty" reflects their disillusion about it. Also, it undermines a woman's "bargaining" position once it comes to marriage. Because of the prevailing gender ideology that evaluates "extra-marital sex" by women differently from that of men, granting men access to their body makes women vulnerable to men's (and other people's) attacks on their moral looseness.

To men, on the other hand, having one or, if possible, several lovers demonstrates a man's virility in a double material sense: his physical and economic capacities to attract and keep lovers. Unmarried men, in the absence of the economic power to generate sustainable wealth and achieve personal autonomy and social control, thus become "gods of small things" (Roy 1997) but in a truncated, almost perverted sense. Thus, as granting sex becomes central to girls' "rent-seeking" strategies, the significance of sexual relations changes from a source of human, and ultimately material, wealth to sex as a short-time assurance of small favors.

Indicative of the female youth's predicaments are their conflicted relationships to female relatives of the older generation, towards whom they tend to bear feelings of envy and incompleteness. Even if girls feel that their parents' conceptions of marriage are outdated, they seek to straddle a line between their own desire for a greater realm of maneuver and their parent's normative expectations, which revolve around the maintenance of the family's reputation and "public face"[28]. Girls' incapacity to produce wealth, be it material or human, is succinctly stated by mothers who frequently blame them for being "useless" and "worth nothing". Allegations

---

27. It is an open secret that some women seek to consolidate their relationship to a particular lover by getting pregnant, by this trying to oblige the man to marry her.
28. The situation of unmarried mothers is particularly revealing about the double-bind in which female adolescents find themselves. Having children sets a woman apart from her unmarried age-mates, but she remains under the control of their parents from whom they continue to be dependent in more than just economic terms. Whenever she pretends to the status of a "complete" woman by adopting the behavior and outfit of a married women, her claim will be challenged and denigrated by her mothers.

such as that they "lack shame" (*"u tè maloya"*) and "go astray" (*"yaala"*, sometimes implying sexual looseness) emphasize their failed accomplishment of becoming a full member of the family in a material and moral sense. In short, the feelings and accusations of incompleteness experienced by girls contrasts starkly with the "dignity" of African women celebrated by the pop singers whose performances girls so much admire[29].

"The World is Made by Talk"[30]: Youth Forms of Sociality in Town

Male social life in town is structured by groups of informal socializing, the so-called "grin" in which men of various ages meet on a daily basis, drink tea, and play cards[31]. While *grins* are heterogeneous in composition, their members generally share a common marital status[32].

Perhaps the most important social significance of the *grin* is that it offers men of all ages a space where they can address their concerns in a sphere outside of the household among friends and peoples whom they trust[33]. Married men discuss worries, such as concerns about financial hardship or marital conflicts, which their role as head of the household prevents them from doing otherwise. To young and unmarried men, *grins* are the place where they can express and exchange opinions outside the control of their parents (Sessay 2001). In 1990, the *grins* of unmarried and unemployed men acquired a central political significance as centers of popular protest and opposition to the government of the former president Moussa Traoré. They constituted the rallying points for the violent confrontations between the youth and military forces, which ultimately led to the overthrow of his regime[34].

---

29. Girls' subjective experience of being incomplete is revealed in their frequent remark *"an'w man dafa"* (literally, "we are not full, complete").
30. *Duniya ye baro ye.*
31. Some authors interpret the *grin* as a neo-traditional form of male "bonding" that is, as a reconstruction of a form of male socializing in the culturally more diverse and anonymous urban setting (CISSÉ 1985). But this interpretation is misleading because the grin has no equivalent in rural areas where young men tend to socialize in working parties (singular *ton*).
32. A characteristic feature of the *grin* is that it cuts across divides of socio-economic background, age, occupation and educational background.
33. The groups are generally based on friendship and neighborhood connections. They are created by a leading figure, the "president", who has the means to provide tea and sugar for the daily tea-drinking ceremony and at whose working place or home the friends gather. Depending on the members' occupations and activities, their meetings start at different times of the day.
34. It is because of their role in the recent political past that the *grins* (and the segments of the disenfranchised urban youth they represent) played are viewed as a threat by the current government of president Alpha Konaré. But it seems that the political force of *grins* are limited, in part because of their highly ambivalent attitudes and actions vis-à-vis the government which they consider to be at the origin of their economic, political and social marginalization. At the same time, they represent a generation that, grown up under the single-party rule of Moussa Traoré, has become used to a state that acts as patron-father. They

Girls' gatherings usually take place around activities that give their socializing a *raison d'être* because many women consider their daughters' meeting and chatting with friends as a sign of lack of discipline. Their meetings are thus more informal and publicly less visible and accessible than the *grins*[35]. They generally meet in the courtyard of one girl's family, or in front of it, yet usually not too far away so that she can always respond to her mother's and brother's requests[36]. Their groups seem to be more homogenous with respect to "class" and educational background. Wherever girls hang out together, they make sure that their mothers will not overhear their conversations.

Common to young men and women's forms of socializing is that they center on, and are constituted by, the very act of conversing. Similar to key role of male beer drinking to Iteso social life (Karp 1980), conversation is the central medium and expression of commensality. The meaning of *baro*, the Bamana term for talk or conversation, is revealing in this respect. It designates talk-as-action and points to its socially constitutive quality. That is, it refers to the capacity of "talk" to create sociality, rather than merely resulting from or reflecting on it. It is often contrasted to a feeling of isolation and longing *(nyanafin)* that emerges in the absence of social company. Metalinguistic commentaries, such as the frequently evoked adage *duniya ye baro ye*, "the world is (made by) talk" similarly illustrate that "just talking" is far from being without aim[37]. Talk adds a social dimension to the texture of everyday life that is crucial to a person's being-in-the-world (Finnegan 1969, Stross 1974). Its socially generative quality is reminiscent of Habermas's conceptualization of "communicative action" which constitutes the "living world" (*"Lebenswelt"*; Habermas 1988). The performative capacity of "talk" to create commensality is also manifest in

---

therefore expect the new government to provide the solution to their problems that is, to distribute jobs and other favors in exchange for the role they played in the overthrow of the former regime (BRENNER forthc).

35. If they are good friends with, or dating, a member of the male group, they may occasionally show up at men's *grin* meetings. But they are rarely considered a member of the group.

36. When girls spend their evenings away from their courtyard, this is considered—and commented upon by neighbors—as a sign of her lack of education. Therefore, many parents will at least try to oblige their daughters to show "shameful" conduct that is, to act according to the public standards of female conduct and thus to protect the family's reputation.

37. In my conversations with girls and young men, the proverb was sometimes cited as a meta-commentary on one's own ability and readiness to engage in dialogue with others. Very often, my interlocutors contrasted the "discursive" character of "African" sociability to (what they perceived as) the "mute" and asocial behavior of "Westerners". But I also overheard numerous conversations in which the adage was cited spontaneously to emphasize the central importance of socializing ("talk") to individual happiness. But a number of proverbs also reflect people's fear of the dangerous implications of speech (DIAWARA 1997b). These various adages thus reflect people's highly ambivalent attitude towards the creative and destructive dimensions of socializing and talk (KARP 1980).

the wider range of semantics of *baro* once it refers to a mixed female-male setting. While occasions for casual interaction between female and male youth are limited during daytime, at night they may and often come together to "have fun" (*"tlòn kè"*[38]) and "talk". In the context of these encounters between young men and women then, *baro* refers to a form of socializing that entails the possibility of a sexual encounter[39].

The fervor with which young men and women discuss problems relating to courtship in their respective single-sex groups illustrates not only its salience but that it should be concealed from the adult world. The riskier it is to discuss matters relating to female-male encounters in a realm beyond parental control, the more hotly debated they are. A common trope is the highly ambiguous image of "money", both as epitome of what is aspired yet cannot be achieved and as an almost personalized force responsible for the erosion of trust, true love and a sense of moral obligation. The image of the financially "insatiable" woman that recurs in young men's discussions illustrates how the new possibilities for engaging in more casual relationships instill feelings of both desire and fear. They tend to blame women for entering into relationships "for the sake of money alone"[40] thus putting a female face to urban life with its limited prospects of self-realization. Young women's portrayal of the situation is even more ambivalent, most likely because the prevailing gender ideology applies unequal standards to female and male "promiscuity". Their denouncement of their partners as being volatile "crooks" or *kalabanci* who "speak a double language"[41] and whose only interest is to have sex, hints at their misgivings about their own dependence on their lovers' provision of material favors. At the same time, there are many women who are ready to hold "women" and their "greed for money" responsible for their own dim hopes in finding a husband. Thus young women, as much as men, express their current misgivings about the foreclosed possibilities to become full-grown members of society through the figure of the greedy woman. As I will argue, local radio creates a new stage and genres that, even if not entirely novel, offer the urban youth new opportunities to express their concerns in such moralizing tropes.

"Hot" Music and "Kuul" Speakers: Talk Radio and the Emergence of an Intimate Public

Listening to music programs broadcast on local, international or national radio is, in addition to talk and tea drinking, the third essential "ingredient"

38. The literal meaning of *"tlon kè"* is "to play around" but it also alludes to sexual play, as in the English notion of "fooling around" (cf. footnote 26).
39. The "sexual" connotation of *baro* is not restricted to urban areas. In the countryside, too, a man's announcement that he wants to "come and talk" with a woman conveys his interest in having a sexual relationship with her.
40. *"olu bè wari ko dòròn"*.
41. *"u be kanfila fò"*.

of daily *grin* socializing[42]. Young men often mention that the common preference for a particular radio station or even a particular program and radio speaker was at the origin of their *grin*. Similarly, what binds many girls together is their preference for a particular musical genre, the pop singers' music[43]. In this sense, local radio stations further new audience communities that come into being in the very process of listening to particular programs or pop music genres.

Local radio stations have been mushrooming in urban Mali since the military overthrow of the former president Moussa Traoré in 1991 when multiparty democracy was introduced under the transitory military regime of Colonel Toumani Touré. The number of commercial radio stations is steadily rising. In spite of differences in their financing structure, their programming does not differ in any remarkable sense from that of community radios and local antennas of the national station[44]. Most local radio broadcasts are relatively repetitive and monotonous, but this does not lessen their high popularity among a broad spectrum of listeners[45]. Young people, in particular men, who before the liberalization of the media market preferentially listened to music and news programs on international radio stations, now most often prefer local radio stations because, as they put it, "they play hot music, that's what we like. They speak to us and our concerns here in Mali"[46].

---

42. Before 1991, when listeners had to chose between the national radio (with its relatively conservative choice of music) and international radio stations, tape recorders were greatly appreciated among young people because it allowed them to play their favorite tapes. Since the multiplication of local radio stations, however, tape recorders have become less important.

43. But girls identified less often the preference for a certain radio station as the reason for socializing with a particular group of friends. Instead, they highlighted "social" criteria, such as the trustworthiness or generosity of friends.

44. Since 1991, when the freedom of expression and free associational life became formally acknowledged civil rights, private radio stations and independent press organs has proliferated at a breathtaking speed. In 1999, there existed—at least nominally—more than 80 local radio stations, most of which were located in towns in the southern triangle of Mali. Ca. 60% of these radio stations were "private", in other words commercial radio stations set up by business men. It is difficult to assess the extent to which these stations were able to be financially independent from sponsors. In the period between 1998 and 2000, the directors of the commercial radio stations constantly complained that receipts drawn from advertisements and other forms of announcement were not sufficient to cover the expenditures (SCHULZ 2000).

45. Music programs featuring Malian pop music, and a variety of international African music styles and of Western pop music genres take up more then 80% of the airtime.

46. Quote from a recorded discussion with a group of 6 "jeunes diplomés sans emploi" (as unemployed young men with an educational degree are called in official parlance), August 1998, Segu. Of course, young men's preference for local radio does not exclude that they temporarily switch to international radio (preferentially Africa Numéro Un (Gabon) and Radio France International) to listen to the news program and particular music and information programs (result of surveys on local radio reception, conducted in 1994, 1998 and 1999).

"Hot music" refers to a broad range of musical styles ranging from international African pop music styles, such as highlife to reggae, salsa, rock music and, more recently, rap and hip hop.

"Hot" describes a rhythm that "makes one move" and, especially in the case of reggae, rap and hip hop, a text that critical and thus "moves" in a political sense. The fact that young people use the French term *"chaud"* to refer to "hot music" is indicative. The "heat" of the music is closely associated with the image of moving, both in a physical and intellectual sense. It also reflects that the various international musical styles they describe as "hot" are defined by their close association with the realm of consumption, media, and a cosmopolitan culture to which male adolescents aspire more than most girls do (Spitulnik ms.: chapter 10). The changes introduced by local radio stations are even more radical for female listeners who rarely listen to international radio stations because they do not play the (Malian pop) music they love for "the courage it inspires"[47]. Local radio stations, and the talk radio programs and women pop singers' music they feature, create a new and unprecedented field of musical consumption for women of all ages.

The private radio stations' association with multiparty democracy and the broad range of musical styles they broadcast are not the only reasons for their spectacular success. They broadcast in local languages and play music and oral traditions that many rural and adult listeners in town approvingly refer to as "our authentic traditions"[48]. Moreover, by greeting people of local renown, skillful radio speakers establish a dialogue that is sometimes imaginary, sometimes materialized in the form of listeners' letters read aloud and commented upon by the speaker. Many listeners establish a personalized, emotionally charged relationship to particular speakers. The latter evoke a local, morally evaluating public by framing difficulties of urban life in strongly moralizing terms, thus creating the impression that the serious predicaments in which people find themselves could be overcome by "good" behavior. The "moral public" is based on the claim to transcend the dividing lines between rural and urban listeners by inviting them to engage in debates over issues raised by the radio speaker (Schulz 1999b, 2000).

---

47. Women listeners (with the exception of those who live in Bamako where they can listen to the "Chaîne 2" of national radio) disapprove of the national radio that in their eyes does not broadcast enough of the pop singers' music which they appreciate most and the lyrics of which they can follow.

48. That local radio stations broadcast in the local vernaculars is particularly important in the northern triangle of Mali (and in some areas of the south) where most listeners do not understand Bamanakan, the national language that predominates in programs of the national radio station. Also, given the fact that until 1992, Bamana and Maninka oral cultures and political histories were promoted as constitutive elements of a national identity, it is not surprising that many urbanites in non-Bamana areas hail local radio stations as institutions that promote "authentic" and locally particular identities in a multicultural nation state.

One of the greatest compliments adolescents pay broadcasters or pop stars is to characterize them as being "kuul"[49]. Most popular are "talk radio" programs in which *kuul* speakers invite listeners to call in or stop by and talk about questions related to the concerns of adolescents and married women[50]. To many girls and young men, it becomes a matter of personal pride and competition to have their statements recorded and broadcast live to their friends who, sitting in the courtyard or *grin*, keep an ear on the radio recorder and wait for their friend to "greet" them personally. A radio speaker's "kuulness" is not just a function of the kinds of topics s/he chooses for debate. Equally important—and this makes speakers really *kuul*—is *how* they talk about it and, most significantly, whether they manage to convey the full complexity of a problem without naming it in too explicit a manner. As much as listeners cherish a speaker's choice of words, the silences, implied allusions and subtle subtexts of her address are as momentous as what she actually utters[51]. Because so many broadcast debates center on issues that emerge in relationship to the other sex, issues that are considered "intimate" and "not to be talked about," a *kuul* speaker's proves her rhetorical and psychological qualities by her ability to let the guests' express their point of view, without ever letting the debate become personalized or "heated"[52]. *Kuulness* as personal quality, conduct and attitude thus stands in contrast to the realm of music; where "heat" and the feelings it sets into motion have a positive connotation. But examples as the pop star Nana Kuul (see footnote 49) show that even a pop star who performs "hot" music may win public acclaim by being "*kuul*".

Kuul speakers present central points of identification in a local and "intimate" public, a public that emerges around the debate of matters of intimacy

---

49. A famous example is the singer Nana Kulubali, who is known by many fans under the name "Nana Kuul". The association with US American radio speech repertories does not seem to be as close as in the case of "the fourth radio" of the Zambian broadcasting station (Spitulnik ms.: chapter 10). "Kuul"ness makes reference to a way of talking that is reminiscent of US American rappers, but implies a wider range of personal qualifications. It adds a further layer of meaning to the semantics of "cool" (*"suman"* in Bamanankan) which describes a man or woman who is laid back, careful and deliberate in her or his actions and thus represents the opposite to someone "hot" (*"kalan"*) who "heats up" quickly and, at worst, is temperamental, impatient, and overly ready to engage in (fistful) arguments.

50. The questions range from rather "innocent" topics such as conflicts in a polygamous household and the pro's and con's of girls' education to those relating to more intimate matters (mostly love relationships).

51. Here lies a continuity with conventions and preferences according to which public speech by professional speakers such as *jeliw* and by politicians in the national arena is evaluated.

52. On a couple of occasions, I witnessed that speakers were challenged by listeners on precisely these grounds. In off-stage discussions, but sometimes even in conversations with broadcasters, the critics complained that the speaker in question "does not have shame" or publicly attacked people "whom everybody in town knows".

and love and broadcasts them to a broader constituency. The "intimate" public is novel, not so much with respect to the topics it addresses or the discursive conventions it follows, but in that it allows for the debate and dissemination at a larger scale of a knowledge that is both intimate and public. Also, its continuities with non-mediated forms of socializing notwithstanding, the "intimate public" is based on a new dimension of "being together" among female consumers. As we will see in the following section, female pop singers enrich this intimate public and contribute to the public intimacy created by local radio broadcasts. And this, I argue, is part of the secret of their success and popularity among female youth.

Intimate Publics, Public Intimacy: Female Youth and Fan Culture

What, then, happens in the process of consuming the pop music? What meaning do female adolescents attribute to the music and how do they relate to the singers? The following statements, made by female adolescents with whom I used to spend most of my leisure time, suggest that an important reason for the attraction of the pop singers is the personal quality of their voice which allows listeners to establish an imaginary and very intimate relationship to them. The remarks convey some of the highly charged, emotional connection listeners feel whenever they hear their favorite stars. They also illustrate that listeners tend not to set apart the singer's personality, voice and lyrics. Taken together, the voice and the song's "moral lesson" create an atmosphere of intimate affection and a relationship that allows the listener to entrust herself to the singer whose "care" and empathy, they feel, is conveyed in the warmth, structural complexity, and "sharpness" of her voice. As a woman[53] explained to me when I asked her to explain to me the reasons of her admiration of a particular star: "You ask me why I like N. so much, what I like about her songs? It's how she sings to me... uuh, you see, [...] it's her voice. It is as if she carried herself over to me, one could say, it makes me feel [as if] I was sitting right next to her."

A distant relative of hers, who overheard our conversation said, in growing exasperation at my incapacity to understand what my friend tried to explain to me: "Can't you hear how her voice cuts everything, it cuts right through the air![54] How she seizes you, she captures you, by the sheer sound of her voice. It takes you and doesn't let you go, indeed!"

---

53. Ca. 20 years old and unmarried, she is the mother of two children.
54. It is important to note that my interlocutor used the image of a voice "cutting through the air" to make me understand the quality of the voice. *Kan magalen* is a more common description of a voice listeners find at once agreeable and far-carrying. *Magale* describes a voice *(kan)* that is not "too sharp" (*"kan gèlènin"*, literally, a "heavy voice") or "too soft" (*"a kan sumalen do"*, literally, "her voice is too heavy").

A girl of fifteen years explained to me: "When I hear her singing, this touches me, well, you know how this is, one cannot even tell [how this affects someone]. I just feel this swelling of pride, the new courage she gives me, I gain new courage to continue with my everyday chores, to hope that some day things will become easier. Some day they will!"

The following quote reveals the close connection that young female listeners establish between the singer's voice and what she "tells you" on one side, and the fact that listening and relating to a singer becomes part of an on-going process of constituting oneself as a *social* being on the other. The quote also betrays young women's experiences of loneliness in the middle of their peers, of occasional desperation, and of their feelings of being "redeemed" by the singer's voice and, even if to a lesser extent, by her "moral advice".

"Sometimes, I feel lonely. It is as if I was sitting alone, even though there are people, other women, friends sitting around me, even though I am sitting with them, chatting, you see. I then think of a good friend I have, we used to hang out all the time. But she left, she's gone off to France, to join her husband, you see, it has been a long time ago that this happened. Before that, we used to hang out, to make the time pass by, sitting together, we talked all the time. So I sit here and think of her, I long for her presence. Longing for her presence takes over, it's all over me. It is then, when I hear D.'s voice, it comforts me. It gives me great comfort, how can I tell you, I cannot put that in words... [she laughs, makes a gesture of embarrassment] Words are lacking, you see? When I hear D.'s voice, it is as if my friend was talking to me. Like her, she makes me feel that there is a value in being a woman, [...] that people, one day, they will realize that I am one of them. I don't know how she [singer] does it, it's something in her voice. She gives me the feeling of being complete. And no longer on my own. Hearing her voice makes me feel she is sitting with me, here, and talking to me."

To young women and girls, then, listening to the pop singers' music is an activity that is both individualized and social in its effects. It is part of a process by which a listener comes to see herself as a social being, constituted through her relationship to the singer and to friends with whom she may talk about the pop star. In fact, many conversations in which girls engage while listening to the pop music broadcast on radio, reflect that *talking* about the pop stars, their dresses, recent travels, family background and private lives is essential to the act of consumption.

As the "world is made of talk", exchange of information and opinions about pop stars, their trendy outfit, dance steps and glamorous life style becomes almost as important as the enjoyment of the aural and, in the case of television programs, visual aesthetics of the song performances.

Girls and young women are generally eager to "collect" detailed information about their favorite pop star's private life, an acquisition that allows them to at least imaginatively partake in her life and glories. In this, their star-related activities bear close resemblances to rituals among female "adoring audiences" in Western industrial societies (Cline 1992; Ehrenreich *et al.* 1992). While most of this information is exchanged and debated in intimate settings, some girls take a great delight in hinting at the breadth of their knowledge whenever they are invited to speak on local radio. As a consequence, the exchange of minute details from a pop idol's personal life becomes part of a public intimate knowledge and contributes to a feeling of shared, "public" intimacy among female listeners. The public intimacy is by no means constituted through consensus alone. I witnessed a number of occasions on which competition among listeners or between a radio speaker and her acquaintances were played out over the air[55]. This shows how competition and strategies of exclusion are constitutive of the new, mass-mediated form of sociality.

The numerous anecdotes that girls relate to each other reveal as much about the pop stars' lives, and sometimes personal dilemmas, as about the girls' desires and their simultaneous awareness that hopes to realize their aspirations are dim. The heroine of the pop star anecdotes is generally very much in control of her life. She impresses her social surroundings by her imposing demeanor, makes a lot of money, chooses her husband herself (and among a range of admirers), and keeps her family and in-laws at bay who criticize her for embarking on a musical career. Girls, in their seemingly obsessive debates of pop singers' private lives, express, with striking explicitness, their longing for becoming an "accomplished" woman[56]. As they turn their pop idol into the alter ego, into the mirror image of their own unattained status of womanhood, this reveals their awareness of their own marginal position, both within the family and society at large.

My argument here is not that the popularity of the singers derives from their capacity to "dissimulate" the serious constraints with which female youth has to grapple in urban Mali. Rather, the pop singers' appeal is closely linked to the fact that they offer their fans an imaginary access to the world of accomplishment and female pride from which they find themselves excluded. We should not mistake girls' devotion to their stars' glamorous lives as an indicator of unconditional empathy or even imitation. Sharing information about the pop idols does not mean that girls fully identify with them. Quite the opposite is true: most of the positions that girls take during

---

55. In one case, the radio speaker (a woman) commented in her talk radio program on the allegations of a friend who had criticized her for being arrogant. In another case, an invited guest digressed from the question the radio speaker asked her and publicly denounced "some envious friends" who had "made up bad stories" about her.

56. A striking difference between the way in which girls and married women talk about the pop stars is that the former only rarely contrast the pop stars to music performed in the countryside (and that is generally considered "traditional"). Married women, by contrast, situate themselves, even though often uneasily, in a continuum ranging from the "modern" pop stars and their sophisticated life style to the "women in the countryside" whom they consider to be more authentic and morally innocent (SCHULZ 2001a).

their discussions and on local radio reveal that they are aware of the distance that separates them from their idols, a distance they do not seek to transcend. Thus, what is at stake in the more or less public circulation of intimate information about the stars is a complex process of engaging with them that creates both imaginary closeness and distance and allows for the on-going construction of a mimetic relationship to the stars (Benjamin 1980).

The pop stars' personal lives is not the only topic in which girls engage. Considerable time is spent on pondering the particulars of a pop singer's attire, "hip" dance steps and body movements which, as I mentioned before, girls know from public concerts and TV music shows[57]. By assessing the "accomplishment" of different pop stars on the basis of their recent acquisitions, girls link notions of personal excellence and achievement to the ability of consumption. A pop star who displays her ability to combine local notions of beauty and accomplishment with international consumer emblems is considered a "complete" woman[58]. That girls talk about outfits they can not see but know from visual broadcasts shows that listening to radio music programs is embedded in a wider field of media consumption. Also, their evaluation points to a process one might describe as "objectification" of personal value; that is, to a tendency towards defining oneself through the acquisition and consumption of goods (Miller 1994: 254, 1995). But, as the anecdotes and girls' preoccupation with the pop singers' marital lives reveal, the new avenues towards personal accomplishment do not fully replace conventional views or ways of becoming a "respectable" person. Nor is the "objectified" mode of gaining respectability a novel mode: the acquisition and distribution of goods, wealth and favors form part of a conventional repertory of strategies to gain "respect" *("dambe")* and a "name" *("tògò")* (Schulz 1999a). But the value of the objects that people acquire is more than before defined by reference to an international market of consumer culture. Also, the most heated arguments are not about a singer's dress and accessories per se, but on the question as to how and where to acquire them. Girls' infatuation with prices and the limited possibilities of purchase is thus a reflection of, and a commentary on, both the growing importance of consumer objects to one's positioning in the community of "complete" women and of the painfully perceived limits of one's own capacity to realize it.

---

57. One favorite topic is the way in which a pop star wraps her headscarf. Kandia Kouyaté, one of the leading stars in the Malian pop universe, is famous for her ingenious ways of wrapping her turban. Her ever-changing headgears generate heated arguments among her followers and fans. They even become a bone of contention for other pop stars who by times go as far as to present Kandia Kouyaté's spectacular headdresses as an indicator of her loose morality.

58. *nin ye muso lakika de ye.* Girls spend even more time on discussing the visual properties of the pop singers whenever they watch their performances on television and on video.

Girls' passion for the pop stars' dresses, their persisting concern about the possibilities of acquiring them can be seen as a sometimes bodily, but more often imaginary appropriation of emblems of a modern, accomplished woman. This points to a parallel to youth fan cultures in Western societies where, as some authors show, the material and verbal exchange of and about pop idol paraphernalia may become as important to the fans as the actual consumption of music (Fritzsche forthc.). Another similarity to "boys groups" fan culture is that most young admirers of the Malian pop singers, too, eagerly partake in the lives and glories of their pop idols, yet also keep a conscious and deliberate distance. However, hidden underneath these similarities lies a substantial difference that is indicative of the marginal place that the Malian youth occupies both in an international and a national culture of consumption. While Western pop music fans generally freely indulge in the collection and exchange of paraphernalia and consumer objects they link to their pop idols, female fan culture in urban Mali consists first and foremost of *talk* about and the *imagination* of purchase. Another crucial difference resides in the ways in which female adolescents engage in pop fan practices to situate themselves vis-à-vis the adult world. Whereas Western pop fan cultures often revolve around the acquisition of "sub-cultural capital" that is separate from mainstream, adult culture (Thornton 1996), a primary concern of Malian female adolescents is precisely to gain access to the world of full-grown adults by displaying the taste and style of "complete" women.

*

My account of female fan practices in Mali was based on the contention that girls' admiration for pop stars should be understood by reference to their current predicaments of "postponed becoming" a full-grown member of the adult world (Seebode forthc.). Female fan-culture, constituted by a discursive and imaginary engagement with the personal lives of pop singers, is far from a mere "imitation" of a "modern" or cosmopolitan femininity. To girls, the stars represent women who are at once modern, cosmopolitan *and* rooted in an "authentically Malian" ideal of femininity. Nor does the fan culture simply reveal girls' impaired possibilities of participating in a transnational constituency of consumers. Instead, their preoccupation with the accessories that the pop stars display can be seen as a mode of imaginatively partaking in the world of womanhood that the pop stars embody, and of engaging with the control the latter seem to have over their lives. *Imagining* establishes an emphatic relationship to pop singers, yet is preconditioned upon female listeners' awareness of the unbridgeable gap between their own life situation and that of their pop idols. This act of imagining bears close resemblance to Gebauer & Wulf's (1995) conception of mimesis as an autonomous bodily practice that is nevertheless social in that it is related to, and acquires significance from, other people's actions. Seen in this light, female adolescents are skilful and experienced media consumers whose practices cannot be appropriately interpreted as instances of escapism (Fritzsche fortc.; also see Radway 1984).

Female adolescents interpret their pop idols' performances in the light of their everyday experiences and create new meanings at the articulation between individual experience and market-driven pop culture. Their fan practices qualify Miller's claim that a distinct feature of the experience of modernity resides in its increasing mediation by objects of consumption (Miller 1987: 19-82). Young women make sense of the dilemmas they confront and of their aspiration towards being a "modern woman" by reference to imported consumer articles. Yet these objects only acquire significance once fans regard them as bearing the personal character of the stars whom they admire and to whom they establish an imaginary relation of trust and intimacy. At the same time, as *talk* about the pop stars' accessories prevails over their actual acquisition, it clearly points to the limits of mimetic appropriation. In this sense, girls' fan practices shed light on the historically specific possibilities, such as imagination made possible by new media, but also the limitations in the current era of global capitalism. Crystallized in these consumer articles, in girls' debates about them are their conflicted relationships to their lovers and mothers. Displaying materialized icons of one's "accomplished" femininity becomes a substitute for the capacity to legitimately procreate and thus to become an accepted member of the adult world. Girls, by exchanging detailed information about the capacity of lovers to provide their girl-friends with gifts, present them as tokens of the value of their relationship to men, and simultaneously carve a space of discussion to which only girls have access.

The fact that fan culture is organized around *talk* illustrates that pop music reception by female urban youth in Mali forms part of a larger field of commercial public culture to which access is restricted (Bennett 1986). At the same time, commercial music culture, enhanced by local radio, creates a space in which girls talk about themselves as "modern" women, and in which feelings of belonging to a peer group with similar tastes and experiences are played out. This "discursive mode of imagining," that is, the combination of debate and imagining, rather than constituting dull or uncritical consumption, is a creative activity which is central to girls' sense of social being.

Female fan practices take place in new, "intimate" publics that are constituted by listeners' debates and their experiences of "being touched" by the singer's voice. Music programs and talk radio programs on local radio create a realm of public and localized intimacy based on a community of common taste. One could argue that the new, "intimate" publics that local radio stations further are more important to female than to male youth. In the absence of "formal" meeting points for girls, the intimate public offers female adolescents a durable "meeting space" outside the household. It remains to be seen whether the "intimate publics" that local radio creates will become more palpable in nature, in other words, whether local radio furthers a development towards the institutionalization of girls' informal socializing.

The combination of listening and debate draws on existing conventions of socializing and gives rise to a form of sociality that is partially new in character and extension. It bears some similarities with the public sphere portrayed by Habermas for eighteenth century Europe: it is based on shared normative expectations and common concerns. It emerges through the debate of the pop singers' appearances and personal fates. Girls' discussions, their engagement with consumer culture, do not lack the rational, argumentative dimension identified by Habermas as the essential characteristic of the bourgeois public. But the particular nature of the issues debated in the "intimate public" renders it incongruent with Habermas's insistence on the fundamentally critical- political dimensions of a "discursive" public. Practices related to the consumption of pop music confirm that the discursive and the performance dimension inherent in a public are intertwined and feed on each other, rather than constituting mutually exclusive orientations or different steps in its historical evolution (Meyer 1994).

Perhaps more fruitful than a comparison to Habermas's normative concept of the public (and more appropriate to his theoretical project, see Postone 1992) is to start with a phenomenological account of social formations constituted at the *interface* of different media. Female adolescents in urban Mali, in their reactions to radio broadcasts, often privilege visual markers of their idols' "completeness". This not only implies that consumers, by highlighting particular dimensions of a polysemic broadcast, chose among competing interpretations and thus actively attribute meaning (Freitag 2001). It shows that new forms of sociality emerge around the consumption of different types of broadcast media. Characteristic of the new, local forms of public sociality is that they are predicated upon commercial culture. It therefore makes little sense to speak of "print" or "visual" public spheres, in other words, to define a public according to the media technology on which it is based.

Department of Anthropology, Free University, Berlin.

824   DOROTHEA E. SCHULZ

BIBLIOGRAPHY

ANDERSON, B.

1983   *Imagined Communities. Reflections on the Origin and Spread of National-
       ism* (London-New York: Verso).

APPADURAI, A

1990   "Topographies of the Self: Praise and Emotion in Hindu India", in L. ABU-
       LUGHOD & C. A. LUTZ (eds), *Language and the Politics of Emotion*
       (Cambridge-New York: Cambridge University Press; Paris: Éditions de la
       Maison des sciences de l'homme): 92-112.

1996   *Modernity at Large: Cultural Dimensions of Globalization* (Minneapolis:
       University of Minnesota Press).

BAKAN, D.

1972   "Adolescence in America: From Ideal to Social Fact", in J. KAGAN &
       R. COLES (eds), *From Twelve to Sixteen: Early Adolescence* (New York:
       Norton): 73-89.

BARBER, K.

1994   "Concluding Remarks. Media, Popular Culture, and 'the Public' in Africa"
       Passages, 8: 23-24.

1997   "Preliminary Notes on Audiences in Africa" *Africa*, 67 (3): 347-362.

1999   *The Religious Disaggregation of Popular Moral Discourse in Yoruba Theatre
       and Video Drama, 1948-1993.* Paper presented to the Conference on "Relig-
       ion and Media in Nigeria", SOAS, London, February 1999.

BENJAMIN, W.

1980   *Gesammelte Schriften* (Frankfurt am Main: Suhrkamp).

BENNET, T.

1986   "The Politics of 'the Popular' and Popular Culture", in T. BENNETT, C. MERCER
       & J. WOOLLACOTT (eds), *Popular Culture and Social Relations* (Milton Keynes,
       England; Philadelphia: Open University Press): 6-21.

BERRY, S.

1985   *Fathers Work for their Sons: Accumulation, Mobility, and Class Formation
       in a Yoruba Community* (Berkeley: University of California Press).

BRENNER, L.

Forthcoming   "Youth as Political Actors in Mali", in P. ROBINSON, C. NEWBURY &
              M. DIOUF (eds), *Transitions in Africa: Expanding Political Spaces.*

CALHOUN, C.

1992   "Introduction", in C. CALHOUN (ed.), *Habermas and the Public Sphere*
       (Cambridge, Mass.-London: MIT Press): 1-48.

CASEY, E.

1976   *Imagining. A Phenomenological Study* (Bloomington-Indianapolis: Indiana
       University Press).

MALIAN GRIOT AND THEIR PUBLIC 825

CASTORIADIS, C.

1975 *L'institution imaginaire de la société* (Paris: Éditions du Seuil).

CISSÉ, M.

1985 "Être jeune aujourd'hui" *Études Maliennes*, 35-36: 94-103.

CLARKE, J., HALL, S., JEFFERSON, T. & ROBERTS, B.

1976 "Subcultures, Cultures, and Class: a Theoretical Overview", in S. HALL & T. JEFFERSON (eds), *Resistance through Rituals. Youth Subcultures in Post-war Britain* (London: Hutchinson): 9-75.

CLINE, C.

1992 "Essays from *Bitch: The Women's Rock Newsletter with Bite*", in L. LEWIS (ed.), *The Adoring Audience. Fan Culture and Popular Media* (London-New York: Routledge): 69-83.

COMAROFF, J. & COMAROFF, J. L.

2000a "Millenial Capitalism: First Thoughts on a Second Coming" *Public Culture*, 12 (2) "Millenial Capitalism and the Culture of Neoliberalism": 291-343.

2000b "On Personhood: an Anthropological Perspective from Africa" *Social Identities*, 7 (2): 267-283.

DIAWARA, M.

1997a "The Mande Oral Popular Culture Revisited by the Electronic Media", in K. BARBER (ed.), *Readings in African Popular Culture* (Bloomington-Indianapolis: Indiana University Press): 40-48.

1997b *L'empire du verbe, l'éloquence du silence. Vers une anthropologie du discours dans les groupes dits dominés au Sahel.* Habilitation thesis (Bayreuth: University of Bayreuth).

DURAN, L.

1989 "The Women of Mali: Tata Bambo Kouyaté" *Folk Roots* 75: 34-38.

1995 "*Jelimusow*: the Superwomen of Malian Music", in G. FURNISS & L. GUNNER (eds), *Power, Marginality, and African Oral Literature* (Cambridge-New York: Cambridge University Press): 197-207.

1996 "'The Songbirds'. Fanned, Fetished and Female. Lucy Duran Goes on the Road with Wassoulou Super Star Oumou Sangaré" *Folk Roots* 149: 40-45.

EHRENREICH, B., HESS, E. & JACOBS, G.

1992 "Beatlemania: Girls Just Want to Have Fun", in L. LEWIS (ed.), *The Adoring Audience. Fan Culture and Popular Media* (London-New York: Routledge): 84-106.

FABIAN, J.

1997 "Popular Culture in Africa. Findings and Conjectures", in K. BARBER (ed.), *Readings in African Popular Culture* (Bloomington-Indianapolis: Indiana University Press; Oxford: James Currey): 18-28 (originally published in *Africa*, 1978, 48 (4): 315-331).

826   DOROTHEA E. SCHULZ

FINNEGAN, R.

1969 "How to do Things with Words: Performative Utterances among the Limba of Sierra Leone" *Man*, 4 (4): 537-552.

FREITAG, S.

2001 "Visions of the Nation. Theorizing the Nexus Between Creation, Consumption, and Participation in the Public Sphere", in C. PINNEY & R. DWYER (eds), *Pleasure and the Nation* (Oxford: Oxford University Press): 35-75.

FRIEDMAN, J.

1990 "Being in the World: Globalization and Localization" *Theory, Culture and Society*, 7: 311-328.

FRITZSCHE, B.

Forthcoming "Vom Nutzen der verhinderten Wunscherfüllung. Einblicke in die Populärkultur Jugendlicher Pop-Fans", in U. LUIG & J. SEEBODE (eds), *Jugendkulturen im internationalen Kulturvergleich*.

GEBAUER, G. & WULF, C.

1995 *Mimesis: Culture, Art, Society* (Berkeley: University of California Press).

GRIFFIN, C.

1993 *Representations of Youth: the Study of Youth and Adolescence in Britain and America* (Cambridge (UK)-Cambridge, MA (USA): Polity Press).

HABERMAS, J.

1988 *Theorie des kommunikativen Handelns* (Frankfurt am Main: Suhrkamp).

1989 *The Structural Transformation of the Public Sphere* (Cambridge, Mass.: MIT Press).

HALE, T.

1998 *Griot and Griottes. Masters of Words and Music* (Bloomington-Indianapolis: Indiana University Press).

HANSEN, M.

1993 "Unstable Mixtures, Dilated Spheres: Negt and Kluge's *The Public Sphere and Experience*, Twenty Years Later" *Public Culture*, 5: 179-211.

HINERMAN, S.

1992 "'I'll Be here with You': Fans, Fantasy and the Figure of Elvis", in L. LEWIS (ed.), *The Adoring Audience. Fan Culture and Popular Media* (London-New York: Routledge): 107-134.

HUYSSEN, A.

1986 *After the Great Divide. Modernism, Mass Culture, Postmodernism* (Bloomington-Indianapolis: Indiana University Press).

KARP, I.

1980 "Beer Drinking and Social Experience in an African Society: An Essay in Formal Sociology", in I. KARP & C. BIRD (eds), *Explorations in African Systems of Thought* (Washington, D.C.-London: Smithsonian Institution Press): 83-119.

KEITA, M. C.

1995 "Jaliya in the Modern World", in D. CONRAD & B. FRANK (eds), *Status and Identity in West Africa. The Nyamakalaw of Mande* (Bloomington-Indianapolis: Indiana University Press): 182-196.

KETT, J.

1977 *Rites of Passage: Adolescence in America, 1790 to the Present* (New York: Basic Books).

LEWIS, L. (ed.)

1992 *The Adoring Audience. Fan Culture and Popular Media* (London-New York: Routledge).

MBEMBE, A.

1985 *Les jeunes et l'ordre politique en Afrique noire* (Paris: L'Harmattan).

MC ROBBIE, A. & GARNER, J.

1976 "Girls and Subcultures. An Exploration", in S. HALL & T. JEFFERSON (eds), *Resistance through Rituals. Youth Subcultures in Postwar Britain* (London: Hutchinson): 209-222.

MEYER, T.

1994 *Die Transformation des Politischen* (Frankfurt am Main: Suhrkamp).

MILLER, D.

1987 *Material Culture and Mass Consumption* (Oxford: Basil Blackwell).

1994 *Modernity. An Ethnographic Approach* (Oxford-Providence: Berg Publishers).

1995 "Consumption as the Vanguard of History: A Polemic by Way of an Introduction", in D. MILLER (ed.), *Acknowledging Consumption: a Review of New Studies* (London-New York: Routledge): 1-57.

MODLESKY, T.

1982 *Loving with a Vengeance: Mass Produced Fantasies for Women* (New York: Methuen).

PIOT, C.

1999 *Remotely Global. Village Modernity in West Africa* (Chicago: University of Chicago Press).

POSTONE, M.

1992 "Political Theory and Historical Analysis", in C. CALHOUN (ed.), *Habermas and the Public Sphere* (Cambridge, Mass.-London: MIT Press): 164-177.

RADWAY, J.

1984 *Reading the Romance. Women, Patriarchy, and Popular Literature* (Chapel Hill-London: University of North Carolina Press).

ROY, A.

1997 *The God of Small Things* (New Delhi, India: IndiaInk).

828   DOROTHEA E. SCHULZ

SCHULZ, D.

1998   "Morals of Praise. Broadcast Media and the Commoditization of *Jeli* Praise Performances in Mali" *Research in Economic Anthropology*, 19: 117-132.

1999a "Pricey Publicity, Refutable Reputations. *Jeliw* and the Economics of Honour in Mali" *Paideuma*, 45: 275-292.

1999b "In Pursuit of Publicity. Talk Radio and the Imagination of a Moral Public in Mali" *Africa Spectrum*, 99 (2): 161-185.

2000   "Communities of Sentiment. Local Radio Stations and the Emergence of New Spheres of Public Communication in Mali", in S. BRÜHNE (ed.), *Neue Medien und Öffentlichkeiten. Politik und Tele-Kommunikation in Asien, Afrika, und Lateinamerika.* 2 vols (Hamburg: Deutsches Übersee-Institut): 36-62 (vol. 2).

2001a "Music Videos and the Effeminate Vices of Pop Culture in Mali" *Africa*, 71 (3): 325-371.

2001b *Perpetuating the Politics of Praise. Jeli singers, Radios, and Political Mediation in Mali* (Köln: Rüdiger Köppe Verlag).

Forthcoming "Political Factions, Ideological Fictions: the Controversy around the Reform of Family Law in Democratic Mali", in *Islamic Law and Society* 10 (2003).

SEEBODE, J.

Forthcoming "Tanzwettkämpfe, Transformationsprozesse und Identität: Tanzstile junger Männer in Nordmalawi", in U. LUIG & J. SEEBODE (eds), *Jugendkulturen im internationalen Kulturvergleich.*

SESSAY, D.

2001   *Freizeitverhalten von Jugendlichen in Bamako*, Bericht zur Lehrforschung in Mali, Juli—September 2000, Institut für Ethnologie, Freie Universität Berlin (research report).

SPITULNIK, D.

2000   "Documenting Radio Culture as Lived Experience: Reception Studies and the Mobile Machine in Zambia", in R. FARDON & G. FURNISS (eds), *African Broadcast Cultures: Radio in Tradition* (London: James Currey).

ms.   *Media Connections and Disconnections. Radio Culture and the Public Sphere in Zambia* (Durham-London: Duke University Press).

STROSS, B.

1974   "Speaking of Speaking: Tenejapa Tzeltal Metalinguistics", in R. BAUMAN & J. SHERZER (eds), *Explorations in the Ethnography of Speaking* (London-New York: Cambridge University Press): 213-239.

THORNTON, S.

1996   *Club Cultures: Music, Media, and Subcultural Capital* (Hanover: University Press of New England).

TRAORÉ, K.

2000   *Le jeu et le sérieux. Essai d'anthropologie littéraire sur la poésie épique des chasseurs du Mande (Afrique de l'Ouest)* (Köln: Rüdiger Köppe Verlag).

MALIAN GRIOT AND THEIR PUBLIC   **829**

WATERMAN, C.

1994   "Celebrity and the Public in Yoruba Popular Music Video" *Passages*, 8: 3-7.

WEISS, B.

1996   *The Making and Unmaking of the Haya Lived World* (Durham-London: Duke University Press).

ABSTRACT

The article combines an interpretation of female adolescents' fan practices with an exploration of new forms of "coming together" made possible the creation of local radio stations in urban Mali.   To understand girls' admiration for Malian women singers who, have become acclaimed stars in national and international arenas, the article explores their fan practices by reference to their current predicaments of "postponed becoming" a full-grown member of the adult world.   Girls' fan practices shed light on the historically specific possibilities of mimetic appropriation, such as imagination made possible by new media, but also its limitations in the current era of global capitalism.   Their consumption of pop music takes place in new, "intimate" publics that are constituted by listeners' debates and their experiences of "being touched" by the singer's voice. Music programs and talk radio programs on local radio create a realm of public and localized intimacy based on a community of common taste.

RÉSUMÉ

"Le monde tel qu'il créé par la conversation": admirateurs des chanteuses, musique populaire et sociabilité urbaine au Mali. — Cet article est consacré à la fois aux pratiques des admiratrices des chanteuses et aux nouvelles formes de "rencontre" rendues possibles par la création des nouvelles stations de radio dans les villes du Mali. De façon à rendre compte de l'admiration des jeunes filles envers les chanteuses maliennes qui sont devenues des vedettes à la fois sur le plan national et international, l'auteur analyse les pratiques des adoratrices de ces dernières en les situant par rapport au problème du report de l'entrée de ces jeunes filles dans l'âge adulte. L'étude des pratiques d'adoration des jeunes filles éclaire sur les spécificités historiquement situées d'appropriation mimétique, telles qu'elles sont rendues possibles par les nouveaux médias, mais également sur leurs limitations à l'époque du capitalisme global. À cet égard, la consommation de musique populaire s'effectue dans le cadre de "publics intimes", c'est-à-dire de discussions d'auditrices centrées sur la façon dont elles ont été touchées par la voix de la chanteuse. Les programmes musicaux de même que les débats radiophoniques créent un domaine d'intimité à la fois privé et public, domaine qui repose sur une communauté de goût partagé.

Keywords/*Mots-clés*: Mali, cultural globalization, gender, griot, popular music, radio consumption, youth culture/*Mali, globalisation culturelle, genre, griot, musique populaire, écoute radiophonique, culture des jeunes.*

Part IV
Historical Approaches

[21]
Tom Jobim and the Bossa Nova Era

SUZEL ANA REILY

Tall and tan and young and lovely,
The girl from Ipanema goes walking,
And when she passes each one she passes goes: Ah!

'The Girl from Ipanema' – or, in Portuguese, 'Garota de Ipanema' – is without doubt the song that turned *bossa nova* into a household term the world over. It was written by Antônio Carlos Jobim and Vinícius de Moraes one afternoon in 1962, as they sat in the Veloso bar – now renamed 'Garota de Ipanema' – on Montenegro Street, where they had watched the young Helô Pinheiro walk past them on her way to Ipanema Beach. The song was first recorded in 1963 by Peri Ribeiro (Odeon) (Machado 1971), and since then over 300 other recordings have appeared on the market, both in Brazil and abroad (Cabral n.d.c, p. 10). When it was first launched in America on the 'Getz/Gilberto' album (Verve),[1] interpreted by Astrud and João Gilberto in 1964, 'The Girl from Ipanema' posed a serious challenge to the Beatles' hegemony over the charts, rapidly moving to second place. With 4.2 million registered performances, it was only in the last four years that its ratings began to fall, but it is still among the world's most widely aired popular songs (Anon 1994c, pp. 124–5).

While abroad it was all being blamed on the bossa nova, in Brazil the style was being replaced by the politically motivated 'modern' MPB (Brazilian Popular Music), which had much less impact on the international music scene. Bossa nova – with its themes of love, smiles and flowers[2] – came and went in just over five years, but it left an undeniable imprint on Brazilian popular music. For some it created a dividing line, distinguishing the pre-bossa nova phase from the post-bossa nova era (cf. Medaglia 1968, pp. 73–4).

A leading figure – arguably the most influential – of the bossa nova movement was Antônio Carlos Jobim, or Tom Jobim, as he was known in Brazil. Along with 'The Girl from Ipanema', he composed and harmonized the tunes for such classics as 'Samba de Uma Nota Só' ('The One Note Samba'), 'Desafinado' ('Off Key'), 'Insensatez' ('How Insensitive'), 'Corcovado' ('Quiet Nights of Quiet Stars'), 'Wave', and the eternal 'Chega de Saudade' ('No More Longing'). Tom[3] himself did not know how many songs he had composed, but estimated that there were over 300 of them; his biographers push the figure more towards 400 (Chediak n.d.b, Vol. 2, p. 15).[4] He featured either alone or as a major contributor on over forty LPs and CDs. His last CD, *Antônio Brasileiro*, was released in November of 1994, and within three weeks it had sold 65,000 copies (Anon 1994b, p. 162).

Tom also composed the sound track for the film *Gabriela* (RCA, 1983), but long before that he had contributed most of the tunes in the musical *Black Orpheus*, made into a film by Marcel Camus in 1959.[5] His repertoire also includes incursions into serious music. He composed several popular symphonies and tone poems, including the *Symphony of Rio de Janeiro* (wih Billy Blanco) (Continental, 1954) and 'Brasília' (CBS, 1983), which received its premier at the inaugural ceremony of the new capital. It is no wonder that he has been seen as Brazil's George Gershwin. Nothing can illustrate Tom Jobim's place in Brazilian popular music more appositely than the tribute paid him by 'Mangueira' Samba School: he was their theme in 1992. Floats representing his musical career passed proudly down the sambad-rome, embraced by the electrifying beats of the percussion ensemble.

When, on 8 December 1994, news reached Brazil that Tom had died in New York after an emergency operation, the country went into mourning. His body was received at the airport in Rio the next day to the sound of his most celebrated tune, 'The Girl from Ipanema' (Anon 1994a). Covered by the national flag, his coffin was placed on an open fire truck, and paraded through the town centre. Thousands turned out to pay their homage, and Rio resounded to his music, a final farewell to one of the most talented musicians Brazil ever produced.

In a tribute to Tom Jobim, this article assesses the role of the bossa nova movement in reformulating the language of Brazilian popular music.[6] Bossa nova was the outcome of an intentional search for a new mode of musical expression among the youths of Rio's privileged classes. But its specificities as a style were defined by the way in which particular individuals used the resources available to them in responding to these new musical demands. Thus, just as bossa nova was a product of an era, it was also a product of the genius of those involved in its creation. Here I shall be looking at how the meeting of minds of the main exponents of the bossa nova movement combined with the lives of Rio's middle-class youths in the late 1950s to generate a musical style which was even capable of transcending national borders.

The new bossa

The term 'bossa nova' first emerged in the lyrics of the song that came to be seen as the manifesto of the movement: 'Desafinado' ('Off Key') (Tom Jobim and Newton Mendonça), first recorded for Odeon in 1958 by João Gilberto. When Newton Mendonça penned these words he had no idea he was baptising a musical style. The term 'bossa' was a slang word to identify something that stood out for its distinctiveness, and it had been in current use since the 1940s, particularly among musicians. The enamoured 'off key' singer was merely claiming that in singing 'anti-musically' he was trying to attract the attention of his beloved: what could be more natural? A few months after João Gilberto introduced the song to the middle-class youths of Rio, the term 'bossa nova' appeared on a poster – allegedly designed by the journalist Moisés Fuks (Chediak n.d.a, Vol. 4, p. 24). It announced a show involving many exponents of the emerging movement and read: 'Today, João Gilberto, Silvinha Teles and a "Bossa Nova" Group' (Tinhorão 1986, p. 235). Ronaldo Bôscoli, the journalist of the movement, picked up on the term and started using it in his stories

(Chediak n.d.a, Vol. 4, p. 24). It caught on, and thereafter it came to designate a distinct musical style, and its former usage faded into oblivion.

That something with a new 'bossa' was taking form in Rio's middle-class music world was not difficult to detect, since the aesthetics of the emerging movement stood in stark contrast to the previous *samba-canção* tradition represented by such performers as Carmen Miranda, Ary Barroso, Lamartino Babo, among many others. While *samba-canção* privileged the quasi-operatic voice of an exotic star dancing merrily in front of a big band, possibly even wearing a pineapple, the sophisticated bossa nova interpreters in black turtlenecks merged their soft spoken voices to a single guitar or at most a four-man band. The ethos of the new style promoted intimacy, the apparent economy of the music masking its complexity. 'Off Key', for example, is highly chromatic, it has a tri-tone in the third phrase and other phrases span octaves with many unexpected intervals. Jobim's altered chordal harmonisation was conceived to make the singer sound 'off key', obscuring the song's tonal centre. The half sung/half spoken vocal line de-emphasised the systematic syncopation of the melody, which was further set against a displaced guitar rhythm, leaving the listener unsure of where to locate the main beats. While proclaiming to be a song that anyone could sing, it could in fact only be performed by those with the most acute sense of pitch and rhythm. 'Off Key' gave as good as it got in responding to the criticism that bossa nova musicians could not sing.

Although 'Off Key' may have acquired 'manifesto' status, it is not considered the first 'true' bossa nova to have been recorded. This place of honour is generally attributed to another of Jobim's compositions: 'Chega de Saudade' ('No More Longing'), with lyrics by Vinícius de Moraes, which had been released a few months earlier by João Gilberto (Odeon). Although precursors to bossa nova proper did exist, possibly as early as 1954,[7] none combined all the features that came to characterise the style as paradigmatically as they were represented in 'Chega de Saudade'. This song was the first recording to unite the three heavy-weights of the movement – Tom, Vinícius and João – epitomising their individual contributions. The melody is far more syncopated than other forms of Brazilian popular music, and it has the characteristic bossa nova modal feeling: the constant modulations and surprising intervals are set against altered and compact chords. These are all features attributed to Tom's compositional procedures, which both drew upon and extended the practices current in popular music at the time.

Vinícius de Moraes's lyrics have a colloquial ethos, following in the tradition of Noel Rosa. Already a well-published and recognised poet at the time, Vinícius nonetheless viewed the writing of lyrics as a distinct exercise. He crafted them in such a way as to make full use of the sound quality of each word, carefully choosing them to co-ordinate perfectly with the accents in the melodic line (cf. Cabral n.d.b, p. 10). The use of words for their sound quality was not new to Brasilian popular music: it was a feature of *emboladas*[8] and some sambas. For example, the samba written by Rubens Soares and David Nasser in 1942, 'Nega do cabelo duro', contains the line *'qual é o pente que te penteia'*, which, when sung, imitates the sound of a shaker. Vinícius, however, used this poetic device in a much subtler manner, more like the symbolist poets of the late nineteenth century. Even if one cannot understand Portuguese, the 'musicality' of his lyrics is still apparent.

João Gilbert's nasal speech-like vocal style, quiet and timid, was ideally suited to the bossa nova aesthetics, enhancing the timbrel craftwork of Vinícius's lyrics.

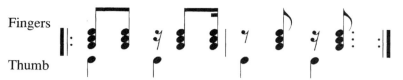

Figure 1. João Gilberto's 'Stuttering Guitar' Technique.

He merged the voice into the ensemble as though it too were an instrument. Again this was not unheard of in popular music: even at the height of the *samba-canção* era, Mario Reis's mellow voice provided a welcome contrast to the dominant bel canto style of other performers. But it was João's guitar technique that attracted special attention: he slotted the chords between the syncopations of the melody, avoiding coincidences, a style that became known as the 'stuttering guitar'. According to Baden Powell, João Gilberto derived the upper snaps of his 'beat' from the rhythms of the *tamborim*, the small hand drum used in samba school percussion ensembles, while the thumb reproduced the thump of the *surdo*, the samba bass drum (Cabral n.d.a., p. 12). He was able to produce chords with up to five tones by using the little finger of his right hand to pluck the highest string, something that had never been done before (Cabral n.d.a, p. 12). In 'Chega de Saudade', the guitar accompaniment centres around the rhythmic phrase presented in Figure 1.

João Gilberto's recording of 'Chega de Saudade' was the first to unite and codify the language that marked the new movement.[9] As Tom Jobim so succinctly put it: 'Bossa nova is serene, it is love and romance, but it is restless' (quoted in McGowan and Pessanha 1991, p. 62).

Rio in the 1950s

Brazilian musicologists have often described the 1950s as an era in which popular music entered a vacuum (cf. Tinhorão 1986), only regaining direction towards the end of the decade, when bossa nova made its debut. To some extent this is true, as no discernible genre exists which bridges the gap between *samba-canção* and bossa nova. Yet this was a period of dramatic change in the country. Rural power bases were losing ground as industry spearheaded the country's economic growth. Juscelino Kubitschek had been elected president in 1955, espousing a platform encapsulated in his slogan: 'fifty years in five'. He promised to lead the country in a developmental drive that would reduce its fifty-year lag in relation to the developed world in a single term of office. A backbone of his platform was the building of Brasilia, through which he intended to bring 'progress' even to the remote interior of the country. National pride was at a high, the urban population resolutely behind him.

In this era of national euphoria the urban middle classes centred their preoccupations on making the most of the modern conveniences industrialisation had brought them. By now the lower and upper social classes of Rio had become spatially isolated from one another (Tinhorão 1986, p. 231), and for the first time in Brazilian history a new generation had grown up with only a superficial experience of inter-class contact, often restricted only to their interactions with domestic servants. Youths that grew up within this context lived a carefree existence of sun,

6   *Suzel Ana Reily*

beaches and romance, secure in their belief that Brazil was finally taking its place on the international scene. The combination of dramatic social change and the prevailing optimism of the era created new aesthetic values for which there were no immediate national models; the search was on to fill this vacuum.

Thus, the 1950s were actually marked by an extraordinary phase of artistic effervescence. There were responses from the world of architectural design through the formalism of Niemeyer's buildings in the new capital; from the literary world through the concrete movement; and from the serious music world which was turning to serialism (Béhague 1979, pp. 343–5). Creative impetus during the Kubitschek regime focused on the formal organisation of the materials under aesthetic treatment. Lines, colours, words or sounds were to be arranged into clearly defined relationships of geometric precision, avoiding all signs of rusticity as well as the exoticising 'folkloric quotations' that had marked earlier nationalist movements.

The spirit of the 1950s also affected the aesthetic values of Rio's middle-class youths. They were searching for a musical style that suited their self-image: it had to be simultaneously Brazilian and non-exotic; it had to be able to speak of guitars and tambourines as well as Rolliflex cameras. Indeed, prior to his departure to the historic bossa nova concert at Carnegie Hall in 1962, Tom Jobim made this statement to a journalist of *O Globo*, a major newspaper in Rio:

We are not going to sell [Brazil's] exotic side, of coffee and carnival. We are not going to wheel out the typical themes of underdevelopment. We are going to pass from the agricultural to the industrial era. We are going to use our popular music with the conviction that it does not only have its own character, but also a high technical level. (quoted in Tinhorão 1986, p. 242)

Bossa nova can indeed be seen as de-exoticised Brazilian music. While drawing on various Afro-Brazilian traditions, the mellow sound of the guitar and the soft percussion highlighted their complex principles of rhythmic organisation rather than their visceral qualities. João Gilberto's timid and quiet voice negated the stereotype of Brazilians as an over-emotive, exuberant race, the natural products of a tropical climate, to portray them as contemplative, intimate and sophisticated. The perfection and precision with which he fitted his accompaniments to the deceptive simplicity of Tom's melodic lines are comparable to the workings of a finely tuned machine. 'Chega de Saudade' was a masterful response to Rio's search for a new medium of popular musical expression. The land of carnival had entered the modern era.

Although this recording finally provided the recipe, the selection of the appropriate ingredients had begun some time earlier. Nightlife for Rio's upper classes had moved out of the large big-band halls to the intimate dark setting of the nightclub, and such establishments were proliferating in the city's affluent neighbourhoods. The nightclub context called for a mellow musical style that could promote the romantic intimacy young dreamy-eyed couples were looking for. Musicians responded by experimenting with the models most readily available to them: be-bop and jazz, particularly cool jazz, fusing them with national material.

The meeting of minds

Experimentation was at the heart of the informal music-making that united a group of young people living in the exclusive neighbourhoods of Copacabana and

Ipanema. Collective composition has been a feature of Brazilian popular music since at least the late 1800s, each nucleus producing a distinct musical style. Towards the end of the nineteenth century, a group of musicians belonging to military bands would gather on Sunday afternoons with their instruments in a northern neighbourhood of Rio, merging their intrumental techniques with the Afro-Brazilian rhythms that surrounded them. The outcome was the '*choro*'. In the early twentieth century another nucleus had developed. This group met at Tia Ciata's house, near Praça Onze, eventually leading to the development of 'urban samba'. Indeed, the first samba ever recorded, 'Pelo Telefone' ('Over the Telephone') (Banda Odeon, 1917), generated a heated row when it was discovered that Donga and Mauro de Almeida had registered what others claimed was a collective composition in their names alone. During the 1930s a group of bohemians began congregating in Vila Isabel, which resulted in the critical and colloquial style of samba epitomised by the partnership between Noel Rosa and Vadico.[10]

In Copacabana there was a group of young musicians, many still in their teens, whose musical tastes were being shaped by Rio's nightclub ethos. Carlos Lyra, Roberto Menescal, Ronaldo Bôscoli, the Castro Neves brothers, Normando Santos, Chico Feitosa, Luís Eça, among several others, met regularly to show each other their latest musical creations. From the local club scene they assimilated the experimental procedures being tested by the 'professionals'. They heard Tom Jobim, Dick Farney, Johnny Alf, João Gilberto and Baden Powell at the 'Cantina do César', the 'Clube da Chave', the 'Plaza', and other night spots, and incorporated these new sounds into their own compositions. Night-long musical exchange sessions occurred frequently at the home of Nara Leão, who later became the muse of the bossa nova movement, interpreting many of the songs that emerged among her colleagues.

While the 'professionals' were moving into studios, the 'amateurs' began organising 'shows', mostly through student associations. A few small clubs in Copacabana's 'Beco das Garrafas' (Bottles Court)[11] began specialising in bossa nova, and this also provided performance space for the movement's exponents, both 'professionals' and 'amateurs'. Carlos Lyra and Roberto Menescal set up a guitar academy, which played an important role in propagating the new repertoire, preparing musicians to confront the demands bossa nova would require of them. The folk distinction between 'professionals' and 'amateurs' which prevailed in bossa nova circles was very tenuous, particularly once the 'show' circuit became a major mechanism for divulging the new style. The 'professionals' were eager to join up with the 'amateurs' for these events as a means of boosting their record sales. Likewise, the 'amateurs' capitalised on the opportunity this gave them of becoming associated with the heavy-weights. Several of them acquired recognition for their musical abilities, becoming major performers in their own right. Indeed, a number of them participated in the Carnegie Hall event, including Carlos Lyra, Roberto Menescal, the Castro Neves Quartet, Chico Feitosa and others. The most successful 'amateur' was Carlos Lyra, who would later lead bossa nova into its politicised phase.

It was through Rio's nightclub circuit that the three most outstanding names of bossa nova chanced upon one another. The first legendary encounter between Vinícius de Moraes and Antônio Carlos Jobim took place in 1956 in a bar in central Rio called Vilarino. Allegedly Vinícius was there with the music critic Lucio Rangel, and Vinícius explained how he had written a musical but was unable to stage it without someone to put music to his lyrics. He had invited Vadico, Noel Rosa's former partner, but he was too ill at the time. Rangel said he knew just the person: it was Tom Jobim, who happened to be in the same bar at the time. They began working together the very next day, and slowly the songs for *Orfeu da Conceição* began to take shape. The play was a tremendous success,[12] and in 1959 it became the film *Black Orpheus*. To comply with the requirements of the French producers, who wanted to guarantee the copyrights, a series of new songs were commissioned. That is when the Brazillian repertoire was graced with the unforgettable tunes 'A Felicidade' and 'Manhã de Carnaval'. The partnership Tom Jobim–Vinícius de Moraes generated a number of classics, including 'The Girl from Ipanema'.

João Gilberto had been in Rio since 1949 when he left his home state of Bahia to join the ephemeral vocal ensemble 'Garotos da Lua' (Boys of the Moon). But it was not until he began performing alone in the 'Plaza' that the distinctiveness – or bossa – of his vocal style and guitar technique were fully recognised. He shared a flat with Ronaldo Bôscoli (Chediak n.d.a, Vol. 4, p. 22), and therefore had close ties with the 'amateurs'. Indeed, he was a frequent participant at the sessions held at Nara Leão's house, where the uniqueness of his 'bossa' was greatly admired. Roberto Menescal, for example, claimed that like other members of the group he followed João everywhere for about ten days, until he grasped his playing technique (Cabral n.d.a, p. 12).

By the second half of the 1950s all the musical elements that would form the essence of bossa nova had become available. There was, however, a significant hurdle still to be confronted: that of gaining the approval of a recording company to test the market with the new style. Tom Jobim had just abandoned his post as artistic director at Odeon, but he used his influence within the company, and was able to persuade them to make a single of João Gilberto's interpretation of 'Chega de Saudade';[13] the flip-side featured João playing one of his own songs, 'Bim-bom'. Folklore has it that when, in July of 1958, the studio in Rio sent a copy of the disk to their rep in São Paulo he was furious, sure that such a record would never sell. He was wrong: it sold 18,000 copies before the end of the year. This may not be particularly impressive, but it was enough to justify forging ahead with the genre, and by November João was back in the studio; this time it was to record the more audacious 'Off Key', soon followed by his first LP, *Chega de Saudade*.[14]

The creators

While the interaction among the main exponents of bossa nova helped socialise the musical ideas being formulated during the phase of experimentation, certain key individuals were particularly influential in defining the parameters that would eventually characterise the genre. The most noteworthy were, of course, Tom Jobim, Vinícius de Moraes and João Gilberto. Given that there were numerous other highly competent musicians operating in Rio's nightclubs at the time, why, one must ask, did Tom's alternatives prevail over those of Dick Farney or Johnny Alf, for example? It may never be possible to answer this question; but it is possible to show how Tom, Vinícius and João complemented one another musically, and how their propositions resonated with the aspirations that propelled the quest in which they participated. Their unique backgrounds and personal creative abilities – dare I say 'talent' – allowed them to draw on material that stood at the border between the popular and the erudite, the national and the international, to produce a sophisticated sound that was simultaneously Brazilian without resorting to the exotic.

Tom Jobim

Antônio Carlos Brasileiro de Almeida Jobim arrived on the scene with a solid classical music training. His introduction to contemporary music circles had been through his *Symphony to Rio de Janeiro*, which was recorded by the conductor Radamés Gnattali in 1954. His passion for music made him drop out of arts college in 1949, where he was studying architecture, to work as a pianist in Rio's night-clubs, but this was also a means of generating an income to support his new family. In 1952 he took a job as piano accompanist at Continental, a major record-ing studio, where he was also provided with an office to transcribe compositions for the studio's musicians who had no musical training. He was, therefore, in a unique position to keep abreast of all the contemporary musical trends. Within a few years he was making arrangements for the studio, which made him a well-known figure in the back-stages of Rio's music circles. It was his collaboration with Vinícius de Moraes in *Orfeu da Conceição*, however, that placed him in the public limelight.

While other bossa nova composers have openly acknowledged their connec-tions with North-American jazz (cf. Schreiner 1993, p. 141), Tom Jobim was always adamant that the only relationship his music had with jazz resulted from their common ancestry: African slaves and the French Impressionists (cf. Chediak n.d.b, Vol. 2, pp. 14–15). Indeed, he claimed he rarely listened to jazz and knew very little about the procedures employed by jazz musicians (Chediak n.d.b, Vol. 2, p. 14). Nonetheless, bossa nova – like jazz – makes extensive use of altered chords, but harmonic changes in the Brazilian style are less frequent; they are generally limited to one or, at most, two chords to a measure, while in jazz there may easily be four (cf. Rocha Brito 1968, pp. 27–8; Chediak n.d.a, Vol. 1, p. 18). For all its similarities with jazz, however, it was appealing to jazz aficionados in America and Europe precisely because it was far more than a mere Brazilianisation of jazz. As Tom himself said:

> Americans took to bossa nova because they thought it was interesting. If it were a copy of jazz, it wouldn't have interested them. They're tired of hearing copies of jazz. There's Swedish jazz, French jazz, German jazz – Germans play a lot of jazz. Actually they just call anything that swings jazz. But, styles that swing are in the United States, in Cuba, in Brazil. That's where they swing. The rest waltzes, with all due respect to the Austrians. (Chediak n.d.b, Vol. 2, p. 14)

The uniqueness of Tom's compositional techniques, then, might best be under-stood in terms of his personal musical background.

Tom Jobim was born in 1927 in the north of Rio, the son of a diplomat and amateur poet. He was only a year old when his family moved to the fashionable neighbourhood of Ipanema where he grew up. When his father died he was eight years old, and his mother re-married a gentle man who was sympathetic towards his step-son's musical inclinations. Tom's grandmother played piano and he had two uncles who were accomplished guitarists: one played in popular styles, the other classical guitar, with a special liking for Bach. His early informal training was acquired through his uncles, and by the time his family bought a grand piano, when he was thirteen, he already played the guitar and the harmonica.

10   *Suzel Ana Reily*

The piano was originally intended for his sister Helena, but she showed no tendency toward music, and her lessons went to Tom. His first piano teacher was Hans-Joachim Koellreuter, a German musicologist who had fled Nazi Germany in 1937. A controversial figure, Koellreuter was highly influential in the Brazilian serious music world: he trained many of the country's best known contemporary composers, such as Cláudio Santoro and Guerra Peixe; he introduced Brazilian musicians to Hindemith and Schönberg's twelve-tone technique; and he led the '*música viva*' movement, the only overtly non-nationalist music circle during the phase of extreme nationalism that marked the Vargas era.

It was through Koellreuter that Tom Jobim first encountered Chopin and the Impressionists, whom he considered major influences upon his music. Indeed, he claimed that 'The One Note Samba' was inspired by Chopin's 'Prelude in D^b' (Anon 1994c, p. 124), but the affinity between another of Chopin's Preludes – the 'Prelude in E Minor' – and one of his well-known songs – 'Insensatez' (How Insensitive) – is far more evident. Later Jobim studied with Tomás Terán,[15] a Spanish pianist whom Villa-Lobos had brought to Brazil in 1930 to teach the new generation of Brazilian pianists, because the composer considered him one of the best interpreters of his music. Villa-Lobos had an especially strong impact upon Tom, as he provided a formula for creating distinctly Brazilian-sounding music using European compositional procedures (cf. Chediak n.d.b, Vol. 2, pp. 14–15).

While the French Impressionists – especially Debussy – are often referred to in the literature on Tom's music, few writers have discussed how they impacted on the Brazilian's style. This is, actually, rather surprising, since a mere superficial analysis of some of Tom's best known pieces evinces the connection. What is, in fact, more noteworthy is that his appropriations of Debussy's compositional techniques are often precisely those commonly found in Villa-Lobos's work: modality, altered chords, unresolved dissonances, and parallelism. Neither Villa-Lobos nor Jobim make use of whole tone scales, which often characterise Debussy's music. Moreover, Villa-Lobos made frequent use of tight tone clusters, which are not endemic in Impressionism, but a marked feature of bossa nova.[16] It appears, therefore, that Jobim's apprehension of Impressionist techniques was received through the filter of Brazil's most renowned composer.

A unique feature of Tom Jobim's music is the way it fluctuates between passages that are clearly rooted in a conventional II, V, I harmonic scheme and others where the tonal centre is nebulous. He created tonal ambiguities in various ways: by using major chords with supertonic functions ('Chega de Saudade', 'Off Key', 'The Girl from Ipanema' among many others) or minor chords with dominant functions ('Off Key', 'A Felicidade' among others) (cf. Rocha Brito 1968, p. 28; Béhague 1973, p. 210); by omitting the dominant chord in a cycle of fifths ('The Girl from Ipanema'); or by using the diminished 7th of the fundamental in the bass ('Dindi'). His more radical deviations completely obscure the tonal centre. The two most common ways in which he achieved this were through melodic and harmonic parallelism, as in the B sections of 'The Girl from Ipanema' and 'The One Note Samba'; and through chord progressions in which the fundamentals either ascend or descend in semitones, as in 'The One Note Samba' (Bm7 – $B^b7(13)$ – Am7(11) – $A^b7(^\sharp 11)$) and 'Off Key' (A7M – $A^b7(^\sharp 5)$ – G7(13) – $G^b7(^b 13)$), where he does more than just hint at dodecaphonic techniques. 'The One Note Samba' is a masterpiece of Tom's harmonic sophistication; despite its twelve-tone allusion, the listener can mentally reconstruct the song's chordal accompaniment, even in its absence (cf. Rocha Brito 1968, p. 30).

Vinícius de Moraes and bossa nova lyricists

The greatest lyricist of the bossa nova movement, Marcus Vinícius da Cruz de Mello Moraes, was born in Rio in 1913 into a musical family. From an early age he was producing lyrics primarily for home consumption, but by 1935 he had published his first book, *Forma e Exegese*, which received first place in the Filipe d'Oliveira Competition, running against Jorge Amado and other prominent literary figures. In 1938 he was awarded a British Academy grant to study English literature in Oxford, but returned to Brazil when England entered the World War. Back at home he worked as a film critic for various newspapers before taking up a diplomatic post in Los Angeles in 1946, followed by another in Paris. He took leave from his diplomatic services for a year in 1956, but returned to Paris for another year, before being transferred to Montividéu, where he remained until 1960. He was sent back to Paris, this time to work on the Brazilian delegation at UNESCO, until 1964. All the while he was publishing one literary work after another, especially poetry, but also plays and film scripts.

From a very early age Vinícius de Moraes had begun taking the occasional stab at song lyrics, and before his twentieth birthday two of them had already been recorded (Cabral n.d.b, p. 10). Nonetheless, his first serious effort was made when he began working on the lyrics for *Orfeu da Conceição*. The endeavour was so successful that he turned his attention to this activity, and during his lifetime he produced the words for nearly 300 songs.[17] He is best remembered for his partnership with Tom Jobim, but he wrote lyrics with numerous other popular musicians, including Baden Powell, Carlos Lyra, Francis Hime, Toquinho and others.

Like Tom Jobim, Vinícius also drew upon numerous sources to create his unique style of lyric composition (cf. Sant'Anna 1986, pp. 215–20). While it evinces the colloquial and situational approach of Noel Rosa's sambas, his lyrics depict the carefree life of Copacabana's youth culture. But his masterful – yet minimal – use of well-selected words for their inherent musicality betrays his literary background, including his familiarity with the French symbolists and the Brazilian modernists, particularly Manuel Bandeira, whose poetry is marked by subjective descriptions of the commonplace. Parallel phrase constructions are relatively frequent in Vinícius's lyrics, which were often underpinned by melodic parallelism, as in 'The Girl from Ipanema'. He also made sporadic use of the techniques of the concrete poets, as in the phrase 'colado assim, calado assim', from 'Chega de Saudade'. Other bossa nova lyricists used this device much more frequently, such as Ronaldo Bôscoli, who ends 'Rio' with the line: 'Sou Rio, sorrio' (I'm Rio, I smile), which parallels certain bossa nova harmonic progressions in which only one or two notes are altered from one chord to the next.

Newton Mendonça, a childhood friend and early partner of Tom Jobim's, produced some of the most ingenious lyrics in the bossa nova repertoire; he is responsible for both 'The One Note Samba' and 'Off Key'.[18] These songs are meta-linguistically constructed, such that their texts are themselves thematically based on what is happening in the music. Newton's mimetic technique was also used

12   *Suzel Ana Reily*

by Carlos Lyra in his song 'A Influência do Jazz' ('The Influence of Jazz'), which parodied the excessive intrusion of North American jazz techniques in Brazilian music by exaggerating their presence in the piece itself. Compositions such as these, which are able to 'conceptualise [within themselves] the theory and practice of bossa nova' (Sant'Anna 1986, p. 217) as a movement, indicate the degree of self-consciousness operating among the musicians of the era.

João Gilberto

The characteristic 'beat' of bossa nova was the special contribution of João Gilberto do Prado Pereira de Oliveira, born in 1931 in the north-eastern town of Juazeiro. He began his career as a crooner in Salvador before moving to Rio. Although he never received any formal musical training, he discovered a guitar technique which played against the melody. He borrowed a procedure common to certain samba and choro traditions, that of altering the passage chords, which gave his playing a contained contrapuntual flare. For each song he devised a particular rhythmic accompaniment, thereby providing other guitarists with a pool of alternatives for their own playing. In his rendition of 'The Girl from Ipanema' on the 'Getz/Gilberto' album, for example, he uses three different patterns over the melodic theme; as they are introduced, the ethos of the piece changes ever so slightly.

The first pattern is introduced with a short vocal 'introduction', and it continues with only minor alterations until the main theme comes up again at the

Figure 2. João Gilberto's rhythmic pattern for 'The Girl from Ipanema'.

Figure 3. Bossa nova percussion accompaniment.

end of the first verse, where he shifts to another pattern, which creates a new set of displacements. This pattern remains while Astrud Gilberto sings through the main theme for the first time, but when she is about to begin the repetition, he shifts to his 'classic' pattern, returning to the second pattern when the main theme re-emerges at the end of her performance. This pattern is then sustained throughout Stan Getz's solo, since its greater density is better suited to counter-balance the volume of the saxophone (see Figure 2).

This polyrhythmic effect is further enhanced by the patterns often used in the percussion accompaniment of bossa nova, in which a brush is scraped across the head of a snare drum in continuous semiquavers while the stick beats out a syncopated rhythm on the rim of the drum (see Figure 3).

João Gilberto is the most enigmatic of bossa nova's principle creators. He has not been keen on being interviewed, and almost everything that is known about him comes from secondary sources, particularly the collection of interviews with bossa nova exponents conducted by José (Zuza) Homem de Mello (1976). While Tom and Vinícius had solid erudite academic backgrounds, João brought his shyness and perfectionism to the scene, almost personifying the style itself.

The bossa nova ethos

Bossa nova was the outcome of the combined efforts of a group of musicians, each bringing to it their unique personalities and musical backgrounds. The style promoted the symbiosis of these contributions; the melody, the harmony, the lyrics, and the interpretation all received equal weighting. In 'Off Key', for example, the timidity of the singer's interpretation is mimicked in the text, which is itself a commentary on the structure of the music and its accompaniment. As Rocha Brito (1968, pp. 22–4) has pointed out, this interdependence of musical elements led to a style of little contrast, as no musical feature was allowed to over-ride the others. Consequently, bossa nova neutralised the centrality of the singer, who, in becoming integrated into the ensemble rather than accompanied by it, lost prominence. In bossa nova the piece took precedence over the performer; what was valued was the group effort, both in terms of composition and interpretation, rather than the 'star' (cf. Rocha Brito 1968, p. 22).

Bossa nova and MPB

By the early 1960s the bossa nova craze dominated the Brazilian popular music scene, and everyone was playing and singing in the same way. Such massification led to over-kill and boredom. Moreover, the mood of the country had changed

14   *Suzel Ana Reily*

dramatically. The optimism of the 1950s had given way to a more realistic percep-tion of the country's predicament: Kubitschek's development programme – par-ticularly the building of Brasília – would have to be paid for, and inflation was rising. By 1964 it had reached the all-time high of 100% a year, legitimating the military coup, which deposed the left-leaning president João Goulart. Student organisations were becoming politicised, and the carefree alienated content of bossa nova no longer reflected their primary concerns. To sustain the interest of their audiences, musicians would have to find a new recipe.

Here Carlos Lyra led the way; he maintained the bossa nova aesthetic, but politicised the lyrics. As José Ramos Tinhorão (1986, pp. 237–45) has argued – with less than a hint of sarcasm – for all its politicisation, bossa nova did not stand a chance of reaching the disenfranchised masses of the country, as it had set out to do, since its sophisticated musical language was far too distant from the sounds of the slums. But his critical view of bossa nova as inherently alienated and alienating has not been adequately challenged. While bossa nova could hardly be perceived as anything but elitist and gimmicky, its performance practice was unquestionably rooted in an ideology of equality among performers. Indeed this may account for the ease with which bossa nova performers were able to switch over from lyrics about the sun, beaches and girls to lyrics depicting life in Rio's slums. Even if it did not reach the popular masses, the new emphasis of the lyrics certainly helped incite sectors of the intellectualised upper classes, propelling them to organise in opposition to the newly installed military dictatorship.

The politicisation of bossa nova would soon lead musicians to start turning to rural Brazil and traditional urban popular styles for new musical alternatives which allowed for a more organic relationship between the music and the lyrics of their songs. This was – without doubt – the recipe of success for Chico Buarque, who took first prize at the II Festival of Brazilian Popular Music in 1966 with 'A Banda' ('The Band'). In this song Chico reproduced the idyllic context of a small town, whose habitual day-to-day affairs were disrupted by the magical music of the local band. Although it has since become a musak classic, it was, at the time, a very welcome change from the prevailing sound.[19]

With the 'regionalist' direction, Brazilian popular music began drawing on a diversity of national sources, and musicians began establishing their own styles. First there were the Mineiros, with Milton Nascimento, and the Bahianos, with Caetano Veloso and Gilberto Gil, followed, in the next generation, by representa-tives of other regions. Today it is impossible to pin-point any specific genre, and call it the dominant trend. But for all its diversity, contemporary Brazilian popular music owes its high standards to bossa nova. Whatever the style, Brazilian intellec-tualised middle-class audiences, the direct descendants of the bossa nova genera-tion, expect to be taxed by their musicians. Only the best wordsmiths, the most precise interpretations, and the most careful arrangements meet with their approval. Hence their pride in their musical heritage, which often lies at the border between popular and High Art.

When Vinícius de Moraes died in 1980, Montenegro Street, which once housed the Veloso bar, became Vinícius de Moraes Street. From now on it will intersect with Tom Jobim Avenue, which runs the length of Ipanema Beach. Could there be a more appropriate recognition of the chance encounter of these two musicians, who changed the face of Brazilian popular music forever?

Endnotes

1. The album received no less than six Grammy awards and sold over a million copies (de Souza 1988, p. 217).
2. The title of João Gilberto's second LP, released in 1960, was *O Amor, o Sorriso e a Flor* (Love, Smile and Flower).
3. In Brazil, some well-known figures – such as Tom Jobim – are popularly referred to by their first names. I shall use this personalised mode of expression throughout this article.
4. There are 101 of his best known songs included in the three-volume songbook compiled by Almir Chediak (n.d.b), which was scrutinised by the composer before publication, and six others are included in Chediak's five-volume collection of 'Bossa Nova' (n.d.a).
5. The film won the grand prize at the Cannes Film Festival in 1959 as well as the Oscar for best foreign film. The best-known song from *Black Orpheus*, 'Manhã de Carnaval', however, was composed by Luíz Bonfá and Antônio Maria, while Tom Jobim and Vinícius de Moraes were responsible for 'A Felicidade'.
6. Like the bossa nova style and much of its repertoire, this article is the product of collective effort. I am grateful to all those who kindly lent me newspaper clippings and their recordings of the music of Tom Jobim and other bossa nova exponents; other people contributed with their musical expertise, and here I would like to thank Martin Stokes and Kevin Dawe.
7. Brasil Rocha Brito (1968, p. 20) argues that 'Hino ao Sol' ('Hymn to the Sun'), one of the movements in the *Symphony for Rio de Janeiro* by Tom Jobim and Billy Blanco, could be considered the first bossa nova. Tárik de Souza (1988, pp. 200–4) has provided a detailed inventory of the precursors of bossa nova.
8. The *embolada* is a tongue-twisting northeastern song genre which is characterised by: melodies with small intervals in rapid rhythmic configurations; stanza–refrain form; humorous themes; an emphasis on the sound quality of words through the use of alliteration and onomatopoeic effects.
9. In 1957 an earlier version of 'Chega de Saudade' had been released. It featured Elizabeth Cardoso on vocals and João Gilberto on the guitar. Here, however, a fundamental ingredient of bossa nova was missing: the appropriate vocal style.
10. Possibly the only visible Brazilian popular style not to have emerged out of organic social interaction was *'samba-exaltação'* (nationalist exaltation samba). This was the style being actively promoted by the nationally owned radio broadcasting station, but nonetheless generated a few masterpieces, such as Ary Barroso's 'Aquarela do Brasil'. It is, no doubt, difficult to imagine a group of musicians sitting with their beers in front of them trying to think up lines to glorify the nation's march toward progress without the affair plunging into sarcasm.
11. The area was called 'Bottles Court' because those living in the sky-scrapers above the clubs resented the noise of the milling crowds below, and in protest they would throw bottles down on them.
12. The set for the play was designed by none other than Oscar Niemeyer, the architect of Brasília.
13. After Tom Jobim left, a friend and musical partner of his, Aloysio de Oliveira, took the job, which undoubtedly helped him persuade the company to follow through with the project.
14. Besides 'Chega de Saudade' and 'Off Key', the LP featured two songs by the 'amateurs' Carlos Lyra and Ronaldo Bôscoli: 'Lobo Bobo' and 'Saudade Fez um Samba'.
15. He also studied under Lúcia Branco, Paulo Silva, Alceu Boquinho, Radamés Gnattali, Lírio Panicalli and Léo Peracchi (Cabral n.d.c, p. 10). Thus, he received instruction from some of Brazil's most reputable musicians.
16. On Villa-Lobos's compositional procedures, see Béhague (1979, pp. 183–204).
17. For a comprehensive list of his output, see Marcondes (1977, pp. 500–2).
18. Little is known about this popular poet, who died prematurely of a heart attack in 1960 without ever knowing the impact his songs would have on the international music scene.
19. Chico Buarque shared the first prize with Geraldo Vandré and Théo de Barros, who presented 'Disparada', which was also inspired by a rural musical tradition, the *'moda de viola'*.

References

Anon. 1994a. 'Homenagem até no desembarque', *Jornal do Brasil*, 10 December Caderno 2:2
Anon. 1994b. 'Vem aí o verbo Tombar', *Veja*, 27, pp. 162–3

16   *Suzel Ana Reily*

1994c. 'Triste é viver sem Jobim', *Veja*, 27, pp. 116–25

Béhague, Gerard. 1973. 'Bossa & bossas: recent changes in Brazilian urban popular music', *Ethnomusicology*, 17, pp. 209–33

1979. *Music in Latin America: an Introduction* (Englewood Cliffs)

Cabral, Sérgio. n.d.a. 'Em busca da perfeição', in *Songbook: Bossa Nova*, vol. 2, ed. A. Chediak (Rio de Janeiro) pp. 10–17

n.d.b. 'O jovem Vinícius', in *Songbook: Bossa Nova*, vol. 3, ed. A. Chediak (Rio de Janeiro) pp. 10–17

n.d.c. 'Tom: revolução com beleza', in *Songbook: Bossa Nova*, vol. 4, ed. A. Chediak (Rio de Janeiro) pp. 10–17

Chediak, Almir. n.d.a. *Songbook: bossa nova* (5 volumes) (Rio de Janeiro)

n.d.b. *Songbook: Tom Jobim* (3 volumes) (Rio de Janeiro)

Homem de Mello, José. 1976. *Música popular brasileira* (São Paulo)

Machado, Paulo Sérgio. 1971. 'História da música popular brasileira: Tom Jobim (vol. 16) (São Paulo) (Record jacket)

Marcondes, Marcos Antônio (ed.) 1977. *Enciclopédia da música brasileira: erudita, folclórica, popular* (São Paulo)

McGowan, Chris and Pessanha, Ricardo. 1991. *The Billboard Book of Brazilian Music* (London)

Medaglia, Júlio. 1968. 'Balanço da bossa nova', in *Balanço da bossa e outras bossas*, ed. A. de Campos (São Paulo) pp. 67–123

Rocha Brito, Brasil. 1968. 'Bossa nova', in *Balanço da bossa e outras bossas*, ed. A. de Campos (São Paulo) pp. 17–42

de Sant'Anna, Affonso Romano. 1986. *Música popular e moderna poesia brasileira* (Petrópolis)

de Souza, Tárik. 1988. 'A bossa nova e o fino da bossa', in *Brasil Musical* eds T. de Souza *et al.* (Rio de Janeiro) pp. 198–219

Schreiner, Claus. 1992. *Música Brasileira: A History of Popular Music and the People of Brazil* (New York)

Tinhorão, José Ramos. 1986. *Pequena história da música popular: da modinha ao tropicalismo* (São Paulo)

[22]

Haitian Dance Bands, 1915–1970: Class, Race, and Authenticity*

Gage Averill

From the emergence of Haitian jazz bands under the American occupation (1915–1934) to the thirty-year reign of the *konpa-dirèk*, the development of Haitian dance music has been broadly conditioned by issues of color and social stratification and the influence of *letranje* (foreigners).[1] The intersection of the issues of class, color, and foreign influence has generated an impassioned and long-standing debate over authenticity in cultural matters, over what is to be considered *natif natal* (native born and truly Haitian). My goal in this paper is to examine the development of Haitian dance band music in order to assess the impact of these social forces.

Class, Race, and Ideology in Haiti

Since it is my contention that the social issues of class and race are essential to an understanding of music in Haiti, a short introduction to the topic is in order.[2]

Class and status groups

Haitians of all classes and backgrounds are quite aware of class distinctions and social stratification, and an elaborate set of terms has been developed to articulate these differences. Figure 1 provides a schematic diagram of how these terms are employed to reflect the Haitian situation.[3] Many of the terms (or at least their English equivalents) will be familiar to the reader, yet it should not be assumed that they maintain their Euro-American meanings in the Haitian context. The term *klas* in

Figure 1. Terminology of social stratification in Haiti

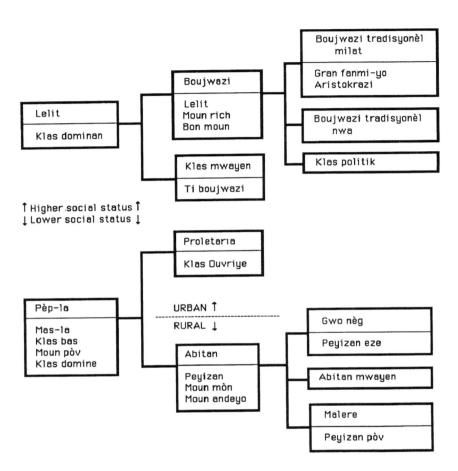

Haiti does not refer to a position determined strictly by one's relationships to the means of production but admits numerous criteria including family background, geographic origins, wealth, access to state power, education, phenotype, and comportment and is thus more akin to the concept of status group. In the top of each box (Figure 1), I have listed the terms that I will be employing throughout this paper, while below them I list alternate or roughly equivalent terms.

Haitians see the country as divided into two basic status groups: those with access to power and money (*lelit*, the elite) and those without (*pèp-la*, the people or masses). *Lelit* is not as exclusive a term as it might suggest and includes both the *boujwazi* (who own businesses, have traditional wealth, or have important positions in the government) and the *klas mwayen* (small entrepreneurs, the lower military echelons, professionals, artisans and state functionaries). The *boujwazi* can be further divided according to whether they belong to the traditional lighter-skinned ruling class (*boujwazi tradisyonèl milat*) made up of well-known families (*gran fanmi*), to the numerically small group of wealthy blacks (*boujwazi tradisyonèl nwa*), or to the *arrivistes* (career climbers), the higher strata of government managers, most of whom are of middle-class origins, who came into power with the black governments after the Second World War (the *klas politik*).

The masses (*pèp-la*) are divided primarily by urban and rural residency into the *abitan* (peasants) and the *proletaria*, or *klas ouvriye* (urban working class). The *abitan* are sometimes referred to by their geographic situation as *moun andeyo* (people from the outlying areas) or *moun mòn* (mountain people), although *moun mòn* can also refer to the most destitute and geographically remote subgroup of peasants—in contrast to the generally more prosperous plains dwellers (*moun plenn*). The highest strata of peasants, those with ample lands and a role in local affairs, are called the *gwo nèg* (literally: big guys), or *peyizan eze* (well-off peasants). Categories are also employed for the middle-level peasants (*abitan mwayen*) and those at the bottom of the rural system, the *malere* (paupers).

The 'question de couleur'

Haitian concepts of class are thoroughly interpenetrated with those of color. Before the triumph of the revolution in 1804, Haitians were divided into two major racial categories which were nearly synonymous with legal status categories.[4] Early generations of mulattos, related by blood to slave holders, were allowed to become *affranchis* (freed slaves) while most blacks remained enslaved until the short-lived abolition of slavery at the time of the French Revolution. The two groups cooperated

to ensure the success of the Haitian revolution, but after the assassination of the black Haitian Emperor Jean-Jacques Dessalines, the country
split in two—the North ruled as a monarchy by King Henri Christophe
and the South as a republic under General Petion. Although the country
was later reunited, an internecine struggle based on racial conflict and
mistrust became a persistent theme in Haitian society and politics.

The basic class contradiction in Haiti was complicated by the exclusion of the black elite from political power on the basis of color. In response, the black elite relied on the color issue to establish a racially-
rooted alliance with the black masses against the politically entrenched
mulatto elite. What resulted was a complex manipulation of the *question
de couleur* to secure and protect group privilege and access to the Haitian
state. In the 1880s, this contest became embodied in the two political
parties. The Parti Libéral, representing the mulatto position, advocated
''power to the most capable.'' The Parti National, a predominantly
black movement, operated under the slogan ''the greatest good to the
greatest number'' (Paquin 1983:51).

The twentieth century was characterized by the growth of the black
middle class (*klas mwayen*) as a social and political force and by the growth
of the proletariat, although it remained a small segment of the Haitian
population. The intellectual avant-garde of the *klas mwayen* was the sector
most responsible for the elaboration of a black racially-based ideology in
Haiti known as *indigénisme* or *noirisme*.

The noirist movement as oppositional culture

Micheline Labelle, in her *Idéologie de couleur et de classes sociales en Haïti*,
describes two well-articulated class/color-based ideologies representing
the competing elite factions (Labelle 1978:15). The mulatto ideology
claims superiority by virtue of European ancestry and its civilizing influences (this was the outlook of the Parti Libéral mentioned above).
The *noirist* ideology, with its roots in the Parti National, called for a
realignment of Haitian culture and society to reflect its roots in black
Africa.

Haitian intellectuals of the occupation period—such as Jean Price-
Mars, Jean-Claude Dorsainvil, François Duvalier, Emmanuel Paul,
Jean-Baptiste Roumain, and Lorimer Denis—shaped the theoretical and
philosophical outlook of the *noirist* movement. The racist theories of the
Frenchman Arthur Gobineau were highly influential among this group
and provided a rationale for their contention that the races were psychologically, biologically, culturally, and historically distinct (Nicholls
1985:53). The putative psycho-biological uniqueness of the African race

was used by the *Griots* (a group of *noirist* writers and scholars) to argue for a non-European approach to culture in Haiti, and (as in some writings of Dr. Duvalier) for a non-European form of government with elements drawn from African kingships. In the "Revue Indigène," in the review (and later a weekly) called "Les Griots," and in the ethnological work of Price-Mars and others, the movement articulated an oppositional culture (see Williams 1973) that challenged the hegemony of mulatto ideology and foreign domination.

Although this movement sought direct political expression (Jean Price-Mars himself twice ran for the presidency), it was more successful in the period before World War II in raising the political consciousness of the *klas mwayen* and even that of the *boujwazi*. During the occupation, the elite grew increasingly resentful of the often racist treatment of *milat* (mulattos) by white U.S. soldiers and responded in 1918 by prohibiting American membership in the exclusive Cercle Bellvue. By the end of the occupation, many of the tenets of the *indigène* movement had been broadly disseminated throughout the population. Thus, the American occupation, which ostensibly favored *lelit tradisyonèl milat*, had the effect of helping to establish the hegemony of the black elite and middle class.

Natif natal

Under the impact of *indigènisme*, a new attitude evolved towards cultural authenticity. If Africa was to be the cradle of Haitian civilization and culture, then those elements in Haiti which were most African were to be regarded as the most authentically Haitian. The *noirists* reassessed the African contribution and found peasant culture, especially the Vodou cult, to be at the center of the meaning of the Haitian experience. An implicit model of authenticity developed that had authenticity declining in proportion to the physical, social, and historical distance from the neo-African peasant experience—one could even say in proportion to the distance from the *poto mitan* (central post of the Vodou temple).

I attempt to represent the meaning of this model in terms of music in Figure 2.[5] I mention the historical, physical, and social dimensions to this model because I believe that all three are collapsed in it or at least implicitly referenced by it. When Haitians speak of the centrality of Vodou to the meaning of being Haitian, they see peasant culture first as a continuation of a historical pattern, as a representation of the Haitian past into the present. Thus, the center of the diagram in Figure 2 has many dimensions including idealized past, rural environment, peasantry, and sacred beliefs, while its perimeter is modern, foreign, elite, urban, and secular.

Figure 2: Conceptual map of authenticity in Haitian music

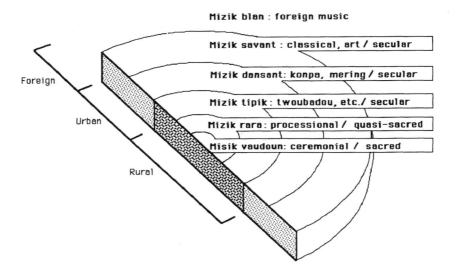

1. Mizik Vodou: the music of the Vodou cult.
2. Mizik rara: music performed by rara bands, associated most closely with the sound of the vaksin bamboo trumpets. These bands are most often seen during the pre-Easter season when they take to the streets.
3. Mizik tipik: a catch-all term used for entertainment music in the countryside, whether for kontradans or played by the Cuban-influenced twoubadou groups. Also called mizik anba tonèl (music under the arbor).
4. Mizik dansant: urban popular dance music.
5. Mizik savant: urban classical or art music for concert or parlor performance.

Indigénisme and its notions of cultural authenticity had revolutionary political implications. The ruling class in Haiti, more European in phenotype and in culture, was positioned as less authentic, less representative of Haiti as a whole, than the middle class and black elite. The cultural implications were no less dramatic. The *noirists* advocated relying on peasant culture as a model for an authentically Haitian culture. The African elements of the Haitian experience would become a cherished part of the folklore of Haiti,[6] integrated where possible into the fabric of the expressive culture of Haiti. This ideology played a significant role in the social transformations that Haiti underwent in the twentieth century and formed a counterbalance to the pressures for modernization and internationalization to which Haiti was simultaneously responding.

There is a parallel here with the argument that Geertz makes concerning the conflicts of identity in newly emerging states:

> Generalized, the "who we are" question asks what cultural forms—what systems of meaningful symbols—to employ to give value and significance to the activities of the state, and by extension to the civil life of its citizens. Nationalist ideologies built out of symbolic forms drawn from local traditions—which are, that is, essentialist—tend, like vernaculars, to be psychologically immediate but socially isolating; built out of forms implicated in the general movement of contemporary history—that is, epochalist—they tend, like lingua franca, to be socially deprovincializing but psychologically forced. (Geertz 1968:242–243)

Haiti was not at this time a newly emerging state but rather one in which class relationships were in flux, in which ideologies were emergent and contested, and in which the hegemony of the ruling class was in question. Haiti's class conflict with its racial overtones thus bears a marked resemblance to Geertz's conflict of ethnic groups in pluralist newly independent states in regard to the competition to provide Haiti with the symbols upon which to construct a collective identity.

The U.S. Occupation: Mereng, Jazz, and Rumba

Indigenist and revitalization movements occur generally under the impact of disruption from outside, and the *indigène* movement was no exception. The arrival of the U.S. Marines in 1915 marked the first time since independence in 1804 that Haiti had been physically dominated by a foreign power. The occupation quickened the pace of technological development, intensified the exposure of Haiti to other musical cultures (notably U.S. and Cuban), and (as I have stressed above) helped to fuel the growth of the oppositional culture rooted in African identity.

210 : *Gage Averill*

The mereng

The pre-jazz music and dance scene for the elite of Port-au-Prince comprised salon concerts and public dances, called *bastreng* or *"douze et demi"* (twelve and a half, the price in centimes of admission for men). The most popular entertainment at these events was a piano or a small string orchestra called *òkès bastreng* with instrumentation including cello, bass, violin, clarinet, and/or trombone. The repertoire included all of the popular European parlor dances (mazurkas, waltzes, *quadrilles*) and the Haitian *mereng* (Fr.: *méringue*).

The *mereng*, a syncretized form with pre-revolutionary roots, is commonly cited as the ancestor of the Dominican *merengue* that was brought to the Dominican Republic during the Haitian occupation of the Spanish-speaking part of the island (1822–1844). In Haiti, the *mereng*, like the *merengue* in the Dominican Republic (Alberti 1975:33) and the *biguine* in the French Antilles, came to serve as the closing dance for the elite *bal* and in time became a staple of the salons and *bastreng*.

At the turn of the century, the *mereng* was both a bourgeois parlor music and an often-satiric song form popular among the proletariat and peasantry. Fidélia characterized the dual class nature of the music as follows:

> Haitian music was divided into two currents. The first current, of a truly satiric nature, was an effective means for the people (especially the lowest people who couldn't do it otherwise) to say with malice or at times brutality what was on their mind to those who kept them in misery. These works were almost all of a political or social inspiration. The second current, composed nearly exclusively of (what is convenient to call) *"méringues lentes"* or *"méringues de salons"*, was the expression of the bourgeois society of the time. They would get together in the salon to listen to the piano. In the afternoon they had tea in the garden or on the veranda. This society was in the position back then to sing of the charms of the country, the joys of life and love, and of all the heady sweetness of tropical island idleness [les douceurs capiteuses du farinente insulaire et tropical]. (Fidélia 1960:3, my translation)

The *mereng* was a subject for elite autochtonous art music. As in Europe, a composite figure—the folklorist-composer—came into being whose goal was to harmonize peasant compositions, to orchestrate them for European-styled ensembles, and to compose new works in a Haitian style. Nineteenth-century art music composers such as Michel M. Montard, Occilius Jeany, his son Occide Jeanty, and others became famous for their *mereng* performed at the *bals du salon* and at concerts by, among others, the Musique du Palais, an army *fanfa* (fanfare, or brass band) that served as the presidential band.

Haitian Dance Bands : 211

The Musique du Palais was perhaps the most important of the numerous military, school, and municipal *fanfa* to be found throughout Haiti. Regimental bands from all over Haiti traditionally spent half the year in the capital, a stay during which the musicians studied theory and technique with special instructors (Dumervé 1962:3). The *fanfa* trained musicians who later excelled not only in art music but also in the dance bands.

Jazz dance bands in Haiti

Through the presence of U.S. troops from 1915 to 1934, through radio, and through journeys of elite Haitians to Paris, Haitians were introduced to jazz bands, the charleston, the fox trot and other novelties of the 1920s and 1930s. Fouchard traces the charleston craze in Haiti to a group of bourgeois Haitian students nicknamed ''le tout Paris'' who brought the dance back with them from school in Paris (Fouchard 1988:119).

Some of the best known Haitian jazz groups of this period were Jazz de Louis Scott, Jazz Guignard (the first group to record, circa 1937), les Jacobins, Jazz de Geffrard Cesvet, and Jazz Hubert. In 1932, Jazz de Louis Scott could be found on Saturday evenings playing at the Sea-Side-Inn in Mariani, while at the Café Latino they were dancing the fox trot and the shimmy (Corvington 1987:281–282). A U.S. Marine observed,

> It was during my stay that American jazz began to sweep through Haiti as it has swept through so many countries. Such gems as ''Charley My Boy,'' ''Yes Sir, She's My Baby,'' and other masterpieces of Tin Pan Alley began to be heard on every hand. The Haitians took to them with vim to the detriment of their native music. (Craige 1933:168)

To these selections, Fouchard has added ''Saint-Louis Blues'' and ''Baby Face.''

Although the jazz band lineup varied considerably, a look at one such group, Les Jacobins (c. 1929), suggests some typical features. The personnel was as follows:

Les Jacobins:

Lafayette Hector	saxophone/clarinette
Roger Smith	piano/clarinette
Elliot Denis	flute/saxophone/clarinette
Joinville Monsignac	piano/drum battery
Pierre Carrié	banjo
Arsène Desgrottes	banjo
Ludovic Vandal	mandolin/banjo
Jean Moïse	trumpet (Herissé n.d.)

212 : *Gage Averill*

The instruments selected for the group reveal influences from such American 'classic' jazz bands as King Oliver's Creole Jazz Band and from the older syncopated dance bands that James Europe popularized in France. Europe's earlier group, the Memphis Students, had incorporated folk instruments such as the banjo, mandolin, and guitar into the dance orchestra along with the saxophone, formerly a symphonic novelty instrument (Southern 1983:344). Jim Europe's World War I regimental band is credited with having stimulated the French appetite for black American syncopated dance music.[7]

The Latin influence

The coming of the *òtofonik* (phonograph player) and the first radio station to Haiti during the occupation favored those genres that had already been widely recorded, especially the Cuban genres such as *son*, *bolero*, and *danzón*. The Cuban groups Trio Matamoros and Septeto Nacional were very popular in this era. A Haitian violinist remarked a decade later that: "The true rhythm of the Haitian *mereng* is no longer in fashion these days, to our misfortune . . . Every day we hear Haitian melodies which are executed to the rhythm of the *bolero-son* or the Cuban *rumba*" (Canez 1942:1).

However, the Cuban influence also filtered into Haitian music with the return of Haitian cane cutters who traveled every year to work the Cuban sugar cane harvests. They brought back with them a guitar-based *típico* song tradition that in Haiti became known as *twoubadou* (troubadour) music. This style filtered into many of the *provins* (outlying areas) and the capital as well. Groups sprang up with names like Trio Orphes, Trio Quisqueya, and Les Quatre Troubadours. A typical group, the Quarteto Jean Legros, had the following personnel and instruments in 1941:

Jean Legros	*gita* (guitar)
Gustave Antoine	*gita*
Antoine Pierre	*malaka* (maracas)
Ernst Rémy	maniba (*marimbula*, a large lamellaphone)
(Herissé n.d.)	

Some *twoubadou* groups also often contained a *tanbou*, a barrel drum similar to the Cuban *conga* drum played with the hands.[8]

Many *twoubadou* musicians went on to become well-known composers and orchestra leaders in Haiti—Dodòf Legros, Jean Legros, and Murat Pierre, for example. *Twoubadou* guitarist Raymond Gaspard became the guitarist for Nemours Jean-Baptiste, the originator of the *konpa-dirèk*. Another star of this young movement was Annulysse Cadet, a banjo player who first performed publicly around the start of World War II and continued to perform into the 1950s, eventually with his own *djaz*, or dance ensemble.

The *twoubadou* tradition persists into the present, and the modern descendents of the *twoubadou* groups can be seen playing at the airport, at restaurants, hotels, and at *fèt patwonal* (patron's day festivals). The groups solicit money from their audiences, and many have large and diverse repertoires ranging from traditional *mereng* to recent commercial *konpa* by popular *mini-djaz* in order to play pieces on command.

That these groups are of relatively recent origin in Haiti is not widely recognized. Because of their semi-rural associations, they are often believed to be quite *natif natal*, in other words, both Haitian and hoary. They are often lumped with a number of other secular, rural ensembles under the rubric *mizik tipik* ('typical' i.e. traditional music) or *mizik anba tonèl* (music played under the arbors).

The Cuban trio style was not the only Cuban genre to play a role in Haitian music. The development of the group Les Gais Troubadours, which started with a group called the Quinteto Estudiantino Haitiano (note the Spanish name), then the Sexteto Estudiantino Haitiano, took place in the late 1930s and into the 1940s and affords us a look into the increasing sophistication of the emulation of Cuban prototypes. Here is the instrumentation and personnel of the group:

Orchestre Les Gais Troubadours (1942):

Hermann Camille	saxophone/maestro
Yves Lerebours	piano
Gaston Madère	bass
André Desrosiers	bongo
Maurice Morisset	battery
Henri Mollenthiel	saxophone
Murat Pierre	saxophone
Michel Desgrottes	trumpet
Dieuville Dugué	trumpet
Kesner Hall	trumpet
Joseph Trouillot	vocals
Ulysse Cabral	vocals
(Herissé n.d.)	

In its instrumentation, it bears a strong resemblance to the early *mambo* groups like Machito and his Afro-Cubans. The trumpet and saxophone horn section is especially significant because it is this group that takes on the function of interlocking arpeggiations that characterize the final *montuno* sections in the Afro-Cuban *sones* and *mambos*. Montuno-like sections using horns became a characteristic of much of the Haitian dance music of the post-war period.

As with the *twoubadou* groups, our attention is drawn to the personnel of this ensemble, because many of the members of this band would play prominent roles in later orchestras. Joe Trouillot, Michel Desgrottes, Murat Pierre, and Ulysse Cabral were four of the most important band leaders of the later 1940s and 1950s. The training that they received in this group, like the training that the *twoubadou* musicians received in theirs, helps to explain the continuing influence of Cubanisms in the period of the Vodou-jazz orchestras *and* the period of the *konpa-direk* and *kadans ranpa*. As a result of the Cuban connection, *boleros*, *guarachas*, and *rumbas* entered into the Haitian repertoire. Even the *pachanga* became popular in Haiti in the late 1950s and early 1960s.

One final Cubanizing influence should be mentioned. A vogue for Dominican prostitutes in the dance halls of the pre-war era helped to establish *panyòl* (Spanish-language) music, such as the Dominican *merengue* and Cuban *son*, as dance hall staples on the *òtofonik* (Fouchard 1988:118). These women were called *fi enpòte* (imported women) or *fi fwontyè* (women of the border).

The radio revolution

Radio HHK went on the air in 1927. Like the rest of the governmental apparatus during the occupation, it was under the direct control of U.S. Marines. The initial programming included a weekly international entertainment broadcast (reaching as far as Canada and Europe) in both English and French. The entertainment was live and the Gendarmerie Band was the first on the air, but the ranks of performers soon extended to many talented members of the elite (Craige 1933:139–140).

Due to a lack of receivers in the country, the occupation government provided public speakers first on the Champs-de-Mars outside the Palace and later elsewhere in the country. A public speaker system was necessary for government educational programs in Creole to reach any portion of their intended audience. Among the most popular broadcasts were the Thursday concerts by the Musique du Palais (Corvington 1987: 307). Thus, even before radio receivers were widely available, radio was on its way to becoming a popular form of entertainment in Port-au-Prince.

Négritude and Music

The cultural mission of the *indigène* movement was formulated during the occupation and had much in common with the romantic nationalist school in Europe and Latin America. The elevation of the peasantry as authentic representatives of the 'soul of the nation,' the study and preservation of peasant culture, and the selective incorporation of symbols drawn from this culture into elite arts firmly anchored this movement in the international context. Certainly, the enduring interest of elite composers with peasant songs (*mereng*) was an earlier expression of some of these same sentiments, a Haitian strain of romantic nationalism. But the *indigène* movement looked deeper into the culture of the countryside for inspiration.

In 1928, Dr. Price-Mars wrote his legendary *Ainsi parle l'oncle*, advocating a thorough integration of peasant Vodou religious music into the concert halls and salons. Price-Mars' suggestion to composers was to study the "plainchant" of the Vodou ceremonies to create a music that would "mark the capacity of the race for an individual art, generating ideas and emotions" (Price-Mars 1983:182–183). This dictum was embraced by the composers Ludovic Lamothe, Justin Elie, and Werner A. Jaegerhuber, among others, who created a small but significant corpus of Vodou-influenced art music.[9]

The Haitian Renaissance

In the post-war years, a political, economic, and artistic revolution took place in Haiti. With the devastation of Europe, the Caribbean playgrounds (especially Port-au-Prince, Haiti, and Havana, Cuba) became the foci of an envigorated Caribbean tourist market. Haitian raw materials fed the booming post-war manufacturing industries, and the election of a black president, Dumarsais Estimé, fueled a renaissance of Afro-Haitian arts. Estimé's election was described by Rotberg as "the victory of the *folklorique* movement of black intellectuals . . . who had long sought political power" (Heinl and Heinl 1978:551). The mulatto elite regarded Estimé with anything from reservation to horror and many considered him a *manje-milat* (eater of mulattos, i.e., a fervent opponent). Under Estimé, and later under Duvalier, the government became dominated by members of the black middle class. The new *klas politik* (political class) emerged to compete with the *lelit tradisyonèl milat* and the *lelit nwa* for power.

In this period, authentic "primitive" painters were discovered by art collectors, the *négritude* literary movement flourished, and large Cuban-styled orchestras proliferated to entertain a growing audience. Certain of the larger hotels and clubs such as Ibo Lélé, Casino International, Hotel Riviera, Cabane Choucoune, and Aux Calebasses had their own house orchestras or ensembles. The most influential bands of the period included Jazz des Jeunes, Orchestre Septentrional, Orchestre Saieh, the Orchestre Casino International, the Orchestre Citadelle, and the Ensemble du Riviera Hotel. These ensembles were known as 'jazz,' or with a Creole spelling, *djaz*, signifying a large urban ensemble that played for dances.[10]

These Haitian orchestras performed a mixture of Latin classics, American jazz tunes, and Haitian *mereng*, now more in favor due to the postoccupation/post-war nationalist currents. The composition of the orchestras in the post-war period generally approximated the following:

> *Bann dèyè* (back group, or rhythm section):
> Piano or accordion
> String bass
> Drum battery or Cuban *timbales* (two single-headed cylindrical
>   drums mounted on a stand)
> Cuban *conga* set or Haitian *tanbou*
> The rhythm section was supplemented with a *graj* (like a Cuban
>   *guiro*) or *tcha-tcha/malakas* (shaken rattles)

> *Bann avan* (front section):
> 3 trumpets
> 3–4 saxophones (tenor, alto, baritone)
> One or more singers

Radio was coming into its own at the same time in Haiti. In 1935, Ricardo Widmaier had launched Radio HH3W, a private station that developed a reputation as a performers' hang-out and that was instrumental in exposing new artists to the public. Among the performers who frequented the station were Annulyse Cadet who headed up the Jazz Annulyse Cadet (c. 1941) and Dodolph Legros (Boisvert 1978:11) who was featured in a *twobadou* group called the Trio HH3W sponsored by the station. Within a few years the station grew into a modern complex with a theatre and a transmitter capable of covering Haiti and points beyond. HH3W became Radio 4RVW (Radio d'Haïti), affiliated with the Columbia Broadcasting System, and began a pioneering series of programs, live broadcasts from the nightclub Cabane Choucoune and the ''*radio-théatres*'' on Sunday morning from the Ciné Paramount. Performers on the station in the 1950s included the Orchestre Saieh, l'Ensemble Weber Sicot, Louis Lahens (later a lead singer with Nemours Jean-Baptiste), Aster-Jazz Latino, and Guy Durosier (Boisvert 1978:11).

Estimé's rule was followed by that of the black general Magloire whose six-year reign was called by one, critic ''*sis ans de kermesse*'' (six years of partying) (Heinl and Heinl 1978:564). Far from being a *manje-milat* (mulatto eater), Magloire was a great friend of the elite and was known as a true *bamboché* (partyer). During the Magloire years, the exclusive club Cercle Bellevue moved to a palatial new complex above Petionville in Bourdon, and dance bands found constant employment in the many clubs and hotels.

Vodou-jazz: Jazz des Jeunes and Orchestre Saieh

Two orchestras dominated the Port-au-Prince music scene in the 1940s and early 1950s and helped to characterize the period as the indigenous era in Haitian music. Orchestre Saieh and Jazz des Jeunes—performing a fusion of big-band swing, *mereng*, and Vodou rhythms—pioneered the concept of a new indigenous dance music. Dubbed Vodou-jazz, this tendency resulted in forms such as *mereng ibo*, *mereng petro*, *mereng raborday*, and many others, all based on traditional rhythms. They were differentiated chiefly by their tempi and the parts for the rhythm section, especially the *tanbou* (usually either conga drums borrowed from Cuban music or Haitian-styled *Petro* drums).

Each rhythm on *tanbou* also had an accompanying timeline called the *kata* played traditionally with sticks on the side of a drum. In the dance bands, the *kata* was often played on a scraper (*graj*) or a Cuban *timbale* set (two single-headed cylindrical drums mounted on a stand). It was common for the groups to use one *tanbouyè* (drummer) but three were sometimes used for a more traditional effect, as there are three *tanbouyè* in the standard battery of a Vodou temple. If a single drummer was used, his function was to reproduce the sound of the traditional three-drum interlocking patterns on one drum.

Although melodies were occasionally borrowed from peasant music, the arrangements and harmonic structure for the Vodou-jazz pieces remained well within the mainstream big-band sound defined by the Cuban mambo bands and the American swing bands.

The composer most responsible for this fusion, Antalcidas O. Murat, worked briefly with the Saieh organization but was much more closely associated with Jazz des Jeunes. Jazz des Jeunes (Jazz of the Youth) was formed in Morne-à-Tuf (a middle-class district in the capital) in 1943 by some friends and included bandleader René Saint-Aude, the *frères* Dor, composer Antalcidas O. Murat, and Pierre Reiché. Murat worked later as a music professor but started out as a trumpet player, folklorist, and composer for Jazz des Jeunes.

The Orchestra Saieh, under the direction of Issa El Saieh, shared some personnel with Jazz des Jeunes, notably the folkloric singer Lumane Casimir and the renowned *tanbouyè* Ti-Roro. Saieh's group was perhaps

218 : *Gage Averill*

best known for its more sophisticated jazz arrangements and more in-
ventive harmonies. The orchestra included singer/saxophonist Guy
Durosier, Raoul and Raymond Guillaume on saxophone, and trumpet
players Alphonse Simon and Serge Lebonde. Saieh strove to go beyond
the military style of playing that was exemplified by the Jazz des Jeunes
horn line (the *fanfa* influence) and make his orchestra sound as good as
a U.S. group.

From time to time, El Saieh would bring U.S. jazz artists such as
Billy Taylor and Budd Johnson to Haiti to give workshops for the group
in harmony and instrumental technique (Précil 1987:17). The arrangements for the band were done by Bobby Hicks, a U.S. citizen living in
Puerto Rico (Interview: Herby Widmaier 1988). Yet Haitian 'folkloric'
music formed an important part of the group's repertoire, and Saieh
himself traveled to meet Vodou *ougan* (priests) and notate cult songs,
much as art-music composers like Jaegerhuber were doing at the time.

Although they played a similar mix of musics, these two orchestras
and the competition between them encompassed conflicts of class, race,
and authenticity that I referred to in the first section of this article. The
difference in sound expressed class and racial differences between the
two groups: Saieh's orchestra drew on a group of musicians with more
boujwa backgrounds and achieved a cleaner sound that was regarded as
son blan (a white sound) or *mizik letranje* (foreign music). It was primarily
for this reason, rather than for reasons of repertoire, that Orchestre Saieh
was considered less authentically 'Haitian' than Jazz des Jeunes (Interview: Widmaier 1988).

During the post-war years, this badge of Haitian authenticity was
instrumental in the greater success of Jazz des Jeunes. In 1949, Port-
au-Prince celebrated its bicentennial with an extravagant exposition centered in the completely rebuilt waterfront area, renamed Cité de l'Exposition. Budgeted at six million dollars, the exposition was an enormous
monetary failure but it helped to launch many of the indigenous arts
movements. Jazz des Jeunes was contracted to perform along with the
newly-formed Troupe Folklorique Nationale and the singer Lumane
Casimir at the new open-air Théâtre Verdure for an audience of Haitians
and tourists (Interview: St. Aude 1988). A few years later, they were
chosen by the government to represent Haiti in Canada and the United
States.

These honors were bestowed on Jazz des Jeunes largely because of the
belief that they best represented the character and soul of Haiti. The
following remark from an article for their fortieth-anniversary concert
in 1988 is typical of the sentiments one often hears from nationalistic
Haitians about the group:

> Jazz des Jeunes is the oldest authentically Haitian orchestra whose reper-
> tory is rich in Haitian colors and whose music is inspired by the soul and
> breath of Haiti . . . After all, when one speaks of Jazz des Jeunes, it is the
> Haitian soul that one causes to vibrate. (Haiti-Observateur, Sept. 9–16,
> 1988:14, my translation)

The music of Jazz des Jeunes was considered a weapon in the struggle
against a Europhile elite. René Beaubrun, writing in the *noirist* journal
"Combite" on December 31, 1957, recognized the combativeness of
Jazz des Jeunes and lauded their "irrefutable contribution to the development of Haitian music, their combativeness in the struggle against
the 'disdainers' from a class of Haitians who reject folklore because of
its popular [lower class] origins."

Murat's composition entitled "Anciens Jeunes," performed by Jazz
des Jeunes (MARC-MDVG 203), was based on the *kongo* and *ibo* rhythms
and extolled the performers in the Théâtre Verdure shows, including
the dancer Claudinette. This piece succinctly states many of the beliefs
of the *indigène* movement. Here are a few verses (my translation):

Ancient Youth

Jazz des Jeunes is the Haitian people's treasured child.
Their pride, their dignity, is to eat their own food.
Living from their garden, they love being ancient,
By extolling the foreign, you betray only yourself.

Haitian folklore deserves to be held in great esteem.
It triumphs in Cuba, Paris, and Colombia,
It makes Africa, source of life, live in us again,
It aided our ancestors at Vertières, Crête à Pierrot.

Yanvalou, rabòday, petro, ibo, kongo, djouba
Are the rhythms of our ancestors, the Arada Negroes
Of all authentic Haitians, real, without pretense,
They have quintupled the beauty of Claudinette.

Like Claudinette, the most beautiful of Haitian women,
Jazz des Jeunes is our cathedral in music.
Claudinette, Jazz des Jeunes, and the Troupe Nationale,
The most beautiful trilogy,
All the art of our magnificent country.

According to Murat, the rhythms of Jazz des Jeunes were "ancient,"
"real," "Haitian," "African," and "authentic." He compares the use
of indigenous symbols in expressive culture to living off of your own
garden (a deeply-ingrained value of the Haitian peasant who seeks independence). Thus, this song depends on subtle connections of meaning
and value in which economic and political independence is linked to

220 : *Gage Averill*

cultural independence, all within a structure intensified by religious metaphors (the images of the cathedral and the trilogy).

The debate over authenticity was cast in sharp relief in "Natif Natal" by Murat, also performed by Jazz des Jeunes (my translation):

Natif Natal

1) In our little country, guys are spouting nonsense
There are those who want to forget they're Haitian.
They want braggards to think chicken shit is butter.
They believe they're foreigners, sad to say.
We have to beware and not let this go too far.
Haiti is ours; to love it is better.
Haiti is ours; to love it is better.
Sun on the rivers, beautiful sky, fruit sweet as honey,
Music, beautiful women, spring waters, this is real.

Chorus 1: Mother Haiti, for you we want to live.
Strong people, the light for us to live as brothers.
Mother Haiti, despite your small size,
In our hearts you are queen.
Long live the nation of Haiti.

2) Cuba has the bolero, guaracha, chachacha;
Mexico has the huapango, mambo, and ranchera;
Argentina has the tango; Jamaica the calypso;
The Joropo is Venezuelan;
The U.S. has blues, fox-trot, and rock-and-roll.
Each people has their own music
Which plays a great role.
But one does nothing in another far-away country.
Beautiful Haitian folklore always carries first prize.

Chorus 2: People who are native born, truly national
Yanvalou, kongo, petro, djouba, ibo,
Well-balanced mereng. They're for dancing.
It's a music without equal, it's an ideal music.

The first four lines are an invective against the mulatto elite for their anti-nationalist ideals, their identification with Euro-American culture, and the premium placed on light skin coloration (this is implied in the metaphor of chicken shit and butter). Verse 2 is an admonition for Haitians to adopt epochalist treatments of traditional music as their national music in order to join the ranks of other countries who lay claim to national styles. In the final chorus, the idea of Haitian authenticity is once again tied into the use of traditional sacred rhythms from Vodou.

The Duvalier Era

The election of Papa Doc

The *konpa-dirèk*, Haiti's pre-eminent dance for the last thirty years, was born in the final Magloire years when his regime was crumbling under charges of waste and corruption. The period after the departure of Magloire was one of tremendous political strife, articulated to an unprecedented extent along racial and class lines. Duvalier had appropriated the ideological mantle of President Estimé and positioned himself as a champion of the black middle class and proletariat (although the urban proletariat leaned decisively toward one of his rivals, the black populist Daniel Fignolé).

François Duvalier's election was greeted by an optimistic collection of *mereng* from *noirist* composers, in praise of the new president. For example, in a *mereng* entitled "Vive Duvalier," Antalcidas Murat (of Jazz des Jeunes) wrote:

> Duvalier is not tyranny
> With Duvalier, we'll have Peace
> With Duvalier, we'll live united
> Long live Duvalier and down with misery [poverty]

Likewise, Jean Legros wrote (in the *mereng* "Dr. François Duvalier"):

> Duvalier, good Father
> Duvalier, good Chief of State
> It's God who puts him here
> In order to save Haiti (L'Institut Musical d'Haïti, 1958:18, 42)

Paradoxically, the racial-based doctrine that Duvalier espoused (*négritude*) played little role in public arts policy after his election. Support for arts that were considered indigenous eroded under the increasingly personalist and arbitrary rule of Papa Doc. Most ideological activity, even that nominally in line with the Duvalier platform, declined in favor of support for the president, pure and simple. The revolution initially linked to *négritude* became a rule by the terror of *macoutisme* (the Tontons Macoutes, Duvalier's personal army). Music more than ever became an escapist medium, sapped of all potentially threatening political and social content. Thus, the Dominican-inspired *konpa-dirèk* of Nemours Jean-Baptiste—lively and perfect for moving the masses at carnival time—found more support from the new regime than the more indigenous Vodou-jazz.

The complex relationship of the Duvalier dictatorship to music during

222 : *Gage Averill*

its thirty-year reign requires a separate study, as many of the issues raised by the use of music by the dictatorship are peripheral to those of race and class. The political problems of the late 1950s and the campaign of terror unleashed by Papa Doc eventually took their toll on tourism, international aid, and consequently the general economy, inaugurating a process of decline from which Haiti would never fully recover. We should not be surprised, therefore, that this era coincides with increasing competition among musical ensembles, with the widespread imitation of a single successful commercial form (*konpa-dirèk*), with a narrow pre-occupation with commercial success, and finally with the appearance of small combos, the *mini-djaz*.

The Dominican influence on a syncretic style

Two saxophonist/bandleaders, Nemours Jean-Baptiste and Weber Sicot, had been profoundly influenced by Dominican music, especially the *merengue* that had reached an unprecedented popularity in the Dominican Republic under Trujillo and that was exported via records and band tours to Haiti.[11] In the early 1950s, a Dominican group called Típico Cibaeño from the Cibao region had a major hit in Haiti. As Herby Widmaier explained:

> That thing hit like a bomb. The Haitians loved the *merengue* because it had a lively beat for dancing. They were doing it in every nightclub, especially down by Carrefour. The Dominican girls were there and would teach the Haitian guys how to dance. (Interview: Widmaier 1988)

In response to this popularity, Nemours Jean-Baptiste, the leader of the Ensemble Aux Calebasses, developed his *konpa-dirèk* in the summer of 1955 as a Haitian adaptation of the *merengue* utilizing a *merengue* rhythm with a slightly modified conga part. A few years later, Weber Sicot responded with his own version that he labeled *kadans ranpa*.

Raymond Gaspard, Nemours' guitarist, is credited with the term *konpa-dirèk* that became the commercial label for the new sound. The term *konpa* refers simply to 'beat,' and *dirèk* (direct) to the harmonic structure inspired by Dominican music. Previously, the Haitian *mereng* was commonly harmonized within I–IV–V7 progressions. In much Dominican and Cuban music, as in the section of the Dominican *merengue* called the *jaleo*, it was common to use a two-chord alternation (often just V7–I).[12] Up to the present, *konpa* musicians have relied heavily on variations of this two-chord vamp in the main section of the piece (the *manman konpa*, or mother *konpa*) but have expanded the repertoire of chord combinations.

Nemours' *konpa-dirèk* was slower than the Dominican *merengue*. Its enormous success can be partially credited to its choreographic simplicity that contrasted with the numerous Vodou-jazz dance steps of the 1940s and 1950s. The close ballroom two-step of *konpa*, called *kare* (square), arrived in the dance halls of Carrefour, just west of Port-au-Prince, and was patterned also on the Dominican *merengue*. Its variants range from stately ballroom styles to more recent adaptations nicknamed *kole-kole* (pasted together), *kole-mayouba* (pasted with the hips swaying), or *ploge* (plugged, an explicit sexual reference), more popular in lower-class (and dimly lit) establishments.

The foreign roots of *konpa* were cause for contempt among Haitian music purists. Historian Jean Fouchard, in his 1973 book, longed for the return of the *mereng*:

> after its long ordeal imposed at the time by the popularity of the . . . imported music with which Weber Sicot and Nemours Jean-Baptiste, who had nevertheless honored the *méringue* with unforgettable compositions, believed it necessary to modernize our national dance. The two ventured to adapt it to a foreign rhythm which they baptised with the bewildering names "*compas-direct*" and "*cadence rampa*" bringing this extravagant addition to their reckless enterprise. Is this really evolution?
>
> It is very arguable, when under the easy pretext of adaptation to the taste of the day, the very structure of our *méringue* is gravely shaken, and its langorous grace, its essential characteristic, is replaced by the jerky rhythms in a style foreign to our traditions. (Fouchard 1973:156, my translation)

One of the attractions of the *konpa-dirèk* for Papa Doc was that it had no previous association with Haiti's elite. It was created and nursed in the middle-class clubs of Carrefour and reflected the consumerist aspirations of the class. It was a middle-class commercial genre par excellence.

Multi-class strategies to the forefront

Fouchard accused Nemours and Sicot of appealing to popular tastes, and he was correct. There was evidence of a substantive change in orientation by the artists concerned—a decline in ideological construction of popular music (the influence of the *négritude* movement) and a concern above all with the mobilization of broad patronage networks for commercial success. Nemours' simple commercial style was perfectly tailored to the needs of the incipient music industry and the (primarily urban) mass audience to which it catered.

Although the performers were most often from the *klas mwayen*, Nemours strove to overcome the class and racial barriers to a mass market

224 : *Gage Averill*

for popular music in Haiti, a market that had been made possible by the extension of the technological media of music reproduction and broadcast, improvements in transportation, and by the relative affluence of the previous decade. He prided himself on his multi-class and multi-color *piblik* (audience), even though performance contexts remained quite segregated. The final barrier remained, however, the brutal poverty of the country that restricted the spread of a consumer-oriented economy and resulted in a very underdeveloped market for music commodities.

In the late 1950s and early 1960s Nemours and his band played on Friday nights for urban teenagers. On Saturday nights they played *swae* (evening, or *soirée*, dances) for the elite at Cabane Choucoune in Pétion-ville. On Sundays they played at Aux Calebasses or Sous Les Palmistes for the middle classes. Only for carnival would there be any significant mixing of classes for music consumption, and even then the different social strata remain spatially segregated. At carnival, Nemours Jean-Baptiste and his chief rival Weber Sicot formed a new kind of middle-class wedge between the elite *cha madigra* (carnival floats) and the proletariat and peasant *bann madigra* (traditional bands of masked revelers). The new orchestras, and the competition between them, captured the public's attention at carnival time.

For *fèt patwonal* and *fèt champèt* (country dances), Nemours bussed the band to the provinces for performances for the *abitan-yo*. Tickets for these rural dances were generally in the $1 range, still a steep price for the peasantry, but concerts were well-advertised by word-of-mouth and inevitably crowded. Often, the peasants would line the dirt roads leading into town to give the band the *bat bravo* (applause) traditionally reserved for dignitaries and heads of state (Interview: Lalanne 1988). Nemours, like Jazz des Jeunes, also appeared on weekly radio shows beamed all over the island on Radio Haiti.[13]

Combo and vocal jazz

Combo jazz of the be-bop era never made significant inroads in Haiti, although there were a few trios and quartets in Port-au-Prince in the late 1950s and early 1960s involving musicians like guitarist Fritz "Toto" Duvalle, pianist Serge Simpson, and bassist George Neff (Interview: Pascal 1988). Vocalist and composer Herby Widmaier had a vocal group, the Starlettes, that was influenced by the pop-jazz vocal combos of the U.S. such as the Hi-Los and the Four Freshmen, although they too performed indigenous music within a modern harmonic style.

After a performance of the Starlettes at the Carrousel in early 1960, a polemic developed that was carried out in a series of editions of the daily "Le Nouvelliste"—a polemic that epitomized many of the issues of race and authenticity in music of the time. The critic Georges Fidélia (Fidélia 1960:2) accused Widmaier of neglecting to explain the bourgeois roots of "Haïti Chérie," which was on the program, and of singing in such a way that his sonority "*n'avait rien de terroire*" (lacked local flavor). He claimed that Widmaier misidentified Vodou songs and that his arrangements "emasculated the Haitian soul . . . under the pretext of modernism." Fidélia complained of the U.S. and Cuban influences in some songs:

> Herby offers us this American imitation of a Haitian melody which in itself is only an imitation of Afro-Cuban music, which is now an out-of-fashion genre even in its country of origin. It's for good reason that we complain of having received this . . . fourth hand. (Fidélia 1960:2, my translation)

Later, Fidélia summarized,

> Herby, in his new technique of harmonization, has the tendency to conserve only the melody whose insufficiency [in comparison to rhythm] has been recognized. Thus, we ask ourselves what remains of essence in the expression of the Haitian soul that won't be diluted in the universality of the too-academic inspiration of this young innovator . . . He thinks that it is important to help Haitian popular music to evolve. But he should worry about the capacity of the audience to follow him. (Fidélia 1960:3, my translation)

Each of Fidélia's remarks concerned authenticity in one way or another: Widmaier introduces foreign pieces, foreign harmonization, emasculates Haitian music, lacks local flavor, excuses bourgeois sentiments, etc. There was much of the revolutionary fervor of the early Duvalier period in Fidélia's stance. Both Fidélia and Widmaier, it should be pointed out, were concerned with authenticity in Haitian music. Widmaier's program for that night included "Haïti Chérie," "Papa Simbi," and "Papa Bon Dieu"—'nativistic' pieces by well-loved Haitian composers (Otello Bayard, Guy Durosier, Raoul Guillaume). Yet his epochalist treatment of these, combined with his light skin and bourgeois status were cause for suspicion and criticism in those years.

Yeye: Haitian rock

Haiti was not immune from the influence of rock and roll. Rock and roll was colonizing the world, and urban youth of the elite in Haiti picked up the torch with enthusiasm, forming groups generically called *yeye* with names like Les Copains (The Buddies), Les Jets, Les Mordues (The

226 : *Gage Averill*

Bitten), and Les As de Pétionville (The Aces of Pétionville). For a short
period, dress, band names, singing styles, and instrumentation were
being patterned on foreign cultural imports. This movement was an
example of a transplantation of an international youth pop culture into
Haiti. *Alamòd* (in fashion) music included the twist, gogo, Johnny Holla-
day (from France), Elvis Presley, the Beatles, and Chubby Checkers.
"Le Nouvelliste," the Port-au-Prince daily, chronicled the hundredth
anniversary party for Barbancourt Rum, at which a new Haitian twist
premiered: the "Barbancourt Twist." As for its reception:

> The enthusiastic clamor that saluted the Barbancourt Twist made the Rex
> Theatre tremble, the audience was literally transported. The ovation seemed
> like it would never finish . . . Twist and peppermint for the youth, *méringues*
> and *pachangas* for everybody. (Le Nouvelliste, April 12, 1962; my trans-
> lation)

In the years that followed, there was considerable pressure upon young
Haitian musicians of the early 1960s not to simply copy foreign styles
but to adapt them to Haitian circumstances, contexts, ideology. I have
already stated that the *yeye* movement, with its strong cosmopolitan component, was spearheaded by boys from the elite class. In 1963, relationships had deteriorated between the United States and Haiti over the
issue of whether Duvalier was going to surrender his office at the end
of his constitutional term. To the contrary, Duvalier orchestrated a campaign to have himself voted in as President for Life. As a result, bilateral
relations continued to deteriorate. Anti-Americanism and the aggressive
nationalism of the times contributed to the pressure for the young elite
groups to Haitianize their repertoire, to avoid becoming culturally dominated by *letranje*.

There was also a pressure to Haitianize from their immediate audience
and the contexts in which they played. The foreign music, which was
popular for listening, couldn't compete with Nemours' *konpa-dirèk* for
dance music. In order to play school graduation parties and like events,
these groups learned to translate the *konpa* favorites into a small rock
combo format by adding conga drums and a bell. The resulting formation and its repertoire was the germ of the ensemble that would soon
be called *mini-djaz*. The term '*mini-djaz*' is popularly attributed to radio
deejay Rico Jean-Baptiste who drew an analogy to the small imported
skirts that were just then becoming popular—mini-skirts. The *mini-djaz*
reproduced the American rock ensemble: rhythm and solo guitars, a
prominent drum battery, and often a solo saxophone.

The Ibo combo legacy

One of the first small ensembles to interpret the *konpa-dirèk* was a different kind of group than the *mini-djaz* that followed. This group grew out of an ensemble that was playing for the Ibo Lélé Hotel, but after a dispute with the hotel's owner about the group playing other venues, they struck out on their own and changed their name to Ibo Combo to evoke a Haitian image. With jazz-influenced musicians such as guitarist Tit Pascal, saxophonist Lionel Volel, drummer José Tavernier, and vocalist André Romain, the group integrated jazz, continental, and Brazilian influences into the music. Their repertoire ranged from *konpa* to jazz standards to bossa novas and slow *mereng*. Their album (Tam Tam ST–102) contained a bossa-nova version of an old *mereng*, a medley of a waltz and a *konpa-dirèk*, and a Haitian *cha-cha-cha*.

For many reasons (its jazz orientation, its parlor *mereng* tradition, its instrumentation), their project fell outside the *mini-djaz* tradition. Partly because of their upper-class image and sound, they never developed the public following of Shleu-Shleu, although they were popular with musicians and helped to introduce a taste for combo jazz and bossa nova sometimes emulated by some of the top *mini-djaz* like Les Difficiles, Les Corvington, and Tabou Combo as well as later groups such as Caribbean Sextet and Zeklè.

The class origins of mini-djaz

In 1965, the neighborhood *mini-djaz* called Shleu-Shleu formed under the direction of the Syrian Dada Jakaman. Their rapid ascent in popularity resulted in Shleu-Shleu becoming the prototype of the *mini-djaz* group that would dominate Haitian music for the next ten years (guitars, percussion, and one saxophone). The musicians were, for the most part, musically untrained, and many learned their instruments after they joined the groups. Some confess to having had no interest in music at all, learning to play only as a means to hang around with the band.

Audiences for the *mini-djaz* tended to reproduce the subtle distinctions in class and racial backgrounds of the performers. These differences were often a matter of neighborhood boundaries. Shleu-Shleu grew out of the middle-class neighborhood Bas-Peu-de-Choses in the capital but was promoted heavily in Pétionville by their mulatto manager, Dada Jakaman. Pétionville, an upper-class suburb of the capital, produced many of the leading groups of the period: Les Difficiles de Pétionville, Tabou Combo (formerly Los Incognitos de Pétionville), Frères Dejean de Pétionville, etc.

Fans of lower middle-class neighborhood groups like Les Loups Noirs from Port-au-Prince and Les Fantaisistes de Carrefour accused Shleu-Shleu and some of the Pétionville groups of elitism. Shleu-Shleu, for example, played regularly at the high-class restaurant Rond Point, for volleyball games at the Collège Saint-Pierre, and in the early days between Nemours' sets at Cabane Choucoune but seldom for the urban poor (Interview: Morisseau 1988). Shleu-Shleu alumnus Jean-Michel "Zouzoul" St. Victor recalled: "It's not exactly that you can call it an elite band, but we had a certain class. We tried to play better parties and find a public that's not going to fight." (Interview: St. Victor 1988)

Until the foreign music boom of the 1960s brought a slight veneer of respectability to the guitar and to guitar-based music, playing with guitars was considered a profession of drunkards and deviants. For the middle class, which has always had upper-class aspirations, the choice of a musical career was a conscious choice of social downward mobility. Even as this situation was changing, resistance on the part of the parents was strong:

> I have to tell you that in Haiti, being a musician was never something that families could accept socially; it was really bad. They thought that playing music meant there was no future for you, because they know that you're a drinker and a womanizer. The first day that my father heard I was playing music, the guy was mad, mad, mad. I can remember my father's words, "Why didn't you just tell me to buy you a conga instead of law books. Then I wouldn't have wasted my money and my time! (Interview: Tavernier 1988)

It might be imagined that in a country as poor as Haiti, the *mini-djaz* were the refuge of struggling lower-class youth with no options outside of music. To the contrary, these were almost all children of the middle-class (and some of the *boujwazi*) who were in school at the time, a luxury in Haiti, and thus slated for jobs as lawyers, doctors, engineers, and bureaucrats. The initial decision to play music was not a rejection of their professional careers but rather a recreational choice.

A few factors were to intervene that would result in many of these young future professionals casting their lot permanently with the *mini-djaz*. The first was the popularity of the *mini-djaz* and the expanding commercial potential of music such that by the early 1970s, an at-the-least meager existence as a band musician could be envisioned. A second factor was the diminishing opportunities for professionals. In the 1960s, as a result of economic decline, repression, and political cronyism, a generation of Haitian teachers, professionals, and civil servants left Haiti for work in Zaire and French-speaking Africa, in the U.S. and Canada, or with the U.N. Haitian schools continued to turn out well-educated

children of the middle and upper classes who had no future as professionals in Haiti. A third factor was the growth of the Haitian communities in the diaspora who were hungry for a taste of *mini-djaz*.

I end this study of class, race, and authenticity in Haitian music in
the period around 1970 because it is then that the migration of bands
to the diaspora and the opening up of foreign markets in the French
Antilles and France introduce powerful new variables into the system.

Conclusion

From revolutionary times onward, Haiti has been fiercely independent
and nationalistic with an understandably strong distaste for foreign intervention. It is the sense of shared history and the opposition of the
categories of *nèg/nwa* (Haitian) and *blan* (foreign, white) that reinforce
nationalism and patriotism that at times of crisis can draw Haitians together to *mete tèt ansanm* (cooperate).

Yet Haiti has always been a country at war with itself. Two broad
social groups (defined by racial and class distinctions) have struggled
against each other since the time of Dessalines and the revolution. In
this struggle, the concept of Haitianness has been redefined more narrowly. The doctrine of *négritude*, a serious political force after World War
II, has helped to marginalize the traditional ruling class of the country,
who were considered politically *and* culturally tainted by their relationship with *letranje*. The concept of authenticity became a weapon wielded
by the middle class in this struggle.

The development of a national popular dance music has taken place
within the framework of this conflict. The Vodou-jazz movement was
the manifestation in dance music of an ideology linked to the black middle class and their assertion of an African cultural heritage. The development of the ideology in the decades during and after the U.S. occupation
helped to pave the way for the political dominance of the class and for
the dictatorial rule of Dr. François Duvalier. It is one of the ironies of
Haitian musical history that the coming to power of his pro-middle-class
regime was accompanied by the eclipse in popularity of Vodou-jazz by
the imported 'apolitical' *konpa-dirèk*.

Under the dictatorship, *konpa-dirèk*, played at first by the Ensemble
Nemours Jean-Baptiste (and the Ensemble Weber Sicot) and later by
the *mini-djaz*, expressed central values of middle-class life in its social
organization and content (commercialism, competition, middle-class
composition, a generalized romantic patriotism in lyrics, etc.) but without the reference to *négritude*. Thus it represents the triumph of one
ideology (middle-class consumerism) over another (*négritude*) and may

230 : *Gage Averill*

speak to the ideological changes that a social group undergoes in its transition from opposition movement to the assumption of power as well as to the chilling effect of a totalizing dictatorship. Despite the triumph of the middle class in Haiti, serious class and color conflicts persist in politics as well as in music. To understand the choices made by musicians and by audiences that have affected the development of popular dance music in Haiti, one must continually reference this set of social antagonisms.

*This article is an expanded version of a paper read at a conference entitled "Race and Class in Latin American and Caribbean Popular Music" sponsored by the Latin American Studies Program at Cornell University. Parts of this article appear in the author's dissertation entitled "Haitian Dance Band Music: The Political Economy of Exuberance" (University of Washington, 1989). I want to thank the organizers of the conference, Debbi Pacini and Martha Carvalho. Many thanks are also due to my colleague Michael Largey and to my dissertation adviser Dr. Chris Waterman for their insights and suggestions. I also owe a great debt to the Mellon Fellowships in the Humanities, which has generously sponsored my research.
The following musicians and music industry personnel have provided invaluable consultations and assistance with this paper: Ralph Boncy, Bobby Denis, Wagner Lalanne, Nikol Levy, Robert Martino, Guesly "Ti-Gous" Morriseau, Alix "Tit" Pascal, Dadou Pasquet, Réginald Policard, René St. Aude, Jean-Michel "Zouzoul" St. Victor, Jean-Claude Verdier, José Tavernier, Herby Widmaier, and Mushi Widmaier.

Notes

1. In general in this paper, italicized [underlined] foreign terms reflect Creole vocabulary and spelling. In choosing to employ Creole spellings whenever possible, I am attempting to reproduce the language as spoken and to be consistent. In Haiti, of course, the use of French for formal discourse and written communication in urban areas is predominant. Some terms, which are restricted almost entirely to scholarly discourse, such as *indigénisme* or *négritude* are retained with their French spellings. Although French has long been the official language (a position now shared with Creole), the great majority of Haitians (80%) speaks only Haitian Creole.

2. For a more complete treatment of the role of class and race in Haiti, see Nicholls (1985) and Labelle (1978). In addition, Buchanan (1980)

provides an excellent analysis of how class and racial distinctions have become models for social organization of Haitians in the diaspora.

3. In addition to class differentia provided by my informants, I have relied heavily on the work of Labelle (1978), Buchanan (1980), Nicholls (1985), and Lundahl (1983) in compiling the terms listed and in assessing their interrelationships.

4. Despite the general classification of Haitians by race into *nwa* and *milat*, Haitians also maintain a very complex and more subtle classification system that relies on skin coloration, various facial features, hair texture, and finally social status to determine whether a person is a *grimò*, *grifon*, *marabou*, *brin*, etc. Nowhere is this better defined than in Labelle (1978) in which she systematically elicits racial classification terms from members of different classes in geographically bounded areas in Haiti.

5. This concept was developed in a discussion with folklorist Michael Largey on our way to a ceremony at a temple near Gonaïves, Haiti, and the *poto mitan* image was his. We were attempting to contrast Haitian attitudes toward his 'object of study' (*mizik savant*, art music) and mine (*mizik dansant*, popular dance music). The details took shape as I went back over numerous interviews and discussions with Haitians from the middle class and elite, many of whom admonished me to go further into the sources of Haitian culture than popular dance music, and effectively provided me with this map. Conversations like this often started out with something like "You know, you must get out into the countryside to see the truly Haitian music, the music of the people. This music (*konpa*) is Haitian, true, but it is very Westernized. You need to see the Vodou music, the *vaksin* of the peasants, the *tipik* music" (Interview: Herisse 1988).

6. For this reason, the *négritude* movement is basically synonymous with the *folklorique* movement and forms the background to Haitian *ethnologie*, which combines the study of archeology, cultural anthropology, sociology, psychology, and development studies (agriculture, etc.) into a study of the Haitian people.

7. Later, James Europe worked with Ford Dabney, a band leader who lived in Haiti for four years during the first decade of the century and who served as advisor to President Florvil Hyppolyte's Musique de Palais.

8. One of the best known *twoubadou* performers from the 1950s, Coupé Cloué, went on in the 1960s to create an individualistic style which he labeled *kribich* (crayfish) and later, after incorporating more components of the *konpa*, *konpa manmba* (peanut *konpa*). Both names were based on off-color word puns, demonstrating an earthiness that is common to the *twoubadou* tradition.

232 : *Gage Averill*

9. The art music community in Port-au-Prince and the corpus of works in Haitian style are the subject of a dissertation-in-progress by Michael Largey of Indiana University.
10. The word jazz has two meanings in Haiti. It may refer to the Afro-American music style, which I continue to spell as 'jazz,' or it may refer to a dance band, in which case I use the Creole spelling *djaz*.
11. The political use of the Dominican *merengue* under Trujillo is discussed in Brito Ureña's book *El Merengue y la Realidad Existencial del Hombre Dominicano*.
12. It has been suggested that the popularity of this chord progression in the Dominican Republic was due to the technical limitations of the early diatonic button accordions sold in the Dominican Republic during the latter part of the nineteenth century with their two-chord accompaniment buttons, featuring the dominant and tonic (Alberti 1974:88).
13. The segregated multi-class audience for *konpa* has changed little over the years. You can see a poster advertising Bossa Combo at Jambala (an elite club) for $15 next to a poster for the same band at Casino (a lower-class club) on the next night for $1.

References

Alberti, Luis
    1975   *De música y orquestas bailabes dominicanas, 1910–1959.* Santo Domingo: Editora Taller.

Anonymous
    1962   "En chantant le Barbancourt-twist." *Le Nouvelliste* (Port-au-Prince). April 12:3.

Beaudry, Nicole
    1983   "Le langage des tambours dans la cérémonie vaudou haïtienne." *Revue des musiques des universités canadiennes*, 4:125–140.

Boncy, Ralph et al
    1987   "Nouvelle musique haïtienne: de Nemours . . . à Beethova." *Conjonction, Révue Franco-Haïtienne*, 176:160–176.

Boisvert, Luc
  1978   "Ricardo Widmaier: pionnier de la radiodiffusion en
          Haïti." *Haiti-Observateur* (New York). 29 September–6
          October: 11–12.

Brito Ureña, Luis Manuel
  1987   *El Merengue y la Realidad Existencial del Hombre Dominicano.*
          Santo Domingo: Editora Universitaria.

Buchanan, Susan Huelsebus
  1980   *Scattered seeds: the meaning of the migration for Haitians in New
          York City* [Ph.D. Anthropology]. New York: Columbia
          University.

Canez, Valerio
  1942   "Notre folkore musical." *Haiti Journal*, 26 November:1,4.

Corvington, Georges
  1987   *Port-au-Prince au cours des ans: la capitale d'Haïti sous l'occu-
          pation, 1922–1934.* Port-au-Prince: Editions Henry Des-
          champs.

Diederich, Bernard and Al Burt
  1986   *Papa Doc and the Tonton Macoutes.* Port-au-Prince: Editions
          Henri Deschamps.

Dumervé, Constantin
  1962   "Batteries sonores." *Le Nouvelliste* (Port-au-Prince). August
          24:2, 4.

  1968   *Histoire de la musique en Haïti.* Port-au-Prince: Imprimerie
          des Antilles.

Fidélia, Georges
  1960   "Autour du Carrousel." *Le Nouvelliste* (Port-au-Prince).
          April 28:2–4.

Fouchard, Jean
  1988   *La méringue: danse nationale d'Haïti.* Port-au-Prince: Editions
          Henri Deschamps. (1973).

Geertz, Clifford
  1973   *The interpretation of cultures.* New York: Basic Books.

234 : *Gage Averill*

Herisse, Jean-Robert "Pòki"
    1988   Personal interview. Port-au-Prince, Haiti.

Herissé, Felix
    n.d.   "Les ensembles musicaux: Jazz." Unpublished manuscript
              in the collection of L'Ecole Ste. Trinité, Port-au-Prince.

l'Institut Musical d'Haïti "Fanfare Glorieuse Occide Jeanty"
    1958   *Chansons populaires composées en l'honneur du chef spirituel de
              la nation*. Port-au-Prince: Imprimerie Serge Bissainthe.

Joseph, Jean Yves "Fan Fan Ti Botte"
    1988   Personal interview. Brooklyn.

Labelle, Micheline
    1978   *Idéologie de couleur et classes sociales en Haïti*. Montreal: Uni-
              versity of Montreal.

Lalanne, Wagner
    1988   Personal interview. Miami.

Lundahl, Mats
    1983   *The Haitian economy: man, land, and markets*. New York:
              St. Martin's Press.

Nicholls, David
    1985   *Haiti in Caribbean context: ethnicity, economy, and revolt*. New
              York: St. Martin's Press.

Paquin, Lyonel
    1983   *The Haitians: class and color politics*. New York: Multi-type.

Pascal, Alix "Tit"
    1988   Personal interview. Manhattan.

Précil, Privat
    1986   "Charles Dessalines, cet inconnu." *Haiti-Observateur* (New
              York). 7–14 February:20.

Précil, Privat
    1987   "Interview avec Guyn Durosier." *Haiti-Observateur* (New
              York). 17–24 April:17–26.

Price-Mars, Jean
    1983   *So spoke the uncle* (Translation by Magdeline W. Shannon
            of *Ainsi parla l'oncle*, 1928). Washington: Three Continents
            Press.

Rodríguez, Demorizi
    1971   *Música y baile en Santo Domingo*. Santo Domingo: Librería
            Hispañola.

Saint-Aude, René
    1988   Personal interview. Brooklyn.

Saint-Cyr, Jean Franck
    1978   *La musique populaire haïtienne, son évolution au cours des années
            1947-1960* [Mémoire de license]. Faculté d'Ethnologie,
            l'Université de l'Etat d'Haïti.

Saint Victor, Jean-Michael "Zouzoul"
    1988   Personal interview. Queens.

Smith, C. C. and Gerard Tacite Lamothe
    1987   "Legends of Haitian music, part 1: Locking horns." *The
            Reggae and African Beat*, 5(2):14-18.

    1988   "Compas! Compas! Compas! Legends of Haitian music,
            part 2." *The Reggae and African Beat*, 7(2):30-37.

Southern, Eileen
    1983   *The music of black Americans*. New York: W. W. Norton
            & Co.

Tavernier, José
    1989   Personal interview. Miami.

Widmaier, Herby
    1988   Personal interview. Port-au-Prince.

Williams, Raymond
    1973   "Base and superstructure in Marxist cultural theory."
            New Left Review, 87:3-16.

[23]

You can't rid a song of its words: notes on the hegemony of lyrics in Russian rock songs

YNGVAR B. STEINHOLT

Abstract

From the mid-1980s, rock music emerged as the leading musical culture in the major cities of the Soviet Union. In writings and research on this 'Soundtrack of Perestroika', attention has been primarily paid to the words rather than the sounds. Russian rock critics and academics, as well as those who participate in Russian rock culture, persistently emphasise the literary qualities of Russian rock music and most still prefer to approach rock as a form of musical poetry – 'Rok poèziya'. This seems out of step with the growing emphasis on an interdisciplinary approach within popular music studies. The aim of this article is to investigate and discuss some of the core arguments that underpin notions of Russian rock music's literary qualities. This may help to uncover some specific national characteristics of rock in Russia, whilst at the same time questioning the need for, and value of, a literary approach to the study of Russian rock.

The rock of our fatherland is founded first and foremost on the Word, on the new verbal subculture. (Andrei Voznesenskiy, Troitskiy 1990A, p. 5)

Introduction

Over recent years, rock music has entered Russian academia. For many years, research on Russian rock music was dominated by Western scholars who regarded it as an exotic and intriguing cultural form. In the work of those scholars, Russian rock first and foremost served as a basis for more or less sophisticated socio-political analysis. Unfortunately, this body of work has done little more than add to already established, and sometimes quite dubious, Western conceptions of rock as a democratically minded counterculture that contributed to the fall of the Soviet Union. The new works on rock that are now published in Russia are therefore a welcome contribution to research in this field.

However, teething troubles are evident within this new body of work. Researchers at the Tver' university are pioneers of research on Russian rock but restrict themselves almost entirely to literary studies. Defining rock as poetry and defending it as a part of Russian literary 'high culture' has been their first priority. Although their fifth volume of articles on Russian rock, entitled *Vladimir Vysockiy i russkii rok* (2001), has started to bring in sociological considerations, lyrics are still its main focus and the music is not discussed by any of the contributors. To defend rock as a worthy cultural form by concentrating on its literary qualities is a strategy that goes back to the pre-Perestroika 1980s, when Zhitinskiy, a member of the Union of Writers, started writing apologies for rock. Russian rock criticism has largely shared these views and helped to enforce them. Thus, the tradition of approaching rock as a form of poetry holds a firm grip on research on rock even today, and it has unfortunately blocked the way for musicological and performance-related approaches.

In this article I wish to examine and discuss the views presented by Russian rock critics, examining and assessing the arguments that are used to defend their approach to rock. Hopefully this might add some nuances to our understanding of the role of lyrics in Russian rock and highlight the need for an interdisciplinary approach to the study of it.

Rock critics and the word

Russian rock critics and writers underline the central position and special qualities of Russian rock lyrics and their priority over the music. Some also emphasise how the themes and function of Russian rock lyrics have traditionally differed from those in Anglo-American rock. Yet surprisingly few of them explain what caused this preoccupation with poetry, and what the specific function and characteristics of Russian rock lyrics might be.

Moscovite critic Troitskiy (1987, p. 34) has devoted part of his chapter on his hometown band *Mashina vremeni* ('Time Machine') to a discussion of arguments for Russian rock's superior lyrical qualities and their origin in Russian culture. The subject of the rock lyric is also discussed extensively and from several different angles by Zhitinskiy (1990) in his articles on rock for the journal *Avrora* which contain the author's discussions about lyrics with musicians, critics and rock club officials. Zhitinskiy may have a limited knowledge of Anglo-American rock traditions and aesthetics, yet he gives a unique inside perspective on Russian rock as understood by a sympathetic minority within the Soviet cultural establishment of the early 1980s. Didurov (1994) writes from his own perspective as a rock poet, presenting his views on rock and poetry in order to explain his own artistic project. His observations thereby offer some valuable points of contrast to those made by the other writers. More popular works, like Zaicev et al. (1990), are generally sympathetic to Troitskiy's views, but their arguments are not as well developed.

In the following discussion, after a brief historical overview of the development of rock music in Russia, I shall follow Troitskiy's 1987 account paragraph by paragraph and discuss his key points in relation to other Russian writings on rock and interviews with Russian rock critics and musicians. I focus on Troitskiy because he is the most prominent rock critic and the only one to have published books in English. The impact of his writings on Western literature has therefore been the most significant. By bringing new examples of lyrics and interviews into the discussion I seek to contribute fresh perspectives to the understanding of the role of lyrics in the Russian rock song.

Rock's becoming Russian: from imitation to self-expression

Russian rock has evolved through much the same stages as those described by Gestur Gudmundson (1999) for Nordic rock music, only in Russia the process started later and met with more serious technical and socio-political obstacles.

You can't rid a song of its words   91

Figure 1. Early 80s Akvarium tea-break. Note the Rutles record in the foreground.

The first Russian rock bands were formed in the mid-1960s. They played mainly cover versions of songs by The Beatles on home-made equipment and sang in English as best they could. Bass guitars were made by stringing acoustic guitars with piano strings, and both bass and guitar were electrified using telephone mikes as pick-ups. Amplifiers were modified home stereo units or were created by students of electronic engineering. Bands performed in small cafés or at student evenings as literal 'Beatle jukeboxes', compensating for the painful scarcity of Beatles records.

Gradually the instruments and equipment improved, but knowledge of the English language did not and repertoires were soon felt to be too narrow, so bands began to write songs in their native tongue. This first learning phase ended at the beginning of the 1970s with the arrival of new musical styles, most notably hard rock. At the same time, the authorities started to crack down on amateur bands, breaking up concerts and confiscating equipment. To gain control over the growing rock scene, the authorities offered musicians the opportunity of joining so-called VIAs (Vocal–Instrumental Ensembles), which normally consisted of six to ten members and, in addition to electric guitar(s) and drum kit, sported horns, strings, balalaikas – and mandatory uniforms. In return for 'going official', musicians were offered a steady income, professional instruments and the possibility of touring and releasing records. However, although the number of underground amateur bands decreased considerably following this new policy, the authorities were unable to exert control over musicians' spare-time activities. Amateur rock thus lived on and new rock styles and genres were imitated and learned.

From the end of the 1970s the number of amateur bands started rising considerably, and with the opening of the Leningrad Rock Club (LRC) in 1981 they found a central base within the USSR's second largest city. The LRC came into being due to a gap in a constantly shifting and often contradictory cultural policy. Repeated initiatives from bands and concert organisers at last met with interest from the authorities who were sufficiently attracted by the opportunity to control and monitor unsanctioned cultural activity to offer them some resources and facilities. The opening of the LRC coincided with the emergence of a new, local rock style. Imitation of Western rock styles had been followed by an integration of rock music with Russian cultural tradition, and by a desire for self-expression on one's own terms. The first Russian rockers had graduated – Russian rock was born.

The rock form which first earned the name 'Russian' by no means reflects the whole history of Anglo-American rock. It consists of a limited number of bands and styles which set the trends for the 1980s. The leaders of this movement were influenced by the do-it-yourself ideals emerging with new wave and punk, but did not necessarily play those musical styles. In Russia, all known rock styles emerged over a relatively short period of time: blues and hard rock remained part of the expressional span, while punk rock had a remarkably limited influence. Punk rock was simply too much to handle for a rock club that led an insecure life under the scrutiny of the authorities, and unlike in Moscow, heavy metal met with little interest in Leningrad where the club was located.

The LRC became almost the sole refuge for rock under the repressive policies of the Andropov and Chernenko administrations. It therefore influenced the musical style that was to emerge with Perestroika and become known as *Russian rock*. (In the following discussion, italics will be used to distinguish Russian rock in general from *Russian rock* as a local style defined by local critics and writers.)

In 1985, 'rock laboratories' opened in Moscow and Sverdlovsk as a rehearsal and performance space. Shortly after that, rock was let loose on the public stage and it started to encounter commercial structures. The ensuing process of acclimatisation proved to be much more confusing, demanding and problematic than expected, but although Russian rock would never again be the same, it has remained true to some founding elements of its tradition, most notably those concerning the lyrics.

Finding a way in the taiga: defining styles, comparing traditions

Before I start discussing Troitskiy's observations on Russian rock, his use of the terms *Western rock* and *Russian rock* need to be defined. Throughout Troitskiy's work, *Western rock* appears to refer to the Anglo-American tradition broadly defined as *rock* with its entire range of different musical styles. In the following discussion I shall continue to use the term in this way and will avoid confusing it with Western rock forms that have specific national or non-Anglo-American characteristics.

When it comes to *Russian rock*, it is important to clarify what sort of rock music critics are talking about when they use this term. Among the bands and songwriters that Troitskiy finds it worth mentioning in his books, *Back in the USSR* and *Tusovka: Who's Who in the New Soviet Rock Culture* (1990), we find, as suspected, no punk or heavy metal bands. Officially approved VIA bands are almost entirely left out. With the exception of the rock band Mashina vremeni, which joined Goskoncert – the state concert agency – in the early 1980s, he concentrates on well-known LRC bands and Moscow rock laboratory bands. The Sverdlovsk scene, associated with Chai-f's Rolling Stones-oriented sound and Nautilius Pompilius' *New Romantic* pop-rock, is left out. So too is Revyakin's (aka 'The Siberian Jim Morrison') band Kalinov Most from Novosibirsk.

Is it, then, correct to call this selection *Russian rock* and compare it to *Western rock* as an entity? The term *Russian rock*, as a rule, describes amateur bands (professional would, in a Soviet context, mean *officially employed*) that were registered in official rock clubs and sang in Russian, and the new generations of bands that followed in their tradition. The definition of *Russian rock* should be kept as open as possible in order to reduce the danger of excluding important musical styles. However, as used by critics like Troitskiy, the term excludes the majority of Russia's VIAs and punk and metal bands.

The term *Western rock* should then refer to the specific Anglo-American traditions that *Russian rock* relates to. The music produced in the rock club environments of Leningrad and Moscow shows marked resemblances to the New York (NY) new wave scene of the mid to late 1970s and the British (UK) new wave, post punk and new pop scenes. These musical traditions or styles should not be distinguished too rigidly, however, because they are mixed together within *Russian rock*.

Troitskiy's discussion of *novaya volná*, a direct Russian translation of 'new wave' (1990A, p. 249–50), associates that style with generational conflict, and suggests that it attracted a new generation that had tired of what it regarded as old-fashioned rock styles and conventions. One is led to believe that this mirrors the opposition of Anglo-American new wave to prog(ressive) rock, but the generational conflict that Troitskiy has in mind is probably of a more local kind. From 1985, a new generation of bands emerged at the LRC, which by then had several older musicians in the ranks of its organisation. The latter had kept the club going through the rock repression years and had learned the value of compromise and caution. When the younger, provocative and outspoken new wave bands took to the stage, they felt muffled by their older colleagues who feared for the club's existence. (In fact, the LRC continued to censor rock music long after the KGB and the official establishment had turned their attention to more serious matters.) They included bands like Televizor and Alisa who were influenced by British trends such as gothic rock and electronic new pop, and they were referred to as the novaya volná.

The term novaya volná thus came to refer to both the Western term 'new wave' and its local variant. The first meaning of 'novaya volná' is represented on the 1982 cassette album *Taboo* which was independently released by the leading band of the LRC establishment, Akvarium (CD 1994), and on a live recording of that band made on 4 June of that same year (CD 1996). These recordings reveal that the band was quite familiar with new wave styles from New York and the UK which incorporated punk, reggae and ska elements. Punk rock was thus a formative influence on the emergence of new wave in Russia, but did not emerge as a style in its own right until later.[1] This is also evidenced in the 1982 concert recording by Akvarium and its crazed-out punk version of *Podmoskovnye vechera* ('Evenings outside Moscow') (*ibid.*).

Troitskiy's definition of novaya volná breaks with the Anglo-American new wave paradigm by including 'new pop' as well. This explains his description of Russian new wave thus: '. . . a maximum of attention to scenic form (like paying

Figure 2. Akvarium's BG at home.

attention to hairstyle, make-up and every possible visual accessory), a laconic and contemporary musical sound – all of which are dictated by the Western wave principles'. However, Russian followers did not always use the same hairstyles and make-up as their colleagues in Anglo-American new pop. Some of the make-up of members of the Russian new wave was reminiscent of the UK glam rock scene or even Genesis-style prog rock. For example, Akvarium's lead singer preferred an early 1970s Bowie look to the mascara and smeared lipstick of Robert Smith. The Anglo-American influences were perhaps more marked musically than visually.

Tver' and Russian rock critics have their own favourite rock poets, who they are reluctant to compare with Anglo-American styles or trends. They include, in particular, the late Aleksandr Bashlachev, whose music is seen as genuine, unspoiled Russian culture. They also include Boris Grebenshchikov of Akvarium, a band that engaged in wide-ranging stylistic experiments during the early 1980s, Yuriy Shevchuk from the rock band DDT, Viktor Coj from the band Kino, and Konstantin Kinchev from the band Alisa, the last two of whom are regarded as the poet representatives of *novaya volná*. In addition, Andrei Makarevich from the band Mashina vremeni will usually be included by fellow Muscovite critics of the older generation. 'Mike' Naumenko from the band Zoopark, whose R&B songs were sometimes direct translations of songs by Dylan or Bolan, is treated with more suspicion, although the re-writing of Western originals in Russian was quite common. Most of these 'rock poets' perform musical styles which to varying degrees resemble NY and UK new wave rock (as performed by the older LRC generation) and new pop (as performed by the younger LRC generation).

The question of authenticity demands some attention. In spite of all the above-mentioned similarities in attitude, sound and style between Russian and Anglo-American new wave rock, there is one fundamental difference: if NY/UK new wave is largely modernist or post-modernist, Russian new wave is more romantically oriented and promotes strong notions of authenticity. The following definitions of authenticity may help explain why:

Authenticity is what is left in popular music when you have subtracted the commercial aspect. The essential contradiction between commercialism and authenticity in rock expresses itself in the music, in its production and its reception. (Michelsen 1993, p. 59)

By claiming authenticity you insist that you are doing something 'that matters'. By avoiding the label of authenticity you are saying that it is not important whether you are doing anything that matters – but it can be important in another way. (Gudmundsson 1999, p. 57)

To LRC bands rock mattered. It was a lifestyle. And *Russian rock* had no commercial aspects to corrupt its sense of authenticity until the late 1980s, although the absence of marketing and commercial distribution networks did not prevent hundreds of thousands of copied tapes from circulating.[2] People knew not only the songs, but also the names of the bands and their songwriters, some of whom were launched to stardom 'in the red' well before commerce set in. Not until the early 1990s were commercial structures strong enough to pose a threat. In a recent interview I conducted in St. Petersburg with Mikhail Borzykin from the new wave band Televizor, he stressed that a big difference between Russian and Western rock in the 1980s was that in Russia, people still believed in the rock 'n' roll myth:

[. . .] we saw rock music as the only way to an inner freedom, a way of thinking that was long since dead and gone in the West. We took everything literally, legends and all. If a UK band messed up a hotel room for the press to produce a scandal they'd live neat and tidy ever after. Here it was done for real: TV sets from windows and all that. And Sid Vicious. Bottle-throwing and pogo bloodbaths were not constructed over here. It was all for real. Here legends were believed and the kids did what they could with vodka and beer. (Personal communication, 22 September 2001)

Role of lyrics – lyrics of spirituality

. . . the lyrics in Russian rock play a more important role than in Western rock. The reasons for this may be the Russian rockers' awareness that they're borrowing music invented elsewhere, their weaker technical virtuosity, and the fact that the commercial and dancing functions of rock never predominated here; more value was always placed on the ideas in a song. (. . .) the purely literary level of our rock lyrics is higher, on the average, than in the West. (Troitskiy 1987, p. 34)

If a comparison is made between the lyrics of *Russian rock* and Anglo-American new wave and new pop, Troitskiy's point about the former's superior literacy loses some of its strength. The limitations of his argument are evident in the above quote. Firstly, what he describes as Russian musicians' weaker technical virtuosity could instead, and this would be fairer to the many fine instrumentalists among them, be interpreted as a combination of the limitations of poor technical equipment and instruments with a preference for the post-punk aesthetics of minimalism and simplicity. The absence of commercialism also makes it more appropriate to compare the music with UK/NY new wave and post-punk rock, where musicians sought to retain wider artistic control of their work by signing to small independent record companies with alternative distribution networks.

Secondly, the fact that the music was not primarily made to be danced to is important. It should be emphasised, however, that this was partly because of the ban on dancing at concerts which prevailed until 1987. Police were normally present at gigs and festivals to ensure order and prevent audiences from acting 'in an uncivilised manner'. This contributed to giving the lyrics an all-important function in communicating with an audience prevented from responding physically and freely to the music. The physical ecstasy of musical empowerment at concerts was inhibited by restrictions, thus strengthening the importance placed on lyrics by Russian critics.

Informants involved with Russian rock music confirm that it was listened to with a special sensitivity for the lyrics, and that when musical qualities were sought, Anglo-American music was preferred. Some see this as historically determined, influenced by a traditional Russian way of thinking which suggests that Russian songs, from folk traditionals to rock songs, are to be listened to, not danced to. The story-telling mode of the folk classic *Chernyj voron* ('Black Raven') may serve as an example here, a song to be listened to and sung in cramped peasant cabins on long winter nights.

In addition, until the mid-1980s, rock hardly existed in the Soviet media. Information on rock music was unobtainable through all official channels. Therefore, the rock lyric became important also as a means for conveying information. According to music journalist and former member of the LRC Council, Andrei Burlaka:

[. . .] before rock music started sounding through the media, the song as a means of communication was crucial to songwriters and bands. Songs were their way of communicating their thoughts, values, tastes and ideas – what books, poets and musicians they admired and so on. There was a lot of information that they wanted to spread and it turned out such information was in great demand, too. (Personal communication, 24 October 2001)

Nevertheless, Troitskiy's claim that *Russian rock* lyrics generally play a 'more important role' than they do in Anglo-American rock music, and that Russian rockers attribute 'more value to the idea of a song', should be treated with caution. Firstly, an *idea in a song* cannot be restricted to its lyrics because the accompanying music should also be taken into account. Secondly, how does one measure the value of music, lyrics and performance to songwriters and their audiences? Nevertheless, although it might be incorrect to insist that lyrics are more important in Russian rock, it may be that their role does differ from that of lyrics in Western rock.

Several theorists, among them Simon Frith (1996, p. 158), have pointed out that in written poetry the printed word and its layout alone control the production of meaning, whereas a song lyric produces meaning through its interaction with voice, music, style and stage behaviour. In this interaction, the lyric may take on a leading or passive role. Ulf Lindberg (1995, p. 63) defines three main types of rock lyrics: *focused lyrics* are those that clearly dictate the meaning of the music; *musified* lyrics are those whose meaning is influenced by the music and the musical qualities of words and lines are as important as their lexical and grammatical meaning; *freely shaped lyrics* are those that contribute to musical emotion and are open to improvisation. This is not to say that lyrics cannot take on both a leading and passive role simultaneously, nor that a focused lyric alone controls the production of meaning. While musified and freely shaped lyrics can be described as characteristic of Anglo-American new wave and indie rock lyrics, *Russian rock* songs tend to favour focused lyrics.

It would hardly be just to claim that a focused lyric is more important or of a

Figure 3. Mashina Vremeni on the TV-show 'Muzykal 'nyi ring', 1986.

higher quality than a lyric playing a more passive role, in that it makes a musical piece more significant and richer in terms of ideas. The domination of focused lyrics within a particular musical tradition can only imply that lyrics play a *different* role within that tradition. Even the lyrics of Akvarium's Boris Grebenshchikov could be described as a combination of both musified and focused, a fact that by no means questions his position as one of the most celebrated Russian rock poets. That rock lyrics have a different, even greater significance to *Russian rock* songwriters and audiences can be agreed without relying upon notions of importance or quality.

From his post-Soviet position, Didurov explains in the following way why lyrics in *Russian rock* get so much attention:

Why, because today our history and the day of today were given back to us. And the word is just as important a part of culture as the living cell to the human organism. Like experience and memory of past generations are encoded in the human cell, a people's history lives in the word. Like a cell reacts instantly to changes in its environment and the organism it is part of, the word responds to changes in the life of a nation, to the cataclysms of its historical environment. (. . .) When the people wake up after the stagnation, it searches for and gives birth to ideas, fights for its rights, remembers that it is both a subject and an object of politics.

Then the word is filled with its hopes, dreams, sorrows, joys and fight, becomes their bearer, tool and weapon.

I am convinced that the way of our rock is special, in many ways original – it is the way of literature, sung in the style of rock, because, generally speaking, the word traditionally lies in the foundation of genuine Russian expression. (Didurov 1994, p. 19)

Apart from the consequences of the silence of the media on rock music during the Soviet-era, the answer to the question of what makes a *Russian rock* lyric more significant to a Russian listener may lie in different ideas about the functions of rock. Western observers with their minds set on concepts of counterculture, Perestroika and the 'democratisation process', have frequently described these functions as primarily socio-political. In my first thesis on the subject (Steinholt 1996), I too started out with this assumption only to discover that the Russian audience from the mid to late 1980s turned their backs on bands that promoted political slogans too openly. This led songwriters to look beyond the socio-political arena for inspiration. Didurov (1994) represents a more sophisticated argument than mere sloganism, yet most of his poet colleagues moved away from political involvement at an earlier stage.

A keyword here is *dukhovnost'* ('spirituality') and it stems from a Russian hippie understanding of rock. It is closely linked to the romantic notions of authenticity described earlier. In the words of Leningrad rock journalist Aleksandr Starcev: 'It seems to me rock is always an art form, and as such should not submit to the conjuncture of the moment, but deal with universal human values' (Zhitinskiy 1990, p. 318). Or, as Boris Grebenshchikov from the Leningrad band Akvarium (henceforth BG) puts it:

Speaking of rock 'n' roll it is impossible not to speak about religion. For this there is a very simple and very atheist reason. Religion is spiritual life and rock 'n' roll is spiritual life. Religion has been taken from us since childhood. Rock 'n' roll is to us the only form of spiritual life. (. . .) Rock 'n' roll leads to religion because religion can explain (. . .) this spiritual life, unlike rock 'n' roll, which in itself explains nothing. Religion is the explanation, rock 'n' roll is the force. (. . .)

We have been torn away from our roots (. . .) the powerful and eternally living folk tradition, as they love to say among us. When this contact was all broken, such a strong hunger came over us, such a thirst that set people howling like wolves. But instead of devouring each other they went back and started growing anew, using any means fit in order to find unity, find understanding and a feeling for one another, find rituals to help us grasp all this, find the feeling for nature. But rock 'n' roll, unlike genuine folk culture, is a very fast-moving thing. Rituals and traditions change every two weeks. Yet its foundation remains the same – a search for unity with God, with the world, with the universe . . . (*ibid.*, pp. 225–6)

Whether rock's function is seen as that of assisting a spiritual awakening for BG or a civic awakening for Didurov, the latter sums up the role of literature in its fulfilment: '(. . .) Russian aesthetic reasoning, Russian understanding of the world were fully realized in language, finding in it the only possible exit – the exit into literature' (Didurov 1994, p. 19).

Literary and musical tradition: from bards to 'bastards'

Rock lyrics here have a direct tie to our poetic tradition and reflect its lexical and stylistic heritage. That's probably explained by the fact that 'serious' academic poetry is really very popular in the USSR. Books of verse often become bestsellers, and the most popular poets – such as Voznesensky or Yevtushenko – sometimes read their works in sold out sport palaces,

You can't rid a song of its words   99

Figure 4. 'Minus 30': Akvarium frozen solid, but looking stylish.

just like rock stars. In the late fifties we already had a recognised school of bard performers, poet intellectuals who sang their verses and played an acoustic guitar accompaniment. (Troitskiy 1987, p. 34)

Historically, the Russian musical underground originates from the pre-revolutionary *gorodskoi romanz* ('city ballad') and *blatnaya pesnya* ('underworld song'). The *blatnaya pesnya* was an urban genre, which had no relation to politics or protest. It included variants of 'cruel song' with a sentimental plea for pity, and songs that revelled in the criminal or semi-criminal milieu. They all depicted a way of life that the Bolsheviks sought to eliminate or refused to recognise, as observed in Stites and van Geldern's *Mass Culture in the Soviet Union* (1995, p. 72). The camp songs, which emerged in the years after Stalin's death, represented a further development of the *blatnaya pesnya* paradigm and provided a setting for the post-war *bardovskaya pesnya* ('bard song'), which included songs written and performed by guitar-playing poets Galich, Okhudzhava and Vysotskiy, to mention but the most famous.

The urban genre *bardovskaya pesnya*, which is also known as *avtorskaya pesnya* ('author's song'), treated themes like religious faith or love for the Motherland in a natural and non-ideological way. Lyrical themes concerning the problems and worries of everyday life or the Russian Character were treated with rich humour or powerful satire. The close relations between the *bardovskaya pesnya* and the poetic tradition meant that the *bardy* were viewed more as lyricists than musicians. Troitskiy (1990A, p. 52) describes their lyrical and musical influence as no less important to Soviet rock than Afro-American influences were to American rock 'n' roll. This is not to say that Soviet Rock remained locked inside the paradigm of the *bardovskaya pesnya*, nor, as I will show below, that rock songwriters themselves necessarily embraced Troitskiy's view. Russian rock bands also utilised elements of the Soviet Avant-garde of the 1920s, the 1950s' mass poetry of the *Éstradniki* (see Troitskiy's reference to the poets Voznesenskiy and Yevtushenko in the above quote), and

Western- and jazz-inspired Soviet subcultures of the 1950s. They also gave more or less ironic renderings of classics from official mass culture.

The height of *bard rok*, which was a musical hybrid combining acoustic rock in the style of Bob Dylan with avtorskaya pesnya, coincided with the emergence of Anglo-American new wave rock. Rather than merely imitating this new Anglo-American style as before, Russian bands began to integrate it to a greater extent with Russian musical and lyrical styles, leaving out what they felt was irrelevant for their purposes. As the Norwegian sociologist Odd Are Berkaak has put it (1989), one doesn't inhabit each other's symbolic universes, but sees metaphorical possibilities in each other's ways of expression in relation to one's own local and contemporary demands of expression.

The rock critic Zhitinskiy (1990, pp. 191–6), curious about the extent of relations between rock and the *avtorskaya pesnya*, conducted short interviews with rock songwriters and representatives of other 'official' and 'unofficial' composers. This is what the rockers answered to the question, 'Has there in your opinion been mutual influences and synthesis between rock music and the avtorskaya pesnya?'. Andrei Makarevich from the rock band Mashina vremeni said that of course there had been: 'On the level of self-expression, rock and the avtorskaya pesnya are very close. Rock music *is* that avtorskaya pesnya, realised in another musical language. The very word *avtorskaya* describes both genres. With Boris Grebenschikov (BG), for instance, the two genres often interact. Obviously with us too'. Viktor Tsui from the band Kino said: 'With me they couldn't be different, because I am an author and I play only rock music'. 'Mike' Naumenko from the band Zoopark said: 'Mutual influence . . . Yes, on the level that practically all bands play and sing their own material and the author normally sings the song. Another question is that the lyrics are not always of the necessary quality, but in any case any attempt in this area may be welcomed. It has already been mentioned, but is well worth underlining once more, that however paradoxical it may sound, rock music is a *folk* music in the most positive sense of the word'. In an interview with *Urlayt*, an underground music paper, part-time solo performer Yuriy Naumov declared: 'I have been raised on Western rock, and when people say that Vysockiy was the first Russian rocker, they might be right, but with me it triggers a protest because my roots are not here. Music set me going, not words' (*ibid.*, p. 265).

These differences in opinion largely concern the definition of *avtorskaya pesnya*. The rockers are not prepared to see it as a genre term that belongs exclusively to the bard poets, but link it to their own work. They see rock as merely a different means of expressing similar thoughts and emotions. They thus distance their work from that of the bards. Furthermore, as Naumenko from the band Zoopark has observed, however influential the bard tradition has been, it cannot guarantee poetical mastery within Russian rock. The rock critic Aleksandr Starcev, reviewing a 1986 rock festival staged at Moscow's Rock Laboratory (*ibid.*, p. 246), complained about 'toothless lyrics' and 'anonymous band leaders'.

In overlooking the similarities between *Russian rock* and UK/NY new wave and post punk rock, Troitskiy gives the impression that *all* factors contributing to the tradition of rock poetry are somehow exclusively Russian in origin. It would perhaps be fairer if he also acknowledged the influence of literate Anglo-American songwriters apart from the obvious examples of The Beatles and The Rolling Stones.

There is little doubt that the songwriters of *Russian rock* are closely connected with the tradition of Russian poetry, whether sung or written (on the other hand,

Figure 5. 'Oh, they walk on the green light': BG on Nevskiy Prospekt 1981.

the music of Anglo-American rock musicians like David Bowie, Lou Reed, Patti Smith, David Byrne, Tom Verlaine, Ian Curtis, Mark E. Smith and Matt Johnson can also be connected with poetic traditions), but they do not make such a big effort to prove it. To them, rock music is a perfectly valuable tradition in its own right and being inspired by a literary tradition is not necessarily a ticket to membership in it. Russian bands have been working to develop rock in their native language. Compared to rock bands in other European countries they were late starters, but from the 1980s onwards they were slowly but surely making progress and were contributing a distinctly Russian rock dialect.

Russian rock of the late 1980s may have aspired to 'high' art traditions because it had not had time to mature into a full-grown movement that set its own standards and borrowed musical influences from wherever it saw fit. It was still constrained by the cultural establishment and struggled to prove itself worthy of inclusion within 'high' culture.

Different thematics: No sex, please – we're Russian?

our rockers don't sing about the same things as Western rockers do . . . In the entire enormous repertory of Time Machine there's not a single clear-cut love song, let alone one about sex. (Troitskiy 1987, p. 34)

It should come as no surprise that Mashina vremeni, the first widely known rock band to 'go official' in pre-Perestroika USSR, did not sing about love, sex or any subject that involved making reference to individuals. The band's endless lyrics about lanterns, candles and isles of hope bear witness to continual compromises with censors. Troitskiy would only need to turn to Mike Naumenko's band Zoopark to find lyrics portraying a landscape of depressed R&B eroticism. But, to be fair, Naumenko was an exception.

Sexual themes are surprisingly rare in *Russian rock* lyrics of the 1980s and when the lyrics do concern sex, they do so in a way that differs from Western rock lyrics. The music also covers a wide range of expression. It may be funny, absurd, euphoric, joyful, romantic, dreamy, sentimental, sorrowful, angry or dark and gloomy; however, it is very rarely sexy. Does this reflect a conscious decision made by the songwriters concerned, or does it indicate the more subconscious influence of Russian literary and cultural traditions, or is it a consequence of the censorship of rock by the Russian authorities during its formative years? The answer possibly lies in a combination of all three factors. Going back to the above-mentioned views of Didurov and BG on the functions of rock, sex appears to be a luxury topic in relation to the ambitious projects of the rock poets. *Russian rock* of the 1980s was more concerned with the academic than with the physical.

The reverse side of this, however, is that the theme of physical love was then left to the lyrical clichés of the *èstrada* ('pop mainstream'). This helped to reinforce the notion that the topic of sex lowered a song's lyrical value. What, then, has become of the heritage that represents the golden age of Russian literature and the fact that the topic of sexual desire concerned so much of the work of writers like Gogol, Dostoevskiy and Tolstoi? Fortunately, the ideals of critics and musicians do not always correspond, as illustrated by the lyrics cited below. The first two examples are songs by the Russian rock band Akvarium: 'Beregi svoi khoi' composed in 1982 and 'Ona mozhet dvigat'' composed in 1985. As a suitable Anglo-American contrast I have chosen to cite some of the lyrics from the song 'Princess of the Streets' by the Stranglers (1977). (I apologise for the fact that my rhymeless translations of Akvarium into English cannot adequately recreate the poetic feel of the songs.)

She's so wise
She's so sleek
She read all that matters, that much is clear
She goes hunting dressed in flowered silk
Watch your ('pride'). (Akvarium 1994, track 4)

She knows how to move
She knows how to move herself
To the full
She knows the trick to the full
Mama, what're we gonna do,
When she's moving herself. (Akvarium 1997, track 12)

She's the queen of the street
What a piece of meat (special treat)

She's real good-looking
She makes me sigh
Blue jeans and leather
Her heels are high. (Stranglers 1977, track 4)

The 'meat' and 'special treat' of the Stranglers are by no means the most provocative Western examples that I could have chosen, and yet the provocative lyrics of The Stranglers attracted a lot of publicity to the band and helped to boost the sale of their records. The hormone-loaded, misogynist, R&B theme of lost love and prevailing lust panted out by singer-guitarist Hugh Cornwell, stands in sharp contrast to the clear-voiced, innocent naïveté of BG from Akvarium, yet the Akvarium lyrics are about as sexually explicit as any recorded and distributed rock song would be allowed to be in pre-Perestroika Russia. In the first and third examples, the lyrics and the music closely complement each other. The overtly sexual lyrics of The Stranglers are accompanied by a heavier beat whilst the music of the Akvarium song is lighter, dizzier, happier. The first example is also accompanied by dirty, curvy guitar riffs, whilst the second example is accompanied by a bouncy boogie-woogie beat. BG's protagonists are not yet personally involved with the woman described in the lyrics, but if they consider making a move the warning rings out: 'Be careful!' / 'Oh, Mama!'.

Akvarium was allowed to perform the song 'Ona mozhet' on a Russian television show in 1986. After the mimed performance the studio audience was allowed to ask the band some questions and an elderly lady in the audience asked rather aggressively who the woman in the lyrics was – the one who knew how to move herself. BG replied dryly, 'Mother Earth', thus elegantly dismissing the question and de-eroticising the lyrics (Vasil'eva 1997, p. 42). In the first example from the song 'Beregi', BG has chosen to emphasise the slang term *khoi*, which in this context appears to connote *pride* or *integrity*. The word is distorted in some renditions of the song in order to highlight its resemblance to the term *khui* ('dick') and thus offer an alternative and more vulgar meaning. However, the lyrics were reputedly altered a great deal when the band performed the song at a private party or in someone's house.

The title of this song, 'Beregi svoi khoi', is taken from Akvarium's 1982 tape album entitled *Tabu*, and although sex before marriage was hardly a taboo in Soviet Russia, neither was it officially sanctioned. The album also contains a mellow reggae song about sitting on a rooftop smoking sensimilla weed, a Soviet taboo indeed. In general, however, rock songwriters were more concerned with humanist ideas. Rock, being a marginal underground movement under constant attack from the cultural authorities, did not need shock tactics like those adopted by The Stranglers which would prompt additional accusations of sexism or drug-abuse. Rock music in itself was provocative enough. Here, another reference can be made to Akvarium's live punk rendition of the popular song 'Podmoskovnye vechera' in 1982, when the woman in charge of the venue found the music an unbearable offence against decent taste and cut the power, thus implementing her own personal criteria for censorship.

To employ a term of Victor Turner's (1969), one main goal of rock is 'communitas', whereby the rock audience becomes united in opposition to society. According to Soviet ideology, societas and communitas play an equal part in the creation of Soviet Man and the creation of communitas was the job of The Party. Rock communitas, with its idealisation of individuality, was seen as a threat against the social order because it was beyond Party control. Rock music thus created a political panic in Russia. Had Russian rock utilised the array of shock effects associated with the UK/NY new wave rock tradition to the full, moral panic would have increased and rock repression might have escalated to a level that was too hard to live with. Consequently, shifting the focus away from rock 'n' roll vulgarity in order to draw attention to rock's more intellectual, high culture qualities was necessary for rock's creative survival.[3] This situation helps to explain the assimilation of musical elements related to the NY/UK new wave rock with the Russian underground tradition of musical poetry.

104   *Yngvar B. Steinholt*

Figure 6. Glam-session: 'Maik' Naumenko with Akvarium, late 70s.

Today, bands like DDT, Alisa and Akvarium, who now represent an older generation of Russian rock musicians, still stick to their ideals. The post-Soviet rock generation experiments more freely with music genres and lyrical themes. The lyrics may be sexy, fascist or anything the musicians want them to be. Today, Russian rock covers the same range of themes and styles as rock in any other non-English speaking European country and is thus free to call itself Russian. Since 1995 the trend has again shifted towards new Russian bands singing in English, but there is no reason to doubt that well-written lyrics in the mother tongue will continue to maintain a strong position in the Russian rock scene for many years to come.

Concluding remarks

The term *Russian rock* points to the emergence of a nationally specific musical style in Russia around 1980. Russian rock critics slightly differ in their opinions as to which bands and artists could be said to play *Russian rock*, but their candidates for this category share the following characteristics: they all sing in Russian; most have refused to compromise by pursuing an official, state-sponsored career; they are also conscious of their Russian roots and do not merely copy Anglo-American trends.

The critics referred to in this article have made no serious attempts to trace the musical, stylistic and lyrical influences of specific Anglo-American musical styles on Russian rock. Instead, they have tended to define Russian rock too narrowly and compared it with a notion of Western rock that is too broad and vague. They have also been eager to distinguish Russia's rock poets from Anglo-American rock styles and have consequently overlooked possible crossovers between the two. Nevertheless, it does seem appropriate to draw some comparisons between *Russian rock* and NY/UK new wave rock, new pop and post-punk. In fact, the Russian term 'novaya volná' (lit. *new wave*) covers the Anglo-American terms 'new wave' and 'new pop'.

Russian rock lyrics are claimed by these critics to be more important than Western ones, but this argument again rests on the wide definition of the Western rock tradition adopted by these critics, and also on their distinction between Russian ('superior') and Western ('inferior') lyrics. Arguably, it would be more appropriate to focus on the fact that Russian and Western rock lyrics are quite different and have different functions. Firstly, in *Russian rock* the tendency towards focused lyrics is stronger. Secondly, the ban on dancing at live concerts encouraged an intellectual rather than physical response to the music and helped to draw attention to the lyrics. Thirdly, because *Russian rock* did not get much media coverage, the lyrics had to play a more active part in conveying information from band to audience. Fourthly, rock's underground status and the absence of a commercial music industry until the end of the 1980s encouraged romantic notions of rock authenticity and the association of lyrics with religion, spirituality, civic awakening and with the Russian literary tradition. All of these factors drew the attention of *Russian rock* songwriters and listeners towards lyrics. In *Russian rock*, lyrics thus play a more active role, which is not to say that the lyrics in themselves are better or more important than, say, those of NY/UK new wave rock.

Russian rock can be regarded as the latest link in Russia's underground song tradition. The influence on *Russian rock* of the bard tradition (*avtorskaya pesnya*) is recognised to varying degrees and with varying degrees of enthusiasm by rock musicians. On the other hand, influences from Anglo-American songwriters working within similar musical styles are not considered seriously enough by Russian rock critics. During the 1980s, *Russian rock*'s literary aspirations were part of a strategy to legitimise rock as a worthy part of official culture alongside 'serious arts' and in contrast to the pop-music estrada. This is reflected in the themes of Russian rock lyrics. In the pre-Perestroika period, bands fought for rock to be recognised as a serious art form. Rockers were careful not to provoke and therefore minimised their use of shock tactics. One of the consequences of this was that sexual themes became devalued and were almost entirely left to the pop mainstream. This helped to give *Russian rock* a certain high-brow intellectual flavour.

During the early 1990s, some Russian rock songwriters felt obliged to reunite their audiences with Russian roots and cultural traditions, particularly at a time when people felt that Russian society was deteriorating rapidly, and to prove themselves as a positive, creative force. Rock therefore remained connected with spirituality or civic awakening, and sexuality and other more profane rock concerns became luxury topics (although they would soon return with a vengeance). Since 1995, 'rock poetry' has been marginalised by the commercial pop-rock mainstream and by the more profane lyrics of Russia's alternative rock scene, although good lyrical craftmanship is still highly valued by the latter.

As the study of Russian rock culture develops, Russian academics will have to begin to develop non-literary approaches to the subject. They will then be able to add a much-needed Russian perspective to the two-dimensional sociological picture that Western scholars have so far painted of rock in the Soviet era. They will also have to appreciate that only a closer examination of the music will enable a full understanding of the similarities and differences between Russian rock and *avtorskaya pesnya*. The cultural synthesis inherent in Russian rock can only be

Figure 7. Chief Russian rock-critic Artëm Troiskiy (left) and rock apologist Andrei Voznesenskiy.

described through an interdisciplinary approach. Following the Russian saying, you can't rid a song of its words, one might add 'neither should you ignore its music'.

Endnotes

1. Avtomaticheskie Udovletvoriteli from Leningrad appeared briefly in 1979, then reformed in late 1982. They are widely regarded as the first Russian punk band. Egor Letov's first punk band, Posev, appeared in 1983, made four tape albums and reformed the year after under the name of Grazhdanskaya Oborona. This band is still active.

2. This 'second economy' cannot be denied its part in music distribution, but its role was secondary, merely an odd form of music piracy. Home copying was by far the most common way of making the music heard. Bands sent master tapes to cities all over the USSR, where they were copied and redistributed locally. The very clear, up-front mix of the singers' voice in recordings of the early to mid-1980s was partly due to the expectation that these recordings would gradually decline in quality after a series of amateur re-tapings.

3. This also suggests that Russian rock played a rather ambiguous role, rather than an overtly countercultural and explicitly anti-Soviet one.

References

Aksyutina, O. 1999. *Pank-virus v Rossii* (Moscow)

Alekseev, A., Burlaka, A., and Sidorov, A. 1991. *Kto est' kto v sovetskom roke* (Moscow)

Baranovskaya, N. 1993. *Zvezdy rok'n'rolla 1: Konstantin Kinchev* (St. Petersburg)

Benson, M. 1987. 'The state of rock in Russia', *Rolling Stone*, 496, p. 20

Berkaak, O. 1989. *Erfaringer fra Risikosonen* (Oslo)

Cherednichenko, T. 1994. *Tipologiya sovetskoi massovoi kul'tury* (Moscow)

Cushman, T. 1995. *Notes from Underground: Rock Music Counterculture in Russia* (New York)

Didurov, A. 1994. *Soldaty russkogo roka* (Moscow)

Dobrotvorskaya, E. 1991. 'Soviet teens of the 1970s', *Journal of Popular Culture*, 26/3, pp. 145–50

Domanskiy, Y. et al. 2001. *Russkaya rok poèziya. tekst i kontekst 5: Vladimir Vysockiy i russkiy rok* (Tver')

Doronin, A., and Lisenkov, A. 1986. 'Chto proku ot roka', *Molodaya gvardiya*, 5, pp. 214–30

Frith, S. 1981. *Sound Effects: Youth, Leisure and the Politics of Rock'n'Roll* (London)
    1996. *Performing Rites* (London)

Frith, S., and Horne, H. 1987. *Art into Pop* (London)

Grebenshchikov, B. 1993. *Polnyj sbornik tekstov pesen Akvariuma i BG* (Moscow)

Gudmundson, G. 1999. 'To find your voice in a foreign language', *Young*, 7/2, pp. 43–61

Kuteynikova, N. 1993. *Bardovskaya pesnya* (Moscow)

Laing, D. 1985. *One Chord Wonders: Power and Meaning in Punk Rock* (Milton Keynes)

Lindberg, U. 1995. *Rockens text: ord, musik och mening* (Stockholm)

Lyrvall, B. 1987. 'Anteckningar från et källarhål: – Møten i Leningrads kulturella underjord', *Nordisk Østforum*, 3, pp. 23–40

Makarevich, A. 1994. *Vsë ochen' prosto* (Moscow)

Michelsen, M. 1993. *Autenticitetsbegrebets historie* (Copenhagen)

Orlova, I. 1991. 'Notes from the underground: The emergence of rock music culture', *Journal of Communication*, 41/2, pp. 66–71

Pilkington, H. 1994. *Russia's Youth and its Culture* (London)

Ramet, P. 1985. 'Rock counterculture in Eastern Europe and the Soviet Union', *Survey*, 29/2, pp. 149–71

Ramet, P., and Zamashchikov, S. 1990. 'The Soviet rock scene', *Journal of Popular Culture*, 24 (Summer), pp. 149–74

Rekshan, V. 1999. *Kaif vechnyi ili kak ya stal Ringo Starrom* (St. Petersburg)

Riordan, J. 1989. *Soviet Youth Culture* (London)

Rokotov, S. 1987. 'Govori! Illyustrirovannaya istoriya otechestvennoj rok-muzyki', *Yunost'*, 6, pp. 83–5; 7, pp. 8–9; 8, pp. 54–5

Romanov, A. 2001. *Istoriya Akvariuma. Kniga fleitista* (St. Petersburg)

Ryback, T. 1990. *Rock Around the Bloc* (Oxford)

Rybin, A., and Starcev, A. 2000. *Mike iz gruppy Zoopark* (Moscow)

Slavkin, V. *Pamyatnik neizvestnomu stilyage* (Moscow)

Smirnov, I. 1999. *Prekrasnyi diletant: Boris Grebenshchikov v noveishei istorii Rossii* (Moscow)

Steinholt, Y. 1996. *Saftutpresseren: Russisk rocktekst i polirisk brytningstid* (Tromsoe)
    2000. 'L'etrange destin russe du punk rock', *Paris-Moscou-Valdivostok*, 1/1, pp. 51–3

Stites, R. 1992. *Russian Popular Culture, Entertainment and Society since 1900* (Cambridge)

Stites, R., and von Geldern, J. 1995. *Mass Culture in Soviet Russia* (Bloomington)

Tolstyakov, G. 1985. 'Sowjetische Rockmusik in den 80er jahren', *Sowjetunion Heute*, 8, pp. 51–2

Troitskiy, A. 1987. *Back in the USSR: The True Story of Rock in Russia* (London)
    1990. *Tusovka: Who's Who in the New Soviet Rock Culture* (London)

Troitskiy, A. (ed.) 1990A. *Rok muzyka v SSSR* (Moscow)

Tsui, M., and Zhitinsky, A. (eds.) 1991 *Viktor Tsui: stikhi, dokumenty, vospominaniya* (St. Petersburg)

Turner, V. 1969. *The Ritual Process: Structure and Anti-structure* (Chicago)

Vasil'eva, N. 1997. *20 let s Akvariumom* (Tver')

Yoffe, M. 1991. *Russian Hippie Slang, Rock-n-roll Poetry and Stylistics: The Creativity of Soviet Youth Counterculture* (Ann Arbor, MI)

Zaicev, I. (ed.) 1990. *Soviet Rock* (Moscow)

Zhitinskiy, A. 1990. *Puteshchestvie rok-diletanta* (St. Petersburg)

108   *Yngvar B. Steinholt*

Discography

Akvarium, 'Beregi svoi khoi', *Tabu*. Triarii AM009, 1994

Akvarium, 'Podmoskovnye vechera', *Èlektroshok: Koncert v GlavAPU, 4 iyunya 1982 goda*. Otdelenie Vykhod B-025, 1997

Akvarium, 'Ona mozhet dvigat'', *Å 25*. Soyuz SZCD 0825–97, 1997

Stranglers, 'Princess of the Streets', *Rattus Norvegicus*. EMI CDP 7 46362 2, 1977

The rise and generic features of Shanghai popular songs in the 1930s and 1940s

SZU-WEI CHEN

Abstract

In the 1930s and 1940s, musicians and artists from different cultures and varied backgrounds joined and made the golden age of Shanghai popular songs which suggests the beginnings of Chinese popular music in modern times. The present article gives a historical description of the rise of Shanghai popular songs and examines their generic features according to Franco Fabbri's five groups of genre rules. Through gramophone recordings, radio broadcasts and films these musical products enjoyed great popularity despite severe criticisms from certain sectors of society. The diversity of musical elements, lyrical contents and forms of performance of these popular songs reflects a collective style of the participating artists and institutions and past audience tastes in a metropolis different from other major cities in the world at that time.

The legendary image

Shanghai, once a wonderland for adventurers and a paradise for gold diggers, has become again today the financial centre of China; it has been claimed that it will be one of the most important economic centres of the world in the twenty-first century. However it is described, the development of Shanghai in the first half of the twentieth century was the epitome of modern China. A considerable number of studies have been made of the growth, transition and boom of the city over the past decades. In addition, topics such as the people's livelihood, cultural interaction, foreign concessions and so on have been widely discussed. Despite this, the popular music that came into existence and developed in the first half of the last century in Shanghai remains largely unexplored. This article is derived from work-in-progress concerning a historical study of Shanghai popular songs which emerged in the early 1930s and is intended to give an account of the rise of these songs and to explore their generic features.

Since the British first moved in and began trade and investment in the middle of the nineteenth century, Shanghai developed steadily and later became so fascinating a metropolis that it attracted other Europeans as well as people from China's hinterland. Although originally Shanghai was only a trade centre, in the early 1930s people from different cultures and varied backgrounds came to live there and contributed to its development. The style of music that developed there was later to be known as Shanghai popular songs and was the origin of the modern Chinese popular music industry. Classically trained White Russian musicians fleeing the October Revolution, Filipino instrumentalists seeking a better living in other shores, Chinese composers, vocalists and artists with various performance skills, all contributed to make the golden age of popular music in Shanghai. Interestingly, this new repertoire was never sung in the Shanghai dialect but in Mandarin Chinese, and since this city was the place where the Chinese popular music industry first started, developed and thrived, they were called Shanghai popular songs. Nightclubs, restaurants and ballrooms, as well as live broadcasts to homes, were the venues for these songs, but we should also not forget the place they had in films. The close cooperation among those different groups of people and the vast and brilliant production they left behind suggest the beginnings of Chinese popular music in modern times.[1] However, few writings emphasise this important point. There is much to be researched about how varied cultural elements and social forces brought about the success of popular songs in Shanghai from the early 1930s to the 1960s.

The first Shanghai popular song, 'Drizzles' (*Maomao yü*), was a tune in a folk style with four verses using what was considered at the time to be overly familiar expressions of love (not customarily used in public) and was accompanied by a band playing Western instruments in a rudimentary form of New Orleans jazz. In a historical recording, this song was sung by a young girl with a high-pitched and untrained voice, sounding like 'a cat being strangled' and to most of us today, perhaps, unpleasantly harsh.[2] However, the commercial success of this combination encouraged its producer to write more pieces in the same format and thereafter involved more musicians and artists in the task. In the ensuing two decades, diverse musical elements were integrated into Shanghai popular songs, such as non-Chinese melodies, elegant, literary lyrics, as well as varied rhythms and a richer instrumentation.

People could now hear the blue notes of jazz and the Western scale interwoven with pentatonic strains and folk tunes. Refined phrases and poetic expressions of longing for a better life and the inclusion of incisive views towards social phenomena, together with romantic clichés in colloquial language, went to produce sophisticated lyrics. The arrangements were marked by the strong pulsation of tango, rumba and foxtrot and the string-dominated sounds of the Hollywood-Broadway tradition presented by a big band or by studio orchestras, as well as simple chordal harmony or regular beats delivered by a couple of Chinese fiddles and percussion. These Eastern and Western musical elements were fused in a harmonically balanced fashion, and so the classic *Haipai* ('Shanghai style') of Chinese popular music came into existence.[3]

As attractive as this music was, Shanghai popular songs declined after the advent of the Chinese Communist regime when most foreign organisations were forced to leave. With the whole entertainment industry moving to Hong Kong, Shanghai popular songs still continued to thrive for another ten years, but their style gradually changed to become practically unrecognisable by the end of the 1960s. Thanks to a small group of enthusiastic supporters in Hong Kong and Taiwan, together with those from the overseas Chinese communities in Southeast Asia, some elderly artists occasionally appear on stage and are still popular among audiences who feel nostalgic for the past. Shanghai popular songs are known in Hong Kong as *shidai qu* ('songs of the times') or in Taiwan as *guoyu laoge* ('Mandarin Chinese old songs') and are now usually heard in a small number of nostalgic radio or TV programmes and played on special occasions such as concerts, reunion events and festivals. The elegant lyrics and charming melodies still elicit admiration among many today.

In recent years some amateurs have set about collecting these now classical songs in the form of recordings and sheet music, while others are writing down life accounts of the artists. However, what seems to be lacking is both a study of how Western and Chinese musical elements mingled and created a new era in the history of Chinese music, and a full discussion of the interaction between the musical elements which made up the characteristic style of Shanghai popular songs.

How did it start?

With prosperity came the need for a variety of entertainment in which musical sounds played an important role. In the 1930s, Shanghai was a metropolis famous for its nightlife and cabarets which outnumbered those of any other city in China. There were American, Filipino, Russian, Indian and other Oriental bands playing American jazz, ballroom dance music or Chinese popular songs in different venues. There were the theme songs of Chinese films and the songs played during the intermission which not only captivated the audiences in the cinema but also often took the whole of Shanghai by storm and were sung in nightclubs and broadcast over the airwaves. Besides dance and cinema, people in Shanghai would attend regular concerts given by the Shanghai Municipal Council Symphony Orchestra, which was the first symphony orchestra started in East Asia. The programmes included European classical music and special performances for children held in theatres, together with outdoor orchestral concerts and brass band marches held in public parks. Those who preferred traditional Chinese music rather than a Western style performance might go to a Chinese theatre to listen to Peking opera or other regional opera styles, or might attend social occasions that favoured the instrumental repertoire.[4] Those with a penchant for political issues could go to the conventions called by the Nationalist Party (KMT) where newly composed songs based on the style of school songs were sung by the participants.[5] They could also join the rallies organised by the leftists and sing the mass songs heard in films or specially composed by leftist musicians and writers.[6]

Almost all the kinds of musical sounds in Shanghai described above could be heard even without being there in person. It was a period of explosive growth for Shanghai's wireless broadcasting industries in the early 1930s and about half of the radio stations of China were established in this metropolitan area.[7] Thus it was easy to pick up the swing of American jazz, the high-pitched tunes of Peking opera or the latest film theme songs by simply turning the knob of a radio. Another popular means to access those sounds was the gramophone record. The first record company in China, Pathé Orient, was established in 1908 with its first released recordings of Peking opera. After a series of mergers and acquisitions between those record companies which owned subsidiaries in China, there were three major record companies operating in Shanghai, which included two transnational capital-controlled companies, Pathé-EMI and RCA-Victor, and one Chinese-owned company, Great China. These majors recorded a wide range of Chinese operatic, folk and popular songs with their own contracted artists, studios and equipment and sold these records in China as well as promoted them to the overseas Chinese. In the meantime, a host of locally-owned *pibao gongsi* ('pocketbook company'), most of which specialised in traditional genres and catered to regional markets in different areas, negotiated recording contracts with local or regional musicians, and rented studios and manufacturing time from the majors to produce their records.[8]

Among these kinds of music that could be heard in Shanghai, two types of songs are worthy of attention: popular songs and leftist mass songs. Seemingly, they were both hybrid genres and composed with already existing musical materials that one could hear in Shanghai as early as the 1920s, such as American jazz, the latest dance music, traditional Chinese melodies and European folk songs. However, to Chinese listeners living in the 1930s, these songs were, on the one hand, brand-new because of the unprecedented pleasure they afforded and, on the other, controversial for their close relation with *genü* ('sing-song girls') and with political issues such as national identity, anti-feudalism and anti-imperialism.[9]

The creation of these popular songs could be traced to the early 1920s when a Chinese musician, Li Jinhui began to compose children's musicals and established the Bright Moon Ensemble to play his compositions as well as to produce gramophone records. Li devoted himself to creating works with a view to instilling the next generation with the spirit of humanist enlightenment, anti-feudalism and nationalism, as well as to promote the use of the official language, Mandarin Chinese. He began composing in 1921 when he was invited to teach in the Shanghai National Language Institute (*Shanghai guoyu zhuanxiu xuexiao*). He wrote several short musical dramas in standard Mandarin Chinese for the pupils of the primary school attached to this institute and organised a group in the school to perform these works. In 1923, he published the first of eleven children's musicals in instalments in a children's weekly magazine. With the enthusiasm and ambition to create a new approach to training youngsters in music and dance, in 1926 he established the China Song-and-Dance Institute (*Zhonghua gewu zhuanmen xuexiao*) but it was shut down after just one year due to lack of funds. Nevertheless, with the financial support of a friend, he set up another institution, the All Beauty Girls' School (*Meimei nüxiao*) in 1927 and continued his training programme.

In order to re-establish his former song-and-dance institute, he reorganised the school into the China Song-and-Dance Troupe (*Zhonghua gewutuan*) in 1928 and started to tour Southeast Asia to raise more funds. Unfortunately, the tour did not succeed financially. Thus, Li's music style changed in 1929 when he found himself stranded in Singapore due to financial difficulties following the overseas performances of his troupe. As he heard the news from Shanghai concerning the commercial success of the songbook containing several love songs he had written originally for the tour, he turned to the creation of love songs so that he could earn travelling fees to go back and raise capital for the institute. Finally he submitted a batch of love songs, including the famous 'The River of Peach Blossom' (*Taohua jiang*) and 'The Express Train' (*Tebie kuaiche*), to the same publisher and then returned to Shanghai. By then his feeling for children's musicals had gone, and sentimental affairs was his new subject matter.

From that time onwards, a large number of love songs were created using a variety of styles, including jazz, Hollywood film music or Chinese pentatonic scales, together with lyrics of classical Chinese love poems or romantic clichés of Tin Pan Alley, and thus began the era of Shanghai popular song. Besides love songs, Li also composed a few theme songs for Chinese sound films (a motion picture with synchronised sound). With the growth of the broadcasting industry, the availability of gramophone records and the popularity of sound films, these popular songs reached almost every cinema, store, street corner and home. Many outstanding female performers who graduated from the institutes created by Li or came from some of the troupes he had founded also had stage careers in broadcasting, recording and in films.

In the late 1930s, several members of Li's famous Bright Moon Song-and-Dance Troupe, established by Li when he returned to Shanghai in 1930, and several Chinese musicians also devoted themselves to the composition of popular songs. These composers included Xu Ruhui, Yan Hua (a member of Li's troupe), Li Jinguang (Li's younger brother and member of his troupe) and Chen Gexin (a conservatory-trained composer and lyricist).[10] It was Li who triggered the development of Shanghai popular songs, and his training institutes and song-and-dance troupes brought to prominence a host of stars who dominated the entertainment industry in Shanghai from the 1930s to 1940s.

Popular and successful as these songs were, they were inexorably criticised by the leftists and the Nationalists as 'decadent sounds' or 'yellow music'. Apart from the explosive growth of the entertainment industry, the 1930s also witnessed Western imperialism, a sequence of territorial encroachments and the military attacks of the Japanese in China. Since Shanghai popular songs were closely linked to the seamy *demimonde* and the capital-controlled commercial activities together with their glamorised female stars, they were regarded as poison to the Chinese people and 'a capitulation to commerce at the expense of the imperative of national salvation' (Jones 2001, p. 74).

A leftist young man, Nie Er, former student of Li Jinhui who studied music under the patronage of the Bright Moon Song-and-Dance Troupe, published a series of critical articles on the decadence of Li's popular music. He sought to create a new form of popular music that would stimulate and inspire the masses. Instead of the love poems and romantic clichés found in Li's popular songs, Nie Er tried to speak out on behalf of the masses in choral works based on didactical school songs, inspired by Soviet style mass music and military marches with lyrics dealing with themes derived from his first-hand experience of the lives of workers, farmers, exploited children and soldiers on the anti-Japan front.[11] He used to work in collaboration with other leftist musicians and writers, such as Ren Guang, Tian Han and An E, who produced films showing the hard living conditions of ordinary people and encouraging the masses to fight for the future of the nation. Nie's musical works were thus widely circulated through films and later made into gramophone records. Although these songs had a connection with the entertainment industry in the sense that they were disseminated through existing media, they were often distinguished from popular songs and referred to as mass songs due to the different message they were meant to deliver.

Therefore, the 1930s saw two types of songs which were created by the rearrangement of existing materials: popular songs and mass songs. Both reached people through the same technology and media of entertainment. The spirit of mass songs became the origin of Chinese communist revolutionary songs which played a leading role in Mainland China until the late 1970s, while popular songs, the subject of this article, however criticised, took Shanghai, or even the whole of China, by storm from the early 1930s and thrived in Hong Kong for another decade after 1949.

A neglected part of the modern history of Chinese popular music

Originating in the late 1920s and early 1930s and developing throughout the 1930s to 1940s as the product of the interaction between Chinese and Western musical elements, Chinese popular music and its producers in the Shanghai era are seldom mentioned in the modern history of Chinese music. Most documentation of and research into China's musical activities under Western influence through the first half of the twentieth century focus on the reformation of education, composition and performance led by the intellectuals and musicians within academies. While mass songs, art songs and choral works and their composers are viewed seriously and discussed in detail by academics, popular songs are mentioned casually or even omitted in most works about the modern history of Chinese music. In a textbook on the history of Chinese contemporary music, Li Jinhui's contribution to children's musicals is recognised (Wang 1994, pp. 87–92), but none of his musicals for song-and-dance troupes nor the popular songs composed later in his life are touched on. Except for Li, no other composers or artists involved in popular music are touched on. In another article about the development of Chinese music in the first half of the twentieth century, Wang mentions Li Jinhui as the pioneer of Chinese entertainment music, and considers that the works written by him and his contemporaries deeply influenced the popular song styles in Hong Kong and Taiwan later in the twentieth century (Wang 2001, p. 189).

Although popular songs are not usually taken seriously in the history of Chinese music, several enthusiasts have examined their origins and written down life stories of composers and artists and their representative works. Liu Xing (1988) traces the beginning of Chinese popular music back to Li's musicals before the coming of sound films and reviews the works of several composers and lyricists from then on to the late 1970s, including those active after 1949 in Hong Kong and Taiwan. Liu Gouwei (1996) also considers Li the father of Chinese popular song. Furthermore, he divides the development of Chinese popular songs into three stages, the eras of Shanghai, Hong Kong and Taiwan and analyses the dissemination of popular songs through radio broadcasts, sound films and television programmes. Kee-Chee Wong (2001) argues that the style of Shanghai popular songs, as well as of those songs produced later in Hong Kong, is unique and different from that of the Chinese songs written later in Taiwan. He also indicates that these 'authentic songs of the times' declined in popularity after the 1960s.

Besides these works, facts and figures about Chinese popular songs can also be found in the biographies and the memoirs of stars and in some compilations of articles which include anecdotes about historic events based upon the author's own recollections. In a collection of several articles originally written for newspapers, Shuijing (1985) discusses composers, lyricists and artists in the Shanghai era together with their styles, and recounts several interviews with some elderly directors and singers. Though without a systematic approach, he also talks about the lyrical content and the patterns of accompaniment, based on the lyrics and melodies he remembers.

Apart from the literature about the development of Shanghai popular songs, it is not until the pioneering work of Andrew F. Jones (2001) that the relation between popular songs and the formation of media culture in China in the 1930s is discussed. While conventional criticisms stress that 'the original innocence of Li Jinhui's early nationalistic efforts to promote children's education is besmirched by his later descent into the tawdry world of commercial media culture', (*ibid.*, p. 94), Jones recognises the fact that 'Li's contributions to Chinese media culture were just as complex and ambivalent as those of his leftist counterparts' (*ibid.*, p. 136) who were later enshrined as revolutionary heroes in the communist pantheon. Although derogated as decadent and pornographic music solely because of the form of performance in which the voices, images and personal lives of mass-mediated females were consumed, Jones believes that Li created a new musical idiom. It is, on the one hand, a renegotiation of jazz music in national terms without entirely dispensing with the pentatonic markers of Chinese national character and, on the other hand, a new culture formed within an emerging transnational economy of musical production and consumption.

Recently, the rapid growth of the economy in Shanghai reminds the Chinese people of the past days of prosperity in that metropolis. A series of reissues of Shanghai popular songs have drawn the attention of the public and mark a revival of and nostalgia for these songs. In Mainland China, two sets of cassettes – a two-cassette set in 1985 and then another four-cassette one in 1993 – have been issued by the state-run China Record Company. Once criticised as unhealthy, these songs are now considered the rich and colourful national heritage of popular music of earlier times by the Chinese authorities, although the songs reissued were selected carefully. Strong consciousness of regional identity in China may provide an explanation for these reissues. To people in Shanghai today, these popular songs can be taken both as a symbol of cultural independence and as a token of a rehabilitated past of this thriving commercial city (Stock 1995, p. 129).

In 1992 and the ensuing five years, EMI (Hong Kong) also released a series of audio CDs which collect a great number of historical recordings from those originally produced by Pathé-EMI in Shanghai before 1949 and those in Hong Kong after the record company moved there up to the late 1960s. Despite the original plan to issue one hundred volumes, this series has been stopped for commercial reasons after the fifty-ninth instalment was released. More compilations of historical recordings were produced subsequently by EMI (Malaysia) from 2000 onwards. A step farther in Southeast Asia, a Singaporean gramophone record collector, Leng-Kok Lee, has been trying to restore historical recordings and so far has published four audio CDs since 2000. Using an advanced audio restoration system, re-mastering the aged recordings and removing unwanted noise from old gramophone records, he makes it possible for us to experience the original aural effect. Though circulated mainly within a limited circle of supporters and fans, the reissue or restoration of historical recordings of Shanghai popular songs by Chinese people in different regions provides valuable source material for musicological analyses and further research.

Shanghai popular songs as a genre

Shanghai popular songs, from the 1930s to 1940s, include songs which had been deeply influenced by Western musical elements as well as those which were still composed and performed in traditional Chinese style. Listeners in Shanghai during this era might have encountered these pieces day and night in wireless broadcast programmes, in films, in cabarets, in the humming of people in the street or through gramophone record playing. Although today we would categorise music which is commercially promoted by mainstream record companies and consumed in great amounts by fans as 'popular', these songs were not referred to as 'popular' by people at that time. These songs were first referred to as 'new songs of the times' or 'contemporary songs' and these terms could be seen on copies of sheet music, the covers of songbooks or in contemporary entertainment magazines released in the 1930s. On the labels of some records we can also find words such as 'social' in English and '*shidai*' ('of the times') in Chinese (Wong 2001, pp. 12–13). Since jazz or other Western style bands were employed to accompany the singing and, in contrast with the traditional repertoire, these songs were new creations, terms such as 'jazz songs' or 'modern songs' were later on widely used. In the light of the usage of these terms, it appears that listeners, publishers and editors had somehow recognised and treated these songs as a specific category distinct from those they considered traditional or folk, such as operatic arias, ballads or short simple strains.

Even today, these songs, generally known as 'songs of the times' (rather than 'new' songs) or 'Mandarin Chinese old songs', are located in a distinct category. For example, in record shops, albums of Shanghai old songs are often shelved together; when young pop stars try to reinterpret Zhou Xuan's hits on TV, elderly fans usually criticise them severely for their inauthentic style and inappropriate accompaniment; when a radio programme plays 1960s Mandarin Chinese classics which were produced in Hong Kong, it is possible to recognise the taste of old Shanghai. We can then say that it is the style and form in which these songs were performed that made them unique and thus easily differentiated from the Chinese popular music prevailing nowadays.

How can listeners today and those who lived in Shanghai at the time tell these songs from other concurrently existing repertoires? What is the uniqueness of Chinese popular music in the Shanghai era and how can these songs be regarded as a specific category of music by the Chinese? To explore the characteristics of this repertoire, I apply the concept of musical genre to Shanghai popular songs. Genre categories are nowadays widely used as a way of organising the music making, selling and consuming processes (Frith 1996, p. 95). In line with these preset categories, all the participants in the music market – performers, producers, shopkeepers, consumers or critics – have an idea in mind of the aural and visual effects they should expect when coming across certain categories of music. At the same time, genre can also be an elusive term, neither a textual essence nor a comprehensive code, because no text will have all the traits of the genre to which it belongs nor are particular texts precisely identical to the categories in which they are included (Toynbee 2000, p. 103). Even so, as the formation of a genre is based upon a set of accepted rules that qualify the authenticity of the musical events making up that genre, it is useful to examine systematically what general features Shanghai popular songs have according to Franco Fabbri's five groups of genre rules.[12]

1. *Formal and technical rules.*   The first group contains rules of musical form and playing conventions, the rules most discussed in musicological literature dealing with genres. From the melodic and harmonic point of view, traditional Chinese music is based mainly on pentatonic scales together with some so-called 'altered notes' out of the pentatonic scale and thus has a distinctive identity. Moreover, in Chinese thinking, a pentatonic scale is already a representation of harmony (Karolyi 1998, p. 153) and therefore, to Western ears, traditional Chinese music lacks complex harmonies and is always played in unison. Some Shanghai popular songs sound quite traditional because their melodies are inspired by or extracted from folk tunes or story-telling ballads. For example, Zhou Xuan's 'The Wandering Songstress' (*Tianya genü*) is derived from *tanci* (a traditional story-telling performance originating in Suzhou) and 'Betel Nut Picking' (*Cai binglang*) is adapted from a folk song of Hunan. However, more Western elements can be observed in other newly composed works. In addition to traditional scales and melody contours, there is frequent use of chromaticisms, the blue notes of American jazz, and the application of Western compositional techniques such as recurring motifs, augmentations and modulations from the tonic key of a song to its relative minor or major. Gong Qiuxia's 'Roses Blooming Everywhere' (*Qiangwei chuchu kai*) is a good case where the first section is in the major pentatonic scale without any altered notes, but it then modulates into its relative minor in the second

section featuring the raised leading tone. It can also be noticed that melodies or cadences are arranged in accordance with the progressions of European harmony, and instrumental introductions and intermezzi are played in part harmony.

From the rhythmic point of view, though both Chinese folk songs and Shanghai popular songs are usually in 2/4 or 4/4 metre, with the accent on odd-numbered beats, there are several popular songs composed in 3/4 metre and performed in the form of a waltz, but few in the 6/8 time of European folk dance. Some songs were originally written in syncopated rhythms with a flavour of American jazz, whereas others remained plain in rhythm, close to the style of Chinese folk songs. Due to their relationship with ballroom dance culture in Shanghai, more rhythmic variations can be heard in the musical accompaniments of these popular songs than in folk music. Since these songs were arranged to be danced, they often took the form of modern dance numbers which prevailed in dance halls or cabarets at that time, such as tango, rumba, waltz and foxtrot. For example, Bai Guang's 'Lingering Dreams' (*Hunying jiumeng*) and Zhou Xuan's 'Recalling My Husband' (*Yi liangren*) are famous tangos; in Bai Guang's 'Autumn Night' (*Qiuye*) and Ouyang Feiying's 'Shangri-La' (*Xianggelila*) we can hear the rhythm of rumba. As for waltz, while Bai Hong's 'Dance of Spring' (*Chun zhi wuqu*) is a Viennese waltz, Zhou Xuan's 'Good Night' (*Wanan qu*) is a slow one. The well-known piece 'Rose, Rose, I Love You' (*Meigui meigui wo ai ni*) sung by Yao Li is arranged as a foxtrot.[13] There are also a great number of rhythmic patterns in traditional Chinese music, but they belong solely to the performance of percussion instruments and have little to do with melodies or dance steps.

It goes without saying that traditional Chinese music or folk songs are performed with or accompanied by traditional instruments, but these instruments are also used in Shanghai popular songs to give them a traditional flavour. A typical combination of Chinese instruments, widely used in the accompaniment of ballad singing or Peking opera, contains a *huqin* (a two-string bowed instrument), a *sanxian* (a three-string plucked instrument) and a drummer's kit consisting of a pair of clappers and a drum. When accompanying a song, the instrumental line usually follows the vocal line in unison with some ornamental variation and fill-in melodies between vocal phrases. Zhou Xuan's 'The Wandering Songstress' and Wu Yingyin's 'Spring Sadness' (*Duanchang hong*) are examples representative of this combination and accompanying style. However, the use of Western instruments in varied combinations is one of the most fascinating features in most Shanghai popular songs. Among a wide range of combinations, some are small groups similar to those of the bands in New Orleans jazz, using a 'front-line' of melodic instruments, such as a trumpet, a clarinet or a violin which might play a fill-in solo phrase, and other 'rhythmic-harmonic backing' instruments, such as a piano, string bass and drums. The earliest Shanghai popular song, 'Drizzles' (*Maomaoyu*), and two late-1930s works, Yao Li's 'Lovesickness for Sale' (*Mai xiangsi*) and Zhang Fan's 'Party Time' (*Manchang fei*), for instance, are accompanied by bands of this sort. There were also larger bands which were comparable to chamber orchestras, such as those string-dominated studio orchestras in Hollywood and Broadway or the big bands of the swing era with expanded brass, reed and rhythm sections. The lush arrangements and sonorous sounds of such an array of instruments can be heard in, to give a few examples, Li Xianlan's 'Evening Fragrance' (*Yelaixiang*), Bai Hong's 'Goodbye Shasha' (*Shasha zaihui ba*) and Ouyang Feiying's 'Misty Rain' (*Yu mengmeng*).

As for the technical capacity of instrumentalists playing in the bands for Shanghai popular songs, it is believed that they had to follow music scores orchestrated by the arrangers when accompanying a singer, but it is not clear if they were expected to improvise as American jazz players did in the fill-in instrumental solo phrases. It is also known that White Russian classical musicians and Philippine instrumentalists were both notable and competent at jazz or Euro-American style music in recording sessions or nightclubs or cabarets, but little is known about Chinese instrumentalists. A famous elderly lyricist, Chen Dieyi, remembers that there was no formal or in-house traditional Chinese musical band, or not so famous as to be remembered, and anyone who played *huqin* might be hired to form a pickup band (Shuijing 1985, pp. 166–7). Perhaps it required more members and close collaboration among them to set up a Western musical band, but two or three players were enough to accompany the singing with Chinese instruments, and it was thus not necessary for record companies to maintain large traditional Chinese bands.

From the vocal point of view, because the singers in the Shanghai era came from different backgrounds, two major singing styles existed at the same time in Shanghai popular songs. Some vocalists were naturally talented and learned to sing by themselves, such as Yao Li and Wu Yingyin; some were trained in song-and-dance troupes, such as Bai Hong, Zhou Xuan and Gong Qiuxia; and others, such as Ouyang Feiying, Qu Yunyun and Li Xianglan, received formal musical training from private tutors.[14] Generally speaking, the nasal, high-pitched voice and the melismatic phrases used in traditional operas or folk songs can be heard in most historical recordings of Shanghai popular songs, while a deeper, more open-throated singing approach or a style like European *bel canto* or *coloratura* soprano, can also be found on several gramophone records. However, some singers changed the manner in which they sang several years after their first appearance as their voices became more mature or they tried to interpret songs in a different way. For example, compared to the immature and strident voice in 'Lovesickness for Sale' released in 1937, Yao Li had developed a warm, rich and elegant style in 'A Broken Heart' (*Yike poxin*), recorded in 1948. While Bai Hong interpreted 'Crazy Musical Band' (*Fengkuang yuedui*) in a traditional Chinese approach, she imitated a *coloratura* soprano style in 'Enchanting Lipstick' (*Zuiren de kouhong*).

More interestingly, in traditional Chinese operas or folk songs, both genders participate in singing, but most of the historical recordings of Shanghai popular songs were sung by female performers. Male performers often served as characters who were secondary in importance to the main female role in duets and choruses, or as vocalists for backing harmonies. Though some male singers also made their own recordings, such as Yao Min, Yan Hua and classically trained Sheng Jialun and Huang Feiran, overall, they left behind considerably fewer works than their female counterparts.

As with the singing style, when looking at the rules governing lyrics we find that there is more than one lyrical form in these popular songs, including classical Chinese texts, refined literary language and vernacular expressions. The language style of a song depends on its lyricist. As the lyricists of popular songs in the Shanghai era usually came from the ranks of scholars, writers (Fan Yanqiao), film directors (Hu Xinling, Wu Cun) and journalists (Chen Dieyi), and most of them were well educated and open to the new culture or brought up with training in classical literature, it is explicable that such different uses of language should have existed. In general, the lyrics of most songs draw on the vernacular idioms and phrases originating from classical works or words only used in writing, and thus the free-form composition of lyrics is similar to what was then called the 'new poems'.[15] A number of them are written in a more literary way with classical words and regular metre, while at the other end of the spectrum some are totally colloquial. The lyrics of Zhou Xuan's film song 'The Little Nuptial Chamber' (*Xiaoxiao dongfang*) were written in a classical poetic form by the director, with eight lines in total and seven words in each line, whereas those of Qu yunyun's 'Young Lady on a Pedicab' (*Sanlunche shang de xiaojie*) were in plain vernacular without any classical idioms or refined words. Interestingly enough, in whatever language a song may be couched, it is possible to find in its lyrics intimate expressions that may be frowned upon if uttered in public.[16]

To sum up, from the point of view of the overall form, Shanghai popular songs mainly use the pentatonic scale with variations based on Western compositional techniques, are mostly sung by female singers in nasal, high-pitched voices, and accompanied by bands featuring Western instruments and arrangements in European-American style. It was a new sound for the audience at that time, and for us today constitutes a particular performance style. However, there were also pieces composed in traditional scales, performed in the style of story-telling ballads and accompanied by Chinese instruments.

2. *Semiotic rules.* The second group of rules refer to the ways in which the meaning of a song is conveyed. To us today, in discussing Chinese popular music of the Shanghai era, these popular songs can be regarded as a musical product which emerged in a particular social context when traditional Chinese culture met Western entertainment, while to those living in the 1930s to 1940s in Shanghai or other areas in China, these modern songs portrayed an imaginary world beyond the hard reality of the country at the time – the encroachment of the Japanese and Western imperialists.

From the point of view of textual strategy, though the true intention of the composers, lyricists or performers of these Shanghai popular songs is not clear, what we can see in these texts is not only fantasy but a representation of the real world in which listeners at the time could find themselves. Songs are meant to express sentiments that can be perceived as the listeners' own feelings, describe events that can take place in the listeners' everyday lives, and draw pictures of a wonderland that listeners might yearn for. For example, the lyrics of Zhou Xuan's 'Recalling My Husband' read:

My husband (*liangren*, literally 'good man') is on the way to the long march
My husband is at the vanguard on the main road
May spring wind send my regards
May spring wind bring him endless happiness

The 'good man' could be any Chinese woman's husband at the front of the Sino-Japanese war and these words could represent the heartfelt wishes of any Chinese soldier's wife.

A close look at various themes in the lyrical content will show that, for a wide range of listeners, the principal communicative purpose of Shanghai popular songs is an emotional one. Sentimental affairs and topics stressing the pleasure of the moment are common subjects in most songs, although the lyrical contents of Shanghai popular songs cover a broad range of issues. Generally, we can see several typical events, such as the dialogue or monologue of courtship, conjugal bliss, the pang of pain of separated young couples, the sorrow of unrequited love or lovesickness, and the desire for affection in this transitory life. In addition to romantic love between couples, there are songs dealing with family or filial love, including subjects such as gratitude for parental love, family reunion, and nostalgia for the homeland during endless wanderings. Compared to romantic love songs, these are usually direct descriptions of events without too many metaphors or double meanings.

Apart from sentiments, ordinary people's livelihood is another theme in popular songs. In some lyrics we may find portrayals of farmers' work, young girls picking tea leaves, people preparing for a wedding, a description of a fishermen's typical day or the beauty and plenty of the land. We may also come across accounts of a broken homeland, of people starving and drifting aimlessly, of homelessness and of dreams of paradise while living in misery. We find incisive views on social phenomena, such as criticism of reckless youth squandering a fortune, the seamy side of the city's nightlife or social inequality. In contrast to these songs full of grumbling and discontent, those calling for the salvation of the nation or service to the society are more positive and constructive. Good examples of this are songs about the coming of spring or of the Chinese New Year with expectations of riches and a better life.

Whether these events are described directly in plain words or with metaphors, the lyrics are often filled with colourful descriptions of natural scenery, as can be seen in many vernacular and literary works. These images may be taken merely as part of the story, serving as a backdrop to create an atmosphere, but sometimes they may be used to suggest something else through their metaphoric meanings conventionally perceived in Chinese society. The name of the seasons, wild life, the weather, celestial bodies and the landscape appear again and again. Spring is frequently used to suggest the revival of nature and the experience of romantic love. Some songs praise the bounty of spring and encourage people to cherish it and work enthusiastically, while others appeal to couples in love. Autumn and winter are usually taken as symbols of depression, solitude and hardship.

Wildlife, such as birds, butterflies, fish and flowers are widely used in songs, and each of them has its traditional meaning in Chinese society. Mandarin ducks, swallows, butterflies in couples or a pair of phoenix usually symbolise conjugal bliss; a swallow departing South or a nightingale calling at night can be associated with unrequited love and lovesickness; fish swimming in water implies the joy of intercourse. The bird metaphor is equivocal and may be contradictory in different contexts. For example, a flock of swallows or orioles are sometimes regarded as a scene of prosperity and sometimes perceived as a horde of women, even, derogatorily, as flirtatious women. As for plants, the peach flower is customarily synonymous with women, but 'peaches and plums' refer to students, especially those who have graduated; a willow by the riverside is a poetic image, but 'flower and willow' is a euphemistic expression for indiscreet behaviour and promiscuity. Roses, though rare in traditional Chinese literature, are common in popular songs and can be interpreted as the female protagonist in the love narrative or as romantic love itself.

Wind, rain, cloud and fog are common metaphoric images for obstructions and gloom, but they may connote differently in works of literature and in popular songs alike. A spring breeze can be interpreted as a touch of freshness in the air and announces the advent of prosperity, but it can also be seen as the stirrings of love. A girl waiting for a spring breeze suggests her longing for love. 'Rain and cloud' are associated with sex, and raining with man's ejaculation. Sun, moon and stars, and land features such as rivers, lakes and hills, are normally used in a straightforward way as backdrops for the narrative. However, 'blue sky and bright sun' and 'red sun' might be politically associated with the Nationalist and the Communist parties, respectively, due to the colour and design of the flags of the two parties.

Since Shanghai popular songs were often played in dance halls and served as dance music no matter for what purpose or in what context they were created, questions are raised as to the meaning of these songs to the hostesses and their clientele in Shanghai. What was conveyed to these people beyond the rhythmic pulses accompanying dance steps? How did people feel about the sentiments, events and images pictured in these songs? For example, Bai Hong's 'No Rain, No Red Flowers' (*Yu busa hua hua buhong*) reads:

You are a dragon in the sky
I am a bunch of flowers on earth
If the dragon does not turn his body over, there is no rain
If rainwater does not sprinkle over the flowers, the flowers do not turn red

In contrast to its monstrous image of something formidable or baneful to Western people, the dragon in Chinese society is conventionally a symbol of the male, of the monarch, and hence of power and wealth. Besides, according to Chinese myths, 'the Dragon King of East Sea' (*donghai longwang*) is the deity in charge of rainfall, and it depends on his mood as to whether there is enough rain for plants to thrive on earth. The allusion presented in the words of this song may, on the one hand, create a picture of how a vulnerable girl needs a powerful man's careful attention, but on the other hand imply sexual intercourse in line with the aforementioned raining as a sign of ejaculation. However, except for these inferences from the usage of metaphor, there is no further proof of how these words might be perceived by a man and the taxi dancer in his arms at a cabaret in Shanghai.[17] It is thus not clear whether the connotative messages conveyed by the songwriter were received by the listeners.

As for the relationship between performers and audience, because not everyone in Shanghai at that time could afford to attend a live performance in the cabaret or to dance with the accompaniment of a band and singers in a dance hall, Shanghai popular songs spread to ordinary people mainly through radio broadcast programmes and gramophone records. Thus most of the audience received these popular songs as disembodied sound, as mediated through records, radio and films rather than as a face-to-face musical experience. The most common approach through which the unseen singers could come to the gaze of their fans was via printed materials, such as copies of sheet music, gossip tabloids and celebrity pictorials where their portrayals or photographs were shown. Another economical and popular way to access these songs and singers was by going to the cinema, where people were able to enjoy the latest songs through high-quality speakers, while at the same time they could watch the look and demeanour of their favourite artists on the screen. Some cinemagoers even went to watch the same film several times because they were fascinated by the songs and wanted to listen to them again (Wong 2001, p. 19). As a result, although some songs were exclusively written for the screen, with their lyrical contents adapted to the narrative and the musical settings arranged in harmony with the plot, other songs, not necessarily relevant to the scenes in films, were added as a publicity stunt in order to promote the films.

3. *Behavioural rules.* The third group of rules cover performance rituals on and off the stage and apply both to artists and to audiences. Due to the lack of firsthand knowledge of the type of audience that these popular songs catered for, as well as the

relationship between audience and performers, it is not clear which were the rules of conversation and codified etiquette current in the popular music scene in the Shanghai era, such as the appropriate behaviour of performers in interviews, the proper response to gossip in magazines, and the guidelines for the spectators during live performances.

According to Yao Li, one of the living elderly singers once active both in Shanghai and Hong Kong, most people at the time would pay more attention to the singing than to the singer's appearance. When giving a live performance in dance-halls, she was always in *qipao* (Manchurian-style female long gown) and never wore any make-up because people usually closed their eyes and just listened to her songs (Shuijing 1985, p. 205). Nevertheless, Yao Li did not mention whether audiences then applauded loudly, shouted 'bravo', encouraged the singer in any other way or even behaved in a manner similar to the ways in which young fans today revere their pop idols in live concerts. A known fact about audience feedback is that in contests sponsored by various entertainment periodicals in the 1930s, readers were asked to send in ballots ranking their favourite singers so that the popularity of the singers could be gauged by the readers' responses (Jones 2001, p. 100). However, more detailed data about behavioural rules must be left in abeyance until more reliable information can be gathered.

4. *Social and ideological rules.*   The fourth group contains the rules which cover the social image of artists and the nature of the music community and its relationship to the world outside. On the one hand, popular singers in this era relied a great deal on record companies for their continuing performing careers; on the other hand, they maintained an ambiguous relationship with the audience. Record companies came to China with a view to opening up a new market for their record players and record-ings. With this new technology, these companies made it possible to store the sounds of stage performances and to sell them in the form of a commodity. To singers, making recordings (either for films or for gramophone records) was the best way to circulate songs quickly in the country and thus to make their names known to a wider audience. Although record companies could reap a great profit for their own sake from con-tracted singers, it was under the support of these companies that the artists could become established and their stage careers last a long time in the entertainment industry. Therefore, it was of vital importance for singers to keep on good terms with record companies.

However, to listeners, a record company was just a commercial institution, similar to countless other companies who promoted Western inventions and ameni-ties in Shanghai at the time; it did not matter which institution released the records. What the audience really paid attention to were songs and singers, who fascinated the ordinary public with their syrupy voices. Despite the fact that entertainers, such as story-telling singers and opera players, had long been stigmatised in traditional society, people were not only attracted by popular singers' musical works but also interested in their personal matters. A Chinese saying goes that 'a whore has no feeling for love; an opera player has no sense of honour and justice' (*biaozi wuqing xizi wuyi*). In spite of being looked down upon in such a way, in the past the players used to comfort themselves with the proverb that 'whoever is human listens to opera' (*fanshi ren jiudei tingxi*). These words indeed shed light on the views of the public on Shanghai popular singers at that time – while entertainment was essential for life, it was low and degrading to provide entertainment.

From an ideological point of view, the Shanghai era saw two extreme attitudes in response to popular music. When this new form of entertainment that fused Chinese traditional and Western musical elements first enjoyed success and popularity, the ranks of scholars, moralists and nationalists derided it and tried to ban it as decadent and pornographic and even denounced it as opium for the masses. They argued that this singing and dancing valued immediate pleasure without thought for the future, and created an illusion of peace and prosperity. Nevertheless, it could not be denied that to those living the harsh reality of Chinese social conditions at that time, popular songs meant escape, while for those chasing flashy and fleshy excitement, cabaret dancing was a fashion and fad as well as a mark of urban superiority. It is possible to argue that on the one hand, Shanghai popular music involved a multitude of commercial activities in conflict with the morality of traditional Chinese society and was incongruous with calls for the salvation of the nation, while on the other hand, these songs filled the needs of sectors of the public for amusement at the same time as the vivid imagery they conveyed reflected most people's longing for a happier life.

5. *Economical and juridical rules.* The last group in Fabbri's rules deals with the commercial activities that guarantee the survival and prosperity of a music genre. The song-and-dance troupe may be the earliest form of commercialisation through which Shanghai popular songs were produced and promoted. The organiser of a troupe wrote songs, trained singers, arranged performances and signed contracts with record companies to make recordings of their stage appearances. For example, Li Jinhui's Bright Moon Song-and-Dance Troupe once signed an exclusive contract and then recorded no less than one hundred records within the course of six months (Jones 2001, pp. 95–6). Another common way of promoting songs was through the music society; these were smaller groups of singers and instrumentalists which usually appeared over the airwaves in programmes sponsored and supported by commercial firms. Some music societies, such as the Great Unity Society (*Datong she*), even promoted their musical works by implementing the use of radio broadcasts with an effective use of printed material – they published periodically collections of songs, as a guide for tunes and lyrics with pictures of their singers on the cover page endorsing the products of advertisers as a means to support the publication.[18]

Besides their work for the song-and-dance troupes and music societies, some Shanghai popular singers also made a living by performing in restaurants and cabarets. For instance, Wu Yingyin had sung in dance halls and nightclubs before she made her first recording. Yao Li, after rising to fame with the success of her radio programmes and records, also performed in top dance halls in Shanghai. In addition to those live performances, films played an important part in the production and dissemination of Shanghai popular songs. Good songs usually helped to promote films and drew a wide range of people and, on the other hand, the songs of commercially successful films were later made into records, published in collections of song sheets, and performed again in broadcasts and dance halls.

The three major record companies active in Shanghai – the British-based Pathé-EMI group, the American RCA-Victor and the local Great China Records – produced popular songs in their own studios with their own contracted artists and promoted them all over China and abroad. By the end of the 1930s the Pathé-EMI group controlled most of the Shanghai popular music market and most composers, arrangers and female singers signed exclusively to Pathé during the most crucial stage of their careers. Existing records indicate that in Pathé most business decisions were made by foreign managers, and song lyrics were usually translated into English to be approved by them before a recording session, whereas Chinese employees provided their musical expertise or worked as compradors responsible for negotiating with performers and local distributors (Jones 2001, p. 64). There was certainly a well-functioning mechanism dealing with copyright of songs and lyrics, as well as recordings, because even now EMI (Hong Kong) still pays royalties to the living elderly singers of the Shanghai era or their descendants when old recordings are reissued (Liu 1996, p. 51). However, because the documents about the organisational structures of these companies were lost or destroyed during the chaos of political change, most facts about the decision-making processes within companies and the legal relationships between artists (including singers, musicians, composers and lyricists) and companies remain unclear.

Concluding remarks

In this article I have given a historical description of the rise of Shanghai popular songs together with the musical background present in the early 1930s. I have described how Li Jinhui's love songs triggered the creation and development of Shanghai popular songs, and that through gramophone recordings, radio broadcasts and films, this new form of musical entertainment enjoyed great popularity throughout Shanghai and other regions of China, regardless of severe criticisms from certain sectors of society. Because these musical works were dismissed as decadent sound and neglected in the history of modern Chinese music, most facts and figures about the popular music industry were not preserved properly and were lost or scattered in Mainland China, Hong Kong and the Southeast Asian Chinese communities because of the political change on the Mainland after 1949.

I have also made a preliminary analysis of the features of Shanghai popular songs from the perspective of musical genre. There is much variety in the musical elements of these songs, though, generally speaking, most combine traditional Chinese melody and singing styles with Western orchestral accompaniment. Despite the fact that these songs tend to be concerned with sentiment and put stress on the pleasure of the moment, other issues can be found in the content of the lyrics as well. Notionally, from the perspective of formal and semiotic features, it is not entirely satisfying to define a genre where songs are mainly in one style but where other diverse stylistic elements are incorporated here and there into the repertoire. However, taking into consideration the social and historical context in which Shanghai popular songs came into existence, it is not difficult to understand why different forms of performance still existed while the main style had been developed through the combination of specific musical materials from the two cultures.

Shanghai was China's first modern industrial, commercial and financial centre, as well as one of the world's most prosperous cities in the first half of the twentieth century. All kinds of modern technology and amenities, such as electricity, gas, running water, telephones, trams and automobiles, were introduced to Shanghai soon after their appearance in other Western major cities; however, Chinese tradition and habits, such as the celebration of traditional festivals according to the lunar calendar and the use of wheelbarrows and sedan chairs as means of conveyance, still existed in people's everyday lives. As Lu Hanchao suggests, 'if Shanghai was a place where two cultures – Chinese and Western – met but neither prevailed, it was not because the two were deadlocked but because both showed remarkable resilience' (Lu 1999,

p. 297). Similarly, while people were intoxicated with the fusion of the Chinese pentatonic scales and the Western instrumental accompaniment in Wu Yingyin's 'Meet by Chance' (*Ping shui xiangfeng*), they never forgot the lasting charm of the *huqin* and story-telling ballad in Zhou Xuan's 'The Wandering Songstress' and never stopped enjoying the resonant *bel canto* singing in Sheng Jialun's film song, 'Singing in the Midnight' (*Yeban gesheng*).

Ever since Li Jinhui began the composition of love songs, arranged commercial performances, and made them into gramophone records, the production and spread of Shanghai popular songs had been dependent on the collaboration between artists (song-and-dance troupes, music societies or other contracted musicians and perform-ers of record companies) and commercial institutions (radio stations, films companies and record companies). Due to insufficient information regarding the details of business practices in the Shanghai popular music industry, it is not clear whether there was someone in an executive position in the music society or song-and-dance troupe or a department in the record company functioning equivalent to the A&R department in today's major record companies, i.e. responsible for the style of musical works and the image of the star. Nevertheless, the musical elements, lyrical content and forms of performance of these popular songs reflect a collective style of these participating artists and institutions and, at the same time, bygone audience tastes. To gain a better view of how listeners and creators together influenced the formation of this collective style would require more information about the producing process and audience reception of popular songs during this era.

As 'historical work on popular music requires careful analysis, a detailed knowledge of context, and a degree of sympathy and imagination' (Gammon 1982, p. 29), the review of the rise of Shanghai popular songs and preliminary analysis of their generic features in this article is just the beginning of a reconstruction of a neglected part of its history. More evidence will reveal a clearer picture of the context in which the various musical events took place and take us a step further in our understanding of this interesting period in the modern history of music in China.

Endnotes

1. In general, the term 'Chinese popular music' indicates popular songs sung in Chinese and produced in China. However, Chinese lan-guage speakers distinguish between songs sung in Mandarin Chinese and those sung in the Cantonese and Taiwanese dialects. In this arti-cle, 'Chinese popular music' refers broadly to popular songs produced in Mainland China, Hong Kong and Taiwan in modern times, while 'Shanghai popular songs' denotes specifically works created in the 1930s and 1940s mainly in that city.

2. The first Shanghai popular song was written by Li Jinhui in 1927. The historical recording (Shanghai Pathé 34278 A & B) mentioned here was performed by his daughter, Li Minghui, and was released by the Pathé-EMI group in Shanghai. It appears that the critical remark 'a cat being strangled' (*niesi mao*) was first made by the noted Chinese writer Lu Xun.

3. The term *Haipai* was originally used by the lit-erati in the late nineteenth century to disparage the more vibrant, liberal and commercially oriented local painting, theatre and literature that was produced in Shanghai and which con-trasted with the supposedly more conservative and traditional *Jingpai* ('Beijing style'). How-ever, in the early twentieth century this designa-tion was gradually accepted by people in Shanghai and applied to them with a positive connotation. For a further discussion of the his-tory and meaning of the term, see Zhang (1991 pp. 1,130–59).

4. There were several amateur groups, such as the Heavenly Cadence Society (*Tianyun she*), the Great Unity Music Club (*Datong yuehui*) and the Midnight Music Club (*Ziye yuehui*), striving to preserve the tradition of serious instrumental music and operatic performance. They also carried out research in the compilation and translation of Chinese music manuscripts into Western notation, and improved the design and manufacture of Chinese musical instruments. These groups usually gave regular concerts in their own right or other programmes in hotels or private banquets by request. Among these

groups it is worth highlighting the Midnight Music Club whose founder, Xu Ruhui, a former member of the Heavenly Cadence Society, conducted his music ensemble which accompanied popular songs written by him; the performance featured Chinese percussion playing frenetic jazz rhythms (Xu 2001, p. 86).

5. School songs were tunes and lyrics collected and published as educational material for teaching singing in elementary school or at higher level. The earliest group devoted to these works was the Music Study Society (*Yinyue jiangxiehui*) founded by Chinese visiting students in Tokyo (Gild 1998, pp. 119–21).

6. By the end of 1935 over a hundred choirs and singing societies had been founded across the various social strata in Shanghai. These societies gathered regularly to sing patriotic songs in hope of boosting the morale of the Chinese people and army (Wang 2001, p. 189).

7. In the mid-1930s, there were eighty-nine radio stations running in China and forty-three of them were situated in Shanghai (Shanghai tong she 1935, p. 564).

8. The reason for being so called is that the most valuable asset to a 'pocketbook company' was usually a 'pocketbook', which held recording contracts with artists, manufacturing contracts with the major companies and a small amount of petty cash.

9. The Chinese word *genü* can be understood literally as those females who sing to earn their living. However, it was usually used as a derogatory term because actresses or entertainers had been traditionally stigmatised in traditional Chinese society, and performers who 'sell songs' to the public might sometimes be associated with courtesans and their sexual services.

10. Li Jinguang, Chen Gexin and another three prolific composers, Yao Min, Yan Gongshang and Liang Yueying, were regarded as the most influential and were later nicknamed 'The Gang of Five' of Chinese popular music by critics.

11. Examples of Nie Er's songs are, 'Song of Dockers' (*Matou gongren ge*), 'Song of Water Chestnut Picking' (*Cailing ge*), 'Songs of the Newspaper Boys' (*Maibao ge*), and 'The Volunteer's March' (*Yiyong jun jinxingqu*), which later on became the national anthem of the People's Republic of China.

12. Fabbri defines a musical genre as a set of musical events (real or possible) whose course is governed by a definite set of socially accepted rules, and further suggests five groups of rules involved in the definition of a genre (Fabbri 1982, pp. 52–81). Although we may see the limitations and implicit contradictions that the application of Fabbri's model to Shanghai popular songs entails, his model is the only one that

provides at present a suitable and systematic approach to genre classification.

In his pioneering work *Yellow Music*, Jones has looked into the media culture around Shanghai popular songs. Through the personal and professional histories of Li Jinhui and Nie Er, he has explored shifting gender roles, class inequality, the politics of national salvation and emerging media technologies. However, the only thing Jones uses to describe the musical features of Shanghai popular songs is 'fusion of American jazz, Hollywood film music, and Chinese folk forms', and all musical works he mentioned were composed no later than 1937, the year in which the Sino-Japanese War began. Through five groups of Fabbri's genre rules, the second half of this article will investigate generic features of not only works produced in the 1930s but also more brilliant works of the 1940s.

13. As a curiosity, we may remark here that this was the first Chinese song with English lyrics that made it in the international market. The interpretation by Frankie Laine (Columbia 39367) became very popular during the 1950s, but most Western listeners had no idea of its Chinese origin when they first came across the song.

14. Seeking higher musical artistry, Ouyang Feiying and Qu Yunyun studied European classical music and art songs under foreign vocalists, Mrs Ford and Mrs Levi. They later gave several concerts with the Shanghai Municipal Symphonic Orchestra (Ouyang 1998, p. 56).

15. The use of vernacular as opposed to classical Chinese in writings and textbooks had been insistently demanded by some intellectuals since the May 4th movement of 1919. As a result, the Ministry of Education acceded to their appeal and officially mandated the use of vernacular in public schools in 1921. Consistent with these demands about using the vernacular, some of the May 4th intellectuals had been writing the so-called 'new poems' (as opposed to classical poems), discarding classical rules of tonal patterns and rhyme schemes for free style and plain words.

16. I am thinking here of expressions such as *lang* ('man') and *ge* ('elder brother') used by females when addressing their beloved men, *nu* (literally, 'slave') used by females referring to themselves, and *jie* ('elder sister') or *mei* ('younger sister') meaning either girls or women.

17. A taxi dancer is a professional dance partner, employed by a dancehall or nightclub to dance with patrons who pay a fee for each dance.

18. This Great Unity Society, where Yao Li and Yao Min played important roles, had no connection to the above-mentioned Great Unity Music Club which was devoted to traditional Chinese music.

References

Fabbri, F. 1982. 'A theory of musical genres', in *Popular Music perspectives*, ed. D. Horn and P. Tagg (Göteberg and London), pp. 52–81

Frith, S. 1996. *Performing Rites: On the Value of Popular Music* (Cambridge, MA)

Gammon, V. 1982. 'Problems of method in the historical studies of popular music', in *Popular Music perspectives*, ed. D. Horn and P. Tagg (Göteberg and London), pp. 16–31

Gild, G. 1998. 'Early 20th century "reforms" in Chinese music', *Chime*, 12–13, pp. 116–23

Jones, A.F. 2001. *Yellow Music: Media Culture and Colonial Modernity in the Chinese Jazz Age* (London)

Karolyi, O. 1998. *Traditional African and Oriental Music* (London)

Liu, G. 1996. *Jinqu wushi nian: Guoyu liuxing gequ shiyong baodian* (Fifty years of the golden songs: a practical treasury of Mandarin Chinese popular songs) (Taipei, Donggong guoji guanggao youxian gongsi)

Liu, X. 1988. *Zhongguo liuxing gequ yuanliu* (The origins of Chinese popular songs) (Taichung, Taiwan, Taiwan shengzhengfu xinwenchu)

Lu, H. 1999. *Beyond the Neon Lights: Everyday Shanghai in the Early Twentieth Century* (London)

Ouyang, F. 1998. *Wo chang xianggelila: Ouyang Feiying huiyi lu* (I sang Shangri-la: a memoir of Ouyang Feiyin) (Taipei, Yuzhouguang chubanshe)

Shangahi tong she (ed.) 1935. *Shanghai yanjou ziliao xuji* (Shanghai research materials vol. 2) (Shanghai, Shangahi tong she)

Shuijing. 1985. *Liuxing gequ cangsang ji* (A record of the vicissitudes of popular song) (Taipei, Dadi chubanshe)

Stock, J. 1995. 'Reconsidering the past: Zhou Xuan and the rehabilitation of early twentieth-century popular music', *Asian Music*, 26/2, pp. 119–35

Toynbee, J. 2000. *Making Popular Music: Musicians, Creativity and Institutions* (London)

Wang, Y. 2001. 'New music of China: its development under the blending of Chinese and Western cultures through the first half of twentieth century, part II', *Journal of Music in China*, 30/2, pp. 187–228

—— 1994. *Zhongguo jinxiandai yinyue shi* (A history of Chinese contemporary and modern music), 2nd edn (Beijing, Renmin yinyue chubanshe)

Wong, K. 2001. *The Age of Shanghainese Pops: 1930–1970* (Hong Kong)

Xu, W. 2001. 'Wode fuqin Xu Ruhui yu Zhongguo zaoqi liuxing gequ' (My father Xu Ruhui and Chinese early popular songs), *Musicology in China*, 1, pp. 63–77

Zhang, Z. (ed) 1991. *Jindai Shanghai chengshi yanjiu* (Modern Shanghai studies) (Shanghai, Shanghai renmin chubanshe)

Discography

Baidai zhongguo shidaiqu mingdian (The legendary Chinese hits of Pathé). EMI (Hong Kong), 59 CDs. 1992–1997

Jinsangzi Zhou Xuan (The Golden Voice Zhou Xuan). China Record Company (Shanghai), 2 cassettes, L-36, 70. 1985

Zhongguo Shanghai sanshishi niandai jueban mingqu (30–40s hits of Shanghai, China). Lee Leng Kok (Singapore), 4 audio CDs, LLK-15062000, 11112000, 11042001, 11042002. 2000–2002

Zhongguo shidaiqu qingge duichang (The love duets of Chinese songs of the times). EMI (Malaysia), 3 audio CDs, 7243 524277 27, 524278 26, 531660 21. 2000–2001

Zhou Xuan. China Record Company (Shanghai), 4 cassettes, CL-51–4. 1993

[25]

Commerce, Politics, and Musical Hybridity: Vocalizing Urban Black South African Identity during the 1950s

LARA ALLEN / University of the Witwatersrand

In 1954 *Bantu World,* a South African broadsheet with an extensive black readership, announced that "a new kind of record has burst upon the market in the last twelve months"; with a "monotonous solid beat, [and] crazy ad-lib solos," the music "rocked like mad—and sales started to jump like mad too." The infectious new style was pioneered by Troubadour Records who, claimed the paper, discovered that "Africans prefer 'beat' jazz with rocking instrumental accompaniment, honking saxophones, and more sophisticated singers like Dorothy Masuka."[1] This music did not, as the paper prophesied, turn out to be a "passing infatuation": it was in fact fundamental to the development of vocal jive, the primary vocal genre popular in South African townships during the 1950s, that ultimately developed into one of South Africa's internationally best-known styles, 1960s *mbaqanga.*[2]

The popularity of vocal jive raises a number of issues, whose examination forms the focus of this article. My investigation into the style's significance for township audiences and the reasons for its commercial success converges on the relationships between three factors: musical hybridity, politics, and commerce. To what extent, for instance, did the hybrid nature of vocal jive contribute to its commercial appeal and political efficacy? Was the style inherently hegemonic, perpetuating government discourses of racial and ethnic purity that championed a return to pre-colonial cultural identity for black people, or did it have a subversive effect? If there was a subversive element, did it constitute political resistance? Did the style's commercial guise render any political aspects more or less powerful? Which aspects of the music and the lyrics were particularly meaningful and enjoyable for audiences, and how did these contribute to the style's commercial and political efficacy? As I shall suggest, the diverse readings of the relationships between these three factors proposed by academics and others during and since the 1950s reflect the various interpreters' positionalities, as conditioned by contemporary intellectual trends and political imperatives.

In order to provide some background and a context for a discussion of these issues, I first set the scene with a case study in the form of several short sketches of the South African music industry during the 1950s. This decade constituted a significant moment in the evolution of black popular music in South Africa because it was the period between the establishment of the mass media for black consumers and the full institutionalization of high apartheid. It was a time of change and negotiation, in which alliances between commercial and political forces formed and dissolved as hybrid styles sought to articulate the experience and aspirations of township audiences. I focus on Troubadour Records, a particularly successful recording company during this period that at times controlled up to seventy-five percent of the African record market (Allingham 1991:4–5), and whose political approach was somewhat different from that of its competitors.[3] Troubadour's top singer Dorothy Masuka receives the most attention here because she is widely acknowledged as the single most influential artist in the development of 1950s female vocal jive, and because she was arguably the most politically-oriented star of the period. I would argue that the issues raised by this case study enjoy broader applicability, for the context in which Masuka functioned, and her musical response to it, well exemplify those, not only of many other female vocal jive artists, but also of a much larger group of musicians who collectively evolved a number of similar hybrid township styles, including male vocal jive, "African Jazz," and *kwela*.[4]

Dorothy Masuka and the Evolution of Female Vocal Jive

Dorothy Masuka's Background

Dorothy Masuka was the first black Southern African woman to launch her singing career primarily as a recording artist.[5] Born in Southern Rhodesia (now Zimbabwe) in 1935, she went to Catholic boarding schools in Bulawayo and Johannesburg. Throughout the 1950s she moved continually between South Africa and Southern Rhodesia, and is now claimed as a national star in both countries. Her background, schooling, and dual cultural nationality significantly influenced her musical development, media image, and career path. While still at school in Johannesburg, she was noticed by a talent scout from Troubadour Records and made her first recordings in 1952.[6] In the same year she ran away from school to perform with the male close-harmony group, the African Inkspots, and one newspaper started to hail her as the "Judy Garland of South Africa."[7] She ran away from school again the following year to perform at the Rhodes Centenary celebrations in Bulawayo. She won the "Miss Bulawayo" beauty contest and, with the Golden Rhythm Crooners, sang for the British Queen Mother.[8] After this second bout of truancy Masuka's mother accepted her daughter's desire for a career in music. As Masuka was still a minor, recording engineer Stewart Cook was sent to Bulawayo on behalf of Troubador to sing a contract with her mother. At the same time Cook made some recordings of Masuka with the Golden Rhythm Crooners, one of which, "Hamba Notsokolo," became one of the biggest hits of the 1950s, launching Masuka into stardom at the age of eighteen. The recording became so popular that Masuka became known as Dorothy "Notsokolo" Masuka.[9]

Working at Troubadour

Despite the undeniably exploitative aspects of the employment conditions experienced by black musicians in South African recording studios during the 1950s (Coplan 1985:178), Dorothy Masuka and other singers recount their time as Troubadour employees with great fondness. Their nostalgia and positive recollections can only be accounted for by measuring their experiences on a relative, rather than an absolute, scale of exploitation. Conditions at Troubadour generally appear to compare favorably with those offered at other recording companies at the time, those experienced by ex-Troubadour artists later in their careers, and with other types of employment available to black women such as laundry or domestic service.

Masuka (p.c.) felt that she was well treated at Troubadour. The directors, Israel Katz and Morris Fagan, and their white employees, "didn't look at people's color," she told me. "They saw me as a little girl, not as a little *black* girl. Just as a little girl. Because they really spoilt me in a true sense . . . they did more for me than my own parents." Indeed, the relationship between the directors and Masuka does seem to have been more akin to that of a doting father and favorite daughter, or benevolent patron and protégée, than that of employer and employee. For instance, instead of receiving a regular salary, or a certain amount per side recorded, Masuka was given money whenever she wanted it: Troubadour paid when she wanted expensive clothes, shoes, and jewelry; gave her a twenty-first birthday party; bought her air-tickets whenever she went to Southern Rhodesia; and ensured that she always had spending money (Masuka, p.c.; Allingham 1991:6).[10] Other aspects of Katz and Fagan's studio policies were similarly unconventional, if not unethical, by today's standards, for they were selectively and opportunistically casual with regard to copyright and musicians' contracts with other companies, as well as about apartheid censorship laws.

Katz and Fagan were relatively liberal in their attitudes toward and treatment of their black employees. Unusually for the era, for instance, they gave talent scout Cuthbert Matumba the freedom to run the studio almost entirely as he saw fit. Matumba could, as a result, make the most of his exceptional marketing skills and his commercial and artistic instincts. Furthermore, contrary to the practices of competing record companies who paid black artists a flat fee per side recorded of a 78 rpm disc,[11] Troubadour maintained a staff of core musicians who were full-time employees drawing weekly salaries. These instrumentalists and female backing singers were at the studio, ready to record from 8:00 am to 4:00 pm every day. (Male backing singers were not employed, instrumentalists being expected to double as singers when required.) Although like other record companies at the time, Troubadour did not pay royalties, their musicians were relatively well remunerated. Mary Thobei, a backing singer at Troubadour during the 1950s, remembered being paid six pounds per week, double that earned by her mother as a domestic servant p.c. Such a salary placed Troubadour's musicians in the top two percent of African wage-earners (Horrell 1959:148–49). Thobei appreciated being able to buy smart clothes, groceries, a weekly train ticket (not often necessary as Troubadour transported musicians to and from the townships in a company van), and "still get change." She also liked the security provided by a salary, sorely missing it when she started working for other record companies in subsequent years. Above all Thobei enjoyed the energy and congenial atmosphere of the Troubadour studio, saying "Troubadour was my happiest place."

Allingham suggests that a great deal of Troubadour's commercial success was due to the speed with which their recordings were released. Songs were frequently composed, rehearsed, recorded, pressed, and released within twenty-four hours. When, for instance, Masuka and Miriam Makeba workshopped songs together on the train from Pimville to Johannesburg, Masuka's versions would be selling long before Gallo Record Company issued Makeba's release (Makeba 1988:66; Allingham 1991:5). Recounting to me the recording process, Thobei related that someone would "come with a number"—basically the melody and lyrics—and the other musicians and singers would "fit their parts in," creating the harmony, rhythm, and form. Matumba and all the musicians would "touch up nicely," make suggestions for improvements and changes until everyone was happy, and then the number would be recorded. There was rarely more than one take; Thobei recalled: "We just test, and from there—microphone. One go, both sides! Those were the 78s. Okay, after that we go for a break. Come back. Start with another number again." As she recalled, when top singers like Masuka were present, they could record four to six songs a day. Troubadour's copious output included versions of its competitors' hits, many of which were more popular than the originals. One such example is Masuka's recording of "Ei Yow (Phata

Phata)."[12] Thobei related that Matumba hastily flew Masuka back from Southern Rhodesia to record the number, which was on the streets and selling well the very next day.

Rehearsing and recording occurred in the studio, a bare rectangular space about forty-five by sixty feet. The musicians were grouped under single microphones in the corners, while Matumba would direct them and the recording engineer from the center (Allingham 1991:5). Masuka remembered sometimes being alone in a corner with her own microphone, but on other occasions sharing a microphone with her backing singers. Although it was somewhat haphazard, Masuka preferred this method of recording to today's system in which musicians lay down tracks on their own; the latter, she told me, "loses the feel . . . because the thing is not together." When everyone records simultaneously, "it's like we are on stage . . . you've got the whole thing there, it brings the artist out." Matumba's mode of direction often included suggesting changes to Masuka's compositions, but he did not make her feel as if her artistic authority was being usurped, or her creativity curtailed. Rather, Masuka regarded his input as helpful and inspiring: "He felt what I was all about you know, and he would put something into it, add something to it."

The Musical Characteristics of Vocal Jive[13]

In terms of style there were three streams of influence on Masuka's musical development. The first to become deeply internalized was probably the *marabi*-influenced Rhodesian urban hybrid style *tsaba-tsaba*, for as a young child she sang tsaba-tsaba songs for customers at her mother's eating-house in return for pennies. This style formed an integral part of the soundscape of Masuka's youth; she told me that she remembers its most famous exponents, August Musarugwa and the Bulawayo Sweet Rhythm Band,[14] travelling around the locations playing on the back of an open lorry to advertise their concerts. Secondly, Masuka cited the traditional musical influences on her music as isiZulu, arguing that the people of Southern Zimbabwe who are now known as amaNdebele are descendants of amaZulu clans who fled the wars of the *Mfecane* period in the early nineteenth century.[15] She mentioned the haunting songs of amaZulu *sangomas* (traditional healers), characterized by descending slides, as a particularly vivid childhood memory. Although not an especially obvious aspect of her style, certain elements in some of Masuka's compositions do echo features of traditional isiZulu music. The suggestion of root movement between two chords a tone apart may, for instance, derive from *ughubu* and *umakweyana* bow music (Rycroft 1971, 1975–76), while overlapping call-and-response relationships between solo voice and chorus is typical of much traditional isiZulu vocal music (Rycroft 1977:222–24).[16]

Not withstanding the contribution of these two idioms, the influences of American blues, jazz, and swing are more strongly evident in Masuka's compositional and performance style. She learnt American songs from gramophone records and the radio from an early age, and as a young teenager evaded school restrictions through various ploys in order to listen to popular recordings (Masuka, p.c.; Allingham 1991:3). Rhythmic patterns are the most important stylistic elements that Masuka drew from American sources. Particularly characteristic are the basic swing rhythm, with accented back-beats or equal accentuation of all four beats in a bar, typically with walking bass. Harmonically and in terms of formal structure, Masuka's initial compositions were more strongly influenced by American models than her later output. Many of her early songs employ relatively extended chord progressions, exhibiting a verse-and-chorus structure rather than the African Jazz-style cyclical repetition of short, four-chord progressions.[17]

By 1956 vocal jive had become standardized and was exhibiting many of the distinctive characteristics of African Jazz. The late African Jazz veteran Ntemi Piliso cited the cyclical repetition of short (usually four-chord) progressions of primary chords (generally not more complex than triads or dominant sevenths) as the definitive harmonic characteristics of this genre (Allen 1993:24). Melodically, African Jazz compositions are built from the repetition (with small variations) and alternation of two or three short melodic motifs (the length of the chord progression) interspersed with solo improvisations. There is usually a rough sequence to the order in which motifs and variations are repeated, although disruptions to the sequence are fairly common and do not disrupt the final effect. By the mid-1950s these characteristics—along with swing rhythm and call-and-response between soloists and choruses—were typical of much vocal jive and other contemporary urban hybrid styles such as kwela. Vocalists and kwela penny whistlers employed similar strategies to vary the repetitions of melodic motifs,[18] and shared the basic instrumental backing line-up of guitars (usually lead guitar and rhythm guitar), acoustic string bass, and drum-set. Structural similarities between kwela and vocal jive facilitated collaboration between penny whistlers and vocalists, the most successful examples being a number of recordings made by Spokes Mashiyane and the Skylarks.[19]

Kwela and vocal jive enjoyed a surge in popularity at the same time, through the same medium—records. The kwela boom started with Mashiyane's first recordings late in 1954, a year after the release of Masuka's "Hamba Notsokolo." The merger of musical elements from different sources was identified by many musicians as one of the primary reasons for the success of vocal jive and related hybrid styles, for such eclecticism expressed the culturally diverse environment of township dwellers (Masuka, p.c.; Albert Ralulimi, p.c.). More specifically, the success of both Mashiyane's and

Masuka's music is commonly ascribed to the fact that their hybrid mix was more distinctively African and local than the American-oriented music of their immediate predecessors. Certainly the record-buying public enjoyed music that expressed a locally-rooted identity, for many numbers incorporating local melodies, current township argot, and topical subject matter became hits. In this regard vocal jive enjoyed an advantage over instrumental hybrid styles in that lyrics, through reference to current events and issues of common concern, enabled listeners to recognize their own interests and experiences more concretely. As particularly effective conveyors of meaning for township audiences, vocal jive lyrics deserve some attention here.

"Singing the News" and the Popularity of Politics

Dorothy Masuka became so successful that Troubadour started to seek similar female vocalists. Their next triumph was Mabel Mafuya, who started recording in 1955 and within a year was being heralded as a star.[20] Mafuya's compositional style was strongly influenced by Masuka, and most of her recordings exhibit the standard characteristics of vocal jive.[21] One of her early hits was a novelty number, "Hula Hoop," but Mafuya told me that she really made her name singing "the latest news." Recordings of songs about news stories, that were strongly encouraged at Troubadour.[22] "Our songs all had a meaning," explained Mary Thobei (p.c); "They reflected what is happening right now . . . Cuthbert used to listen to the news, you see. Then he would come there and say, 'Did you hear about in the news they said this and that and that?' It ended up we are going to record that."

Partly as a result of efforts by the African National Congress (ANC) to increase its support base, the mass of ordinary township people became more politically conscious and active during the 1950s (Lodge 1983a), and, in turn, the commercial viability of politically oriented recordings increased considerably. In 1956–57, for instance, Mabel Mafuya produced several hits about bus boycotts,[23] and Nancy Jacobs, star of Trutone Records, launched her career with her recording of "Meadowlands," which commented on the forced removal of Sophiatown residents to a section of Soweto.[24] Jacobs also enjoyed success with a song about a controversial court ruling that a racially white woman was culturally and socially black, and was therefore not infringing the Immorality Act by living with a black policeman. This recording, "Regina Brooks Khumalo lo Harry Mekela," reportedly sold two thousand copies on the day it was released.[25] Within a few weeks Troubadour released their version of the story, entitled "Regina" and sung by Mabel Mafuya.[26] In a similar manner, other companies attempted to capture some of the market for songs about the bus boycotts and forced removals.[27] Such was the popularity of these songs that journalists complained on several occasions that topical subject matter was enough to make a song a hit, regardless of its musical merits.[28]

Vocal jive lyrics customarily consist of a few lines, repeated and alternated. The lines of lyrics and melodic motifs coincide with the length of the four-chord harmonic cycle. While each line relates to a central theme, there is usually no narrative story, allowing for the repetition and alternation of lines of text without disturbing the sense of the song. The lyrics generally state the subject simply, without providing commentary, explanation, or narration. Thus the lyricist's skill lies in the ability to imply layers of significance in a few lines, leaving audiences the challenge of deciphering deeper meanings— a poetic strategy typical of South African hybrid musical styles (Blacking 1995:218; Erlmann 1996:204–06). A literal translation of Masuka's "Mhlaba," for instance, reads: "In this world we are having problems, black people are sorrowful; black people are having problems, black people are sorrowful."[29] However, the song's meanings reach beyond direct translation. Masuka explained that she recorded the song because, "I didn't understand why I should be barred to go to that restaurant, why I should be barred to be with that person" (Allingham 1991:6). Similarly, Thobei (p.c.) interpreted "Mhlaba" as saying, "In this world we are having a very tough time. Black and white are fighting each other. Now what are we supposed to do? Because now we are being treated like slaves." Both the semi-improvisational, mosaic-type structure of the lyrics, and the inference that there are deeper levels of meaning that may be reached by the listener, are distinctive characteristics of lyrics in traditional and popular, musical and poetic forms throughout Southern Africa (Gunner 1979; Berliner 1981; Vail and White 1991).

The ability of cryptic lyrics to accommodate multiple interpretations is particularly useful in a repressive political climate.[30] On occasion, a song's surface meaning thinly veils a coded message, whose interpretation can be reinforced by the performance context. For instance, one press report claimed that Mafuya's recording "Udumo Lwamaphoyisa" (A Strong Police Force) was sung by "look-out boys" to warn shebeen queens and illicit drinkers of police presence and the possibility of a liquor raid.[31] One of the most famous examples of the successful covert expression of anti-government politics through multiple readings, reinforced by a song's use within a particular context, is "Meadowlands," written by Trutone talent scout Strike Vilakazi. Relying on a literal translation, the government interpreted the song as supportive of their removals programme. Black record buyers, however, interpreted it as meaning the opposite, and "Meadowlands" became a protest anthem against the Sophiatown removals (Sampson 1956:228; Kavanagh 1992:i; Allingham 1994).

In a similar act of creative cooptation and resignification by ordinary people of an oppressive practice, anti-establishment sentiments were believed by some to be encoded in the dance accompanying one of Masuka's most famous recordings, "Ei Yow (Phata Phata)." A contemporary press report claimed that the movements of the phata phata dance originated in Johannesburg's main prison. The dancers shuffle along in a line simulating prisoners queuing for food, sometimes with their hands raised above their heads. In another step the male dancers stand in a row with their arms extended out to the front, palms to the floor, while the women pat each in turn in a manner resembling security-search body-frisking, after which the men do the same to the women.[32]

Political criticism was more easily expressed in some forums than in others. Despite his success with politically topical songs, for instance, Strike Vilakazi did not receive the support from Trutone's directors that Cuthbert Matumba enjoyed at Troubadour. Matumba knew that Katz and Fagan, who were constantly in search of commercially successful ventures, would routinely tolerate the release of politically sensitive or subversive material. Their attitude was illustrated in an episode relating to one of the company's early overtly political recordings, Masuka's "uDr. Malan Unomthetho Onzima" (Dr. Malan's Government is Harsh).[33] The recording sold well and was even played on the South African Broadcasting Corporation's African re-diffusion service before it was banned.[34] When security police arrived at the studio to demand the master tape, Katz and Fagan attempted to defuse the situation by claiming that the number was a praise song (Allingham 1991:6), and that such recordings were not political, but merely functioned as "the newspaper of the world." Another song entitled "Chief Luthuli" again brought the police Special Branch to the studio, although several other seditious recordings eluded the censors entirely (Thobei, p.c.).

Dorothy Masuka and Politics

While Masuka's early songs were largely inspired by personal experience—love, parting, and the difficulties of township life—she increasingly sang about social hardship and politics, particularly as more oppressive apartheid laws were introduced and enforced towards the end of the 1950s.[35] Masuka's last recording for Troubadour, inspired by the assassination of Congolese leader Patrice Lumumba, provoked another security police raid. Fortunately Masuka had flown to Bulawayo immediately after making the recording; however, she had become a "wanted person," a status that prevented her from returning to South Africa for over three decades (Masuka, p.c.; Thobei, p.c.; Allingham 1991:6–7). Masuka's commitment to the anti-apartheid movement dominated the next period of her career and life. Her ability to set political lyrics to music that was simultaneously "modern" and African was appreciated by the South African ANC and pro-independence movements elsewhere in Africa. Under the protection of these organizations, Masuka spent the early 1960s travelling through Central and East Africa with musical troupes performing pro-independence songs. When the colonial authorities in one country became aware of her activities, she would be spirited over a border into another country. After this period she spent several years in exile in London and New York, housed and supported by ANC sympathizers, after which she lived in Zambia and Zimbabwe until 1992, when she finally returned to South Africa (Masuka, p.c.).

Discourse about Politics, Commerce, and Hybrid Music

What then are the active ingredients of vocal jive that had particular significance for township people? The above sketches suggest that the ordinary township residents who constituted the bulk of the recording industry's buying public enjoyed music that expressed a locally-rooted identity reflective of their everyday lives. Within a style that referenced a sophisticated, cosmopolitan outlook, they also evidently appreciated being able to recognize themselves, for they voted with their money for local melodies, current township lingo, and topical subject matter. But the significance of vocal jive runs deeper than its ability to articulate cultural identity for its audience. The interpretation of musical hybridity in South African townships during the 1950s is complicated by a number of key relationships, specifically that between commerce and politics, the connection between the forces driving hybridity and its meaning, and the position of interpreters in relation to their subjects.

The political significance of vocal jive is complex in itself. It is, for instance, important to understand the overtly political vocal jive lyrics discussed above in the context of two caveats. First, the recording of blatantly subversive political material by Masuka and her colleagues was exceptional.[36] For the most part vocal jive lyrics did not directly address political issues; more often the subversive challenge was disguised through reference to the individual struggles of ordinary people, which were understood to result from political injustice. Further, the increasingly repressive political climate towards the end of the 1950s and the demise of Masuka's South African career discouraged other vocal jive artists from performing openly anti-apartheid material. Secondly, the impetus to release topical songs referring to sociopolitical injustice during the mid-1950s (before the first major apartheid clampdown, resulting in mass arrests and prosecutions for treason) was as much commercial as political, for such songs sold well. Moreover, the fact that sales were not necessarily proportional to the gravity of the issue being referenced demonstrates the limits to which political popular consciousness may be deciphered from the marketplace, for any political function of popular music is likely to be mediated by what many argue is its primary function, entertainment. For instance, the topical recording by Mabel Mafuya that received the most publicity concerned the death of heavyweight boxer Esekiel Dhlamini (known as King Kong) who, while serving a twelve year sentence for murder, committed suicide by drowning himself in a prison dam.[37] Similarly, although the circulation of the magazine *Drum* rose dramatically with the introduction of features on social injustice (especially issues containing exposés about brutal treatment of farm labourers, prison conditions, and the Defiance Campaign), even more popular was an issue featuring a story on the rumoured appearance of a *tokoloshe,* a mischevous imp in isiZulu cosmology (Sampson 1956:121).

While the intention of political lyrics may be relatively clear, the meanings or effect of non-verbal phenomena such as musical hybridity can only be inferred. It is not surprising, therefore, that Africanists, like scholars of other cultures, have debated whether hybrid cultural forms tend to uphold hegemonic ideological patterns (Waterman 1990:9) or are potentially subversive and serve the interests of the oppressed (Comaroff 1985:97–98). This dichotomy seems especially appropriate in cases where hybridity is "used by members of one definable social grouping in their struggles against another" (Kaarsholm and James 2000:202), and where, for example, cultural hybridity is either an ideal of the governing establishment, or of resistant communities. Throughout much of Africa hybridity functioned as cultural resistance during colonial or white rule, and has often been central to post-independence cultural policy insofar as it expresses the "cosmopolitanism" of ruling black elites (Turino 2000). In South Africa during the 1950s, hybridity could reasonably be interpreted as an articulation of resistance to government policies promoting traditional, ethnically-specific aspects of African culture.[38] Most artists and audiences may not necessarily have intended or experienced hybridity as resistant in this sense, and strictly speaking "resistance" is intentional. However, the musical eclecticism of vocal jive was politically significant in that its merger of Western and African elements to form a non-tribal, internationally-oriented, urban African cultural identity was at odds with policies of racial segregation promulgated by British colonials and Afrikaner settlers, and consolidated under apartheid.[39]

In many interpretations of popular culture the goals of commerce and radical politics are perceived as antithetical, for the urge towards profit generally does not coincide with radical political agendas. However, even in particularly repressive political contexts, commercial popular culture can arguably function in a seditious manner. As James Scott has argued, when people cannot contest the terms of their subordination openly, they voice dissent behind the backs of the powerful through "hidden transcripts"— critiques of the dominant public discourse in the form of jokes, songs, or gestures, often expressed even while adopting a strategically acquiescent public pose (1990:x–xiii). While hidden transcripts may function as outlets for frustration, thereby defusing tensions that could lead to radical revolt, as Terence Ranger points out, popular culture—informal, festive and apparently escapist as it often is—has frequently provided one of the only channels through which African people have been able to articulate and respond to their experiences (1975:3). Arguably, the opportunity to voice dissent more than compensates for any dissipation of radical energy.

Throughout Africa the flourishing of hybrid popular music forms has for decades been facilitated by advances in communications technology (Merriam 1955:32, 1959:82–84; Kubik 1998:322). During the 1950s the South African music industry established a mass market among African consumers, and vastly increased the dissemination of popular culture through commercial media.[40] The rise of the mass media created new domains of cultural production through which township people could create, interpret, and understand their world. In this way popular culture not only reflected but actively constructed social reality (Fabian [1978] 1997:19). Music recordings could be particularly effective politically because, of all the products of the 1950s mass media, they most closely represented the cultural identity of ordinary township people. This effectiveness was partially a result of easy access, in that the ability of township people to enjoy recorded music, unlike consumption of newspapers, was not impeded by low levels of literacy; nor was access to recorded music limited to those able to attend a show, as was the case for stage performances. The relative success of particular recordings thus provides a taste-index of township audiences.

Although South African record companies did not keep sales figures during the 1950s, a sense of the types of songs that became hits may be deduced from other sources. In particular, newspaper advertisements indicate those compositions considered worthy of extra publicity by record companies, and many recordings were reviewed in the contemporary press;[41] further, musicians I interviewed tended to remember hit numbers particularly vividly. While it is generally problematic to assume that high sales reflect the un-manipulated taste of an audience (especially from perspective of the present, when marketing exerts enormous influence over consumption), musicians and producers went to considerable lengths to provide a product appreciated by ordinary township people, suggesting a high correspondence of public taste with hit numbers. For instance, Cuthbert Matumba conducted regular street-level market research by broadcasting new recordings from a van in busy places (such as outside a train station during rush hour) and gauging public reaction. Only those numbers that elicited a particularly favorable response were specifically promoted (Ralulimi, p.c.).

The inscription of contested cultural identity in the non-verbal elements of vocal jive and other contemporary music styles is manifest in the politically-inflected interpretations that characterize the ongoing debate over the meaning of this musical hybridity. From the emergence of vocal jive in the 1950s, the discourse around hybridity among musicians and their contemporary cultural commentators highlighted internal tensions within urban black culture. There was, for instance, dissent between those oriented towards international, particularly American, forms of sophistication, and those dedicated to the advancement of distinctively local African identity and pride. Some black intellectuals were aware of the potential support hybrid styles could offer to the philosophy of African nationalism, in opposition both to tribal identities and white Western culture. "New Africanists" such as Walter Nhlapo lauded hybrid urban music such as tsaba-tsaba as African cultural heritage, an angle later reworked by Todd Matshikiza in an article about marabi and early African Jazz.[42] Herbert Dhlomo (n.d.) grudgingly acknowledged the role played by record companies in nurturing African national consciousness in "Bantu forms of art, drama and music" through the dissemination of syncretic musical forms. On the whole, however, spokespeople did not represent the recording industry and the hybrid musical product it nurtured particularly positively. Journalists, belonging as they did to a small intellectual elite, did not devote much column space to local styles. Instead, they promoted emulation of highbrow Western art forms or African-American culture, the latter largely based on Hollywood projections of jazz, Harlem, and the Chicago underworld. Musicians who played music that aspired towards America rather than reflecting the local-oriented tastes of ordinary township people tended to dismiss hybrid South African styles as inferior, sometimes charging that record companies produced a second-rate product using second-rate musicians. (Besides differences in taste, some of this animosity resulted from competition over employment opportunities amongst artists.) Many established jazz musicians did not take recording seriously, regarding it as an activity to resort to only when in need of ready cash (Dolly Rathebe, p.c.). African Jazz, particularly in its recorded form, was disparagingly termed *mbaqanga* (isiZulu for stiff maize porridge) by modern jazz musicians because they played it in order to earn quick "bread money."[43]

Academic discourse of the period was similarly fraught with tensions over the significance of hybridity. Ethnomusicologists working in Southern Africa who were primarily dedicated to the documentation and preservation of pre-colonial African musics lamented the impact of Western styles. For instance, David Rycroft, although later revising his stance somewhat (1977), in the late 1950s asserted that there "is little to be said in praise of most South African 'town music' today" (1958:54), which constitutes "an impoverished cultural practice" in which "indigenous practices become weakened and new, imported techniques are adapted and oversimplified" (1959:29). In a similar vein Hugh Tracey, who devoted considerable energy to the preservation and dissemination of traditional Southern African musics, believed that popular styles, by African and world standards, were eroding artistic integrity, bringing urban Africans to the brink of cultural genocide (Tracey 1963a, 1963b).[44] Significantly, in support of his vision of the development of African music, Tracey cited not the ethnic divisions of apartheid policy, but the conviction expressed by "the new political leaders in Africa today" that "there must be a return to the integrities of indigenous skill if their composers, musicians and artists are to do justice to what they consider to be their distinctive national personalities" (1963b:40).

Within two decades, however, a number of researchers were taking a contrary view and reading musical hybridity as a valuable and authentic cultural expression of township inhabitants (Coplan 1979, 1982a, 1982b, 1985; Andersson 1981; Ballantine 1993). These writers, who were inspired by the political imperatives of the anti-apartheid struggle that influenced much post-1976 intellectual endeavor, highlighted the political complexities involved in promulgating both "pure" traditional music and hybrid styles strongly influenced by traditional styles such as 1960s mbaqanga (Andersson 1981:18; Coplan 1982b:125). David Coplan also voiced particular concerns about the political implications of what he saw as black artists' loss of "cultural autonomy" to white cultural brokers (Coplan 1979, 1982a:372, 1985:139).

A reading of the significance of the hybrid nature of vocal jive from a current perspective has points of intersection and difference with those offered over the past fifty years. Against the interpretations by Tracey and Rycroft discussed above, and in agreement with Coplan and Andersson, I would stress how the hybridity of styles like vocal jive exemplifies African musicians' ability to assimilate external influences and adapt their own traditions to serve contemporary expressive ends (Waterman 1990; Ranger 1975; Barber 1987). As an expressive response to the social, cultural, political, and economic upheavals caused by colonization, urbanization, and industrialization, hybrid styles are part of a "long conversation" with the West (Comaroff and Comaroff 1997:59), in which contemporary African realities are addressed and expressed through the selective appropriation of elements of foreign cultures.[45]

I would further suggest that in the 1950s musicians, producers, and audiences enjoyed more agency regarding the shaping of recorded and staged performances than is generally acknowledged by much research of the 1970s and 1980s.[46] Given the intensely political environment of the late 1970s, issues relating to racial inequality were understandably uppermost in the minds of both researchers and informants.[47] However, contrary to the portrayal of black musicians as engaged in a struggle to escape the dictates of white-controlled commercial and state structures (Coplan 1979, 1985:148, 243–44), my findings presented here suggest that, although the record industry was entirely owned by white capital, white owners and shareholders generally did not try to shape or control the nature of the cultural product, providing it was commercially successful. Furthermore, musicians neither regarded themselves as artistically helpless against the domination of big business agendas, nor did they indicate resentment of the ways in which producers molded their performances. The latter were largely regarded by musicians as members of a team engaged in a mutual quest for a hit.[48] Paradoxically, then, it was the very commercial quality of recording companies that allowed not only black creativity but also social critique to flourish.

My emphasis on the differences between this and other readings of the significance of vocal jive is not intended to discredit previous interpretations, but to reflect the unavoidable effects of positionality, given the highly polarized nature of South African society and cultural attitudes therein. I do not, of course, think my own work exempt from the influences of the intellectual and political priorities of my time and place. National politics have tended to exert significant pressure on the ways in which South Africanist scholars have engaged with academic debates and issues.[49] My own intellectual background, that of the liberal South African university environment up to the mid-1990s, is one that commonly sought political significance in cultural forms, particularly in relation to issues of race, class, and the struggle against apartheid.[50] However, the experience of conducting fieldwork after the first democratic elections in 1994 removed such clear-cut frameworks, revealing a messier reality, peopled by individuals looking after their own interests rather than purportedly acting for the greater good of a wider social group.[51] My interpretation is affected by the fact that the mood prevalent in the music industry during the late-1990s engendered responses highlighting individual economic self-interest more than had been the case during the 1980s, when scholars and musicians focused on the effects of racism and capitalism. The period from the first democratic elections in 1994 to 1999 was a time during which the celebration of cultural hybridity was a national ideology, encompassed in President Nelson Mandela's promotion of Bishop Desmond Tutu's vision of a "rainbow nation" (Tutu 1994). However, to the disappointment of many musicians, significant government funding of the performing arts, equivalent to that enjoyed in many newly independent African countries from the 1960s to the '80s (Nketia 1998:43), did not occur in the post-election period. Thrown back on their own resources for economic survival by a dearth of government support, musicians have tended to interpret present as well as past musical developments more in terms of commercial motives than socio-political ones.

Recorded popular music of the 1950s flourished within explicitly commercial structures driven by the profit motive. Yet an interpretation of commercial popular music as a hegemonic, conservative, and alienating entity does not explain the complexities of the South African recording industry during this period.[52] The recording industry, by providing a space for the articulation and affirmation of urban African identity, functioned in opposition to a state policy that sought to shape South African life according to specific "traditional" ethnic identities. Hybrid styles such as vocal jive embodied the urban, non-tribal, partially Westernized experience and identity of township dwellers, whose existence the government wished to deny. Furthermore, songs with topical lyrics sold well. Therefore, material that, to varying degrees of explicitness, was critical of government policies was continually released. Apart from obviously seditious material that attracted police attention, recording companies managed to evade recrimination by presenting their product as the innocuous candy-floss of popular culture. By nurturing the development of hybrid musical styles that expressed an identity rejected by the government, and by allowing dissident lyrics, the recording industry provided the mass of ordinary township people with a powerful means to voice cultural resistance, whether overtly, or more often, in a covert, ambiguous, contingent, fluctuating manner. Ultimately vocal jive and other urban hybrid styles of the 1950s functioned neither as panacea nor cultural weapon, neither as pure resistance nor complete acquiescence; rather, they provided, in Hall's terms, "the ground on which the transformations are worked" (1981:28). Urban styles of the period also demonstrate that the meaning of musical hybridity is often contradictory and always in flux, being open to multiple readings subject to the positionality of interpreters.

Acknowledgements

This research was largely undertaken as a Junior Research Fellow at Girton College, University of Cambridge. I would like to thank Sue Benson, Deborah James, and Roger Parker for their helpful comments on previous versions of this paper. I would also like to thank Rob Allingham, Mabel Mafuya, Dorothy Masuka, Joe Mogotsi, Albert Ralulimi, Dolly Rathebe, and Mary Thobei for granting me interviews from which I have quoted. Financial aid from the following is hereby acknowledged: the Patrick and Margaret Flanagan, and Elizabeth Allan Scholarship Funds; the Cambridge Livingstone Trust; Queens' College Cambridge; Girton College Cambridge.

Notes

1. *Bantu World* (Johannesburg), 20 February 1954.

2. *Mbaqanga* was popularized internationally during the mid-1980s by Mahlathini and the Mahotella Queens.

3. Allingham's assessment of Troubadour's domination of the recording industry is based on interviews that he conducted with sound engineers and other personnel who were involved

in the industry during the 1950s (Allingham, p.c.). Other major companies producing recordings for black South Africans included Gallo Africa and its subsidiary Gramophone Record Company (GRC), and Trutone, a local subsidiary of EMI.

4. For discussions of African Jazz, kwela, and male vocal jive, see Coplan 1985, Allen 1999, and Ballantine 1999. "African Jazz" was the term most commonly used in the 1940s and early 1950s to describe the fusion of American big-band swing with local styles such as *marabi* and *tsaba-tsaba* by South African swing bands. The other commonly used term, mbaqanga, now risks confusion with a different style of the same name that emerged during the 1960s.

5. Unless otherwise indicated, the following biographical information is drawn from interviews with Dorothy Masuka in 1996 and 1999, and Rob Allingham in 1991 and 2002; and from the television documentary *Into the Light with Dorothy Masuku*, directed by Helen van der Merwe, commissioned in 1995 by NNTV, South Africa. Dates of other interviews (cited as "p.c.") are as follows: Mabel Mafuya, 1999; Joe Mogotsi, 1999; Albert Ralulimi, 1990; Dolly Rathebe, 1996; and Mary Thobei, 1995.

6. *Bantu World,* 26 April and 28 June 1952; *Drum* (Johannesburg), August 1952. During the 1950s producers were called talent scouts; they also fulfilled the Artists and Repertoire portfolio.

7. *Bantu World,* 10 May, 14 June, and 27 June 1952.

8. *Drum,* November 1953; *Bantu World,* 16 January 1954; Masuka, p.c.

9. *Bantu World,* 30 March, 16 April, 7 September, and 10 December 1955; *Drum,* January 1955; *Golden City Post* (Johannesburg), 22 April 1956.

10. Although unusual in South Africa where most musicians did not do as well as Masuka financially, ad hoc payment of artists was common practice elsewhere in the world at the time. Such practices were particularly prevalent when social inequality made avoidance of formal royalty payments easier, such as in the production of "race records" in the United States, and of music for local audiences in the Congo (Ewens 1994).

11. Reports of the size of the fee vary, but the average payment during the early 1950s was £2.10, rising to between £7.50 and £10 per side towards the end of the decade (*Umteteli wa Bantu* [published in Johannesburg by the Chamber of Mines], 3 September 1955; *World* [formerly *Bantu World,* renamed in 1956], 25 May 1957, 6 September 1958; Dolly Rathebe, p.c.; Makeba 1988:52).

12. CDZAC 60. As it would be difficult for readers to source the original 78 rpm recordings, wherever possible I refer to recordings that have been reissued on compact disc.

13. The following conclusions about the basic musical characteristics of vocal jive are formed on the basis of discussion with musicians and analysis of 360 vocal jive songs, including twenty-seven by Masuka.

14. Also known as the African Dance Band of the Cold Storage Commission of Southern Rhodesia.

15. *Mfecane* refers to the period of warfare and destruction wrought by uShaka during the expansion of his amaZulu kingdom.

16. See, for example, "Five Bells" and "Baya Goli," on CDZAC 60.

17. "Hamba Notsokolo," for instance, consists of two sixteen-chord progressions that are repeated and alternated; its original flip-side, "Mama Ngi Niki," is a twelve-bar blues. The structure of "Hamba Notsokolo" is, in fact, akin to that of many Manhattan Brothers compositions, which frequently consist of a local melody alternated with a newly composed section, added to make the song less repetitive (Mogotsi, p.c.; Allingham, p.c.).

18. Typical examples of such variation in Masuka's repertoire include: singing different words to the same melody; varying the backing singers' riff that accompanies a reiterated lead vocal melody; introducing small variations in the solo part; alternating a motif between the solo voice and the chorus, or between solo voice, chorus and solo instruments; and lead vocal or instrumental improvising over repetitions of the motif by the chorus. Such variation strategies may be heard in "Mhlaba," "Mali e Shebeen," "Zono Zam," "Ei Yow (Phata Phata)," on CDZAC 60.

19. For example, "Miriam and Spokes' Patha Patha" (TELCD 2303), and "Uile Ngoan'a Batho" (CDZAC 61).

20. *Bantu World,* 17 September and 10 December 1955; *World,* 7 January, 4 February, and 13 October, 1956.

21. "Nomathemba" (on CDZAC 61) is typical of Mafuya's style.

22. *World,* 11 May 1957. The importance of topical songs in the African diaspora has long been recognized (see, e.g., Merriam 1959:51).

23. "Evaton" (AFC 400), and "Alexandra Special" and "Azikhwelwa" (AFC 429), both with the Alexandra Casbahs.

24. CDZAC 61. For a history of the Sophiatown removals, see Lodge 1983b.

25. *Bantu World,* 14 December 1955.

26. *World,* 17 January 1956.

27. Recordings about the bus boycotts include: "Azikhwelwa" (NV 3084) by the Boksburg Lillies (see *Golden City Post,* 2 October 1957); "Five Pence Special" (TJ 145) by the Scotland Brothers with Margaret Masimong (see *Drum,* August 1958); and "Azikhwelwa, Hadi Palangwe" (TJ 124) by the Sophiatown Gaieties. Recordings referring to the removals include "Let's Pack and Go" (GB 2852; *Drum,* February 1959) and "Sophiatown is Gone" (TELCD 2315), both by the Skylarks.

28. *Bantu World,* 17 December 1955; *World,* 7 January 1956 and 25 March 1957.

29. CDZAC 60.

30. See, for example, the interpretation of chimurenga songs during the Zimbabwean struggle for independence (Frederikse 1982; Pongweni 1982, 1997; Sherman 1980).

31. *Ilanga Laze Natal* (Durban), 6 June 1959.

32. *World,* 29 August 1959.

33. *Ilanga Laze Natal,* 11 August 1956; Masuka, p.c.

34. Re-diffusion was a cable radio service incorporated into houses when areas such as Orlando in Soweto were built.

35. For example, "Marshal [sic] Law" (AFC 510; *World,* 20 December 1958), and "Kunzima'" (AFC 529; *World,* 24 June 1959).

36. These songs may be seen as the culmination of what Ingrid Byerly has described as the first wave of increasingly overt musical resistance to apartheid (1998:9–10).

37. *World,* 11 May 1957, 13 December 1958; *Ilanga Laze Natal,* 6 June 1959.

38. Kaarsholm and James argue that readings of popular culture as resistant are frequently flawed because they posit a monolithic "people." As they and others have observed, popular culture is often not produced by a single social group but is forged through interactions between groups, resulting in a merger of resistant and dependent aspects and exposing intricate dependencies that bind unequals together (2000:200–03). However, the successful mass-politicization of ordinary township dwellers by the ANC during the early 1950s created, for a brief moment, a "people" united in their opposition to apartheid. Vocal jive, and particularly those songs with overtly political lyrics, articulated this opposition.

39. John Blacking similarly argues that, apart from the lyrics, the music of South African protest songs communicates political significance through the merger of Western and African elements (1980:198).

40. The media's recognition of the cultural voice of ordinary people paralleled the political shift of the ANC from an elite to a mass-based organization during the late 1940s and early 1950s.

41. However, caution is needed when attempting to gauge the success of recordings from newspaper reviews. The musical taste of the majority of township dwellers frequently differed from that of journalists who generally considered American culture superior to local forms.

42. *Bantu World,* 11 January 1941; *Drum,* August 1957. The New Africanist movement that arose during the 1940s proposed that black artists and intellectuals develop African national cultural forms based on elements drawn from indigenous cultures rather than emulating European culture. H.I.E. Dhlomo defined the New African as "detribalised, sophisticated, socially-

progressive and hard-hitting" (*Ilanga Laze Natal,* 11 April 1944). For a comprehensive discussion see Couzens 1985, particularly pp. 265–72.

43. *Drum,* August 1957; Coplan 1985:161; Moloi 1987:215.

44. See also comments by Andrew Tracey in Andersson 1981:16.

45. This process has been variously described as "hybridization" (Comaroff 1985), "creolization" (Fabian [1978]1997:19; Hannerz 1997:15), "syncretism" (Coplan 1982b; Barber 1987; Waterman 1990), "confluence" (Hampton 1980), "shock absorption" (Diawara 1997:46), and even "cannibalization" (Jewsiewicki 1997:103).

46. My conclusions are relevant to the recording industry catering for an urban black audience during the 1950s. A different argument, beyond the scope of this article, would need to be presented for a study of the period from 1960, when the grip of apartheid tightened. Particularly influential were the establishment of Radio Bantu and the negative effects of segregation laws on live performance. See Hamm 1995.

47. The particularly charged political environment in which Coplan was working, for example, is indicated by his assertion in 1979 that politically-inflected music "is presently too sensitive for scholarly analysis under any circumstances" (1979:149).

48. The relative normalization of South African society after the first fully democratic elections in 1994 makes it possible to acknowledge that even in highly racist environments race may, on occasion, be subordinate to profit. A remarkable parallel exists between the approach of South African recording companies in the 1950s, particularly Troubadour, and that of white American radio DJs of the same period who continued playing black R&B in the face of racist complaints, because it was popular. As record producer Jerry Wexler explained, "It was all about making money. It wasn't black or white, it was green—they were following the green dollar" (in the documentary film, *That Rhythm, Those Blues* [WGBH/Boston, WNET/New York, KCET/Los Angeles, 1988]). I would like to thank Peter Manuel for bringing this parallel to my attention.

49. See also Nketia (1998) for a survey of the close relationship between the work of African musicologists and their political and intellectual environments throughout the continent during the colonial and post-colonial eras.

50. Research into music expressing the concerns of this era includes Coplan 1985, Erlmann 1991, Ballantine 1993, and Allen 1993.

51. These observations are based on time spent with musicians as a participant observer, and over sixty formal interviews with musicians and other music industry personnel conducted between 1995 and 1999.

52. However, writing about the development of Radio Bantu after 1960, Charles Hamm asserts that recorded music was used by the state to support capitalist relations of production and to legitimize apartheid (1995:210–48, 249–69). For a similar approach to the interpretation of the political role of the mass media under apartheid, see Tomaselli et al. 1989.

References

Allen, Lara. 1993. "Pennywhistle Kwela: A Musical, Historical and Socio-Political Analysis." M.Mus. diss., University of Natal, Durban, South Africa.

——. 1999. "Kwela: The Structure and Sound of Pennywhistle Music." In *Composing the Music of Africa: Composition, Interpretation and Realisation,* edited by Malcolm Floyd, 227–64. Aldershot: Ashgate.

Allingham, Rob. 1991. *Hamba Notsokolo and Other Original Hits.* CD notes, Gallo Music Productions CDZAC 60.

——. 1994. *From Marabi to Disco: 42 Years of Township Music.* CD notes, Gallo Music Productions CDZAC 61.

Andersson, Muff. 1981. *Music in the Mix: The Story of South African Popular Music.* Johannesburg: Ravan Press.

Ballantine, Christopher. 1993. *Marabi Nights: Early South African Jazz and Vaudeville.* Johannesburg: Ravan Press.

——. 1999. "Looking to the USA: The Politics of Male Close-harmony Song Style in South Africa during the 1940s and 1950s." *Popular Music* 18(1):1–17.

Barber, Karin. 1987. "Popular Arts in Africa." *African Studies Review* 30(3):1–78.

Berliner, Paul. 1981. *The Soul of Mbira: Music and Traditions of the Shona People of Zimbabwe.* Berkeley: University of California Press.

Blacking, John. 1980. "Trends in the Black Music of South Africa, 1959–1969." In *Musics of Many Cultures: An Introduction,* edited by Elizabeth May, 195–215. Berkeley: University of California Press.

——. 1995. "The Music of Politics." In *Music, Culture, and Experience: Selected Papers of John Blacking,* edited by Reginald Byron, 198–222. Chicago: University of Chicago Press.

Byerly, Ingrid. 1998. "Mirror, Mediator, and Prophet: The Music *Indaba* of Late-Apartheid South Africa." *Ethnomusicology* 42(1):1–44.

Comaroff, Jean. 1985. *Body of Power, Spirit of Resistance.* Chicago: Chicago University Press.

Comaroff, John L. and Jean. 1997. *Of Revelation and Revolution: The Dialectics of Modernity on a South African Frontier, Volume Two.* Chicago: University of Chicago Press.

Coplan, David. 1979. "The African Musician and the Development of the Johannesburg Entertainment Industry, 1990–1960." *Journal of Southern African Studies* 5(2):135–64.

——. 1982a. "The Emergence of an African Working-Class Culture." In *Industrialisation and Social Change in South Africa: African Class Formation, Culture and Consciousness 1870–1930,* edited by Shula Marks and Richard Rathbone, 358–75. London: Longman.

——. 1982b. "The Urbanisation of African Musics: Some Theoretical Observations." *Popular Music* 2:113–30.

——. 1985. *In Township Tonight! South Africa's Black City Music and Theatre.* Johannesburg: Ravan Press.

Couzens, Tim. 1985. *The New African: A Study of the Life and Work of H.I.E. Dhlomo.* Johannesburg: Ravan Press.

Dhlomo, H. I. E. n.d. "Evolution of Bantu Entertainments." MS., Killie Cambell Africana Library, Durban (Reference KCM 8290 Z).

Diawara, Mamadou. 1997. "Mande Oral Popular Culture Revisited by the Electronic Media." In *Readings in African Popular Culture,* edited by Karin Barber, 40–47. Oxford: James Currey.

Erlmann, Veit. 1991. *African Stars: Studies in Black South African Performance.* Chicago: University of Chicago Press.

——. 1996. *Nightsong: Performance, Power, and Practice in South Africa.* Chicago: Chicago University Press.

Ewens, Graeme. 1994. *Congo Colossus: The Life and Legacy of Franco and OK Jazz.* North Walsham: Buku Press.

Fabian, Johannes. [1978] 1997. "Popular Culture in Africa: Findings and Conjectures." In *Readings in African Popular Culture,* edited by Karin Barber, 18–28. Oxford: James Currey.

Frederikse, Julie. 1982. *None But Ourselves: Masses vs. Media in the Making of Zimbabwe.* Johannesburg: Ravan Press.

Gunner, Elizabeth. 1979. "Songs of Innocence and Experience: Women as Composers and Performers of *Izibongo,* Zulu Praise Poetry." *Research in African Literatures* 10(2):239–67.

Hall, Stuart. 1981. "Notes on Deconstructing 'The Popular.'" In *People's History and Socialist Theory,* edited by Raphael Samuel, 227–40. London: Routledge.

Hamm, Charles. 1995. *Putting Popular Music in its Place.* Cambridge: Cambridge University Press.

Hampton, Barbara. 1980. "A Revised Analytical Approach to Musical Processes in Urban Africa." *African Urban Studies* 6:1–16.

Hannerz, Ulf. 1997. "The World in Creolization." In *Readings in African Popular Culture,* edited by Karin Barber, 12–17. Oxford: James Currey.

Horrell, Muriel, compiler. 1959. *A Survey of Race Relations in South Africa 1957-1958.* Johannesburg: South African Institute of Race Relations.

Jewsiewicki, Bogumil. 1997. "Painting in Zaire: From the Invention of the West to the Representation of the Social Self." In *Readings in African Popular Culture,* edited by Karin Barber, 99-109. Oxford: James Currey.

Kaarsholm, Preben, and Deborah James. 2000. "Popular Culture and Democracy in Some Southern Contexts: An Introduction." *Journal of Southern African Studies* 26(2):189-208.

Kavanagh, Robert M. 1992. *South African People's Plays: Ons Phola Hi.* Johannesburg: Heinemann.

Kubik, Gerhard. 1998. "Intra-African Streams of Influence." In *The Garland Encyclopedia of World Music: Vol.1, Africa,* edited by Ruth M. Stone, 239-326. London and New York: Garland.

Lodge, Tom. 1983a. *Black Politics in South Africa since 1945.* Johannesburg: Ravan Press.

———. 1983b. "The Destruction of Sophiatown." In *Town and Countryside in the Transvaal: Capitalist Penetration and Popular Response,* edited by Belinda Bozzoli, 337-64. Johannesburg: Ravan Press.

Makeba, Miriam, with James Hall. 1988. *Makeba: My Story.* Johannesburg: Skotaville.

Merriam, Alan. 1955. "The Use of Music in the Study of a Problem of Acculturation." *American Anthropologist* 57(1):28-34.

———. 1959. "African Music." In *Continuity and Change in African Cultures,* edited by William R. Bascom and Melville J. Herskovits, 49-86. Chicago: University of Chicago Press.

Moloi, Godfrey. 1987. *My Life: Volume One.* Johannesburg: Ravan Press.

Nketia, J. H. Kwabena. 1998. "The Scholarly Study of African Music: A Historical Review." *The Garland Encyclopedia of World Music: Vol.1, Africa,* edited by Ruth M. Stone, 13-73. London and New York: Garland.

Pongweni, Alec J. C. 1982. *Songs that Won the Liberation War.* Harare: College Press.

———. 1997. "The Chimurenga Songs of the Zimbabwean War of Liberation." In *Readings in African Popular Culture,* edited by Karin Barber, 63-72. Oxford: James Currey.

Ranger, Terence O. 1975. *Dance and Society in Eastern Africa, 1890-1970: The Beni Ngoma.* London: Heinemann.

Rycroft, David. 1958. "The New Town Music of South Africa." *Recorded Folk Music* 1:54-57.

———. 1959. "African Music in Johannesburg: African and Non-African Features." *Journal of the International Folk Music Council* 11:25-30.

———. 1971. "Stylistic Evidence in Nguni Song." In *Essays on Music and History in Africa,* edited by Klaus P. Wachsmann, 213-41. Evanston: Northwestern University Press.

———. 1975-6. "The Zulu Bow-Songs of Princess Magogo." *African Music* 5(4):41-96.

———. 1977. "Evidence of Stylistic Continuity in Zulu 'Town' Music." In *Essays for a Humanist: An Offering to Klaus Wachsmann,* edited by David Rycroft and Klaus Wachsmann, 216-60. New York: The Town House Press.

Sampson, Anthony. 1956. *Drum: A Venture into the New Africa.* London: Collins.

Scott, James C. 1990. *Domination and the Arts of Resistance: Hidden Transcripts.* New Haven and London: Yale University Press.

Sherman, Jessica. 1980. "Songs of Chimurenga." *Africa Perspective* 16:80-88.

Tomaselli, Ruth, Keyan Tomaselli, and Johan Muller, eds. 1989. *Broadcasting in South Africa.* London: James Currey.

Tracey, Hugh. 1963a. "Editorial." *African Music* 3(2):1.

———. 1963b. "The Development of Music." *African Music* 3(2):36-40.

Turino, Thomas. 2000. *Nationalists, Cosmopolitans, and Popular Music in Zimbabwe.* Chicago: University of Chicago Press.

Tutu, Desmond. 1994. *The Rainbow People of God.* London: Doubleday.

Vail, Leroy, and Landeg White. 1991. *Power and the Praise Poem.* Charlottesville: University of Virginia Press.

Waterman, Christopher. 1990. *Jùjú: A Social History and Ethnography of an African Popular Music*. Chicago: University of Chicago Press.

Discography of reissued recordings

Makeba, Miriam, and the Skylarks. 1991. *Miriam Makeba and the Skylarks Volume 1*. Teal Records, African Heritage, TELCD 2303.

———. 1991. *Miriam Makeba and the Skylarks Volume 2*. Teal Records, African Heritage, TELCD 2315.

Masuka, Dorothy. 1991. *Hamba Notsokolo and Other Original Hits from the 50's*. Gallo Music Productions CDZAC 60.

Various Artists. 1994. *From Marabi to Disco: 42 Years of Township Music*. Gallo Music Productions CDZAC 61.

Name Index